Praise for the first book c

BEHIND THE LINES

(which detailed the chaotic beginnings of the CRB, CN, and Belgium food relief)

Kirkus Reviews Best Books of 2014
"An excellent history that should catapult Miller to the top tier of popular historians."

Foreword Magazine INDIE FAB Book of the Year, History Finalist

Colorado Authors' League Writing Awards, General Nonfiction Finalist

Colorado Independent Publishers Association EVVY Awards,
Award-winner in History, Cover, and Interior Design

"This valuable narrative reprises a dramatic chapter of world history that rarely takes center stage in history books. . . . [T]he pages fly by, thanks to Miller's consistently smooth prose and careful scene-setting. He effectively captures the human drama, with exquisite descriptions of how characters looked . . . and why they behaved as they did. . . . Miller writes that his goal was to write for people 'who never read history books'; he accomplishes that splendidly, while also creating a work that scholars will admire. . . . An excellent history that should catapult Miller to the top tier of popular historians."

—*Kirkus Reviews* (Starred Review)

"Miller's excellent research is extensive and strongly supports his thesis that Hoover and the CRB were instrumental in saving the lives of untold numbers of Belgian civilians."

—*Publishers Weekly*, Book Life

"Miller, fascinated with this largely forgotten slice of history, has published . . . a fascinating look at the first five months of the relief campaign."

—*Denver Post*

"The impressive research and generally crisp writing transforms what could have been an arid study into a dramatic and at times inspiring narrative."

—*Westword*, Denver's alternative weekly

"One of the historian's jobs is to take all the shards—all the accounts, statistics, stories, and documents of a particular time—and make them click into place like a pattern in a kaleidoscope. Jeffrey B. Miller does this admirably in *Behind the Lines*."

—BlueInk Review (Starred Review)

DEDICATION

To my grandparents,
Milton M. Brown and Erica Bunge Brown,
who started it all.

To Susan Burdick—my north star, my
inspiration, my friend, my one true love.

ALSO BY JEFFREY B. MILLER

Stapleton International Airport: The First Fifty Years,
Pruett Publishing, Boulder, CO, 1983.
The first history book about a major U.S. airport.

Facing Your Fifties: Every Man's Reference to Mid-life Health,
co-author, Dr. Gordon Ehlers, M. Evans & Co., New York, 2002.
Included as one of only three health books in *Publishers Weekly*'s
"Best Books of 2002."

Behind the Lines, Milbrown Press, Denver, Colorado, 2014.
Covering August 1914 to December 1914, it detailed
the chaotic beginnings of the Commission for Relief in
Belgium and the Comité National.

ABOUT THE AUTHOR

Jeffrey B. Miller has been a writer, editor, and author for more than 40 years. His career includes starting six magazines (city, regional, and national), being editor in chief of five in-flight magazines, and serving as director of communications for AAA Colorado, where he supervised its magazine, public relations, public affairs, traffic safety programs, and website. He lives in Denver with his wife, Susan Burdick.

A band of Yanks in German-occupied Belgium help save millions from starvation as civilians resist the harsh German rule.

August 1914 to May 1917.

Jeffrey B. Miller

MILBROWN PRESS
DENVER
www.WWICrusaders.com

Special discounts are available for quantity purchases.

Published in the United States of America.

Milbrown Press is an imprint of JBM Publishing Company.

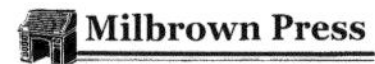

Jeff Miller
Milbrown Press
1265 South Columbine St.
Denver, CO 80210
(303) 503-1739

www.WWICrusaders.com
jbmwriter@aol.com

ISBN: 978-0-9906893-8-6 (paperback)
ISBN: 978-0-9906893-5-5 (ebook)

Library of Congress Number: 2018906957

Front-cover photograph: public domain; Herbert Hoover Presidential Library and Archives.
Back-cover photograph of Belgian girl eating a slice of bread: public domain; *War Bread*, E. E. Hunt (Henry Holt & Co., 1916).

Text design by Pratt Brothers Composition
Front cover design by Laurie Shields Design

Contents

Section III
Crises, 1916

Section IV
Farewell, January to May 1917

Epilogue

Author's Note

One of my professional goals has always been to write a history book that would be read by people who say they "never read history books." Through the years I've been inspired by the best history storytellers—writers such as Barbara W. Tuchman, David McCullough, Doris Kearns Goodwin, Laura Hillenbrand, and Erik Larson.

To me, the best history writing captures moments in time that come alive and can be seen, felt, and otherwise experienced by those who read them. If, at the end of my book, readers feel they have met and become familiar with the main characters as living, breathing people, then I've done my job.

I can't speak for the reader, but for me, after years of research, these main characters are very much alive. I want to be beside first-year Rhodes scholar David Nelson as he walks alone toward the Belgian border not knowing what to expect. I want to hear Hugh Gibson's impassioned arguments as he tries to stop the execution of Edith Cavell. I want to warn Eugene van Doren that the Germans are coming for him. I want to help Erica Bunge start the dairy farm that will provide milk for Antwerp's children. And I want to have a beer and intense conversation with war-correspondent-turned-compassionate-relief-worker E. E. Hunt.

But does my vision of these people, places, and events match up with what other history scholars have written? Is my book "accurate"?

I think of history in fluid terms. To me, capturing one moment in time is like capturing one moment in the bend of a river. What does the bend really look like? It all depends on your perspective. The pebble on the submerged riverbed sees it differently than the reeds on the right bank, the trees on the left, the bird gliding overhead, the fish battling upstream, or the bit of driftwood floating by.

After years of research and study (see Acknowledgments for details), I determined that the interwoven histories of the Commission for Relief in Belgium, the Comité National, and German-occupied Belgium during World War I demanded one book to detail the complex and chaotic beginnings of their stories. In 2014 my narrative nonfiction book written for general readers, *Behind the Lines*, was published. It covered August 1914 to December 1914. I'm happy to report it received numerous positive national reviews and acknowledgments, including selection as one of *Kirkus Reviews'* Best Books of 2014. The *Kirkus* Starred Review ended: "An excellent history that should catapult Miller to the top tier of popular historians." (I'm still waiting for the catapult.)

Later, I decided it was best for readers to have one volume that fully covered the topics in a rich, narrative style filled with personal stories. *WWI Crusaders* is that book. It contains:

Section I: Beginnings, 1914, which summarizes *Behind the Lines* in slightly different ways and with new material;
Section II: Conflicts, 1915;
Section III: Crises, 1916;
Section IV: Farewell, January to May 1917, which takes the characters up to the last Americans who leave Belgium after America's April 1917 entry into the war;
Epilogue, which wraps up the main topics and tells what happened to the major characters through the rest of the war and later in life.

I might not have written what some academics would consider a scholarly history book. My formal training is in journalism and magazine writing. I have possibly bent—or even broken—a few of the academic rules of history writing. If I have done so, my only defense is that I did so to make the reading experience smooth and enjoyable for general readers.

An example is attribution within the text: If an item is historically common knowledge and/or in multiple sources, I did not attribute it in the text because it slows down reading and is needlessly disruptive. However, the item is sometimes quoted to show I did not phrase it in that particular way or that I did not make it up. And it will be properly attributed in the endnotes at the back of the book—the source is confirmed, just not in the text.

Another example is the spelling of certain words, which have changed in 100 years. I felt it was best to stay true to the time period and its original documents, so I used French for place names, with first reference indicating the Flemish spelling in parentheses.

I also know that when it comes to the book's scope and coverage, I have barely touched upon the varied Belgian, English, French, or German activities during the war. Simply put, I had not the time, the space, nor the expertise to do so. It helps to know that there are numerous great books that have covered each nationality's activities far better than I could ever do.

With those caveats in mind, I hope you enjoy *WWI Crusaders*, my loving tribute to the men and women of Belgium and the CRB during World War I.

This book contains my vision of who those people were and what they did. It is my vision. It is my perspective of the bend in the river.

German-Occupied Belgium and Northern France during WWI

Three major zones were created by the Germans after the invasion: 1. The Occupation Zone (shaded) included the majority of Belgium and was controlled by the German civil government which was ruled by Governor General Baron von Bissing. 2. Two Army Zones named Etape were controlled by each regional military authority. The French Etape contained six districts: Longwy, Charleville, Vernins, St. Quentin, Valenciennes, and Lille; the Belgian Etape had two districts: West Flanders and East Flanders. 3. Within each Etape district was a thin strip of land right behind the trenches that was called the Operations Zone (indicated by the dotted line just to the right the trench line). Not part of the German occupation was Free Belgium, a tiny piece of land between the trenches and the French border where King Albert and his Belgian Army were stationed through the majority of the war. (© Jeff Miller 2018; map drawn by Bill Nelson.)

Reader Aids

Primary Groups and People in the Book

The Relief Organizations

The Commission for Relief in Belgium (CRB)

Founded on October 22, 1914, in London by Herbert C. Hoover and a small group of Americans, the CRB was a volunteer relief organization attempting to do something that had never been done before: feed an entire nation trapped in the midst of a world war. Its major responsibilities included the securing of financing for its massive operations; buying and shipping of goods; warehousing, processing, and release of supplies to local communes; supervising operations to catch abuses by Belgians and Germans; and handling multiple government relations and guarantees necessary for relief to continue. Supervision within Belgium and northern France was done by a small band of American "delegates" to meet British demands that no food would go to the Germans. These mostly young men had to maintain strict neutrality as they watched the Belgians suffer under the harsh German rule.

The Comité National de Secours et d'Alimentation (CN)

The CRB counterpart in Belgium, the CN, was led by Belgian financial giant Émile Francqui. The CN handled the storage, preparation, and distribution of relief supplies through provincial committees, 2,600 communes, and more than 40,000 Belgian workers to feed more than 7 million Belgian civilians every day.

In early 1915, a portion of northern France trapped behind German lines was added to the CRB's responsibilities, bringing the total number of civilians in need of food to nearly 10 million.

It was critical that the CRB and the CN work well together, despite Hoover's and Francqui's dislike and distrust of each other.

The Americans

Milton M. Brown

A 1913 Princeton graduate, Brown became a CRB delegate and entered German-occupied Belgium in early 1916. He was given the task of running the newly formed

CRB clothing department. He faced continual opposition from the CN, which had developed its own extensive clothes-processing network independent of the CRB.

Hugh Gibson

The secretary to the U.S. Legation in Belgium, Gibson was 31 and nearing the middle of his diplomatic career when the war broke out. He earned admiration and respect for his hard work, dedication to helping the Belgians, and unfailing sense of humor. He and his boss, U.S. Minister Brand Whitlock, rarely saw eye to eye on issues.

Prentiss Gray

After years of working in his father's steamship company, Gray was one of the few CRB delegates who had the critical shipping experience that the CRB needed. He would become the assistant director of the CRB Brussels office and later be one of the last Americans to leave Belgium.

Joseph C. Green

A scholar who was fluent in French, Green joined the CRB in the autumn of 1915 and within a few months was accused by the Germans of being a spy. Later, he would become the head of the CRB's Inspection and Control Department. His efforts would enrage Francqui and cause a major crisis between Hoover and Francqui.

Herbert Clark Hoover

A highly successful 40-year-old U.S. mining engineer, Hoover was living in London before the war and searching for a way to get into public service or politics. When war erupted, he organized assistance for stranded American tourists trying to return home. When Belgian representatives came to London looking for a way to avert seemingly inevitable starvation within their country, he volunteered to help and started the CRB. (He later became the 31st president of the United States, in part due to his humanitarian work during and after World War I.)

Edward Eyre Hunt

A sensitive and artistic magazine journalist in America, E. E. Hunt became a war correspondent so he could see the war up close. When he did get a clear vision of what was happening—especially in Belgium—he joined the CRB to do something concrete for those in need. He became the CRB's chief delegate to Antwerp Province, where he helped create and develop food-relief processes.

David T. Nelson

In late November 1914, Nelson was a first-year Rhodes scholar ready to embark on six weeks' winter break from Oxford. When the 23-year-old from North

Dakota heard that Hoover was looking for volunteers to go into German-occupied Belgium as neutral observers to ensure the food would not be taken by the Germans, he signed up. When he first entered Belgium, he was pro-German.

Walter H. Page

The U.S. Ambassador to Britain, Page became America's patron minister of the relief program (the other two neutral countries that were relief patrons were Spain and the Netherlands). Page would provide critical support to Hoover and the CRB during numerous crises.

Maurice Pate

One of the youngest CRB delegates at 21, Pate was mature and levelheaded as he faced multiple problems within Belgium and northern France. His experiences in the CRB would lead him to a lifetime of service, most notably on behalf of children as the founding director of UNICEF after World War II.

William Hallam Tuck

In 1915, Tuck sailed for Europe with plans to join the British Army. Onboard he met a few CRB men who convinced him to speak first with Hoover in London. Hoover convinced the 25-year-old to join the CRB. With a strong sense of honor, Tuck was committed to Hoover's demand that all delegates stay neutral. More than a year later, the Germans would do something that tested Tuck's promise to the breaking point.

Brand Whitlock

When Whitlock was appointed minister of the U.S. Legation in Belgium in early 1914, he was looking forward to working on his novels at the traditionally noneventful post. He would be thoroughly tested by the war and the potential starvation of nearly 10 million people in Belgium and northern France. In the end, he would become a figure who was both respected and ridiculed, beloved and belittled.

The Belgians

Edouard Bunge and His Three Daughters

A wealthy Antwerp merchant, Bunge was vice president of the provincial relief committee for Antwerp Province, owner of Chateau Oude Gracht on the Hoogboom estate, and widowed father of five daughters. Three of them—Erica, Eva, and Hilda—were living with him when the war broke out. In early 1915, he and his 23-year-old daughter, Erica, developed a dairy farm that sent milk every day to the children of nearby Antwerp.

Abbé Vincent de Moor

A man of the Catholic faith, de Moor was not only a priest but a clandestine operative for British Intelligence. He became partners with Eugene van Doren on an underground newspaper that would inspire a nation but lead to the imprisonment of many and the execution of a few.

Émile Francqui

One of the most powerful financial men in Belgium before the war, Francqui would lead the Comité National. He and Hoover had met before and disliked each other immensely. With his passion for his country and his domineering personality, Francqui would create continual problems for Hoover and the CRB.

Eugene van Doren

A Belgian cardboard manufacturer, van Doren so hated the Germans that he took up clandestine work for Abbé de Moor before helping to develop the idea for an underground newspaper, *La Libre Belgique*. His work and the newspaper would inspire the nation and would lead to a German reward of 10,000 francs for the capture of those responsible.

The Germans

Baron Moritz Ferdinand von Bissing

A 70-year-old Prussian military officer who had been born into the German landed gentry, von Bissing had had a distinguished military career before being appointed by the Kaiser to be governor general of Belgium. Demanding in his adherence to rules, regulations, and the hierarchy of authority, von Bissing was determined to bend Belgian citizens to his will. The underground newspaper *La Libre Belgique* mocked and taunted him constantly, and as a result von Bissing was practically obsessed with the capture of those responsible. The governor general also became a major stumbling block for the CRB and CN.

Baron Oscar von der Lancken

A sophisticated, multilingual diplomat, von der Lancken had spent 10 years as a counselor in the German Embassy in Paris. Brought to Belgium by von Bissing, von der Lancken was named head of the political department of the German civilian government and was responsible for relations with the CRB and CN. He was no great friend of Americans.

WWI CRUSADERS

"The German Chancellor might cynically refer to Belgium as a 'pawn' in the 'imperial' hands, but to us, who saw [the German occupation of Belgium] and lived it, she was a suffering, sentient being, quivering and bleeding under hoof and pistol butt."

BRAND WHITLOCK, U.S. Minister to Belgium, *Belgium*, Vol. II, 686.

"[The world] had lived, for months, under the impression that 'things were not so bad' in the conquered [Belgium]. After the outcry caused by the atrocities of August, 1914, there came a natural reaction, a sort of ant-climax. Fines, requisitions, petty persecutions do not strike the imagination in the same way as the burning of towns and the wholesale massacre of peaceful citizens. It had become necessary to follow things closely in order to understand that, instead of suffering less, the Belgian population was suffering more and more every day."

ÉMILE CAMMAERTS, *Through the Iron Bars*, 45.

1

Left or Right

"No One Slept throughout the Night"

Before the August 1914 start of World War I, the Belgian village of Virton was a thriving administrative and commercial center in Luxembourg Province. A Walloon, or French-speaking, municipality of 3,500 residents, Virton was known for its hilly streets, massive St. Lawrence's Catholic Church, and remnants of medieval walls. Located just south of the better-known Ardennes region and less than five miles north of the French border, Virton was the principal town of the small Belgian region known as Gaume, which boasted a warmer microclimate than those around it. Gently rolling green hills and lush pockets of forest were peaceful dividers between picturesque ancient towns and villages.

When the war came, it did not pass lightly over Virton and the surrounding villages. During the invasion, more than 200 men, women, and children were dragged from their homes and executed in one of the worst massacres of the time. Many houses were partially or completely destroyed. Across Belgium the Germans outlawed all movement outside a person's neighborhood without a properly authorized *Passierschein* (safe conduct pass). A constant barrage of *affiches* commanded Belgians in all matters of life. These placards came from either the local German commander or from Belgium's German governor general, Baron von Bissing. Any disobedience was met with harsh fines and sometimes imprisonment.

Nearly two and a half years of occupation had passed when the stories of the "slave raids" crept into Virton long before the German *affiche* was posted. When the official proclamation appeared on the town's walls in late 1916, people read the notice of their turn in the upcoming deportation of Belgian men more with horrified resignation than surprise. It ordered all men between 18 and 55 from the town and the surrounding villages to appear the next day at Virton's Saint Joseph's College. The men were to be there at 7:00 a.m. with blankets and three days' rations. Nothing was said about what would happen to them or where they would go.

"No one slept throughout the night," wrote Joe Green, an American civilian who witnessed the event. "The women were busy mending and packing clothes and blankets. The men were settling their affairs. The notaries' offices were crowded with men making their wills. The priests and the burgomasters [mayors] and the leading citizens moved all night from house to house, giving words of encouragement and advice, and promising to look after the wives and children left behind."

Green was 29 years old, with thick dark-brown hair and a heavy moustache that reinforced his intense look. An air of seriousness rarely left him, and his temper could be like a firecracker—quick and explosive. He did not suffer fools lightly. And yet, that evening in Virton as he walked among the people he was sworn to help feed, he had to contain his anger and sense of injustice—he was the provincial chief delegate of the American-led Commission for Relief in Belgium (CRB) and had sworn on his honor as a gentleman to remain neutral when serving in German-occupied Belgium.

The next day dawned heavy, with low-lying pewter clouds and snow that changed back and forth to rain as it fell quietly. The sense of dread and foreboding was heightened by a reminder of the fighting to the south as the big guns thundered off in the distance toward Verdun.

Those who did not obey the *affiche* were taken from their homes by German soldiers wielding rifles with fixed bayonets. Protests, explanations, and pleadings were lost on the German soldiers, who responded with rough handling and rifle butts to motivate the Belgian men. Women and children stood by helplessly as they watched their husbands, fathers, or brothers forced into the street. They joined others—the ones who had heeded the *affiche*—trudging toward Saint Joseph's College. Most of them were workmen dressed in traditional Belgian corduroy pants, coarse shirts, and peasant caps. If it had been farther north in Flemish territory, many would have had on *sabots* (wooden shoes), but this was Walloon country, so heavy work boots were what most wore.

By 7:00 a.m. the streets around the college were clogged with people. Green was watching and tried to remain calm as "the men, each with his sack on his back, were herded like cattle, village by village. The women and children, kept at a distance, stood in compact masses, wailing, moaning, wringing their hands. Order was kept by the Uhlans, especially brought from France for the purpose."

German *uhlans* were lance-carrying cavalry who had become infamous from stories of their brutality during the invasion. When it came to crowds, these cavalrymen knew how to control restless, desperate people. They would ride up and down, using their horses to cut wide swaths through the throng, clearing a path, breaking up little knots of people, always keeping them moving so a crowd could not gather in one place. Each *uhlan* carried a long lance that had a pennant near the end and a steel, razor-sharp tip. He would carry the pike loosely in hand, not resting in the stirrups, and would brandish it at will above the heads of the women and children.

In Virton, the men who were corralled outside Saint Joseph's College were called in groups by village. As they stepped forward, they were shoved and shouted at by the soldiers and formed into a single line that led through the gate into the courtyard of the college. There the Belgians found a long table and four German officers—the men who would decide their fate.

No time was given for any meaningful review or analysis of the health, employment status, or general fitness of each man. Any objections Green might have made were ignored. "Scarcely any questions were asked. There was no time for questions. The examinations averaged less than ten seconds per man." Each man showed his identity card, which had his name, age, and profession. He then waited for the last officer to make his pronouncement, a one-word command in German: *links*, left, or *rechts*, right.

Left was freedom. Right was forced deportation.

Green watched as "those who passed to the right disappeared, waving a last farewell" as an "agonized shriek went up from some woman in the crowd." And as more men disappeared, the crowd become more agitated. Women kept trying to break through the barricade of soldiers to "say one last word to a husband or a son."

The horrifying scene continued to unfold as the young American bore witness. The women were "pushed back roughly into the crowd, often with kicks and blows. In a short time all the women in the front rows of the crowd were being beaten by the soldiers, both with fists and with the butts of guns. This indescribable scene went on for over half an hour, in plain sight of the groups of [Belgian] men, many of whom were weeping unrestrainedly from rage and helplessness. Finally an officer came out of the court[yard] and put an end to the worst of the brutality."

As the rain and snow continued to fall, the men marked for deportation were herded by German soldiers with fixed bayonets to the train station. Cattle cars were waiting, and the men were shoved in. Each car had a recommended capacity of only eight horses or 40 men, yet the Germans were known to force up to 60 men into one car. The Virton men probably fared no better.

By nightfall the Virton train, packed with its human cargo, was gone. As the train had pulled away from the station, the men had no doubt been singing, like many before them, the Belgian and French national anthems, "La Brabançonne," and "La Marseillaise." Any women and children lining the tracks who had been watching carefully might have seen a few small scraps of paper tossed from the moving cattle cars—hastily scribbled notes from deportees wanting to send one last message to loved ones.

In the end, about a third of the men from Virton were taken and, as Green stated, "almost none under the age of 25 . . . escaped." The nearby village of Ethe was hit the hardest—only 17 "able-bodied men remaining out of a population of 1,500. The women and children will be unable to cultivate the fields next spring. In one family in particular, four little girls are left alone. The mother was shot at the beginning of the war. The father and elder brother are now carried off to Germany. The Industrial School at Ethe lost 36 out of its 40 remaining students. This in spite of the formal promise of the Germans that none of the students would be taken."

Green was shocked and horrified and would never forget what he saw that day in Virton. He ended his official account: "The deportations go on. The Province of Liège, Greater Brussels, and many other localities have not yet passed through the ordeal. Belgium waits."

He was much more forthright when he wrote his parents about the deportations, dropping any pretense of neutrality: "They are carried out with the last degree of brutality. They are utterly unwarranted by the situation in Belgium and they may simply be regarded as the latest and worst manifestations of that systemized German barbarity which must be crushed."

Ultimately, the slave raids would touch most of Belgium, ensnare more than 120,000 men (counts vary widely), and herald a new, harsher existence for the civilians under German occupation. "These deportations," Green explained to his parents, "have done more to break the spirit of the Belgians than all that has happened in the last two and a half years put together. . . . Now an impenetrable gloom, apparent on every face, is settling down on the country."

As one British newspaper reported, the past demands and difficulties of the German occupation had at least allowed civilians to live peacefully in their own homes. With the start of the deportations, however, "now the fear of exile hangs over every man's head, and every woman and child in the land knows that at any moment German soldiers may knock at the house door, and, at the point of a bayonet, drive husband, father, or brother away without a moment's warning, to be swallowed up in the slave army which goes to Germany for no one knows how long, and to return—if ever—no one knows when."

Brand Whitlock, U.S. minister for the legation in Brussels, wrote in his official report on the deportations: "Appalling stories have been related by Belgians coming to the Legation. . . . Even if a modicum of all that is told is true, there still remains enough to stamp this deed as one of the foulest that history records."

And "left" or "right" became words that defined the brutality of the forced deportations. None who were taken then, however, could have guessed that those two words would foretell even greater terror only 24 years later as they became forever linked with the horrors of World War II's Holocaust.

But back in World War I Belgium, the genesis of the deportations—and how the Belgians and a small group of Americans that included Joe Green reacted to them—were all part of a much larger story that had its roots in the early stages of the war. That larger story was of the American-led Commission for Relief in Belgium (CRB) and its Belgian counterpart, the Comité National de Secours et d'Alimentation (CN), which joined forces to try and save nearly 10 million Belgian and northern French civilians from starving to death.

Food relief on such a massive scale had never been attempted before—by governments or private citizens—and was considered impossible during times of war. Would the Allies allow food into occupied Belgium? Would the Germans keep their hands off it? Would the Americans be able to raise the funds and organize the purchase and shipment of the massive amounts of food needed to feed a nation? Could the Belgians organize the food preparation and distribution to millions of residents?

Those questions and many more were all backdropped by additional hurdles—the Allies' military opposition to the relief, a harsh German occupation, the deportation of Belgian workers, Belgian passive resistance to the German rule, and even infighting between the CRB and the CN.

In the end, all those forces and events would cause a tumbling together of extraordinary people into a chain reaction of life-and-death situations far from the trenches and killing fields of World War I.

And hanging in the balance were millions of civilian lives.

By September 1914, Belgians throughout the country had no choice but to join the soup-kitchen lines as the country quickly consumed its dwindling supplies. (Public domain; *In Occupied Belgium*, Robert Withington, The Cornhill Co., 1921.)

SECTION I

BEGINNINGS, 1914

A column of German foot soldiers during the invasion that began August 4, 1914, and launched World War I. (Public domain; *Fighting in Flanders*, E. Alexander Powell, Charles Scribner's Sons, 1914.)

King Albert of Belgium was 39 years old and little-known to the world before the start of World War I. Cardinal Mercier wrote, "As the simplest of his soldiers, [King Albert] stands in the trenches." He became known as the symbol of stouthearted, heroic Belgium. (Public domain; *A Journal from Our Legation in Belgium*, Hugh Gibson, Doubleday, Page & Co., 1917.)

The ancient university town of Louvain in ruins after the Germans ransacked it on August 25–30, 1914. (Public domain; multiple sources.)

2

Setting the Stage

Major Events of the War

On August 4, 1914, the armies of German Kaiser Wilhelm II invaded neutral Belgium on the way to their ultimate goal, Paris. The invading force was quickly surprised by the fierce resistance of the small Belgian Army and the sporadic acts of self-guided *franc-tireurs*, or guerrilla fighters. German soldiers' reactions to such opposition were swift and brutal—burning, looting, and mass executions in many towns and villages, including Louvain, Dinant, and Visé. To avoid such devastation, the Belgian capital of Brussels declared itself an open city that would not oppose the Germans as long as they marched in peacefully, which they did on August 20.

Belgium's neutrality—which had been sanctioned by all the major European powers in the 1839 Treaty of London—was a significant factor in the war. Germany's flagrant violation of Belgium's neutrality led to Britain entering the war to officially honor its commitment to that neutrality. Sides were quickly established: the Allies, or Entente Powers (Britain, France, and Russia), against the Central Powers (Germany, Austria-Hungary, and the Ottoman Empire). The United States declared its own neutrality on August 4, with President Woodrow Wilson detailing the American position in an address to congress on August 19. The American government officially wanted nothing to do with what it saw as a strictly European dispute.

In September on the Western Front, the British and French were finally able to halt the German advance—which came within 25 miles (40 km) of Paris—and then push it back slightly. This success, however, came at a heavy price: In the war's first major battles—the First Battle of the Marne and the First Battle of the Aisne—more than 2 million men took part, with nearly 500,000 killed or wounded. The stalling of the German offensive also led to months of the "Race to the Sea," in which each side swung west to outmaneuver the other until both sides had reached the coast of the North Sea.

Meanwhile, the thought-to-be impregnable city of Antwerp, defended by a ring of 54 fortresses, was taken by the use of long-range artillery that simply stood miles back and blasted the forts to rubble. The city was bombed for three consecutive days before it surrendered on Saturday, October 10.

In a final stand along the Yser River, Belgian King Albert and his remaining troops stood firm to save critical English Channel ports. Knowing he could not hold out forever, the king ordered the opening of sluice gates during high tide at the seaside town of Nieuport. The subsequent flooding created an impassable barrier two miles wide and shoulder deep from the sea to the town of Dixmude. This watery obstacle protected a thin slice of Belgium between the Germans and the French border where the king remained with his men, waiting for the day his country would be liberated. The trenches dug there comprised the most western section of the Western Front and became known as the Yser Front, or the Western Flemish Front. The Belgian Army, along with parts of the French Army, manned the trenches. King Albert established his headquarters just south of the trenches and just north of the French border, near the town of Veurne.

Nearby, but further inland, the little town of Ypres lent its name to one of the most massive battles of the war. The First Battle of Ypres pitted the Germans against the British in a fight that raged from October 20 until the third week of November, with hardly a movement of the line either way. Altogether, the battle took the lives of nearly a quarter of a million men.

By late November/early December, the Race to the Sea and the First Battle of Ypres were over, and both Allied and German soldiers began to dig in, establishing the 400-mile front of trenches from Switzerland to the North Sea that would barely change through four years of war.

During December 1914, many of the men on both sides were sick and tired of the war and spontaneously created mini-truces and cease-fires up and down the line, culminating in the incredible Christmas Truce of 1914. Later stories told of opposing soldiers exchanging greetings, newspapers, food, and drink. Men from both sides sang songs together and reportedly even played soccer matches in the no-man's-land between the trenches.

The world would never again see such fraternization during World War I. And the bloodshed—which up to that time had shocked the world—would be equaled, and then some, in the remaining years of the war.

German-Occupied Belgium

By the end of 1914—with the fall of Antwerp, the establishment of the 400 miles of trenches, and the creation of the water barrier protecting a thin slice of free Belgium—the Germans began to settle into the occupation of Belgium and a small section of northern France that lay within their domain.

Even though the Germans had known their neighbor to the west for thousands of years, they seemed to have little sense of how independent, strong-willed, and resistant the Belgians would be to occupation.

Belgium was no stranger to invading armies. In fact, it was known as the cockpit of Europe, referring to the cockfighting ring where two fierce roosters would battle to exhaustion or death. In the past, Belgium had always been a region without its own country—pieces of which had belonged at times to France, Germany, Holland, Spain, and Austria. Its people were eyewitnesses to many other nations' battles across their land—most notably the Battle of Waterloo, on the outskirts of Brussels, where Napoleon had his final defeat in 1815.

Before the war, Belgian nationalism was thought to be nonexistent because the country had been formalized only in 1830 and because there were stark socioeconomic and linguistic divides between the Walloons, who lived primarily in the south and spoke French, and the Flemings, who lived in the north and spoke Flemish (a Dutch derivative). Few in Europe felt that such a country could possess strong nationalistic feelings.

That assumption was smashed quickly with the German invasion. According to Hugh Gibson, secretary of the U.S. Legation in Brussels and a man who had a front-row seat to the August 1914 invasion, "even the Belgians themselves were surprised at the depth and sincerity of the patriotism that was revealed."

The surprise was on both sides. As Gibson explained, "The Germans, of course, were convinced that no real national sentiment existed and the spirited defense of the Belgians quite upset their calculations. Several German officers have spoken to me complainingly of the behavior of the Belgians as though they had in some way misled and swindled Germany by endeavoring to maintain their neutrality and independence."

Reflective of this little-realized nationalism was a Belgian story told of two "wizened city clerks" living under the German rule in occupied Brussels. As they discussed the war, one asked the other, "When and how will the Germans be beaten?" The other man "shrugged his shoulders and declared solemnly, 'They were beaten when they set foot for the first time in Belgium.'"

Before the war, Belgium, with 7.5 million residents and a landmass slightly smaller than Maryland, was the most industrialized country in Europe and was the most densely populated with 652 people per square mile (the United Kingdom had 374, Germany 310, France 189, and America 31). The country imported more than 75 percent of the food it consumed and more than 78 percent of the cereals necessary for making bread, which was a vital part of every Belgian's diet.

American journalist Arthur Humphries explained, "To the Belgian, bread is not only the staff of life; it is the legs. . . . At home in America, we think of bread as something that goes with the rest of the meal; to the poorer classes of Belgians the rest of the meal goes with bread."

Prior to the start of hostilities, Belgium's high import rate of food was not a problem because of the country's well-developed industrialization. Belgian industries—from coal to armament plants to lace-making co-ops—exported enough to balance the tremendous amount of food imports the country needed.

That all changed when the Germans invaded. Suddenly the factories and mines were closed and thousands were out of work. Much of the harvest was destroyed, requisitioned, or left rotting in the fields for lack of workers to harvest it. And the Germans never even considered providing food to the conquered Belgians. In fact, the invaders simply took food and material wherever and whenever they wanted, despite the world's shocked reaction to their lack of responsibility. With winter only a few months away, a Belgium food crisis was coming closer every day.

But as one observer noted, "Famine sweeps over a country like a blighting wind—yesterday even its approach was unsuspected; to-day it is everywhere." By September, food in Belgium was expensive and getting harder to find, but it was still in markets, restaurants, and unharvested fields that could be scavenged. Farmers retained at least some of their livestock and worked hard to produce whatever they could, no matter how small the quantity.

On the international stage, full alarm bells regarding a pending food crisis had not yet been sounded by the press (that would only happen in October, when it became a cacophony), but within Belgium, some people and organizations had begun taking action even before the war's first shots were fired. On August 1, the Belgian government had bought the entire wheat supply on the market in Antwerp and stored it for the coming need. Some began stockpiling on a local level as well.

The Genesis of Belgium Food Relief

Overall, the country was better prepared than some for such a food crisis. It boasted numerous wealthy individuals of the upper class and merchant class who traditionally helped out during tough times. The general population was ready to sacrifice and volunteer if called upon, and the country had an extensive network of canals used for mass distribution of goods. But by far the most important element to aid Belgium in this particular situation was the country's commune system of governance.

While there was a federal government in place, much of everyday life and everyday affairs were handled by the more than 2,600 local communes throughout Belgium. Each hamlet, village, and town had a commune that kept track of all residents; acted to represent, protect, and adjudicate when needed; and provided charity for those who could not provide for themselves. In larger cities there were multiple communes to handle different districts. The greater Brussels area alone had 16 communes that dealt with its 700,000 residents.

These communes worked so independently from one another and from the higher levels of government that they continued to function relatively well even after the Belgian government fled to Le Havre, France, and King Albert stayed with his troops on the Yser River.

Additionally, the German occupation government dealt more with the larger cities and regional levels of government. One American historian noted: "The whole machinery of the Belgian central government had been broken down or swept away by the invader. . . . Only the communal administrations remained fairly intact and possessed the liberty of action to permit them to meet the crisis brought on by the shortage of food and the tremendous increase in destitution. It was a happy circumstance for the Belgian population that the local government was so well organized and so relatively independent in normal times."

Because of this, the communes were the perfect vehicles for massive food distribution—if only an adequate and steady supply could be found.

The first Belgians to feel the effects of the war and therefore require assistance were the August refugees. Those who had left their homes in advance of the German armies or had been forced out by the invaders sought food, clothing, and shelter from anyone who would give it. Many headed to Brussels. One American war correspondent reported, "Waves of refugees, many of them utterly destitute, all of them in a state of abject panic and demoralization, thronged into Brussels as the Germans advanced. Day by day their numbers and their distress increased. Relief measures were imperative unless the fugitives were to starve by the roadside or be driven in desperation to plunder right and left." Tens of thousands had already made it into Holland and France, but many more were still on the move because the fighting in Belgium was still fluid and would not be contained to trench warfare until November.

By late August and early September, however, the food situation was obvious to anyone who could read the signs. According to one later history, "It was practically impossible to purchase more than a pound of flour or sugar at a time, and almost all stocks of tinned goods were sold out, bought by anxious people who besieged the shops in the desire to get hold of a private stock before all was gone. The price of food rose to exorbitant figures."

Communes all over Belgium attempted to deal with the coming food shortages. In Brussels, a group of wealthy individuals came together to form the nongovernmental Comité Central de Secours et d'Alimentation (Central Committee of Assistance and Provisioning) for the purpose of supplying Brussels with food.

The major instigator and its elder statesman was 76-year-old Ernest Solvay, the country's richest man, a distinguished and respected businessman, and a world-renowned philanthropist.

The committee's president and forceful leader was 51-year-old Émile Francqui, a major force in the financial world and director of the Société Générale de Belgique, arguably the most important financial institution in Belgium.

Somewhat surprising, in the organizational meeting of the Comité Central, there were three Americans: two businessmen living in Brussels, Dannie

Heineman and William Hulse, and the secretary of the U.S. Legation to Belgium, Hugh Gibson. According to one historian, they were there because 41-year-old Heineman had "suggested to Francqui and others that it would be of great utility to the proposed [Comité Central] to invite the [neutral] American and Spanish Ministers . . . to act as patrons; in this way the committee would be given a neutral character and protection against requisition of its stocks of supplies might be assured."

Francqui, ever the pragmatist, liked the idea and knew that in this case Belgian self-reliance could not achieve all that was needed. As such, Brussels-based U.S. Minister Brand Whitlock and Spanish Minister Marquis de Villalobar y O'Neill became patrons of the Comité Central. The first official meeting of the Comité Central took place on Saturday, September 5. It was quickly established that four major jobs had to be accomplished before food could arrive in Brussels:

1. The Germans had to agree to allow the food in and to not requisition it.
2. The English had to allow food through the blockade that it was establishing to cut off Germany from world trade.
3. Processes had to be developed for determining how much food was needed to feed Brussels; then the food had to be bought, shipped, and transported into Belgium; and then it had to be distributed to the 16 communes of Greater Brussels.
4. Some entity had to be found to pay for such a giant undertaking.

It was a daunting task, but the stakes were too high not to try. Those in positions of prominence began using their contacts and special avenues of influence to apply pressure to the governor general of Belgium, Field Marshal Baron Wilhelm Leopold Colmar von der Goltz, to formally guarantee that the Germans would not requisition any imported food.

The task was a little easier than some would have imagined. At this stage of the war, the German thought process was straightforward: they would not feed the Belgians; there was little left to take from Belgium; they needed every man at the front; peaceful Belgians did not require many soldiers to control; and Belgians would remain peaceful if they were fed.

This logic dictated that a neutral effort to bring food to the Belgians would serve German interests. On September 17 a letter from von der Goltz to Whitlock served as a hands-off guarantee. He agreed "not to requisition the shipments of wheat and flour destined for the alimentation [the provision of nourishment] of the Belgian civil population." However, he also stated that von der Goltz and his civil government would decide on and supervise distribution. While that stipulation was totally unacceptable to Francqui and the Comité Central, it was felt that that battle could be waged later if all other hurdles of food importation had been overcome.

At the start of the war, Herbert C. Hoover was a 40-year-old mining engineer who was a no-nonsense, ambitious, roll-up-your-sleeves-and-get-it-done kind of American. He would go on to organize and build the Commission for Relief in Belgium (CRB), which would become the largest food and relief drive the world had ever seen. During four years of war, nearly 10 million Belgians and northern French would be saved from starvation by the efforts of the CRB and its Belgian counterpart, the Comité National. (Public domain; Herbert Hoover Presidential Library Archives, West Branch, Iowa.)

Americans Get Involved in Belgium Relief

The Comité Central gave the task of finding and securing food for importation to Millard K. Shaler, an American mining engineer living in Brussels before the war. Armed with travel permits and permissions from the Germans, Shaler reached Holland but found no available food for purchase, so he went on to England. There he was able to buy 2,500 tons of wheat, rice, and beans but could not secure permission to export the food to Belgium.

The reason was clear—he was a private citizen representing a Brussels citizen group that had no formal diplomatic backing. That did not get him far in cutting through the red tape of British rules and regulations. He tried to speak with the Belgian minister in London to obtain official Belgian government support. He never got past the reception desk. Shaler sat stymied in London for the rest of September and into October, telling anyone who would listen that the Belgians needed help right away.

Meanwhile, another mining engineer, Herbert Hoover, who had been living in London before the war, was wrapping up months of volunteer service as the head of a group he had founded to assist the 100,000 to 150,000 American tourists stranded by the war (an accurate count was impossible).

Hoover was a no-nonsense, ambitious, roll-up-your-sleeves-and-get-it-done kind of American who was highly skilled at tackling complex problems and organizing massive operations. He also had little patience for trivial things, such as fashionable clothes, as evidenced by one colleague's dry remark that "his dress never varies—he merely writes to his tailor, 'Send me another suit,' and seldom gives himself the bother of a try-on."

Photos of Hoover at the time show a man with dark hair parted nearly down the middle, a high forehead, a strong jaw, and a downward-turned, set mouth. It could be seen as a fighter's face that had so far successfully avoided many a punch. There was also a feeling of restlessness and impatience within the strong gaze and solid pose, as if the moment the camera was clicked, the man would bound away to tackle important issues.

In August 1914, Hoover and his wife, Lou Henry Hoover, were living in London with their two young sons, Herbert Jr., 11, whose birthday fell on August 4 (the day World War I began), and Allan, 7. Besides managing his worldwide mining operations, Hoover was in London trying to secure European nations' participation in the upcoming Panama-Pacific International Exposition to be held in San Francisco in 1915. He and Lou both realized their mission was stillborn the moment the war started.

Additionally, though, Hoover, who would turn 40 on August 10, was contemplating what he should do in his next stage of life. He was restless and not content to sit back and manage his mining operations. An orphan at an early age, he had been raised as a Quaker and was instilled with a "Quaker conscience" of morality that led to a strong desire to serve humanity, but he was unsure how to do so.

Options included the presidency of Stanford University and the purchase of a California newspaper as two different pathways into public service and politics—two areas that deeply interested the mining engineer. He was a wealthy man, but as one associate later wrote, "He didn't want to become just richer. He wanted sincerely . . . to do public service and help people, but in a wholesale way. I don't think he was terribly sympathetic to the fellow selling lead pencils on the corner, but I think he was very desirous to create a society where that fellow wouldn't be selling lead pencils on the corner."

Within days of the war's start and hearing of stranded American tourists, Hoover had organized the Committee of American Residents (also known as the Relief Committee, or Residents' Committee) to help his fellow countrymen. By late September/early October, he was winding down the work when he was approached by his closest friend and confidant, Edgar Rickard, who was also a mining engineer and editor of a mining magazine.

Rickard suggested Hoover meet Shaler. Hoover did so and was, as a later history stated, "immediately impressed by the seriousness of the Belgian situation." He "promised to help if any means could be devised to send in relief." Hoover took the next few days to work the project over in his head while also consulting many of his close associates who were still part of the Residents' Committee. They included Rickard, Colonel Millard Hunsiker, Clarence Graff, and John Beaver White, all of whom agreed that something had to be done to help the Belgians avert a major crisis.

While Hoover was determining what he would do, Hugh Gibson arrived in London from Brussels with dispatches from Whitlock and to personally brief the U.S. ambassador to Britain, Walter Page, on the critical food situation in Belgium. Shaler quickly enlisted Gibson's aid to help reach the so far unreachable Belgian minister in London. In short order Shaler, with Gibson's aid, had the official backing of the Belgian government in his request to the British government to allow the food shipment through.

During this time, it became apparent to most of those involved that the coming food crisis would affect not only Brussels but the entire country, and that food relief was not a temporary issue but one that would last as long as the war. While most of the general public felt the war would be over soon, there were enough unknown factors that those working on the Belgian problem began seeing it in a longer time frame than first imagined. Overall, the scope, magnitude, and duration of the project began to grow with every conversation and every day that went by.

Regardless of the relief's ultimate size and how long the war might last, the first hurdle to overcome was the approval from Britain to ship what Shaler had already bought.

It was no small task. Arguments about the shipment were raging at the highest levels of Britain's government. To some British officials, Shaler's request of one ship of food was seen as a worthwhile humanitarian endeavor that seemed to be of limited scope. To other officials, that same shipment was seen as aiding the enemy and setting a dangerous precedent for more shipment requests.

An added element was legitimacy. A few days earlier, the shipping request had been a request from an individual, Shaler, representing the nongovernmental Comité Central. After Gibson's interceding, however, Shaler's request was backed by an official representing the Belgian government—the same government that had stood and fought the Germans and in so doing had given the British and French enough time to marshal their own forces.

But how far would the debt of honor and treaty obligations take this shipment request?

On Monday, October 5, a break came. The British Board of Trade informed the Belgian minister that approval for the shipment had been given. But as historian George Nash explained, "At this point a misunderstanding occurred that was to shape the entire outcome of the relief mission and, indeed, the course of world history." The English made a "procedural suggestion" to the Belgian minister that the food be sent from the American Embassy in London to the U.S.

Legation in Brussels. But the Belgian minister, when conveying British approval, told Ambassador Page that this was a *condition*, not a suggestion, and asked if America would accept this responsibility.

Why was this of such major importance?

As Nash states, "It was an extraordinary, probably unprecedented, request in the history of warfare: that a neutral government, far from the scene of battle, oversee the provision of foodstuffs to the capital of a belligerent country under enemy occupation."

Page had no idea how to reply. He had been moved by the personal accounts from Gibson and Shaler of the pending food crisis, but faced with what he thought was the British demand for direct U.S. patronage, he felt he could not officially act without instructions from Washington. The ambassador immediately wrote a cable to the State Department outlining the situation and asking that he be allowed to participate in such a necessary shipment to Brussels. He also added that if the State Department agreed to this, it should also seek additional guarantees from the German government in Berlin to reinforce the guarantee from Governor General von der Goltz in Brussels.

A long two days later, working faster than its usual snail's pace, the State Department contacted James W. Gerard, the U.S. ambassador in Berlin, and outlined the situation, asking that Gerard request German government approval of the plan and confirm von der Goltz's guarantees.

Meanwhile, Hoover—who was in the thick of things long before he ever officially took on Belgium relief—was in nearly constant discussions with Shaler and others. According to one historian, when he met for the first time with Page on Saturday, October 10, "the idea of the Commission for Relief in Belgium first took tangible form." Page later told others that this was the meeting at which Hoover asked if the ambassador would support him and his associates if they needed diplomatic assistance once they took up relief work for Belgium. The ambassador "approved heartily of the plan and promised to render all possible assistance." He also told Hoover that representatives from other Belgian cities, such as Liège and Charleroi, had come to see him, asking for assistance to cut through British red tape and gain American support. Page told Hoover that from then on he would refer all Belgian delegations to him. Hoover would ultimately meet with representatives of multiple Belgian cities.

During the following days, Hoover had a lot to think about on a personal level. There was his immediate family of Lou and their two young sons. What about his mining interests all over the world? He knew that if he chose to tackle the job of feeding an entire nation ensnared within a war zone—something that had never been attempted before—he would have to turn his back on his businesses, and his family would take second position so he could focus solely on the humanitarian relief. Was such sacrifice worth an effort that had no guarantee of success?

Two days later, on October 12, Hoover met again with Page, and this time he had a more concrete relief plan that dealt with the entire country of Belgium, not just individual cities.

Arguably, that is the moment Hoover was all in, committed to taking on Belgium relief.

A later account dramatically told of how Hoover struggled over what he should do and what would happen to his mining interests if he took on the relief program. That account tells of him coming to his breakfast table one morning—ten days later on October 22—and telling his visiting friend and journalist Will Irwin that he would take on the project and "let the fortune go to hell."

That certainly makes for a dramatic story perfect for publication, and it quite probably did happen as reported, but Hoover's activities in the relief process days prior to making such a proclamation argue that he was already deeply committed to taking on the relief. In fact, his prewar contemplation of entering public service, coupled with his months of thorough and wholehearted tackling of American tourist aid, reflected a man primed for taking on Belgium relief.

When he sat down with Page on October 12 with a nationwide plan for Belgium relief, he was a man already dedicated to the cause. There was still no reply from the State Department to Page's October 6 cablegram, so what Hoover was suggesting was all predicated on the ultimate U.S. acceptance of responsibility for the Shaler shipment. If that happened, other shipments would have to follow immediately if Belgium was to be saved. It was assumed these additional shipments would also fall under the protection and patronage of America and be allowed through the blockade by the British.

To organize these relief efforts, Hoover recommended to Page that a central nongovernmental American committee be formed and authorized (with the patronage of America) to administer the entire program. That program would include everything from handling and spending all funds raised worldwide (which was already starting) to the purchasing, shipping, and distribution of all food in Belgium. Hoover also recommended that the new committee absorb the American committee then in Brussels and that Dannie Heineman be asked to take charge of the work of distributing food in Belgium as vice-chairman of the new committee.

Page immediately approved the plan although his hands continued to be tied by the lack of news from the State Department.

Hoover didn't wait for State Department approval to act. He immediately began a worldwide publicity campaign to bring to light the Belgian people's suffering and potential starvation. Hoover knew that the only way he could get governments to agree to any part of the Belgium food-relief plan was to gain worldwide public sympathy and support for the Belgians. Governments would find it difficult, if not impossible, to go against a relief program that was heartily supported by their citizens.

"The greatest hope," he wrote, "of maintaining the open door for the importation of foodstuffs into Belgium and the retention of native food, was to create the widest possible public opinion on the subject. We believed that if the rights of the civil population in the matter of food could be made a question of public interest second to the war itself, then the strongest bulwark in support of the Commission would have been created."

Hoover's understanding of this concept, and of the way the world's news media worked, would serve him and his cause extremely well from the very beginning.

Finally, on October 17, the German government in Berlin agreed not to impede or requisition any food imported by the neutral Americans into Belgium. That was followed two days later by the State Department's approval of the Shaler food shipment.

The ever-impatient Hoover knew that the key to the whole situation was the German guarantee, so on October 17, before the State Department's approval, he generated a major story that went out over the newswires. It announced "a comprehensive scheme for the organization of an American committee with the purpose of taking over the entire task of furnishing food and other supplies to the civil population of Belgium, so far as American relief measures are concerned, under the official supervision of the American Government." This committee would also "concentrate and systematize" all funds and food donated to Belgium relief, and Page had "consulted" with Hoover, who "would be one of the leading members of the committee, which would also include leading Americans in Brussels." While the release did mention the committee was a "proposal," there was little doubt that creation of the entire committee was a fait accompli.

Hoover was going to save Belgium, and no one was going to stop him.

The CRB and the CN Are Born

Even with a determined Hoover steering the proposed relief, there was one more critical person needed before the Belgium relief program could be fully established—Émile Francqui.

As the concept of Belgium relief began taking shape in London, Dannie Heineman back in Brussels had come to the same conclusion as those in London: Brussels food relief had to become Belgium food relief, or the entire country would ultimately starve. It took him days to convince Francqui, the Comité Central, and the two neutral patrons, Whitlock and Villalobar.

On Thursday, October 15, the committee met and decided to extend its operations to the entire country—even before the members had heard that Shaler's initial food shipment was approved. It was an audacious but critical move if Belgium was to be given any chance at all. The Comité Central immediately petitioned and received von der Goltz's approval to expand the program nationwide. The next step was to send a delegation of Francqui and Baron Léon Lambert, accompanied by Gibson, to London to secure British and American approval of the program.

And thus, two major forces of nature—Herbert Hoover and Émile Francqui—were about to collide. In a surprising coincidence of life, they had met before at the turn of the century in China when they were on opposite sides of a major court battle. To say they disliked each other was a vast understatement. Now, in a fascinating twist of fate, their ability to work closely together would dictate the survival of a nation.

Reportedly, when Francqui was told before the London meeting that Hoover was the man leading the American relief for Belgium, he had shouted: "What! That man Hoover who was in China? He is a crude, vulgar sort of individual." Those were some of the worst insults a Belgian of prominence could toss at any man. While it's true that the recorder of that scene did not personally witness it, the words sound so Francqui-esque that it's more than likely they accurately reflected the Belgian's reaction, if not his exact words.

As for Hoover's personal reaction when he first saw Francqui again, he left behind no immediate personal recollection of how he really felt. Whitlock, who was not in London to witness their first meeting, wrote that "gossips" reported both men had stood silently for a long moment staring at each other; then, as if breaking a spell, they had shaken hands and gotten down to business. While they would each take strategic opportunities in the coming months and years to disadvantage the other—to the serious detriment of the relief—they never betrayed their public appearance of polite teamwork.

At this first gathering in London, they both were pragmatic enough to realize they could not do the job without each other. Hoover had seen the entire operation as solely American because he had a neutral country's freedom and diplomatic influence to obtain the food and ship it into Belgium. But he also realized he lacked a practical way of distributing the food once it entered the country. Francqui, who believed the entire operation could be run by Belgians, knew he had the foundations of a nationwide distribution network, but he also knew the belligerents would not allow Belgians to have the necessary freedoms to buy and ship the food into Belgium.

On October 22—the day Hoover reportedly stated "let the fortune go to hell"—he and Francqui formally agreed to a cooperative relief program between the American Commission for Relief in Belgium (soon changed to the more-inclusive Commission for Relief in Belgium, CRB) and the Comité Central de Secours et d'Alimentation (soon to be transformed into the nationwide Comité National de Secours et d'Alimentation, CN, when Francqui returned to Brussels). As to the overall concept behind the two organizations, both Hoover and Francqui agreed that relief would have two prongs: provide food at a slight profit for those who could pay; and provide outright charity for those who couldn't. The profit from one should pay for the other.

In essence, both men wanted to reestablish commerce in a country where it had died. They wanted to restimulate the food chain so that it could become self-perpetuating while also providing funds for the charity portion of the relief.

Taking the most important commodity—wheat—as an example, this meant that the wheat imported by the CRB for Belgian mills would be paid for by the millers, who would pay Francqui's group. The millers would be paid for the flour by the bakers, who would pay a portion of all sales to Francqui's group. The bakers would be paid for the bread by those who could afford to pay. Francqui's CN would collect the funds from various points of Belgian sales, provide subsidies for certain portions of relief, and ultimately pay, through complicated transfers not yet agreed to, the CRB for the original imported wheat. Prices for everything would be set to provide a small profit, and the whole system would be primed by the operating capital that came from donations and governmental subsidies that Hoover and Francqui hoped to secure.

But how much food was needed per month to feed more than 7 million Belgians? An initial goal was set by Francqui of 80,000 tons per month. It was a significant amount, but as Hoover was quick to say, Belgium normally imported at least three times that amount, more than 250,000 tons a month. The estimated 80,000 tons per month would translate to approximately 10 ounces of food per person per day, or according to Hoover, "considerably less than one-half of a soldier's ration."

The organizational concepts behind the CRB and the CN sounded deceptively simple, more a matter of logistics than anything else: The CRB would buy and transport food to the neutral port of Rotterdam, where the supplies would be transferred onto canal barges and hauled to various central warehouses via Belgium's extensive canal network. Once at these distribution centers, the food would be transferred from CRB supervision to CN responsibility. The CN would prepare and distribute the food through its extensive communal network to more than 7 million Belgians in a ration system that would sell the food to those who could pay and give free sustenance to those who could not pay.

The whole operation hinged on two critical agreements with the belligerents: British approval to allow such imports through its blockade, and German guarantees not to take any imports for themselves.

In theory, the entire relief program as envisioned by Hoover and Francqui was straightforward and clear-cut.

In reality, nothing was further from the truth.

CRB Delegates—A Necessary Prerequisite

Because the English did not trust the Germans to keep their hands off any imported food, they stipulated that an unspecified number of Americans be in Belgium to act as U.S. Minister Whitlock's "delegates" to guarantee the Germans honor their no-requisition commitment and to supervise the food until it was turned over to the CN for distribution. From this one stipulation was born the CRB delegate, an ultimately fascinating and multifaceted category of volunteer who would become, to most Belgians, the true heart and soul of the American side of relief.

But finding and recruiting American CRB delegates was not an easy task. Where could Hoover find U.S. volunteers ready to drop everything for an extended period of time, work for free, go into the unknown world of German-occupied Belgium, and do a job no one could explain in detail? And with a transatlantic crossing taking a week or two, coupled with recruitment time, it might be months before American men with the right experience could be found and brought over. But Hoover needed people immediately.

There were two pathways from which Hoover found willing recruits.

The first pathway was serendipity. By November, 10 to 15 men had floated into the CRB like driftwood onto a beach and become delegates. Jarvis Bell was in Rotterdam working with Captain John F. Lucey; Edward Curtis was the courier between Rotterdam and Brussels; Frederick W. Meert, who had attended universities in Belgium before the war, took charge of Belgium's Brabant Province; Robinson Smith, author of *The Life of Cervantes*, appeared one day in Brussels and became chief delegate of Hainaut Province; James Dangerfield, who had worked two years in Ghent, became a delegate in Flanders; and E. E. Hunt, a freelance war correspondent, would soon join the group through contacts in Holland.

Others would join them in a similarly random fashion through the next month, with most of them being young, adventuresome, and usually from good universities. They included George S. Jackson (Harvard), Amos D. Johnson Jr. (University of Kansas), T. Harwood Stacy (University of Texas), Carleton B. Gibson (University of Alabama), Floyd S. Bryant (University of Nevada and Oxford), William M. Sullivan (Brown and Oxford), Frank H. Gailor (University of the South and Oxford), and William H. Sperry (no university listed).

These first responders who had come to the CRB through serendipity were businessmen and artists, war correspondents and book authors—bound together and driven by the common desire to aid a nation in trouble. Some had lived in Belgium for years, started families, and loved the country like a second home. Others had helped Hoover with his American tourist relief program in London before volunteering for the CRB. A few were simply in Europe, had heard of the proposed relief program, and volunteered to help.

While each one of them was critical at the time for helping the organization move forward, they represented a haphazard way of recruiting that was not practical or reliable for the huge relief program on the horizon.

The same could be said for the second pathway from which Hoover found recruits; it was nearly as unorthodox—Oxford University. The school term was almost over, and numerous American students (most in the Rhodes scholar program) were about to start six weeks of winter break.

One student, 25-year-old Perrin C. Galpin, had seen articles about the CRB and its need for volunteers to go into German-occupied Belgium. He had written to Hoover and was immediately enlisted by the CRB's executive team in London to recruit more students. Galpin had no difficulty finding willing participants, as their youthful spirit of adventure was aroused by the thought of walking into the unknown to help a starving people trapped in a brutal occupation. As the student organizer, Galpin even decided which students would go—in direct contradiction to later assertions that Hoover had approved every delegate.

By early December, 25 Oxford students had signed up and entered Belgium. These idealistic, enthusiastic, rather naïve young men—one of them was only 19 years old—had to deal with battle-hardened German officers and conservative, buttoned-downed Belgian businessmen as they tried to figure out what they were supposed to do. Their entry into international humanitarian relief work was by no means an easy one.

Before the first group of 10 students left Britain, they met with Hoover. Edgar Rickard wrote to Galpin that "Mr. Hoover gave them a nice little talk," and added, "We think these chaps are going to prove quite adequate for the work." At the meeting, which was documented by journalist and CRB member Ben Allen, Hoover told the young men: "When this war is over, the thing that will stand out will not be the number of dead and wounded, but the record of those efforts which went to save life. Therefore you should in your daily service remember that in this duty you have not only a service to render to these people, but that you have a duty to this Commission, and above all have a duty to your own country."

Their biggest challenge, Hoover believed, was to maintain a total sense of neutrality no matter what they saw, heard, or felt. He told the young men: "You must forget that the greatest war in history is being waged. You have no interest in it other than the feeding of the Belgian people, and you must school yourselves to a realization that you have to us and to your country a sacred obligation of absolute neutrality in every word and deed."

How those student volunteers would react to Belgium—and how Belgium would react to them—was a huge unknown. That was just one of many uncertainties that plagued Hoover, the CRB, Francqui, and the CN as 1914 came to an end. Every day seemed to bring new challenges that threatened to shut down the operation. How would the relief be funded? Would the military men from both sides who opposed the program allow it to survive? Where would the food come from? Who would provide ships? Where to find a steady stream of reliable CRB delegates? Could the American delegates remain neutral in the face of the Germans' harsh rule? Would Belgian civilians fight back against the occupation, and, if so, how? And would Hoover and Francqui truly put aside their animosity?

It was anyone's guess whether or not the relief—and the people of Belgium—would last through the winter, let alone the war.

3

The Students Head into Belgium

Arriving in Rotterdam on Saturday evening, December 5, 1914, the first 10 Oxford students who had agreed to become Commission for Relief in Belgium delegates were a bit stunned by how quickly events had transpired. A few days before, they had been university students (mostly Rhodes scholars), and now they were in neutral Holland preparing to go into German-occupied Belgium to do a job that was anything but clear.

"What we were to do, no one exactly knew," said Emil Hollmann, one of the first 10, who was 24. "We had visions of sitting on the top of box cars or sleeping on the decks of small canal barges in their long journeys from Rotterdam into Belgium. . . . We expected to see German savages prowling around ready at the slightest provocation to scalp women and children and perhaps provoke a quarrel with us for the same purpose!"

They had more questions than answers. Neither Hoover nor anyone else had been able to say what the work would entail. The CRB was—by the necessity of attempting such massive relief for the first time—making it up as it went along. And because conditions within sealed-off Belgium were sketchy at best, especially when it came to infrastructure, few outside the country knew what to expect within the country.

For instance, Millard K. Shaler, the American mining engineer who had arranged for the first food-relief purchase and had become a member of the CRB executive team, had made a statement widely circulated in the British press back in November. He had said that each delegate "will see that the shipments of food supplies arrive intact, and who must be informed of any infraction by German troops of the guarantee given by Baron von der Goltz. When this delegate, covered by the American flag, learns of such infraction, he will verify it, and immediately call attention to it, when the Ministers of Spain and America will make the proper representations to the German authorities."

Reality would prove that definition woefully inadequate.

The 10 newly minted CRB delegates from Oxford were Carlton G. Bowden (23, University of the South); Emil Hollmann (24, Stanford University); David T. Nelson (23, University of North Dakota); Tracy B. Kittredge (23, University of California, the only non-Rhodes scholar); Walter C. Lowdermilk (26, University of Arizona); Scott H. Paradise (23, Yale University); Richard H. Simpson (25, University of Indiana); George F. Spaulding (24, University of Arizona); William W. Stratton (22, University of Utah); and Laurence C. "Duke" Wellington (24, Williams College).

All 10—and the next wave of 15 who would follow a week later—had been chosen by a fellow Oxford student, 25-year-old Perrin Galpin, who went to Belgium in the second wave. As Hoover telegraphed Galpin back on November 30, "We propose to leave the selection of the ten men entirely in your hands as we have confidence in your ability, and, furthermore after our conversation on Friday you are aware of the conditions which we impose."

Practically speaking, Hoover simply didn't have the time to choose delegates as he dealt with much larger issues and crises. He knew these young men weren't the ideal candidates for such a job, but he had no real choice. The time and distance from America made it impossible to wait for the perfect CRB delegates. For that matter, what constituted a "perfect" delegate was still unknown.

It all meant that the efforts to find the right volunteers had the built-in probability that not all CRB delegates would work out. Numerous CRB delegates admitted later there were some bad seeds, but they always maintained the bad seeds were few and far between. In reality, they were more than some would imagine, but it's difficult to get an accurate count because the successful delegates rarely referred to those who had washed out by name, and CRB histories simply never mention them.

What is known is that at least six of the first 25 Oxford students to enter Belgium were never listed by the CRB as having served as delegates. The assumption is that they either did not complete their agreed-upon service or did so to such an unsatisfactory degree that the CRB did not want to include them in official records.

Thought of failure was never mentioned on the Sunday morning, December 6, when the first 10 Oxford students gathered at the CRB office in Rotterdam. Failure, however, could quite possibly have been on the mind of Captain John F. Lucey, the director of the CRB Rotterdam office, as he looked at the youthful, expectant faces waiting for word of where they would be assigned and what they would do in Belgium. Lucey was many years and multiple jobs away from the inexperienced naïveté of most of the Oxford students facing him.

When the CRB was first formed in London in late October, Lucey was one of Hoover's executive volunteers. Hoover had immediately sent him to Rotterdam to begin the arduous task of setting up the main CRB shipping office between the outside world and German-occupied Belgium.

Hoover couldn't have picked a better, more resourceful, and hardworking man. Born in County Kerry, Ireland, Lucey and his family had moved to America when he was very young and settled in New York City. From a young age, Lucey had been independent. He first took a job as a newsboy and left home in 1888 when he was only 14, heading west and becoming a newsagent for the Santa Fe Railroad between Albuquerque and Los Angeles. At 18 he joined the army. Later, he took part in the Alaska gold rush, then turned to the new industry of oil. First working in the California oil fields as a roustabout, he then moved into management before starting his own firm, Lucey Manufacturing Corporation. With hard work and a lot of traveling, both in America and overseas, he was able to turn his company into the second-largest oil-well supply company in the world in 12 short years.

A good-looking, clean-shaven man with a prominent Roman nose and dark hair swept back and tight to the head, Lucey stood over six feet tall and had the erect posture of a military man. He liked being addressed as Captain Lucey. An outdoorsman who loved golf, he was in perfect health at 40 years old and was "endowed with an enthusiastic and optimistic nature" that had never left him through his various experiences. He had slogged through Alaskan snow, wrestled with drilling pipes and roughnecks, and survived boardroom brawls in the cutthroat business world. Successful and financially independent, Lucey probably felt there was nothing he couldn't do, and if he did fail, he knew it would be simply a matter of trying again until he found a way to succeed. He also shared an important trait with Hoover: impatience.

By November Lucey had been able to set up the CRB Rotterdam office in a 100-year-old mansion, secure permission from the Dutch government to import all the supplies needed for Belgium relief, and arrange with the German Consulate in Rotterdam to provide safe-conduct passes for the needed food and for the canal barges that would carry most of it into Belgium. The Dutch government also provided free use of the state telegraph lines to the CRB and even agreed to carry free of charge a certain amount of food per day from Rotterdam south to Liège once the system was set up.

A substantial clerical staff was also growing for what Lucey envisioned would be a blizzard of paperwork necessary to ensure Hoover's demand for scrupulous accounting of all transactions and activities. Out on the docks, stevedores, cranes, and modern floating elevators would transfer the cargoes from the oceangoing vessels to canal barges that would take the supplies throughout Belgium. (Most Belgian trains were not available because of use by the German military.)

Lucey's first major success came on Monday, November 2—only eight days after the official founding of the CRB. It was then that the first food, stowed in eight canal barges, or lighters, was ready to go. Towed by four tugs, they slowly made their way out of Rotterdam harbor bound for Brussels. The holds of each barge were sealed, and a large sign stated in English, "Consigned to the American

Minister in Brussels for the Comité National de Secours et d'Alimentation." On the door of each lighter captain's cabin was a copy of von der Goltz's guarantee and his request that German officials give the shipment safe conduct. The crews were all neutral Dutch who carried with them individual German passes allowing them to travel to Brussels and back. This was a "Flotilla of Mercy," as one English newspaper christened it.

By early December the CRB Rotterdam office was already the bustling and rapidly growing shipping arm of the CRB. A large staff of Dutch, Belgian, and American clerks was scattered throughout the building, and Dutch and Flemish barge captains and dock laborers were always waiting in line for an audience with someone who could either put them to work or solve a problem they had encountered while employed by the CRB. The halls and various offices were filled with a nearly constant cacophony of ringing phones, clattering typewriters, and buzzing conversations.

When the 10 Oxford students showed up at the Rotterdam office on Sunday, December 6, people were already hard at work and Lucey was there to greet them. One CRB delegate described Lucey as a "nervous, big, beardless American . . . who left his business . . . to organize and direct a great trans-shipping office in an alien land for an alien people." With the 10 students, the captain spent little time on the preliminaries, getting straight to work on instructing them as to what he knew of Belgian conditions, what he thought they would be doing, and what he felt needed to be done.

One of the students, David T. Nelson, wrote his parents about the meeting saying, "You will be surprised when you hear the magnitude of this undertaking, and of the extraordinary difficulties under which it must be carried on."

Nelson went on to outline in general terms what some of those difficulties were: "Many of the canals are useless for navigation; the military have right of way on all railroads; and lastly the very fact that a war is in progress renders everyone liable to suspicion, arrest, and detention."

In a confident tone that marked so many Americans of the time, Nelson stated, "The Americans have been hampered so far by lack of men and lack of supplies, but when our men get established throughout the country, and the organization is perfected, we will be able to handle the situation, for we already have some thirty or forty ships on the way to Holland."

Nelson had turned 23 on September 10 and had been born and raised in North Dakota by parents who had emigrated from Norway. He was about five foot 10 inches with a full head of hair and a face that at rest was as unreadable as the prairies he had grown up around. But his smile was open and straightforward, and he was known to be trustworthy and hardworking.

David T. Nelson had just turned 23 when he started at Oxford University as a Rhodes scholar. He would be in the first wave of Oxford students who would go into Belgium in early December 1914. (Public domain; John P. Nelson.)

After graduating in 1912 from Luther College in Decorah, Iowa, Nelson spent the next year as principal and teacher at the high school in Hannaford, North Dakota. He then moved to Bisbee, North Dakota, and taught in a one-room school while studying Greek in his spare time to prepare for his year as a Rhodes scholar. During the summer of 1914, as the world braced for war, Nelson rode around North Dakota on his new Indian Motorcycle, saying his goodbyes to relatives and friends.

In Rotterdam during the first meeting with Captain Lucey, Nelson was so impressed with the operation and with Lucey that he wrote his parents, "One feels prouder of being an American after meeting and talking with him." The young first-year Rhodes scholar already knew, before he had started doing any relief work, that "our work goes on day and night, seven days a week." He even predicted that for the Oxford students this would not be a six-week jaunt, as they had signed up for: "This job is not a three month's or six month's job; it is a one or two year's job, for even if the war should stop today, the Belgians must be fed until they can gather in the next harvest." And he was already clear on his intentions, even before experiencing one day in occupied Belgium: "I shall very likely stay by this work for six months or longer, if I can arrange matters at Oxford." He had become a convert to the cause and even ended one of his letters to his parents by stating, "I hope North Dakota, which is prospering because of this war, will be generous in her aid to the Belgians."

Nelson's Difficult Entry into Belgium

Lucey assigned Nelson to be the CRB delegate in Liège, a large city in southeast Belgium. He would first travel by train to the Dutch town of Maastricht with Emil Hollmann, who had been assigned to Maastricht. Lucey had tasked Hollmann with establishing a central station and a forwarding and transshipping office at Maastricht because all supplies for the provinces of Liège and Limburg, and a lot for Namur, would come by rail or canal barge via Maastricht.

As the two men prepared to leave Rotterdam, Nelson wrote his parents that they needed to be careful when writing him. All letters should be sent to Rotterdam in care of Captain Lucey. As for content, Nelson warned "under no condition to write anything which might be called into question by the authorities. The Germans have been very obliging, but when the lives of so many are at stake, we cannot afford to take any chances. Besides, we have to deal not only with the Germans, but also with the British and the French, who from the strictly military point of view are not in favor of the work we are doing, and have even placed considerable difficulties in our way."

Nelson's entry into Belgium would not be the easiest, and it reflected just how confusing the situation still was. When he and Hollmann reached Maastricht on Tuesday, December 8, Hollmann began working on his assignment while Nelson began to arrange for another food train from Holland to Liège in Belgium. To complicate matters, Nelson discovered that the train would not be allowed through the border due to the decision of some Dutch stationmasters south of Maastricht.

Nelson—quickly learning that one of the most important characteristics for a CRB delegate was improvisation—decided he needed to talk directly with those stationmasters. He found a ride the next day in a motorcar from Maastricht south seven miles to the small Dutch town of Eijsden (not to be confused with the Belgian town of Eisden, which was north of Maastricht), where the train's permits were being held up. Once there, "after scouring the town I got to the burgomaster's chateau and managed to secure a man who could speak English as well as Dutch, French, and German. You need all to deal with a Dutch official. A Dutchman is without question the slowest person on earth." The volunteer he found to help him with the difficult Dutch officials was a "very nice fellow; count or something, I heard them call him. He thanked me very much for what we Americans are doing and wouldn't hear of my thanking him."

Once Nelson and his volunteer had convinced the stationmasters to allow the train through and secured clearances, permits, and scheduling for the oncoming train, another problem arose. The motorcar that had given him a ride had left, and he had no way to get to his next stop, the Belgian village of Visé, which was across the border and about five miles south of Eijsden. There were no motorcars to be had, and the Dutch stationmaster in Eijsden would not allow him to ride on the train that would come through later. "Verboden, you know," Nelson was told.

The only thing to do was walk. But he had his valise with him, and it was too heavy to carry such a distance. With little confidence he'd ever see it again, the CRB delegate left his suitcase at the station to be forwarded to him whenever possible. "I shall entertain no hope till I actually lay my hands on it again."

Ever the pragmatist, Nelson took a moment "to eat a little lunch before starting on the walk, as rations may be rather scarce in Belgium." At the café, none of his three languages helped: "The waitress at this little café knows no English, and so little French or German that it is painful to try to get anything, but I finally got her to bring forth some bread and cheese and cold meat and, of course, beer. I didn't have to mention that." In the café he had written a letter to his family. He signed off, "Well, now for the Germans—with much love to you all. Dave."

On that cold Wednesday afternoon, December 9, as the sun was getting low in the sky, Nelson—sans suitcase and carrying only the clothes on his back, his wallet, his ever-present little Lefax notebook, identity papers, and permits to enter Belgium—began his lonely walk into German-held territory.

The Second Wave Hits

The same day Nelson was walking into Belgium wondering what he had gotten into, the second wave of Oxford students, 15 in all, departed England for Rotterdam. The group was informally shepherded by Galpin, who had been the primary organizer and decision-maker of the Oxford men in the first two waves. Galpin had always wanted to go but had not included himself in the first 10 because he was unsure he could give the CRB the minimum amount of six weeks Hoover had asked for. But Hoover and others kept at him to go to Belgium, and his thoughts continued to return to the importance of the work until he agreed to go.

While in Rotterdam, waiting to leave for Belgium, Galpin wrote his brother in a final letter home: "Since tomorrow we leave civilization as represented by a good country with cheap cigars that is not at war [Holland], I suppose that this will be the last news from me . . . for some time. . . . Tomorrow we meet militarism in person and then may learn a little of a new phase of existence." Galpin, just like the other new recruits, was taken aback by the sheer magnitude of the endeavor. "The amazing size of the work appalls me more and more for it is worldwide in its organization as you probably know. But I will leave all superlatives to the official press agent."

Lucey assigned Galpin the task of overseeing all CRB delegates in Belgium. Galpin wrote his brother: "My job will be the general supervision and control of the eleven different distribution centers in Belgium. I will have headquarters in Brussels where the system is working ok, and with a motor and a traffic man to go with me." Galpin would quickly find out that this job, and the jobs of the others, wasn't as well-defined and established as he thought.

Galpin and most of the 15 men were sent on to Brussels rather than assigned to a specific province. When they reached Brussels, they met up with many of the first 10 from Oxford. The CRB had arranged for all of the Oxford students in Brussels to stay at the Palace Hotel in the lower, older part of town. *Baedeker's Belgium and Holland* tour book described the hotel as "a new and luxurious establishment opened in 1909" that boasted a bathroom with each room and a "high-class restaurant and frequented taverne." After the city's surrender, the Germans had requisitioned most of the rooms for their officers. For the Oxford students, the luxurious establishment was a far cry from the countryside camping and sleeping on top of train cars that they had initially expected. The Brussels hotel also instantly exposed them to more German officers than they had ever thought they'd see in their six weeks' work.

But the hotel was not where the new CRB delegates wanted to be. They were ready to work, but CRB executives in Brussels had not yet determined how best to utilize them. In these early days—with American engineer Dannie Heineman's Brussels office often focused more on German relations and Comité National matters than getting the Oxford men moving—the newly created CRB delegates in Brussels didn't have much to do.

As one CRB history related, "In those first days everything was in a very chaotic condition. It was naturally impossible to create a smoothly working organization to handle so tremendous a task in the short space of a few weeks. When the first batch of Rhodes scholars arrived at Brussels . . . no one in the Brussels office seemed to know what they were to do, save that they were to represent the Commission in some matter in the provinces. The only emphatic instructions which they had received were that they were to be punctiliously neutral in every word and deed and were to avoid any sort of friction with the German authorities. This had been intimated to them at London, repeated emphatically and eloquently at Rotterdam by Captain Lucey, and reiterated tearfully but sternly in Brussels by Jarvis Bell. They spent several days, or even weeks, alternating between the Palace Hotel and the Rue de Naples [CRB office] before they were all assigned to their posts and given their instructions."

Heineman's lack of focus in getting the delegates into the field was a serious issue that Captain Lucey and Hoover were concerned about. Hoover would deal with it shortly.

Nelson's Perspective on the Germans

One person who wasn't sitting around waiting for something to do was David Nelson. With no suitcase and little besides the clothes on his back, Nelson was imagining the worst as he approached the Dutch-Belgian border.

What happened next caught him off guard. Nothing. "It was a distinct surprise to me after the picture I had formed of being stopped and obliged to show my papers at every cross-road." Customs officials quickly passed him through to Belgium and the town of Visé. He walked among the ruined parts of town before going to the train station. There he ended up chatting with the German stationmasters before taking a train to nearby Liège. From the station in Liège, he caught a ride with a German merchant in his motorcar to the city's Grand Hotel, which sat on one of the major squares, *Place Saint-Lambert.*

Nelson would find that he was not the lone American in Liège. Albert Heingartner was the U.S. Consul in the city and would help the CRB wherever and whenever possible. George S. Jackson—a Harvard grad still in his twenties who had joined the CRB and entered Belgium in November—was already working as the province's CRB chief delegate and would be supervising Nelson.

Jackson and Nelson had their hands full, for Liège was one of Belgium's major cities, and as the capital of Liège Province, it boasted a university, a bishop, and more than 175,000 residents. *Baedeker's Belgium and Holland* declared that Liège "lies in a strikingly picturesque situation. The ancient and extensive city rises on the lofty bank of the broad Meuse. . . . Numerous factory-chimneys bear testimony to the industry of the inhabitants, while the richly-cultivated valley contributes greatly to enhance the picturesque effect."

Because Liège was at the confluence of the Meuse and the Ourthe rivers, an island was part of the city center. It was connected to the right bank by five bridges and to the left bank by six bridges and a small iron footbridge. The main part of town, with its principal buildings and churches, was on the left bank, while numerous factories and the homes of workers and artisans were on the right bank.

Before the war, Liège had been a prosperous city due to the surrounding coalfields and the numerous manufacturing industries that had grown up over generations. In an unusual turn, one of the city's major businesses had for years utilized laborers' homes. As explained by Baedeker's, "One of the chief branches of industry is the manufacture of weapons of all kinds, which have enjoyed both a European and a Transatlantic reputation since the end of the 18th century. The pieces are made and mounted by the workmen in their own houses. These mechanics, 40,000 in number, work at their own risk, for a piece containing the slightest flaw is at once rejected." Additional industries in and around the city included zinc foundries, engine factories, and cycle and motor works. The city was also home to the royal gun factory, the cannon foundry, and the Société de St. Léonard, which made steam locomotives.

The people in such a highly industrialized city were not only hardworking but also surprisingly free-spirited and resentful of any authority that tried to restrict them. In a history that included numerous invasions by various countries, the residents of Liège "frequently manifested a fierce and implacable spirit of hostility towards those who have attempted to infringe their privileges."

Couple such spirit with the city's valuable industries, and it wasn't surprising that 12 fortresses encircled the city within three to five miles and made Liège one of the most daunting fortifications along the Meuse. It was the first major city the Germans had attacked in their August invasion, primarily because it sat within the Meuse Valley, which they needed to traverse to reach France. Liège's forts and 30,000 troops had slowed down the Germans for a critical 12 days in August, but they were ultimately no match for the German Army and five days of constant bombardment by massive Big Bertha artillery of the encircling forts.

As Nelson noted, however, much of the city was still intact. "When I entered Liège I was surprised to find that the city had not suffered at all from the bombardment. It may be that in the outskirts some traces may be found; I have not yet been around the city to any extent. But the main portion of the city is absolutely intact with the exception of a few buildings opposite the University which were destroyed because of a riot, and of course the bridges, several of which were torn down by the Belgians. The Germans, however, are repairing them rapidly."

For Nelson, the first experiences with Germans were what he had hoped for. Unlike most of the CRB delegates, he was self-proclaimed "pro-German" and found it difficult to believe many of the stories he had read about German atrocities. He wrote his parents that during his journey into Belgium he was "stopped by no 'haughty German officers,'" as he had been forewarned about. At Visé, he wrote that two German stationmasters, once they learned he was American, had "brought forth cigars and a bottle of German beer, and we talked, with slight interruptions, for two hours or more. (I speak wretched German and worse French, I might add.)"

After nearly a week in Liège, Nelson wrote to his parents more about the Germans: "I have found them uniformly courteous. They mind their own business strictly and give the Belgians great freedom when one considers the tenseness of the situation." The city curfew was at seven in the evening, but Nelson said the Germans were relatively lax about enforcing the exact time, and that "whenever I have observed them in cafés or elsewhere, [they] pay for all they get."

The only thing he didn't like about the Germans was their loud cars. "The military autos go by early and late and their horns make an infernal noise, for they have right of way and must give everyone warning to scatter."

Near the end of his long letter, Nelson wrote: "I suppose you will say that my pro-German sympathies have not vanished yet, but frankly, after seeing what has so far come under my observation, I can honestly say that I now feel justified in not believing the atrocious stories that reached America from London. . . . And I say this not because this letter will come under the eye of the German censor . . . but rather because I think that justice should be rendered where justice is due."

It was Monday, December 14, the start of the first week in Belgium for Nelson, and his feelings for the Germans were practically the same as when he had left America three months before. And they would not begin to change for a few more months.

A German Christmas in Belgium

In fact, two weeks later on Christmas day, Nelson wrote his father a long letter that was filled with how he spent a very German Christmas. While he had celebrated the night before with the Belgian family he was staying with (Belgians celebrated more Saint Nicholas Day, December 6, than Christmas), on Christmas day Nelson took off the first day from work since arriving in Liège. He seemed to long for a Christmas that was closer to his Scandinavian heritage. He found it with all things German. He first bought *Die Woche*, a German weekly publication, and then "to complete the German part of it" he went to the Canterbury café and ordered "my mug of 'Münchener,'" which he termed "the last word in beer." He told his family there were only two places in Liège where he had found Münchener, and the Canterbury was one of them. It was also "much frequented by the Germans and in fact is German-owned and operated."

Best of all, in the center of the café was a "Weihnachtsbaum," Christmas tree, that Nelson described as "decked out with Christmas tinsel and ornaments and lighted with electric lights." He wrote that "the Germans have their Christmas-trees wherever they are stationed. It is almost touching to see how they cling to their old customs in spite of the war. It is one of the most admirable traits of their character."

As the afternoon wore on, Nelson sat at his table drinking his beer, reading his German paper, soaking in the Christmas atmosphere of the café, and finally writing his father a letter detailing how he was spending the day. It had been three weeks without a letter from any of his family—a situation he had not faced at Oxford, as a letter had usually arrived at least every few days from his parents or siblings. "One loses all sense of time while here," he wrote in his journal, "and it seems weeks between mail." Hearing no word from his family was something that bothered him, and he mentioned it in nearly every letter he wrote.

His Christmas letter was no different: "If you have received my former letter from Liège you have been better off than I. To date I haven't had a word from America or England either since I left Oxford the 3rd or 4th of December." But this was wartime, he knew, and he was cut off from the rest of the world by what Hoover called a "ring of steel." No doubt Nelson's father felt the longing in the young man's words when he signed off the long letter: "Well—I have monopolised this table for an hour and a half now, and perhaps it is time for me to leave. With much love to you, mother, Hafe, Karsten, Hegges and all. Your son, David."

It would be a while longer before the CRB delegate who was so far away from home finally turned his back on the cheerful café, with its fine German beer and decorated Christmas tree, and headed out into the cold night to begin his lonely walk back to his Belgian host family.

Within a few months, however, Nelson would change his perspective on the Germans. As he became more involved in the CRB work, became better acquainted with the Belgians, and had much closer contact with the Germans in a new position in northern France, his feelings about them would be cast in a much different, much harsher light.

4

Brussels

War Settles Heavily on the City

Occupation fell over Brussels like a black mourning shawl.

Before the war, the city was the "proud Paris of the North," boasting an air of gaiety and refinement that was heightened by magnificent architecture. The charming old section of town had crooked little streets and the stunning *grand place* (main square), which Baedeker's tour book proclaimed was "one of the finest medieval squares in existence and, whether seen by daylight, when lighted up at night, or by moonlight, produces a striking effect." The square was anchored by the city's inspiring *hôtel de ville* (town hall), "one of the noblest and most beautiful buildings of its kind in the [region]." Begun in 1402, the building's facade was in the Gothic style, and its 370-foot-tall tower was completed in 1454.

The city boasted fashionable cafés, luxurious restaurants, wine rooms, and simpler brasseries (taverns) that offered a wide variety of food and drink. And shopping for Belgian lace, chocolates, and *haute couture* was a leisurely pastime for many tourists. On the edges of the old part of town were beautiful, broad, tree-lined boulevards where ancient city walls used to stand. To the west, along a slight ridge, was the fashionable upper section of town, and to the south and southeast were the "new quarters" of town, which included *Quartier Leopold,* named after the country's first king.

By the winter of 1914–1915, occupied Brussels was a totally different city. It had started the moment the German Army had marched in. That first day, as Hugh Gibson described it, "all telephone and telegraph wires were cut. All railroad traffic was stopped. The post office was taken over by the military and the postal service came to an abrupt end. The newspaper offices were closed, the presses seized and a ban was placed on all printing."

Gibson had known the city only a short while before the war. He, like his boss, U.S. Minister Brand Whitlock, was new to Brussels but, unlike Whitlock, he was not new to diplomatic service. The two were totally different men who had very different backgrounds.

Thirty-one-year-old Hugh Gibson was the secretary of the U.S. Legation in Belgium when the war broke out. He was energetic, passionate, and filled with a lively, cutting sense of humor. He always seemed to be the busiest person at the legation. (Public domain; author's archives.)

At 31, Gibson was energetic, passionate, and filled with a lively, cutting sense of humor that was never far from the surface. Photos showed him to be a slight, well-groomed, impeccably dressed, and stylish man. A broad forehead was part of an open face, with eyes wide open in perpetual curiosity and a slight, upturned smile that gave him an impish look.

Gibson had been born in Los Angeles to a banker father and a schoolteacher mother. In his early years, he was a "delicate child" who had contracted polio but was one of the lucky ones who did not suffer any lasting ill effects. Because of his health issues, however, he spent most of his early years being privately tutored by his mother, Mary, who believed in a woman's right to vote and passed that belief on to her son. They were very close, especially after his father died when Hugh was 18. While the family was not rich, the father had left enough money for the pair to travel for a year throughout Europe and to finance Hugh for four years at the École Libre des Sciences Politiques in Paris. In 1907, while in his early twenties, he graduated with honors and returned to America where he joined the Foreign Service.

Like many others in the diplomatic corps, he began by pinballing from job to job, serving as secretary of the U.S. Legation in Honduras (1908); second secretary of the American Embassy in London (1909–1910); private secretary to the assistant secretary of state in Washington, D.C. (1910–1911); and secretary of the U.S. Legation in Havana, Cuba (1911–1913).

In April 1914, he arrived in Brussels as the new secretary to the legation. He had been promised it would be a quiet post where he could take a breather from the more stressful positions he had held. On July 4, 1914, only one month before the start of the war, Gibson wrote in his journal, "After years of hard work and revolutions and wars and rumours of war, the change to this quiet post has been most welcome and I have wallowed in the luxury of having time to play.

"For the last year or two," he continued, "I have looked forward to just such a post as this, where nothing ever happens, where there is no earthly chance of being called out of bed in the middle of the night to see the human race brawling over its difference."

The post to Belgium had been everything Gibson had wanted—at least for a few months. Then his innate curiosity and "longing for something more active began to manifest itself." He wrote to the Department of State that he was "ready whenever there might be need of my services to go where there was work to be done."

Less than a month later, the war began and the quiet post was transformed into the eye of the raging storm that was World War I. Gibson quickly rose to the challenge. During the invasion, he risked his life to travel around Belgium as a neutral observer concerned about the growing number of reported German atrocities, and he acted as impromptu courier of diplomatic dispatches in and out of the war zone. His reputation grew as "his wit and fearlessness were the talk of Brussels." In a very short time, he had made a good name for himself. He was nothing if not hardworking, and as one observer commented, Gibson always seemed to be the busiest person in the legation.

His earlier desire for a less stressful post was seemingly overshadowed by his sense of duty, innate curiosity, and obvious desire to be in the thick of things. Only three days after the invasion began, Gibson wrote his mother: "This is undoubtedly the most interesting post in all Europe now and our Legation is the most interesting Legation in the post. I would not be anywhere else for anything on earth."

Just like Gibson, the U.S. minister to the legation, Brand Whitlock, had come recently to the post, only seven months before the war started. Born in Urbana, Ohio, the 45-year-old had had a successful career as a journalist, working as a reporter in Chicago before entering politics and becoming mayor of Toledo, Ohio, in 1905. He had been reelected in 1907, 1909, and 1911.

Whitlock was tall and slender, with a long, thin nose and eyes that had the "tense look of constantly straining to see something too close to him." With his rimless pince-nez (glasses with a nose clip rather than earpieces), he had the appearance of a scholar or professor, and just like one, he longed for the solitude of a writer's garret. When President Wilson had appointed him to lead the U.S. Legation in Brussels, it was just what Whitlock had hoped for.

The post was known as a quiet one, with more diplomatic show than substance. That suited Whitlock perfectly, for all he wanted to do was have time to write literary novels. If he had known what the next four years would be like—and what history would call on him to do—he probably would not have taken the position.

And while Whitlock was as yet little known in Belgium, he would, during the next four years, become a figure who was both respected and ridiculed, beloved and belittled. But in the spring and early summer of 1914, Whitlock saw Brussels and all of Belgium as a blessed island of solitude and peace for his work as a novelist.

Forty-five-year-old Brand Whitlock had taken the appointment of minister of the U.S. Legation in Belgium in June 1914 because he thought it would be a quiet, uneventful post. Less than two months later, the Germans invaded Belgium. (Public domain; Robert Arrowsmith papers, Hoover Institution Archives, Stanford University, California.)

That had all changed on the day the Germans marched into Belgium. Whitlock had walked through Brussels and noted "the dim, familiar streets seemed strangely deserted, and yet, almost palpably, panic, fear, stalked through them."

In the coming days and weeks, as Gibson rode in and out of trouble, crossing active battle lines and staring down German officers, Whitlock had been trapped in the legation, swamped by thousands of American tourists who had suddenly been stranded in the middle of a war with little or no resources to get home because of the transportation and financial chaos created by the conflict. "All our patience was absorbed by the crowds of Americans that filled the corridors of the Legation day and night. . . . Many of them were without money; their traveler's checks suddenly worthless, they were at their wits' end."

Whitlock made one major mark in those early days that many would never forget. He, along with the Spanish minister in Brussels, Marquis de Villalobar y O'Neill, had helped to convince city leaders—most notably the larger-than-life Burgomaster Adolphe Max—to declare Brussels an open city and save it from the destruction that had befallen so many other places by then. It had been days and nights of tense negotiations, but in the end the ancient monuments, medieval churches, and broad, tree-lined boulevards of Brussels (compared favorably by many to Paris) were spared from bombardment and devastation as the Germans had marched in on August 20.

Even with that notable accomplishment, Whitlock—unlike his eager assistant, Hugh Gibson—would probably have named numerous places he'd rather be than in Brussels in August 1914.

Both Americans, however, would have agreed on one thing—the city they had both come to love had changed drastically with the occupation.

Gibson complained of the loss of freedom. "It was forbidden to enter or leave the city save with a military pass which was almost impossible to secure. We were thus pretty thoroughly cut off from the world. Most of the conveniences which we had come to take for granted in our modern life were stopped without warning, a hundred restrictions were put upon us and several millions of people had to adapt themselves over night to an entirely new and abnormal mode of life under the menace of German cannon that swept the streets and a truculent soldiery which in its anxiety to inspire terror did more to provoke trouble than to avoid it."

As one British woman still living in Brussels wrote, "We go to bed very early now—nothing to be done, and to save gas. All cafes are closed at nine, and it is like the city of the dead from then on—not a cat to be seen anywhere. There is no traffic in the streets even in daytime, as the Germans allow no motors of any description, or bicycles, and there are no horses, as they took them all away—only a stray old broken-down horse vehicle to be seen occasionally."

Whitlock saw something else. "We began to note a new phenomenon," Whitlock wrote, "new at least to Brussels—women begging in the streets. Hunger, another of war's companions, had come to town."

Another American observer walking around Brussels also saw beggars wandering the streets: "Women holding young babies in their arms stood on all the curbs, begging openly, or selling matches and shoestrings." On the streetcars, which had resumed service, the Belgians did the only thing they could do in protest: they "proudly turned their backs, or refused to sit beside the hated [German] uniforms." It was the same in the cafés, where many residents preferred to leave "rather than sip beer or coffee beside the enemy."

Thousands of other Belgians "besieged the [German] Pass Bureau for permits to travel. The soup kitchens and bread lines were thronged. There was no work to do. The rust of idleness was on everything. An occasional aeroplane from the Allies dropped little celluloid tubes containing encouraging news, but the Germans, waging a successful war, insolently published all the news, even the official reports of the Allies."

The *grand place* (main square) "echoed to soldiers' steps, and the rue de la Loi, beside the Parc, was closed to all but Germans. The splendors of Brussels dripped ooze, her park walks were churned up by the hooves of German war-horses, and even the alleys 'reserved for children's games' were appropriated for the drilling of raw cavalrymen."

Added to the city's sense of occupation was the entire country's feeling of desperation. A renowned Belgian playwright and poet, Émile Cammaerts, wrote in *Through the Iron Bars* about the transformation wrought by the occupation. He believed it was "roughly divided into two periods"—before the October surrender of "the great fortress," Antwerp, and after. Before Antwerp's fall, it was a time when "the hope of prompt deliverance was still vivid in every heart, and when the

A line of people in Brussels waiting for the daily ration of bread and soup. (Public domain; Herbert Hoover Presidential Library Archives, West Branch, Iowa.)

German policy, in spite of its frightfulness, had not yet assumed its most ruthless and systematic character."

After the fall of Antwerp, throughout Brussels and the entire country "the yoke of the conqueror weighed more heavily on the vanquished shoulders, and [it was] when the Belgian population, grim and resolute, began to struggle to preserve its honour and loyalty and to resist the ever increasing pressure of the enemy to bring it into complete submission and to use it as a tool against its own army and its own King."

The Germans—famous for their precision, eye for detail, and desire for control—even went so far as to change the time in Brussels and throughout occupied Belgium. Before the war, Belgium had had only one time zone, Greenwich Mean Time, while Germany had set its clocks one hour earlier. When the Germans took over, they insisted that the country convert to German time and that all town clocks be set to the new time.

Immediately, towns all over Belgium reported faulty tower clocks that couldn't be repaired. Most Belgians exercised passive resistance as they began referring to all appointments in Belgian time, as opposed to German, or "hour of the clock," time.

Gibson put it all into humorous perspective when he had an early run-in with the time differences. He was to meet a German official at the man's office, but when Gibson showed up, no one was there. The next day, Gibson talked with one of the official's assistants, who told him: "Oh, I see, you came at half past six, Belgian time! Of course [Baron Oscar] von der Lancken expected you at half past six, German time!" When Gibson was asked when he would like to reschedule, his sense of the absurd came through, at least mentally, when he later wrote: "I felt inclined to set eleven in the morning and then wander over at three in the afternoon, with the statement that, of course, I did everything according to New York time."

Even Gibson's humor could not change the harsh reality of occupation. As time wore on into the winter, the Belgians began to feel a more permanent and oppressive sense of occupation. Joining the ever-present German soldiers were German bureaucrats and civil service personnel, who came to the city to run the German civil government of occupation. They filled the streets, crowded onto trams, and took many of the seats in the city's cafes—unwanted and unwelcomed people who most residents hoped were only short-term visitors, not new residents.

Adding to the feeling that the city was being taken over was another new sight, German *affiches*. These posters were plastered daily around Brussels and all over occupied Belgium and usually were written in three languages: German, French, and Flemish. Belgians were used to the occasional local government placards, which gave residents neighborhood information, but these German posters were new. They carried war news or rules and regulations of the occupation and, according to Whitlock, "played as large a part in the life of Brussels just then as had newspapers before the war. They might not always provide news, but they could provide sensation, and if written by the proper hand, send a thrill through the community."

The first *affiche* was posted on the first afternoon the German Army began marching into Brussels and was indicative of what was to come. It was signed by the commanding general of the army, General Fredrich Bertram Sixt von Armin, and began innocently enough with a call for residents to stay calm and continue going about their business. That changed quickly, however, when it stated: "Resistance and disobedience will be punished with extreme severity. The owners of houses where ammunition and explosives are found may expect to be shot and have their houses burned. Whoever offers armed resistance will be shot. Whoever opposes the German troops, whoever attacks them, whoever is found with arms will be shot."

Regarding these *affiches*, one sarcastic Belgian source explained that now civilians learned their news by "facing the wall—you know the wall, everyone has his own wall in his own neighborhood—on which the military Government, which is really too kind, pastes every morning news which is skillfully doctored with the sole object of amazing, first of all the Germans, then the Flemings [Belgians speaking Flemish], and finally the Walloons [Belgians speaking French]."

PROCLAMATION.

Inhabitants of both sexes are strictly forbidden to leave their houses so far as this is not absolutely necessary for making short rounds, in order to buy provisions or water their cattle. They are absolutely forbidden to leave their houses at night under any circumstances whatever.

Whoever attempts to leave the place, by night or day, upon any pretext whatever, will be shot.

Potatoes can only be dug with the Commandant's consent and under military supervision.

The German troops have orders to carry out these directions strictly, by sentinels and patrols, who are authorised to fire on anyone departing from these directions.

THE GENERAL COMMANDING.

An English translation of a German affiche *(French for "poster") displayed in occupied Belgium. It reflects how completely the Germans wanted to control civilian life.* (Public domain; Joseph Green papers, Seeley G. Mudd Library, Princeton University, New Jersey.)

There was no escaping the Germans and their arrogance. "Above the prostrate Belgians, like another race or another caste, roared and flashed the brilliant, careless, militaristic Teutons, their lives hedged about with glory and sudden death."

The city's occupation—and transformation—was just beginning and about to get worse.

Von Bissing Becomes Governor General

Nothing would have as much negative impact on the citizens of Brussels and the entire country as the arrival of the new governor general, Baron Moritz Ferdinand von Bissing. On December 3, 1914, he replaced von der Goltz. The changing of command came with a one-sentence *affiche* that was plastered all over Brussels and the rest of the country: "His Majesty, the Emperor and King, having deigned to appoint me Governor general of Belgium, I have to-day assumed the direction of affairs." It was signed "Baron von Bissing, General of the cavalry."

Von Bissing was a 70-year-old Prussian military officer who had been born into the German landed gentry. In 1865, at 21, he had become a lieutenant in the German cavalry and had taken part in both the Austro-Prussian and the Franco-Prussian wars. As a young major in 1887, he had become the aide-de-camp to the crown

On the right, next to an unidentified man, is the sword-carrying Baron Moritz Ferdinand von Bissing, who became governor general of Belgium on December 3, 1914. He would rule Belgium ruthlessly. (Public domain; *A Journal from Our Legation in Belgium,* Hugh Gibson, Doubleday, Page & Co., 1917.)

prince, who later became Kaiser Wilhelm II. After a distinguished military career, von Bissing had retired in 1908 but was recalled to lead the VII Army Corps from August through November 1914. He had then been promoted to *Generaloberst* and appointed by the Kaiser to be governor general of Belgium.

A few days after von Bissing's appointment, Brand Whitlock was officially presented to the governor general by Baron Oscar von der Lancken, newly appointed head of the political department of the occupation government. Whitlock was joined by his Spanish counterpart, the Marquis de Villalobar, and his Dutch counterpart, Mynheer van Vollenhoven. The three men formally met von Bissing in the richly appointed salon of the residence of the Belgian arts and sciences minister. For Whitlock it was an inauspicious moment because the man they were meeting, "justly or unjustly, was destined to stand forth to the world as the symbol of one of the darkest, cruelest and most sinister pages of its miserable history."

As Whitlock recorded it, the man who stood before them was "old, and thin, with thick graying, black hair brushed straight back from his forehead and plastered down as with water or with oil on the curiously shaped head that was so straight and sheer behind. His face was hard and its leathern skin, wrinkled and old and weather-beaten, was remorselessly shaved as to chin and throat and high lean cheeks, leaving the thick, heavy moustaches of a Prussian *Reiter* [horseman] to hide somewhat the thin lips of the stern mouth and then flow on, growing across his cheeks to bristle up fiercely by his ears."

The German was "scrupulously clean, one might almost say scrubbed. . . . His brow was high and the lean face tapered to the wedge of a very firm jaw; the visage of an old Prussian dragoon of the school and mentality of Bismarck." Whitlock noted that from such a face "there gleamed a pair of piercing dark eyes that seemed black until one saw that they were blue; they were keen, shrewd eyes, not wholly unkind."

He was not so much dressed as adorned with the accoutrements of a Prussian cavalry officer: "A great heavy sabre that clanked against his thin legs . . . a well-worn uniform . . . blue trousers, caught with straps below the long, pointed boots that were made of soft leather and furnished with great silver spurs. His tunic was light gray and short, and its shabbiness was somehow accentuated by the Iron Cross of the first class that he wore, and by the enameled star of the Order of the Black Eagle, fastened by a cravat about his collar and dangling heavily out at this wrinkled old throat."

While von Bissing was able to speak French, he did not like to, so with the three ministers he "expressed himself with a rough voice in German" and made von der Lancken stand by him translating into French. He shook hands with each man and spoke a few personal words to each before "the brief audience, which had been invested with the formality of a private presentation at Court, ended." Whitlock and his companions "drove back in the bleak afternoon, with its lowering clouds and gusty winds, under the impression of a strong and possibly a hard personality."

The aura of imperial, harsh royalty that swirled around von Bissing was one that many people had. According to CRB delegate E. E. Hunt, von Bissing's new position "carried with it the dignity and authority of royalty. His proclamations were written in the first person: 'I command. . . . I ordain. . . . I decree.' They say that in his youth Governor general von Bissing was a chum of the Kaiser's and that the Kaiser used to pay the bills at a time when his friend's personal fortune was too small to permit even of the ordinary expenditures of a dashing young army officer. If that is true General von Bissing has advanced a long way since then. He lives in a Belgian palace, he rules a nation, and he stands on a par, under the War Lord [the Kaiser], with the petty monarchs of some of the oldest German states."

Under the baron's harsh rule, the occupation took on deeper and darker tones. As one history explained, "Times had changed, and within the past few weeks changed considerably . . . since von Bissing's arrival [December 3]. . . . Brussels had become to all intents a vast concentration camp under a harsh and tyrannical rule."

This meant that to enter or leave the city required a pass, which was difficult and costly to obtain from the Germans. All citizens had to carry an identity card bearing a photograph, and Belgian men 18 to 40 had to register and regularly report to the German Kommandantur (commandant's headquarters). Day and night the streets were patrolled by armed soldiers as well as by the Belgian city police force. Reportedly, the Germans also employed three special brigades of secret police that used *agents provocateurs* and Belgian informers.

As for the CRB and food relief, von Bissing would initially see the humanitarian effort as a way to gain greater control over his domain. As one modern-day Dutch historian, Johan den Hertog, wrote, "Bissing's prime objective was to make

Belgium a satellite state with a German leader—he naturally saw himself as a suitable candidate. This ideal was easily reconciled with the food aid. A turbulent, resentful Belgium would not want to be governed by Germans. So he was prepared to guarantee, up to a point, that CRB supplies as well as the domestic harvest would reach the local population. Far more dangerous, in his view, was the Comité National's prominent role in distributing the food."

Before von Bissing's arrival—from October through November when von der Goltz was governor general—the Germans had been generally helpful to the work of the CRB and the CN. But as one CRB history records, "As the work of the Commission grew in volume and importance the attitude in general and von Bissing in particular became less accommodating. The change was due in part to the fear that this neutral body was becoming too powerful in territory where, theoretically at least, German rule was absolute, and in part to disapproval of the enthusiasm with which the Belgian people greeted the Americans wherever they went on their tours of inspection. Whatever the cause, the German tendency to deny the Americans reasonable freedom of movement raised a serious issue, for without that freedom, the Commission could not discharge its responsibility of guaranteeing the proper distribution of relief."

The issues would soon lead to a clash of wills that would threaten the entire relief effort.

Von Bissing's relationship with the Belgians was just as antagonistic. As Whitlock noted only seven days after von Bissing's appointment, the governor general decreed that the Belgians must pay 40 million francs a month, or 480 million francs a year, as a "contribution of war." (This was the equivalent of $96 million 1915 U.S. dollars; the Belgian peacetime budget was only $120 million–$160 million.) To determine how to raise such a sum, the governor general convened a special session of the provincial councils of Belgium for Saturday, December 19, and set guidelines: the session would last only one day; all deliberations were to be held in secret; and the sole objective was to determine a method for raising the money.

Von Bissing's harsh rule had just begun.

It would not be long, however, before certain Belgians would make him realize his job would not be an easy one.

Francqui Builds His Network

When Francqui and Lambert had returned from their trip to London back in October, they had immediately set to work establishing the Comité National de Secours et d'Alimentation (CN) as the organization responsible for providing relief to the entire nation and the rallying organization for all the local communes. They established a hierarchy that flowed from Francqui and his executive committee down to newly created provincial committees that worked more directly with the long-established 2,600 local communes.

The CN was divided into two departments, a commercial one (d'Alimentation; provisioning) that dealt with all the issues around providing food for those who could afford to pay, and a charitable one (de Secours; charity) that handled all the issues revolving around those people who could not pay. Under the de Secours benevolent department were five divisions created to work on providing the following: 1. Money; 2. Food; 3. Clothing and Shoes; 4. Work; and 5. Houses and other buildings. Beneath all these, a large number of charitable committees grew up for the aid and protection of a number of groups: refugees; families of officers and under-officers deprived of their income by reason of the war; doctors and pharmacists; artists, children, and orphans of war; the homeless; damaged churches; unemployed; foreigners; and lace makers. Additionally, the CN was patron of the Belgian Commission for Information for Prisoners of War and the Interned; the Central Committee for the Aid of Invalids of War; the Canteen for Prisoners of War; and the Belgian National League Against Tuberculosis.

By strong force of will, Francqui set up the CN organization in record time. He was a man who would have accepted nothing less.

Francqui was truly a man of action. At 51, he was a major force in the financial world and was director of the Société Générale de Belgique, arguably the most important banking institution in Belgium. He had been a driven, ambitious man all his life and had literally come up through the ranks to achieve his fame, fortune, and power.

An orphan at a young age (just like Hoover), he was sent to military school at 15. When he was an officer of 21, he was appointed by King Leopold II to be one of a group to organize and run the Congo Free State. After that the king sent him to China to negotiate the awarding of a contract to Belgium for the large Hankow-Canton railway concession. While he was there from 1897 to 1902, his "main rival in these negotiations was Herbert Hoover," according to a history provided by the modern-day Francqui Foundation. As fate would have it, Francqui and Hoover—two powerful men of distinction—had met earlier, battled before in a courtroom, and disliked each other intensely. And yet years later they were being called upon to work side by side. Historians would probably agree that none but the highest cause could have convinced these two men to work with each other. Even then, it would be a marriage both of them would probably consider rocky at best and made-in-hell at worst.

Unlike Hoover—who wanted full control from behind the scenes—Francqui was a man who wanted full control from center stage. He was known for running businesses and meetings as a dictator who brooked no questioning of his

Émile Francqui was a major force in the Belgian financial world and a man who disliked Herbert Hoover intensely. Francqui became president of the Comité National, which was the Belgian counterpart to Hoover's CRB. (Public domain; CRB portrait book, Herbert Hoover Presidential Library Archives, West Branch, Iowa.)

commands and took no prisoners if anyone dared to cross him. His physical appearance—big, burly, with mustache and cleft chin—was as imposing as his business methods. One man called him "the iron man of Belgium." E. E. Hunt described him as "a type familiar to Americans: a big-business man in the prime of life, self-made, brusque, bourgeois, sometimes intolerably rude, but always efficient, and the man of the hour in Belgian financial affairs. He resembles an American trust magnate, with more than a spice of Gallic salt in his composition. He has no small ambitions, no cheap ideas of glory, and no sentimentality or cant."

While Francqui managed the nearly impossible by getting the Comité National up and running in a matter of weeks, this did not necessarily mean, however, that the communes fully embraced the concept of the Comité National or of Francqui and what some people perceived as his grab for power.

Belgium's political situation before the war had always been highly charged, if not explosive. Factions included the Catholics, Protestants, those speaking French (Walloons) in the south, and those speaking Dutch-derived Flemish (Flemings) in the north, as well as socialists and every other usual political party.

The language issue had been a major one. Most educated Flemings were bilingual, able to speak fluently both French and Flemish, but in many cases they resented speaking French. Many French-speaking Belgians in the southern portion of the country had only limited understanding of Flemish. While Flemish is very similar to Dutch in the written form, it has many differences in the spoken form. CRB delegate E. E. Hunt, who took the time and effort to learn Flemish, descriptively explained, "It is a warty, hard-fisted, tough-muscled language which has been out in the weather until it has got well sunburned; a splendid language for oratory—and profanity!"

Hunt also addressed an American misconception about the language issue. "The Flemish Movement," he wrote, "is not a separatist movement, as is commonly supposed in America. It is a democratic, and in my opinion, a just assertion of the predominant influence of the Flemish stock in Belgium."

The war had brought a superficial end to the bickering between the Walloons and Flemings because, as Hunt stated, "the Flemings are as loyal as any other portion of the people to the ideal of a free and united Belgium." But taking a break from arguing the language issue did not mean the underlying issues and their attendant emotions had disappeared. They still simmered just below the surface that was shown to the Germans, and they had to still be considered by Francqui, who was trying to create a unified organization in the Comité National.

Additionally, religion played a significant role in Belgian life. The majority of Belgians in 1914 were Catholic, and the religion was a driving force in the country, more so in the Walloon south than in the Flemish north. In fact, religion was such a strong influence in Belgium that it mitigated many of the differences that existed over language. And in the critical arena of politics—which seemed to dominate nearly every Belgian's body and soul before the war—the Catholic party had been in power for nearly 30 years.

A later CRB delegate, Earl Osborn, reported, "It takes quite a while for an American to realize that in Belgium political beliefs are the standard by which men judge each other and on which they form their friendships and enmities; the first question that a man asks about another is whether he is a liberal or a Catholic."

All of these differences in Belgian life were reflected in the country's foundation—its local communes. In the end, if the Comité National and its system of provincial committees were going to succeed, they had to have the support of the local communes.

Outwardly, most communes knew they didn't have the power the Comité National was mustering, and they couldn't even begin to achieve what the CN wanted to do, but that didn't mean they had to like it. Those not solidly behind the CN sat back and bided their time, hoping Francqui and his group would somehow slip up without jeopardizing the feeding of the country.

One of the first steps of the CN was to determine how much food was needed to sustain more than 7 million Belgians. A start was to determine how much food would sustain a human being each day and then use that to determine how much was needed of what—most importantly wheat for making the all-important bread that was a critical component of many Belgians' diets. It was understood that whatever figure was arrived at, it would ultimately be subservient to what could actually be provided.

In the beginning months, both the CN and the CRB grappled with this issue. The CN received guidance from Dr. Mikkel Hindhede, a Danish physician, nutritionist, and manager of the National Laboratory for Nutrition Research who was also working at the time with the Solvay Institute of Sociology in Brussels.

Another famous nutritionist—this one from America, but not a medical doctor—was also working at the Solvay Institute of Sociology when the war broke out. His name was Horace Fletcher and he had developed the concept of thoroughly chewing any food—including liquids, he maintained—at least 32 times before swallowing as a way to good health. "Fletcherizing" your food with every bite had become a health and diet fad in the early 1900s and had made Fletcher a millionaire. When Belgium fell under German occupation and the CN and the CRB began, the 65-year-old Fletcher volunteered his services as a CRB delegate. Among the mostly young men of the CRB, Fletcher became known as the wise "dean" and, according to E. E. Hunt, "was one of the our most loyal, most enthusiastic, and most inventive workers. He looked like an angelic boy, masquerading with white wool for hair and eyebrows." Another CRB delegate referred to Fletcher as "a merry, rosy, little old gentleman."

From Fletcher, Dr. Hindhede, and numerous other nutrition experts, the CN initially determined that what was needed when it came to all-important bread was a minimum of 250 grams (slightly more than half a pound) per person per day. As Hunt stated, this was considered "extraordinarily low" by many experts. That amount was used as a goal from November 1914 through the first month of 1915, but by February 1915, it was seen that this amount of bread was simply too low for a daily ration. The figure was increased to 325 grams (less than three-quarters of a pound) of bread, which required 250 grams of flour to produce.

As for the overall food importation goal, Francqui and the CN had informed Hoover on October 26 that starting December 1, the minimum foodstuffs required would be 60,000 tons of grains, 15,000 tons of maize, and 3,000 tons of rice and dried peas, or a total of nearly 80,000 tons a month—a significant amount, but less than a third of the 250,000 tons a month that Belgium had imported before the war. And 80,000 tons only equated to a meager 283 grams (10 ounces) of food per person per day.

Even that amount, however, was difficult to obtain during the first three months of CRB/CN operations: November had seen a total of only 26,431 tons imported into Belgium; December, 58,000 tons; and January 1915, 70,000 tons.

It was anyone's guess if the 80,000 tons a month could be obtained and then maintained for the duration of the war.

5

Antwerp and Environs

The CRB's Chief Delegate in Antwerp Finds His Way

On Friday, December 11, 1914, E. E. Hunt arrived in Antwerp as the new CRB chief delegate for Antwerp Province. As the month progressed and the trench warfare was being established outside of German-occupied Belgium, Hunt began waging his own war to establish a functioning, effective, and efficient food-relief program for the nearly 1 million people within the city and province of Antwerp.

There were no blueprints or manuals for the job, no experts to instruct him on what needed to be done or how to work with the members of the Antwerp provincial committee or the Comité National. No one—Belgian or American—knew precisely what to do or how to do it, for such an effort had never been attempted before, even in peacetime. The basics were obvious. Food shipments that were starting to appear in Belgium via canal barges from Holland had to be processed, paid for, and distributed in a fair and equitable way, regardless of anyone's status, position, politics, or religion. And the Germans could not touch any of it, even though they ruled occupied Belgium with an iron hand.

For Antwerp, Hunt was the right man at the right time for the job.

At first glance, Edward Eyre Hunt was an unobtrusive man of slight build, average height, dark hair, mustache, and deep-set, thoughtful eyes. At 29, he was a Harvard graduate who had stayed on campus after graduation and worked in the English Department for two years, then headed to New York City, where he had worked on the editorial staff of *American Magazine* for a couple of years. He was a passionate, introspective, and sensitive young urbanite looking for something meaningful to write about.

The few months prior to Hunt joining the CRB were instrumental in preparing and fortifying him for the coming year as a neutral relief worker in German-occupied Belgium. He had come to Europe as a freelance war correspondent, arriving in Rotterdam on Tuesday, September 8. From there he had traveled into

Edward Eyre (E. E.) Hunt was an American war correspondent who went from impartial observer to involved participant when he became the CRB's chief delegate for the city and province of Antwerp in December 1914. (*One Generation,* Erskine Carmichael, M.D., self-published, 2013.)

Germany, where he spent most of the month observing, interviewing, and reporting on everything from German officials and their policies to children playing in the streets. By October 6, Hunt had found his way from Germany into Antwerp. It had not been an easy journey, and at one point he was arrested by the Belgians for being a spy, but the trip would later seem like a joyride compared to what he was about to experience.

Shortly after Hunt arrived in Antwerp, the Germans began a three-day bombardment of the city. Hunt had been in a townhouse that had taken a direct hit, had picked his way through debris-covered streets overflowing with panicked refugees, and had watched in stunned silence as thousands shoved their way onto Antwerp's main wharf, trying to flee the city.

After three days of incessant bombing, the city capitulated and Hunt saw his wartime story shift from the city and the victorious German soldiers marching in to the refugees fleeing north to Holland. For the Germans, there was no desire to stop anyone from fleeing Antwerp as long as they weren't young men of fighting age. Let the women, children, and old go.

Hunt followed. On Saturday afternoon, October 10, he joined the steady stream of thousands of frightened Belgians too exhausted to do much more than trudge along in the footsteps of those before them. Women, children, and old people moved like a slow tide rising through the Belgian countryside, ever northward toward the freedom and safety of neutral Holland, 20 miles away.

Walking with the refugees through the rain and into the night, Hunt finally reached the border, where the bewildered and beleaguered Dutch sentries stood helplessly as they watched the endless stream of ragged and beaten people pour into their country. Hunt waited for hours with hundreds of others to catch a train to the closest city, Bergen op Zoom. When he finally reached Rotterdam at 3:00 a.m. on Sunday, October 11, Hunt cabled New York the story of Antwerp's fall. He hoped he had conveyed the true sense of defeat, despair, and heartfelt courage he had witnessed in Belgium and on the journey to Holland.

It was sometime during October, in this transformative period between summer and winter, that Hunt received news from America that his fiancée had suddenly died. He would grieve privately. In fact, he recorded nothing of the tragedy—who she was, what had happened—in his well-known later book, *War Bread,* or in any personal journals available to the public. Within all that material, there is only one comment he wrote at the end of a letter to one of his magazine agents: "My fiancée's death leaves me still pretty ragged. Your letter helped."

With Hunt's generally heightened sensibilities and sensitivity, it's not too surprising that as he went about gathering, experiencing, and writing each new war story, he began to change. He was becoming more involved, more emotionally affected by what he saw happening around him. Hunt was moving, consciously or unconsciously, from objective journalist to passive observer to budding relief participant.

After Hunt's walk from Antwerp to Holland, he delivered food supplies by motor launch to refugees on the Dutch border, then spent much of the rest of October and November writing articles on what he had seen and done in Belgium and Holland. While trying to maintain journalistic impartiality, Hunt could not escape the emotional impact of war. On November 23 he wrote one of his agents, Miss Holly: "I could write you endless 'human interest' things if I had the strength. The war is bedlam and takes life from all of us over here." On the same day, he wrote to another agent, Mr. Forman, "I've so much to say, and so little mental or emotional vim behind it just now, that sometimes it all looks very dark."

As he worked on his articles and continued researching and interviewing people about the war, the Belgian refugees, and life in Holland, he naturally came into contact with the U.S. minister to Holland, Henry van Dyke, and through him Captain John F. Lucey, the CRB director of the Rotterdam office overseeing the transfer of relief supplies to barges bound for Belgium.

The story these men told Hunt of the CRB struck a chord within him, not only as a journalist but also as a person. "As an American citizen I was deeply interested in the budding work of the Commission for Relief in Belgium. . . . I learned that Americans were urgently needed in Belgium to oversee the distribution of food in each of the provinces and to certify that all of it went to the Belgians. Men were wanted who knew both French and German and who had business training, and they were wanted at once."

Before he committed to the CRB, however, he took a quick trip into Belgium to see the work and the situation for himself. As his group drove between Antwerp and Brussels in a misty rain, Hunt was touched by what he saw. The "landscape lay blurred and drenched—a vista of burned villages and muddy roads. It was a country seen through tears."

Hunt's journey into Belgium had a profound impact. He returned to Holland, but not for long. "On December eleventh I was again in Antwerp, this time holding

Mr. Brand Whitlock's power-of-attorney as chief delegate of the Commission for Relief in Belgium in charge of the fortress and province—a territory as large as the State of Rhode Island, and with a population of more than a million."

To hell with freelance journalism; Hunt was now in the volunteer relief business.

Hunt's first order of business was to figure out just how he and the CRB fit into the Belgian situation. He found this was much more complicated than he had first thought.

E. E. Hunt and Belgian Politics

As Hunt worked with diverse groups of men in the numerous Belgian committees and communes, he quickly realized that he was standing in a hurricane's eye, surrounded by the swirling winds of Belgium's social, religious, and political attitudes. He knew he would have to understand and acknowledge the powers of each to effectively fashion a coordinated relief effort.

Belgium had become a nation less than 100 years before, which meant, as Hunt learned, "the commune, not the nation, was the Belgian fatherland." At odds were "Republicanism against Monarchy, Clericalism against Anti-Clericalism, Flemings against French-speaking Walloons, Socialism against Capitalism. Business, society, every department of life, was divided and subdivided into self-contained cliques. The bitterness of the struggle and the disunion were almost unbelievable."

While the Germans had changed all that and converted the country's fierce generational parochialism into "tenacious patriotism," Hunt acknowledged that wasn't enough to wipe out the divisions. "Even in the midst of war men could not be expected to lay aside fundamental principles." The Belgians "still feared and distrusted their fellow Belgians. War exaggerated certain of their suspicions, instead of allaying them."

The CRB was supposed to be above all that. It was, in theory, working for all Belgians, no matter what their religion, political affiliation, or social standing.

That concept was tested when in late December the members of the city district of Turnhout had told Hunt privately they did not want to be on the Antwerp provincial committee; they wanted to deal with Brussels directly or just with Hunt when it came to providing relief supplies to their district. They had not yet received any food from Antwerp and did not trust that a provincial committee could represent them and their needs to the headquarters in Brussels. As Hunt wrote, the town of Turnhout was "rustic, old-fashioned, and Clerical" and did not trust the "merchants of Antwerp." In fact, the Turnhout delegation was not even clear on what the CRB was supposed to do. As Hunt put it, "It looked on us as an association of benevolent grain-dealers, selling flour to a body of Antwerp business men, who, in turn, would resell it to the Turnhout delegation, of course at a profit to themselves!"

The issue came to a head at a provincial committee meeting. "There was an exciting moment when all the Turnhout delegates were on their feet at once, speaking Flemish instead of French, as they usually did when much excited, protesting . . . and adding that they were appealing to Brussels for complete separation from Antwerp." The room began to feel uncomfortably small, and, as Hunt said, "one of the gentlemen wept in the excess of his feeling, and choruses of recriminations, which I could not understand, were exchanged between the groups." The Turnhout group threw across the room to their colleagues a damning question: "When had Antwerp, rich and pious in the Middle Ages—now subject to tradesmen and freemasons—when had it been generous to Turnhout?"

The representatives of Turnhout were so adamant in their beliefs that they petitioned the CN and the CRB in Brussels to permit a division of the province. Hunt was equally adamant that his province not be divided. He wrote multiple reports about the issue and why it was not a good idea to allow the secession of Turnhout. With major communication difficulties still existing throughout Belgium, Hunt's reports did not reach Brussels in time to affect the decision.

Because the CRB office was still under Dannie Heineman, who often seemed to take more of a Belgian perspective than an American one, the CRB Brussels office decision came down, allowing Turnhout to break away from the Antwerp provincial committee.

Hunt refused to accept the verdict. He pleaded his case with greater intensity. Within a few days, "more as a favor to me than for any sounder reason, Brussels consented to reverse this judgment." Hunt immediately assigned one of the new delegates, Richard H. Simpson from Indiana—who had initially worked in the Belgian municipality of Hasselt and wielded a cane more for show than for aid in walking—to deal exclusively with Turnhout as a way of alleviating the city's fears of not being properly represented.

Hunt did not stop there, however. He knew that there was truth in what the Turnhout representatives had been saying. The city of Antwerp had too much control over what was happening in the entire province of Antwerp. Hunt decided to take a bold next step in an attempt to address some of their concerns. It was time to take on the powerhouse of Antwerp.

The city had been running relief efforts since the beginning of the war, before the CRB had shown up. City officials had always seen the work as a municipal matter. These officials, however, were "party men. They belonged to the Liberal or Socialist party. No Catholics were among them." And while they had done an admirable job and had "shared with their neighbor communes what food and money the municipality controlled," they saw no reason "why they should surrender their favored position at the center of supplies when food began to come from America instead of the municipal warehouses."

As Hunt stated diplomatically, "As an American delegate I was pledged to a different point of view."

To correct the situation, Hunt realized that "the Antwerp Provincial Relief Committee must be divorced from the Antwerp Town Hall and the group of party men who had so ably ministered to the wants lying close at hand." The separation began, as Hunt noted, rather comically. His youngest assistant, 19-year-old Bennett H. (Harvie) Branscomb from Alabama, was designated as delegate to the city. One of his first jobs had been to reprimand the local committee for the reports they had been handing in. As Hunt wrote, standing before some of the most prominent men of one of the greatest Flemish cities, Branscomb had held up one of their reports and spoken in a quiet, southern drawl: "We cannot and we will not send another such report as this to Brussels. Reports must have our signature as American delegates. We will not give our signatures to tardy and un-businesslike reports."

The men were taken aback. The controller of Antwerp supposedly told a friend, "I have been accustomed to handle millions of francs every day, and now these young Americans come and ask me what became of such-and-such bag of flour last week!"

If they were surprised by Branscomb's remarks, they were shocked by what Hunt announced at the next provincial committee meeting. He told the assembly that he had transferred the entire relief work for the city of Antwerp from the town hall to offices in Edouard Bunge's Bank of the Union of Antwerp at 2 Marché aux Grains and had designated a new delegate, Thomas O. Connett, to serve as the representative for the city. Hunt added that Connett had been instructed to create a census of all bread and flour consumers in the district.

While the transfer was completed in four days, "such precipitate action appalled some of our supporters in the Committee," Hunt reported.

After some time, however, their reaction became muted and then turned to praise once they saw what Connett was able to do. As Hunt noted, the "quiet, unobtrusive young Cambridge student, about twenty-two years old," with the help of numerous bank clerks, "had card-indexed the city of Antwerp and reorganized the system of control over food distributions with a saving of about one-fifth of the supplies."

Despite their youth, the American delegates were getting things done. As Hunt noted, "None of us was out of his twenties. We were beardless boys in the assemblies of our elders, but young or old, we were equal participators in a thrilling undertaking and we intended to do our part."

While December had been a little rocky for Hunt and his handful of delegates in the province of Antwerp, they had made a respectable start.

During the war, the Chateau Oude Gracht on Hoogboom estate was home to Antwerp merchant Edouard Bunge and three of his five daughters: Erica, Eva, and Hilda. The palatial four-story chateau became an island of respite for the American CRB delegates. (Author's archives.)

A Belgian Family Welcomes the Delegates

In his role as vice president of the provincial committee of Antwerp and board member of the Comité National, Belgian merchant Edouard Bunge met multiple times with Hunt, both in formal gatherings and individually. Although Bunge was considered progressive in his business and societal thinking, he still found it a little disconcerting that Hunt moved to challenge the conventional wisdom of the provincial committee and the local commune leaders. Overall, though, Bunge heartily approved of Hunt and the other CRB delegates he met. It was natural for Bunge to automatically extend an open invitation to any delegate to come out to his sprawling Hoogboom estate and the palatial four-story Chateau Oude Gracht, 20 miles northeast of Antwerp, for moments of much-needed relaxation or to stay the night if journeying around the province.

Hunt, along with many other delegates from around Belgium, took Bunge up on his invitation. It was at Oude Gracht that Hunt met three of Bunge's daughters: Erica, Eva, and Hilda. While two other sisters (Dora and Sophie) had married and moved away before the war, the three remaining daughters lived with their widowed father and maternal grandmother at either Oude Gracht or their large townhouse in the city. The family was served faithfully by a large number of servants and estate workers.

The Bunges had had an eventful time during the invasion and siege of Antwerp.

From left: Hilda, Eva, and Erica Bunge. All three Belgian women volunteered in a hospital and a children's canteen. In late 1914, Erica Bunge and her father, Edouard, began working on how to do more to feed the children of Antwerp. (Author's archives.)

When the war began, the three sisters had volunteered at temporary Antwerp field hospitals, at the city's soup kitchens, and in the children's canteens run by an organization named Les Petites Abeilles (the Little Bees). During the three-day bombardment of Antwerp in October, the sisters and their father had stayed in the city at their townhouse. Erica, Eva, and Hilda had continued to work at a nearby hospital.

On the morning of October 7, 1914, as shells whistled across the sky, the three women walked to the hospital and were shocked by what they found.

In hospitals all around the city, many of the wounded had been evacuated. Unfortunately, the most severely wounded were left behind because moving them might have killed them, and it would have slowed down the Belgian and English soldiers' retreat. But this meant that those who remained were left to the mercy of the Germans. Every Belgian had heard stories of German "mercy," so it was understandable that some of those left behind became extremely agitated. As E. E. Hunt recorded, "There was panic in some of the wards. Mutilated men dragged themselves from their beds and pulled on what garments they could; they screamed and implored the nurses not to let them fall into the hands of the Germans. Some begged revolvers so they might shoot themselves."

At the hospital where the Bunge sisters worked, 50 severely wounded men had been left behind. The Bunges weren't too surprised by that, but what shocked them was the fact that all "the regular nurses, the stretcher-bearers, the director, even the doctor . . . the entire male personnel of the hospital had fled." The only staff left were the directress, one Belgian nurse, and two English nurses who had refused to go with the retreating English soldiers.

With shells still flying overhead, the Bunge sisters and the four other women got to work calming the patients, cleaning festering wounds, rebandaging where necessary, making comfortable where possible, and tidying up from the hurried exit of the others. Most importantly, though, they wanted to find the best place for the wounded to ride out the bombardment. They agreed on the basement. It took tremendous effort and no small amount of brute strength, but they somehow managed to get all 50 badly wounded men—20 of whom were British soldiers—down to the relative safety of the cellar.

The wounded in the cellar survived the three-day bombardment, as did the Bunges.

When Hunt and the other delegates became acquainted with the Bunge sisters in December 1914, they quickly found that Erica, the eldest of the three at 23, was known as the practical, business-minded one who was forceful and confident—handsome rather than attractive. Eva was the studious, intellectual sister and looked the part with her wire-rimmed glasses and tightly pulled-back hair. Hilda was acknowledged as the prettiest Bunge girl, with a rather adventurous spirit and no desire for long, involved political conversations. Before the war the three had been avid readers, and Erica and Eva in particular had been fascinated and engaged in what was happening internationally. When the occupation began, like most other young Belgian women, they had put away their colorful dresses and wore only dark or subdued colors to mourn their country's situation.

Erica had learned much about business through her discussions with her father and had over the years evolved into a trusted business adviser to her father. She felt she was quite progressive in her social, religious, and political attitudes, but she could be surprised by the brash and straightforward-speaking young Americans.

At Chateau Oude Gracht when delegates were in attendance for dinner, Erica insisted there be no separation after the meal so that the entire group of men and women could adjourn to the parlor for conversing, playing piano, reciting literary passages, or listening to the gramophone. And there was always her nightly game of billiards with her father, who would occasionally invite a delegate to join them.

Many times at Oude Gracht, the conversations were about the war, German atrocities during the invasion, or the occupation. It was during those discussions that Erica and Eva especially could get quite frustrated with many of the Americans. Their frustration lay in the fact that Hunt and most of the other Americans generally refused to talk about their feelings regarding the war, the Germans, or the occupation. They were honor bound as gentlemen to be neutral, and most of them strove hard to maintain that neutrality in all their dealings, whether formal or informal. Erica had no qualms about telling anyone who would listen how she felt about the Germans, using the disparaging term "dirty Boche," (no literal translation). Edouard would many times frown when she did so, but he always held his tongue.

The Bunge sisters were, however, at times naïve about some aspects of life simply because of their privileged position as part of the wealthy merchant class. As one delegate, John Simpson, known by his American nickname "Pink," later recalled, "[The sisters] thought we were marvelous, a curious lot, and they evidently liked us pretty well because some of them married Americans. They were very wealthy people, and the idea that I, for instance, obviously a college graduate, that I had done menial tasks—of course they didn't believe it to begin with, that I was a farm hand and pitched hay for a dollar a day, and so on. And then I told them about selling the *Saturday Evening Post.* I had my Saturday route to dispose of 150 copies of the *Post*—bought at 3 cents, sold at 5 cents—to make some pocket money.

"And one of these girls would say to another, 'Do you know the latest from Pinkske? He now claims that he was a newsboy.'

"'Oh,' the other one would say, 'don't believe a word he says. You can't believe anything he says.'"

They certainly knew what a newsboy was, but as Pink said, "their picture of a newsboy was some waif standing on the Bowery in New York in a driving snow storm peddling papers."

The lighthearted moments at Chateau Oude Gracht did not diminish the Bunge family's feelings about the war and the Germans. What they had seen and experienced during the Antwerp siege and surrender reinforced their desire to do more for their country. The three sisters continued to work in the soup kitchens and children's canteens, as the temporary Antwerp hospital where they had worked was shut down by the end of December because the patients had been moved or were released. The three had completed a Red Cross course in nursing and Erica wrote in her diary with hopeful enthusiasm, "If the Allies come back, we are ready, and what a joy it would be to take care of our own wounded again!"

Erica and her father began to talk about how they might do more to help the people of Antwerp.

By spring the two of them would have an answer that few would have expected possible in war-ravaged Belgium. And it would involve the Belgian-Dutch border, something that had been changing and evolving since the war's beginning.

The Belgian-Dutch Border Tightens

When the war had started, the border between Belgium and Holland had been overrun with tens of thousands of refugees and retreating Belgian soldiers. Some estimates had the number as high as half a million who fled north to the Netherlands or south to France. The Dutch and Belgians put aside their traditional dislike of each other as Holland opened its collective arms to the refugees and the Belgians responded with grateful appreciation. Many Dutch homes spontaneously took in as many as they could, while tent cities, some housing as many as 25,000 people, sprang up nearly overnight.

For refugees identified as Belgian soldiers, the crossing into neutral Holland meant they would be interned for the remainder of the war—prisoners, some might say, in a gilded cage. The high stacks of guns, ammunition, and other accoutrements of war at the border posts attested to the fact that many soldiers had walked into Holland as soldiers and were stripped of their weapons at the border.

But the roads leading to Holland were also littered with helmets, packs, uniforms, and other equipment, which spoke to another fact—many soldiers had shed all signs they were soldiers so they would be officially identified as civilians by the Dutch when crossing the border into the Netherlands. For many of these soldier-civilians, the hope was to one day return to Belgium or to rejoin the fight via Britain or find their way to the thin slice of Belgium that was still free and fighting under valiant King Albert.

No matter what the refugees desired, however, they all waited to see what would happen next when it came to possibly returning to their homeland. They didn't have long to wait.

In December 1914, after the German occupation of Belgium had had a few months to settle in, the new governor general, Baron von Bissing, issued a proclamation promising no retribution to those who wanted to return to their homes. More importantly, those Belgian men of military age were promised they would not be taken prisoner or held accountable for their past military service.

The Germans' seemingly benevolent beckoning for Belgians to return home was viewed by many as a blatant attempt to curry favor with worldwide public opinion. To the refugees, it was a welcome call to go back home. Tens of thousands quickly collected the small amount of possessions they had and began walking home. This time, however, there was no panic in their footsteps, no fear in their eyes—just a hope that their homes were still intact.

Such a fluid border in those first five months of the war would not be seen again until the end of hostilities. After von Bissing's December 1914 refugee proclamation, the Germans began tightening the border, and by early 1915 Belgium was effectively sealed off to all those who did not have an official pass issued by the German authorities.

On the other side, the Dutch were also interested in a secure border. As modern-day Belgian historian Jan Ingelbrecht states, "The Netherlands, once the panic [of initial war] was over, supported by all means the return of as many [Belgian] people as possible, but not without a minimum level of guarantees for the returning refugees. Once that was completed, the border was closed and guarded by both parties."

This did not stop the continued clandestine attempts to get people and goods in and out of Belgium.

People trying to get *out* of Belgium included Allied soldiers and downed airmen trapped in enemy territory, as well as young Belgian men eager to join the Belgian or Allied armies.

People trying to get *into* Belgium without proper paperwork were either Allied spies or smugglers dealing in food or material outlawed by the Germans. Smugglers also knew that the imprisoned Belgians wanted one other item nearly as much as food—information; information about the war and the free world. As such, the Germans were determined to stop its entry into occupied territory. One Belgian historian explained: "The access of the population to neutral press or news coverage in any form whatever was to be prevented. Letters, mail and newspapers were smuggled as well, to the displeasure of the occupier who kept the local residents in ignorance as much as possible."

The Secret Press in Belgium stated the issue more strongly: "The sentinels had orders to fire on the sellers of newspapers who sought to cross the frontier, and they did not hesitate to do so. . . . In December, 1914, the German sentinels shot two news-vendors at Putte." Putte was a small border village that was only a few miles north of the Bunges' Chateau Oude Gracht. Even at the risk of death, smugglers kept crossing the border, due in large part to the substantial money that could be made on the Belgian black market.

No matter the direction desired—in or out of Belgium—the easiest way for those without proper documentation to cross the border was to bribe a German sentry. As Hunt stated, "Few could run the border without collusion with the German sentries." Many of these guards were Landsturmers—older Germans (many from Bavaria) used for noncombat duties—who were not so prone to follow every rule and regulation, especially when simply looking the other way might mean good Dutch chocolate, butter, tobacco, or even hard cash.

A sympathetic description of these older soldiers was given by Scott Paradise, one of the young Rhodes scholars who had joined the CRB in December. "The old Landsturmers, with their dingy uniforms, their long beards and their gentle eyes, seem sadly out of place guarding the railroad tracks in the cold rainy nights. One of them once remarked to us, to our great astonishment, as he read our passes, 'Haven't you any English or American newspapers? I'm so damned lonely I don't know what to do,' and this in perfect Yankee."

Border bribery with these Landsturmers was more likely to be successful at the smaller, lesser-used crossings than at the larger sentry posts on the major roads.

Much riskier was attempting to cross the border fence, or swimming across in places where the border was a river or canal. Both had the serious risk of being shot by guards during the frequent patrols.

German Governor General Baron von Bissing issued a proclamation after a little more than a month in office that showed how seriously the Germans took illegal border activity. "Persons capable of military service have lately attempted on various occasions to cross the Dutch frontier in secret in order to join the enemy army." He decreed that no one was allowed "circulation in the regions bordering the frontier" and any who attempted to cross would "run the risk of being killed by the sentinels on the frontier." Those caught would be sent to Germany as prisoners of war. "This applies equally to members of the family of any Belgian capable of military service as above who do not prevent the latter from entering Holland." Von Bissing's message was clear—the innocent would also pay the price for the guilty party's actions.

But how to properly secure 280 miles (450 km) of Belgian-Dutch border? Much of it traversed the Campine, the sparsely populated landscape just north of Antwerp. Baedeker's tour guide called the Campine "moorland" and "monotonous," while others termed it a desolate, flat land dotted with scrub pines and purple heather. It would be a nearly impossible task for the Germans to closely monitor and seal such a land.

In the spring of 1915, however, the Germans would begin using a new technology with deadly force to ensure no one illegally crossed their Belgian border.

6

Brussels

Hoover Sees the Belgian Situation Firsthand

Despite the inability of the CRB to import the target of 80,000 tons a month in the first three months of operations, much had been accomplished. Hoover was making giants leaps in London, organizing the office, purchasing initial food shipments, securing guarantees from both the British and the Germans, and gaining worldwide sympathy for the cause through a strategic public relations campaign. And Captain Lucey was making great strides in Rotterdam, setting up the transshipping operations.

That could not hide, however, the problem that resided in the CRB Brussels office. Reports were coming into Hoover from London personnel and from Lucey in Rotterdam that those in Brussels were not being cooperative and were unresponsive to critical queries such as canal operational conditions, statistical information about those in need, and exact food requirements. With no telegraph or postal service between Rotterdam and Belgium, Lucey was flying blind as to what food to send to whom. The establishment of regular courier service between Brussels and Rotterdam through CRB delegate Edward Curtis was begun, but even with that, any information from Brussels was difficult to obtain.

Officially, the CRB Brussels office was run by Dannie Heineman, the American engineer living and working in Brussels when the war broke out. He had helped start the Belgium relief effort and had naturally become the first director of the CRB Brussels office. According to one historian of the CRB, Heineman "had been engaged for two months in gathering together food for Greater Brussels, and he went on now from the same offices with hardly more than a change in name. He was now [Brussels] director of the Commission for Relief in Belgium and not, as before, chairman of a subcommittee under Francqui's direction. Many of the chief men of the Comité National probably failed to realize the significance of this change in name. They continued to regard the Commission as a subordinate agent of the Comité National, just as Heineman's food-supply subcommittee had previously been. They were consequently inclined at times to object to any interference on the part of the Commission in the control of food distribution."

With no real CRB staff support yet and his loyalties mixed between his CN friends and CRB associates, Heineman just kept doing what he had been doing—finding food for those in the greatest need. But that did not help the then-international efforts of the CRB to organize and coordinate relief. It seemed at times as if the Brussels office was more like an extension of Francqui's CN than an independent CRB operation.

Hoover decided it was time to visit Brussels and get things more to his liking. He wanted to "see for himself the exact conditions in Belgium and to hasten the organization of the Brussels office." Whitlock explained that Hoover came to Brussels because the CRB "had already been functioning, but there were many defects in the C.R.B. and it was to remedy these that Mr. Hoover had crossed the North Sea and come to Belgium."

Leaving London on the evening of Thursday, November 26, Hoover quickly and personally experienced some of the harsh realities of being in a war zone. He was strip-searched twice, once as he was leaving England by British Intelligence agents and once at the Belgian border by German sentries. In great understatement, Hoover said later that his first trip to Belgium had felt like entering a prison and that "possibly the rather rough search of my person by the German guards strengthened that impression."

Hoover's first impression of Belgium and Brussels stayed with him the rest of his life. "German soldiers stood at every crossroads and every street corner. The depressed, unsmiling faces of the Belgians matched the mood of the dreary winter landscape. There were no children at play. The empty streets, the gaunt destroyed houses, the ruins of the fine old church of St. Pierre and the Library at Louvain, intensified the sense of suspended animation in the life of the people."

Arriving on Sunday afternoon, November 29, Hoover entered into a series of meetings and conferences that would last for much of the next two days. Most of the meetings were held at the legation offices and, at various times, included Whitlock, Gibson, Francqui, Shaler, and Heineman. From the meetings, Hoover was "more impressed than ever of the need for the immediate extension of the Commission's services in Belgium. . . . No effective office service had been organized and Hoover urged that this should be created as quickly as possible."

Hoover knew after reviewing the Brussels operation that what was needed was a strong, independent CRB office in Brussels, and he was not sure Heineman was the best person to head such an office. Hoover felt Heineman was at times more focused on helping and working with Francqui and the Comité National than on guarding and nurturing the CRB. Whitlock related in his journal that at a conference with Hoover and Francqui, where they talked about possibly replacing Heineman, the three "agreed that we had great need of him since he had influence with the

Germans." Francqui might like having allies around, such as Heineman, but only if they managed their responsibilities appropriately and did not get in his way.

As Hoover's first trip to Brussels was winding down, he knew he wanted Heineman out, but he needed the man's good German relationships too much to simply remove him. And he knew it would take some time to find the right kind of individual to be director of the strong Brussels operation he envisioned. Being a man of action, however, Hoover had to do something, even if it was incomplete or untested.

His solution was to bring in a current CRB man, Jarvis Bell, from Rotterdam to take charge of the CRB's administrative side of the Brussels office while Heineman stayed on handling German relations. The idea, no doubt, was to let nature take its course between Bell and Heineman and see who came out on top.

Within weeks, the matchup would show that nature could get ugly at times.

The day Hoover left Brussels—Wednesday, December 2—he finally came face-to-face with the people he was trying to help. Already, more than 400,000 meals a day were being served to Brussels residents from more than 130 canteens (also known as soup kitchens) throughout the city. That meant approximately 200,000 people—a third of the city's population—were receiving a ration of bread, soup, and coffee twice a day from their local soup kitchen. Brussels was divided into 21 districts, and each had a local committee that organized its own distribution. Bread and soup were delivered directly to those committees before 10 o'clock every morning. These facilities were supplied by 14 huge municipal kitchens that were run by many of the city's out-of-work chefs.

As reported by one British newspaper, "At the Central Kitchen 36 cooks and 50 assistants start at 2:30 every morning to make the soup. The cooks are divided into two squads and are supervised by a special committee. . . . While delivery is being made, by means of 14 trolleys, the cooks bone the meat and cut up the potatoes for the next day's soup."

On the morning of Hoover's trip around Brussels, it was cold, and there was a "dismal rain," according to Whitlock. The entourage included Hoover, Bell (probably as a way of confirming his new position), Francqui, Gibson, and others. They took a trip through the city on a journey that followed the food from Comité National preparation through to distribution. The group first visited one of the municipal kitchens, which was in a large hangar of an express company that no longer existed. It was a bustle of activity as cooks prepared the food and attended to gigantic cauldrons where the soup was cooking. The soup itself contained potatoes, meat, rice, onions, and leeks. Once the soup was ready, it would be transferred to manageable containers that were then carried by dogcarts or horse carts to nearby canteens.

The next stop for the group was a soup kitchen. The one they visited was located in an old concert hall on the Rue Blaes in the *Quartier des Marolles*. When

From the start of the war through December 1914, many Belgians were uncertain where or when their next meal would come. (Public domain; Herbert Hoover Presidential Library Archives, West Branch, Iowa.)

the motorcars pulled up out front, Hoover and the group saw hundreds of people standing in line. As Whitlock reported the scene, "They stood with the divine patience of the poor, there in the cold rain, shivering in shawls and old coats and wooden shoes, with bowls or pitchers and each with his number and his [ration] card, issued by his commune."

Hoover seemed touched by the quietly spoken "merci" as each person received a bowl of soup, a loaf of bread, and a little coffee and chicory. Whitlock wrote that each thank-you "somehow stabbed one to the heart, and brought an ache to the throat, and almost an annoying moisture to the eyes. One felt very humble in those human presences. . . . I knew what was going on in Mr. Hoover's heart when he turned away and fixed his gaze on something far down the street."

What struck an even stronger emotional chord were the canteens where the children and babies were fed. Before the war, children and babies of the poor had been fed at a few canteens operated by Les Petites Abeilles, or Little Bees. When Francqui and the CN were developing their soup kitchen organization in September, they decided to simply subsidize and expand the Little Bees operation. By the time Hoover showed up in Brussels, there were 32 such canteens feeding children and babies every day.

Hoover left Brussels with a new, even stronger resolve, if that was possible. He had seen the human side of the suffering. It was a picture that would stay with him forever. Whitlock wrote that when Hoover came to say goodbye, he "was very much moved by the sight of suffering he saw today, and very cordial and very fine. A remarkable man indeed."

A Chance Meeting Leads to Clandestine Activities

While Hoover had seen one side of Belgian suffering, he could only guess at how the German occupation must have been gnawing at others like a festering wound that couldn't be reached.

During the invasion, the Germans had been ruthless in their responses to any violent opposition. It would be no different with the occupation. Immediately after the invasion, Gibson reported that "huge red posters were put up throughout the country announcing that all villages where hostile acts were committed would be burned to the ground; that punishment for the destruction of roads, railroads and bridges would be visited upon the nearest village regardless of its guilt; that persons approaching places where [military] balloons and airplanes descended would be shot without warning; that hostages would be taken in every street of the town to be put to death in case of disorders; that the entire population would be held collectively responsible for the acts of individuals and that the innocent would be mercilessly punished with the guilty."

From such decrees and the swift brutality shown by the Germans to any overt act against them, any Belgians who wanted to take physical action against the occupiers realized they could do so only covertly, or innocent people would suffer.

For most civilians the only relatively safe avenue to show disdain for the Germans was passive resistance. While many Belgians were creatively subtle in expressing such resistance, a special few chose a more provocative—and highly dangerous—form that would be aimed squarely at the symbol of German oppression: Baron von Bissing.

The first proof the German governor general had of a major underground adversary came in a perfumed pink envelope carried by a pretty Belgian girl in early 1915.

But the story of that adversary started back at the time of the invasion with a chance meeting of two seemingly unlikely clandestine operatives—Eugene van Doren, a middle-aged Brussels cardboard manufacturer, and the Abbé Vincent de Moor, vicar of the Church of Saint Albert in a northeast suburb of Brussels. On August 20, both men had coincidentally gathered with others on a hillside near their homes to watch the Germans march into Brussels. Because van Doren was significantly taller than most, he caught the eye of the abbé, and the two men shared a silent moment of disgust and anger at the serpentine line of Germans

Eugene van Doren, a 38-year-old Belgian cardboard manufacturer, became a driving force in the underground against the German occupation. (Underground News, The Complete Story of The Secret Newspaper That Made War History, Oscar E. Millard, Robert M. McBride and Company, 1938.)

marching into their beloved city. That led them to speak to each other, and from that quick exchange an unlikely partnership in underground activities began. More importantly, their work, and the work of those who followed, would inspire an entire nation longing for heroes.

But their actions would also infuriate the Germans and lead ultimately to the imprisonment of many and the execution of some, including a heroic 23-year-old Belgian girl, Gabrielle Petit, who gave up a chance for freedom and said goodbye to her fiancé so she could work in the underground. She was to be one of 11 women the Germans tried, convicted, and executed by firing squad in Belgium during World War I.

As for Eugene van Doren, according to one history he was unusually tall for a Belgian, slim, and with sloping shoulders. He had a scholarly look that was accented by close-cropped hair and pince-nez (glasses with a nose clip rather than earpieces). At 38, with a wife and five young children, van Doren was a successful cardboard manufacturer. His home was near the abbé's Church of Saint Albert, and his factory was located in the northwest part of the city. A man of strongly held political beliefs, he had blue eyes that were, according to one history, "mild and thoughtful, but . . . they quickly reflect his feelings and occasionally flash with unexpected fire. His mouth, extremely mobile, smiles easily, and he has a ready laugh, when his eyes gleam boyishly." Altogether, he was a passionate, enthusiastic man who was never afraid to show both, and yet from his physical appearance he was the least likely of heroic figures.

In contrast, the Abbé Vincent de Moor was nothing like what most thought of as a priest. He was, according to one account, "broad-minded, iron-willed, fearless, and as strong as a horse," with black hair and the "jaw of a fighter. There was devil in his dark eyes and his mouth was like a steel trap. But the hard mouth frequently softened into a broad smile which, with the twinkling eyes, gave the aggressive features an unexpected and wholly attractive gaiety."

The Abbé Vincent de Moor (pictured in a later army uniform) was vicar of Saint Albert Church in Brussels and underground partner with van Doren. He also worked with British Intelligence against the Germans. (Public domain; multiple sources.)

Van Doren's initiation into underground activities began shortly after their first meeting. The Abbé de Moor (already experienced in clandestine operations) instructed his enthusiastic protégé, van Doren, whose passionate desire to strike any blow against the Germans had to be controlled and guided or it would have led to a quick capture. Initially, the priest had the businessman help stranded Allied soldiers who needed to be fed and clothed, given money, and ferried to various safe houses until they could be smuggled out of the city on their way to the Dutch border. Van Doren also carried letters for the underground network *Mot du Soldat* ("Word of the Soldier"), which passed letters back and forth between Belgian civilians and their loved ones fighting with King Albert outside of German-occupied Belgium.

As van Doren was drawn deeper into underground activities, he wasn't too surprised to find that his newfound friend, the abbé, was also an agent working with British Intelligence. Van Doren was sure the abbé was involved in multiple clandestine activities. In fact, de Moor had more than a handful of identify cards, all under different names.

But the student was an apt pupil. By October, van Doren was fed up with the constant flood of German *affiches* proclaiming the greatness of the German armies. He suddenly got an idea and bought a small duplicating machine called a "jelly press," and he and de Moor began creating "ironical little sheets illustrated with insulting caricatures pillorying the Kaiser and his troops. These they slipped into letterboxes as opportunity offered as they went about their more serious business."

These little bulletins were not something new in Brussels or Belgium. Since the occupation, other brave civilians had been producing leaflets, flyers, and/or information sheets that criticized the Germans or relayed outside news of the war. According to one history, "Day by day numbers of persons buy French and English newspapers and copy, upon the typewriter, the most significant passages. These leaflets are secretly distributed, either gratuitously, or in return for a trifling sum which more often than otherwise finds its way to the Red Cross or the National Committee for Relief and Alimentation [Comité National]."

The difference between van Doren and the other leaflet producers was that the cardboard manufacturer kept thinking bigger and acting on those thoughts. It was at this early stage that van Doren—without de Moor's knowledge—took on another partner, Victor Jourdain, the father-in-law of his sister. Jourdain was a 74-year-old heavyset man with blue eyes and "an expression of permanent irritation and a gruff voice that often reached the listener as an indistinct mumble through the bushy white moustache that drooped over his mouth onto his clipped beard." He had an air of "grandfatherly grumpiness."

But Jourdain was also a talented and highly skilled writer and newspaper editor. For 30 years he had captained the *Patriote*, considered by many the most influential newspaper of the Catholic press, with 100,000 readers. When the Germans had entered Brussels, he closed down the *Patriote* in concert with all other Belgian publications, and he and his ill wife, along with their daughter, Julie, lived above the shuttered newspaper offices.

Van Doren enlisted Jourdain's aid in producing his little bulletin—while keeping the newspaperman's identify a secret from de Moor.

In many ways, the cardboard manufacturer still saw his underground activities as more of a game than a dangerous pursuit. He did, however, begin to take some precautions, a few of which would later save his life and those of others.

At his home in a Brussels suburb, van Doren found a good hiding place to store his bulletins and other anti-German work. In the loft was a disused chimney that had an inspection plate on it. When it was time to hide things, van Doren would carefully remove the plate, tie all his papers together, lower the bundle on a long rope down the chimney hole, and replace the inspection plate.

For Jourdain, van Doren drilled three deep holes in the top of the editor's thick attic room door so he could roll up his papers at a moment's notice, insert them in the holes, and tap into place wooden plugs for nearly perfect hiding. Van Doren also installed a "discreet buzzer" in the attic that could be set off by someone in the living quarters below to warn Jourdain of any German raid.

To transfer Jourdain's material undetected through the city to a printer, van Doren came up with another idea. He began using a walking stick that had a hollowed-out compartment for rolled-up paper.

To carry the printed bulletins undetected, van Doren found carriers who developed their own unique hiding places, from under priests' cassocks and women's dresses, to inside shirts, suits, and jackets. Some who felt lucky even blatantly carried the printed copies in small boxes as if making a delivery of a legally allowed item.

German Action Stimulates Greater Underground Efforts

As van Doren and his team were taking such precautions, the Germans did something in the autumn of 1914 that would change the focus and drive of his burgeoning underground network. In some of Belgium's largest cities, the occupiers began to print a French-language newspaper as a way to control and manipulate the civilians. In Namur it was titled *L'Ami de l'Ordre* (*The Friend of Order*). In Brussels, the paper was titled simply *Bruxellois.*

When Jourdain read the first issue of *Bruxellois,* he was incensed, which stimulated his journalistic and patriotic feelings. Suddenly, he was a new man, with a new purpose in his life. He poured out his anger and frustrations in an essay that van Doren printed and circulated through the growing network he and de Moor were building.

After von Bissing became governor general in December, the occupation grew tighter and more restrictive. Then another German-controlled French-language newspaper, *La Belgique* appeared under the auspices of the governor general. This new affront fueled the desire of van Doren, Jourdain, and de Moor to do more in attacking the hated Germans and to find a way to bolster Belgian spirits.

They got their chance in early January 1915, courtesy of the spiritual leader of the Catholics in Belgium, Cardinal Désiré Félicien François Joseph Mercier, who resided in Malines in the Flemish province of Antwerp.

The cardinal had been born in Braine-l'Alleud, 20 miles south of Brussels; had been educated in Louvain; and was "proud of being a Walloon," according to U.S. Legation Minister Whitlock.

He was a very tall man, well over six feet, and stood out in any crowd. When Whitlock first met the cardinal, he was impressed because Mercier "entered, advanced, tall and strong and spare, in the long black soutane with the red piping and the sash, not with the stately, measured pace that one associates with the red hat, but with long, quick strides, kicking out with impatience the skirt of his soutane before him as he walked, as though it impeded his movements."

CRB delegate E. E. Hunt, when describing Mercier, focused more on his face. It was "thin, scholarly, ascetic, with sparse, grayish-white hair above it . . . and his forehead so white that one feels one looks on the naked bone. His eyes are deep-set, the eyes of a man who sees a great deal. There is a pleasantly humorous look about the corners of the firm mouth, but the expression of his face in conversation is that of a man who knows what he thinks, measures what he says, and feels in advance the exact effect of every remark he makes and of every look he casts upon one."

Mercier had become archbishop of Malines in 1906 and a year later was elevated to cardinal, so that he was both a bishop and a cardinal.

In late August, as the Germans had swept through Belgium, he had had to leave his beloved country and go to Rome to select a new pope, who became Benedict XV. While in Rome, Mercier had heard about the arrest and imprisonment of numerous Belgian priests and civilians, the destruction of many towns and villages, and most distressing of all, the burning of Louvain and its great university, where he had been an instructor years before.

The cardinal had immediately traveled to Brussels and paid a visit to Governor General von der Goltz to ask for the return of Belgian priests and teachers who had been deported at the time of the invasion. He also talked about the refugees who wanted to return home but were afraid any fighting-age men would be arrested or deported. Mercier—who had already negotiated an agreement with the German governor of Antwerp, General von Huhne, that all returning Belgians would be left alone—was able to get von der Goltz to accept and apply the agreement nationwide.

Even with that significant victory, Mercier watched in growing concern the increasing harshness of the German occupation, especially when Baron von Bissing took over from von der Goltz in early December. During that month the cardinal and the new governor general had fought in a spirited correspondence that had done little to quiet either man's objections to the other's actions. The cardinal's growing anger and frustration, fueled by what he saw and heard from people all over Belgium, would lead him to a major act of resistance that would stimulate and engage the work of van Doren, Jourdain, and de Moor.

Each year Cardinal Mercier would write a Christmas pastoral letter that was read by priests at each congregation throughout the country. Because the cardinal was known as a straightforward speaker who did not hold back his opinion, most Belgians hoped he would be forthright in his first letter under German occupation.

The cardinal did not disappoint. His long missive was a civilian call to passive resistance. It began by describing some of the horrors of the August invasion but did acknowledge that Belgians should "abstain from hostile acts against the enemy army." But then Mercier proclaimed that the German occupation government was "no lawful authority. Therefore, in soul and conscience you owe it neither respect, nor attachment, nor obedience."

This was no humble speech from a person locked within a brutal German occupation; this was a spiritually free man calling upon Belgians to remember the past, accept the present, and hold in their hearts the knowledge they were unjustly imprisoned and would someday be free.

Von Bissing was furious. He immediately had Mercier's printer arrested, confiscated all copies of the letter, and put the cardinal under house arrest. Von Bissing understood that while the Christmas pastoral letter was a powerful indictment of the Germans and a call to action for Belgians, it meant nothing if the Belgians had not seen or heard it.

While the first reading had been limited in its reach, the pastoral letter still became the talk of Belgium. One writer explained that most Belgians had not heard the entire letter, nor read any of it, so "the result was that comparably few people actually knew the contents of the Letter about which everyone was talking."

That gave editor Victor Jourdain an idea. He asked van Doren if he could find a printer to do the job and then distribute copies to as many people as possible. Van Doren agreed immediately and worked with the Abbé de Moor to get it printed and distributed. After a precarious start—in which one printer's operation was shut down and de Moor came close to capture—a second printer was found, and the huge job of printing and distributing 25,000 copies was completed. (The rest of the world read the cardinal's inspiring words in late January 1915, when a copy was smuggled out of Belgium and printed.)

It was a major success for the small underground team, as it was for a handful of other groups throughout the country that also took the risk of printing and distributing the cardinal's letter. One history records that "a dozen editions were printed in French, and three in Flemish; it was also distributed by means of type-writing. . . . At the establishment of a single printer in Brussels the German police confiscated 35,000 pamphlets."

An Underground Newspaper Is Born

For Jourdain, this was just the beginning, as he followed up with his biggest, best idea. It was a natural extension of his anger at the Germans and his earlier impassioned essay reacting to the German-sponsored newspapers. The elderly editor told himself: If the Germans were going to publish such lies, he needed to counteract their propaganda with an underground newspaper that told the truth. It would be called *La Libre Belgique* (*The Free Belgium*). He would write, edit, and pay all costs while van Doren would be responsible for all production, printing, and distribution.

When Jourdain approached van Doren with the concept, he did not mince words when it came to the potential danger. "Your part is going to be more difficult . . . more dangerous too. You've got to find a way of getting the paper printed regularly and distributed . . . not by hundreds but by thousands. You'll need help, but that's up to you. I don't want to know who you choose. . . . All I say is be careful who they are. They mustn't know of my existence. The fewer in the secret the better."

With childlike enthusiasm, van Doren was all in and couldn't wait to tell his friend and underground partner, de Moor. Even though van Doren knew he could not divulge that the famous editor Jourdain was at the helm of the new publication, that did not dampen his excitement as he nearly ran to see the abbé. Van Doren was sure that when he told the abbé the exciting news, his priest friend would immediately and enthusiastically embrace the idea. As the book *Underground News* later described the scene, de Moor surprised van Doren when he initially said he wasn't sure he would do it.

"I'm sorry, Eugene, but I must think it over. I don't think you realize what you're taking on. Within a week you'll have the Kommandantur, the police and all their spies after you."

"I know that," van Doren retorted. "So much the better. I'm not afraid, if you are."

De Moor seemed to set his large jaw, then spoke quietly, "I've got responsibilities that don't permit me to take fool risks unless they're worth while." He was thinking of all the other, much more important, clandestine activities he was involved in, such as payments to Belgian railroad workers for troop movement information. Taking on a highly dangerous newspaper could jeopardize all his other work.

Van Doren stormed out of the abbé's room. The priest knew "perfectly well that van Doren had not stopped to think of all the difficulties and grim possibilities of the job he was undertaking so blithely. The running of a clandestine newspaper in occupied territory was daring to the point of folly. . . . True, too, that he had helped van Doren with his offensive little pamphlets. But that was only a prank that he could stop at a moment's notice."

On reflection, however, de Moor thought of all that van Doren had done for him, how he had "taken on every venture the Abbé had suggested to him, without a thought to his own safety."

A short time later, the priest was at van Doren's door. "Well, hot-head," de Moor started, "after due reflection I've come to offer your vast organization the benefit of my services. Now tell me what it's all about."

Before a first issue could be produced, however, van Doren and his associates would have to find a printer and distributors willing to take on such a dangerous job. And they had to tighten up their operation, set up security measures, and prepare for a project that had no end in sight, for once it was started, according to one account, it had to be "continued at all costs if the enemy were not to be allowed a victory which would be worse than if the attempt had never been made. It was a tall order."

7

London

"The Supreme Test of the Man"

Hoover was strongly affected by his first trip into Belgium. He arrived back in London on December 3 and found that his wife, Lou, had just returned from America. Despite the fact they had not seen each other for months, Hoover immediately took the time to write up an extensive report about his trip, covering everything from canal blockages to how many sacks of wheat were left in Brussels warehouses. Ever mindful of the need to keep Belgium in the public eye, he released the report to the press, and it was picked up by numerous British and overseas newspapers, including the *New York Times.*

In Britain, the *Daily News & Leader* was one of the newspapers that published it. In the article Hoover reported, "Of a population of about 650,000 remaining in Brussels an average of 218,000 were on the adult canteens and 31,000 babies on the baby canteens last week, or more than one-third of the total population." But these statistics were fleshed out as he recalled the visit to the Brussels canteen: "I can imagine nothing more pitiful than the long lines of mothers we saw, with children in their arms, waiting their turn at these canteens."

Instinctually knowing what sound bites were before they existed, Hoover declared, "The clock has stopped in Belgium," which meant that "practically every Belgian soul will be dependent upon the Commission for bread within thirty days."

The practical, no-nonsense businessman summed up his trip by saying, "It is difficult to describe, without appearing hysterical, the condition of the civil population of Belgium. I do not know that history produces any parallel of a population of seven million people surrounded by a ring of steel."

What Hoover had to accomplish was extraordinary, and he had to work on multiple levels simultaneously, as if he were playing a three-dimensional chess game. Hoover was dealing with several problems:

- Personnel upheavals in his executive staff of the Brussels office.
- CRB delegates not sure what their jobs were and either overreaching or underachieving.

- German continual requisitioning of Belgians' foodstuffs.
- British demands to stop German requisitioning or all support would be withdrawn.
- Lack of a consistent financial structure to support the ever-growing relief program.
- No method of shifting funds back and forth from occupied Belgium without transferring actual currency or gold. The money that was made by selling imported CRB food had to somehow find itself back outside of Belgium so it could pay for more food.

While there was still much to do, much had been accomplished. According to Tracy Kittredge—a Californian and one of the first 10 Oxford students into Belgium who later wrote a history of the CRB (which was never officially published)—"By December 1 the German government had agreed not to requisition any imported foods, to temporarily suspend the requisition of native cereals, and to grant the Commission liberty of action within Belgium." The Germans had even indicated they might be agreeable to allowing the Belgians to keep all their projected 1915 harvest if the Allies allowed the CRB to continue the relief work.

In addition, the Allied governments had allowed the work in the first place; the British government had granted an initial subsidy of £100,000; and the Belgian government had advanced large sums to the CRB.

Even with these positive movements, though, victory was far from assured. As CRB delegate Robinson Smith wrote in an article about Hoover, "The supreme test of the man was in those first months of the Belgian Relief. Then he had no certain government support, his responsibility continued to the actual feeding of the people, and the whole thing was new."

Part of the problem was that people simply didn't know exactly what the CRB was. According to Kittredge, "The chief significance of the Commission, and most of the difficulties, arose because of the fact that it was a diplomatic compromise, not only in the beginning but throughout the whole of its activities. As a tremendous business organization, it had to carry on its work in a way satisfactory to [warring nations] that were struggling with each other for life and death. It was only Mr. Hoover's ingenuity in persuading or bullying the various [warring nations] into making the concessions demanded by the other groups that made possible the continuance of relief work."

Kittredge went on to explain, "In carrying on these negotiations, the Commission acted from the first as a semi-diplomatic body, sometimes dealing with the governments concerned through its diplomatic patrons, more often acting through personal interviews or correspondence of members of the Commission, and especially of Mr. Hoover, with the competent officials of the various governments. The Commission's work was based on a loose sort of contract between the belligerent governments, with the Commission acting as a negotiator and a depository and the executive agent for enforcing the contract. Such a position has probably never been occupied by a similar body."

British Opposition to the CRB

In December 1914 it was anyone's guess if the CRB would survive from day to day. Since Hoover's return from Belgium, he felt, according to historian Nash, as if "the British posture toward his relief project was hardening." Opposition was gaining momentum as individuals such as First Lord of the Admiralty Winston Churchill, Chancellor of the Exchequer David Lloyd George, and Secretary of State for War Lord Herbert Kitchener insisted that any relief to Belgium was assisting the enemy. Their contention was that the CRB's work helped the Germans for several reasons:

- The food simply replaced what the Germans were requisitioning.
- Any imports to Belgium indirectly helped support the heavy monetary war levies the Germans were placing on Belgians.
- Without the CRB the Germans would, no doubt, feed the Belgians.
- It relieved the Germans of feeding the Belgians, so it prolonged the war.

Additionally, and well outside the public's earshot, there was another argument circulating among the British military leaders. In a startling statement, Hoover later told Whitlock that "Kitchener had made the cynical and brutal statement that if the Belgians were to be let to starve it would then require more German troops to subdue the revolutions that would break out as a result of hunger, and thereby so much weaken the German forces." In other words, Belgian starvation would create such havoc that the Germans would have to pull troops from the Western Front to maintain order.

Much of this was laid on the table at a hastily arranged meeting between Hoover and British Prime Minister Herbert Henry Asquith on Friday, December 4. Hoover later wrote a memorandum recording what happened at the meeting in which he indicated that Asquith was not very sympathetic to the Belgian cause. He felt the Germans were obligated to take care of the Belgians, and food relief would relieve them of their obligations. He saw no way that the British government could sanction such assistance to the enemy.

By all accounts, Hoover stood up to Asquith. He even hinted—if not downright threatened, depending upon which source is consulted—that the British government could not afford to oppose the relief work because it might jeopardize favorable American public opinion toward the British.

Hoover told Whitlock later that before the Asquith meeting he had sent a long cablegram to his journalist friend and CRB executive Will Irwin in New

British Prime Minister Herbert H. Asquith initially did not believe his government should sanction or financially support Belgium relief. (Public domain; multiple sources.)

York, exposing the Kitchener argument. Hoover had, as he told Whitlock, instructed Irwin to "hold this until I send a cablegram releasing it, then blow the gaff, and let the work of revictualing [supplying] go up in a loud report that shall resound over the world to England's detriment."

Walking into the meeting with Britain's prime minister, Hoover supposedly had the cablegram in his pocket, according to Whitlock's account. That message represented the huge hammer of public opinion. Hoover had known from the very start that it was critical to have public opinion on his side for the CRB and Belgium relief to have any chance of success. None of the governments involved would ever agree to the work without the specter of negative public opinion hovering over them. Believing this, Hoover had been carefully constructing that hammer since October, and as proof, Belgium and its plight were never far from the front pages of the world's major newspapers. World opinion was then strongly on the side of aiding Belgium in any way possible. It was time to see if such media-generated public opinion had the power he thought it did.

Hoover wasted no time in preliminaries. Once Asquith finished stating that his government would not support Belgium relief, Hoover launched his counteroffensive, as described later by Whitlock.

"You have America's sympathy only because America feels pity for the suffering Belgians," he told Asquith. He then pulled the Irwin letter from his pocket and showed it to the prime minister. "I will send a telegram at once, and tomorrow morning the last vestige of pity for England in America will disappear. Do you want me to do it?"

Asquith was stunned. He told Hoover he was not used to being addressed in such a way, adding, "You told me you were no diplomat, but I think you are an excellent one, only your methods are not diplomatic." Hoover supposedly "expressed regret" to the British head of state, but, as historian Nash commented, "It did not sound like the most penitent of confessions."

Three things about this story indicate that the meeting probably didn't take place so cinematically: the prepared cablegram to Irwin has never been found;

Hoover was, at times, prone to dramatic retelling for the public relations (PR) effect; and Whitlock was a born storyteller with a flair for literary drama.

No matter the details of what happened in the meeting, the end result was indisputable—Asquith became more supportive of Belgium relief and the CRB.

CRB Publicity Helps to Drive World Opinion

On a smaller, everyday scale, Hoover continued to chip away at the arguments opposing relief in every possible way, in every meeting and correspondence with the British government, and in every contact with the press. He knew Asquith had changed his mind in large part because the British people were supportive of helping the Belgians in any way possible. Much of that public support came from the direct efforts of Hoover and his CRB publicity team. Whenever possible, Hoover engaged the press to keep the plight of Belgium in the forefront of the minds of the world. At every opportunity he issued press releases; reported activities of the London, Rotterdam, and Brussels offices; and forwarded messages or information the CRB had received from inside Belgium. He also gave speeches whenever and wherever possible, despite the fact that he didn't seem to like public speaking and was not known as a strong, large-group orator.

As Hoover later recalled to an associate, "I employed myself from the first of December until Feb. 17th [1915] in constant proselytizing with Englishmen of importance, and with the Cabinet ministers on this issue. In the meantime, we have worked up a sentiment in the United States, Canada, Australia and other countries in favour of the feeding of the Belgian people to such an extent that it became a worldwide movement of interest, second only to the war itself. We carried on the most active campaign of publicity by every device we could invent in England as well as in those countries."

In early December, Hoover publicized letters that were still coming in from various Belgian communes asking for assistance. On Thursday, December 3, the British *Daily Telegraph* ran an article titled "A Plea From Belgium 'We have nothing here.'" It opened, "The following letter, received yesterday by the Commission for Relief in Belgium . . . from the authorities of the Belgian town of Dendermonde, is typical of the pathetic requests which arrive daily from every part of Belgium."

The letter reported that 1,200 homes in the town had been destroyed during the fighting. While many residents had fled during the fighting, people had come back: "With a few exceptions, most of the returned men are workers, and as all the works are closed, now, nobody can work in this country. Consequently, you will quite well understand the situation. We have nothing here. We need most food, beds, clothing, and coals. Even if we could buy a quantity of about 150 tons of wheat at a very low price we should be happy to do so, so that we may be able to feed the hungry poor workpeople."

Only three days later, the London *Sunday Times* ran a major article, "'One Huge Cemetery.' Desolate Belgium. Pitiful Sights." It was a report of what Theodore Waters of the American *Christian Herald* had seen when he had followed a cargo of food that the paper's subscribers had donated to the CRB. Waters said, "In Antwerp I saw over one thousand poorly clad women, one in bedroom slippers . . . standing shivering in the snow and slush, waiting for food to be doled out to them, and this under the shadow of a big hotel where well-fed, well-clad soldiers drank and made merry."

Waters rode in a two-horse carriage from Antwerp to Brussels. On the road "we overtook thousands of refugees tramping dejectedly along, weary and forlorn, returning to villages and towns where there is not now food enough to sustain those who are already there."

Most striking to the American journalist was the fact that "the country was one huge burying ground. Always between the ruined houses we could see graves. Graves, graves, graves! In some would be stuck a bayonet with a Belgian soldier's cap hanging on it. Above other rough [graves were] white crosses rudely inscribed, 'To the memory of a Belgian soldier.' On one grave was a child's shoe, poor little marker of its parents' grief. Graves, graves, orphans, orphans, a country desolate; its trees felled in rows to make way for the gullets, its crops long gone to seed, and sticking leanly up through the snow, dead things in rows like markers in a miniature cemetery."

These accounts of Belgium's misery were, for the most part, true and heartrending. They also served well Hoover's greater purpose of building public sentiment and sympathy so that the relief work could go on.

Four days after the Waters article appeared, Hoover came up with a smart PR move. He sent a telegram to King Albert asking that one man, representing all the American press, be allowed to visit the king at his battlefield command in the little sliver of free Belgium along the Yser Front. That journalist happened to be Ben Allen, Hoover's trusted friend who was helping CRB founding member Edgar Rickard in the CRB publicity department. Four days later, the king agreed to the interview, and Allen crossed the English Channel. He had to wait days to interview the king, but on December 20 he got his chance. From that trip and that interview, the worldwide media learned more about the suffering Belgians and their tall, dashing, heroic king.

Hoover himself was becoming prominent, and on Friday, December 18, he gave a major speech at the American Luncheon Club in London, which was covered by numerous reporters. He was introduced by U.S. Ambassador Page. It was probably one of his first important public speeches.

The *Bristol Times Mirror* covered the event and quoted Hoover, who declared: "The Commission had under charter 32 cargo ships for the transport of foodstuffs, and had delivered into Belgium something like 50,000 tons of food, with a gross value of about £500,000. For future delivery, cargoes aggregating a gross value of about two million sterling were arranged."

But just in case listeners thought the organization was growing too big to need continued individual help, Hoover put those figures into context: "Large as these figures might appear, when contrasted with the required monthly budget of £1,200,000, they were adequate only for a short period."

Hoover also made sure to speak directly to those who thought the Germans were still taking Belgian food. "I wish to make clear with emphasis that the Germans are not interfering with this foodstuff. Not one mouthful, so far as we know, has gone down a German throat yet, nor do I believe we will ever be confronted by such an event."

While Hoover wanted Belgium to be in the press as much as possible, he also wanted the information to come from him or the CRB publicity office. Three days before Christmas, multiple newspapers throughout Britain ran an extensive report from William Stratton, one of the CRB delegates inside Belgium. This was probably a Hoover-inspired and CRB-distributed report because of its widespread publication, because of its use of Hooveresque language and statistics, and because the delegate who penned it continued to work for the Commission long after the article had been published, which probably would not have happened if it had not been sanctioned or if it had been critical of the CRB in any way.

Stratton was 22 years old, from Utah, and one of the first 10 Rhodes scholars to go into Belgium as a CRB delegate. In the British newspaper *Morning Advertiser,* Stratton's inside-Belgium report began with a description of the lines of the needy in Brussels. "Each morning, between the hours of 11 and 12, some 200,000 persons received their portions of soup and bread, the lines forming and moving through the distribution depots with perfect precision and regularity."

Stratton admitted that "a few—very few—persons of the humbler classes have been driven by hunger to seek food by breaking into the houses left vacant by rich Belgians, who have gone to England for the duration of the war. In some cases they have even been driven by their hunger to the point of rioting with the German troops stationed over them. Fortunately thus far these incidents have been followed by no serious consequences, largely owing in those cases with which I am familiar, to the reasonableness and the good sense displayed by German commanders."

Then, sounding like Hoover when he would imply dire consequences to gain advantage over opponents, Stratton warned about the rioting: "If this sort of thing continues—and it may be more or less expected as long as there is hunger—there is no knowing what may be the result. It might be most terrible."

There was nothing like the vision of food riots to keep the sympathy and charity coming. With this kind of exciting copy, the newspapers never seemed to tire of running stories about Belgium. And Hoover never seemed to run out of stories to send them.

Financing Belgium Relief Becomes Critical

In late November/early December, Hoover faced two major issues regarding the financing of the ever-growing CRB:

1. Where to find steady financial support. Donations from around the world were substantial, but they did not begin to cover the nearly £1.5 million per month that was needed to ship approximately 80,000 tons of food per month into Belgium.
2. How to get the money that was made from selling the food *inside* Belgium to the CRB *outside* Belgium so more food could be bought. The Germans would not allow any physical transfer of currency or gold in or out of occupied Belgium. Some kind of exchange had to be developed.

The first shipments into Belgium in late November had established an initial structure and process. The CRB-imported food was sold to the Belgians in a chain that included consumers, local communes, provincial committees, the Comité National, and the CRB within Belgium. Everyone in the chain paid whenever possible, and at a price slightly above cost so that the profit could pay, at least in part, for those who needed charity.

Unfortunately, no matter the line of sale, the result created the same problem: money generated from the imported relief was stuck in Belgium. Somehow, the money had to get back out of Belgium and into the CRB's hands so it could purchase more food.

The key to solving the exchange problem came from Aloys van de Vyvere, the minister of finance of the exiled Belgian government operating out of Le Havre, France. Hoover had met with him in late November, and van de Vyvere had told him that the Belgian government had certain financial obligations within Belgium that it could no longer pay. These included salaries to Belgian state employees, civil service pensions, old-age pensions, allowances to soldiers, and military pensions. Together, these obligations totaled 10.5 million francs per month.

Hoover's plan was a surprisingly simple and straightforward monetary exchange. The money generated in Belgium by the imported food could pay the Belgian government's salary and pension obligations, while the equivalent of those payments *inside* Belgium could be advanced to the CRB *outside* Belgium by the exiled Belgian government. It was a financial exchange without the physical transfer of any currency or gold in or out of Belgium. While additional subsidies would be needed to fully fund the CRB's efforts, the exchange would provide the critical vehicle needed to exchange any large sums in and out of Belgium.

Such an exchange, however, did not solve another underlying problem: the exiled Belgian government did not have the large sums that the exchange—and the CRB—needed. Hoover believed the problem could be solved by Allied subsidies advanced to the Belgian government as loans. In essence, the Allies would subsidize the CRB through those loans.

By the end of 1914, the Germans had agreed to Hoover's monetary exchange concept. The biggest hurdle, however, was getting the British to agree to the substantial government subsidies needed to fully fund the exchange plan and the CRB. On this critical financial issue, Hoover was focused solely on convincing the British government (as opposed to the French government) because the British government was "the banker of the Allies," and Hoover hoped it would be possible to convince the British to "formally authorize exchange operations and to furnish an adequate and regular subsidy in order that the Commission could maintain the necessary program of importations."

The British would not be an easy sell. A major concern was that the Germans were still requisitioning supplies throughout Belgium. The British refused to support food relief that they thought would simply be replacing what the Germans were taking. Hoover was told he would get British support for his CRB program only if the Germans would agree to stop taking Belgian supplies.

Hoover set to work. Finding no sympathetic ear or help from von Bissing in Belgium, Hoover decided to go over von Bissing's head—a move he no doubt knew would incense the governor general and rattle Whitlock (both of whom felt that traditional protocol should always be followed). When it came to securing continued relief for the Belgians, Hoover couldn't care less about von Bissing's or Whitlock's feelings. Hoover turned to James Gerard, the U.S. ambassador to Germany stationed in Berlin, and asked that he petition the German civil government for a nonrequisition guarantee in Belgium.

While that process was continuing, von Bissing threw a different wrench into the diplomatic works. As Brand Whitlock noted, only seven days after von Bissing's appointment, the German decreed that the Belgians must pay as a "contribution of war" 40 million francs a month—480 million francs per year. A later history of the CRB explained that the sum "was to be guaranteed by the Deputations Permanentes of the various provinces, and to be paid to the Germans in the form of notes issued by the Société Générale de Belgique [Émile Francqui's bank] on the security of the promises of repayment of the Deputations Permanentes."

Besides the burden this indemnity would place on the Belgians, it had an additional negative effect. "The announcement of this war tax was a further serious embarrassment to Mr. Hoover in his negotiations to secure subsidies from the allied governments."

But Hoover's take on von Bissing's war tax was typically pragmatic. Money was one thing; food was altogether another. He and Ambassador Gerard had received a New Year's Eve present in the form of a German government guarantee that no more Belgian foodstuffs would be taken, effective January 1, 1915. To Hoover, the new monetary war levy was not on the same par as the just-received foodstuffs guarantee. "If the Germans take money out of Belgium," Hoover said, "it may indirectly cause great hardship, but it does not starve the Belgians, because the whole problem of feeding Belgium is that of actual material foodstuff required, which we propose to introduce into the country in sufficient amounts to supplement the stores which are already there." A CRB history explained that with the Germans agreeing to "leave to the Belgians their own products, Hoover felt that the matter of money indemnity was of less importance."

Unfortunately, the Allies did not see it Hoover's way. Despite the securing of a nonrequisition guarantee, the British were "much incensed at the German levy and were not disposed, so long as the Germans continued to exact money from Belgium, to assist the Commission by subsidies."

Hoover would have another battle on his hands.

Hoover Turns Again to Deal with Brussels

While the head of the CRB was gaining great Belgian publicity around the world and making small inroads with the British government, he was also learning in December that things were going to hell in Rotterdam and Brussels.

Captain Lucey might have had excellent executive abilities, but he also could be a maverick with a loose and informal style. Because he sometimes felt that it was better to break the rules and later apologize rather than to pass up an opportunity to move the relief efforts forward, Lucey had undertaken many initiatives that had rankled not only the Dutch but also the Germans, the Belgians, and even some Americans in Brussels.

Additionally, as Hoover had seen in his first visit and learned from reports by Lucey and others, the CRB Brussels director, Heineman, was too involved with, and tied to, the Comité National and his own business affairs to fully comprehend the necessity of a strong, independent CRB presence in Brussels and across Belgium. And he was still using his own office at 48 Rue de Naples as the CRB main office.

Meanwhile, Hoover's November decision to have Bell handle administrative duties in Brussels while Heineman stayed in place to deal with the Germans was not working well. The two men fought constantly and were driving Whitlock crazy. Within a few weeks, Whitlock had had it with dealing with long conversations with Bell over who was in charge of what. Whitlock called for Bell's removal and in a letter to Ambassador Page in London complained, "By some sad fate everyone who comes in here feels that he must assume command of the entire situation, oust everybody from all authority, and establish as it were, a government of occupation."

Bell's removal did not solve anything. Kittredge wrote in his CRB history, "During the month of December the Commission offices in Belgium were gradually coming into working order, but chaos still reigned in the Rue de Naples [Heineman's office that was also the CRB head office in Brussels]." As CRB delegate Robinson Smith remarked dryly in a later article, the CRB was then "an organization without one."

The situation was so bad that Kittredge wrote, "The provincial [CRB] delegates, coming in after strenuous days spent in touring about their provinces in motor-cars, found little tangible assistance at Brussels. . . . [They] usually left Brussels in despair and went ahead on their own initiative to work out plans of distribution in co-operation with the provincial committees. The delegates on going to Brussels would often wait for hours in the corridors of the office, without being able to find anyone who was at all concerned about their difficulties. Every time they would ask for advice, the almost invariable answer would be: 'We will go into the matter; won't you call in to-morrow?' The exasperated delegate would walk out with his problems unsolved and return to his province to win his own battles as best he could."

It was time that the CRB assert itself against what Hoover perceived to be the CN's continual efforts to take on the entire operation. By the end of December, Hoover needed to deal with the "new administrative difficulties that had arisen."

Hoover seemed to be able to solve any problem laid before him, whether it be in London, Rotterdam, or Brussels. According to Kittredge, "Everywhere that he went he found anxious problems to be solved, involved situations to be disentangled, seemingly irresistible obstacles to be overcome, but almost invariably in a very few days he was able to find a ready and satisfactory solution."

For Hoover, this Brussels problem was a do-or-die situation that needed drastic action. He told a friend later, "We have had great trials over [on] this side through the conduct and attitude of the Belgian Committee [the CN] and part of our Commission who were in control in Brussels. Things got on to such a footing, that it was brought home to me, that unless an immediate revolution took place we might afford one of the greatest scandals of the War and be in a position that would damn the balance of our lives. After many sleepless nights, I went to Belgium and found everybody dead against me."

8

Brussels

Francqui Runs the CN Show

By the end of the year, Émile Francqui had whipped the Comité National and the provincial committees into the shape *he* wanted. Just like Hoover—but with totally different, dictatorial methods—he had either cleared the field of competitors or brought them under control and established himself as the driving force behind the CN. With the military precision he had learned from being a Belgian Army officer in the Congo, he ran the weekly Comité National meetings. They illustrated perfectly the kind of man and executive he was.

The CN weekly meeting was held every Thursday in the Brussels office of the Société Générale de Belgique bank, which Francqui controlled as its director. The men gathered in the large, ornate parlor room. Furnished in the Empire style, it was a vision of cream and gold gilding. Two tall rosewood clocks stood as sentinels, one on each side of the wide double doors. At each end of the room were large mirrors, and hanging from the ceiling was a massive glass candelabrum over a T-shaped wooden table covered in green baize that had turned gray with age. Watching over any proceedings were white marble busts of King Albert and Queen Elizabeth and large paintings of two previous Belgian kings, Leopold the First in coronation attire and Leopold the Second in a general's uniform, in ornately carved wooden frames.

For CRB delegate Hunt, the room conjured up much more than its furnishings. "There is a suggestion of the French Revolutionary period about the room. It is decorated in the style of the Empire, but one feels *avatars* of *sans-cullottes* [incarnations of revolutionaries] may lurk behind the upholstered chairs, and that one breathes an atmosphere of conspiracy and subterranean activity."

The practical, hardened businessman Francqui would have dismissed such a notion. The only occurrences and conjuring to happen in that room were what he wanted said and what he wanted done.

The 40 men who entered the room every Thursday for the CN meeting would not have necessarily agreed with that, but few would have questioned Francqui publicly. They were generally older, prominent, influential businessmen, high government officers, or political leaders, and all were dressed in business formal attire. Most boasted impressive beards and bald heads. Hunt gave intimate details of some of them in his book, *War Bread*:

- Paul van Hoegaerden, "the vigorous, vociferous president of the Liège Provincial Committee, with a trick of pulling at his collar as if its tightness impeded the flow of his harsh, metallic words; his able son Jacques, secretary of the Liège [provincial] Committee, one of the few younger men in the National Committee."
- Fulgence Masson, "vice-president of the Hainaut [provincial] Committee, wise in counsel, quick in action, his round face humorous as a clown's."
- Louis Franck, "president of the Antwerp [provincial] Committee . . . with black Assyrian beard and sparse hair, piercing eye and clean profile, always smiling his enigmatic, optimistic smile."
- Michel Levie, with a "Michel Angelo profile . . . president of the light railways of Belgium."
- Chevalier de Wouters d'Oplinter, CN vice president, "quiet, efficient."
- Firmin van Bree, CN vice president, "swarthy as the pirate Black Beard."

Francqui usually entered the room after all others were there. The big, heavyset chairman of the CN would go quickly to his seat. As Hunt reported, "He seats himself, raps on the table for quiet, and without waiting for it, begins to chant the order of the day, his heavy Bismarckian head sunk forward, his voice running like a millrace [the channel carrying the swift water that drives a mill wheel]."

Francqui would read quickly and humorously, according to Hunt, and include weekly information provided by the CRB; notifications of new rules imposed by the relief's patrons because of German orders; information about shipments that had arrived in Rotterdam or that were in route to the provinces; a financial report; an agricultural report; and any instructions to the provincial committees.

Hunt described these meetings as "stage-plays purely. No Germans are present, but the sense of oppression is always there, and to break it the assembly seems to take on an attitude of mock-seriousness and to shoulder its deliberations lightly."

Everyone in the room knew that the real work had already been done by Francqui and a small executive group behind closed doors. It was generally considered for the best because Belgium before the war held numerous financial, social, political, and language factions that few men could have tied together. Francqui was one of those who could, and most of the men accepted it as the best for Belgium during the war. Hunt explained, "Great financiers are usually dictators, and Mr. Francqui is no exception to the rule. But the situation seems to call for a dictator . . . the real work goes on behind the scenes, and the committeemen are not sorry to have it so."

Another CRB delegate, Arthur Maurice, described Francqui as being "dominant over all, like a martinet of a school teacher among his pupils."

9

Elsewhere in Belgium

Harassment by German Sentries Leads to Trouble

As 1914 came slowly to a close, many Belgians could not see much to be cheerful about, even during the Christmas season.

For the Germans, the 1914 Christmas spirit did not seem to touch many of their sentries who were posted throughout Belgium. They continually stopped, searched, and generally harassed the CRB delegates as the Americans tried to make their way around Belgium. Even though the German soldiers had been dealing with the Americans and the concept of massive food relief for at least two months, they still didn't seem to gain much in understanding nor acceptance of the interlopers.

The delegates carried with them multiple documents, including a U.S. passport, a letter in German stating the carrier was a member of the CRB, and always a *Passierschein* (a German safe conduct pass) for that particular trip. If they were lucky, the *Passierschein* had been signed or authorized by the governor general himself, and those coveted items became known to the delegates as G-Gs. The passes usually stated that the Americans were not to be detained, searched, or questioned without cause.

Unfortunately, many times the passes were not even looked at, while the sentries ordered the Americans out of their automobiles and interrogated them extensively. In some cases, the Germans actually took apart the CRB cars to search for contraband. Any complaints about treatment or questions about the guards' authority to take such actions could mean rough handling or jail. Once in jail, the only way out was to somehow get a message to someone in the CRB or the American diplomatic corps, who would then secure release from a German officer higher up the chain of command.

To Hugh Gibson, such behavior was part of the "German love of bullying . . . an essential part of the German system. Under that system every German is overbearing to some other German unless he happens to be of the very lowest form of animal life—and then life isn't worth living. The whole system is to cringe before your superiors and bully your subordinates. It is done without any sense of shame or decency and is accepted even by the sufferer as perfectly natural.

"It is a common thing in Belgium to see a sentry stop a motor filled with officers, explain that he has orders to examine the passes of all that pass that way—and then to see one of the officers rise up in his car, red in the face with rage, curse and revile the soldier in a way that would cause a mutiny in any other army and then roar at the chauffeur to drive on. The sentry would usually shrug his shoulders and slouch back to his sentry box as though it were perfectly natural that an officer and a gentleman would so violate all discipline and be guilty of such contemptible injustice."

The Americans were, however, not totally blameless when it came to sentry post incidents. A day after Christmas 1914, Gibson wrote about two new Rhodes scholar delegates and a stenographer who were entering Belgium for the first time. They had been pulled out of their car at the frontier and searched. While the three had been warned back in Holland that it was illegal to transport letters in or out of Belgium, the men were still found carrying numerous letters to and from a variety of people. They were immediately tossed in the local jail. There, they made their situation even worse. The stenographer had written a letter to his girlfriend back home, which he decided he should tear up while in jail. "Of course that meant that he was caught red-handed 'destroying documents' and the whole crowd was in bad," according to Gibson.

The CRB car was confiscated, and the men were then brought to Brussels under guard. Before Gibson and Hoover, who was in Brussels at the time, headed over to the political bureau to try and talk them out of jail, Gibson had some choice words for those to be rescued: "It is astounding how grown men can be such fools. We shall probably succeed in getting them off but it is almost more than they deserve."

Hoover was continually faced with such youthful indiscretions as he tried to get the young delegates to understand they must remain absolutely neutral in both thought and deed if the relief was to continue.

So, while some of the fault in the Germans' sentry stops and searches lay with the Americans, most often it was the pigheadedness of German sentries who refused to review or honor the passes that the CRB men held. Official complaints to von der Lancken and even to von Bissing didn't seem to do much good, despite von Bissing's order to all troops within his domain to allow CRB delegates through without stopping, searching, or questioning. The governor general was sure no troops under his command would ever go against such a directive.

The issue would come to a head in mid-January 1915 with a comically sad event for a young German officer. The incident would be a catalyst for a major confrontation between von Bissing and Hoover.

SECTION II

CONFLICTS, 1915

Rotterdam harbor: A U.S. cargo ship in the process of off-loading sacks marked "Kansas Sun Wheat Four" into a canal barge. (Public domain; Herbert Hoover Presidential Library Archives, West Branch, Iowa.)

10

The Mechanics of Relief

By New Year's Day 1915, the CRB had had only two full months to build its operations and put into place the basic processes by which it could ensure proper supervision and handling of all relief supplies until they were officially handed off to the Comité National in Belgium.

Four critical components were necessary for food to be purchased and delivered into the hands of the needy:

- Reliable international shipping
- Steady transportation into Belgium
- A distribution system that was fair and equitable to all
- Permanent financing

By the start of 1915, partners and procedures for shipping food from England to the Netherlands had been established. Barge transport of food from the Netherlands into Belgium was working, despite numerous challenges. And the distribution of food within Belgium was efficient, despite political spats. But permanent financing—a critical element of Hoover's plan—remained elusive, and in three weeks a major challenge would blindside Hoover and jeopardize the fledging relief organization.

Shipping—A Fundamental Problem to Find and Protect

From the beginning, the securing of international ships to haul the purchased food from around the world to Rotterdam was one of the CRB's greatest difficulties. It was wartime, shipping was at a premium, and the British had established a blockade of German ports and declared the North Sea a war zone. Into such a scenario, one man, Herbert Hoover, had had the audacity to ask a belligerent nation to allow ships to carry food to the enemy's occupied territory. It was only because the food was destined for the Belgians and the operation would be handled by neutral Americans that the British allowed such action.

This did not mean shipping was no longer a problem. Quite the contrary. The first two vessels permitted through to Rotterdam by the British were the *Coblenz* and the *Iris*. Their red-tape delays had shown how difficult providing a steady, reliable flow of food into Belgium would be once the CRB was fully ramped up. Hoover, with the diplomatic help of Ambassador Walter Page, suggested to the British government that one Brit be appointed as liaison between the CRB and various British departments to smooth the way and to help cut through any red tape.

Lord Eustace Percy was appointed to the new position by his boss, Foreign Secretary Sir Edward Grey. As Hoover said of Percy, "His fine idealism, high intelligence, and capacity for hard work were rare in any country. His sweet personality endeared him to all the members of the C.R.B. He knew all the paths through the red tape of government. He quickly developed a friendship for the Commission, and he never flagged in supporting us among his official colleagues. Had he been a member of the Commission he could not have been more loyal to its purposes. Much of the success of the Commission was due to him."

Percy was able to help in the first shipping challenge that came from the British. The government initially permitted only neutral shipping to be used, which severely limited the number of ships available for charter. Early in 1915, however, Hoover—with the help of Ambassador Page in London and Ambassador Gerard in Berlin—was able to obtain an agreement from the German government that any ship flying the newly created CRB flag and carrying relief for Belgium was immune from being stopped, seized, or sunk. With the German guarantee, and with Percy's help, Hoover was able to secure from the British the right to charter English shipping.

The number of ships the CRB needed was relatively small but would grow as the CRB enlarged its organization. The target of bringing approximately 80,000 tons of foodstuffs each month into Belgium required approximately 20 vessels, depending on each ship's tonnage capacity. But to guarantee the monthly amount on a consistent basis, at least two months' worth of foodstuffs would need to be in transit at all times—a total of 50 to 60 ships under CRB charter at any one time.

As the CRB grew, the war dragged on, and the international shipping situation became more competitive, the Commission ended up buying some vessels to complement the charters. At one time, more than 75 vessels, either owned or chartered, were flying the CRB flag.

Before the CRB fleet had reached such a size, however, it had to face another challenging situation. In early February 1915, Germany declared a war-zone blockade around the British Isles that included merchant shipping even from neutral countries. The German government said the new situation was in response to the British blockade of German ports—the militarists on both sides wanted to starve their opponents into submission.

Each CRB ship was outfitted with large signs on both sides to alert German U-boats that it was not an enemy vessel. (Public domain; *A Journal from Our Legation in Belgium,* Hugh Gibson, Doubleday, Page & Co., 1917.)

The German blockade would be enforced by a deadly submarine fleet, which was instructed that a state of unrestricted warfare existed—meaning commanders no longer had to warn merchant ships before striking. Many of the German submarines worked out of the Belgian port of Ostend, giving them greater range and access to British sea lanes than if the U-boats had been based in German ports.

Upon hearing the news, the CRB rushed to reconfirm with the Germans that they would honor their initial agreements of CRB ship immunity. Hoover, who was then in Berlin for another CRB issue, had a meeting with German Chancellor Bethmann-Hollweg and asked for confirmation that the CRB flag would be honored by submarine commanders.

"I told him the story of a man who had a bulldog which he assured his neighbor would not bite." Hoover said. "But the neighbor replied: 'You know the dog would not bite, but does the dog know it?'"

The chancellor agreed to remind the submarine commanders that CRB shipping was off-limits; Hoover was not totally convinced that that resolved the issue. He would be correct and the issue of unrestricted submarine warfare would become an international crisis in less than three months.

Meanwhile, it was determined that each CRB ship about to sail had to apply for and receive numerous passes and permits. From America, each ship was first given a certificate from the U.S. Customs Service stating its cargo and destination. The German ambassador in Washington would then use that certificate to issue a permit that, in turn, would secure a safe-conduct pass from the German consul of the port of departure. The British consul at the port would also issue a certificate to the ship.

On board, each vessel was provided with the CRB's large flag that proclaimed, "Commission Belgian Relief, Rotterdam," and two huge cloth signs, five feet high by 100-feet long, that were attached to each side of the hull declaring the ship was sailing under the Commission for Relief in Belgium. Electric lighting signs were also created to be used at night.

Another stumbling block for shipping was competition in the charter marketplace. In the early stages of the relief during October, November, and December of 1914, other relief organizations such as the Rockefeller Foundation and individual Belgium relief groups in America were collecting money and purchasing food to send to Belgium. But they faced the same situation with shipping as the CRB and ultimately ended up bidding against one another for ships, thus driving up the cost.

Hoover, not wanting any competition in Belgium relief—mostly for practical efficiency, but, no doubt, also to satisfy a personal desire to be the sole provider of Belgium relief—quickly found ways to drive the others from the arena. Once that was achieved, the CRB entered into arrangements with two major English shipping firms, Birt, Potter & Hughes and Trinder, Anderson and Co., which agreed to set up the CRB's shipping department for free.

Other issues that arose in late 1914 and early 1915 included obtaining war-risk insurance coverage; securing special sea routes from both sides to safely traverse minefields and stay as clear of U-boats as possible; and dealing with the British insistence that all CRB vessels stop at British ports before reaching Rotterdam since the Germans adamantly stated they would not guarantee the safety of any CRB ships that *did* stop at English ports. (This was resolved by Gerard, the U.S. ambassador to Germany, who got the German government to back down.) These and other issues were tackled as they arose by Hoover, Lord Percy, Page, Gerard, and the CRB shipping director, John Beaver White.

Even after resolving the startup issues and establishing general permissions, approvals, and procedures, shipping would be a never-ending issue that faced numerous crises—none bigger than the German *promise* of immunity, which was never a *surety* of safe passage.

Transportation—Following the Wheat

With the CRB's massive program of relief, tight controls were necessary not only to manage such massive amounts of foodstuffs but also to satisfy the ever-increasing Allied demands regarding the usage and distribution of all imports.

Rotterdam was the central transshipping point for all relief supplies destined for Belgium. A major international seaport before the war, Rotterdam was well prepared for the influx of relief vessels, with its modern equipment for loading and unloading, its full complement of stevedores, and the hundreds of canal barges available for carrying supplies into Belgium's extensive canal system.

The importation goal for the CRB and CN had been established by Francqui at approximately 80,000 tons of food per month—far less than the 250,000 tons per month that Belgium had imported before the war. And 80,000 tons only equated to a meager 10 ounces of food per person per day. The 80,000 tons included 3,000 tons of rice and dried peas, 15,000 tons of maize, and 60,000 tons of grains, primarily wheat.

Wheat was the most important import because it was the primary component of bread, and bread was a critical staple of the average Belgian's diet. The processing of the wheat shipments, and how the wheat was distributed and converted into bread, set the standard for how all other imported products would be handled and controlled.

Using as an example an average-sized vessel carrying approximately 9,000 tons of wheat, such a ship could be unloaded at Rotterdam in 36 hours of nearly nonstop work. When the vessel first arrived in port, it was greeted by giant floating elevators and a multitude of lighters, or barges, ready for loading. Floating elevators would come alongside the supply vessel and pump the wheat that was in bulk out of the ship's forward hold and into the lighters. In the ship's stern, or back, the lighters would pull alongside and stevedores would come aboard, climb down into the aft hold, and shovel the wheat into sacks. The sacks would then be manhandled over the side and placed in the lighter's hold.

Once full, each lighter's cargo size would be recorded and then the hold would be secured with a Dutch and CRB seal. Even the barge's depth in the water would be recorded as a way of spotting any unauthorized removal of wheat. A shipment number would be painted onto a large square of cotton and placed prominently on the barge. All the barge's details would then be transferred to the CRB Rotterdam office, which was within eyesight of the harbor, and a battery of clerks would dutifully record the information and begin tracking the precious wheat.

The destination of each barge was carefully planned out from a complicated process that had started inside Belgium. Weeks before, local communes would have determined how much bread per week they needed to feed all the people who were enrolled in their local ration system.

Because each loaf of bread had been standardized as to size and weight, it was already known how much wheat was needed to make each loaf, so a quick calculation could determine the amount of wheat needed.

This was not as easy as it sounds. In German-occupied Belgium, needs changed rapidly, Robinson Smith, chief delegate in Mons for Hainaut Province, noted, "Two weeks ago there were stores of native wheat in certain parts of the province of Hainaut; enough to last fifteen days; the Commission therefore did not send

The scenic look of a Belgian prewar canal, this one through the city of Tournai southwest of Brussels. The canal-barge tugboat is waiting for the footbridge to be raised. (Public domain; multiple sources.)

into those parts. But those fifteen days are past and at once those parts have to be placed on the same footing as the rest of the province." And before that, he said, "Three months ago only the millers feared the exhaustion of supplies; everyone had his bread, why worry. Ten days ago the provincial committee here at Mons said they were being saddled with too much rice: it was too much of a charge for the province, the population were not used to its consumption. Last night there was a not a sack left in the warehouse."

When the commune's wheat needs were estimated as best as possible, this information was then sent to the provincial committee, which processed all communal orders and transferred those to the Comité National, which conveyed all provincial orders and its own recommendations to the CRB offices in Brussels, Rotterdam, and London. While the London CRB office would make any adjustments to its wheat buying to match the newly received needs, the Rotterdam office—knowing what wheat was currently available and projected to arrive in the next month—would match the kind of wheat (bulk or sacked) on hand with what was needed where.

But the uncertainty of specific needs at specific times led to the development of a warehouse system within Belgium to complement direct shipping to communes. Approximately 40 CRB warehouses were established throughout the country so supplies could be brought in prior to knowing exactly where the need was greatest.

Once the Rotterdam office knew where the wheat barges should go, it would secure from the local German diplomatic offices all the necessary authorizations for the barges to be sent into Belgium.

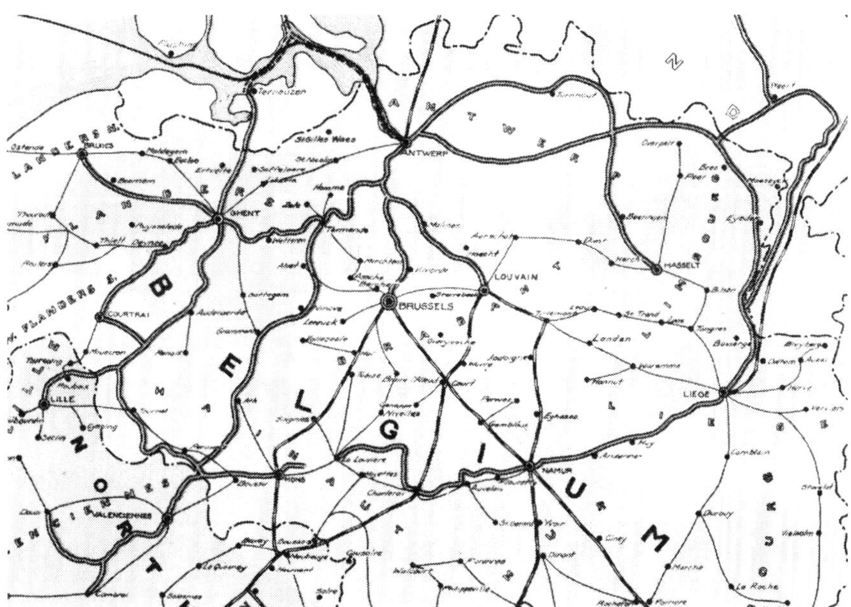

A closeup view of the canal network within Belgium. Solid double lines indicate canals, smaller two-toned double lines are railways, and single lines are roads. (Author's archives.)

Loaded down with paperwork and wheat, the barges would then be pulled by tugs toward Belgium. When they reached the border, or frontier, each barge would be checked to confirm the seals were still in place and the barge's depth remained the same. CRB personnel positioned at the frontier would telegraph the Rotterdam office when the barges had passed Dutch and German checkpoints and were in Belgium. At all subsequent control stations along the way, more telegrams would be sent so the Rotterdam office had continual updates on where each barge was before reaching its final destination.

Belgium, like Holland, had a vast network of canals that covered practically the entire country. There were three main arteries from Holland into Belgium, with some continuing into France. Before the war, these canals had been freely used, but with the German occupation they were under tight controls and some were highly restricted because they were in the Etape Zone, a subzone of the German Army Zone, which was controlled by the military, not von Bissing's civil government.

The first major canal was from the Dutch towns of Terneuzen and Sas van Gent to the Belgian city of Ghent (which was in the Etape). This was a large canal that could handle big barges carrying 1,200 tons. At Ghent, the cargos from the larger barges had to be reloaded into 300- and 400-ton lighters to go north to Ostend and Bruges or south to Courtrai (Kortrijk in Flemish), Tournai, Mons, or Charleroi, with branches leading to the French cities of Lille and Valenciennes.

The second major canal ran from the Dutch town of Roosendaal to Antwerp and from there to Brussels or Louvain. It was also large enough to handle 1,000-ton barges. At Antwerp, small canals led to Mons and the surrounding area. This second major canal was doubly important because most of Belgium's chief flour mills were around Brussels or Louvain. Much of the imported wheat ended up heading down this canal to the mills for processing before leaving again as flour in smaller lighters along smaller canals.

The third major canal came from Rotterdam to the Dutch town of Weert and into the Belgian province of Limbourg (now spelled Limburg). It branched west to Turnhout and Antwerp, south into Holland again at Maastricht, and then back into Belgium to Liège and Namur. Depending upon the water levels, lighters could be sent from Namur along the Sambre River to Charleroi, or south on the Meuse River to Dinant, and ultimately to Charleville in France.

The extensive Belgian waterway network meant that all the major centers of all the provinces (except Luxembourg) could be supplied from Rotterdam. Depending upon the final destination, however, a barge could take days if not a week to complete its journey. Before the war, tugs were used to haul barges through the larger canals, while horses were used to pull them through smaller ones. With the advent of war and the requisition of most horses by the military of both sides, horses were in short supply. That meant in some cases that men were hired to haul the barges by hand through the smaller canals, and in a few cases women were used as well.

When a barge reached its destination, a CRB delegate would normally be there to record the breaking of the seals, the checking of the shipment size, and the unloading—all of which was carefully recorded and transmitted back to the Brussels and Rotterdam offices.

Usually at this point, the CRB would officially hand over responsibility for the shipment to the Comité National, which was officially in charge of distribution. But because the CRB had agreed to Allied demands of true accountability throughout the entire process, Hoover insisted that CRB delegates continue to observe and supervise throughout the process to catch any oversights and/or abuses. (Such CRB meddling in what the CN considered to be its own affairs was a constant bone of contention between the CRB and the CN, and it would cause innumerable conflicts, both large and small, throughout the history of the relief.)

With the wheat barge that had just reached its destination, if there were any shipment discrepancies discovered during unloading they were quickly investigated by the CRB delegate on hand and the outcome was reported.

Opportunities for theft during shipping were minimized by the rules, but the potential still existed. CRB delegate Joe Green—who would ultimately head the critically important CRB Inspection and Control Department—related, "Thefts by the unloading gangs were of common occurrence. I made it a rule that each gang was to be collectively responsible for any thefts occurring while it was at work, and on one occasion when four workmen with a cart were carrying off sacks of maize, I discharged the entire gang and stuck by my refusal to reemploy the men under any consideration. That action had considerable effect upon the honesty of other gangs with which we contracted."

Another point of possible problems was with the lightermen and their families, who lived aboard the barges. "Lightermen were also notorious thieves," Green continued. "When the barge had been entirely unloaded, it was the duty of the chief [Belgian] surveillant to search it from top to bottom to see whether any sacks had been hidden away for the use of the lighterman and his family. From time to time the American representative was supposed to accompany him in these searches, in order to see that they were properly carried out. No part of the barge, even the sleeping cabin of the family, was sacred. On one occasion I discovered and confiscated a large sack of grain hidden under the bed of the lighterman's daughter."

The result of such a find could be devastating to the lighterman and his family. Any such theft resulted in the barge being placed on the CRB blacklist, and if a similar incident happened again the lighterman would no longer get any CRB contracts for carrying relief supplies. In war-ravaged Belgium, where industry and commerce were basically dead, the cutting off of any steady work could spell financial disaster.

For the wheat barges that reached a mill and turned over their cargoes to a miller to be ground into flour, the controls became even tighter. The miller had to account for everything, from the initial cleaning of the wheat, to the grinding that created bran (used for cattle), to the refuse. He even had to account for whatever flour he might find when he cleaned his mill.

Because of the extraordinary wartime situation and the agreements that had been made with the Allied governments, any wheat that entered the mill had to be CRB wheat. If there was indigenous wheat available, it would first have to be sold to the CRB before being delivered to the mill, where the same rigid rules used for imported wheat would apply.

Since the beginning of the occupation, most of the country's smaller mills had been shut down and only larger ones were kept open to grind the CRB wheat. Most Belgian provinces had six to 10 large mills in operation, with the exception of Luxembourg Province, which received its flour from Brussels mills. Each mill had a provincial committee bookkeeper to manage the large amount of paperwork involved in ensuring compliance with all regulations.

These mills and what they produced were so important to the relief effort that they were prominently marked with CRB placards to protect them from German soldiers who might want to buy or requisition flour. Additionally, German soldiers guarded each one at night. Even the wagons that delivered the flour from the mill to the bakers were protected by CRB placards. The CRB warehouses were similarly protected. The placards themselves were so valuable that they were numbered and recorded, and if one went missing it was immediately reported to Brussels.

The flour was as tightly controlled when it reached individual bakers, and that control even included machinery to shake the empty sacks of flour to get the last bit from each. Bakers had to present their finished loaves to a central warehouse, where each loaf was weighed. That, according to CRB delegate Robinson Smith, was because a baker, if left to his own devices, would "sift out the fine white flour left to make his loaf; and his loaf was almost never due weight. He did in many cases mix potato flour with the gray flour left to make his loaf; and his loaf was almost never due weight." Such abuses, according to Smith, had been going on "from time immemorial," so to prevent those activities the standardized loaves and warehouse checks were put into place. For the most part, those safeguards worked and curbed much of the baker abuse.

How much flour a baker received was dependent upon his customers. Within each commune, each family received a ticket good for 330 kilograms of bread per head per day from a baker the family had chosen. A hundred kilos of flour, when mixed with water, would produce 135 kilos of bread. The baker would, therefore, receive only enough flour to produce enough bread for the tickets allotted to him by his customers.

As the CRB controls were put into place, and as all settled into their respective roles in the relief system, many delegates were surprised how ingenious the Belgian bakers continued to be in their attempts to scam the system. And the battles that raged between the two forces brought out the most creative side in each.

This was especially true for E. E. Hunt as he took on the work of chief delegate for the city and province of Antwerp and tackled the systemic problem of unscrupulous bakers. Many of them would end up lamenting the day Hunt came to town.

Distribution—Following a Recipient of Relief

CRB delegate Smith, working in Mons and covering the large Hainaut Province, put the relief effort's ultimate goal in perspective when he stated in early 1915, "It is not starvation the Commission wishes to forestall, but an approach to starvation."

That was echoed by an old peasant woman Smith met on his travels around the province. The CRB delegate asked her if anyone had died of starvation in her commune. She answered straightforwardly, "No, we have too much to die, and not enough to live."

What compounded the situation was that conditions for individual Belgians were changing all the time. One day a person was able to pay for food; another day he or she was laid off from a job and could no longer pay. This meant the

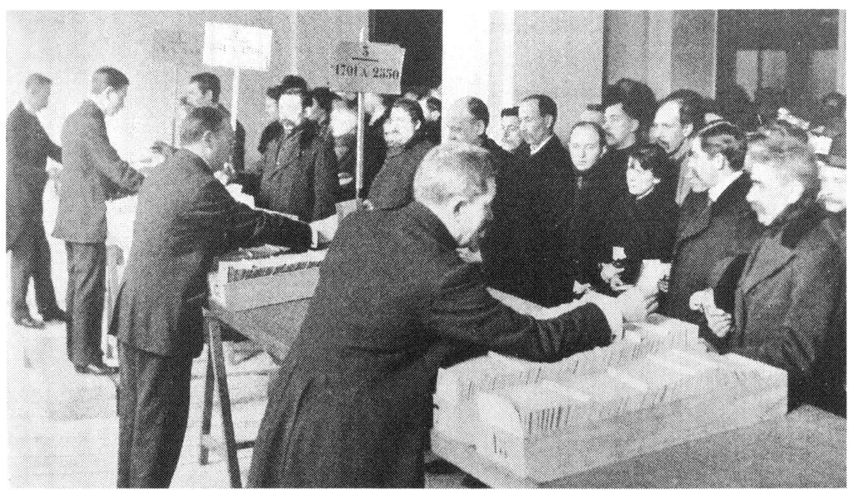

Each Belgian recipient of food relief had to have a ticket that was issued by the local commune or provincial committee. (Public domain; *The Millers' Belgian Relief Movement, Final Report, 1914–1915,* William C. Edgar, Miller Publishing Co., 1916.)

relief system had to be flexible enough to handle rapid changes. Fortunately for the Belgians, their commune form of government already contained much of that dexterity, and it ultimately evolved with the help of the input from provincial committees, the Comité National, and the CRB to accommodate the needs of more than 7 million Belgians.

Smith helped the world understand how the system worked when he wrote a series of articles outlining the major components of the relief work. His articles were full of operational details but they were also PR appeals for Americans to keep giving money to the cause. He humanized the explanation of how the soup kitchens worked by telling the story of an unnamed man living in Brussels who had a wife and three children.

The man suddenly found himself out of a job after his factory ran out of raw materials and shut down. With little savings, he applied for relief for himself and his family at his commune's local soup kitchen. The same day he applied his application was investigated to verify what he had said. Because this was done locally in his commune where many people knew one another, his need was quickly confirmed and he was issued a blue ticket with a large numeral "5" plainly stamped on it to indicate five recipients. The ticket was good for 30 days.

Once the man had the ticket in hand, he showed up every day at 11:00 a.m. at the soup kitchen with a large pitcher or other container. He was given five half-liters of meat-and-vegetable soup and five small loaves of bread, which he carried to his nearby home.

Each portion of the soup he received cost two cents to make, while the bread cost six cents per loaf. Initially, the man was proud and found a way to pay five cents a day, but after some time he could no longer pay and the color of his ticket changed to indicate full charity.

His commune paid half the cost of the meal, with the other half coming from provincial and CN subsidies and money collected from those who could pay. In addition to the daily soup and bread, the man received a ticket for a weekly supply of potatoes and coal. The communal personnel who did the actual work—from investigating cases to punching tickets to ladling out the soup and handing out the bread—were all volunteers.

To the Americans, the entire system was a marvel of efficiency and, as Smith reported, showed its value by how non-existent lines were, regardless of how many were served. "There is no eternal standing in line," Smith related. "Twelve hundred are dealt with in an hour at any table of any one station; there is no crowding or cursing or need of police."

Many of the other communes and provinces around the country had slightly different systems, but that was allowed as a way of acknowledging the fact that all provinces, communes, and Belgians were not the same.

The CRB Relief Difference

Smith took the time in his articles to give readers an understanding of the overall picture of relief and how it was different from other forms of aid in times of suffering.

He began by saying that the establishment of the CRB gave the delegates a true understanding of what relief really meant. "Relief means the putting into operations of such an extensive and well-ordered distribution of supplies that everyone will automatically and inevitably be taken care of." Smith clarified by saying this kind of relief "does not mean a house-to-house visiting. . . . What Belgium needed was forty huge warehouses into which the Commission food could pour by train and barge from Rotterdam. This the Commission prepared for, this the Commission achieved."

Smith explained that the CRB's massive efforts were different "radically from other large ventures in relief." He recalled the "spontaneous, magnificent" responses to American disasters still in the minds of many U.S. readers—the 1889 Johnstown flood that killed more than 2,200 people, the 1900 Galveston hurricane where 6,000 died, and the San Francisco earthquake of 1906 that took the lives of more than 3,000. "These charities, called so quickly into being," Smith wrote, "were for the moment. They were of no avail unless their relief was brought to bear at once, as it was." As for the Red Cross, it was pledged to aid combatants on all sides during a war. Its military relief operations were different in goals, scope, and duration.

The CRB was an organization specifically targeted to feed an entire nation caught in the middle of the largest war the world had ever seen—something that had never been attempted before. Or even thought to be achievable. As Smith explained, with the CRB, "the need was pressing, the only hope of coping with it was on deliberate, permanent lines. The Commission acted from the first as if it had come to stay."

And Hoover fashioned it in a completely different way from how other relief efforts had been established. He organized it like a big business, which had opened it up to criticism that Smith acknowledged and described. "Many people still think of it as a huge American concern, eager to sell its goods. Every delegate has that anxious down-town look for a new customer, precisely as if he were to get a certain percentage or rake-off from a sale."

"But that is where the difference comes in," Smith declared. "Though organized like a big business, where every account is scrupulously examined, every expenditure tallied, there is absolutely no diversion of funds [away from relief] . . . though the Commission acts like a commercial house in reducing its expenses to the very lowest and in bringing its efficiency to the very highest, it is in its motives and spirit wholly an experiment in ideality, and that is what lends to the work such an absorbing, not to say exciting, interest."

Moving quickly into hyperbole, Smith went on to say, "Almost every dream of the idealist comes true. People, for once in the world's history, are governed by purely unselfish motives."

To explain further, Smith stated, "The Commission has a fairly free hand: what it says is law; and that law is never the slightest in favour of one class or party or province. It considers solely the general good. And every time it acts that way, the Commission succeeds. It is bound to win out. Given a fair field, justice and reasonableness are sure to win."

To prove his point, he told a couple of stories when the CRB tried to make a "distinction" or distribute food in an unequal way and had failed. "It tried to give a little more food to the man that worked than the man out of work. But the man that worked, worked only three days a week, and the days he was home and still got more, the other man made trouble for him. We tried at the beginning to give more food to children over twelve than to those under, until one day a woman came and said that her daughter Marie Louise was big enough to be fourteen. After that every day-old baby in Belgium received as much as an adult. Its mother was weak and deserved it."

The Belgian Unemployed

When it came to Belgium's industry and commerce, the German invasion and early months of occupation had completely shut down and shut off those two vital economic generators from the outside world. Additionally, the Germans had dismantled many factories and heavy equipment and taken them back to Germany and requisitioned much of the nation's livestock and stored supplies.

As Antwerp chief delegate E. E. Hunt put it, "A great part of machinery of peace-time can be converted into machinery with which to manufacture implements of war. Above all soldiers need food and consume it in immense quantities. Finding all these things at hand in Belgium, the Germans proceeded to commandeer them right and left. . . . Belgium was gutted." By early 1915, when the CRB and the CN had secured German guarantees not to touch any imports or Belgian crops, there wasn't much left to take.

The human by-product of the German actions—especially in the most industrialized country in Europe—was large numbers of men and women thrown out of work.

Added to these unemployed, or *chômeurs,* were Belgians who could have worked for the Germans but refused. They cited The Hague Conventions of 1899 and 1907 (multilateral treaties regarding the conduct and laws of war) that declared people in occupied territory could not be forced to do work that would help the conqueror's war efforts. While it's true that most Belgians employed in essential services such as transportation, water, and power did return to work after the invasion, resentment was building and would soon lead to action by some.

Because of Belgium's well-organized communal system of governing, the unemployed immediately become one more subject of a list in the extensive number of lists that were compiled by each commune. The communal lists then became the basis for pensions and benefits and for the ration card program that was the foundation of food relief. Additionally, the unemployed lists had been earmarked to use for a public works program that the Belgians had developed to put the unemployed to work during the occupation. Unfortunately, the Germans had quickly quashed much of that concept.

Many wealthy Belgians did their part to try and absorb some of the unemployed. In their offices they sometimes brought on extra personnel, and on their estates whenever they could they added more household staff, increased grounds personnel, and even occasionally created work projects that were acceptable to the Germans.

Antwerp merchant Edouard Bunge was one who did his fair share and more. Besides continuing to house, feed, and employ 100 workers and their families on his Hoogboom estate and in Chateau Oude Gracht, he also created a works project to build canals throughout the 740-acre property as a way of employing those who had no other work. To any inquisitive Germans, these canals were irrigation ditches to help maximize farm yields—a worthy endeavor during the occupation. The Germans never seemed to catch on that those canals more or less meandered through the property and never seemed to be completed, no matter how many men were employed.

The CRB did its part to aid the unemployed. It ultimately hired thousands of Belgians in ancillary relief work—everything from chauffeurs for the delegates' cars to stenographers, typists, translators, general office personnel, and even mechanics to keep the motorcars running. To help monitor and supervise the relief distribution, the CRB was provided by the provincial committees with certified lists of the unemployed.

Those lists of *chômeurs* were substantial and growing every day as the war dragged on. In pre-war Belgium, the total number of civilians working in commerce and industry was nearly 1.8 million. With the start of the occupation, the first enrollment of classified unemployed across the country totaled 760,000, and when dependents of those unemployed were added on, the total came to nearly 1.4 million people.

Initially, the *chômeurs* were not an issue with the Germans because they were included in the total population covered by the CRB's and the CN's relief efforts. In fact, one of the major tenets of the CRB, according to Hoover, was that no one could be denied food because of employment status. The concept was that all Belgians must be allowed access to relief—then, and only then, those who could pay would pay, and those who couldn't pay (such as the unemployed and dependents) would receive charity.

Through 1914, the Germans generally went along with the unemployed being part of general relief. They issued statements assuring the Belgians and the world that Belgian men of military age and the unemployed would not be singled out for forced labor or for the nearly inconceivable idea of deportation. As one Belgian historian reported, "At least ten times in the course of 1914 and 1915, the Germans had given their pledge word not to deport Belgians to Germany or not to interfere with their personal liberty."

One of those pledges came in a letter from Baron von Huene, then military governor of Antwerp, to Cardinal Mercier, on October 18, 1914. That pledge was read by priests to their congregations throughout the province as a reassurance after the fall of Antwerp. It stated, "Young men need have no fear of being deported to Germany, either to be enrolled in the army or to be subjected to forced labour." A few weeks later, as reported by Cardinal Mercier, that same promise was extended to the entire country under then Governor General von der Goltz.

But time, a stalemated war, and the realities of the military's need for bodies were strong inducements to change German minds.

11

London

Northern France Becomes an Issue

On January 2, 1915, Hoover received a telegram in London from James Gerard, the U.S. Ambassador to Germany, the man who had already helped Hoover and the CRB secure German nonrequisition guarantees of food. This time, Gerard informed Hoover of the need for food among the French citizens trapped behind German lines in the narrow strip of northern France between the trenches and Belgium's southern border. More than 2 million people lived in that area and word had reached Gerard that they were about to starve—the mayor of Roubaix had said 250,000 residents would be starving within a few days if nothing was done. The ambassador wanted to alert Hoover to the tremendous need and to the fact that he had already telegraphed the State Department requesting an arrangement be made with the German and British governments to allow the importation of 1,000 sacks of flour a day for three cities (Roubaix, Tourcoing, and Lille) within the French territory.

The State Department's reply, which Gerard copied to Hoover, said that the British had no objections to the importation of food into northern France just as it had none with the CRB's importation of food into Belgium. So, the cable continued, "The question how far it is desirable that the Commission should extend its activities to districts in France, now in German occupation, seemed to be one primarily for submission to the French Government."

Hoover and the CRB had heard stories about the food situation in northern France for the past few months before receipt of Gerard's telegraph. In fact, in November and December 1914, the CRB and CN had agreed to feed those living in and around the two northern French towns of Maubeuge and Givet-Fumay because they had been placed under von Bissing's civil government control. (After making the exception to feed Maubeuge, the CN's Émile Francqui had opposed feeding Givet-Fumay because he felt it should be the responsibility of the French government to do so, but the entire CN voted to provide relief.) For administrative purposes, Maubeuge was attached to Hainaut Province, while Givet-Fumay was attached to Namur Province. Beyond these two areas, however, Hoover and the CRB could do no more because of the lack of resources and governmental approvals.

Personally, Hoover had had to face a distasteful episode regarding food for France. In January he had received a visit in the London office from an American ready to supply food for the French city of Lille, which was in the German Army Zone. While Hoover never publicly named the man, he was identified by Kittredge in his history of the CRB as the former American consul at Lille, which would indicate it was Christopher J. King.

The man came to Hoover and stated he had been retained by merchants in Lille to bring in 10,000 tons of grain monthly. He said he had the money and was authorized to act as the import agent. He had already made a visit to the British Foreign Office and was planning on approaching the French government. As Hoover wrote to Louis Chevrillon (soon to be appointed CRB delegate in France), the man "proposed to us that we should join him in selling wheat to the people of Lille at 70 to 80 centimes per kilo cost to us, about 38 delivered to Lille), and that we should divide the profit with him and among ourselves individually."

Hoover was incensed. "We threw him out of the office," he told Chevrillon. "The gentlemen in this organisation are here for humanitarian reasons. We are giving our time and paying our own expenses and do not propose to take advantage of the fact that we have a food monopoly to damn our immortal souls, nor do we propose to have any dealings with such characters as this."

All of this meant that Hoover was well aware of the needs of northern France when he received Gerard's telegram. Within a few days, he telegraphed back to the ambassador stating that "we have had this called to our attention repeatedly." He wrote that the CRB was prepared to take on the "extra labor entailed in finding the foodstuffs and transporting them through Belgium into this section, provided of course the Germans agree." With that said, however, Hoover also felt that the French had to support their own people and would have to "make a substantial subscription to our funds for Belgian work." He also informed the ambassador that "we are already sending some food into one section of France, but other sections we have been unable to undertake, as we have no resources with which to do so."

One of the major stumbling blocks to opening up northern France to CRB relief was how the territory—and Belgium—was divided up and governed.

When the 400-mile-long Western Front trench line from Switzerland to the North Sea was established in November and December of 1914, the land then occupied by the Germans—nearly all of Belgium and a thin strip of northern France—was divided up into zones. (See the map in Reader Aids.)

The Occupation Zone consisted of the majority of Belgium (excluding East and West Flanders) and the French districts around Maubeuge (16 miles south of Mons) and Givet-Fumay (31 miles southeast of Charleroi). The vast majority of the work of the CRB and CN was focused in this zone. Governmental responsibility for the Occupation Zone fell to Governor General von Bissing and his German civil government.

Within this region all local administrations, including communal officials, the police, and the judicial system, still functioned as they had before the war, but under the watchful gaze of the Germans. Even with von Bissing's restrictions, Belgian residents living in the Occupation Zone did maintain a certain number of personal liberties and freedoms.

The Army Zone lay between the trenches and the Occupation Zone. It was a strip of land approximately 50 miles wide that ran from Verdun to the North Sea. It was controlled by the several German armies that served in the region. The Army Zone was divided into two smaller subzones—the Operations Zone, which started at the front lines and extended inward for approximately 12 miles, and the Etape, or Etappen, which was the remaining strip of land between the Operations Zone and the Occupation Zone.

One CRB history explained control of the Army Zone in terms of its two smaller subzones: "Subject only to the higher authority of the Supreme Command, the several German army commands imposed absolute rule in the Operations and Etape Zones. The application of military law was more drastic in the Operations than the Etape Zone, but in neither did anything remain of civil institutions or personal freedom. The armies assumed proprietorship of property, of food, of currency; they arrested all French male citizens of military age; they forbade the inhabitants to leave their own communes, and in general restricted the conduct of private affairs to such an extent that the people had scarcely any greater liberty than actual prisoners of war. Although the systems of administration were not identical in all the Army Zones, there were but few variations except in the Flemish provinces, where the Germans mitigated the severity of their rule on the theory that the Flemings might be persuaded to break away from their allegiance to the Belgian State."

While most of the Etape part of the Army Zone was comprised of northern France, by the end of 1914, parts of Belgium were also included—East and West Flanders and the western part of Hainaut Province around Tournai. That was, however, in a state of semi-flux, as CRB delegate Tracy Kittredge explained: "Later on, this line was modified several times, Tournai being first, in the spring of 1915, put into [the] occupation district under Governor-General [von Bissing], and again included in the etappen in August 1916. The district around Mons, and the southern part of the province of Luxembourg, were also included in the etappen in December 1916."

No matter what adjustments or modifications were made to the dividing line, however, overall life in the Army Zone was brutal, harsh, and unforgiving.

Initially, the CRB and the CN had had little to do with either of the army subzones, except the areas of East and West Flanders, which were included in the initial relief guarantees secured by von Bissing and agreed to by the military commanders in the areas. These two regions followed the same basic regulations, and they were subject to the CRB/CN relationship established throughout occupied Belgium, which dealt with food distribution, control of mills and bakers, and the setting of rations and prices for food.

If the CRB was to take on northern France, it would have to deal much more directly with the military authorities, not with von Bissing. Hoover had no choice—people were near starving—so he had to try and provide food for the residents of northern France. Whether the German military and Allied governments would agree to it was something else altogether.

But first Hoover knew his most urgent priority was to maintain and secure the work that was already being done in Belgium—definitely not a sure thing, as he would quickly find out.

Hoover's Financial Showdown with Lloyd George

With the start of the New Year, financing for Belgium relief was still not yet secured. The British government had not backed away from its concerns over German war indemnities levied on Belgium.

In a January 13, 1915, meeting with British Foreign Secretary Sir Edward Grey, Hoover came face-to-face with that objection. The meeting did not begin well when Grey reportedly stated "half-humourously" that Hoover better not hope to get financial support from the British as long as the Germans were levying indemnities in Belgium.

Grey quickly learned this was not the time to joke with Hoover. The American shot back with a "terse statement of the case." He reminded Grey that he had been told earlier that the British could not support Belgium relief because the Germans were requisitioning Belgian food. So Hoover had petitioned the German government through U.S. Ambassador Gerard and had secured from Berlin a guarantee that no more food would be requisitioned in Belgium. With that success, Hoover said the CRB was "entitled to [financial] support from the British Government, and he was disappointed that further stipulations were now raised." He pointedly asked Grey, if he was able to get the Germans to drop the war indemnities, would the British give financial aid or once again add more stipulations?

Grey immediately replied that he "personally thought" the CRB would have earned financial support if the levies were removed, but he could not vouch for others.

Hoover left the room not knowing if he could get the Germans to give up the war indemnities and if the British would come through with financial support and acceptance of his monetary exchange. When he hadn't heard from Grey for nearly a week, Hoover wrote him asking for news and stating bluntly, "I am rapidly drifting into the most intense financial difficulties, having large payments to make at the end of the week, while I am just simply busted."

Grey's reply was to set up a meeting for Thursday, January 21, with David Lloyd George, the Chancellor of the Exchequer. As Hoover wrote later, he thought the meeting was to discuss "the question of the exchange of money with Belgium." Without the exchange plan he had developed, the food relief would not be able to function on the scale necessary to feed the entire nation. Hoover knew that Lloyd George was an opponent of the CRB, but he also felt that the work and the CRB agreements had advanced far enough that this meeting would be about pounding out details regarding his financial exchange plan. Nothing more.

He was in for a rude surprise. As historian George Nash stated, "A routine appointment now turned into a battle of survival."

Sitting with Lloyd George was Attorney General Sir John Simon, Lord Alfred Emmott of the Committee on Trading with the Enemy, and Lord Eustace Percy of the Foreign Office, who was also Sir Edward Grey's assistant and liaison on CRB matters.

Hoover, not knowing he had walked into an ambush, began by detailing the substantial costs already associated with importing food and how he and his team had hit on an exchange plan that would not involve "any transfer of any actual gold or silver into Belgium." Hoover was ready for a lively discussion on the pros and cons of this exchange plan.

Instead, Lloyd George—the man who controlled Britain's purse strings—told Hoover outright that he was totally opposed to any relief to Belgium because, "indirect as it was, it was certainly assisting the enemy, and that this assistance would take place in several ways." The imported food would simply be requisitioned by the Germans. The food would give the Belgians "more resources generally" to help them pay German war levies. And overall, because the war would be won by economic pressures, Lloyd George believed the first one to cave under such financial weight would lose the war. By helping the Belgians with food, the CRB would be relieving the Germans of an economic obligation that it would no doubt take up if the CRB was not in place.

Hoover reported that the chancellor of the exchequer "expressed the belief that the Germans would, in the last resort, provision the people of Belgium; that our action was akin to the provisioning of the civil population of a besieged city and

British Chancellor of the Exchequer David Lloyd George was totally opposed to the CRB when he met Hoover on January 21, 1915. It would be a defining moment for Hoover, the CRB, and the Belgian people. (Both photos: public domain; multiple sources.)

thus prolonging the resistance of the garrison; that he was wholly opposed to our operations, benevolent and humane as they were; and that therefore he could not see his way to grant our request."

One of Britain's toughest politicians, known for his strong stands on issues, had just told Hoover he was going to shut down the three-month-old CRB.

It would be a defining moment for Herbert Hoover, the CRB, and the Belgian people.

Hoover took a breath and turned to his powerful opponent. He quietly but forcefully laid out his case for the Belgian people, answering Lloyd George point-for-point.

Regarding the requisitioning of food, "the Germans had given an undertaking that after the first of January no such requisitions would be made." He also insisted that, to date, the Germans had "impressed none of our actual food."

As for the point that the food indirectly helped the Belgians deal with the war levies, Hoover was adamant: "We were introducing no new money into Belgium, but were simply giving circulation to the money already existing, and that there was no danger of the Germans taking the money which we collected for foodstuffs because that money was in the possession of the American Minister."

Hoover was also confident that all of his dealings so far with the Germans had shown they would never feed the Belgians. He said that he and his fellow Americans had at first undertaken the job "with the greatest reluctance and our first move was to satisfy ourselves that this [Belgian] population would starve unless America intervened and converted the hitherto negative quality of neutrality into one of positive neutrality."

The Germans' reasoning for not feeding the Belgians, Hoover explained, was that they had no legal obligation because they had *conquered*, not *annexed*, the country. As Hoover put it, the Germans believed "there was no clause in The Hague Convention obligating the Germans [as conquerors] to provision the civil population of Belgium; on the contrary, it incidentally provided that the civil population should support the military."

Furthermore, the Germans felt that because the Belgians imported most of their goods, it was the British who were starving the Belgians with their blockade. The Germans reasoned that if the Allies would agree to open the port of Antwerp for international trade with neutral countries, the Belgians would be fine.

Hoover pointed out that the Germans had not changed their position even after a small amount of rioting in Belgium, and that the northern French behind German lines were, in some cases, already starving.

Hoover added, "I did not offer these arguments as my own but to illustrate the fixity of mind by which the German people justify their action in refusing to feed the Belgians, and asked [Lloyd George] if he could conceive for one moment that with this mental attitude of conviction on their part that they were right and the Allies were wrong, they would be likely to feed the Belgians."

Lloyd George, according to Hoover's memorandum of the meeting, "denounced the whole of this as a monstrous [German] attitude."

Hoover, to further strengthen his case—especially when it came to the argument that relief would prolong the war—tried to stir a sense of British pride and greatness within those listening. The American maintained that the British had undertaken the war "for the avowed purpose of protecting the existence of small nations, of vindicating the guaranteed neutrality by which small nations might exist, for the avowed purpose of guaranteeing to the world the continuance of democracy as against autocracy in government." It would, therefore, be an "empty victory if one of the most democratic of the world's races should be extinguished in the process and ultimate victory should be marked by an empty husk."

Hoover wrapped up his argument with a final declaration that "the English people were great enough to disregard the doubtful military value of advantage in favor of assurances that these people should survive, and I felt the obligation went even further than mere acquiescence in our work and extended to an opportunity to the English to add to their laurels by showing magnanimity toward these people, a magnanimity which would outlast all the bitterness of this war."

When Hoover finished his impassioned remarks, a silence fell upon the room. Lloyd George paused before speaking, and to the always impatient Hoover, the pause was no doubt nearly interminable.

In an instant it was done: "I am convinced," Lloyd George stated. "You have my permission." Standing up, he said he had to leave but was sure the group would "settle the details of the machinery necessary to carry it out."

He then turned to Hoover and said "the world would yet be indebted to the American people for the most magnanimous action which neutrality had yet given way to."

In that moment, as one history later stated, "Hoover scored the most signal [significant] triumph of his diplomatic career, for, by his clear concise statement of the situation and his eloquent advocacy of the cause of the Belgians, he won over Lloyd George, who had previously been an opponent of the Belgium relief work, and enlisted him as a hearty supporter of the Commission's activities."

Additionally, the chancellor of the exchequer "was alert to the humanitarian aspect of the relief operations and more than some of the members of the Government he appreciated the force of world opinion which had been mobilized behind the Commission's activities."

And because Lloyd George would go on to become prime minister in 1916, the impact of Lloyd George's conversion was huge. "From this time on the attitude of the British Government became much more sympathetic toward the Commission and it gave, not only its approval, but its money and its ships and its constant co-operation to the Commission."

The CRB's Military Opponents

Hoover's success with Lloyd George did not mean all within the British government were on the side of the CRB. The military leaders and politicians who had initially voiced opposition to the CRB—referred to here as militarists—still felt the humanitarian relief was hurting the war effort.

In fact, Hoover felt that from "the first day of our existence," militarists not only from Britain but from Germany and France were against the CRB and "periodically demanded its suppression."

Hoover had realized early on that it would be the civilian governments of the warring nations that would be more receptive to moral arguments and public pressure regarding humanitarian aid to the Belgians. He was sure civilian governments would find it difficult, if not impossible, to go against a relief program that was heartily supported by their citizens.

On the other side, the German militarists felt that the Belgians could take care of themselves if the English food blockade was lifted and free trade was reestablished between Belgium and the rest of the world. It was, therefore, the Allies—

and specifically Britain—that were responsible for whatever happened to the Belgians. While the English blockade remained, the German militarists saw no reason why they should be "called upon to feed these relatives of the Allies by depriving their own women and children."

As Hoover put it, they "argued that the threatened starvation of these people, who were the allies of Britain and France, would, in the end, secure relaxation of the food blockade against themselves. They maintained that the opening of a door in the blockade by way of the C.R.B. weakened this pressure." The militarists also felt sure the CRB delegates were spies for the Allies and bitterly resented the Belgians for having resisted their invasion and having squashed their plans for a quick victory.

The German military governor of Belgium, General von Luttwitz, summed up the militarist position "with some show of feeling" when he told Hugh Gibson, "The allies are at liberty to feed the Belgians. If they don't, they are responsible for anything that may happen. If there are bread riots, the natural thing would be for us to drive the whole civil population into some restricted area, like the Province of Luxembourg, build a barbed wire fence around them, and leave them to starve in accordance with the policy of their allies."

Hoover wrote that the French and British militarists were "also violent in their opposition to the Commission." Their stance was that it was the duty of the Germans to feed the Belgians and if the CRB wasn't around they would be forced to do so. They also believed the food relief "relaxed the pressures of the Allied food blockade against the German people."

To help sway and keep the British civilian government on the CRB's side, Hoover worked the press expertly, providing its members with a constant flow of article ideas and public relations articles about Belgium's plight and the humanitarian activities of the CRB and the CN.

To directly counteract the militarists' belief that the Germans would feed the Belgians if the CRB wasn't around, Hoover suggested to famed American war correspondent Frederick Palmer that he go to Germany and report on what he found. Palmer did so, and when Hoover received what the journalist had written, he forwarded it on to Sir Edward Grey. Hoover knew the articles would be circulated throughout the British government and especially to the two highest-ranking militarists against the CRB: Lord Kitchener, secretary of state for war, and Winston Churchill, first lord of the admiralty.

Palmer was straightforward in his assessment that Germany would never feed the Belgians on its own. "Food required to keep Belgians from starving this winter would feed five army corps a year. Any German Governor who diverts that amount from Germany's supplies will have to reckon with German public opinion. . . . The one valuable life, the one person to be fed [by Germany], is a fighting soldier or one who may recover to fight again. If she gives her military prisoners only enough for bare existence, will she spare any gratuities to Belgium? She will not, no matter how many governors say so.

"Germany can think of Belgium only with angry bitterness. Not humanity, but do-or-die patriotism governs her emotions. They blame the Belgians for spoiling their plan of campaign. Nothing is too bad for the Belgians. Let the Belgians take care of themselves represents German public feeling. . . . Belgium needs food. It can come only from the outsiders. The Belgians are sure of getting it only under outside direction."

In Germany's case, the general public might not have been behind feeding the Belgians, but Germany's civilian government knew that allowing the CRB to provide food relief would gain worldwide goodwill—something that they thought necessary to keep neutrals such as America out of the war. As long as the German civilian government held power over its military, the CRB had a fighting chance of staying alive.

Hoover summed up in two paragraphs why the CRB was allowed to exist. He wrote, "It was the civilian leaders in each belligerent government at war who prevented the militarists from having their way. Aside from any feeling of compassion, there were practical war policies at stake.

"These civilian leaders of both combatants were feverishly anxious either to bring the neutral nations into the war on their side or to prevent them from joining the enemy. For these purposes, they kept up an enormous flow of propaganda. But a deep sympathy for the Belgians has spread over the whole neutral world [in large part due to Hoover's news media efforts]. To the Foreign Offices, their foreign policies were more important than one Relief Commission, no matter how obnoxious. It was upon this slender thread that the fate of the C.R.B. often hung."

As for the English militarists, unlike Lloyd George, most of them did not change their minds, but judging their country's public opinion about Belgium and the CRB, some began looking for backdoor ways of getting rid of the CRB.

In short order a clandestine investigation, complete with informers inside Holland and Belgium, was initiated. Its goal was to uncover within the food-relief process any German abuses, CRB missteps, or Belgian corruption.

It would not be long before damaging accusations arose.

12

Brussels

German Sentries Still Cause Problems

The continuing problem of CRB delegates being harassed when stopped by German sentries came to a head in mid-January 1915. Gibson reported that the delegates were "being stopped at the frontier, thrown into prison, stripped and searched like common criminals and generally treated as we would be ashamed to treat an enemy." Additionally, the issuance of passes became a problem, as E. E. Hunt in Antwerp stated: "Our monthly passes for automobiles became more difficult to get. Twice or thrice we were forced to lie idle for a day or two on account of the failure of Pass Bureaus to provide our passes promptly." Others waited a week or more to get passes. Officially, the CRB and the U.S. Legation "complained rather bitterly of it," but were "laughed to scorn."

In a meeting with von Bissing, Gibson said the governor general refused to believe any of it and told "us that such things simply did not happen; that people who traveled with the sort of passes our men had were treated with the greatest respect and deference and that we were either misinformed or exaggerating." In another gathering with CRB men, von Bissing repeated that he was confident the passes given to the delegates were good—so good, that the men were treated like emperors.

That's when someone in the meeting had a brilliant idea. Why didn't a German officer dress in civilian clothes and travel with CRB Brussels Director Dannie Heineman, who was leaving for Holland the next day? The officer could see first-hand how the sentries acted. The governor general thought it was a splendid idea and quickly one of his young staff officers named Beutner volunteered to go along. According to Gibson, Beutner was the son of a German imperial cabinet official and was a "very decent young officer." To ensure the best results, the Germans gave Beutner passes that would be accepted by any German who read them and that were signed by the governor general. Many of the Americans thought because of these G-G passes, the contest wouldn't even be fair.

As recounted by Gibson in a letter and a speech, the scene unfolded rather differently than von Bissing and von der Lancken would have hoped:

Two German Landsturmers—older Germans used for noncombat duties such as sentry duty. (Public domain; Roger Van den Bleeken, Archives Heemkring, Houghescote vzw, Kapellen, Belgium.)

When the car rolled up to the guardhouse at the frontier a sentry came out and gruffly ordered them to get out. Beutner held up his pass and gently explained that they were authorized to cross the frontier without stopping to be searched. Neither the soldier nor the N.C.O. [noncommissioned officer] in command of the post would read the pass.

After more arguing, Beutner was seized by the legs and dragged out onto the road, then ordered to go into the guardhouse and wait until an officer was ready to deal with his case.

There was nothing to do but obey and Beutner went meekly into the guardhouse and sat down. After fuming for a few minutes while the soldiers searched other people, Beutner got up from the bench where he had been ordered to sit, approached the N.C.O. and began arguing that he must read the passes and let them go. The man refused.

Presently an officer came in to investigate. Beutner got up, clicked his heels, announced his identity, held up his pass and said that he was ready to leave.

The officer snatched the pass away from him with a sneer, saying that it was probably a forgery and telling him to sit down and hold his tongue.

This was a little too much and Beutner wrathfully proclaimed that the whole proceeding was an outrage.

That was the spark that set off the magazine.

The officer seized Beutner by the throat and began to choke him, calling to the soldiers to come and help. Four or five of them beat him up enthusiastically, some of them thumping him from behind with their rifle butts until he was reduced to a state of pulp.

He was then pushed into a military motor more dead than alive and taken back to Antwerp in a military car. There he was held for several hours before being sent back to Brussels, still under arrest.

And there for the first time an effort was made to find out who he was and whether his pass was any good.

As can be imagined, von Bissing, von der Lancken, and the rest of the German command in Belgium did not take the story well. "Of course," Gibson related, "there was a great uproar and a court martial was convened to try the guilty ones but we never heard what happened to them."

The Americans and Belgians had a slightly different reaction.

"This was the sort of thing," Gibson said, "that other people had been putting up with for some time and within an hour everybody in Brussels was chortling over the fact that one of the Boches [derogatory name for Germans] had got a taste of it."

As for Beutner, Gibson reported, "The first time I saw Beutner his face was so swollen that he could hardly talk and his disposition was still more inflamed, but the thing that pained him most was as he said, 'Gibson, you remember that big fellow with the black beard who [I told you] kicked me from behind? That was a professor of ethics in the University of Munich!'

"While we were all mighty sorry for Beutner we could not keep our faces straight when we heard the story. We have hopes that the incident may result in our getting more considerate treatment in the future."

For one delegate, at least, the event was especially good news. Twenty-four-year-old George Spaulding who had graduated from the University of Arizona and was a Rhodes scholar, had been one of the first 10 Oxford students to enter Belgium in early December. He had been assigned to serve as a delegate in the Hainaut Province with another Oxford student, 26-year-old Walter Lowdermilk. After five weeks of them living in Chateau Mariemont (offered by the owner) and working throughout the province, they both had decided to return to Oxford.

Spaulding had kept a diary of his time in Belgium and had heard that the Germans at the border were getting very strict and "suspicious of notes of any kind, fearing they might be in code. Finally, we heard that most of our representatives who went out [of Belgium] in autos were made to strip and sometimes spend hours waiting."

Spaulding was about to destroy his diary for fear it would be discovered when the story of Beutner's border travails circulated throughout Belgium. He decided to risk smuggling out his diary, successfully betting on the belief that the sentries would be reticent to do anything toward American CRB delegates, at least for a few weeks. "This [Beutner incident] happened only a few days before our departure; and consequently we were met with great courtesy and leniency. This explains why my diary was not confiscated and I have no jail tale to tell."

While the treatment of delegates by German sentries did improve markedly, the Beutner affair would soon stimulate von Bissing to take serious action against the Americans.

Friction Grows between the CRB and CN

For many Belgians—especially Émile Francqui and members of his Comité National—a few things had become apparent by January 1915:

- The war would not be over quickly.
- The initial food crisis had passed; long-term food relief was needed.
- The world—and many Belgian civilians—saw the Americans as the sole proponents of relief.
- Some American delegates were taking executive actions in their provinces.

None of these points sat very well with Francqui and his associates on the CN, and those points began to create friction between the CRB and the CN.

Because of the initial war crisis, the Americans had been welcomed into the humanitarian relief process, especially when it came to establishing the international agreements and the purchasing of food outside of Belgium. "At first there was little difficulty," Kittredge wrote in his CRB history. "The country had been so near the threat of famine, the work of the organisation was so difficult and so engrossing, that the Comité National and the Commission alike threw themselves wholeheartedly in the work of organisation."

But as Hoover's publicity machine began to generate worldwide press about what the CRB was doing in Belgium, and as the young American delegates became highly visible symbols of relief as they motored around Belgium bringing barge loads of foodstuffs into every province, the Belgian people took notice. Francqui and his associates were stung by their countrymen's feeling that the entire relief work was being done by the Americans when, in fact, it was Francqui, the CN, and the provincial committees who had admirably set up the complex systems for food preparation, rationing, and distribution.

And then there was the issue of the role the delegates played in Belgium. "The Comité National did not intend that the Commission or its representatives should have any executive voice in the control of the distribution of food or of relief in Belgium." This was especially true with the young, upstart American delegates. As Kittredge put it, "The activities of certain of the American delegates began to rather annoy and irritate certain of the members of the Comité National and of the provincial committees. These Belgians of prominent position and of standing in the community naturally found no very keen pleasure in having their ideas overruled and the conduct of their organisation controlled by striplings from across the seas who, though capable and amiable enough, yet had as a rule but little practical or business experience."

This was not to say that there was any objection to the Americans being in Belgium. Everyone—even Francqui—welcomed them because they lent diplomatic weight and protection to relations with the Germans. They just didn't want the "striplings" making any decisions or taking executive actions within Belgium.

The delegates' duties in the provinces had been a point of contention between the CRB and the CN—and even among the delegates themselves—since the beginning of relief efforts. Despite a December memorandum from Hoover that outlined many of the duties and responsibilities, the reality was that the individual "power, influence and duties of the provincial delegates differed according to the efficiency of the provincial committees, the difficulties of the local situation and the personality of the delegate," according to Kittredge.

Within the ranks of the CRB, this boiled down to two opposing points of view. Kittredge explained, "On the one hand was the group led in the beginning by [E. E.] Hunt and Robinson Smith, that believed that the work of relief should be essentially an American affair; that the responsibility for the direction of relief operations rested on the American members of the Commission; that its methods should be those of American business efficiency; and that consequently the head delegate in each province was to be regarded as the manager of relief operations in his province."

On the other side of the discussion "were the majority of provincial delegates and all of the successive directors of the Commission in Brussels. They agreed the work of the Commission was indispensable to the success of the relief operations, and that the American delegates should exercise such supervision and control as to make sure that the food-supplies and benevolent funds were efficiently handled, that they were fairly distributed and that they went solely to the Belgian civil population. But, according to this second point of view, the actual work of distribution was essentially a Belgian domestic problem; the work could be best done by Belgians who, because of their acquaintance with local conditions, habits and ideas, were in a position to conduct the work in a manner agreeable to the Belgians themselves."

Most critical of all, Hoover and the majority felt that "it was not the duty nor the function of the Americans to reform the Belgians or revolutionise their business methods and their social habits." Therefore, "the delegate should use his power with extreme discretion, should act as a diplomatic intermediary between the Germans and the Belgians and between the various conflicting groups of Belgian committees."

It was easy to know which side Francqui and the CN took—the latter. The few delegates like Hunt and Smith who supported the former were causing quite a concern for Francqui and his group, despite Francqui's occasional compliments about these young men.

While Hoover and most of the delegates understood they were not there to change Belgian ways, this awareness did not mean they agreed that they served no useful function within Belgium. They knew their presence was necessary for the relief to function at all because of the responsibilities imposed upon the CRB by the allied governments. Hoover had personally agreed to, and the CRB had officially accepted, the job through the Allied guarantees of buying, shipping, and supervising the distribution of food and clothes down to the commune level, with no German requisitioning of foodstuffs. Hoover and his young—and sometimes strident—delegates would accept nothing less.

This point was not lost among the everyday operations of the young delegates out in a war-ravaged countryside dealing with Belgian businessmen of varying social, religious, and political affiliations. As Kittredge honestly assessed, "In the end, as in the beginning, no definite decision was ever reached as to the exact function of the delegate. . . . His position continued to depend largely upon his personality and upon that of the heads of the province to which he was assigned."

The disagreements between the CRB and the CN, which Kittredge termed "rather painful misunderstandings," developed from a CN viewpoint that would basically never change: Francqui and some of the other members of the CN felt the entire relief work was a domestic issue that they were quite capable of handling themselves, and thus there was no need for CRB delegates to be wandering around their country supervising relief operations.

In this regard, the Belgians and Germans agreed. The Germans felt relief efforts could be handled by the CN under German supervision and they "regarded the Americans of the Commission as rather troublesome intruders, who were not to be allowed to have an active voice in the distribution of food and who were to be induced to be content with seeing that the food did not go to the Germans."

By the summer of 1915, resentment toward the CRB would bubble up again into a full-blown crisis that was led by Francqui but supported by Baron von Bissing.

Van Doren's Game Becomes Dangerously Real

Once van Doren and the Abbé de Moor committed to publishing and distributing *La Libre Belgique,* they knew there was no room for errors.

The most obvious component of their operation that needed to be improved and reinforced was distribution. Since their earliest days, they had circulated their anti-German materials by wandering the city and dropping off individual copies in residential mailboxes. Or they would give the materials to friends who would do the same. Such methods, however, were too open to the possibility of chance observation and capture. The men understood that to stay with the "haphazard letterbox distribution was out of the question; it would be too costly, too dangerous and, with the comparatively small number of copies they could handle, ineffective." They would have to build a distribution network that would be efficient, effective, and protect them from capture as much as possible.

To do so, however, meant they also would need to separate the editorial side of the operation from the printing side, and both of those from the distribution side.

By January 1915, the inner circle of critical people numbered only five: van Doren; the Abbé de Moor; Victor Jourdain; his daughter, 35-year-old Julie

Victor Jourdain was a renowned Belgian journalist who was founding editor of the underground newspaper La Libre Belgique. (Public domain; *Histoire de La Libre Belgique Clandestine,* Pierre Goemaere, Bureaux de *La Libre Belgique,* Bruxelles, 1919.)

Jourdain; and Father Paquet, Jourdain's confessor and "one of the most active charity organizers in the city." Paquet, according to one history, was "a big, benevolent-looking Jesuit past middle age. He spoke little and he had a steady, level gaze that people found disconcerting or soothing according to their individual conscience." Julie Jourdain lived with her elderly father and helped him in all aspects of the work while also attending to her sick mother.

Van Doren was the critical link because he was the only one who knew the four others of the inner circle. The abbé did not know that the two Jourdains and Father Paquet were involved, and they did not know de Moor was working with van Doren and active in other underground activities.

After much discussion among the inner circle, the distribution model they settled on was to individually build separate distribution circles, or circles of trust, from one central point, "something like a planetary system of which van Doren was the sun. Van Doren would remain unknown to all except the vital contacts with the next circle, and even to these he would pose as a simple distributor supplied by someone supposedly nearer the source."

As one writer later commented, "The whole system may seem open to criticism. . . . No doubt any thriller writer would be able in five minutes to evolve a method surer, safer and in every way more efficient. But as a piece of pure improvisation, based largely on speculation in the first place and accomplished by tentative groping in the dark, it was a creditable achievement."

Once the team understood the concept of these circles of trust, they began to build them outward, away from themselves. Julie Jourdain gave van Doren a list of people she felt he could rely on to circulate small amounts of whatever was produced. She also carefully began contacting convents and Catholic schools, beginning with the well-known Jesuit St. Michael College, where her sons attended school, "and going from one to the other with a recommendation from someone in the previous establishment."

Altogether, the team realized quickly that "laying the foundations of the distributing system was a laborious business. It demanded considerable patience and sometimes eloquent persuasion" to enlist people who were frightened or reluctant to tempt the fates and the German authorities.

Finally, after much preparation and hard work, the first issue of *La Libre Belgique* was ready for distribution. Consisting of only one large sheet that was folded vertically to create four pages, it was a modest affair. Printed all in black-and-white, it had no illustrations, and articles were either summaries of Allied war news or commentary on the occupation. But the front page had a bold, proud title banner and below it was the statement "Bulletin de Propagande Patriotique—Réguliéérement Irrégulier" (Patriotic Propaganda Bulletin—Regularly Irregular). The price was "elastic—from zero to infinity."

Two quotes just below either end of the title called on the Belgian people to maintain a calm resolve toward the occupation. To the left was the last official statement from Brussels Burgomaster Max before he had been sent to jail: "Let us temporarily accept the sacrifices imposed upon us and patiently await the hour of reparation." To the right was a quote from Cardinal Mercier's banned December 1914 pastoral letter: "Toward those who dominate our country by military force let us show the regard that the general interest requires. Let us respect the rules they impose upon us so long as they touch neither the liberty of our Christian consciences nor our patriotic dignity."

With a heart and spirit much bigger than its body, the little newspaper declared proudly that its editorial offices were located in an "automobile cellar" and audaciously announced its telegraphic address to be "Kommandantur, Brussels"—Governor General von Bissing's headquarters.

The newspaper's mission was just as bold and defiant. The front-page lead article, written by Victor Jourdain, stated proudly, "The aim of *La Libre Belgique* is to strengthen and encourage Belgian patriotism until the hour, still unknown but certain of the deliverance of our great-hearted and glorious little country. . . . To give our readers the opinions of competent military observers, and keep them informed of the progress accomplished by the Allies and of the increasingly desperate situation of Germany. . . . To show to young men of age to carry arms the path of duty and bring to their ears the echoes of the call of King and Government. . . . To combat defeatism and refuse calumnies hawked by the censored press against Belgium and her Allies. . . . To denounce Germany's constant violations of the Hague Conventions and counteract her manoeuvres to divide Belgians one against the other by reviving the language quarrel."

On February 1, 1915, the first issue was printed and ready for circulation. As van Doren sat proudly holding the issue, he decided to do something special and extremely risky—make sure von Bissing received a personal copy. De Moor liked the idea so much that he put a few twists in it and enlisted his sister to play the role of a veiled girl delivering a perfumed envelope to von Bissing.

The entrance of the headquarters of German Governor General von Bissing. (Public domain; Roger Van den Bleeken, Archives Heemkring, Houghescote vzw, Kapellen, Belgium.)

A Belgian Gauntlet Is Thrown Down

The delivery, as recorded by the book *Underground News*, took place on Monday afternoon, February 1, 1915, less than two months after von Bissing had assumed his role as governor general. Passersby would have noticed the veiled, "smartly dressed" young woman who purposefully walked toward the imposing building that once housed the Ministry of Agriculture. She definitely stood out from all the German soldiers who swarmed in and out of the entrance like worker bees buzzing to and from a giant hive.

Most Belgians knew that inside was the office of the governor general, supreme ruler of occupied Belgium. From his high-ceilinged, palatial office, the battle-hardened Prussian officer Baron von Bissing would send out daily edicts, declarations, and pronouncements that ended up as *affiches* plastered all over the city and country. Few Belgians would ever willingly walk into such a place.

As the young woman approached the entrance, she paused a moment and "looked coyly at the stalwart sentry posted at the door," then boldly walked past him into the massive building. Her high heels echoed through the entrance hall as if warning of her approach. She walked up to a young orderly who sat at a table.

"Is the Freiherr von Bissing in?" she inquired in hesitating German with an attractively soft accent. "It's a very personal matter . . ." she added with a hint of shyness, taking from her handbag a delicately perfumed, pink envelope.

A grin spread slowly over the orderly's face, and his eyelids flickered.

"Yes, Fräulein," he said. "His Excellency is in. What can I do for you?"

"You would be very kind to hand him this," she said sweetly. "It is very important. It is for him personally."

"I will hand it to His Excellency myself, Fräulein. Is there any answer?"

"I shall be calling back tomorrow," she said, and thanking him, walked demurely away.

Not long after, the orderly handed von Bissing the pink envelope. When the governor general opened it, he found the inaugural issue of the four-page, poorly reproduced newspaper with the bold title *La Libre Belgique* [*The Free Belgium*]. Looking closer, von Bissing and his waxed moustache must have bristled at the sight of the provocative subtitles, quotes, and articles.

On the same day, the little underground newspaper was also sent to the Kaiser, who was then at the German military headquarters in Spa, a town just 80 miles southeast of Brussels. There is no record of whether the Kaiser actually saw the paper or if it was simply thrown out by an underling.

When von Bissing received the first issue, it reportedly "annoyed him. No more. He had given the unfortunate orderly a dressing-down for being a fool, and issued instructions to the secret police to see that there was no repetition of 'this offensive nonsense.' With that he dismissed the matter. . . . He attached little importance to this manifestation of a spirit against which he had been forewarned."

That would change quickly as, without fail every week, a new issue of *La Libre Belgique* somehow found its way to von Bissing's door. It would not be long before the paper—growing every week in circulation and stature—inspired the nation, became the bane of the German secret police, and generated a 50,000-franc reward for the capture of its editors. For the governor general, the little newspaper quickly became a personal obsession, and he vowed to many, including the Kaiser, that he would crush the paper and silence its creators.

Van Doren, Jourdain, and de Moor had little idea just how rapidly they would come to feel the heavy hand of the German secret police.

Von Bissing Cracks Down on the CRB

The beating of young Captain Beutner by German soldiers and the CRB's continual complaining about sentries not honoring passes did result in a few changes for the better. It was agreed that the delegates would begin carrying a CRB "passport" as well as their own U.S. passport. Additionally, any CRB couriers would be required to hang around their neck a large pouch (nearly a foot-and-a-half by a foot-and-a-half) with clear plastic on the front so that sentries could easily see and read all relevant documents for that particular trip.

But a good argument could be made that the embarrassment von Bissing felt regarding the lack of German adherence to proper passes drove him to come down harder on the CRB and its delegates.

From left: An unidentified man and CRB delegate Frederick Dorsey Stephens wear the large, obvious passes that were created because some German sentries were ignoring normal-sized German-issued passes. Note the small U.S. flag flying from the car's left bumper. (Public domain; *The Millers' Belgian Relief Movement, Final Report, 1914–1915,* William C. Edgar, Miller Publishing Co., 1916.)

Less than two weeks after the Beutner affair, in early February 1915, von Bissing suddenly decided it was time to restrict the movements of the delegates, and even limit the number of Americans allowed into Belgium to supervise the relief. This was viewed as a potential major blow to the burgeoning CRB and would, if implemented, severely curtail relief efforts.

It was less than four full months since the CRB and its delegates had begun work in Belgium. Initially, the German government had been receptive to issuing passes and had allowed the delegates freedom to move about the country. But that attitude began to change as the CRB and the relief work grew in food tonnage, delegate numbers, and overall importance. There was a fear that this neutral organization was getting too powerful in a country that was supposed to be ruled absolutely by the Germans.

Early delegate Kittredge stated, "The Germans naturally looked with no great favour on the idea of having a considerable number of Americans travelling about freely in a conquered territory so close to the theatre of military operations. The Commission, with its delegates in every province, was more than once suspected . . . of being a great espionage machine."

What made it worse—much worse—was the fact that the delegates, wherever they went, were heartily greeted by the Belgians, who cheered as they roared by in their motorcars. As Kittredge explained, "It was undoubtedly galling to the Germans, who regarded themselves as absolute masters of the country, to see Americans, who were not in the least afraid of them and who were beyond their control, dashing about the country in automobiles."

Each automobile used by the delegates was adorned with a "CRB" in large letters on the front of the radiator or on the sides of the engine hood. At least one American flag, if not two, flew from the front fenders. Many Belgians who had rarely, if ever, seen an American flag suddenly knew it from afar and would stop to cheer and wave as the delegate motorcars approached.

To most Belgians the American flag quickly came to represent not only food relief but also international acknowledgment of their plight and a kind of independence from—and rejection of—the hated German occupation. Brand Whitlock wrote that for Belgians the American flag "came to express their hopes, their ideals, their aspirations."

At one point in the late winter of 1914/1915, according to Whitlock, there were more than 8,000 American flags flying atop provincial warehouses, communal storehouses, mills, and the motorcars of the delegates.

Such prominence of the flag was more a natural outgrowth of how relief had begun than a planned action. As the first shipments of food supplies had entered Belgium in 1914 and the first American delegates had followed in their wake, it was natural that American flags were used to indicate to both the Germans and the Belgians that the food in the barges and the men riding in the motorcars were part of a neutral humanitarian effort. As the food went on to be delivered to provincial and commune warehouses, those facilities were also earmarked by American flags because the Americans felt the food was their responsibility up until final distribution to individual civilians. (Later this concept was adjusted to responsibility up until that point when the food was turned over to the CN or provincial committees.)

"We had flown our flag over our warehouses and storehouses in every city and village in Belgium," chief delegate E. E. Hunt reported. "It gave the Belgian people a feeling of security to see the stars-and-stripes in their midst. It made them feel that the weight of the United States was behind their bread supply."

Initially, the flags were accepted by all and honored by the Germans. But in early 1915, as the relief settled into a more long-term effort and Belgian civilians reacted so positively to the flag, the Germans began to resent its use. It got to the point where German officers would stop CRB cars and warn the delegate "there was but one flag in Belgium and that was the German flag."

In meetings with von Bissing and von der Lancken, Brand Whitlock was told that the American flag posed the possibility of spurring violence from German soldiers and officers who resented its use in a country that they controlled. They insisted to Whitlock that it must be taken down in all places.

In a move that would be highly criticized by many delegates, Whitlock followed their instructions and ordered the delegates to remove the flags from their vehicles and any Belgian-controlled facilities. By spring he would go on to negotiate with the Germans to have the flag removed from all but the provincial warehouses. Taking the place of the flag on the motorcars and elsewhere, would be the CRB's own flag.

Whitlock wrote a long letter to CRB Brussels Director Albert Connett detailing his feelings about the situation. He was mainly in agreement with the Germans and simply could not abide by the "promiscuous use of our flag during the last few months and recently the flag has been so generally in evidence that it is in danger of losing all official significance whatever." He felt strongly that the American flag should only be used by diplomatic personnel. In a surprisingly strong tone not normally used, he told Connett to tell all the delegates that "they are in no sense diplomatic officers and have no diplomatic functions to discharge. They are not here to protect anybody's interests nor are they to interfere in any way as between belligerents [Belgians and Germans] or to receive complaints of any sort except those relating to the food that has been sent for the relief of the civil population."

Their only job, as far as he was concerned, was that "they represent the Minister [Whitlock himself] with a power of attorney that entitles them to give a receipt for goods that are consigned to me and this done, their duties end, except naturally, that they are to see that no misappropriation of the food is made."

Whitlock's take on the use of the American flag and the delegates' duties was more in line with how Francqui, the CN, von Bissing, and the Germans felt than how Hugh Gibson, the delegates, and Hoover perceived the situation.

The German and CN resentment didn't stop there. According to Kittredge, there was "considerable objection" by the Germans and "a few of the leaders of the Comité National" not only to the "excessive use of the American flag" but also "of everything American in the relief work."

Besides the flag-removal action, another smaller event took place about the same time that could be seen as one more indication of the CN's resentment toward the CRB. The CRB, trying to be sensitive to numerous sides, asked the CN to change the name of the stores that sold sundry items that were not appropriate for mass distribution. These shops were called "American Stores," and the CRB asked that the word "American" be removed. As Kittredge explained, "The Comité National interpreted this request very broadly, and in sending out instructions to the provincial and local committees, directed them to discontinue and to remove

The Belgians prominently displayed the American flag wherever possible, including this children's cantine in Brussels, until the Germans demanded that most American flags be taken down. (Public domain; *Fighting Starvation in Belgium,* New York, Doubleday, Page & Co., 1918.)

all signs from local depots and magasins [warehouses] bearing the name of the Commission for Relief in Belgium."

Even though the CRB references were soon put back in all appropriate places, "this was the first incident," Kittredge stated, "of a series of events which in the course of the succeeding months made many of the members of the Commission feel decidedly uncomfortable and embarrassed, because of the change in the attitude of the direction of the Comité National."

Regardless of the CN trying to remove signs of the CRB, and Whitlock's insistence on fewer U.S. flags flying, the fact remained that the delegates continued to travel nonstop around the country, seemingly immune to German authority. The entire food-relief program became in the minds of many Belgians a great benevolent organization that was run by an enthusiastic band of young crusaders and functioned outside of, and somehow high above, all the horrors and pettiness of the war and the Germans.

Such a belief in the CRB delegates reinforced German concerns. They "soon became aware of this feeling among the people and regarded it as very dangerous," according to Kittredge. In the German mind, it was the duty of the Belgian people to be submissive to their conquerors, and the CRB and its delegates seemed to give added resolve to the Belgians' passive resistance.

It seemed obvious to many in the CRB that von Bissing's February command that the CRB limit its personnel and restrict delegate movements within Belgium was an extension of the German resentment and concerns about the American presence in what they perceived to be their country.

To Hoover, von Bissing's demands were simply unacceptable. He was certain that the CRB could not "discharge its obligations in Belgium without an adequate force of Americans to act as delegates in the provinces in close touch with the details of the work. These delegates could accomplish nothing without automobiles to carry them about their districts and passports permitting them to use the automobiles. It was necessary, in order to assure the success of the work, that the Commission representatives should enjoy complete liberty of movement and of action, and as great facilities of communication as were possible."

When von Bissing's new demands were issued, Hoover was in Brussels, having just come from Berlin, where he had unsuccessfully tried to get the German government to help subsidize the relief work.

On Thursday, February 11, 1915, Hoover went to see Governor General von Bissing in a somewhat unusual evening meeting. He stated later that Whitlock went along, but Whitlock did not mention it in his journal and even implied that Hoover had gone alone. Whitlock's lack of focus on such a critical issue and meeting was somewhat understandable—a few days before he had learned about the death of his younger brother Frank, who had been studying medicine and had died suddenly in Philadelphia. "For days I have been under an intolerable depression, and the news of the death of Frank was the last straw. . . . I cannot write; I cannot do anything except what literally has to be done each day."

For Hoover, it was his first sit-down with the old Prussian cavalry officer. Hoover was not impressed: "Von Bissing was a small-sized man, and my impression was that without his uniform, high boots, and helmet he would have looked most insignificant. My impression of his mental processes would also be included in that term."

There's no record of what von Bissing thought of Hoover, although later the German reportedly said about the American and his perceived neutrality, "I fully trusted Mr. Hoover although I knew quite well that he was in constant touch with the French and British governments, and that he was at heart with our enemies."

At that initial meeting, Hoover pleaded his case, but von Bissing remained firm. He angrily told the American that the delegates already had too much liberty of movements and that they were running all around the country to the great concern of the military. He stated that the CRB must change quickly and decrease its requests for passes because the government of occupation was soon going to impose even more restrictions on the delegates.

"The Commission," he stated emphatically, "only needs a few men in the central warehouses, who should remain in these warehouses and not move about the country; the Belgians can attend to all the work of food distribution."

Hoover pointed out how the CRB had international responsibilities to both the Allied governments and the German government to ensure all the guarantees were followed and that the food continued to be distributed fairly and exclusively to Belgian civilians. The only way to do that was through complete freedom of movement so the delegates could inspect the entire scope and process of the humanitarian aid, as well as help speed along the shipments of food.

Von Bissing refused to accept any of Hoover's points and barely seemed to listen to what the American was saying. Part of the problem could have been the simple fact that they did not share a common language—von Bissing spoke German and French; Hoover spoke only English—and had to converse in the unwieldy situation of translators.

"We did not get anywhere," Hoover said with great understatement. Realizing the governor general was not going to budge, Hoover left, already working out in his mind how he was going to get around the old Prussian.

The next day he went to see Whitlock, who wrote that Hoover was still "boiling with rage" about the meeting and von Bissing's unwillingness to see the importance of the work and the need for unfettered independent delegates. To compound his rage, Hoover had also been to see Dr. Marx, who was a German official in the bureau that issued the passes. At one point during their conversation, the man had asked him point-blank: "What do you Americans get out of this, I should like to know?"

Hoover was furious. He constantly faced this same insinuation with many German officials—that the CRB and its delegates were in the relief business for monetary or political gain. This was probably due in part to the generally held opinion that America was a country of shopkeepers and businessmen who were only interested in bettering their own bottom line.

"It is absolutely impossible," Hoover shot back, "for you Germans to understand that one does anything from pure humanitarian, disinterested motives, so I shall not attempt to explain it to you."

Hoover's next move was to write an extensive letter to von Bissing, in hopes that a dispassionate, logical explanation outlining the CRB's problems might have a better chance of success than a personal meeting, which was complicated by language barriers and personal opinions.

The day after his meeting with von Bissing, Hoover presented the letter to von der Lancken. In the long missive, Hoover reiterated how the British government had agreed to allow the imports of food only after serious pressure by the Americans and only on the condition that the Americans would be allowed the freedom in Belgium to supervise and control the food distribution.

Hoover also pointed out that of all the many passes that had been issued to date, none of them had been "misused," and that the volunteers were men "worthy of the fullest confidence and that they are gentlemen who would scorn the imputation of espionage or other improper conduct on their part"— neglecting, of course, to mention the few troublesome delegate-pass infractions that had already taken place.

Hoover also pointed out the magnitude of the relief; each month 99,000 tons of food were being handled. He reminded the governor general in his letter that the American public, the American government, and the Allied governments depended upon the CRB's assurances that everything was being done properly and with the agreed-upon guarantees. He could not assure them of that without the proper freedom of movement.

Then it was time for a ploy that Hoover would use many times during the challenging life of the CRB. He threatened to pull the CRB out of the relief work. In his letter he wrote, "Although I feel deeply the responsibility, I am compelled to assure Your Excellency that unless we can establish a basis of confidential and friendly relations and trust from the German authorities, we shall be compelled to withdraw and the flow of the stream of foodstuffs into Belgium from outside countries must necessarily cease."

Hoover would use the same tactic many times, on many different people and governments, but he would do so only when he knew he was in a position of power and that the recipient had little probability of taking him up on it. He was confident that even if von Bissing didn't back off because of the threat, the German government in Berlin would.

Hoover immediately followed his threat of withdrawal by restating how important the work was, not only to the Belgians but also to the Germans. "We feel that while our service is personally beneficial to the Belgian civil population it is nevertheless of the utmost importance to the Germans from every point of view."

Hoover ended the letter by suggesting that a good idea would be to appoint one man in the pass bureau to handle CRB passes exclusively so they could be dealt with expeditiously.

Von der Lancken listened to Hoover's points and read the letter. Realizing how important the issue was, he promised to personally take up the matter with the governor general.

Hoover left Brussels for London with the hope that his letter would have the desired effect.

13

London

Hoover Stands Up for Northern France

Upon arriving back in London in mid-February 1915, Hoover knew he had to directly confront the problem of northern France. His concern had grown as repeated efforts to convince the French government to support the relief fell on deaf ears. The French position was that Germany was responsible for the care and sustenance of those it had conquered and should be held accountable to do so. Because Hoover had had to confront that same belief in the British government when arguing for Belgium relief, he knew it was meaningless and doomed to fail.

On February 17, 1915, Hoover took direct action, as he had already done so many times with the British. He wrote to Raymond Poincaré, president of the French Republic. In a long letter he outlined the brutal living conditions in the German Operations and Etape Zones, told of the limited efforts the CRB had made, and made a personal appeal to gain the support of the French government. His first sentence conveyed the urgency he felt and the unusual method of delivery for his missive by a 50-year-old prominent American forester and politician well-known in France: "I deem it my duty to lay before you the position of the French civil population north of the German lines, and I am asking Mr. Gifford Pinchot, one of our members, to deliver this letter to Your Excellency in person."

Hoover told of French representatives who had come out of the region and begged for food from the CRB. He told of CRB delegates who had gone into the two army subzones with German permission to investigate the situation and had found great need.

In mid-January Hoover had extended the food relief into one area of France because "our investigation indicated that unless foodstuffs were introduced into this section the actual deaths from starvation, which had set in, would quickly decimate the population before outside arrangements could be made."

This meant, Hoover pointed out, that the limited amount of CRB food imported for the Belgians had to be reduced even further to provide for the French. This had not stopped the Belgians from agreeing to "divide their last morsel with this population until something could be done."

But the generous gesture could not be continued for long, he stated, and he drove the point home with stark truths: "It is no use dividing the food between the Belgians and the French in order that all may die. We have no right to take money provided to feed the Belgians and give it to the French."

He went further and declared that he had already directed that no more food would be sent over the frontier from Belgium into France after March 1, which was less than two weeks from the date of the letter.

Hoover's frustration was evident when he wrote about how the CRB's efforts to get the French government to finance the relief had gone nowhere. The French objection was that the Germans should feed the civilians.

Hoover addressed that thought plainly and forcefully: "I have nothing to say except that, not only do [the Germans] not do it, but they state emphatically that they do not intend to do it, that they have insufficient food supplies for themselves and do not propose to prejudice their own people."

Appealing to the president's humanity, he wrote, "If Your Excellency could see the mobs of French women and children which surround every German camp from daylight to dark to gather the refuse from the German soldiers, Your Excellency would then believe that these French people will pay the last penalty unless someone comes to their rescue."

He finished with a sentence full of repressed emotion: "In conclusion, before taking the heavy responsibility of saying to these people 'you shall not have bread,' I make this last appeal to the French people themselves in the name of their own country-women and children."

A few days later Hoover sent a follow-up telegram to Pinchot at the American Embassy in Paris outlining a bold course of action if the French would not agree to support the relief. It was a hardball move that he had used successfully against the British government—agree to support the relief or worldwide public opinion will be called down upon the French government.

Hoover explained to Pinchot, "If French Government is not prepared to give us positive reply I propose make statement to press of the world that we have up to now fed the people along the border, that our resources do not permit us to continue, that we have applied to the French Government for aid, that we do not believe this is a proper appeal to the world's charity, that the responsibility for the death of these people rests on the French nation itself; and I propose to do this simply to free this Commission from responsibility as to what will follow on withdrawal of our present supplies."

Two days later, on February 27, 1915, Pinchot wrote a memorandum to Hoover of a conversation he had had with M. Ribot, the French minister of finance. In it, he stated that he had yet to give Hoover's letter to President Poincaré and that his interview with Ribot lasted not more than five minutes. But what an extraordinary five minutes.

In that time, the French finance minister stated clearly that the French government would not give formal approval to any financing of aid to its people through the Belgian budget (as Hoover had proposed). However, unattributed money would be provided to the Belgian government and the Belgian government "would be asked no inconvenient questions," such as the origin of the funds.

The reason the French would not give money in their own name was "because to do so would be to put into the hands of the Germans the argument that since the French Government was permitted to feed its citizens therefore the German Government should be permitted to feed the people of Germany." The Allies had already been restricting many goods from going or coming from Germany and on March 1, 1915, the British and French would announce a blockade that would effectively stop all goods from entering or leaving Germany. It was a retaliatory blockade for the February 4, 1915, German "War Zone" declaration, which declared that the North Sea was a war zone and ships within it, whether or not they be neutral, could be sunk without warning.

Ribot told Pinchot that the 400,000 French civilians already receiving aid from the CRB should go on being fed and that the CRB should expand the relief and simply ask the Belgian government for the necessary funds as needed, but "not," the minister stipulated, "to keep the French in the invaded provinces in luxury, but to give them what is necessary to prevent them dying of starvation."

Hoover—probably initially frustrated and angry that Pinchot had not yet delivered his letter—had to be relieved by what Ribot had said. Armed with this rather unorthodox assurance that financing would be ultimately available, Hoover moved forward in two areas: He began to stockpile French flour without reducing the Belgian ration; and he began negotiating with the German military command to provide relief inside the army subzones.

Hoover already knew from trips he had made to Berlin and Brussels earlier in February that the Germans were amenable to expanding relief into northern France. He would tell the Germans that the additional food was being provided by "charitable institutions which we represent." It was a "fiction," as one later CRB history noted, that was necessary "because of the unwillingness of the French Government to admit openly that it supported financially the feeding of French civilians in the occupied regions lest the Germans use this fact as an additional argument against the legality of the Allied food blockade of Germany."

In the end, it took more than a month to get all the necessary agreements and financing lined up. These included nonrequisition guarantees from the German government in Berlin and the German military in northern France, approval to import from the British government, and the secret financing arranged from the French government to the Belgian government.

When it all came together, the handful of CRB delegates who went into northern France to supervise the relief would encounter many more difficulties and hardships than their counterparts working in Belgium. By far the most frustrating and intrusive in their lives was what the first delegates referred to as their German "wet nurse"—a term "to indicate jokingly the relationship that existed between them." It would quickly be shorted to the less-descriptive "nurse."

Hoover Takes Drastic Diplomatic Action against von Bissing

As Hoover was struggling to bring northern France into the relief program, he received von Bissing's reply to the letter he had left the governor general when he had departed Brussels and returned to London in mid-February. In that letter, he had threatened to pull the CRB out of Belgium relief if the CRB and its delegates were not given greater respect and unfettered freedom of movement.

Dated February 20, 1915, the governor general's letter had been written only after officials of the German occupation government had conferred with Dannie Heineman as to what the CRB wanted. Heineman was the American who had been so helpful in organizing early relief and had been the first CRB director in Brussels. However, by that time he had been removed as director because Hoover thought his efforts and sympathies were too closely aligned with the interests of Francqui and the CN and not enough with the CRB. Because von Bissing had a close association with Heineman, the German had had his staff work with Heineman and not the current Brussels director, Albert Connett. That meant the needs of the CRB were not properly conveyed to the Germans working on the issue.

Von Bissing started his reply by agreeing with Hoover that the work was important and that the Germans would support it. But then he had a long list of conditions that were to be met, including: the number of delegates must be restricted as much as possible; the current number of 30–40 delegates would be cut to 25 by April 15; the frequent changes in delegates would be stopped as much as possible; delegates would be given passes for only their province and to Brussels; only four members of the Brussels office would be allowed to have passes for the entire country; and only six passes a month would be issued for trips to Holland.

Upon reading the letter, Hoover said it was simply "reiterating a number of intolerable restrictions." He and the rest of the CRB were frustrated and angry at von Bissing's lack of understanding of what they were doing and what was needed to do the job properly. They were certain 25 men could not adequately supervise the work across the entire country. They also knew that if they agreed to such demands, it would be recognizing the Germans' right to control the CRB, something that was unacceptable to Hoover and to the British government.

Hoover knew from von Bissing's reply that he and the CRB had little, if any, influence over the German occupation government in Belgium. He also knew this was a major turning point in his organization and in the life of the relief work. If he failed to win the day on freedom of movement for his delegates, it would subjugate the entire humanitarian aid to German authority. That was intolerable to Hoover and unacceptable to the Allies, and it was a primary reason why he had threatened to pull out if the restrictions were not lifted.

If the British Foreign Office only knew about von Bissing's letter and demands, it would force the issue, in Hoover's favor he hoped. While that would temporarily mean hot water for Hoover, it would also justify his going over von Bissing's head and pleading the case to the German civilian government in Berlin, which had the power to override the governor general.

But how to alert the British Foreign Office to the situation? Hoover could not simply show the letter to the British because that would be a major breach of his adherence to strict neutrality and to international protocol during wartime.

In a not-too-surprising development, the British Foreign Office did somehow find out about von Bissing's letter. Officially, there has never been a full explanation of how that happened, although Hoover does point the finger of culpability at the British government's covert investigations of the CRB in Belgium. Throughout the war, there were heated disagreements between Britain's military, which was opposed to the relief, and the civilian government, which generally supported relief. As a result, the military had instigated investigations of the CRB in an effort to discredit the organization.

Hoover referred to that when he wrote, "The British Foreign Office, being informed of [von Bissing's letter and demands] through their Intelligence, promptly objected." It's just as likely, though, that von Bissing's letter, or the gist of it, was intentionally leaked to the British by someone in the CRB's London office.

No matter how the issue arose, the hot water came quickly; Hoover was called into the Foreign Office. The mining engineer wrote Whitlock on March 6, "I have had a severe drilling this week, from the English Government with regard to our whole organization in Belgium." He told the legation minister that the British government was adamant the CRB could not do its job with a reduction to 25 delegates and with heavy restrictions on movement. Hoover ended his letter without telling Whitlock to try to change von Bissing's mind, but the implication was there. Whitlock did meet with the governor general but to no avail.

With Whitlock's ambivalent, at best, support for the delegates, and outright disagreement at most, Hoover also had to battle with his own Brussels director, Albert Connett, over the issue. Connett, a well-known American engineer, had started in February, and his belief about the need for delegates was more in line with Francqui's and even the Germans, than Hoover's. He was "unfavorably impressed with the youth of the delegates in Belgium" and did not see the necessity to have a large number of them roaming about Belgium.

When Hoover wrote Connett from London to convince him of his position and included a letter from Ambassador Page that stated the delegates in Belgium should be numerous and more actively involved in the distribution, Connett sent back a rather shocking reply on March 8. He wrote that he had initially intended to call the delegates together and instruct them to follow the new guidelines as outlined in Hoover's and Page's letters. "However," he then wrote, "after a night's sleep and a frank talk with Mr. Francqui, I changed my mind. We both are confident that the Ambassador's letter was inspired in London Wall Buildings [Hoover's office] and not in Grosvenor Gardens [Page's office]."

After such an insult—regardless of how true it might be—it's no wonder Connett lasted as director only until April.

Facing pressures from all sides, Hoover once again decided it was time for strong action. On Tuesday, March 9, three days after sending his letter to Whitlock, Hoover went over von Bissing's head and bypassed diplomat Whitlock. He wrote a telegram to James Gerard, the American ambassador to Germany in Berlin, outlining the situation and asking for help. "We have been notified by Governor-General, Brussels, to reduce our staff in Belgium to twenty-five members by early April and that passes to these gentlemen will only be issued under great restrictions and apparently through the intermediary of Mr. Heineman. We are entirely discouraged by this attitude of local authorities. Do not believe that it can be in line with intention German Government toward us and trust you will take it up with them."

Hoover's line "trust you will take it up with them" was uncharacteristically diplomatic. That was out of necessity. While Hoover's end run around von Bissing and Whitlock was highly undiplomatic, his interaction with Gerard had to be as diplomatic as possible. The fact remained that Hoover was still a private citizen, pleading the case of a private company to a diplomat whose country had no official function within the CRB and Belgium relief. The ministers of America, Spain, and Holland who had agreed to be patrons of the CRB had agreed to do so more as private citizens than as representatives of their governments. Hoover had to walk a fine line of not pushing the ambassadors too far in his requests, or they might simply walk away, or claim they no longer had time from their other official duties to help the CRB. As for Whitlock, his case was different because he was inside Belgium—he had no choice in the matter but to be involved.

That was not the same situation with Gerard. Hoover had to tread more lightly with the U.S. ambassador to Germany because he had not yet come to know the man well. So in his telegram, he outlined to Gerard what the bare minimum would be for the CRB to function properly. "Fundamental fact is that in order for us to give proper executive control to distribution of this foodstuff, to properly account to its donors, and above all to give credibility to our assurances to the Allied Governments as to their guarantees, it is absolutely necessary for us to have the right to at least fifty people, to put any such number of staff into Belgium as may be reasonable to meet our own emergencies. Their passes must be issued directly on certification of Mr. Whitlock and on liberal basis of movement."

Hoover ended by asking Gerard to pass the telegram to Whitlock and Connett. He knew that Whitlock, Connett, and von Bissing would not take it well.

14

Antwerp and Environs

By early January 1915, E. E. Hunt had been officially on the job just a month. The Brussels CRB office had sent him three young delegates: Bennett Harvie Branscomb, 19; Oliver Cromwell Carmichael, 23; and William Willard Flint Jr., 22. Two more delegates arrived in January—Richard Harvey Simpson, 25, and William W. Stratton, 22—to replace Branscomb and Flint, who had left only a month after their arrival so they could return to Oxford and their studies. On February 1, Hunt received another delegate, Thomas O. Connett, 21, whose older brother, Albert N. Connett, was then the new Brussels director. Hunt, at 29 years old, was the elder statesman of the group, with Branscomb, as the youngest, celebrating his 20th birthday a month before on Christmas Day, 1914.

All of Hunt's early CRB delegates to Antwerp were what he termed "Rhodesters," American Rhodes scholars taking their winter break from Oxford. They had only agreed to work the six weeks of their break, and Branscomb and Flint stayed true to that plan when they left Hunt's group and Belgium in late January. The others would stay longer as their emotional commitment to helping the Belgians became stronger than the pull of their student plans.

In these early days, details big and small were still being worked out. As more delegates joined the CRB—volunteering their time and energy to the work—it became obvious to Hoover and the other executives that they deserved compensation for at least any expenses they incurred while in Belgium. It was finally established that each man would receive 20 francs a day, or 600 francs a month, to cover his expenses. But the policy was never officially announced throughout the network, and a few delegates heard only rumors about it.

One such delegate was Stratton. He officially wrote Hunt, as chief delegate, on February 3, 1915, urging him to "use your influence at Brussels toward ascertaining who, if anyone, knows anything about the 20 francs per day that is supposed to be paid to Americans in Belgium for defraying personal expenses. I have been broke since God knows when; the landlady has threatened to throw me out and has already interdicted me from the use of the bathroom and laundry until my bill is paid. I do not know how or where the Relief Commission could do any more useful work than in my case."

In the bottom left corner of Stratton's letter, fellow delegate Richard Simpson had added, "Endorsed: Absolument d'accord. Same here. R.H.S."

Hunt quickly remedied the situation, Stratton paid his bills, and the delegate's housing situation would be later rectified in a luxurious way.

The Antwerp CRB Delegates Deal with Bread

As for the work in Antwerp Province, Hunt knew he and his team had multiple jobs, but two were primary: "see that the Germans strictly observe the guarantee against requisitioning food supplies," and ensure that "every Belgian man, woman, and child receives his daily bread."

Hunt meant bread both metaphorically and literally. While the CRB imported multiple kinds of produce, the critical one in most Belgians' eyes was wheat, which would then be milled into flour for the making of bread.

The system of distributing wheat and flour to make the bread was straightforward. The CRB imported wheat that was delivered to mills, which existed in each of Belgium's provinces. There were ten mills in Antwerp Province, and each, as Hunt explained, was under the management of CRB delegates and the local Belgian committees. "The mills," Hunt stated, "were also considered Commission warehouses, under the protection of the American flag, and deliveries to the communes were made direct from them."

While the distribution system was generally straightforward, there were numerous places along the line where abuses could—and did—take place.

Hunt and his team were constantly following up on complaints regarding the bread ration and even the quality of the bread. The largest number of complaints and the biggest battles over bread were fought with the bakers.

Once the wheat was milled into flour, the flour was distributed. In the country districts, the flour was provided directly to consumers, who baked their own bread. In the cities, however, with their much larger populations, this wasn't possible. So bakers were contracted to receive flour and produce a certain amount of bread every day that would be sold to those who could afford it and given to those who were part of the charity arm of the relief.

These city bakers were notorious for taking any opportunity to scam the system to their betterment. Admittedly, as Hunt reported, part of the problem stemmed from the system itself. The CRB had a near monopoly on flour, but it did not establish a monopoly on baking.

"The bakers," Hunt explained, "were in keen competition with each other, under conditions of terrible strain. Many of them were delivering bread to clients who could no longer pay, and the Commission all the while was paring off the profit on bread-making to keep the price as low as possible for the ultimate consumers. At the same time the Dutch were smuggling flour and bread over the Belgian border," while part of the Dutch government was attempting to restore business between the Dutch and Belgian communes along the border.

The problem of baker fraud was so widespread and, to a certain extent, so endemic to Belgian bakers that something on a large scale had to be done. "To insure honest bread at honest weight and an honest per capita distribution, the Commission began to card-index all consumers in Belgium." That meant millions of people had to be identified and filed in a system that was all hand done. It was a huge job but was absolutely necessary to ensure the maximum efficient and effective distribution of relief.

In Antwerp, before card-indexing, Hunt and his crew had developed bread requirements by taking the estimated city population and dividing that number "among the big and little bakeries," so that they had "a rough-and-ready method for distribution." He and his team also "closely followed up complaints from the ultimate consumers."

When the word came down from the CRB Brussels head office that they needed to implement a card index, Hunt immediately knew that the process would "take time but would ultimately be best for the system." In the city, Hunt would have to deal with 185 bakeries and 46 pastry shops, indexing each establishment's customers, which would have to be cross-checked for verification. He had given the project to new CRB delegate Thomas O. Connett, who began the process with help from the bank director and clerks where the CRB offices were located.

A week later, in mid-February, Hunt asked for a progress report. Connett told him 12 bakers' lists had been completed so far.

"What do they show?" Hunt asked.

"Every one of them is fraudulent," Connett replied. "They've padded their lists of customers—given names of refugees who are in Holland or England, or purely fictitious names. And we've been furnishing them with flour for three weeks on a basis of lies! It makes me sick!"

"What do you want to do? Fine them?"

"We've done it: that is, I've insisted on fining the biggest baker in the lot, but the Belgian committeemen object." Hunt asked why, although he probably already had guessed the reason.

"They say all the hundred and eighty-five lists are padded, and they think it's too hard on that one to fine him alone!"

In the end, it took three weeks of full-time work for Connett and his team of bank clerks to create a verified list of consumers from which the CRB could accurately project wheat and flour needs. Still, it was worth the time and effort because, as Hunt explained, Connett "had card-indexed the city of Antwerp and reorganized the system of control over food distributions with a savings of about one-fifth of the supplies." That was a significant savings when every gram had to be tracked and recorded as it was imported, inventoried, and processed.

Once this revised system was in place, fraud and abuse were mightily decreased but never completely removed. Hunt was proud to report that "in spite of petty fraud, every Belgian was being fed." He also had a special weapon that was always at his disposal—provincial committeeman J. G. Delannoy.

This was a Belgian whom no baker wanted to cross. Delannoy was tall, big, and boisterous, a socialist who always wore an old-style frock coat and high collar. His appearance at the CRB offices was like an actor in a melodrama making his entrance in grand style: "Buzzing through his teeth the tune of the Socialist *Internationale,* Mr. Delannoy would burst into the Commission offices, roaring greetings right and left, smacking the desks with his great hands, conquering ears and hearts by his onslaught, and speaking an extraordinary mixture of English, French, and Flemish—a strong, meaty *potpourri* of languages."

Seemingly larger than life, Delannoy, according to Hunt, was "one of the most valued members of the Provincial Committee, respected and admired, even by his political enemies; a man of little fear and no favor, with a *penchant* for strong-arm methods."

One memorable case reaffirmed Delannoy's reputation. A baker with the last name Ixe had been found to be participating in some fraudulent activities. The CRB office was about to recommend a hefty fine. Hunt recorded in his book *War Bread* a complete vignette of what happened next.

When Hunt told Delannoy the news, the Belgian thought for a moment then said, "Mynheer 'Unt, I will explicate. It is the charAKter of the Flemish pupils (people) to make fraudeur (fraud)."

"Let's not discuss Flemish character," Hunt replied.

"No, no, no, no, no, no, no, no! Listen. I, Delannoy, moi, je, ik, I have make fraud—not now, no!—but in peace. I make fraud by the Garde Civique—Civil Guard—militia! You know what is the Garde Civique?"

"Yes. It is like our National Guard."

"Eh bien! I desert, I skip drill, I make fraud."

"The deuce! You're one of the 'straightest' men I ever met."

"But no. I make fraud by the Garde Civique. It is the charAKter of the pupils. Like you Americans; you pay not the customs moneys in New York; isn't it?"

A long silence!

"It is the charAKter of the Flemish pupils; always they make fraudeur. But, Mynheer 'Unt, I will see Ixe; n'est-ce pas?"

"Deal gently with him, for Heaven's sake. Don't massacre him. We don't love him, but we don't want him killed."

"I will kick him down the stair."

No one officially recorded the outcome of the meeting between Delannoy and Ixe, but the lack of paperwork on the case implies that the poor baker probably no longer "make fraud," as Delannoy would say.

The Threat of Epidemics Becomes Real

While the CRB was officially concerned with only the importation of food, the delegates could not ignore what was happening in all the communes, small villages, and little towns where they worked. Hunt, like many other delegates, quickly saw how the stress of war, the lack of a complete and healthy diet, and the ensuing cold in the winter of 1914/1915 was a recipe for the spread of diseases.

"Belgium needed far more than bread," Hunt said. "Thousands had neither clothes nor dwellings; millions were out of work; people of all classes were cold and idle and ill. The Commission for Relief in Belgium could not long remain a simple doling out of rations, for food was almost useless without other things as well—clothing, fuel, dwelling houses, money, and good health."

By early 1915, clothes were starting to be shipped in, aided in large part by the Rockefeller Foundation, which helped the CRB by establishing a station in Rotterdam to sort and ship clothing donations received from America for the Belgians. As the concept grew from idea to plan to implementation, large quantities of clothes would soon begin coming into the country.

Much more acute from a health standpoint was the fact that by the beginning of 1915 two epidemics had already been reported in Antwerp Province—typhoid and black measles. Hunt reported that 75 cases of typhoid were known and others suspected in the town of Willebroeck (now spelled Willebroek), 12 miles (20 km) south of Antwerp. The province's chief delegate took it upon himself to help the situation.

Hunt knew of two American women working in the Rockefeller station in Rotterdam. They were Dr. Caroline Hedger and Miss Janet A. Hall, both of whom had served with the Chicago Health Department as representatives of the Chicago Woman's Club. They had volunteered to work in Rotterdam and had come over in 1914.

"At my request these ladies came to the province of Antwerp as volunteer health officers," Hunt related. No one had told him to do so, no one had asked him to deal with typhoid, or any other health issues in Antwerp Province. Hunt had simply seen the need and acted, gaining the approval of the Belgians and the travel permissions from the German authorities for both women.

They arrived in Willebroeck with their own supply of typhoid vaccine. For two weeks they lived above a tavern in a small suite of rooms where "mould was so thick on the walls that one could scrape it off with one's fingers," Hunt said. With a literary flair, he noted that the winter was "cold and damp as an icy sponge," and in the two weeks the ladies were there, they "never once were thoroughly warm, although they were admirably dressed."

They started work immediately, helping local physicians and going into every house where typhoid had been reported or was suspected to be. They inoculated as many people as possible and ended up donating $3,000 worth of anti-typhoid vaccine to the CRB. That was used to help eradicate it in other areas where the disease had shown itself.

Hunt's action and the women's efforts not only helped Belgium; they also helped the CRB realize that health issues were a major concern, especially as the war dragged on. Quickly the delegates—both those already on the job and those arriving—were inoculated with four separate injections for typhoid.

A greater concern was also shown for other opportunistic diseases, such as tuberculosis, which had found footholds within Belgium and northern France as the long-term lack of plentiful food began to take its toll. (CRB delegates were not immune, as illustrated by one delegate, Major Robert M. Dutton, who served with the CRB from April 1915 to November 1916. He left Europe and headed home complaining of a pain in his right side. It would turn out to be tuberculosis and he would die in a Colorado sanatorium on February 19, 1918, at the age of 48.)

From Hunt's early actions and other health-related situations arising in early 1915, Hoover and the executive team realized that bringing health experts into Belgium to report on conditions would help on multiple levels. That would become an ongoing process throughout the life of the CRB.

The Bunges Offer Respite to the Delegates

As Hunt's efforts to provide relief for the Belgians became more intense, he found he needed occasional respites from the work to maintain his energy and enthusiasm. He would escape to a nearby monastery for some quiet reflection. He also took time to visit—alone and with other CRB delegates—numerous wealthy Belgians who had volunteered their country estates as retreats for the Americans. One of the ones he frequented was Chateau Oude Gracht, where the Bunge family lived.

There, he and the other delegates could relax in many ways, including participating in inside pursuits such as reading in the ornate and extensive library, playing billiards, engaging in conversation with the Belgians and other guests, or listening to the gramophone in the large parlor. Outside, depending upon the fickle Belgian weather, the delegates could take long walks through the fields and forests of the Hoogboom estate, play tennis on the clay courts, take a rowboat out on the lake, or wander around the nearby farm buildings. And always at night there would be splendid dinners in the large dining hall, with multiple courses, various wines,

Many CRB delegates spent downtime on the Bunge estate, which was 20 miles northeast of Antwerp. (Photo taken after WWI.) (Author's archives.)

and servers tending to the guests under the watchful eye of the tall, stately Isidore, Oude Gracht's *maitre d'hôtel* (head butler).

From these days of relaxation away from the war, Hunt began to get involved in the lives of the three Bunge women, particularly Erica. On Sunday, January 17, 1915, Erica wrote in her diary that she had had a special event with the help of Hunt.

"I have a dog of my own now!" Erica declared. "She is a pretty and delightful collie. Mr. Hunt and I went to get her this evening. I will name her Ninia. She is a beauty and a love. She refuses to go to the basement and for the moment she sleeps under the telephone."

A month later, Erica once again wrote in her diary about the delegates. It was evident that she was very much a young woman not always focused on work. "The Americans (Hunt, Oliver Carmichael, Richard Simpson and Thomas Connett) are here again. Hunt is the nicest of all, but he was strange tonight. I feel a little guilty and I'm sorry I was sarcastic. He is very sentimental, and so depressed! Why did he talk so much to Eva? Would I be jealous by any chance? May God preserve me from that! He is so nice, I like him very much! Ninia is a love. Mr. Hunt loves her and she licks him, which is a pleasure to see!"

The CRB delegates found rest and relaxation with the Bunges at the Chateau Oude Gracht. From left to right, E. E. Hunt and the Bunges: Eva, Edouard, Hilda, and Erica. (Author's archives.)

The 23-year-old Erica ended on a note of longing that belied her confident public persona. "I wish I were ten years older! My character and my personality would be more stable, more balanced. I get angry and I'm very silly sometimes, and afterwards I regret it! If only I were more sure of myself!"

Such internal conflict and questioning didn't stop Erica from wanting to somehow become more directly involved with helping her country. She was reminded of the war all the time, even on the tranquil Hoogboom estate, where she could often hear the sounds of the large artillery fire from the front. As she wrote in her diary on Sunday, January 3, 1915, "Right up to Christmas we could hear the cannon. Since today it has started rumbling again, having stopped from the 25th to Jan. 2nd."

A Dairy Farm Is Started on Hoogboom Estate

In January, Erica and her father, Antwerp merchant Edouard Bunge, continued thinking about what more they could do to help their country, and specifically the people of Antwerp. They had already done a lot.

Edouard was the vice president of Antwerp's provincial committee, sat on the board of the Comité National, donated office space in his bank building for

E. E. Hunt and his staff, and turned his large townhouse into a residence for the CRB delegates. The wealthy merchant had also personally used some of his fortune for the benefit of the general public. Knowing a large stock of coffee owned by the Brazilian state of São Paulo was sitting in an Antwerp warehouse, he and the CN received permission from the German authorities to buy and distribute it. Bunge paid for the coffee himself and turned it over to the CN, which portioned it out to the provincial committees. They, in turn, made it available to the general public.

Edouard Bunge at Chateau Oude Gracht. (Author's archives.)

As for Erica, she—along with her sisters Eva and Hilda—had worked in a makeshift Antwerp hospital during the invasion and had also found time to volunteer at soup kitchens and children's canteens. After Antwerp had surrendered and the German occupation began, all the British soldiers they had been tending were transferred to the military hospital in the city. The three had been sorry to see them go and worried about what would become of them. Either the British wounded would stay under the care of German hospital staff, or, if they got better, they would be transferred by rail to a military prison camp in Germany. Neither option held much promise of a bright future. By the end of December 1914, the hospital had been closed, and the Bunge women focused more on their volunteer work at the soup kitchens and children's canteens.

Even with such work, Erica wanted to do more, and she and her father would talk often about what they might do. They were aware that the hardest hit by lack of nutrition were newborns, who desperately needed fresh milk for proper development. Father and daughter decided they would explore ways of creating new sources of fresh milk for the children of Antwerp.

The obvious answer was to create a dairy farm, but could it be done under the German occupation? The Germans had restarted the local tramlines in and around Belgian cities, so Edouard and Erica knew they could create a reliable transportation network to bring milk from the farm to the tramline at nearby Cappellen (now spelled Kapellen). From there it was a 20-minute run into Antwerp, where members of the city's relief committee could distribute the milk to children's canteens and hospitals for newborn babies.

But would the Germans allow the Bunges to import dairy cows from Holland, bring in fodder for the herd, and create the facilities necessary to ramp up their estate's very limited current dairy production? If the Germans did agree to all that, Hoogboom estate would be an ideal location.

Edouard Bunge had purchased the estate on March 31, 1913, but the family had not moved in until June 1, 1914, two months before the war started. Previously, he and his family had lived at Calixberghe castle in Schoten, 6.5 miles (11 km) south of Hoogboom estate.

His new property was 300 hectares, or 741 acres, and contained a north and south farm with their associated buildings, a small train connecting the two farms, numerous houses throughout the property for the families employed on the estate, and a four-story castle that came to be known as Chateau Oude Gracht (Flemish for "old moat" or "old canal"). With a history going back hundreds of years, the estate had gained its name from the little ancient village of Hoogboom, which was adjacent to the property and provided many of the estate workers.

As one local history recorded, every day Edouard "took a walk or ride through the domain, paying attention to every tree, bush or animal. He always walked around with plans to make improvements or changes so that everyone could fully enjoy the beauty of nature; new homes were built and the old ones were improved so that the service staff had optimal accommodations. An oven was made for each house built and a pigsty, so that each family could provide for their own needs."

The estate produced game and wood from the forests, while the two farms produced various crops, milk, eggs, beef, pork, and lamb. Wool from the sheep was also sold regularly.

The southern farm was within walking distance of the chateau along a cobblestoned lane. The path crossed a wooden bridge spanning one of the property's numerous canals that fed the lake. The farm was the size of a small village. Buildings lined three or four converging cobbled roads, and there were long barns for cattle, horses, and sheep. Clustered around these were the houses of the estate supervisor, the forester, and the gamekeeper, as well as numerous small cottages for the farm tenants. All were red brick with thick thatched roofs, and they sported shutters and doors painted red and white. The south farm focused on spring and summer crops such as corn, potatoes, beans, and beets. It also had more farm animals such as chickens, pigs, and sheep.

The northern farm—located on the far northern part of the property known jokingly as "Siberia"—was connected to the summer farm by a small rail line and it focused on autumn and winter crops. It had fewer buildings and workers than the south farm did and planted crops that could handle the wet, cold Belgian weather. Major tubers and taproots hardy enough for the winter climate included scorzonera (Flemish: schorseneer; when cooked it's like a poor man's asparagus); black radishes (Flemish: rammenas; the color of charcoal but with less bite than a red radish); Jerusalem artichokes (Flemish: aardpeer; looks like ginger root); winter purslane (Flemish: winterpostelein; a hardy leafy green with a spinachlike taste); and root parsley (Flemish: wortelpeterselie; similar to a parsnip).

When Bunge had bought the estate, he had continued to employ all those working on the farms and in the chateau, but he also convinced a handful of Calixberghe people he greatly respected to come with him. They included estate supervisor Hendrik Verheyen, who lived on the property with his wife and three children; estate forester Louis Willems, known as "de Witte," who lived in the forester house with his wife, three sons, and five daughters; and his personal butler, Isidore, who lived in Chateau Oude Gracht and became its *maitre d'hôtel,* responsible for the smooth running of the household, including the supervision of the annual cleaning of the 1,100-piece chandelier in the formal salon.

When the war had come, so had Belgian soldiers to the Bunge estate. Erica wrote in her diary on Monday, August 10, 1914, that after gaining Belgian military permission, she had traveled from Antwerp to Hoogboom estate to take stock of the situation. "I went to Hoogboom, we were stopped nine times to show our permits. I arrived just in time. A detachment of [Belgian] Artillery is on our place, Commandant Nyssens, eight officers and junior officers, two orderlies, a stableman, and one cook are living in the chateau. We made ready 14 rooms, they all seemed very happy with the good beds and the baths. The soldiers have permission to bathe, to catch rabbits and other things; a good post! There are 400 infantry soldiers, a Commander and some officers, and the whole estate belongs to them! I hope they will respect it."

Two days later, her diary entry reflects her sense of dread as to not knowing what was happening with the war and her assessment of what was happening on the estate. "No official news. . . . Where are the Allies? . . . The waiting is awful, we cannot do anything. . . . We have 600 [Belgian] soldiers on the estate, 400 infantry and 200 artillery. Fifteen are in the chateau. 450 grams of meat a day, one loaf of bread, and the rest, 150 kilos of potatoes are taken per day. Soon there won't be anything left."

On Friday, August 14, 1914, she wrote again of war and the property. "Still no news, we are desperate. The poor soldiers. We don't know anything new. The great battle must not have been fought yet. The [Belgian] Commandant [at Hoogboom] believes that the Germans will march on Antwerp and will try to take the forts. It would be awful. And we have to wait. . . . There has been a lot of work done digging trenches [on Hoogboom] by the infantry. Pereken [the name she called her father] is very tired, beaten down. . . . What will become of us? Personally I'm not afraid, it's so heartbreaking to think of those who are fighting."

The war-preparation work on the estate had been massive, primarily because the property was so close to Holland—parts of it were less than five miles away from the border. With the Belgian military's belief that the Germans might invade Holland and then swing south into the area (the Germans did not invade Holland), the soldiers had built 48 bunkers and dug numerous trenches in strategic areas in the northern part of the property closest to the border. In front of each trench, all the trees and bushes had been felled so that the defenders could have a good line-of-sight view of any attackers. The Belgians had done such a good job of clearing the land that on a clear day someone standing in the area could see the church tower of the little town of Putte, which straddled the Belgian-Dutch border less than five miles away.

When the German occupation of the country began in September/October, Hoogboom estate escaped unscathed (besides what the Belgian soldiers had done), leaving all its facilities intact and all its workers safe and in place. The estate, however, could not fully function as it had before the war because of the Germans' confiscation of horses and other draft animals and restrictions on motorized vehicles, gasoline, and other necessities of modern farming.

All in all, if a dairy farm was going to be started to help the little children of Antwerp, Hoogboom estate had much going for it:

- Proximity to the Dutch border, making for relative ease in purchasing and importing dairy cows and fodder.
- Two existing farms with multiple facilities already in place.
- Access to a tramline going directly into Antwerp.

Most importantly, the estate had Edouard and Erica Bunge—one to finance the dairy, the other to run it.

On Wednesday, March 3, 1915, a meeting of the Antwerp Economic Food Committee, comprised of influential Antwerp men, came together to address the issue of the milk supply for the city and most notably for the children. While there were still dairy cows in the area, their numbers had dwindled, and because fodder for them was scarce, the production of milk was way down.

As the men discussed what could be done, one of them, Mr. Friling, announced that his friend and neighbor, Edouard Bunge, had come forward with a proposition. He would provide 100 dairy cows and daily shipments of milk to Antwerp, if the group would provide the fodder necessary for maintaining such a herd. Even though 100 dairy cows would not solve the city's milk shortage, it would go a long way toward feeding the very young. The group quickly agreed.

A Dutch cattle trader was contacted to arrange the purchase and export license. The Dutch government needed proof, however, that the Germans would not requisition the cows or the milk. The German military governor for Antwerp, General von Hune, agreed to the project and provided a letter in April stating no dairy cows or milk would be taken by the Germans.

The purchase of dairy cows took place at a price of 1,300 francs per animal (equivalent to a little less than a year's wage for one farm worker), and the cows were delivered to Hoogboom estate. Edouard Bunge and his business partner, Georges Born, paid the entire price.

Erica Bunge stepped in to run the operation; estate supervisor Verheyen became the dairy farm administrator; Dr. Bonroy, the director of the Industry School of Antwerp, volunteered as scientific and technical adviser; while a man named Van Wallendael took on the purchasing of feed and monitoring of the stables. Hélène Born, a close friend of Erica's and daughter of Georges Born, volunteered to assist Erica.

Erica was more qualified for the position than many young Belgian women. At an early age she had shown an interest in business and had quickly become a business confidant of her father's. Years before the war, the family was not surprised when she announced she wanted to go to agricultural college in England—a rarity for women in the early 1900s. When the Bunges moved into Chateau Oude Gracht, Erica began to use her agricultural degree and participate in the management of Hoogboom estate's two farms.

When the dairy farm idea came into being, Erica was excited at the prospect of running the operation with Verheyen's help. First, however, facilities had to be built to handle the larger herd. New structures to be built included the following:

- A large, modern stable for 100 head of cattle.
- A smaller structure that contained a stable for 15 head of cattle, a storage room for all vehicles and equipment, a stable for four horses, and two saddleries.
- A building that housed Erica and Verheyen's office, a laboratory, a room for cleaning the milk cans, a hall for filling the milk cans, the cooling equipment for the milk, and a locker room for the dairy farm's staff.

Three existing structures were incorporated into the new buildings to form the foundation of the dairy farm. When the new structures were completed, Bunge and Born had paid more than 260,000 francs for their construction.

On Tuesday, May 11, 1915, the dairy cows crossed the border in a long line of wagons that arrived safely at Hoogboom estate. With the Bunges' existing small herd, the total livestock of the dairy farm came to 130 dairy cows, one bull, three pull oxen, four horses, and 30 to 40 heifers and female calves.

Erica and Verheyen would have their hands full getting the operation running. It remained to be seen just how much milk the cows could produce and if the milk could be reliably shipped to Antwerp every day.

15

Elsewhere in Belgium

Getting Down to Work

After David Nelson's melancholy Christmas in the German café, he settled into the work and life in Liège. He and the chief delegate, George Jackson, were joined by another delegate Dr. William H. Percy, who had been an instructor at Columbia Medical School before sailing for Belgium on December 4. Percy lived with Nelson in a pension that Nelson wrote his sister "is fine—just like we were in a home."

On New Year's Eve, Nelson celebrated by taking to his bed with a bad cold. The situation was made much more bearable, however, because that day he had finally received his first mail from outside of Belgium. He had received a letter from his sister and a cousin and one from his mother that had included a photo of her. Nelson was touched by his mother's photo and wrote back, "I think it is fine—Thank you so much for it." The next day, the first day of 1915, he felt "fairly well again this morning and will be over it in a day." He headed off on an inspection tour within the province that included stops in Visé and Hasselt.

The workload was immense, and Nelson's early days as a Liège delegate were so filled that he wrote his family that they "have left me little time for writing." As his shorthand notes from one day indicate, he was nearly constantly on the move: "Spent the morning at Maastricht [Holland; one-hour drive from Liège]. Verhoustraeter helped me obtain passes etc. Maastricht to Eysden [Belgium]—terrible with inspectors over Joseph's pass [the pass for his driver]. Eysden to Visé—Visé to Hasselt—Beer with Provincial Attorney—Brother's wine cellar of 40,000 bottles—Hasselt to Maastricht." The day included a bit of drama as Jackson, the chief delegate of the Liège team, didn't know where Nelson was and later that night described "his thrills of fear at [the] thought of my being shot as a spy."

Nelson spent many days motoring around Liège Province, visiting towns and villages to talk with commune officials about food-relief needs, inspecting mills and how the flour was distributed, going to Maastricht to confirm food shipment

David T. Nelson found the work as a delegate challenging as he motored around Liège Province visiting towns and villages. (Public domain; Hebert Hoover Presidential Library and Archives, West Brand, Iowa.)

documents and approvals for transit into Belgium, and assessing the situation with the Germans to see if they were honoring the guarantee not to touch any imported food. He, Jackson, and Percy also made weekly trips up to Brussels to meet with other CRB delegates to talk out problems and share ideas. Nelson complained to his family that he was spending a tremendous amount of time in his car. "This past week and a half . . . I have almost lived in the car."

Nelson had a driver, Joseph, who was available nearly every day and night, regardless of time or weather conditions. Like most of the other cars used by delegates, Nelson's was an open touring car. It was not the best for dealing with the infamous wet and cold Belgian weather—as Nelson wrote his family in late January, "Belgium has no climate, it has only weather." Multiple layers of thick clothing and heavy blankets were de rigueur for most motorcar trips during the winter and many other times during the rest of the year.

Belgian weather wasn't the only problem when it came to motoring around Belgium. On one trip Nelson made to Brussels, "We drove through Hainault, Tirlemont, and Louvain and were able to get a very good idea of the condition of the country. The fact that we had four blow-outs on the way up [covering only about 55 miles, or 89 km] made the trip interesting in more ways than one."

Blowouts and motorcar breakdowns weren't the only obstacles. There were numerous German checkpoints positioned throughout the country and at all the border crossings into Holland and into Germany. The soldiers at these posts would stop everyone to confirm each person had the necessary travel documents and usually searched most people and vehicles.

Even the officially sanctioned CRB was not immune to checkpoint problems—in fact, some of the delegates felt they were searched more than others because they were part of the CRB. Especially during the early days of food relief, most regular soldiers did not know what the CRB was, causing a lot of unnecessary suspicion, while some officers who knew the CRB's mission felt that the supposedly neutral delegates were not only providing food relief to the Belgians but also secretly providing valuable war information to the Allies.

And then there were simple self-inflicted errors that caused problems at the checkpoints. Nelson wrote his father that an official CRB courier (probably Edward Curtis, who was the first CRB courier) had been arrested by the Germans at one of these checkpoints. "His pass had expired," Nelson explained, "and instead of applying for a new one which would certainly have been granted, he conceived the brilliant idea of changing the date of expiration himself. He did so; his forgery was detected; and now he is out of employment. He was fined 100 marks and was told that he could not drive his car again for a month—a very nominal penalty, considering the nature of his offence."

At the border posts, one of the worst offenses in the eyes of the Germans was for CRB delegates to carry in or out of Belgium personal correspondence (their own or others) or publications, such as Allied newspapers or Belgian underground material. Nelson was lucky in mid-January when he was crossing from Belgium into Holland heading for Maastricht and realized that "I came through this morning with a letter and two postcards (my own, however)—but they never took them out of my pockets. The soldier was about to go over me carefully but hadn't more than started when the officer in charge told him, '[Das] ist gut; er ist staatseingelörige [*sic*] Amerika" [It's OK; he is an American citizen] and it didn't take the flunky more than five seconds to make a couple of passes up and down my body for weapons of any sort and it was over."

Nelson's German sympathies had not yet changed, as evidenced by what he added when he wrote his sister about the incident: "Germans, as a rule, treat us very finely. They even stretch the rules in our favor now and then."

Along the same lines, Nelson then went on to show a weariness toward how he felt the Belgians exaggerated stories of German atrocities. In the same letter, which he wrote while in Holland, he stated, "The [food] train I came up here to look after is due in half an hour so I shall have to close." Then he added with a note of frustration, "Back again to German patrols and sentries, and Belgians ready to believe any tale created by an imaginative fellow-country-man. Tales of atrocities begin to grow tiresome. The American Consul at Liège showed me a letter written by an apparently sane Belgian business man which he left at the Consulate for forwarding. It described how the Germans seized a Belgian, put out his eyes, cut off his hands and feet, pierced him with fifty bayonet thrusts, and then buried him alive, head foremost. Some imagination. I haven't met a Belgian yet that spoke from personal observation—none of them have been eyewitnesses apparently."

The stories might have been tiresome to hear, but what could not be denied was that the ruins of war were impossible to ignore, especially with the amount of traveling Nelson was doing. On one trip he wrote in his journal, "In the afternoon visited Herve, which is one-fourth destroyed and in great want. Met the Vicar there who gave us much information. Passed through Battice on way home. Battice is completely ruined. I saw only three or four houses standing."

Seeing ruins was one thing, but meeting and getting to know Belgians was another. On Wednesday, January 13, Nelson wrote of going with a Madame Olivier to visit some of the poor of Liège. He reported that they were mostly in need of shoes and something to eat. Among those he saw were a "girl about to become a mother," a "soldier's wife with three bright children," a "young mother with one child living in a single room—bed in one corner," and a "Walloon [French-speaking] wife of coal-miner who was cross and refused the mittens [that were offered]."

A few days later, Nelson, Dr. Percy (by that time known as "doc"), chief delegate Jackson, and a man named Kaufman (never identified) drove to the Belgian town of Spa, renowned for natural mineral springs that were believed to possess health-giving properties. The town had for centuries bathed both the sick and healthy and was the inspiration for the generic term "spa." With the German invasion and occupation, Spa's hospitals became a major German convalescent center.

The CRB delegates were given a tour of the hospitals caring for convalescent typhoid patients. Nelson was impressed and felt the doctors and nurses "certainly give them the best care." The tour was led by a German doctor, "who treated us very nicely," Nelson reported, "but spoiled it by saying at parting: 'I hope you will give us a good mark when you get home.'" While Nelson was still pro-German, he did not like how some Germans seemed to consciously act to influence the neutral Americans' opinion about Germans.

The Christmas Ship Arrives

Three weeks later, on Sunday, February 7, the delegates returned to Spa for a very different event. They had been invited by the town's burgomaster (mayor) to be present at the distribution of Christmas gifts that had been sent to Spa as part of the cargo of an American Christmas ship, USS *Jason*. The ship, also dubbed USS *Santa Claus*, had brought from America 5 million gifts weighing 12,000 tons and including everything from toys, sweets, and nuts to girls' and boys' clothes, according to Britain's *Daily Mail* newspaper.

The initial idea of sending Christmas gifts to Belgian, French, and English children affected by the war was started in Chicago but had quickly spread across America. Donations of all kinds had flooded in, and the USS *Jason* was quickly filled. After crossing the Atlantic, the first stop was Britain, where a portion of the gifts was unloaded. The ship then continued on to Europe. While the ship had sailed in December, it had taken months for each recipient country to sort through its portion of the cargo, divide it up into individual gifts, and then divide those into groups for as many cities as possible.

On Sunday, February 7, 1915, it was finally Spa's turn to give out its portion of gifts. Belgian gratitude was such that Nelson, Jackson, and Kaufman were the honored guests at the event. They were surprised to walk into the town's major hall and find the place decked out with banners, American flags, and boughs of evergreen. An excited and enthusiastic crowd filled the hall and greeted them with cheers as an orchestra struck up "Hail, Columbia," considered by many Europeans to be America's national anthem. As the stirring tune was reverberating through the hall, the burgomaster led Jackson and Nelson up to a dais on one side of the hall. When the room finally quieted down, the burgomaster gave a short speech in French thanking the Americans for such generosity.

Nelson was happy to tell his family that he could understand the speech, but because of both delegates' "very halting French," neither chose to "attempt a reply." This didn't faze the crowd as "many in the audience wept," then broke into cheers and shouts of "Vive L'Amerique," as the orchestra struck up "Yankee Doodle." After that lively tune, the crowd greeted a schoolboys choir that sang "La Brabançonne," Belgium's national anthem. Many in the crowd sang along with great gusto, especially because the tune was by then outlawed by Governor General von Bissing. Once the thunderous applause had died away, the distribution of gifts began. "Altogether," Nelson wrote his family, "it was a very touching ceremony."

Only three days later, Nelson was involved in another unusual event. This time he played chef at his boardinghouse as a direct result of the American food relief. Americans were sending over a large variety of foods, many of which were unfamiliar to, or normally not used by, Belgians. These items included canned corn and canned sweet potatoes.

"As these are unknown in Belgium," Nelson wrote his family, "the [Belgian] Provincial Committee came to us to find out how to prepare them. I told them to send me a can of each of them and I would show my landlady how to prepare them after which she could write out the [recipe]." With a note of pride, Nelson wrote, "Knowing my abilities as a cook it is entirely superfluous to tell you that we had some excellent corn and sweet potatoes for supper. To-morrow morning I get the [recipe]."

This kind of culinary activity was happening all over Belgium, as the delegates within their provinces had to explain how to prepare certain food.

Belgian Patriotism

Food wasn't the only item that was suddenly imported into German-occupied Belgium. Because Belgian patriotism was outlawed by von Bissing, patriotic expression toward America quickly took its place, much to the consternation of the Germans. Belgians who were no longer allowed to wear their country's flag colors suddenly began wearing knots of ribbons of red, white, and blue on their lapels, hats, coats, blouses, and scarves. Displays of Belgian flags were no longer allowed, but nothing had been said about American flags, so little American flags started showing up as adornments on doorways, windows, and pieces of clothing. The

Belgians became more and more passionate about using displays of Americana to express their own suppressed patriotism and anti-German feelings.

In Liège the citizens wholeheartedly embraced this way of passively antagonizing the Germans. Such spirit came naturally to them. They were famous for their fighting spirit, which had sprung from a heritage of hearty coal miners and heavy industry workers. As a contemporary Baedeker's tour book explained, "Indefatigable industry and a partiality for severe labour are among their strongest characteristics, but they have frequently manifested a fierce and implacable spirit of hostility towards those who have attempted to infringe their privileges."

The Germans and their occupation were just the latest manifestation of an army attempting to conquer a people who felt they had never truly been conquered before. Even though the Germans had taken over in August 1914, active resistance was still taking place occasionally, as evidenced by Nelson, who wrote in his journal in early January that 30 people had been captured "trying to blow up the main bridge east of town." While such outward resistance had nearly ceased in the face of brutal German reprisals, passive resistance was quite alive and well in Liège, as shown in another incident that Nelson recorded.

By February, word had spread throughout Belgium that Monday, the 22nd, was the birthday of America's first president, George Washington. Local celebrations were planned around Belgium to honor America. As Nelson wrote to his family, in a leadup to the big day, many Liège citizens had begun wearing small American flags "as a little appreciation of the American Commission's work." Nowhere better could that be seen than on the city's main street, Boulevard D'Avroy, which ran north from the Parc d'Averoy to St. Paul's Cathedral and its soaring 300-foot-high tower. Even in wartime, the broad boulevard was still a favorite during good weather for evening promenades, where families would stroll under large, leafy plane trees. With many then out of work, the street drew people all day long.

On Thursday, February 18, the plane trees were bare, and the winter wind carried the chill of the cold waters of the nearby Meuse River through the city. But that did not stop many of the out-of-work residents from strolling the boulevard. And most of them, as Nelson recorded, were wearing some form of the American flag. Word spread that this day could be a patriotic display to the Americans and a slap in the face to the Germans even though it wasn't yet Washington's birthday. The number of strollers grew.

All was peaceful at first, until suddenly a squad of soldiers appeared. Walking south, they too noticed the many American flags adorning the passersby. To the Germans—just like the Belgians—the little American flags were not simply displays of a neutral country's flag. To the soldiers, the emblems somehow represented disrespect for their own government, which they felt was benevolently governing a conquered people.

Some of the soldiers moved from person to person and "with great rudeness pulled off the flags from a number of men and ladies, and threw them to the ground."

The civilians were quick to react. "In just a moment all was excitement; the quick Liègeois swarmed in the streets; the Germans feared a riot; the call was sounded; all the officers hurriedly left for the Kommandantur." As the small band of soldiers, probably no more than 20, retreated to the German headquarters, the growing crowd milled around, angrily telling and retelling what had just happened—each person wanting to tell what he or she had seen or experienced.

The Belgians did not have long to wait for a German response.

In short order, according to Nelson, 250 men—with fixed bayonets and rifles at the ready—came marching swiftly down the boulevard in a show of force meant to intimidate. Their boots slapped loudly on the pavement, creating an urgent beat that roiled out in front of them and smashed headlong into the crowd.

The Belgians parted reluctantly to let the soldiers through.

As Nelson told his family, "It was merely a demonstration to let people know they were on the job, but it shows how quickly trouble starts. Nothing came of it all; the incident was evidently the result of the hot-headedness of a few soldiers." In the end, the occupation government within Liège realized this was not a battle worth fighting—an announcement was later made, and as reported by Nelson to his family, American flags "could be sold and worn freely and the people are now so doing."

To most citizens of the city, this was a victory, made sweeter by every time they displayed the American colors.

A few days later, the celebration honoring President Washington was held without incident.

A Motorcar Tale Leads to Chauffeurs for All

Because the delegates assigned to the provinces had to travel extensively as part of their duties, motorcars were a necessity. In the early days of the CRB, the cars were a wide variety of makes and models because they were loaned to the Americans by wealthy Belgians who could no longer drive them—the Germans had prohibited any personal use of vehicles by civilians. By early 1915, however, the CRB had begun receiving a fleet of well-known American Overland light touring motorcars donated by the Willys-Overland Motor Company.

Initially, maintenance issues, tires, and even gasoline were the responsibility of the individual delegates in the field. As existing supplies were used up and as the CRB grew in size and the Brussels office became more organized, this individual method became unworkable. After negotiations with the British, the CRB gained approval to import parts, tires, and gasoline for its sole use. A CRB motor

Belgian chauffeurs became mandatory for CRB delegates after some incidents involving the devil-may-care young Americans. In the front seat with the Belgian driver is Gilchrist Stockton; in the back seat is Richard Simpson. (Author's archives.)

pool was established in Brussels by the Belgian Armand Dulait, who became an unofficial—but highly efficient and greatly appreciated—member of the CRB. He and his transportation department maintained the growing fleet of 40 motorcars countrywide, drew up rules for their use, and even employed and supervised the group of chauffeurs used throughout Belgium.

Driving the cars had been a different story than supplying the parts and gas. Before the CRB got fully organized in Belgium, the earliest delegates—many of them young daredevils—drove their own cars. According to delegate Kittredge, "Most of them drove with more speed than skill and the results were sometimes disastrous and always expensive."

Some of the problem had to do with the countryside itself. The terrain could be incredibly challenging, especially because Belgium was known for its year-round rainy weather. Many roads were cobblestoned and many had large swaths of mud on each side that became legendary in the minds of the American delegates.

Kittredge picturesquely wrote, "When [a delegate] thinks of Belgium there will come to his mind a narrow cobblestone road between two bottomless seas of mud, stretching down between two long lines of trees, and on this road a battered Overland car bouncing its way past obstinate carts and, occasionally, over unsuspecting chickens, dogs and even pigs."

Tracy Kittredge, 24, was probably the driver in a single-car incident that he later wrote about humorously in his CRB history. (Public domain; author's archives.)

As reports came into the Brussels office of motorcar mishaps, a decision was made to do something about it. In February 1915, Philip Chadbourn, a 25-year-old North Carolinian with a finely waxed handlebar mustache and a preference for bowties, was instructed to visit all the CRB provincial delegates and instruct them to use their cars with all due caution and to never exceed 30 miles an hour.

His first stop nearly became his last.

Chadbourn and his chauffeur began by driving 50 miles (80 km) east of Brussels to Hasselt, the capital of the province of Limbourg. At the time, two delegates were stationed there: Scott Paradise and Tracy Kittredge. Both were 24 years old and both had been in the first group of 10 Oxford students to join the CRB in December 1914. Kittredge, who would later write an unofficial history of the CRB, related in that history the following motorcar story without revealing if he or Paradise was the driver, although the intimate details provided would seem to indicate Kittredge was the driver.

The day after Chadbourn arrived in Hasselt, it was decided that he and one of the delegates, along with the delegate's Belgian secretary, would tour the regional warehouses. The chauffeur who was supposed to drive them was unable to do so because of blood poisoning in his hand. The Hasselt delegate—presumably Kittredge—said he would drive instead.

They were motoring along quite nicely at the prescribed speed when they came to a sudden fog bank. It clung tightly to the narrow cobblestoned road and lent an air of mystery to just how deep and wide the mud was that crowded both sides. Things would have definitely gone quite differently if a German military car hadn't suddenly emerged from out of the fog like some mythical beast. Roaring along at full speed, it had no intention of slowing down and expected anything in its way to speed up or get out of the way.

Kittredge, knowing just how hellish the mud could be, chose to speed up. Very quickly, he and his passengers were hurdling along at more than 50 miles an hour, just barely staying ahead of the German staff car. They and their car were taking a beating as they thudded along on the uneven cobblestones, but it was better than diving into thigh-high mud.

Just as quickly as it had appeared, the German car suddenly turned off onto a side road. Before the group could cheer, however, out of the fog came a worse vision. Directly ahead was a 90-degree turn and straight beyond the turn were the tracks of the vicinal (local) railway.

"The distance was too short to stop," Kittredge declared, "the angle too acute to turn." There was nothing left to do but take his chances with straight ahead. "After hurtling uncertainly over the railway track, the motorcar "skidded between two trees and turned a double somersault into a ditch ten feet deep on the other side."

As the car started its first aerial maneuver, Chadbourn and the Belgian secretary were thrown far ahead and landed in a yielding mudbank.

Kittredge struggled to get free of the steering wheel. He finally dropped away from the car in one of its flips. He landed in a ditch just in time to look up and see in horror the motorcar in slow motion coming down on top of him.

In a second it was over.

The car had landed on both sides of the V-shaped ditch. Kittredge, at the bottom of the V, lay looking up at the vehicle inches from his face.

That foggy, muddy, Belgian day, none of the three was hurt.

As Kittredge concluded the story, however, Chadbourn "said little to the local delegate, but when he returned to Brussels two very strict and emphatic letters were sent out to all delegates providing that henceforth the car should only be driven by chauffeurs and not by delegates and the speed-limit should never exceed twenty miles an hour."

The new regulation served numerous purposes, not only saving delegates from themselves, but also giving much-needed employment to Belgians and displaying to the Belgian public and the Germans the proper level of respect and professionalism that the CRB hoped to achieve in Belgium.

16

Northern France

The Army Zones Create a Unique Situation

While the need for food was as strong in northern France as it had been initially in Belgium, the situation was much more complicated in northern France because relief had to take place in one of two German Army Zones. (See map in Reader Aids.)

Most of Belgium was in the Occupation Zone, which was controlled by von Bissing and his civil government. The land closest to the battle lines was in two Army Zones (one in Belgium, one in northern France), which was administered by the regional German armies. Each Army Zone was subdivided into an Operations subzone that was the thin strip of land closest to the trenches, and the Etape, or staging area, that comprised the rest of each zone. The Army Zone within Belgium contained two districts: East and West Flanders. The Army Zone within northern France contained six districts: Longwy, Charleville, Vervins, St. Quentin, Valenciennes, and Lille.

The commanders in each of the six French districts had complete authority and severely limited the movements and actions of those involved in relief. Communications were so highly restricted that civilians were effectively cut off from anyone outside their neighborhood. There was no postal service, no communication allowed between communes, and even commune meetings were rarely permitted.

This imposing militarized zone did not seem to bode well for Hoover and his executive team, who had to secure relief guarantees from the German General Staff in Charleville before regular food shipments could begin. They only had to think about the difficulties they had faced with Governor General von Bissing in occupied Belgium to believe that the German high command would be even more formidable.

What they found surprised them. The German military was much more open to working with the CRB to provide food for the civilians within the Army Zone than von Bissing seemed to be. Major von Kessler, the primary person in Charleville that the CRB had to deal with, was helpful and responsive. As Kittredge noted, "Major von Kessler always maintained a sympathetic and friendly attitude toward the Commission, and in general the Commission did not have to encounter in its work in France the continual suspicion that was directed against it by many of the higher authorities in Belgium. In France its work went on for the most part very smoothly and without the dozens of petty annoyances and aggravating incidents that continually arose in the territory of [von Bissing's] General Government."

This didn't mean there weren't difficulties and crises that would occur—including the arrest and ultimate rejection of Hoover's pick for chief delegate for all of northern France—but the initial setup of relief guarantees came about relatively smoothly. On April 13, 1915, an agreement was signed by Major von Kessler, representing the supreme command of the German Army, and Oscar T. Crosby, then CRB director in Brussels representing the CRB.

The need in northern France had been so great, however, that the first shipment had gone out in early February. It was a trainload of flour from Namur to Charleville and the commune of Sedan. The food was personally escorted by two young CRB delegates.

In dramatic and unnecessary collegiate fashion, 22-year-old Rhodes scholar John L. Glenn rode "perched on the engine to make sure the food reached its destination," while 23-year-old friend and fellow Rhodes scholar Carlton Bowden raced along in his Overland car to help pave the way. The flour was presented to the mayors of both towns with the insistence that cash be paid for the temporary one-off delivery. As Kittredge later wrote, "The American delegates returned to Namur with the Overland weighted down with the money which they had received." A few more sporadic shipments were made before the official agreement for provisioning was signed and regular shipments were developed.

As for the CRB delegates who would be assigned to work in the Etape, there was much for the German high command to consider. Some of the places where relief personnel had to work were within eyesight of the trenches, where they could observe men training, see battle preparations, and watch general troop movements. Such unique frontline positioning was not lost on the German commanders, who subsequently demanded that strict military procedures and regulations be followed and that American personnel be subject to close observation and searches at anytime.

Similar to how relief was organized in Belgium, the actual distribution of food to the more than 2 million northern French would be handled by locals. Those workers would be part of a newly formed organization, the Comité d'Alimentation du Nord de la France, commonly referred to as the Comité Francais (CF). The CF resembled the CN in Belgium, but a major difference was that the actions of the CF were severely restricted by the military government. Because of those limitations, a central committee of the CF was headquartered in Brussels, but it was more an accounting group than an executive committee. Overall coordinating control was maintained by the Brussels CRB office. Within the Army Zone, the CF had committees at the district, regional, and communal levels that coordinated the distribution. Because the members of these committees were restricted even more than the CRB delegates, much of the communications between the groups was aided by the American delegate, who traveled extensively throughout his district.

Another major difference between relief in northern France and Belgium was that in northern France there were no neutral diplomats involved (such as Whitlock and Villalobar), and no German officials (such as von der Lancken) representing the German civil government. This meant the CRB delegates had to deal directly with the military authorities within each of the six districts and with the overall German military headquarters located in Charleville. And any problems or crises that arose had to be dealt with directly between the CRB and the German military.

To the German high command, all these differences demanded greater supervision, management, and control of the CRB delegates working within the Army Zone. This led to the condition that each CRB delegate working in the six French districts be accompanied by a German officer who was fluent in English and French.

Officially designated as a *Begleitsoffizier* (escorting or accompanying officer), they were chosen by the German General Staff primarily for their command of English and French. Their job was to protect the delegates from petty annoyances (usually from the local German forces), observe—and report if necessary—all interactions with the local French, and aid in any negotiations that were necessary with the local German authorities.

In early April 1915, the first CRB delegates to northern France met their German accompanying officers in Charleville, France, where the German General Staff had its headquarters. Not knowing how the job would play out, the CRB executives had sent in as many men experienced in Belgium relief as they could spare—at least eight out of the initial 10 had at least a few months experience with the CRB.

Carlton Bowen, Frank Gailor, David T. Nelson, Hardwood Stacy, and Richard Simpson had started with the CRB in December 1914. Lewis Richards had lived in Brussels for years before the war and had joined the CRB in January 1915, as had Frederick Dorsey Stephens. H. G. Chasseaud had started with the CRB in February 1915, and W. H. Chadbourn had begun in March 1915.

The only man assigned to northern France who was completely new to relief, having started in April 1915, was Robert Dutton, but at 45 years old, he was nearly twice the age of the others, a graduate of the Naval Academy, and a seasoned war veteran. Early in his career he had transferred from the navy to the marines, had been at the Battle of Manila Bay during the Spanish-American War, and had later been stationed in China. He retired in 1905 as a major after failing the physical. In 1915 he had volunteered for the CRB, and his first post was northern France.

When the first CRB delegates assigned to northern France met their accompanying German officers, there was a lighthearted spirit that was illustrated in a comic photo taken then. Lieutenant Rumelin struck a dominating pose over Americans Stacy, Stephens, Nelson, Dutton, Richards (couching), Simpson, Gailor, Van Brée (a Belgian), and Bowen. The lightheartedness would not last long. (Public domain; Herbert Hoover Presidential Library Archives, West Branch, Iowa.)

A group photo taken in Charleville in late April to commemorate the start of relief shows the Germans in their uniforms of jodhpurs, polished Hussar boots, and peaked caps with polished bills, while most of the Americans are in three-piece suits and shiny leather shoes (Chadbourn and Chasseaud are not present). The mood seems causal, almost lighthearted, as a few hold cigarettes or cigars and some offer up slight smiles. Only the faces of Dutton and a few of the German officers reflect a more thoughtful, serious attitude. Not surprisingly, the only Belgian in the photo, Firmin Van Brée representing the CN—and described by Hoover as "a favorite of all our Americans, and their friend and defender in all their troubles"—stands stiffly and without expression as German officers pose so close as to be touching.

Another photo was taken that day. It was a comically staged one and the handwritten caption reads: "A mock-atrocity photo at Charleville, German General Staff Headquarters, April, 1915." In that photo one of the younger German officers, Lieutenant Rumelin, is on one side of a wrought iron fence striking a domineering, imperial pose with an outstretched arm holding a long riding crop that extends over the eight Americans and one Belgian who are behind the fence in various positions of supposed submission. Stacy appears to be holding up his hands in surrender, Richards and Van Brée are crouching down and holding the bars as if in jail, and Major Dutton is trying to join in the fun but seems not sure how best to do so; Bowen is simply leaning against the fence smoking and looking bored, while Nelson and Gailor appear to be waving to the camera. By far the most creative expression comes from Stephens. He seems to be performing what the British call "cock a snoot" and the Americans call a five-finger salute, as he holds his thumb to his nose and extends all five fingers. Or, as others might interpret it, he is simply performing a half-hearted wave.

No matter what the poses, the air was one of jesting and joking.

Few of the men would be laughing as the true impact of life together in northern France became a reality.

No Job for the Faint of Heart

The German edict establishing relief in northern France was taken to the extreme by the fact that the accompanying officer would live with the CRB delegate in a requisitioned house within the district. The two men—along with usually a couple of support staff for the officer—would eat together, sleep in the same house, and travel together in the officer's large Mercedes Benz staff car. CRB delegates were not allowed to have conversations—business or personal—with any French without the German officer being present. No personal or business mail could be sent by a delegate without first having it pass through the hands of his German officer. And, officially, there was never any free solo time allowed for the delegate.

This was no job for the faint of heart or those with a weak mental constitution. U.S. Legation Minister Whitlock explained, "These [accompanying officers] never leave the delegates day or night; it is an intolerable relation, and at the end of three weeks the delegates come back to Brussels, so nervous and unstrung that they burst into tears. Mature men will not accept the posts, only young men with the love of adventure. Nothing of course more impossible, more hellish, could be imagined than to be forced to live with one of those German officers, even the best of them."

Delegate Kittredge wrote, "In general it was the American delegate's duty to keep an eye upon the situation, to keep his ears open and his mouth shut. . . . He had first and last to get on well with the German officer. If he had the confidence of this officer, he enjoyed much greater liberty and was given much more information about what was actually going on than would otherwise have been possible and in general."

It's no wonder that the delegates assigned to northern France used humor to mitigate the personally stifling situation. Behind the officers' backs the delegates called them "nurses," and one unnamed delegate called his "my man Friday, for we felt like Robinson Crusoe on his desert island."

The same delegate explained that "in the French zone of action we could have no friends. . . . It had been agreed that we were to superintend in all centres of distribution, but we were superintendents who were superintended—we were suspects. Each of us had a German officer as a constant companion. . . . We could never speak to a Frenchman freely or alone; the big ears of the German officer were always wide open. In the course of our rounds we passed the night in the same hotel with him, and sometimes in the same room; we took our meals at the same table; at the meetings of the French committees the German officer never left our side. We were as inseparable as a man and his shadow. We were young, and we were not there to grumble. As long as the Germans kept their word and did not lay hands on any of the imported wheat, it was our business to keep silent. It was also part of our instructions from Hoover; 'You have nothing to do there except to see that the wheat arrives, that it is made into bread, and the bread eaten by those for whom it was meant. If it is hard to say nothing, remember that silence is the price of food for those people.'"

The strain of the job was so intense that it was quickly decided that all of the delegates working in northern France would come once every week back to Brussels for a Saturday meeting. They and their German officers would normally leave on Friday in time to be in Brussels by Saturday morning, then drive back Sunday evening or Monday morning.

These meetings became vital for two reasons. One was that they afforded direct and uncensored communications between the delegates and the CRB Brussels office, which would have been impossible if the delegates had stayed at their French posts. Just as importantly, the Saturday gatherings helped relieve the personal pressure each delegate faced during the week. Kittredge was blunt in his history when he wrote, "The nervous strain of the work in France was so great that even with the weekly visits to Brussels most of the delegates in France found themselves physically unable to remain much longer than six months at a time in a French post. In fact quite a number had nervous breakdowns after only a month or two in France." (Kittredge used "nervous breakdown" more to describe physical or mental exhaustion than as it's widely used today to indicate mental illness.)

David T. Nelson, the 23-year-old Rhodes scholar from North Dakota who had been a delegate in Liège since December 1914, was one of the first to agree to go into northern France. He wrote his mother in late April, "I was offered the chance to come down here and as I saw nothing better to do and had received the permission of the [Oxford] college authorities to stay on in the relief work, I agreed to go."

He would become a delegate in the district named Vervins, which was also the name of the town in which he lived. It was 50 miles (80 km) south of the Belgian city of Mons. To placate his mother's concerns, he mentioned that his position was "behind the German lines—not so very near the fighting lines, but close enough to get an idea of the magnitude of the German organization."

He was not the lone American in Vervins; Major Robert M. Dutton was named the chief delegate for the district. Dutton would last much longer than Kittredge's six-month time frame for northern France delegates. In fact, he would last nearly a year and then go back into northern France for a second tour of duty. But the time spent there and in the CRB would end up having a devastating effect on his health. (He would later die in America of tuberculosis that his family believed was contracted while working for the CRB.)

Nelson, the rugged individualist who had walked solo into Belgium not knowing what to expect, did not last three months in northern France. But the time spent in such close proximity to the Germans, and what he observed of their war effort, would radically change his pro-German views forever.

On the other side of the coin, for some of the German accompanying officers life with a CRB delegate seemed to demand alcohol—a great deal of alcohol.

17

Brussels and Environs

Whitlock Reluctantly Deals with CRB Passes

Much to the displeasure of Governor General von Bissing, Hoover's end run around both von Bissing and Whitlock had worked. Hoover's March 9, 1915, telegram asking Ambassador Gerard in Berlin to petition the German government to rescind von Bissing's order limiting the movement and number of CRB personnel had been successful.

As von der Lancken told Whitlock on Thursday, March 11, "Von Bissing is a touchy gentleman and was offended by Hoover going [over his head] to Berlin." That meant the Germans would fall back on strict protocol. Von der Lancken explained to Whitlock, "Of course, we can give no official recognition of the Commission for Relief. We recognize only the Comité National de Secours and the patronage of Villalobar and yourself."

Whitlock was also put off by Hoover's move but acknowledged, "The work is enormously difficult and there is the necessity of raising ten million dollars a month. We have to have somebody like Hoover to look after the details." The minister's frustration over how diplomatically difficult it was to provide relief came through when he told von der Lancken, "It would be easier to feed milk to a lamb in a cage between a lion and a tiger than to feed the Belgians between the Germans and the British."

Whitlock went further than that when he wrote that night, "The Germans have never understood the organization nor comprehended the difficulties of this work; assurances, patronages, and so forth are all very well, but it takes money to buy food and to buy food enough to feed nearly seven million of people takes a good deal of money."

Whitlock, who had turned 46 the week before, was tired, frustrated, and depressed that he had to continually deal with the Germans, who, he wrote, were like a "tribe that has wandered down into modern times out of the middle ages."

While the Germans might not have fully understood the CRB, they did understand the importance of chain of command. And von Bissing had been told by the

German government in Berlin to give in to what the CRB needed and wanted. He agreed to more delegates and greater freedom with passes.

As Hoover put it, "Gerard at once obtained directions from Berlin asking von Bissing to relax. The General was amazed." As for Whitlock, Hoover wrote, "At the same time, Whitlock was upset at my direct appeal to Berlin, so I wrote him a placating letter on March 18. In any event, this attempt by von Bissing to limit the American staff had been squelched—for a while."

That did not mean the Germans were happy with the situation. An early unofficial CRB history explained, "It was exceedingly humiliating to them to feel that they, the rulers of an occupied territory, should have to have the observance of their promises watched over by an agency from outside, whose activities they were often inclined to regard with jealousy and suspicion. To the German military commander any order of the German army command was as definite and as exactly executed as the will of God. . . . So, to them any inspection by the American representatives of the Commission to determine whether these orders were observed was a quite unnecessary and even impertinent intrusion into military matters of a purely domestic nature in which no interference could be admitted nor tolerated."

As a result of relaxing the restrictions, the CRB Brussels office developed an extensive pass department that worked exclusively on ensuring speedy processing. One of the critical men in the department was Hermancito "Germàn" Bulle, the Mexican chargé d'affaires at Brussels, who was considered a CRB member since the beginning and became a unique diplomatic secretary representing the CRB to the German occupation government. He was a short, stocky, jolly man, always quick with a funny comment or smile, and was completely devoted to the relief work. Through Bulle's leadership and help, the department even took on the task of securing passes for members of the CN and provincial committees.

While passes would occasionally become an issue later, von Bissing's begrudging acceptance of what Hoover wanted in March 1915 effectively took care of the problem.

That meant the governor general had been reined in, for the moment. It would not be long, however, before he turned his controlling sights on a new target within the humanitarian relief.

La Libre Belgique Becomes a Target

After the first issue of *La Libre Belgique* was placed in von Bissing's hands, he had assumed his security forces would find the culprits responsible, and he would never see the publication again. That, as he quickly found out, was not the case. Week after week the impertinent little paper always ended up in his possession, as it would with all the German high officials in Brussels.

Sometimes the paper would show up in von Bissing's daily stack of dispatches, or be delivered by an unsuspecting orderly, or be in an envelope postmarked from Germany. At times it would be delivered with the vegetables or coal. But, as Hugh Gibson wrote in his journal, "It appears without fail upon the desk of the Governor-General—in that sanctum guarded like the vaults of the Bank of England."

For the U.S. Legation secretary, who was supposedly remaining absolutely neutral, *La Libre Belgique* became a secret joy to read. "My copy reaches me regularly and always in some weird way as in the case of the Germans. I don't know who my friend is that sends me the paper. Whoever he is I am much obliged."

Von Bissing did not feel the same. "The exasperating regularity with which it turned up in his correspondence, the unexpected places in which he found it in his own house and the persistent attacks made upon himself, began to get on von Bissing's nerves," according to one history. Gibson went so far as to remark that the governor general was said to "have a tantrum every time it appeared."

Additionally, the little rag of an underground paper—that had had a tiny initial print run of only 1,000 copies—was inspiring Belgians and counteracting the propaganda work of the German-controlled newspapers. Gibson wrote that "the messages of confidence and patriotism they contain are widely discussed among the people and do a lot toward keeping up the courage that is so necessary." It also helped that "the Germans rage publicly, which only adds to the pleasure that the Belgians get from their little enterprise."

Von Bissing quickly determined something had to be done quickly. He ordered the German secret police to find the culprits immediately.

They went about their duty with gusto. They sent out raiding parties to newsagent shops and bookstores. They tore apart the offices of all the shuttered Belgian newspapers to see if any of them were responsible for the underground paper. Even the smallest printshop or newsstand known to the Germans was checked out.

At the same time, van Doren and de Moor were being inundated with requests from their distributors for more and more copies. "The response had been better than they had dared hope." The first issue's 1,000 copies had been increased to 1,500, and by the third weekly issue the press run was 2,000, with a reprint order of 2,000 for the first two issues. These numbers, however, were not an accurate reflection of how many people read the newspaper, "for each copy was passed from hand to hand, and by the time it was returned to its original owner (if ever) it had been read by twenty or thirty people." The little paper was becoming the whispered talk of everyone in Belgium.

"Within a month of its appearance," one history related, "there was not a soul in Brussels who had not heard of it and seen at least one copy. And although, officially, Brussels was practically isolated from the rest of the country, copies of the paper had by devious ways reached every town of importance in occupied territory. The title was on everyone's lips." Much to van Doren's amusement, he even had friends offer him their copy of the newspaper.

With the excitement of such success, van Doren was feeling relatively confident of the tiger he had by the tail as he strolled into the fashionable arcade Galerie Saint Hubert on a day in early February 1915. Located in the northeastern part of Brussels's "Lower Town," the arcade had been built in 1847 and was still a marvel in 1915. With a soaring glass ceiling and a tiled, marble floor, the passage connected Marché aux Herbes with Rue d'Arenberg and Rue de l'Ecuyer and was, as one tour book declared, a "spacious and attractive arcade with tempting shops." These stores were some of the city's most stylish and expensive, which not only attracted Brussels's elite but also those who wanted to get a taste of a life they could not afford. The indoor arcade was especially appreciated in a country where good weather was rarely expected or seen.

The book *Underground News* described the unfolding scene in great detail. Van Doren wielded his hollow walking cane in his usual jaunty way as he entered the arcade and turned to stop in front of an antique store. Pretending to study some fine items in the window, he used the reflection to watch the stationery and newspaper shop directly behind him. The store he was watching was owned by a newsagent named Massardo who was already a distributor in the underground network and had secured the printer for *La Libre Belgique.*

Van Doren was there that day to deliver the material for another issue that Massardo would pass along to the printer, who was—as part of the team's security measures—unknown to van Doren. In return, Massardo thought van Doren was just another distributor whose name was Mr. Willem.

Still pretending to stare into the antiques shop window, van Doren waited patiently for the one customer in the paper store to leave. The Abbé de Moor had taught the cardboard manufacturer that he should always wait to enter a place until at least one person had come or gone. It was a necessary precaution because after the Germans made a raid they usually kept even innocent people in the place to try and apprehend more of the guilty who would walk in unsuspecting.

When the customer left, van Doren glanced up and down the arcade to see if anyone looked suspicious. Seeing nothing to alarm him, he turned and walked into the shop.

Behind the counter was Madame Lucie Massardo. She told him with a meaningful smile that her husband was out on business. That meant, van Doren knew, that Massardo was meeting with someone to pick up the most recent contraband Allied newspapers, which he would sell to only his most trusted customers.

Even with no others in the shop, the two acted as if they were being watched. Van Doren discretely opened up his cane, removed the rolled-up manuscript pages, and slid them across to Madame Massardo. Just as carefully, she picked them up, turned away, and demurely hid them in her loose-fitting blouse. Once the transfer was complete, van Doren smiled and walked out of the shop.

Lucie Massardo and her husband owned a stationery and newspaper shop in Brussels. She did much to aid Eugene van Doren and the underground newspaper La Libre Belgique. (Public domain; *Histoire de La Libre Belgique Clandestine,* Pierre Goemaere, Bureaux de *La Libre Belgique,* Bruxelles, 1919.)

He had taken only a few steps when suddenly he heard a frightening sound—a car pulling up at the end of the arcade. No one but the Germans and the CRB could use cars. Trying not to react quickly, he turned slowly, while still moving away from the shop's entrance. With a sense of horror, he saw a handful of German *polizei* (policemen) jump from the car and march down the arcade right toward him. The thundering sound of their hobnailed boots echoed loudly through the arcade, making every onlooker freeze in fear.

Van Doren nearly panicked then, wanting desperately to run away as fast as he could. Instead, he fought the urge and deliberately began a slow walk toward the other end of the arcade. When he reached the far end, he couldn't help but turn. "As he feared, a Polizei [was] standing at Massardo's door." He could only imagine what was going on inside the little shop.

The oncoming sound of heavy boots swept into the paper shop moments before the bell above the door tinkled. Madame Massardo had already pulled the copy from her blouse and thrown it into the coal chute when the sound of the bell caught her emptying the chute into the stove. As the *Underground News* described:

She looked up, feigning surprise. "Bonjour, Messieurs. Cold, isn't it?"

The officer in charge shoved her into the counter with unnecessary brutality.

"Stand back," he ordered. "What have you put in the stove?"

"Lucie Massardo's heart was thumping in her throat and she was pale beneath her sallow skin, but her dark eyes blazed. "Brute! What do you put on a fire?" she retorted.

The German opened the lid of the stove and fingered the coal but only succeeded in burning himself, for the sides of the stove were red hot. He swore savagely. "Search this place!" he ordered his men. "You, for the Kommandantur," he said to the woman, pointing to the door.

Luckily for everyone, Lucie's husband had not yet returned to the store when the raid occurred, so the Germans found no contraband in their search. After a long night of interrogation at the Kommandantur, in which Lucie "strenuously denied knowledge even of the existence of the *Libre Belgique*," she was released at six in the morning.

When van Doren heard the news, he was overwhelmed with relief. Despite the close call, the Massardo family agreed to continue to work for the underground paper.

The printer, however, was not so courageous. When he heard of the raid, he refused to print any more issues.

Furious at the printer and not sure what to do, van Doren turned to the one person he hoped could solve the problem—the Abbé de Moor. De Moor did not disappoint. Within a day he had checked with numerous contacts and found through a Jesuit priest a printer who agreed to meet with van Doren about the job. His name was Arthur Allard and he was a mild-mannered, middle-aged man who van Doren came to realize was a "fine craftsman and a stout patriot." Before the war he had owned a small printing business that also employed Allard's two brothers, Louis and Philippe.

Van Doren—as Mr. Willem—had no trouble convincing Allard to take on the job of primary printer for *La Libre Belgique*. The man quietly promised secrecy at all costs and agreed to the work without knowing the names or addresses of anyone else involved. He was doing it for his country and to strike a blow against the hated Germans—that was enough for him. This new partnership would turn out to be a positive turning point for the fledging underground newspaper.

Van Doren and Allard quickly fell into a production routine worthy of any spy novel. It began with van Doren going to see Jourdain once or twice a week to collect the handwritten text and layout for the next issue, along with Jourdain's money to pay for the printing. Using his cane to conceal the material, van Doren would go home and type up the copy, finalize the layout, and add any instructions necessary for Allard.

Van Doren had previously established a drop site where he would transfer the finished copy to Allard. It was at the tram stop on the Rue de Linthout, about halfway between his home in a northeast suburb on the Rue Victor Hugo and Allard's home in a southeast suburb on the Rue des Cultivateurs. At a prearranged date and time, they would meet and if no one was around they would make the transfer quickly in the street.

If either man felt uncomfortable, they would make the transfer on a tram: "At other times the two men met without a sign of recognition and mounted the first available tram. Standing side by side on the platform . . . van Doren slipped the envelope into Allard's overcoat pocket and a few stops further on picked up the parcel Allard had placed on the floor and jumped off the tram. Neither man spoke, and the exchange was made so neatly and naturally that, unless someone had been warned and was watching the two men, detection was almost impossible."

With the transfer system in place and working smoothly, frequency increased to twice weekly, and circulation rose to 5,000 copies per issue. Van Doren developed a harness under his coat so he could carry multiple packages totaling more than 2,000 copies.

But such expansion meant that van Doren could not spend time circulating individual copies, a job he left up to de Moor and the abbé's distribution network. That included, according to one history, "Catholic colleges, convents and an ever-increasing number of institutions, whence hundreds of copies of the papers were distributed in ones and twos by unknown hands." De Moor had a list of more than 1,000 addresses that received the paper regularly. Besides his usual distributors, he also enlisted the help of his father, brothers, and sister.

By the end of February 1915, de Moor faced the fact he could not handle the ever-increasing job of distribution director and maintain his other duties as a Catholic priest and as an agent for British Intelligence. He found help in a young architect, Philippe Baucq, whom he knew from another secret organization: the group headed by nurse Edith Cavell, a group that was helping Allied soldiers and young Belgian men get across the border into Holland. Coincidentally, Baucq was a neighbor of van Doren's who only thought van Doren was a sub-distributor in the employ of de Moor.

Baucq was a force to be reckoned with. He was stocky and strong and had the close-cropped hair of a military man. He sported a large mustache that curled up on both sides and a goatee that made his jaw appear even larger and firmer than it already was. He was also courageous to the point of recklessness. In one instance, he had been seen with a bundle of envelopes containing the newspaper under his arm as he walked up to a house where a German sentry was posted. He coolly strolled to the letter box and dropped in an envelope, then winked at the soldier as he left.

By the end of February, Baucq had quadrupled the list of recipients and had established a network of sub-distributors who expanded the growing reach of *La Libre Belgique*. He quickly became a critical member of the burgeoning underground team.

He would not live to see Christmas 1915.

18

London

The Dog Attacks

Back in February, with the advent of the Germans' blockade of Allied ports and unrestricted U-boat warfare, Hoover had to rely on the promise by the German government that the U-boats would honor the neutrality of CRB shipping. He had personally told German Chancellor Bethmann-Hollweg the story of a man who said his dog did not bite, with the punch line, "Does the dog know it?"

On April 10, 1915, the dog bit. Less than two months after the chancellor had given his word he would instruct his submarine commanders not to attack ships displaying CRB signage, the properly labeled CRB ship *Harpalyce* was torpedoed and sunk by a U-boat. It had already off-loaded its precious food cargo in Rotterdam and was heading back to Norfolk, Virginia. Attacked without warning at 10:00 a.m. in the English Channel, it sank quickly. Fifteen of the 44 crew were lost, including the captain, chief officer, fourth engineer, chief steward, one European cadet, and 10 Chinese crew.

Hoover was incensed. "I simply find myself totally unable to express in sober language a proper characterization of this action," he told Ambassador Page. "It is absolutely in its complete barbarism without parallel in the last century. I count myself as not being given to hysterics over the abnormal events of modern warfare but if this action can be reconciled with any military necessity, or, to put it on its lowest plane, of any military advantage, then we can but abandon any hope that civilization has yet accomplished anything but enlarged ruthlessness in destruction of human life."

He also had to deal with the practical problem the sinking had created. "Every contract we have made for ships and insurance based on this agreement is shattered, the work brought to a standstill, and the lives of 10,000,000 people imperiled."

Official German inquiry into the sinking brought German denials. While they admitted a U-boat had sunk a vessel on the day, time, and place where the *Harpalyce* had been torpedoed, they insisted they could not identify it as such, and they said the ship had no CRB markings or signage. That directly contradicted the photos the CRB had of the ship in Rotterdam while unloading and the signed statements by officers of a rescue ship who said they saw the signage before it went down.

There was nothing left to do. The Germans closed the inquiry. Hoover later wrote, "But this was only one of the tragedies we were to endure."

The Dog Bites Again—with Much Greater Consequences

While the sinking of the *Harpalyce* brought little official condemnation other than from Hoover, less than a month later another U-boat attack and sinking of a very different ship created worldwide condemnation.

On May 7, 1915, at 2:10 p.m., on a clear day 10 miles off the coast of Ireland, German submarine U-20 torpedoed without warning the majestic passenger liner *Lusitania*. A second blast following close behind was thought to have come from within the ship. In less than 20 minutes the ocean liner was gone, taking with it 1,193 souls while 767 men, women, and children somehow survived. One hundred and twenty-eight of the dead were Americans.

Worldwide condemnation was swift and universal.

Many in America, including ex-president Teddy Roosevelt, called for the United States to enter the war. Presidential adviser Colonel Edward House, who was in London at the time, cabled President Wilson that America was now put in the position of having to decide if she stood with civilized or uncivilized warfare.

Wilson, who had stood firmly to keep America out of the war, remained steadfast in that principle, even in the face of strong opposition. His response to Germany was to send three sternly worded protests (on May 13, June 9, and July 22). His Secretary of State, William Jennings Bryan, resigned in protest over the second letter, believing Wilson's statement had been too provocative and unbecoming of a president of a neutral country. Wilson appointed the State Department's second-in-command, Robert Lansing, to be the new secretary of state. The third letter, on July 22, was a strong threat that ended, "Repetition by the commanders of German naval vessels of acts in contravention of those rights must be regarded by the Government of the United States, when they affect American citizens, as deliberately unfriendly."

The German response to the international outrage was to first declare the *Lusitania* had been armed—a charge quickly disproved—and that it had been carrying munitions bound for the Allies, a charge strongly denied at the time but decades later proven to be true. Ultimately, the concern over America entering the war on the side of the Allies prompted Kaiser Wilhelm and German Chancellor Theobald von Bethmann-Hollweg to issue an apology and to curb the policy of unrestricted submarine warfare.

For the moment, at least, the German civilian government had maintained its control over the military, which had few, if any, reservations about continuing such maritime warfare.

In early May 1915, Lindon Bates Jr. headed for Europe to become a CRB delegate. His death during the sinking of the Lusitania *would eventually lead to major problems for Hoover.* (Public domain; multiple sources.)

Even though the sinking did not drag America into war, it did help alter public opinion regarding the importance of American neutrality and drew the country that much closer into the European conflict.

For the CRB—and Hoover personally—there was a direct connection to the sinking that would later have a major impact upon him and the relief organization.

Onboard the doomed ocean liner was passenger Lindon Bates Jr., also known as Rox. He was the son of the CRB's vice chairman, who was also the director of the New York office and a decades-long personal friend of the Hoover family. The younger Bates had grown up knowing the Hoovers and had followed in the footsteps of both Hoover and his father by becoming an engineer. He was already well-known and well-respected, having authored books on technical and economic topics. He was aboard the *Lusitania* heading to London, where he would take up relief work with Hoover and the CRB.

Traveling in first class with Bates were family friends Amy and Frank Pearl, along with their four children (ages five, two-and-a-half, one-and-a-half, and three months) and two nannies, one English and the other Danish. Bates was in stateroom E69, and the Pearl group had nearby staterooms E67 and E51. One deck up from their rooms was the first-class dining room, and two decks up was what many called the promenade deck, where fellow saloon passengers would take the air.

On May 7, Bates was standing at the rail with Amy Pearl when the torpedo struck. Amy was thrown away from the rail and into a bulkhead, which broke her wrist. During the ensuing onboard pandemonium, Bates was seen helping Amy, assisting others to lifeboats, and telling some others how to manage the boats to get them over the side correctly. He was last seen giving his life preserver to a frightened woman passenger before heading back down into the ship to look for the Pearl children.

Seven weeks later, on July 31, 1915, only 14 days after what would have been his 32nd birthday, Bates's body washed ashore 230 miles from where the ship had gone down. The courageous young man would have been especially saddened to know that two of the Pearl children also had not survived.

Through the long weeks before the body was recovered, both Hoover and his wife, Lou Henry Hoover, were extremely supportive and loving to the devastated Bates family. Herbert sent numerous cables to his friend, updating him on the search and reiterating his friendship and support. He also offered assistance to the younger son, Lindell, who went to Ireland to physically search the shoreline for his brother's body.

Lou Henry Hoover sailed home from London and spoke movingly at the memorial service in New York. She said she was there for womanhood and childhood, since it was "for women and children that he laid down his life." She told the assembled mourners that she had known Bates and his family for decades and watched him grow from a schoolboy to the fine young man who volunteered with the Commission for Relief in Belgium.

She closed by stating quietly, "Such a death is not death, it is resurrection, for greater love hath no man than this, that he lay down his life for others."

King Albert of Belgium sent a cable of condolence to Lindon Bates Sr.: "I learn with deep affliction of the death of your son, traveling to aid our distressed people and express to you my most sincere sympathy."

From all accounts, Rox had been an exceptional young man who had acquitted himself well during the sinking. He was much like his father.

Lindon Wallace Bates Sr. was an internationally known civil engineer who had had a hand in the building of the transcontinental railways and the Panama Canal, reportedly developing the important three-lake plan. He even had a connection to Belgium, having helped improve the port of Antwerp, which was then the world's third-busiest in movement of vessel tonnage. He had worked on huge engineering projects all over the world. He was also an old and trusted friend and associate of Hoover. In October 1914, when he was in America, Bates read about the CRB that was being formed around Hoover in London and cabled his old friend his support and best wishes. Hoover had cabled back and asked if Bates was interested in working in the CRB. He was, he replied.

At the time, Bates's availability dovetailed nicely with Hoover's desire to counteract the New York-based Rockefeller Foundation and the Belgian Relief Committee, both of which were building their own Belgium relief programs in America. Hoover asked Bates to start a New York office, form a committee of "leading New York men," and take on the title of vice chairman of the CRB. Hoover also wanted the New York office to establish a strong publicity campaign to drive contributions and to gather general support for the entire relief program. Bates jumped into action and took on all jobs with enthusiasm, never knowing that he had been Hoover's second choice for the position.

Lindon Bates Sr. was a well-known mining engineer and a personal friend of Hoover's who became director of the CRB's New York City office. The death of his son would contribute to his turning against Hoover. (Public domain; Herbert Hoover Presidential Library Archives, West Branch, Iowa.)

Bates did a good job of creating the New York office and helping Hoover ultimately drive the two other relief groups into roles of just fundraising and supply-gathering for Belgium relief. By the end of 1914, Hoover, with help from Bates and others, had consolidated the CRB's American power position and gained the public perception that it, and it alone, was in charge of Belgium relief. In a letter to Bates, Hoover detailed the CRB success over the two other groups, then followed with a strong summary: "You can always bear in mind that the people who are going to control this Commission are the people who control the money and the people who control the international agreements, and that we have both of these things in our grip."

When it came to publicity, Hoover had had one of his best men and oldest friends, journalist Will Irwin—who had been in London in October 1914 when the CRB was formed—take on the management of the press department of the New York office. Working in cooperation with his counterpart in London, William A. M. Goode, Irwin developed the New York department into a fine-tuned machine that generated "daily and weekly news releases to papers and press associations and prepared pamphlets and handbooks for the use of the [CRB] committees in the field. Weekly and monthly publications carried articles on Belgium relief, and both magazines and newspapers donated advertising space for appeals for contributions for which the Press Department furnished the copy."

One of the most successful ideas was the "Famous Authors' Service," which was conceived of and instituted by Irwin and coordinated with Goode and the London office. The idea was to approach famous authors on both sides of the Atlantic and ask them to contribute Belgium-related stories to be syndicated during a three-month period in the leading newspapers of America. Contributors included John Galsworthy, George Bernard Shaw, and Thomas Hardy.

By early 1915, Bates was fully in charge of the New York office, which was a strong advocate for the work being done by Hoover and the CRB in Belgium, and for Bates and the CRB in New York. Bates was convinced of the importance of, and need for, the CRB, and those feelings had spread through his entire family.

His wife, Josephine, and his sons, Rox and Lindell, all did various jobs for the CRB. When Bates Jr. decided he wanted to go to Europe to work directly with the CRB and Hoover, there was nothing the father could say or do to keep him in New York. Bates senior was a proud father as the son booked passage to Europe on the *Lusitania*.

On the loss of their son, the Bates family was nearly inconsolable, especially the father. Unfortunately, despite the Hoover family's love and support, at some point in the grieving process Bates turned on his old friend.

But the schism between these two men had begun to appear even before Rox's death. It was noticeable in their underlying strategies for charitable giving, their different approaches to publicity, and, finally, in their perceptions of who was in charge.

Before Rox's death, difficulties had arisen in the coordination between the London and New York offices. To resolve those problems, Hoover had asked Captain Lucey—who had established the Rotterdam office and organized the Brussels operations and was returning to America in February—to join the New York office to try to work with Bates. The friction between the two men was such that Lucey left soon after arriving.

In April, Hoover tried again, sending over Colonel Hunsiker, one of the CRB's founding directors. He, too, "encountered difficulty through Mr. Bates' opposition to his arrangements" and did not last long.

By the end of May—a few weeks after the *Lusitania* had sunk—some of Hoover's most trusted advisers in London were calling for the reorganization of the New York office because of Bates's reluctance to follow all of Hoover's instructions.

The differences between the two men came into greater focus when Bates could not fully understand Hoover's complex solution to the CRB's long-term financial situation.

CRB Financing Leads to Misunderstandings in America

By the late spring of 1915, the CRB and its relief efforts were resting on a relatively strong financial foundation. Hoover had miraculously arranged for sufficient and steady Allied financing for both Belgium and northern France. He had also found a way around the major hurdle of currency not being allowed in or out of Belgium. A complicated exchange was agreed upon by all governments in which the exiled Belgian government provided funds to the CRB for the purchase of food that was then brought into Belgium and sold to the CN and the Belgian people, with the proceeds going to pay the Belgian government's obligations inside Belgium for items such as salaries and pensions to state employees and retired military personnel. The Belgian government, having no access to revenues, took out British loans that would be paid back at the end of the war. For northern France expenses, the French government had agreed to secretly fund its portion of relief through payments to the Belgian government, which, in turn, gave the money to the CRB.

As simply put as possible, this meant money flowed from Allied loans to the Belgian exile government, then to the CRB, which purchased food that was sold inside Belgium, then the money from those sales went to pay Belgian workers and military personnel—who were then able to pay for food. A key component of the process was that the food was sold at a slight profit, which went to pay for those who could not pay anything.

"To be sure," one CRB history stated, "a vast number of individuals who would otherwise have been completely destitute were thus enabled to pay for their rations, but there existed a large and growing number of destitute who were entirely outside this circle. These were entirely dependent upon the charity of the world."

Initially, as the CRB had struggled to gain acceptance in late 1914, funding for relief had come in charitable donations and occasional lump sums secured by Hoover's begging, borrowing, and negotiating with anyone who would listen to him. Finally, in March 1915, with the creative financing system finally in place, the CRB received its first monthly subsidy, indicating it had achieved a more secure and stable position.

This did not mean, however, that the CRB no longer needed charitable giving.

Donations were still a critical part of the relief equation. The established financing was not enough to meet all the foodstuff needs of nearly 10 million civilians. And the Allied subsidies were only for food, not for clothes, which were becoming more important as the war dragged on and old clothes wore out.

Just as significant, there was also the psychological importance of individual donations—a person who gives, or continues to give, has a personal stake in where the money is going and how it's used. That kind of engagement, Hoover knew, was necessary to keep public opinion firmly on the side of humanitarian aid to Belgium and northern France. And public opinion, he knew, was the force that kept the Allied and German governments supportive of the CRB.

Unfortunately, when the highly complex funding arrangement was revealed in the American press, some of the articles had incorrectly portrayed the plan. These articles gave readers the erroneous impression that financing for Belgium relief had been solved by the Allied governments and there was no longer any need for American charity. There were also some Americans who saw only that the CRB was making a profit on selling food, without fully understanding that all profits from the relief to those who could pay went back into the program to support the destitute.

The American public's valuable attention was additionally sidetracked and diffused from the need for Belgium relief by the May 7 sinking of the *Lusitania,* which brought on months of news coverage devoted to how America should react to such an atrocity.

The result was that, throughout the spring of 1915, charitable giving from America had dropped drastically. The people were no longer responding as quickly or as generously to appeals made by the New York office. Something had to be done.

In London, Hoover knew that the right kind of media exposure and publicity could generate tremendous giving. He understood the power of the press and the importance of public opinion in keeping the humanitarian relief program alive. He had worked hard—mostly in England—to develop good worldwide publicity and had had tremendous success keeping Belgium's plight at the forefront of war news around the globe. That had led to unprecedented giving.

Analyzing the American situation, Hoover realized he had to have greater control of the message being sent out from the New York office and that the message had to change.

Across the Atlantic, Bates's view of the CRB's newly stabilized financing had led him to a different take on the situation. He cabled Hoover on April 19, 1915, with a somewhat surprising idea—end requests for donations by June 1. He stated that the time was "near or has come on behalf of all whose generosity has been invoked and which has enabled the situation to be bridged to put the future responsibility squarely up to all the warring nations. The question imminent is how far it is fair and proper to continue appeals in this and other neutral countries. The fall and winter [of 1914/1915] conditions warranted and demanded world humanity . . . but as these disappear or governments assume or become capable of carrying the burden, such [donation] appeals should cease . . . say by June 1st."

Hoover responded immediately, feeling like Bates did not fully understand the situation. "Many reasons why cannot abandon benevolent side." His reasoning was that the financial arrangements were basically an exchange (money from outside Belgium to pay for food and pensions inside Belgium) did not cover all relief, most notably for the destitute. Hoover was also about to make a major appeal for donations in Britain and other countries, so, as he wrote Bates, "obviously cannot close [U.S.] appeal [the] way you suggest while appealing [to] other countries." He ended with what he felt was his most compelling reason why requests for donations would always be appropriate: "In any event destitute always with us."

Bates's vision was more and more at odds with Hoover's. The New York office had become a strong presence in America, and Bates felt it was on par with the London office when it came to influence, prestige, and decision-making. He also began to believe that he and Hoover were on an equal footing when it came to running the CRB.

Hoover disagreed. To him, the New York office provided three important services to the relief effort: serving as a central clearinghouse for donations, purchaser and shipper of foodstuffs, and publicity generator to keep the relief in the forefront of American minds.

As Bates had gone about his job, however, he had gathered around him too much power for what Hoover considered to be a satellite office of the London headquarters. This was most obvious when it came to publicity. While Hoover had to agree that Bates and Irwin had generated tremendous press in America, he also knew that publicity in and of itself wasn't good enough or could even have a detrimental effect if the wrong message was conveyed. To maximize impact and results, publicity in any form had to be driven by a strong, focused message. As time went on, the publicity messaging coming out of the New York office was not aligned with the publicity messaging of the London office.

Like nearly every other aspect of the CRB, publicity was something Hoover wanted complete control over. Because he knew that he could not control what the press ultimately printed, he was adamant that whatever came out of the CRB offices for the press had to be coordinated and in sync with what he wanted said. That became more and more difficult as the New York office moved away from what Hoover and the London office wanted said.

Hoover knew the time was coming when he would have to confront the situation and his old friend.

19

Elsewhere in Belgium

A Delegate Is Steamrolled into Oblivion

None of the improvements von Bissing and his staff made regarding the expediting of delegate passes helped Robert Warren, a CRB man from the second wave of Oxford Rhodes scholars who was arrested in late April 1915 at the border of Holland and Belgium.

Warren was the victim of a German system in which the local military command seemed at times to act independently of higher authority and could steamroll someone into oblivion, even when the person was a citizen of a neutral country serving at the acceptance of the German occupation government. On a more personal note, Warren's story also shows just how isolated and ultimately alone these young men could become in a world totally controlled by the Germans.

Warren was only 21 years old and had attended Yankton College, a small liberal arts school that had been founded in 1881 as the first institution of higher learning in the Dakota Territory. Clean-shaven with dark, wavy hair and prominent ears, Warren had the studious, serious look of a student, which was accentuated by heavy eyebrows and a tight, small mouth. In his official CRB photo, his stare seems intense and focused on trying to project his maturity and honesty. For the portrait, he wore a wool three-piece suit with starched collar, pinstriped white shirt, and thinly knotted polka dot tie. While Oxford might have influenced his wardrobe, he appears in the photo to be as serious and straightforward as his CRB official reports, which were clear, concise, and with no embellishments or unnecessary adjectives.

Since early December 1914, Warren had been a delegate working in Hainaut Province and living in Mons. In mid-April 1915, he decided to return to his studies at Oxford and was in Brussels preparing to leave Belgium for good. It was then that CRB delegate administrator and fellow Oxford student Perrin Galpin told him that delegates were needed in the slice of northern France trapped behind German lines.

The story of what happened to Robert Warren, 21, showed how isolated and ultimately alone many CRB delegates were in a world totally controlled by the Germans. (Public domain; Herbert Hoover Presidential Library Archives, West Branch, Iowa.)

Warren immediately volunteered to postpone his return to Oxford and serve in northern France. Because the CRB director in Brussels, Oscar Crosby, felt the London office had to approve the reassignment, and that could take a week or more, Warren asked if he could use the travel pass already issued to him and spend his waiting time in Holland. Crosby agreed, and Warren left Friday morning, April 16. He had no trouble getting through the border.

The young delegate stayed for a week at the Hotel Weimar in Rotterdam. His first duty was to visit the CRB office, where he told Director Carl Young of his situation and how he was awaiting word from Brussels to either go back to Oxford or return to Belgium for posting in northern France. While at the office, he collected 50 letters from friends and family and several packages that were delayed Christmas presents. He also met Ridgley R. Lytle, another Rhodes scholar who was an incoming CRB delegate about to enter Belgium for the first time. Together they spent Sunday traveling to The Hague, where they called on the American minister to Holland, Henry van Dyke.

During his week's stay in Rotterdam, Warren also visited numerous cafés, took in two moving-picture shows, and spent time reading, walking along the many tree-lined canals, and waiting for news from Brussels. He rarely talked with anyone other than CRB men although he did share a word or two with people in cafés, on train station platforms, or in railcar compartments.

"Throughout my stay in Rotterdam, I talked but little to anyone except members of the Commission. Such casual conversations as I may have had with strangers and the hotel people were merely exchanges of common place. . . . I may state positively and can take oath that at no time and in no manner did I do or say anything which would have the slightest importance from a military standpoint for anyone."

Such mundane details of his week in Rotterdam did not seem important at the time.

On Friday morning, April 23, a week after he had left Brussels, Warren received a telegram from Crosby saying that if he still wanted reassignment to northern France he was approved by London and should return to Brussels.

"I'll go," he telegraphed back, then went straight to the German Consulate office in Rotterdam and received a pass to travel to Brussels. The rest of the day, he spent writing letters to friends and family about his sudden change of plans.

He left for Brussels Saturday morning, first taking a train from Rotterdam to the Dutch border town of Roosendaal, where there was a perfunctory Dutch customs checkpoint. He then boarded another train to the Belgian border town of Esschen, where the German military took over examining those who wanted to enter occupied Belgium.

"On arriving at Esschen, I went into the station to have my baggage examined. I paid duty on some tobacco and on opening my two valises for a second examination, was taken into custody by an officer and led to a small room for personal examination."

At that time, all his papers and documents were taken, after which he was asked to sign a statement that his papers were authentic. He did. He was then personally searched, which came up with only one inappropriate item—his hotel room key that he had forgotten to return. The Germans kept that, along with all his documents, which included his passports (one CRB, one U.S.), German travel pass, and identity papers stating that he worked for the CRB.

Up to that point, nothing had happened that was too much out of the norm for CRB delegates dealing with German harassment at borders and sentry posts. Usually, however, once a delegate's papers were thoroughly studied, the German in charge would let the delegate proceed with his trip.

Warren wasn't so lucky. Suddenly, the German officer handling the exam turned mean. He accused the young delegate of saying goodbye to someone at the station that morning. That person was overheard saying he was going on to Flushing, the Dutch town where ferries came and went from England. The implication was that Warren had been dealing with a spy, which meant he was a spy as well—a serious offense.

Staying outwardly calm, Warren now knew the cause of his troubles—one of the thousands of German counterespionage agents who was scattered throughout Holland and Belgium had probably followed him during his stay in Rotterdam, had seen or overheard things he felt were suspicious, and had talked to the German authorities. As long as Warren kept his head, he was sure he could straighten things out. He knew he had done nothing wrong.

He quickly denied the accusation, then added that even if he had, it would have been nothing of importance. Saying goodbye to someone at a train station was not a crime.

The officer shot back in German, "Speak the truth!" He told Warren that they knew all that he had said and done while in Holland, so he might as well tell the truth now.

Warren again denied the charge. At that point, the interview turned into a full-blown interrogation.

"I was closely questioned regarding date and place of birth, family connections, residence, time spent at Oxford, reason for coming to Belgium, date, length of time spent here, number of trips taken to Holland from Belgium, passes used, routes taken, purpose of trips."

His answers were all written down and he was told to sign the resulting statement. He did.

Warren then turned on his accuser. "I officially requested he inform the American ambassador at Brussels, Mr. Brand Whitlock, that I had been arrested. It was my right as an American citizen."

The German refused, stating that the American was a prisoner, and prisoners had no rights.

"I officially requested he contact the Commission for Relief in Belgium and told him that in my documents I had a letter, signed by CRB executive Captain Lucey and stamped with the CRB seal, that stated I was a member."

The German refused again.

Nothing Warren said made a difference. Soon, he was taken to the waiting room of the train station and placed under guard for the night. As he sat in the empty room, waiting for dawn, he wondered how long it would take for someone to start looking for him. Director Crosby in Brussels was so busy it might be days before he even realized Warren hadn't shown up. Director Young in Rotterdam had already moved on to a hundred other jobs after saying goodbye to Warren. No one he could think of was actively thinking of him and his whereabouts.

As he tried to sleep on the hard wooden benches, he took stock of his situation—he was 21, a prisoner of the German Empire, and no one knew where he was. He was truly on his own and had no idea how he was going to get out of his predicament.

Morning brought no resolution. The same officer escorted him by train to Antwerp, where they went straight to the offices of the German political department. There, numerous conferences were held with various people and Warren was repeatedly asked the same kinds of questions he had been asked back in Esschen.

"I urgently requested they tell Mr. Whitlock, or some officer of the Commission, in Brussels or Antwerp, of my arrest."

Again the requests were refused.

The Germans said someone would have to go to Holland to investigate the entire matter. Warren gave them the address of the CRB office in Rotterdam and the personal address of Young, the director, repeating his plea to tell someone at the CRB what was happening.

Warren was then escorted by armed guard to Antwerp prison and placed in cell 16.

"I was permitted to speak to no one except prison officials." With nothing else to do but stare at the walls and wonder what was going to happen, Warren wrote two letters, one to E. E. Hunt, the CRB chief delegate in Antwerp, and one to CRB Director Crosby in Brussels. He convinced a prison guard to take them and hoped they'd be posted. He would have written another letter to Harry Diederich, the American consul general in Antwerp, but he didn't know the man's address.

The young CRB delegate spent the rest of Sunday afternoon and evening in his cell.

Monday came and went with no news.

Tuesday the same, with no word as to what was happening.

He wondered how long the letters might take to reach their destinations and how long it would take for someone to get him out of there. As each day passed, he wondered if he might never get out.

His thoughts would have darkened even more if he had known neither of his letters ever got through.

Finally, on Wednesday morning, April 28, at nine o'clock, he was taken back to the German political department and stood before a new officer.

To Warren's great relief, also in the room was Diederich, the American consul general, who told him that an unofficial, unnamed source (probably a sympathetic Belgian from the prison staff) had told him on Monday about Warren's situation. It had taken more than a day to start the process of getting him released.

Warren was escorted to an Antwerp hotel for lunch and kept there under guard until 5:30 p.m. But he was still not out of the woods. He was then taken back to the political department, where he once again faced the German officer from Esschen, who had either made the trip to Holland or had received more information regarding Warren's case.

The German stated that the proprietor of a café in Rotterdam, a certain Mueller, had said he had observed Warren having multiple conversations with a certain person in his café in the evening and then seeing the same person off at a train station on Saturday.

Warren—standing there in the same suit, shirt, and tie he had put on four days before—had no idea when this ordeal would ever end. He once again wearily denied all charges.

"I told him I knew of no Mueller, nor the café he mentioned. I admitted to the bare possibility that I had exchanged words with someone at the Rotterdam station

Saturday, but, I swore he was someone I didn't know, had never seen before, and that whatever I might have said was nothing more than ordinary small talk."

The officer also produced a handful of letters addressed to Warren that he had somehow gotten from the CRB Rotterdam office. They had been opened and read. All of them were personal letters from friends and family in America.

"I protested against this action, but no attention was paid to my protest."

A statement was drawn up recounting all of what had been said. Warren signed it.

And with that, just as it had begun, the whole ordeal was suddenly over, with no words of explanation or words of apology.

"I was released in the presence of the American consul at 8 p.m. Wednesday, April 28th, it being understood, however, that I was to remain at Brussels till further notice."

Even though Warren had initially agreed to be a delegate in northern France, he never made it there. He returned to Oxford. No reason was ever given for why he didn't go into northern France. It could be that the London office had already filled all the new posts by the time Warren was freed from jail. Or maybe Warren was simply fed up with the Germans after what they had just done to him.

The whole experience must have been a frightening one—to know that he had done no wrong, that he had certain legal rights as a neutral in occupied Belgium, and yet the local Germans in command had taken total control of his life. Warren must have also thought how easily the entire incident could have gone the other way and he'd still be in jail.

Either way, he and all the other American CRB delegates knew one thing for certain—Warren had been treated far better than any Belgian would have been in the same situation.

The "Strike of Folded Arms"

German policy regarding the Belgian unemployed, or *chômeurs,* began to change in early 1915. The process came in fits and starts, and the German civilian government was not as inclined as the military in wanting to get Belgians to work for it.

The first moves were not to *force* Belgians to work; they were to entice *volunteers.* "Every effort was made to induce the people, by offers of high wages and other advantages, to work for the Germans." Some skilled workmen were offered wages as a high as £2 per day (equivalent to $200 in U.S. dollars today).

The German offers to work, however, fell mainly on patriotically deaf ears. Most preferred to live either on Belgian half wages or on the monetary assistance of the CN and the food assistance of the CN and CRB. The Belgians saw any work performed for the Germans as war work that was directly against their country, against the Allies, and against the stipulations of The Hague Conventions. Across Belgium and northern France, few accepted the German work offers, as most began what some termed the "strike of folded arms."

While this labor resistance was tolerated for a while, by the spring of 1915 the Germans were losing what little patience they had had, especially when the unemployed in Belgium and northern France were living off the food relief of the CRB and CN while Germans had to be brought in to do the work.

A famous Belgian playwright, poet, and author at the time, Émile Cammaerts, wrote, "It became more and more evident that Germany, whose man-power was steadily decreasing, would no longer tolerate the resistance of the Belgian workers, and would even attempt to enroll in her army of labour all the able-bodied men of the conquered provinces."

Even in Germany there were numerous articles that called for the German authorities to put all captive peoples to work—forcibly if necessary—as a way of replacing those who were serving in the German Army.

On one side were the German militarists. Their thinking was obvious—if the Belgians and northern French could be forced to work in jobs currently being done by Germans, then those Germans would be free to join the armed forces.

On the other side was the German civilian government in Berlin. It seemed reluctant to implement forced labor, most probably over a concern that worldwide opinion would be strongly against any such action.

As these two forces wrestled with the issue, a few incidents around Belgium in the spring of 1915 showed to anyone who was watching that much more severe, systematic, and unilateral actions were not far off.

Among the first labor groups to feel the impact of a shifting German mindset were Belgian railroad workers. The group was so large that as the war continued, the Germans had to use 40,000–45,000 of their own men to replace the Belgians who refused to work. In military terms, that number of men was huge—the equivalent of two or three German infantry divisions.

What made matters worse was that when German railroad workers took over, "things went badly," according to one historian. "Ignorant of the Belgian system of signaling, unfamiliar with some very new types of locomotives, the Germans were unable to avoid a series of mistakes and accidents."

Renowned for their efficiency, the Germans would not let that situation remain for too long. The Germans wanted the Belgian railwaymen back to work and they were going to do everything in their power to see that happen.

One of the first battlegrounds was the village of Luttre, 10 miles (16 km) north of Charleroi in the country's southern Hainaut Province. Luttre was part of the municipality of Pont-à-Celles, and while it might have been small in population, it was large in stature as a transportation link. The little village lay beside a major canal that connected the southern part of the country to Brussels, and it also boasted a train station on important rail lines from Charleroi to the north.

In April and May 1915, the railroad workers of Luttre refused to work for the Germans, which led to a quick escalation of events. At first the men had been offered high wages if they would return to work under the Germans. They refused. When that didn't work, the men were threatened with deportation to Germany. They refused.

German frustration ran high, but because von Bissing and his government were not yet fully committed to mass deportations, they didn't immediately act on their threat. Instead, they rounded up most of the men and locked them in railway carriages and cattle cars. The workers sat there for nine days as the Germans took some of their family members as hostages and billeted the hated *uhlans* (German cavalry) in their homes.

At one point, the leader of the railway workers was arrested, locked up, and later brought before his men and ordered to tell them to give up their resistance. He did address the men, but it was not what the Germans wanted to hear. The leader actually told his men it was a matter for "their own consciences." The Germans threw him back in jail.

In the end, 190 men were deported to Germany while 60 more were arrested on June 5.

The entire situation in Luttre was for all intents and purposes a disaster for the Germans. They convinced no one to return to work, they ended up having to provide more Germans to man the positions left by the deported workers, and the story lent significant fuel to the smoldering fire of Belgian resistance.

A new fire flared nearly simultaneously when a similar situation occurred farther to the north. This time, however, the event took place on a much larger stage in the city of Malines (Mechelen in Flemish).

No small village like Luttre, Malines was one of the principal cities of Belgium. Situated on the tidal River Dyle, the city was home to nearly 60,000 residents. Malines was more than 1,000 years old and boasted a *grand place* that was ringed by picturesque gabled houses of the sixteenth and seventeenth century and held the city's fourteenth-century *hôtel de ville*. Among all the architectural treasures in the city, however, the most famous was the magnificent Saint Rumbold's Cathedral, which had been started at the end of the thirteenth century, completed in 1312, and rebuilt after a massive fire in 1342. A tower that had been planned as the tallest in all of Christendom was incomplete at 318 feet and gave the cathedral its distinctive flat-topped tower. Starting in 1560 the church had been the home of the Catholic archdiocese of Malines, which covered all of Belgium, and was then home to the outspoken Cardinal Mercier, which made the city the spiritual center of Belgium's Catholics.

The ancient town was also a major rail link to practically all points in Belgium and boasted the oldest railway line in Belgium, built in 1835 between Malines and Brussels. A major stop along three heavily used railway routes—Liège-Louvain-Ostend, Antwerp-Brussels, and Malines–St. Nicolas—the city also boasted extensive railway workshops that were constantly busy maintaining much of the country's rolling stock.

In late May, the railroad repairmen of Malines refused to work for the Germans. Before the war, they had been employees of the Belgian state, which owned the country's railroads. When the German occupation had begun, the railway men had refused to work for the Germans then, and a few hundred German workmen had been brought in to do their jobs. But these Germans had been recently sent back to their posts, and the authorities had commanded the Belgian workers to return to their jobs.

As Cammaerts stated, "The patriotic duty of these Belgians was evident enough: by resuming their work, they released German soldiers for the front and increased the number of coaches and engines, of which the enemy was in great need for the transport of troops." The men refused to work.

The Germans then forced the burgomaster (mayor) to provide a list of 500 railway men, and they were promptly rounded up, arrested, and marched to the workshops under armed guard.

When the workmen refused to work, Baron von Bissing took drastic measures. He cut off the entire city from the rest of Belgium. In a proclamation dated May 30, 1915, he "forbade anyone to enter or leave the town, and isolated it from all communications with the rest of Belgium." Additionally, "the whole population was punished by confinement indoors from 6 p.m. each evening." The reasoning for his actions was clearly stated in his proclamation: "The town of Malines must be punished as long as the required number of workmen have not resumed work."

The men still refused to work. And Cardinal Mercier protested strongly and loudly directly to von Bissing.

The standoff was finally broken when the Germans backed down and brought back their own workers. It was a huge psychological success for the Belgians. They had beaten the Germans on the battlefield of workers' rights.

The Belgians should have known by then, however, that von Bissing would not take such a defeat lightly. The consequences of the worker victory in June 1915 would ultimately lead to a series of actions and events that would culminate in much more brutal German operations against the Belgians and northern French a year later.

Von Bissing Attempts to Divide the Nation

The governor general had been heavy-handed when he tried to convince Belgian workers to work for the Germans.

He was subtler when it came to *Flamenpolitik* (German for Flemish policy), whose goal was to divide Belgium into two separate territories, the Flemings, or Flemish-speaking people to the north (centered around Flanders and Antwerp), and the Walloons, or French-speaking people to the south (concentrated in Brussels and the south).

Before the war the country, which had only existed for a little more than 80 years, had struggled with the language divide. The French-speaking Walloons had more control over Belgium's affairs than the Flemish-speaking Flemings, and French was the predominant language used throughout the country in politics, education, and commerce.

The Germans—and von Bissing in particular—wanted to exploit that difference. The ultimate goal, according to the governor general, was not to have the Flemings gain an independent state but to make it easier for Germany to absorb the Flemish territory into the German Empire. "Among the German interests in Belgium," he wrote, "is also the Flemish movement, which has already made good progress. . . . We have among the Flemings many open and very many still undeclared friends, who are ready to join in the great circle of German world-interest."

Von Bissing stressed, however, that the German occupation must "repress boundless hopes on the part of the Flemings. Some of them dream of an independent State of Flanders, with a King to govern it, and of complete separation. It is true that we must protect the Flemish movement, but never must we lend a hand to make the Flemings completely independent. The Flemings, with their antagonistic attitude to the Walloons, will as a Germanic tribe constitute a strengthening of Germanism."

With the invasion, however, the multilingual Belgians had surprised even themselves by coming together, Walloon and Fleming, into a stubborn front opposed to the Germans. While they were appreciative that the Germans ran all their official *affiches* in three languages—German, French, and Flemish—that did not mean they would take the bait of division.

As one Belgian historian at the time explained, "Not being able to stir the people against the Allies or against their own Government, the German Press Bureau attempted to revive the language quarrel to provoke internal dissensions." His scorn was obvious when he went on to write, "Germany, who had never troubled much before about the Flemish movement and Flemish literature, suddenly discovered a great affection for her Flemish brothers who had so long been exposed to [what the Germans called] 'the insults of the Walloons.'"

Von Bissing and his civil occupation government strategically gave preferential treatment to Flemings and acknowledged them and their authority whenever possible.

A year later, von Bissing would unveil his most aggressive move to drive a wedge between Walloons and Flemings.

20

Antwerp and Environs

Hunt Gets a New Antwerp Delegate

In May 1915, chief delegate Hunt received a new delegate to work with him in his Antwerp Province. Hunt had been such a good organizer and administrator—and the Belgian provincial committee ran so smoothly—that the CRB Antwerp office had become a revolving door for new delegates to gain some quick training before being sent elsewhere. In fact, some CRBers joked that "Antwerp training" was easy because the well-oiled machine left little to actually do.

Hunt, of course, never let an opportunity go by to dispute such a label, and he could definitely look back with great pride on what he had accomplished since he started the office in December 1914. That included training a few men who would go on to be some of the CRB's best delegates, such as Gilchrist Stockton and John L. Simpson. Another who would later earn his way onto that best list was new delegate Gardner Richardson, who joined Hunt and his group on Tuesday, May 11, 1915.

Richardson, 31, was considered one of the older delegates (as was Hunt at 30). But he cut a distinctly different figure from the slight, young-looking Hunt. Richardson's bald head was accented by a ring of dark hair while a full mustache, prominent Roman nose, and strong jaw gave him a stalwart presence. A Connecticut man who had graduated from Yale like many of his family before him, Richardson went on to work for years at his uncle's weekly newspaper, *The Independent*, which covered religion, politics, and literature from its headquarters in New York City.

When the war came, Richardson had joined the American Ambulance Corps in Paris and was there when he read about the CRB. He wrote to Hoover, who invited him to join, and he arrived in Brussels in early May 1915. He was immediately assigned to Antwerp Province, which normally had five men (Hunt as chief delegate and four other delegates), but was then down to only Hunt and Stratton.

Richardson joined the two CRBers who were living in a luxurious Antwerp mansion at 21 Rue Marie-Thérèse. The residence had been presented earlier as

Gardner Richardson, 31, was older than many other CRB delegates and went on to serve with distinction. (Public domain; author's archives.)

a gift to Hunt and the CRB. That had happened about the time Hunt had received Stratton's February letter regarding expenses and landlady problems. Stratton had been overjoyed to find that a long-term solution to housing had appeared—Edouard Bunge, the vice president of the Antwerp provincial committee, and by then a friend and trusted adviser to Hunt, had graciously offered his city mansion, along with a small group of servants, as residence for Hunt and his delegates. The home was where Edouard and his daughters—Erica, Eva, and Hilda—along with their servants, had lived during the three-day bombing and then surrender of Antwerp in October 1914.

"From the windows," Hunt said of the townhouse, "we overlooked a little park, and the capped, thoughtful statue of the artist Quinten Metseys. The lintel of our doorway was gashed, where an incendiary shell, striking in the street, had ricocheted and burst."

Hunt and his team did not have much time to enjoy their home, however. There was too much to be done.

"We patrolled the province in our automobiles," Hunt explained, "attended committee meetings—there were one hundred and seventy of these meetings each week, so our range of choice was large—carried on extensive correspondence in four languages [English, French, Flemish, and German]; compiled exhaustive reports on official matters; and held the scales of justice as level as we could in a country which reeled and slipped in the bloody path of war."

Richardson would quickly find out firsthand about those reports on official matters.

Richardson Reports on the Unemployed

If Richardson had been warned about the ease of "Antwerp training," he would have been surprised at what was thrown at him no sooner than he arrived on the job. Hunt immediately put him in charge of preparing a substantial report on the unemployed, or *chômeurs*—a critical topic that was taking on greater and greater significance throughout Belgium.

The numbers were already large and growing. In Antwerp, the second-largest city in Belgium, by the end of 1914 the total population was slightly more than 1 million and the unemployed numbered 213,397, with that figure increasing all the time.

As the war had dragged on, Émile Francqui and the Comité National had developed a national plan to provide unemployment relief—not only to supply the necessities of life but also to provide some kind of employment through public projects.

While the issue of Belgian unemployed was not a direct responsibility of the CRB, it was nonetheless important that the CRB delegates understand how the unemployed were treated and what CN rules and regulations applied to them. Hunt explained, "In the plans for *chômeur* relief, then, the Commission was not involved, but as a matter of administrative fact the Commission and the National Relief Committee [CN] were married partners, and neither could act without involving the other." That's why Hunt wanted Richardson to report on the situation with the unemployed.

Richardson took less than a month to complete his report, which was dated June 11, 1915. He led off with a quick summary of the "Object and General Plan," which was twofold: "the actual feeding of the families" and "the furnishing of useful occupation to the workers."

The unemployed throughout Belgium, Richardson wrote, received small monetary assistance through the CN plan. Nine-tenths of each benefit came from the CN through the provincial committees, while the remaining one-tenth came from the local communes themselves. Bachelors received 12 francs ($2.40) a month. Heads of households received 12 francs a month, an additional 6 francs ($1.20) a month for a spouse or housekeeper, and 2 francs (40 cents) a month for each child under 16 who was not working. Unemployed women who had worked in industry received the same benefit as men. These unemployment benefits were small, considering a Belgian bricklayer before the war earned nearly four francs a day. But the benefits were complemented by the CRB and CN relief of at least one meal a day, if not two, of bread and soup through the communal soup kitchens.

Each of the 165 communes in Antwerp Province had to create and maintain a current list of the unemployed, in accordance with rules set up by the CN. Most importantly, each commune had the right "to require from each *chômeur* the labor, equivalent in value to the relief granted to him and his family, and with the approval of the commune, has the right to specify the public work to be carried out."

The public works generally were in maintaining and improving roadways, canals, and streets, as well as the cultivation of crops on vacant lots and unused public property. Antwerp Province was not alone in this endeavor; throughout Belgium public works were being designated as a way to keep the unemployed working. Initially, the Germans allowed it.

One acknowledged problem in this plan, however, was obvious when it was realized that most of the unemployed were inside workers and most of the public projects were outside work. "This problem," Richardson wrote, "is gradually working itself out by compromise on the part of the workers and the ingenuity of the committees."

Richardson also explained in his report that the CN already had 22 regulations regarding the *Secours* (assistance or charity) portion of relief, which had been drawn up and ratified by the CN—official name, Comité National de Secours (charity) et d'Alimentation (provisioning). He summarized the most important points:

- The provincial committee must strictly supervise the communal committees.
- The communal committees must be made up of experienced business people, must keep detailed lists of the unemployed, and must monitor for fraud.
- Only fully unemployed are considered for work, and they must be over 16 years old, of either sex, and must have been previously employed in industry or commerce.
- No distinction is to be allowed regarding those who have held public or private jobs, who have worked in a factory or at home, or who belong, or do not belong, to any organization.
- Every *chômeur* must be given an identity card, which shows facts about the person and his family, as well as what aid is being received.
- The aid must be paid in goods and not cash.

The last regulation had evolved as difficulties had presented themselves. Richardson explained that, initially, the unemployed were paid in cash for aid and/or any work done. But "abuses were at once observed," he wrote. "Heads of families spent the money for other objects than food." So the system was changed to one that gave out tickets for food, but "while an improvement, this did not entirely obviate the abuses, for the [tickets] were sold for cash and were then used by persons not entitled to them."

This led to the final system, one that provided each person with a nontransferable identity booklet with coupons attached. "This booklet must be presented in person and the goods received by the *chômeur* from the communal store. The only possible abuse is now the selling of the food, which offers fewer opportunities for malpractice than the cash grant or the [ticket] system."

Richardson's summary acknowledged both the good and potential bad. "In general, the theory of the relief work is excellent, for it makes the men work for what they get, and enables the communes to keep their districts from running to decay. In practice there are abuses, but it may be said that such abuses are found under similar conditions elsewhere, from accident insurance claims to U.S.

pensions, and that the committees are making actual progress in systematizing the work and in correcting regulations which have offered the most opportunities for abuse in the past."

Unfortunately, the public works part of the program was destined to be quashed by the Germans. As Hunt explained it, before the CN unemployment plan, the Germans had been able to "secure a certain amount of labor from the Belgians, and would probably have secured more had the unemployment relief remained unorganized . . . but the [national] system of communal relief for the unemployed practically closed all doors against them. Thereafter Belgians could work without working for the Germans."

And who among the highly patriotic Belgians would work for the Germans if they didn't have to? The dramatic examples of the railroad workers' strikes in Luttre and Malines were strong answers to that question.

"The Commission was thoroughly alive to the danger," Hunt noted. "The plan of relief for the unemployed was a Belgian plan, the administrators were Belgians, and the recipients of course were Belgians. We were neutrals; Belgians were belligerents. We needed constantly to be on our guard against unscrupulous patriots who might use us to club the Germans."

It would take a while for the Germans in command to fully understand the consequences of giving Belgians money to work on Belgian projects, but when they did, things would change dramatically and to the detriment of all Belgians.

As for Richardson's report, it no doubt contributed to a quick reassignment to a much tougher position. Just a month after he turned it in, Richardson accepted the challenging assignment of chief delegate of Valenciennes District in the Army Zone of northern France. It wouldn't take long before he had made his mark there.

The Emotional Toll on the Delegates

Few of the delegates publicly acknowledged the internal, emotional stress the job created within the Americans. Hunt was one of the few, and as a trained and experienced journalist, he brought a literary bent to his efforts.

"The conditions of war soon grow to seem normal," he wrote in his book, *War Bread*, "but there is an emotional and physical strain about them which eats at one's heart."

"Belgium was like a military prison and an asylum for the insane, rolled into one. Always, just under the surface of life, one felt the tearless, voiceless, tragic resistance of an unconquerable people."

Such emotion, while beautifully expressed, could still indicate a depth of feeling and internalization that could end up having a strong and at times disabling effect.

As Kittredge had related in his history of the CRB, the stress experienced by many delegates in northern France led to "quite a number [who] had nervous breakdowns after only a month or two in France." (Kittredge's expression of "nervous breakdown" was used more to describe a state of mental and physical exhaustion than what is widely used today to indicate mental illness.)

These were young, and in many cases inexperienced, men facing battle-hardened German officers who scorned and mocked them, buttoned-down Belgian businessmen who mistrusted them, and half-starved women and children who looked at them as saviors. Every day the Americans awoke to a place where few spoke English, news of family and friends was rare, and the work was a tedious mixture of bills of lading, stock taking, endless meetings, and incessant demands for written reports.

When the delegate ventured away from his office, he did not find much to cheer him. In the cities, towns, and villages the people were muted, subdued in their dress and emotions, and ever watchful for the German soldier, secret policeman, or spy who might be observing a little too closely or listening a little too intently to their innocent conversations. And many times the Belgian weather seemed to match the worst moods—dark, cloudy, cold, and rainy.

"Until late in the spring [of 1915]," Hunt said, "when a special censorship for the Commission members was arranged with the Germans, we received no letters or newspapers from any one outside of Belgium. We had no new books. We knew little about the progress of the war. Home was almost a myth."

It was a country that in many ways appeared normal from afar, but on closer inspection was revealed to be an emotional prison that wore one down day by day.

In such a stifling world, Hunt noted, "breathing spells were not many, and we sometimes longed for escape from Belgium as a convict longs to break prison."

As the months went by, the strain of the work would show itself, especially during the Thursday Brussels meeting of all the delegates when they could finally talk honestly among themselves. Those weekly meetings were important release valves, as were the evenings that were spent together in collegiate camaraderie prior to the meetings.

"When we spent the night in Brussels," Hunt recalled, "Amos D. Johnson's house at 12 Galerie de Waterloo roared with our fun and the recitation of each others' Odysseys: how [Carlton Bowden] and [Frank Gailor] refused to salute the German colonel at Longwy and how the colonel almost died of apoplexy in consequence; how Robinson Smith, translator of *Don Quixote*, gently but firmly refused a gold watch tendered him by the Provincial Committee of Hainaut, until the Committee had adopted his scheme of bread locaux communaux; how [C. H. Carstairs] was soon to marry a Belgian girl, and how other delegates were suspected of being matrimonially minded . . . how somebody tried to ram a Zeppelin shed, and should have been shot in consequence . . . of one of our fellow-citizens who said to Cardinal Mercier, 'You're a Catholic, ain't you? . . . Well, I'm a Presbyterian myself; but I ain't got no prejudices' . . . the competence or incompetence of our respective chauffeurs and automobiles, and the greatness of Hoover."

Such a spirit of camaraderie was critical to the morale of the delegates, and yet the Thursday delegate meetings were discontinued in February by new director Albert N. Connett. Kittredge minced no words when he stated that Connett "soon grew impatient with the attitude of some of the delegates and was frankly bored by the discussions at the delegates' meetings. After attending one, he decided it was useless to hold any further meetings and no more were held during the time that he was in Belgium." (Connett lasted only until April, after which the meetings were reinstated.)

Tempering the February 1915 loss of the Thursday meetings were Brussels office luncheons, where food was brought in and any delegate in the vicinity could join in. Kittredge explained that a lunchroom had been established in the Brussels office in January 1915 and "it soon became a gathering place, at luncheon time, for the heads of departments and provincial delegates." This was where the delegates could have "bicker sessions" and laugh and argue. "It was there that Hugh Gibson would delight the company with his inimitable witticisms and caustic comments upon the general situation and particularly upon the German administration. It was there that the developments in Belgium were discussed from day to day and the problems of the Commission informally thrashed out."

But that wasn't all that the luncheons served to do. They also were where the delegates came to know one another "in a companionship which made of the body a real fraternity, a group of men actuated by unwavering loyalty to their chief and by self-sacrificing devotion to the interests of the people whom they had come to Belgium to aid."

By far, though, the most important release for delegates was the occasional permission to leave Belgium for some much-needed R&R in Holland. This was Hoover's doing, according to Hunt, as he had "arranged a series of vacations for delegates, because the men could not stay long in the work and remain well in body and spirit."

"Crossing the border to Holland was like a spiritual experience," Hunt explained. "The sudden sense of freedom was as strange and real as mountain air after a long stay in the city, and one's heart sang like a lark, merely to be quit of Belgium."

On Hunt's first escape to Holland after months on the job, he was emotionally pulled up short by a group of children. "A crowd of Dutch children in a frontier village screamed at the motor-car and flung their caps under it, as children do the world over, except in Belgium. It was a bitter reminder of the repression and fear in the little land behind me."

Many of the delegates beyond the headquarters in Brussels worked either alone or with only one other man. Most of them found their own unique ways or places of escaping, even momentarily, the pressures of the job and the prison they lived in.

One of Hunt's special places was the old Premonstratensian Abbey of Tongerloo (now spelled Tongerlo), 26 miles (42 km) southeast of Antwerp, just off the main road to Hasselt and Liège, where he would "try to forget everyday affairs. The avenues of venerable linden trees, the gaunt halls, the white-gowned canons and gray-gowned acolytes and novices, the sanctity and repose of the place were irresistibly soothing."

There were also the short, sporadic times spent at the numerous Belgian country chateaus that had been flung open by their owners to the Americans. They were homes like the Bunges' Chateau Oude Gracht on the Hoogboom estate, where the men could play tennis, take long walks in the woods, and have evenings of music in the salon, quiet reading in the well-stocked library, or a fiercely competitive game of billiards upstairs with Edouard Bunge and daughter Erica.

Hunt would often go to Chateau Oude Gracht to relax. On one visit in the spring of 1915, "I ran out of the chateau for a lonely, happy, night walk. The cool spring air was marvelously clear and the new beech leaves were like lattice-work against the blue-black sky. Rhododendrons and azaleas were in blossom, hidden in the dusk like tropical birds. The thrilling smells of turned earth and young growing things were in my nostrils. A lake behind the castle lay mirror-still, and I stopped beside it, listening to the guns—the everlasting guns.

"Seventy-five miles away, along the Yser, in the spring dusk, men were killing and being killed. Each explosion could be heard: a toneless stab in one's head, not like a sound, but like a wound; a thrust that twisted and tortured into one's consciousness and could not be forgotten.

"But from across the lake, from the depths of a little wood came a new sound. Cannon-thunder was a commonplace to us. If nights were quiet we heard it even in the heart of the city like Antwerp; we heard it every Sunday in the country. The new sound was a bird voice. The first nightingale of the year had begun to sing, clamorous and violent and glad. It rioted in music, and then at last the song sank gurgling into silence.

"And again came the remorseless drumming of the Yser guns."

Hunt's Impact on the Bunges

Such experiences and visits to the estates of wealthy Belgians were many times calming and relaxing interludes for the American delegates. But they were not done in a vacuum. Their Belgians hosts were many times young women, and they had just as many problems, concerns, and anxieties as the American delegates. And with most eligible Belgian men dead, in a prison camp, at the front, in an Allied country, or trying to find work in a decimated economy, these wealthy Belgian women had little exposure to male companionship and looked forward to any American's visit.

At Chateau Oude Gracht, Erica Bunge was one such Belgian woman. Outwardly she was a strong and independent woman who was attempting to get a dairy farm organized to help feed the youngest children of Antwerp.

Internally, however, she was still a 23-year-old woman who could not help but be impacted by the constant comings and goings of numerous American delegates. In her diary she had numerous entries of who just arrived and who was leaving, and she assigned nicknames to certain American friends. Gardner Richardson was "Uncle Dick," Richard Simpson was "Snips," and John Simpson (who would come in late 1915) was "Pinkske."

She gave no nickname to E. E. Hunt, but he was obviously her favorite, the one she sought out and the one who hurt her feelings when he did not spend enough time and attention on her. Most hurtful to her was when he would be more attentive to either of her sisters, Eva and Hilda, and yet Erica disliked herself for being jealous. Numerous entries record the strong feelings of a young woman.

In March 1915 she wrote in a joyous, cryptic way, "I'm playing with fire! I'm afraid, and then I like it! I really don't know what to do! Tomorrow is the first day of Spring! . . . I am a fool and can't help it! . . . Playing again! But . . ."

The next month her entries are filled with jealousy and frustrations regarding incidents with Hunt.

"If you want to be indifferent, well that's alright but what I do object to is your rudeness and sneers! I don't know what happened, I can't think except that Hilda must have said something about me that made you change your countenance towards me instantly.

"On Sunday morning you came down early, Father and I were at breakfast and everything went off all right and as usual. Then the others came down and suddenly Hilda and you got up (after a whispered conversation) and walked out. We did not see you again until lunchtime! Why? . . . I walked with all the others and we went everywhere and couldn't find you two. Well, that's quite all right, why shouldn't you walk with 'little sister'?"

By Monday things had not improved in Erica's mind. She wrote that Hunt was "stiffer still! You never said good-morning to me, didn't take Ninia out for a walk. You were just here and most impolite at table."

She concluded the entry, "I considered you a friend and treated you as such and I have always been loyal to you, that's how you are? I wonder what is the matter? Are you jealous because of me liking Mr. [Richard] Simpson? So you want to make me jealous and angry? I wish you would tell what it is! I am sorry!"

Even with such frustrations, Erica knew where her war priorities lay and that the most important one was getting the dairy up and running.

When the purchase and shipment of the 100 dairy cows from Holland had been arranged, Erica, along with someone else (possibly her dairy farm assistant, Hélène Born), decided it was important to supervise the transportation of the cows.

She secured from the Germans travel permits to go from Chateau Oude Gracht to Holland and back. Hunt, as chief delegate of the CRB in Antwerp, loaned the women a CRB car and driver.

Hunt's seemingly generous gesture got Erica into trouble with the Germans. When she drove back into Belgium, the German border guards confiscated her passport, and she was told she had to report in person to the Antwerp travel permit department the next day. When she did, she was told that what she had done was illegal. The CRB driver could only drive CRB personnel, and she and her companion were not members of the CRB. She told them she was a member of the Commission d'Economie Alimentaire of Antwerp Province and showed the pass that had been issued to her and her friend. The German officer confirmed her membership via a phone call to the Commission.

As Erica later wrote in her diary on May 15, 1915, the German, once he confirmed her travel permits were in order, stated that "we were allowed to sit in the car because of the pass, the driver was allowed to drive the car, but not with us in it! Ridiculous! . . . Well, there are no names strong enough for the Germans." Happily, the trip had already taken place, so no further action was taken on the part of the Germans.

It was time for her to focus on getting the dairy farm fully functional.

The Germans Create a Deadly Border

The Bunges had been lucky to get the Germans to agree to the purchase and importation of the dairy cows in early 1915. As the winter turned to spring 1915, the Germans had decided that the border between Belgium and Holland had to be strengthened. Too many young Belgian men were escaping to Holland and then joining King Albert on his little slice of free Belgium. Too many smugglers were coming and going with food items, mail, international newspapers, and other commodities desperately wanted by Belgians willing to pay black-market prices. And spies found it relatively easy to slip back and forth, gathering and providing information to the Allies.

The Germans faced two primary challenges in trying to stop the flow of people, materials, and information through the border: the checkpoints and the land itself.

The checkpoints along the 280-mile (450-km) border were at major and minor roads. The major checkpoints—which monitored foot traffic, vehicles, and trams—were manned by German officers and soldiers while some of the small posts were initially maintained by the Belgian customs officials who had guarded them before the war. By early 1915, however, it had become obvious that many of the Belgians at the checkpoints were too easily bribed to look the other way at strategic times.

An unidentified victim of the German electric fence, which sealed off Belgium from Holland and the rest of the world. No date or location is known. (Public domain; Roger Van den Bleeken, Archives Heemkring, Houghescote vzw, Kapellen, Belgium.)

One such checkpoint was at Putte, the little village less than five miles north of the Bunges' Hoogboom estate. The border actually cut the little town in half so that one side was in neutral Holland while the other was in German-occupied Belgium. A British historian at the time reported, "In order, it seems, to close the last possible loophole of escape, the Belgian Customs officials at Putte-[Cappellen], on the frontier north of Antwerp, who had hitherto been allowed by the Germans to continue their functions, were removed from their posts, and German soldiers were sent in their place."

Even with the checkpoint changes, however, bribery was still a problem, as the German soldiers used for such noncombat duties were old men called Landsturmers who were nearly as prone to accepting bribes as the Belgians had been, and were even more inclined to do so as the war dragged on. Some of them chose to walk over to Holland and give up their guns, preferring internment in a Dutch camp to staying in the German Army.

When it came to the other border challenge, the land, that was not as easily addressed. Known as the Campine, it was an inhospitable, wind-swept countryside of wetlands, moors, dwarf pines, and barren hills of sandy heath. It was difficult to monitor and harder to guard.

One of the German switching houses, where the electricity for the electric wire could be shut off. It also served as a bunkhouse for soldiers. (Public domain; Roger Van den Bleeken, Archives Heemkring, Houghescote vzw, Kapellen, Belgium.)

An idea to deal with such terrain came from a Prussian army officer, Captain Schutte, who was working with German Intelligence in Belgium. He suggested an electrified wire barrier be built along the entire border. The concept was tried in early 1915 along part of the Swiss border and had been "enthusiastically received by the army command," according to one Belgian historian.

By April 1915, work had begun on installing what the Germans called "Grenzhochspannungschindernis," or border high-voltage wire. Many Belgians came to call it the "dead thread."

The main electricity for the wire came from feeder lines that tapped into already established power stations or large facilities nearby. But the border's extreme length dictated that a *schalthaus* (switching house)—run by gas generators and used as rest stations for the Landsturmers—be built every two kilometers to keep the electricity at a sufficient level. That level was 2,000 volts—enough to kill.

As the Germans began to install the electric wire, they faced continual passive resistance from most of the Belgians they tried to engage. Maurice Lippens, the owner of a factory near a western section of border, took a strong stand few would have followed. He refused to provide electric current for the section of wire near his facility. He was deported to Germany.

A German guard was posted every 200 meters (656 feet) along the Belgium-Holland border. Because of the notoriously bad weather, the guards would build simple shelters. (Public domain; Roger Van den Bleeken, Archives Heemkring, Houghescote vzw, Kapellen, Belgium.)

To lower the cost of construction and to make it easier to monitor, the Germans did not follow the exact border. Certain bulges and parts of the country were cut off, and only about 196 miles (316 km) of the 280-mile (450-km) border would be electrified.

The Germans also reconfigured the border barrier around the new electric wire. A large swath of no-man's-land was established so that the entire border became comprised of a line of traditional barbed wire, an open space, the electric wire, another open space, then another line of barbed wire. In populated areas, the width of the open spaces around the electric wire was relatively narrow, while in the less densely populated frontier regions the open spaces were wide enough to accommodate roving patrols of German cavalry. The electric wire itself stood on tall poles with barbed wire on each side. Altogether an imposing and frightening barrier.

In a number of villages, the electric wire ran straight through the residential center while some villages were entirely excluded from the newly configured border.

In the little village of Putte, where the border had dissected the town, it was decided that the electric wire would run to the south of the village, which would still remain within the border. This meant the town sat in the middle of a large section of no-man's-land and became a very small, completely enclosed zone. People coming from Belgium had to go through a checkpoint at the first line of barbed wire, at the electric wire in the middle of town, and then at the last string of barbed wire before finally entering Holland.

The entire electrification project took months to complete, but before it was finished specific instructions on how to traverse it and what would be allowed were posted on June 28, 1915, by the German military commander in Antwerp and signed by Governor General von Bissing.

Even before the German *affiche* had been posted, those who wanted to cross illegally were devising ways around the border.

What no one was sure about was the electric wire. Electricity had only come to Belgium less than 30 years before, and many in rural areas had little, if any, experience with electricity. Was the German border wire truly live or just a ploy by the Huns to scare people from trying to cross? If it was live, would the wire give only a shock or would it kill? Did a person have to touch it to be shocked, or was the electricity able to jump out of the wire?

As one Belgian historian noted, electricity for many Belgian homes before the war "still remained a total unknown and a barrier which was deadly by touch was not far from science fiction." The Germans posted numerous *affiches* explaining the dangerous nature of the new wire. These warnings were posted in three languages—French, Flemish, and German—because the Belgians were not the only ones who needed to be cautioned. "The German soldiers had not necessarily much knowledge of high voltage with deadly consequence. They were sometimes the first victims of accidents."

The one thing Belgians were sure of was that from then on only the serious-minded would take the risk of trying to cross the border.

21

Brussels and Environs

The CRB Is Drawn into the Workers' Fight

As the railway men of Malines were facing off against the Germans in May and June, the CRB was drawn into the railroad workers conflict. Hoover would have much preferred that the CRB stay out of it. As he saw it, the duty of his neutral band of relief workers was to stay as far above the fray of local events and war-related incidents as possible. His own job was to feed a starving nation—in the end, nothing else truly mattered. As for the specifics of the Belgians and their strike of folded arms, Hoover later wrote, "The Belgians had every moral and patriotic right to embarrass the Germans by any device they could invent, and it was none of the C.R.B.'s business."

He would, however, be drawn into the workers' fight during a trip to Belgium in June 1915. On that trip he was informed by his inspection team and the new Brussels director, William Poland, that the Allies, in concert with the Belgian exiled government at Le Havre, France, were implementing an underground scheme that would jeopardize the relief work. The CRB men had discovered that the Allies were smuggling money into Belgium to subsidize Belgian railway employees and other skilled workers so they would not work for the Germans. While Hoover felt what was done clandestinely was none of the CRB's business, he believed the scheme was "foolish and would invite reprisals."

According to the principles of the CRB, the railroad men and their families would be given food under the established rationing system, regardless of employment status. Besides, Hoover stated, the Germans had plenty of men of their own to handle all railway operations necessary for their military needs.

What concerned Hoover most, however, was "if the Germans believed the C.R.B. was connected with it, they might raise serious questions about our fidelity to our undertakings to preserve rigid neutrality."

Hoover could have chosen to ignore what he knew, but he could not do that as a man who was painfully honest and forthright. He knew his path was clear: "At once we made a record of protest in Belgium and later at Le Havre, which might clear our skirts if any such charge arose." Hoover and the CRB were now covered if the Allied intervention was ever discovered. He did not, however, inform the Germans of what was happening—he surely knew how dangerous that would have been to the entire relief program, and it would have overstepped his scrupulous regard for neutral boundaries.

While Hoover stated later that the Germans never mentioned the Allied intervention with the railway workers, that didn't mean he wasn't sure they didn't know. In a book written after the war, he immediately followed that statement: "But von Bissing quickly began a series of measures—to coerce the Belgians to work for the Germans—which did concern us." The "but" implied that Hoover saw a connection between the Allied actions and the increased pressure by von Bissing to get workers to resume work.

Von Bissing wrote to Brand Whitlock on June 26 and included this statement: "Concerning the relief to be granted to those out of work, the presidents [of our relief provincial committees] shall take care that the latter do not hinder the resumption of work by the laboring population. Moreover, relief cannot be given to workmen who refuse remunerative labor."

Hoover later wrote that his interpretation of the statement was that, "This made food for the Belgian workmen contingent upon working for the Germans." It was a totally unacceptable position as far as the CRB and the CN were concerned, and it was one that would put the entire relief effort in jeopardy.

Outside of Belgium, von Bissing's statement—and the entire workmen's situation—did not escape the ever-vigilant British. British intelligence services and the Foreign Office were continually monitoring and investigating potential infractions by the CRB or by the Germans in the relief agreements and operation. To the British militarists, who were inherently opposed to any Belgium relief, von Bissing's statement, once it was discovered, was one more piece of evidence to support shutting down the CRB and all imports into Belgium.

On July 17, Sir Edward Grey wrote to the ambassador patrons of the CRB in London and stated that no food would be allowed to go into Belgium if used for coercing workers into helping the Germans. Hoover and the London-based ambassador patrons turned to their counterparts in Belgium to approach von Bissing to try and change his mind.

In Brussels, Whitlock and Villalobar were able to obtain a statement dated July 29 from von Bissing's political department head, Baron von der Lancken. It declared that the governor general would "never make use of the Comité National to force the Belgian population to employ itself in the service of the German Army contrary to the stipulations of The Hague conventions."

As Hoover noted dryly, "This was not entirely satisfactory, but we concluded to await further developments."

By then, von Bissing had been stymied by the railroad workers and others who had refused all coercion to return to work. And he was receiving continual pressure from the CRB, CN, and Cardinal Mercier, who opposed his actions against the workers. He felt it was time to set the record straight on where he stood.

Less than a month after his July 29 statement, the governor general issued two decrees, on August 14 and 15, 1915, that were published in *Gesetz und Verordnungsblatt* (*Law and Regulation*) in Brussels on August 22.

One section stated, "Anyone who without adequate reason refuses to undertake or continue labor in the interest of the public, for which he is called upon by German authorities and which is in the line of his professional activity, shall be punished by detention or imprisonment for not more than one year." Such severe punishment would also be handed out to anyone who aided or abetted a refusal to work or tried to convince anyone not to work.

Von Bissing did add, "Any reason for such refusal based on international law is to be accepted as adequate." To many, that statement was added merely to show the world German fairness, when in fact it would never be honored.

If there was any good news, it was that the proclamation dealt only with men working in Belgium, meaning the concept of forced deportation to work outside of Belgium was not mentioned—yet.

A month later, von Bissing's decrees raised major issues with the British when the Foreign Office found out about them and received a published report by the Belgian Commission of Inquiry about what had happened to the railway workers in Luttre earlier that summer. As a result, on September 22, 1915, Foreign Secretary Sir Edward Grey "blew up in a letter to Ambassador Page," according to Hoover.

The long missive detailed the numerous German actions that had already taken place against Belgian workers and said that it was not necessary to "dwell on the measures of deliberate starvation, imprisonment, deportation, and torture to which these workmen have been subjected." Grey stressed that regardless of what the Germans said about honoring international laws, he believed they would not abide by them.

Grey's biggest concern was that the Germans were using the relief to coerce the Belgians into working for them. He thought they were basically using food as a weapon, and that "it is alleged on good evidence that, in order to give effect to that policy, the relief committees, communal soup-kitchens, etc., have in many cases been forbidden to give relief to classes of workmen whose labour the German authorities desire to enlist in their service."

He stated strongly that Belgium relief could not continue if German actions against Belgian workers and the relief program persisted. Grey—indicating he had learned from Hoover that the threat of publicity could aid a cause—made a strong threat: "I feel that, were this correspondence to be published—and it will, I fear, soon be my duty to ask Your Excellency's consent to its publication if present conditions continue—the people of this country will draw from it the conclusion that no further assistance should be given on their behalf by His Majesty's Government to a relief organisation whose activities are in danger of being so controlled by the enemy."

Grey wrote that he wanted Page to pass on his letter to the three CRB patrons (Whitlock, Villalobar, and Dutch representative van Vollenhoven) in Brussels so they could take the necessary steps to see that the Germans "abstain from all interference in the work of relief which [they] have so recently promised to leave free and untrammelled."

The war of the words was escalating, but as Hoover said, "Protests from the British Foreign Office had little effect on von Bissing." The threat to shut down relief on this issue would not be acted on, as other issues kept changing the game.

Von Bissing Restricts the CN

As spring 1915 had turned into summer, the governor general had grown more and more frustrated with Belgium relief efforts. He had watched as the program, which had begun relatively modestly, had grown into a huge operation that was taking on more and more significance in what he considered to be his fiefdom. The CRB and the CN had naturally taken on greater power and decision-making in the process of growing such massive humanitarian aid, and they had never considered consulting him or asking his permission for such expansions of their authority. They simply had done what was needed to be done to keep the food coming and to equitably distribute the food.

In March, von Bissing had vented his frustration by trying to limit the movement and number of CRB personnel. That had been stymied by Hoover's end run to Ambassador Gerard and the Berlin civilian government, which had overridden the governor general.

On June 26, 1915, von Bissing's frustration rose to the surface again. This time he tried to gain greater control over the CN. Making sure not to acknowledge the CN's authority by writing directly to Émile Francqui, von Bissing wrote instead a long letter to Brand Whitlock, the primary neutral patron of relief. He stated that it had become "clear that the sphere of the Comité's activity has assumed an extension which had not been foreseen at the time of its creation." The time had come, he declared, that "the activity of the Comité be clearly delimited and that the mutual relations of the administration under my orders and of the sub-organization of the Comité be regulated." The Germans were going to take over.

He outlined how a member of his civil government would sit in on each of the Belgian provincial committee meetings and review all committee correspondence. In relating to local committees, the provincial committees would not be allowed to send any information, ask for any statistics, or make regulations without first consulting with the German civilian in charge. All policing powers that the CN had taken on regarding millers, bakers, and others in the distribution chain were "revoked since the administration under my orders is alone qualified to exact these measures."

Von Bissing did toss a bone to both the CN and CRB by stating that the two organizations "have the right to make inquiries and statements regarding the abuses committed by the millers, bakers, etc., but their right is limited to making these statements. They are allowed to communicate these afterwards to the competent [German] authorities," but that was as far as they could take such matters.

No matter how far apart the CRB and CN were in their internal squabbling about who was responsible for what, they could both easily agree that von Bissing's new regulations were totally unacceptable. Meetings in Brussels between Baron von der Lancken, Whitlock, and Villalobar were held to work through the issues. At the same time von Bissing's letter was sent to the two relief patrons in London, Ambassador Page and Spanish Ambassador to Great Britain Rafael Merry del Val. They, in turn, forwarded the letter to the British Foreign Office for advice.

The process took nearly a month but on July 17, 1915, Foreign Secretary Sir Edward Grey replied to Page. He voiced the British government's objection to von Bissing's efforts to control relief and restated the nine conditions by which relief would be permitted. He explained that the British government believed in the "spirit of non-interference" with the CRB and the CN and that it would insist that "the German authorities shall also act [in the spirit of non-interference], toward the Commission for Relief in Belgium and the Comité National in all matters which fall within the functions of those bodies. It is on this spirit, and not on the strict belligerent rights of either government, that the whole work of relief is based, and the introduction into these discussions of any such claims of right cannot but be fatal to the continuance of that work." In other words, the Germans had to lay off trying to control the CRB and CN or the food relief would be shut down.

The British government's objections were taken to von der Lancken, who held two long conferences with Whitlock and Villalobar. Nearly two weeks after Grey's letter had been written, Baron von der Lancken wrote to Whitlock on July 29 formally stating that the governor general agreed to the British conditions outlined by Grey.

Von der Lancken wrote, "The Comité National and the Commission for Relief in Belgium shall be able to enjoy all liberty of action necessary for them to be in a position to fulfill the mission which has devolved upon them through the agreements entered into between the Governor-General and the representatives of the neutral Powers."

With the acknowledgment by von Bissing of the integrity and authority of the CN and CRB, one would have thought any problems between the CN and CRB would have been shelved, at least for a moment or two.

Far from it, as the CRB found out right away.

Delegate Duties and the 1915 Harvest Lead to a Battle for Control

As von Bissing's attempt to control the CN was raging, so too were other issues—issues between the CRB and CN as to who had control over relief. In the spring, the CN had quietly supported German insistence that the number of American flags be reduced, and the CN had overreacted to a CRB request to remove the word "American" from its "American Stores" by implementing the removal of all CRB references throughout Belgium (quickly restored).

By June and July, two more items came to the fore—delegate responsibilities and the 1915 Belgian harvest—and they would highlight how Francqui and the CN wanted to take complete control of relief.

Delegate responsibilities had already been an issue with von Bissing's February attempt to decrease the number of delegates and curtail their movements. Hoover had successfully countered the governor general by getting Ambassador Gerard to appeal directly to the German civilian government in Berlin, which had backed Hoover and his request for more delegates and greater freedom of movement. Francqui and the CN had done nothing significant to aid Hoover in this fight.

But the definition of what a delegate was supposed to do was changing, primarily under pressure from Francqui, the CN, and some provincial committees. They continued to press for a change in delegate duties, from the irritating active, administrator-like role some delegates had assumed to a more passive, advisory role.

Efforts had been made by the CRB and CN to clarify the issue, but by the summer of 1915 the CN still saw some of the delegates as overstepping their bounds of responsibility. Conversely, Hoover and the CRB came to realize that the delegate issue was not yet fully resolved and that the tussles with Francqui and the CN had been only "the first phase in a much more vital conflict affecting the whole matter of control of relief."

Soon delegate responsibilities would once again become an issue at the same time as an agreement was finally reached over who was to get the 1915 Belgian harvest.

As to the harvest, Governor General von Bissing had thought little about the subject beyond his belief that Belgium was under his absolute control; therefore, any crops grown in Belgium would be the property of the German Empire.

But earlier in the year, the British had announced that importations of food into Belgium would not be continued if the Germans did not agree that the 1915 Belgian harvest would be used to feed only the Belgians.

Hoover, working through multiple diplomatic channels and multiple individuals, had put pressure on von Bissing to give the harvest to the Belgians. As the months had slipped by without any German assurances, the British had taken a stronger stand. In May, Foreign Office liaison Eustace Percy had written Hoover that relief would be shut down by the middle of August if the Germans did not agree to give up all rights to the harvest.

Francqui had weighed in on the issue, but definitely not in the way that most would have thought. His contention—spelled out in a letter to Hoover on May 6—was that the Germans would probably not give up requisitioning the harvest. But that, he stated, should not stop the British from allowing relief to continue because the original agreements regarding nonrequisition had applied only to imported foodstuffs, not to native crops. Therefore, Francqui believed, the British "had no right to make new conditions for the continuance of the relief work."

Hoover told Francqui that this argument basically justified the Germans' claim to take the harvest for themselves, thus giving up the harvest before an argument could even be made to keep it. As Kittredge noted dryly, "At first in the matter of harvest negotiations Hoover and Francqui were working rather at cross purposes."

What followed was a series of meetings and negotiations in Brussels in June between Hoover, Francqui, the patron ministers, and representatives of the German government, most notably Baron von der Lancken. They covered multiple topics, including the CN's integrity and authority issue (resolved in July) and who would receive the 1915 Belgian harvest.

With Kittredge's usual frankness, he stated that during these June meetings, "Francqui showed a greater tendency than before to work directly with the German authorities and to eliminate the Commission from consideration. His attitude seemed to have been at this time that the Comité National was able to carry on the work of relief; that the British Government could be induced or coerced into accepting the assurances of the Comité National or of the patron Ministers that all was well in Belgium; that the Commission should therefore become a mere purchasing agent for the Comité National, and that in Belgium it should be made use of as an additional protection of a diplomatic sort; but that for all practical purposes the Comité National alone was to direct the relief operations."

Francqui knew he could count on the support of patron minister Villalobar, who had no great love for Hoover, and he was probably confident that he and Villalobar could sway Whitlock to their perspective. The Belgian also saw that in this one regard, he and von Bissing were in accord—they both wanted Hoover and the CRB gone from Belgium.

The differences between the two sides were manifest in what the British envisioned versus what the Germans finally established.

The British had stated in a July 7 letter from the Marquis of Crewe to Ambassador Page that the first stipulation to any crop agreement was "that the purchase and distribution of the harvest in Belgium shall be under the management of the Commission for Relief in Belgium and the Comité National, in the same manner as the imported foodstuffs."

That stipulation was slightly strengthened and repeated by Sir Edward Grey in another letter on July 17: "The whole yield of the present harvest of breadstuffs in Belgium shall be acquired by the Commission for Relief in Belgium and the Comité

National, and shall be held, controlled, and distributed by them alone, precisely in the same manner and under the same guarantees as the imported foodstuffs."

Such definitive statements would have been ones that Hoover and his associates would have stressed throughout all of the crop meetings and negotiations.

And yet, in a decree from von Bissing on July 23 that finally acknowledged the 1915 harvest would be given only to the Belgians, the governor general stated unequivocally, "I assign to the Comité National de Secours et d'Alimentation the sole right to purchase for cash, the requisitioned stocks and whatever bread grains remain."

Hoover, undoubtedly, saw Francqui's editing pen on von Bissing's words that the CN had "sole right to purchase." Francqui would have probably rebuffed Hoover's objections by simply stating that Belgian crops in Belgium deserved to be handled by Belgians.

The only way that von Bissing's arrangement was at all palatable to Hoover and the British was that a Central Harvest Commission (later known as the Central Crop Commission) had also been decreed by von Bissing to handle the harvest, and the CRB had representation on it.

Regardless of Hoover's feelings, the important fact was that the 1915 harvest was finally earmarked for Belgians. Hoover later found out that von Bissing had come around, once again, because of pressure from the German civilian government in Berlin, which had been stimulated by U.S. Ambassador Gerard. Gerard was becoming an indispensable weapon in Hoover's diplomatic arsenal.

A direct benefit of the agreement was that during the peak months of harvesting, the CRB could naturally decrease the amount of imports, but it wasn't by much. The CRB still had to import 54,000 tons each month to maintain the bread ration in Belgium. (Not to mention the new amount of foodstuffs needed to feed more than 2 million northern French, which had been taken on in April. The 1915 harvest in northern France was ultimately negotiated to go to the French as well.)

The most important benefit to the harvest agreement, however, was that it led the British to allow continued CRB imports into Belgium until the 1916 harvest—contingent, of course, on the honoring of all relief agreements. One more year of humanitarian work was tentatively secured.

Even with such good news, Hoover and the CRB still faced the growing number of slights, problems, and challenges from Francqui and the Comité National. They were becoming intolerable.

It was time for what would become a signature Hoover maneuver.

Should the Retirement of the CRB Be "Considered"?

According to Kittredge, "With the organisation of the central crop commission, there was indicated more clearly than ever the purpose of the Comité National to eliminate the Commission from all voice in affairs in Belgium."

Hoover, in later writings, said little about this time and the challenges he and the CRB faced when it came to the infighting with the CN. It's left to the ever-frank Kittredge to state the case: "Many important decisions had been taken by the Comité National in Belgium without consulting the Commission or heeding its advice and counsel."

While Hoover might not have said much about these particular CN conflicts in any of the later books on the CRB and his life, he nonetheless felt them deeply, and proof of that is in what he did to finally counteract them. He played what he felt was his final, most dramatic card—pulling out the CRB from all relief work. It was not so much an option as it was a strategy that Hoover would use sparingly during the next few years, but always when he felt the odds were stacked in his favor regarding the outcome.

It could be easily argued that Hoover—with his sense of commitment, integrity, honor, and belief in the humanitarian work—would never have willingly left the Belgians and northern French and that his threat was never more than a bluff.

An example was during the harvest negotiations, when Hoover had somewhat offhandedly used the threat to von der Lancken by writing, "It is perfectly immaterial to the C.R.B. whether or not these negotiations reach a successful consummation, except as to their interest in the people of Belgium. . . . If it is not the wish of the German Government to facilitate this matter . . . the Commission . . . would be only too glad to retire from the entire situation, which will involve Northern France as well as Belgium."

That statement was totally disingenuous—Hoover cared deeply about the outcome and would not have forsaken all relief for a bad outcome to this issue. But the way he made the threat in a letter could have been easily explained away if von der Lancken had called him on it.

On the other hand, what Hoover did after the harvest question was settled was much more forceful.

Hoover had come to Brussels in the middle of July to conclude the harvest agreements. He had brought with him two of his executive team, John Beaver White and Edgar Rickard, because he knew Francqui and the CN were working to undermine the CRB. What they found, according to Kittredge, was that "Francqui's attitude was apparently not to be changed and that he intended that the Commission should no longer have any real authority in Belgium. Hoover recognised that this would make impossible the accomplishment of the purposes for which the Commission existed, that if it could not have an effective control in Belgium it would be perfectly useless as an organisation."

On July 20, 1915, Hoover and his team sat down with Francqui and the executive committee members of the CN for a major conference in Brussels. The description of what happened in *Public Relations of the CRB* neglects to mention any CN problems and Hoover's threat to pull out. The authors of the book give the section a muted, rather innocuous subtitle, "Adjustment of Functions of C.R.B. and C.N. July 1915."

Hoover's handling of the situation was unlike his usually direct approach to problems. In a document that's identified as a *procès-verbal* (report, or minutes), Hoover didn't simply announce the CRB was pulling out because the CN was trying to run the show. He asked the group "if the time had now arrived when the retirement of the Commission from the relief work in Belgium should be considered." He then went on to list four positive events and situations that had led him to that question.

1. Initially, because the military authorities had not allowed freedom of movement for Belgians, the CN and its committees needed the CRB to establish communications links within the distribution network. Now the situation was "improved" because of the "more liberal attitude of the military authorities in these particulars," and therefore the CRB wasn't needed that much anymore.
2. The financial situation had been resolved so "no further appeals for the charity of the world in support [of Belgium] is necessary, or if necessary, they could be made by the C.N."
3. The Germans had kept to the agreements not to requisition any imported foodstuffs, so all the agreements in place should satisfy the Allied governments that the "whole line of guarantees can quite properly be transferred from the Commission for Relief in Belgium to the Comité National."
4. With the harvest agreement, the CRB's role in "conserving native food supplies has become less important."

Hoover summed up by saying the "sole object" of the CRB was to help the Belgians because they weren't free to help themselves. With the improving "political situation," he basically said the Belgians could get along without the CRB. The organization would retire gradually, with the plan of leaving by the middle of October, thereby completing one full year of service.

For Francqui—a man who led meetings like a dictator running a show he had scripted—it must have been very difficult to sit through Hoover's presentation. With Francqui's preference for behind-the-scenes preparation before any major meetings, no record has been found to indicate what, if anything, went on prior to the meeting and whether Francqui even knew what Hoover would do.

The official record says that Francqui and the CN protested each of Hoover's reasons for pulling out and stated "it was impossible" that the CRB "should retire." The Belgians gave six points to their contention that the CRB must stay. The last point summed up their official stand: "The Comité National is certain that it could not go on without (1) the political and moral support of the Commission; (2) that the executive work could not continue without the co-operation of the

Commission; and (3) that the finance, purchase, and transport operations are impossible at the present time by Belgians alone.

"Therefore, the Comité National not only protests at the idea of withdrawal, but specifically requests the Commission to continue its activities without idea of cessation."

The turnaround was abrupt and startling to any who had been following the rising tide of CN challenges to the CRB. And one wonders why Francqui, when faced with what he had probably wished for, turned it down.

In all probability, it was because Francqui was more than anything else a pragmatist and he knew the Allied governments would not allow Hoover and the CRB to pull out nor accept the CN taking over the CRB's responsibilities. And he knew that with the Central Crop Commission and with other areas, he and the CN were making headway at diminishing the role of the CRB in everyday operations. He would continue to work behind the scenes to continue that movement.

Certainly none of the Americans in the meeting cared to question Francqui's reversal.

The meeting then confirmed that the "ravitaillement [relief] and care of the destitute in Belgium shall continue as a joint undertaking." A long list detailed the administrative relationship between the two groups. The CRB would retain representation on the CN's executive committee, and the delegates would sit as members on the provincial and local committees.

A noticeable change was the timetable for when the CN took charge of the imported foodstuffs. In the beginning, the CRB had retained control of the food until its actual distribution. But from the time of the meeting forward, the CN would take official charge of the food shipments once they reached the provincial warehouses (with mills being considered provincial warehouses).

As Kittredge noted, however, that change meant "the whole question of the activity of the provincial delegates was left unsettled, except that it was provided that they should co-operate as closely as possible with the provincial committees."

As a way of resolving that and other issues, after the meeting a CRB internal memorandum regarding the organization and its delegates was prepared and circulated in-house. Much of it had to do with the CRB delegates working with the provincial committees and their newly adjusted role. The Hunt concept of delegates taking executive action was definitely out. The memorandum stated clearly, "We are here to help, not to order." Kittredge noted, "The view of a number of the provincial delegates, that efficiency in the work could only be secured if the delegates were to be given authority to take executive action, was thus definitely overruled."

The delegates were instructed that there were three areas they were responsible for: providing help and general services to the provincial committees wherever possible; ensuring all guarantees were met as to German nonrequisition and the fair distribution of food to all; and maintaining transportation and statistics so that food could keep coming in and the CRB would be able to report on all operations.

As to relations with the provincial committees, the memorandum repeated that "the attitude of the delegates shall be entirely of the order of inspection and advice and not of executive action." As to relations with the Germans, the instructions were just as clear and vague at the same time: "The relation of the delegates to the local German authorities shall be purely one of a friendly intermediary."

While the memorandum did clarify much of the CRB's duties and its organization, according to Kittredge it did something else as well: "This memorandum did, however, strengthen the hands of that group in the comité exécutif [executive committee] of the Comité National which objected to any sort of American interference in the actual work in Belgium. The conflict of authority and the incipient friction between the two organizations was therefore postponed rather than removed."

In the end, all the delegates could do was to feel a sense of relief that the major issues between the CRB and CN, and the CRB and the Germans, were seemingly resolved, at least for the moment. E. E. Hunt stated at the end of the entire affair of crop negotiations and CRB/CN discussions, "The tension at headquarters relaxed abruptly and a fairer and franker attitude toward the Commission and the National Committee took the place of earlier distrust. It is safe to infer that much of this was due to Herbert C. Hoover."

Even with the lessening of tensions, for one delegate at least, it meant the time was coming to move on. E. E. Hunt had done an incredible job in establishing operations in Antwerp Province, and his executive actions had done wonders to streamline and build an efficient operation, but his methods were at that point outdated and not officially welcomed anymore.

La Libre Belgique Grows

As Hoover was fighting for the life of the CRB, a handful of Belgians continued to fight to maintain an underground voice and presence within the harsh German occupation. Van Doren, Victor Jourdain, the Abbé de Moor, Philippe Baucq, and the countless distributors of *La Libre Belgique* continued to produce weekly issues of the one sheet, four-page underground newspaper that buoyed the spirits and hearts of the Belgian people while frustrating and infuriating the German occupiers.

The first 13 issues were written solely by the elderly journalist Victor Jourdain. By the spring of 1915, articles began appearing from other writers. The first was by a monsieur Le Comte, who had read the Germans' white paper on invasion atrocities and was so angry at its inaccuracies that he wrote a strong repudiation titled "Das ist nicht wahr!" ("This is not true!"). Le Comte, like many other Belgians, felt the newspaper was produced by Jesuit priests, so he took the article to a priest he knew at St. Michel College. That priest innocently passed it on to the Abbé de Moor, not knowing his role in the publication. De Moor turned it over to van Doren, who took it to Jourdain. A week later the article was in the newspaper. That was the start of a long list of other contributed articles by volunteer writers and regular columnists who were recruited over a long period of time.

The Germans kept up their raids of known printers and newsagents, looking for anything that tied those establishments to the underground paper. A reward of 50,000 francs was posted for the apprehension of the editor or editors. Thousands of informers across Belgium were instructed by the German secret police to find out who was responsible. One history related that the paper "was made the subject of an uncomplimentary report from His Imperial Majesty's General Staff. Within two months it had become almost an obsession at the Kommandantur [German headquarters in Brussels] and the nightmare of the chief of the secret police."

Because Allard's printing press was out in a Brussels suburb southeast of downtown, it had so far escaped attention, but van Doren knew the press was a critical part of the paper that had to be protected. He decided that the composing, or typesetting, of the newspaper, which took the most time and was done by Allard, should be completed someplace other than where the printing press was located.

Van Doren went to his trusted friend, the Abbé de Moor, who talked to a master at St. Michel College. The institution was the primary Jesuit school in Brussels and was becoming more and more involved with the newspaper as its priests and students became distributors. A master, Father Dubar, suggested that the college's barber, de Becker, might have an answer. The barber was caretaking a house on the Avenue Verte and had his barbershop in the front basement. He lived in the back and the rest of the house was unoccupied. The barber agreed to allow Louis and Philippe Allard to move in with their typesetting equipment so they could compose each issue. The house was not far from the Allard printing press. Van Doren and the others believed that the Germans would not look in a barbershop for an underground newspaper.

Once that operation was established, van Doren carried each issue's set type from the composing room in the Avenue Verte to Allard's press in the Rue des Cultivateurs. Because the lead type was heavy, he had two boxes made that were divided into compartments just large enough to hold a column of type. When the boxes were full, they weighed close to 50 pounds. The tall and lanky van Doren would carry them for the 20-minute walk to the printing press, usually preferring to walk rather than wait for the unreliable trams.

One day, though, van Doren decided to take a tram. He had boarded and was standing near the exit with his two boxes on the floor beside him when two German secret police hopped aboard. As the Belgian knew, the Germans could have asked to see inside his parcels at any time, looking for smuggled food, contraband, or even copies of *La Libre Belgique*.

Trying to remain calm, van Doren decided to bluff before they could act—at the next stop he got off and asked them politely, "Would you give me a hand with my parcels, gentlemen? They're rather heavy."

With relations strained at best between Belgians and Germans, the two hesitated for a moment, then one nodded and handed van Doren the parcels. The Belgian thanked them profusely as the tram pulled away.

Such luck continued for a while. All was going well, with the paper's print runs getting larger and larger and the circulation reaching more and more people throughout occupied Belgium. Then von Bissing made a move that would have serious consequences.

The governor general and his secret police became sure that the newspaper was produced by Jesuit priests. The writing was in their scholarly style; the literary and academic references indicated highly educated, religious writers. A plan was conceived to entrap the creators of *La Libre Belgique.*

One day in April, a stranger approached the Abbé de Moor with a letter of reference from the rector of St. Michel College. He told de Moor that he represented the exiled Belgian government in Le Havre, France. The government wanted to give the editor of the underground newspaper a significant amount of money to keep his efforts alive.

A highly suspicious de Moor told the man that he sometimes received copies of the publication but knew nothing else. The two agreed to meet again in a few days, so that de Moor could have time to ask around and look into the situation.

The abbé quickly checked with the rector and came to the conclusion that the man must be a spy. The next time they met, de Moor had a woman friend and her child follow the stranger after the meeting. The spy went straight to the luxurious Palace Hotel, which had become the favorite location for German officers when in Brussels.

De Moor was heartbroken. He knew the Germans were closing in on him and he would have to flee. He put off the German spy for a few days as he wrapped up all the loose ends of his various underground activities. He met one more time with van Doren and expressed how hard it was to leave the businessman whom he had come to know and respect in their nine months of working together. The priest warned van Doren, "They're getting warm. And if you're not very careful they'll be making it hot for you." He also said he had arranged for another person to be the new central depot for *La Libre Belgique.*

When the abbé met with the spy again, he told the man that the newspaper was actually run by a group of barristers and led by one of the most distinguished members of the Antwerp bar. He said he had set up a meeting for Sunday, May 1, between the man and the newspaper's leader in front of the Antwerp cathedral after high mass.

When the spy showed up at de Moor's home on Sunday to take him to the meeting, the priest was already safely in Holland, having reportedly crossed the border illegally the night before by swimming the Campine canal.

Van Doren had been shocked by de Moor's departure, but he knew the paper had to continue. When de Moor's new central depot did not work out, van Doren went directly to St. Michel College and talked with Father Dubar, who agreed to become the main depot for copies of *La Libre Belgique*. The college was thought by van Doren to be a perfect place because of the constant comings and goings of priests, parents, and pupils, which would make for less chance of discovery.

From that point on, fewer people knew of van Doren and his pivotal role in the operation; most knew him by an alias and as simply another distributor. Additionally, only van Doren and Father Paquet had direct ties to editor Victor Jourdain; the printer, Allard; and the distribution leader, Philippe Baucq. The innermost circle had shrunk by one, which slightly increased the odds of the full organization never being completely exposed.

By June 1915, with the overwhelming demand for more and more copies of the newspaper, there was a greater need for those willing to circulate the publication. This was especially true when trying to get copies from city to city throughout Belgium. The major rail lines were not open to the general public and the little intercity electric or steam trams that remained in service were heavily watched and searched constantly by the Germans. Most copies of the newspaper had to be carried by walkers who could take days to get from place to place. It was hard, dangerous work, but many people volunteered to do it.

One of them was a young woman, Gabrielle Petit, an orphan who had previously escaped to England with her fiancé before choosing to return to her country and work for various underground networks. Auburn haired with brown eyes, she was 22 years old but reportedly looked much younger. Since she had returned from England, she had worked with the letter-smuggling service *Mot du Soldat* ("Word of the Soldier") and helped the group headed by English nurse Edith Cavell by ferrying Allied soldiers and young Belgian men to the Holland border.

Petit's connection with *La Libre Belgique* came about through an uncle who was associated with *La Libre Belgique*. He arranged for her to meet Philippe Baucq, who quickly enlisted her in his group of walking carriers. She began working for Baucq in June 1915 as she continued to help the other underground groups whenever and wherever possible.

As Petit enthusiastically embraced her work for *La Libre Belgique*, van Doren became more and more concerned that Allard's printing press would be discovered. A month had passed since de Moor had left, and nothing much had happened to disrupt the operation, but still van Doren worried. He finally made an incredibly bold decision. He would set up a printing press in the empty cardboard manufacturing

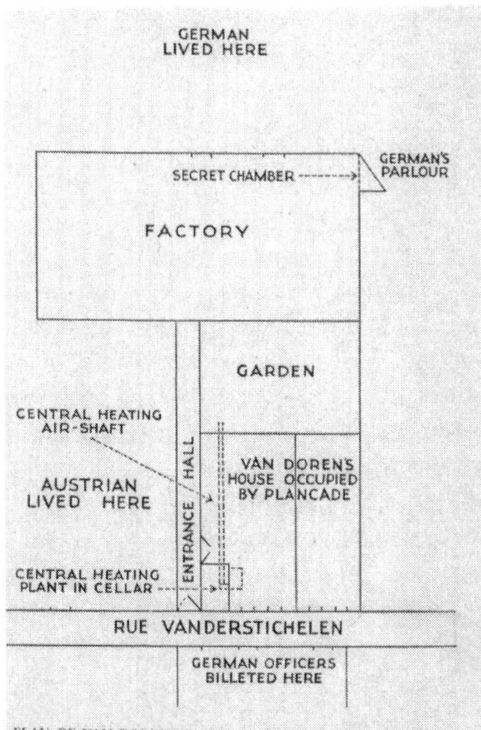

Eugene van Doren made the audacious decision to hide—and operate—a printing press in a secret chamber within his abandoned factory. (A page from *Underground News: The Complete Story of the Secret Newspaper That Made War History,* Oscar E. Millard, Robert McBride and Co., 1938.)

building he owned in a northwest suburb of Brussels. The factory was at the back of a piece of property with a house at the front. Before the war, the house had been rented to his factory workers and was still being used by a man named Theodore Plancade. If van Doren could succeed in building a secret press in the empty factory, he felt it would be the safest, most secure location he could find for a printing press.

When he couldn't find a press to buy, he turned to Allard and convinced him to sell his, with Victor Jourdain paying for it. Van Doren told Allard to break it down to its smallest pieces and wrap them up. Then, with a Herculean effort, van Doren and Plancade transported the pieces of the nearly one-ton printing press to the factory and reassembled them and installed the press in the building.

It took more than a week to get the press set up and they had to improvise to do so. As one history explained, "A gas engine on the ground floor was connected up by masked shafting to operate the press on the floor above." Once that was complete, a brick wall was built around the press to create a small seven-foot by 13-foot secret space. The bricks had to be brought in a few at a time so as not to alert neighbors or those who might be watching. The wall was then whitewashed and dirtied to match the building's other walls. Access was only through a hole in the ceiling that was concealed by old lumber and boxes. Ventilation was through a removable brick to the outside. They sound-proofed the entire room by securing mattresses to the walls. To get from one end of the room to the other, they had to climb over the press.

No matter how uncomfortable it was to operate, however, it worked, and without anyone outside knowing what was going on.

The obstacles had been impressively huge—not least of which were van Doren's living on a busy street with a German policeman permanently stationed at the end of the block, the presence of a German civilian living next door, and the potential hazard of several German officers living across the street. "On the face of it," one history noted dryly, "a more ill-chosen hide-out for a secret press would have been hard to find."

As van Doren and Plancade—his newly charged printing assistant—printed issue number 29, van Doren decided he needed to do something special to celebrate the new press. And to aggravate von Bissing even more.

Issue 30 turned out better than van Doren had hoped, and it enraged von Bissing to new heights. On the cover was the publication's first illustration, a doctored photo of a seated von Bissing holding a copy of *La Libre Belgique*. The headline over the photo read "His Excellency the Governor Baron von Bissing and an intimate friend." The caption cut even deeper: "Our dear Governor, sickened by the lies of the censored papers, seeks the truth in *La Libre Belgique*."

To guarantee von Bissing did not miss the issue, van Doren sent a copy to the governor general's private residence, to his wife in Berlin, to the Brussels Kommandantur, and to the chief of the secret police on the Rue de Berlaimont. (Nearly a year later, the issue would become famous when the front page was reprinted by the *New York Times* in an article about *La Libre Belgique* on May 21, 1916.)

Understandably, the issue was an instant success with Belgians across the country. As for von Bissing, one writer noted, "The exasperated Governor's wrath was so intense that its repercussions were felt among the lowliest underlings in the Government's service, who in their turn did their best to take it out on the civilians by a thousand petty tyrannies." However, simply "knowing the cause of [the Germans'] peevishness the Belgians only laughed the more."

The celebration would not last long.

German Raids Catch Two Important People

Within a month, St. Michel College's barber, de Becker, went to Father Dubar and told him that a man he had been shaving had spotted one of the Allards walking through the shop to get to the composing room. The man began saying to others that he knew who was printing the underground newspaper. Father Dubar quickly went to van Doren and told him the bad news.

Van Doren was sure he didn't have much time before the Germans got wind of the story and would come to search the barbershop. He decided to shut down the composing room immediately. De Becker left the city for an unscheduled vacation.

To shut down the composing room, van Doren had two large black tin trunks delivered to the shop, and he and the Allard brothers loaded them up with all the

NUMÉRO 30 — THE HERBERT HOOVER ARCHIVES — JUIN 1915

PRIX DU NUMÉRO — élastique, de zéro à l'infini (prière aux revendeurs de ne pas dépasser cette limite)

LA LIBRE BELGIQUE

Acceptons provisoirement les sacrifices qui nous sont imposés... et attendons patiemment l'heure de la réparation.
Le Bourgmestre ADOLPHE MAX.

FONDÉE LE 1er FÉVRIER 1915

Envers ce personnes qui dominent par la force militaire notre pays, ayons les égards que commande l'intérêt général. Respectons les règlements qu'elles nous imposent aussi longtemps qu'ils ne portent atteinte ni à la liberté de nos consciences chrétiennes ni à notre *dignité patriotique*.
Mgr MERCIER.

BULLETIN DE PROPAGANDE PATRIOTIQUE — RÉGULIÈREMENT IRRÉGULIER

NE SE SOUMETTANT A AUCUNE CENSURE

ADRESSE TÉLÉGRAPHIQUE : KOMMANDANTUR - BRUXELLES

BUREAUX ET ADMINISTRATION ne pouvant être un emplacement de tout repos, ils sont installés dans une cave automobile

ANNONCES : Les affaires étant nulles sous la domination allemande, nous avons supprimé la page d'annonces et conseillons à nos clients de réserver leur argent pour des temps meilleurs.

AVIS.

On nous fait à nouveau l'honneur de s'occuper de notre modeste bulletin. Nous en sommes flattés, mais nous nous croyons forcés de répéter ce que nous avons déjà dit pour notre défense. Ce n'est certes pas nous qu'on peut accuser sans manquer à la vérité, de provoquer nos concitoyens à la révolte. Nous ne manquons pas une occasion de prêcher la patience, l'endurance, le calme et le respect des lois de la guerre. Aussi profitons-nous de cette occasion qui nous est offerte pour répéter l'avis que nous avons déjà inséré :

RESTONS CALMES!!!

Le jour viendra (lentement mais sûrement) où nos ennemis contraints de reculer devant les Alliés, devront abandonner notre capitale.

Souvenons-nous alors des avis nombreux qui ont été donnés aux civils par le Gouvernement et par notre bourgmestre

SON EXCELLENCE LE GOUVERNEUR Bon VON BISSING ET SON AMIE INTIME

NOTRE CHER GOUVERNEUR, ÉCŒURÉ PAR LA LECTURE DES MENSONGES DES JOURNAUX CENSURÉS, CHERCHE LA VÉRITÉ DANS LA « LIBRE BELGIQUE »

M. Max : SOYONS CALMES!!!

Faisons taire les sentiments de légitime colère qui fermentent en nos cœurs.

Soyons, comme nous l'avons été jusqu'ici, respectueux des lois de la guerre. C'est ainsi que nous continuerons à mériter l'estime et l'admiration de tous les peuples civilisés.

Ce serait une INUTILE LACHETÉ, *une lâcheté indigne des Belges que de chercher à se venger ailleurs que sur le champ de bataille. Ce serait de plus* EXPOSER DES INNOCENTS *à des représailles terribles de la part d'ennemis sans pitié et sans justice.*

Méfions-nous des agents provocateurs allemands qui, en exaltant notre patriotisme, nous pousseraient à commettre des excès.

RESTONS MAITRES DE NOUS-MÊMES ET PRÊCHONS LE CALME AUTOUR DE NOUS. C'EST LE PLUS GRAND SERVICE QUE NOUS PUISSIONS RENDRE A NOTRE CHÈRE PATRIE.

L'ORDRE SOCIAL TOUT ENTIER DÉFENDU PAR LA BELGIQUE.

Le 3 août, le Gouvernement allemand remet à la Belgique une note demandant le libre passage pour ses armées sur son territoire, moyennant quoi l'Allemagne s'engage à maintenir l'intégrité du royaume et de ses possessions. Sinon, la Belgique sera traitée en ennemie. Le roi Albert a douze heures pour répondre. Devant cet ultimatum, il n'hésite pas. Il sait que l'armée allemande est une force terrible. Il connaît l'empereur allemand. Il sait que l'orgueilleux, après une telle démarche, ne reculera plus. Son trône est en jeu, plus que son trône : les sept millions d'âmes — quelle éloquence prennent les vulgaires termes des statistiques dans certaines circonstances! — qui lui sont confiées : il voit en esprit ce beau pays indéfendable : ces charbonnages, ces carrières, ces usines, ces filatures, ces ports, cette florissante industrie épanouie dans ces plaines ouvertes qu'il ne pourra pas préserver. Mais il s'agit d'un traité où il y a sa signature. Répondre oui à l'Allemagne, c'est trahir ses consignataires, le

PRIÈRE DE FAIRE CIRCULER CE BULLETIN

In 1915, long before Photoshop existed, the underground newspaper La Libre Belgique *faked an image that made a mockery of Governor General von Bissing by showing him reading the paper. It enraged the Prussian military officer.* (Public domain; Herbert Hoover Presidential Library Archives, West Branch, Iowa.)

typesetting equipment. He then told the brothers to clear out, never come back, and deny everything if the Germans came to their home.

Van Doren then waited for Philippe Baucq, who was coming to help him move the trunks. By then it was dark and van Doren sat in the empty barbershop, wondering if Baucq would get there and if they'd be successful. Every once in a while he heard the tramp of German boots down the street and anxiously waited for pounding on the door and shouted German commands.

Finally, Baucq showed up, dressed as a street vendor and pushing a fruit and vegetable cart. They quickly loaded the two trunks and covered them with a tarpaulin. They knew they couldn't take the precious cargo to the new printing press, which was four miles away, and they didn't want to take it to any known associate's house for fear they might be followed. That's when Baucq, according to one history, turned to van Doren and told him to go home. "This is my party," he said to his friend, "leave this one to me. You're too big and respectable for this job."

Van Doren knew he was right and reluctantly headed home.

Baucq began to stroll down the street like any other pushcart vendor out late, either coming from a market or going to a market. He would spend half the night wandering the streets until he found a safe haven with a woman who worked for *Mot du Soldat*. A few days later he moved the trunks to the attic of a sympathetic Belgian policeman.

Meanwhile, van Doren, with the help of Father Dubar, made arrangements with another printer to do the typesetting and some of the printing. With the work of that press combined with his own, van Doren was able to increase the circulation and have three issues come out in two weeks.

Even though the group had so far survived unscathed, van Doren was on constant alert. When several of Baucq's sub-distributors were arrested with copies of the paper, van Doren warned Baucq that he was no longer safe and needed to exercise much more caution. Baucq always brushed off the warnings with a stout-hearted declaration of "Funk!"

As van Doren knew, Baucq was also working in Edith Cavell's network, helping to hide and guide Allied soldiers and young Belgian men to the Dutch border. Neither man knew that the secret police were closing in on the Cavell network as well.

The Germans came for Baucq late one summer night.

He had arrived home earlier that night, Saturday, July 31, with two big packages of issue number 37. He had placed them in the bedroom. At 10:00 p.m. he went to the front door to let out his dog. Suddenly, he was blinded by a powerful flashlight as two German soldiers rushed in. Baucq was stocky and strong and fought hard. As he struggled to get free, his daughter ran to her parents' bedroom and tossed the two packages out the window, where they fell on a German *polizei* guarding the back of the house. Soon Baucq was restrained and a detective was holding a gun on him. He, his wife, and daughter were taken to the Kommandantur. The next day the women were released while Baucq remained in jail. He would stand trial in October.

The loss of such a critical person was a major blow to van Doren's small group. It would call for a reorganizing and regrouping.

A little more than a week later, on Tuesday, August 5, 1915, another person was apprehended by the Germans. Edith Louisa Cavell was the 49-year-old English nurse who had been asked before the war to train nurses in modern nursing methods at Dr. Antoine DePage's clinic in Brussels. When the war began, she showed her compassion by treating the wounded of both sides. For such work, the Germans had allowed her to continue to practice and teach after the occupation began.

As she did so, she became drawn into another side of war, not only by her own compassion but also by the example and urgings of aristocratic friends such as Princess Marie de Cröy and the Countess Jeanne de Belleville. Soon Cavell was secretly hiding Allied soldiers and young Belgian men and helping them get to Holland. The network, which ultimately took her name, became so large that the Germans couldn't help but hear of it. In early August they staged multiple raids and rounded up numerous members, including the princess, the countess, Cavell, and Baucq. Tricked into believing the Germans knew everything in detail, Cavell confessed to all that she had done.

She, like Baucq, would stand trial in October. Unlike the Belgian, however, Cavell and her story would become famous around the world, while he would remain largely unknown to most.

Despite that difference, they would share a common fate that none of the others would.

22

Northern France

From April 1915—when relief efforts had started in northern France—to the end of 1915, the work had progressed to a point where people were surviving. While the figures weren't as large as in Belgium, they were still substantial. The six northern France districts and their civilian population figures were:

	Communes	*Population*
Lille	107	622,696
Valenciennes	339	591,155
St. Quentin	511	450,424
Vervins	431	222,646
Charleville	339	150,476
Longwy	406	112,218
Total	2,133	2,149,615

Two French areas that contained a combined total of 130,000 civilians—one around Maubeuge and one around Givet-Fumay—had been assigned for provisioning to Belgium's Hainaut Province and Namur Province, respectively. (In December 1916 the region of Maubeuge was taken out of von Bissing's general government control and became part of the Army Zone, where it was merged into the St. Quentin district.)

After much study and analysis, a minimum ration per person per day "on which this population can be kept alive" included:

Flour (bread)—190 grams	Salt—10 grams
Rice—20 grams	Sugar—10 grams
Legumes—20 grams	Lard—30 grams
Coffee—20 grams	Bacon—30 grams

Even though the first shipments of food had starting going into northern France in April, all items were still not being fully delivered by summer and early fall. Because food had to be bought and shipped from North and South America and those orders were in addition to the orders already placed for Belgium relief, it took two to three months after purchasing for delivery to be anticipated in northern France.

Within each district, the CRB delegates were trying to do their work as they struggled to adjust to their German *Begleitsoffizier* (escorting or accompanying officer). The turnover of CRB delegates was higher in northern France than in Belgium, primarily because of the living conditions the delegates had to endure while stationed with—and practically attached-at-the-hip to—their German officer, or "nurse."

The German "Nurses" Become Personalities

Most of the German officers who worked and lived with the delegates in northern France ultimately became fodder for inside delegate jokes and stories that rarely indicated how difficult the situation was between the Germans and Americans. The partial list below of names attached to districts gave no insight into what these men were like.

District	*Delegates*	*German Officer*
NORTHERN FRANCE ETAPE		
Lille	Lewis Richards	Capt. Bahr
Valenciennes	T. Hardwood Stacy	Lieutenant Paul Neuerbourg*
	G. H. Chassaud	Capt. Bahr
St. Quentin	F. Dorsey Stephens	Lieutenant Fritz Neuerbourg*
	Frank H. Gailor	Lieutenant Fincke
Vervins	David T. Nelson	Capt. Weber
	Major Dutton	
Charleville	John L. Simpson	Capt. Count von Wengersky
		Otto Karl zur Strassen
Longwy	Carlton G. Bowden	Capt. Rumelin
BELGIUM ETAPE		
Flanders	Julian A. Van Hee	Lieutenant Schroeder
	Scott H. Paradise	
	E. C. Thurston	
Tournai	Maurice Pate	Lieutenant Willis

* Brothers; multiple different spellings of their last name, but Neuerbourg is correct.

The first group of German officers who became accompanying officers to the CRB delegates assigned to northern France. Number 1, Lieutenant Neuerbourg; 2, Major Kesseler; 3, Count von Wengersky; 4, Lieutenant Schroeder; 5, Lieutenant Neuerbourg; 6. Lieutenant Schall; 7, Captain Weber; 8, Lieutenant Rumelin; 9, not identified. (Public domain; Herbert Hoover Presidential Library Archives, West Branch, Iowa.)

Joe Green, who would become the head of the CRB's Inspection and Control Department in 1916, wrote an essay about the accompanying officers. In it, he expressed candidly what many delegates thought of these German "nurses." (The veracity of parts of his statements could never be fully verified and in some cases are contradicted by other delegate comments.) Standouts included:

CAPTAIN BAHR. Green said, "He was fairly tractable when he was drunk, but absolutely unbearable when he was sober. Fortunately, he was drunk ninety per cent of the time. Our representative always supplied him with the necessary liquor from Brussels." This didn't mean he was a bad sort, however.

Delegate Arthur Maurice reported, "Of all the German officers with whom the men of the CRB were thrown in contact, unquestionably the most genuinely liked was Captain B. [Bahr]. . . . Every one who had been associated with B. spoke of his fairness and his kindness. He had something of the politeness of the heart. Under his good manners you never detected the sneer. I am sure it was not there. In that he was the exception. But despite his uniform, of which he was immensely vain—the girls in the Bodegas [CRB warehouses] used to amuse themselves hugely playing upon his weakness—and the clanking sword which was too long for his short legs, and over which he was always stumbling, he never gave the impression of being a soldier."

But Maurice also acknowledged Bahr's fondness for drink. He would usually start around noon with a bottle of champagne and continue from there so that "by two or three o'clock in the afternoon he was dreaming that he was in Paris, sipping a liqueur at the corner table of the Café de la Paix, and looking down the Avenue of the Opera."

CAPTAIN VON WENGERSKY AND CAPTAIN OTTO KARL ZUR STRASSEN. Green stated, "They were so horribly disagreeable and so insulting to most of the Americans that Charleville was generally considered the worst post in the C.R.B. service. Few of our men could survive it more than three months." In fact, five out of the seven delegates who served in Charleville lasted fewer than three months. Brand Whitlock, however, gave another view of Count von Wengersky. He said the German was "a fine-looking man who, after his twelve years' residence in London, wore a monocle and had a manner that was distinctly English." As a liaison officer between the General Staff and the CRB, von Wengersky, according to Whitlock, "rendered loyal service to the cause. Mr. Hoover and Dr. Kellogg [a CRB Brussels director] had always spoken of him with respect."

LIEUTENANT (LATER CAPTAIN) RUMELIN. "Long and thin," Green wrote, "with a slight limp which he exaggerated for the effect. [Carlton] Bowden always maintained that this 'wound' was sustained by a fall into an empty canal one night when the Lieutenant was somewhat the worse for wear. Bowden could handle him beautifully, and he really managed the district of Longwy as long as he was stationed there."

LIEUTENANT WILLIS. According to Green, Willis was "the son of a British army officer who fortunately is not living. His mother was Austrian. He was a pleasant, rather well-appearing individual, who made a great display of his anti-British feeling. He used to call the Belgians in his district 'my niggers.'"

LIEUTENANT FINCKE. Green wrote, "He was said to be the nephew of some magnate at Hamburg. As a Ravitaillement [relief] officer he was utterly useless. He was drunk the great proportion of the time and he was a fool whether drunk or sober."

One delegate wrote that Fincke was "debonair" and could dance a jig, but also mentioned his heavy drinking that would get him into trouble, followed by great regrets the next morning. To another delegate, he was young, "witty and philosophical" and nicknamed Winkie. That came from a ritual Fincke supposedly performed on many a morning. After a long night of heavy drinking, he would wake up usually with nothing on but his Hussar boots. Ragged and greatly hung over, he would stumble to a mirror, look mournfully and regretfully at his disheveled image, then extend a finger, wave it at the mirror, and mumble, "Winkie, Winkie, you naughty little Hun!"

LIEUTENANTS PAUL AND FRITZ NEUERBOURG (BROTHERS). Green said, "I always thought them rather decent fellows. Paul had lived many years in England and had married an Australian. His wife and son were in London throughout the war, and various members of the C.R.B. including Mr. Hoover, often carried messages back and forth between the husband and wife. On one occasion we even took a pair of good London boots over for Neuerbourg, because he could not find what he wanted in the occupied territories." (There is no evidence that Hoover carried any personal messages across any borders, which would have been an illegal act that Hoover was constantly warning others about.)

Both Neuerbourg brothers had weary, hangdog eyes, brows that drooped like tired dough and a little black toothbrush mustache that would become a famous style 20 years later on Adolph Hitler.

One of them would prove to have strong moral fiber when tested.

LIEUTENANT SCHROEDER. Green wrote, "He was a nasty little specimen, half German and half Chilean, and combining the worst characteristics of the Spaniard and the Prussian."

Nelson and His Pro-German Views

In Vervins, where Nelson and Dutton had begun the work on April 26, 1915, the German officer was Captain Weber, a short, stocky man. His family owned the famous Leipzig illustrated magazine called *Illustrirte Zeitung*, which had begun publishing in 1843. As Nelson described Captain Weber, he had "traveled through practically all the parts of the world worth seeing—furthermore he speaks excellent English." Green described Weber as "a solemn, bullet-headed-looking man. He was supposed to be rather hard to get along with, but he did good work."

Nelson, the rare CRB delegate who was more pro-German than pro-Allies, seemed to be the perfect fit for the well-traveled Weber. In his letter to his mother, Nelson casually relayed that Weber would have complete control over his communications to Belgium and the outside world. It didn't seem to bother him as it did some of the other delegates. He was also clear to his concerned mother about potential danger: "So far as actual fighting is concerned we see nothing of it for we are about forty miles behind the lines. And even when one is within ten or fifteen miles of them one is reminded of war only by the sound of guns and the presence of the soldiers and army automobiles."

He was sure he would be in the northern France position for some time. "My stay here," he wrote his mother, "will of necessity be indefinite."

With Nelson's already proven grit and determination, with his pro-German feelings, and the well-bred Weber as accompanying officer, it seemed a sure bet that Nelson would be at his northern France post indefinitely.

He lasted less than three months.

On July 12, 1915, Nelson left Vervins and moved back into Belgium to Mons, where he became a delegate for Hainaut Province. He served there until October 1915, when he left the CRB and returned to his studies at Oxford.

While there is no official or unofficial explanation for his move from Vervins to Hainaut, strong indicators of what happened in Vervins can be found in a long letter he wrote his father on October 5, 1915, when he had reached Rotterdam and was finally able to write freely his thoughts and opinions of what he had seen and experienced. "In spite of many happy hours spent [in Belgium], there is a feeling of relief at being finally in a country untrammeled by militarism."

He asked his father, "Did I tell you, or rather did Mr. Chasseaud [a CRB delegate who had arrived in 1915 and left Belgium before Nelson] write you for me that I have changed my views on the war?"

He reminded his father of his initial pro-German stance: "When I left the states and even long after I was in Belgium, in spite of my sympathy for the Belgians, I continued to find the German cause justifiable. I wasn't absolutely sure and I came [to Belgium] partly to be able to better study the situation."

Nothing he had seen or experienced in Belgium had changed his mind. "I know that I can say that my change in opinion is not due to a sentimental sympathy for the Belgians, or to the influences which have been brought to bear upon me by being continually among them."

The change had started during his time in northern France and his close association with Weber. "I began to find that my view of the case was not theirs [the Germans]." With a few opportunities to travel with Weber into Germany, Nelson had "the opportunity of meeting several large German manufacturers as well as other prominent and well-informed Germans."

From these interactions, "I received an awful jolt," Nelson wrote. "It was slowly forced upon me against my desires and against my long-standing preconceptions that Germany was on the aggressive, that Germany had really set out for her 'place in the sun,' that instead of waiting to win it by peaceful and lawful methods, she had decided that the time was ripe to clinch it by war. Militarism was in command of the government and militarism had hypnotized the people when last August [1914] the ultimatums were sent out to Russia and France."

He then went on to praise the German war machine as "the most powerful, the most perfect organization that I have ever seen. I have had the opportunity of seeing what it could do and has done to places like Liège, Namur, Antwerp, and Longwy. It has been called a machine and it deserves the name; it is a machine directed by master military minds, minds which have gauged its every potentiality and have known for years what could be expected of it."

Nelson was convinced—and felt many others thought the same way—that if Germany had only fought Russia and France, it would have been "overwhelmingly victorious." Germany's "miscalculation" had been to think England would have stayed neutral. He also felt the Germans had underestimated Belgian resistance by about 25 percent "not more," but coupled with England's entry into the war had "meant the saving of France and the allies."

He added a strong caveat to his thoughts. "I do not incriminate the whole German people, man, woman, and child; I do not think the bulk of the Germans had shrewdly calculated the chances of such a war and then decided to plunge France and Russia in ruin that Germany might dominate. The bulk of the Germans had nothing to say."

He laid the blame for the war squarely on the shoulders of the German military, but he knew that argument was one his father and other Americans might not buy. "A military party [in America] can not dominate a nation like Germany to that extent. It does sound incredible to us Americans; it sounded incredible to me; I refused for a long time to believe it."

But, he explained, "I found the evidence too strong. I was forced to believe it. . . . Germany was more prosperous, was more powerful, was better organized, was more highly developed in industrial lines than any one of her neighbors, but Germany was ambitious. Germany, military and aggressive, forgot her duty and led by militarists turned to conquest. It cannot be called by another name."

Nelson ended his description of his change in perspective by explaining why he had written so much. "I have dwelled at some length on this change of opinion because I want you to be sure of my position. I don't want you to say to yourself that I have been won over simply because I have been so long closely connected with those who are enemies of Germany."

And with that, Nelson stepped away from the CRB relief work and resumed his studies at Oxford, already realizing that his 10 months of humanitarian service had changed him forever.

23

London

Changing Times Dictate a Change in PR Messaging

By the summer of 1915, Hoover was still facing the New York office's misconception about CRB long-term financing. In a June 1 letter to Alexander J. Hemphill, the new treasurer of the New York office, Hoover wrote once again to explain the financial situation, which had caused misunderstanding with the American public. He acknowledged the difficulty of explaining how the CRB's provisioning department was making a profit. "The fact, however, does remain," he wrote, "that this method of organization has been the salvation of Belgium and that every concession which we can obtain on the purchase of foodstuffs which we resell increases our profits, and that these profits go direct to the support of the destitute."

Regarding the American articles that had misled the public, Hoover was straightforward in his concern, but also implied that the New York office's publicity department was partially to blame by not explaining the situation better to the media. "I regret intensely that any misconstruction should have been put on the matter in America, and apparently nothing of the kind originated here, as is evidenced by the great support we have had from England and her Colonies as a result of these explanations. . . . In other words we believe that, complicated as our system is, it is capable of intelligent representation and that a frank and open statement of the whole of our methods commands the most intelligent support."

Analyzing the American situation, Hoover realized he had to have greater control of the message, and the message had to change. That change was all about the recipients of relief and how relief had evolved from crisis to long-term aid.

Initially, the PR message Hoover had wanted to tell the world was that the humanitarian relief was all about helping *save a nation* in the midst of a crisis.

Once it was accepted that relief would be needed for a long war and relatively stable funding had been established, Hoover realized the PR message had to be repositioned to communicate that they were helping *save the destitute.*

The London office, Hoover told Bates in a long letter, had at first "appealed for foodstuffs for a starving nation, but we have since built up an economic machine by which this is no longer a legitimate undercurrent of appeal and we long since abandoned it everywhere except that these phases of the matter seem to crop up in the American mind. The only legitimate, honest appeal which we have the right to make to the public now is for food, money, or clothing for the *destitute* [Hoover's emphasis] in Belgium. Any other basis of appeal is subject to refutation at once as dishonest, and must lead us into criticism."

He acknowledged that in the beginning, "in order to bring vividly before the world the right of the Belgians to import foodstuffs, we engaged in a wide propaganda of newspaper publicity. This material had great news value and was freely used and in the main served to create a public opinion in support of the Commission's objectives." But those days were over, he said, and the "material no longer has news value and is no longer received by the press . . . and is degenerating into personal puffs [articles about personalities, not the Belgians or relief]. It is a useless waste of money, time and energy to pursue it, and lacks dignity apropos the position we have arrived at."

Then came the heart of Hoover's message to Bates. "Announcements of importance must be made from London. The political phases which surround the Commission are so delicate and only to be balanced by the London office."

He finished with once again reiterating "but, above all things, the American campaign has got to be gotten off the basis of 'saving a famished nation' and gotten on to the support of the destitute."

An added benefit to changing the focus from nation to destitute would be that it better described the newer, full scope of relief, which had begun to also feed the more than 2 million northern French.

As Hoover was trying to get his critical message across to the New York office, another wedge came between Hoover and Bates. Since the loss of his son on the *Lusitania,* Bates had become harder to manage and, as far as Hoover was concerned, Bates's ego had stoked the belief that he was practically co-leader of the CRB. He also seemed driven for more and more "personal publicity." The underlying cause, Hoover felt, was his tremendous grief over the loss of his son, which, when added to his CRB work, created "great nervous strain. . . . His mind, while not precisely unhinged, seems to have been greatly shaken and he seems to have developed a number of curious obsessions." Kittredge's history of the CRB stated it more directly: "In the late summer of 1915 it became apparent that Mr. Bates, because of overwork and his personal sorrow, was showing signs of an imminent breakdown."

The wedge came on August 28 in the form of a major article in the prestigious *Saturday Evening Post.* It highlighted the workings of the New York office and Bates's role in the humanitarian relief. Written by Frank Marshall White and titled "No Dividends: Big Business Works for Charity," it practically gushed over Bates and how important he was to the entire relief effort. The CRB, the article maintained, had risen rapidly to be "one of the most efficient business machines of the world . . . due primarily to the genius of Lindon W. Bates." If that wasn't enough, the article stated that the "enormous executive burden" was "borne almost entirely by Mr. Bates and Mr. Hoover," putting the two of them on what appeared to be equal footing.

There was no excuse for such a piece, especially because parts, if not all, of the article had been reviewed by the New York office prior to publication. Bates had known about the article and let stand many inaccuracies regarding the inflation of his position and his efforts.

Hoover did not sit still. He shot off a long letter to Bates on August 31. He curtly informed his old friend that the article had "46 absolute untruths and 36 half-truths of a character which is entirely misleading." He went into detail on explaining his thoughts about a few of those errors. He saved his strongest statements for the element of publicity. The CRB, he declared, "has not been founded to advertise its Chairman, Members, or employees." Any such articles that simply promote CRB individuals would give readers the misconception that the CRB was merely an "advertising bureau" for its members. He stated in blunt fashion that all CRB publicity had to be truthful and helpful to the Belgian people; all else was "below the dignity and purpose of this whole effort."

In an official letter he sent to Bates on August 31, Hoover dealt more with what was needed than his own anger. What Hoover wanted was more charitable donations from America, which would not only bring money but show critical public interest in the cause. Unofficially, he also wanted to somehow remove Bates or decrease his power. He saw one way of possibly achieving both goals and brought it up in his letter. "Our experience of actual results in soliciting benevolence proves that beyond all question of doubt the only real fruitful method of securing what we want is through strong decentralized committee organization. The thing which produces money and material is the personal interest and solicitation of people of standing in each community."

Using an example that fit perfectly and gave a not-so-subtle knock at America's efforts so far, Hoover wrote, "Practically our most successful field to date has been the Australian Colonies where we have issued but one [press] document and that was originally an appeal from the London office. The whole of the work has been done by closely knit and able local committees and has produced so far practically as much money out of the five millions of people as has been produced out of the whole ninety million in the United States." Such hands-on community involvement, Hoover contended, could show great results "without any daily newspaper dope."

He offered up his own idea for America's reorganizing the relief efforts. Back in the founding days of relief, Hoover had sent out appeals to every governor to set up a committee to support donations. The new idea was to go back and set up local committees to work with the state groups so that the relief was felt all the way down to the most personal level. Hoover would also "set up the chairmen of all state committees and have them co-operate with us in forming a national body in support of this Commission . . . to elect from their members an executive body; that the Commission for Relief in Belgium should undertake to pay the whole of the out-of-pocket expenses of the central organization . . . its sole function to be to collect money and material and hand them on to us."

This would effectively take New York out of its number-one power position and shift much of the power into the hands of the executive body of state committees.

Hoover also recommended that Bates stop all weekly newssheets for the press and focus on providing good information to the local committees.

Not content with just words, Hoover told Bates that he was sending over to New York John Beaver White—one of the founders of the CRB—to take up "the whole question of publicity and organization of the charitable side in America, as he knows our experience here and can keep before you our actual psychological changes in tenor at this end." Hoover had hopes that White could somehow check the errant Bates.

Lastly, he thought to fight fire with fire. Hoover sent his Bates letter to a journalist friend, William C. Edgar, the editor of the respected millers' weekly trade magazine, *The Northwestern Miller*. Early on, the millers as a group had collected a shipload of flour, beans, peas, oatmeal, and barley for Belgium relief, and Edgar had followed the shipment all the way into Belgium. His report on what he had seen had praised the CRB and the work being done. Edgar was also the editor of the Minneapolis-based literary magazine called *The Bellman*. When Hoover sent Bates's letter to Edgar, he did not ask that anything be written in his defense, but the hope was certainly there.

Edgar did not fail. His response to Hoover's letter was quick and cutting. In the September 25 issue of *The Bellman*, he wrote the article "Small Work by Small Men," which denounced the *Saturday Evening Post* article, pointing out its errors and exaggerations.

Hoover had to have felt somewhat vindicated by Edgar's article, and he hoped that his own strong words to Bates would set things right.

To Bates, these efforts only meant a greater sense of mistrust and a suspicion that Hoover wanted him gone.

All-out war between the two was little more than a month away, and it would even get President Wilson involved.

24

Elsewhere in Belgium

A New Delegate Comes to Hainaut Province

In late August/early September 1915, William Hallam Tuck joined the CRB. Like some of the other delegates before him, he had had plans to take a more active role in the war than as a delegate for the CRB. After graduation from Princeton in 1912, Tuck worked as a chemical engineer. When the war broke out, he followed the news closely and finally made the decision in the summer of 1915 to become personally involved. He booked passage on a steamship bound for Britain with the sole intent of joining the British Army.

The SS *St. Louis* sailed from New York in early August with a scheduled arrival in Liverpool of August 15, 1915. Tuck had a compartment in first class, and he found among his fellow passengers three men who would change his life forever. Laurence "Duke" Wellington, who had turned 25 just before sailing, had been one of the first 10 Oxford students who had entered Belgium in December 1914. He had been with the CRB until May 1915, when he had left to return to America. Wanting to return to a job he felt was of critical importance, Wellington not only rejoined, but he had also convinced a friend, Francis Wickes, to sail with him on the *St. Louis* and become a CRB delegate. Also onboard was William Poland, a 47-year-old civil engineer known for managing international railroads. He was also a newly recruited CRB delegate who would ultimately play a major role in the CRB as director of the Brussels office and director of the London office.

During the Atlantic crossing, Tuck interacted with these three men on a daily basis and was quickly fascinated by Wellington's Belgian stories and with the CRB's ability to attract professionals such as Poland. He was told to seek out Herbert Hoover when he was in London to learn more about the humanitarian relief.

Intrigued, Tuck did so and was told by Hoover not to enlist but rather to join in the fight to feed Belgium and northern France. Hoover, as usual, was convincing, and the young man signed up immediately.

On the other side of the coin, Tuck obviously impressed Hoover and all the others he met with his serious demeanor, superior command of French, and his seeming ability to be not only diplomatic but also firm in upholding any principles he believed in. It was as if he was tailor-made for Hoover's demand that delegates remain true to the tenet that absolute neutrality in act and thought must be maintained at all times.

The initial opinion of Tuck in London quickly spread across the CRB rumor network in Belgium. The word was that he would make an outstanding delegate. E. E. Hunt, as chief delegate of Antwerp Province, wanted him and expressed it through a jovial, collegial comment he later wrote to the dean of Tuck's alma mater, Princeton: "Tuck had just arrived a short time before I left. Everyone was so very much impressed with his maturity and his familiarity with the French language. . . . He was 'rushed' by about every province in Belgium. It was really amusing to see how we fell over each other in our frantic attempts to get Tuck, and how like a freshman being rushed for a college fraternity he proved to be."

This, though, was no freshman. Tuck was a 25-year-old with the poise and presence of a much older man. In his official CRB portrait, he stood ramrod straight, arms crossed, mouth firmly set, and level glaze directed at what could easily be imagined to be a distant point of conflict that must be resolved. His starched white collar is high and stiff, his clean-shaven jaw is strong, and every hair of his light brown hair lies neatly tight to his head—a man totally buttoned down, sure of himself, and ready for whatever might come his way.

Belying Tuck's serious personality (or maybe confirming it) was the nickname some CRBers later gave him—Friar Tuck, after the jolly, rotund parish priest of Robin Hood fame.

When Tuck first arrived in Belgium, though, he was all business and was initially posted to Namur Province as a delegate. Probably reflecting not only his ability but also the administrative difficulties with finding and retaining good delegates, Tuck was promoted within a month to chief delegate. Then, a few weeks later, he was transferred to the large and important Hainaut Province, where his territory would include a piece of northern France.

He spent a few weeks being trained by the more experienced Joe Green, who was director of the CRB's Inspection and Control Department and had come down from Brussels to temporarily run the province until someone could be found to replace Robinson Smith. Once Green left, Tuck became the chief delegate and would remain there for most of his CRB work.

Tuck quickly settled into his job in the Walloon province of Hainaut. He lived in the city of Mons. With approximately 30,000 residents, Mons was the capital of the province and the center of the chief coal-mining district in Belgium. According to a prewar Baedeker's tour book, the residents were known as *borains* (coal-borers) and more than three-quarters of the 125,000 coal-miners in Belgium lived in Hainaut Province.

Like other CRB delegates, William Hallam Tuck, 25, changed his plans and joined the CRB after meeting Hoover. (Public domain; author's archives.)

The city of Mons had begun as a hilltop fortress built by Caesar during his campaigns with the Gauls. Over the centuries the town spread out over the hill, and later fortifications were converted to a "pleasant promenade." The late-Gothic Cathedral of St. Waltrudis was built from 1450 to 1589 while the *hôtel de ville* was constructed in 1458–1467 but never completely finished. As with most other Belgian cities, municipal life revolved around the medieval *grand place.*

Tuck secured lodgings with a Belgian lawyer (probably Georges Heupgen), whom he described as "a delightful man. He had two sons at the front. He understood our work and appreciated it—above all he had the same keen admiration—almost reverence—for Mr. Hoover that we in the Commission for Relief in Belgium all have. He helped us in our work and smoothed over difficulties that we were tackling the wrong way, which only a Belgian could have done."

Working with another delegate, Charles Carstairs, Tuck faced all the challenges and duties that most of the delegates in the provinces confronted, although his territory was one of the largest, with 1,340,000 inhabitants.

Early most mornings, on the way to the CRB office, he or Carstairs would stop by the local canal dock office, where they were told which barges were being unloaded that day, how much of what had been shipped by rail, and when future shipments were expected. A continuing stream of telegrams would announce the progress of all barges from Rotterdam, and a large canal map on a wall had pins with flags so they could visually track every barge. One of the two delegates had to sign all bills of lading and other shipping documents.

At the CRB office they would usually find a stack of mail that they'd deal with using their Belgian secretary and stenographer. As Tuck quickly found out, his office was not like a typical business office back home. He noted that it "resembles a consulate. English citizens apply to [the CRB delegate] for information concerning departure of special trains of English subjects to Holland—aged inventors submit extraordinary designs of new and lightest of aeroplane motors, with the request that the American Representative smuggles them to France or England for the Allies! People arrive with the request that they may be allowed an extra bread ration for one reason or another, and lightermen who have come all the way from Rotterdam to Mons come to complain, in loud Dutch, against treatment accorded them by the Regional Store House Employees, who have refused them their bread rations. One of these men was very much worried because he had been told by one of our employees that he and all his tribe of inland watermen were a cross between pirates and gypsies and had the vices of both classes!"

Tuck and Carstairs also had to attend numerous meetings.

The weekly provincial committee meeting was attended by all the critical players in the relief, and it was where Tuck felt he was the "youngster of 25." He sat opposite the president of the provincial committee, whom he described as "a splendid lawyer and statesman of the Hainaut—of the Henry Clay type—quick and full of wit and a splendid speaker." Beside the president was the German governor of the province, whom Tuck recorded was "one of those who had shown tact and been willing to take counsel from the Belgians in his work of administrating their province." As for the rest, Tuck wrote that "as you look around the table you see men of very different walks of life. Members of the Catholic, the Liberal and the Socialist Party—German, French and Belgian all untied to discuss the one topic—how best to feed the people."

Twice a month Tuck would preside over a meeting of 40 Belgians from around the province. These men reported on what was happening out in the field, where the relief actually took place. They told him of how well the provincial committee's instructions were being followed, if there had been any illegal requisitions by German troops, and about the general well-being of the local citizens. Tuck would inform the group of any executive decisions that had been made at the national and provincial levels. Overall, the American found this meeting particularly interesting and instructive because the attendees were men "at the pulse of the whole work," and through them "the meaning of the work and its importance to the people is brought thoroughly home."

Chief delegate duties also included extensive traveling around the province and any pieces of northern France that had been assigned. Every Tuesday Tuck and/or Carstairs would motor in their Overland cars around their territory, visiting the regional depots, some of the nearly 500 communes in their jurisdiction, and the mills that ground CRB wheat.

The milling of wheat into flour for bread was critical to the entire relief program. As Tuck explained, "It is my duty to see that this [CRB] wheat is ground at the best mills, where the work is well and cheaply done—that no favoritism is shown in allotting this work to the few mills which still grind, and that the flour that is sent out from these mills goes directly to the Belgian Civil Population and to no one else."

The level of detail was at times surprising. If there were complaints about the quality of bread from the general population, "extra samples of flour are taken to be tested for milling and per cent humidity. This work is generally done at Mons by a very well organized Chemical Department who receive samples of wheat, flour and bread regularly from all Mills and certain Bakers." The department would post daily results of tests on flour and wheat so that "we are able to tell whether the yield which we insist that the Bakers shall obtain can be reasonably demanded of them, for this very naturally depends on the humidity of the flour furnished them by the Mills." The chemical engineer in Tuck must have been happy to know such testing was an important part of the job.

At the end of each month, Tuck and each of the other chief delegates had to prepare a territory-wide report showing the exact amount of flour and other foodstuffs on hand in their regional depots. These provincial reports were forwarded to the Brussels CRB office for use in its reporting to Rotterdam to determine future shipments.

A definite bright spot in all the paperwork and meetings was a weekly trip to Brussels. Every Thursday delegates in the provinces were invited to come to Brussels to attend the weekly Comité National meeting, share a lunch with all the other delegates at the CRB office, and then attend a 2:00 p.m. general meeting of delegates.

While the CN meeting with the domineering Francqui was not high on any delegate's list of enjoyable activities, the CRB lunch, filled with youthful jesting and camaraderie, and the more serious delegate meeting definitely were. And if Hoover was in town, the delegates' meeting would be a packed house, with few if any absentees. That was because, according to Tuck, "we hear news of ships chartered, ships sunk, grain purchased—we get firsthand knowledge of the attitude of the British and French and German Governments and if [Hoover] makes a trip to the [German] General Head Quarters in France we know that something is in the wind."

Tuck believed that "the work of the CRB is continually in peril of being stopped. We have one and only one defender—that is Mr. Hoover. . . . In one month he may see members of the French Staff, the British Cabinet, members of the Belgian Government at the Havre, the German Government of Occupation in Brussels and the German Authorities in Berlin. If there ever was a Civilian who played such a part, and among warriors, he has yet to be found."

While Tuck's assessment of Hoover was accurate, it neglected to mention another critical component to the relief—the CRB delegates themselves. It was men such as Tuck who, through their hard work and strict adherence to neutrality, made the fragile system work.

But a little more than a year after Tuck joined the CRB, he would come face-to-face with human misery that would test all of his commitments to himself and to neutrality.

25

Antwerp and Environs

More Than Food Is Needed

As late summer turned to autumn 1915, as the war dragged on, and as the food issues were dealt with by the CRB and CN, the Americans in Belgium came to realize that food was not the only critical item needed for survival. It was becoming obvious that clothes and shoes were wearing thin and retail shops across the country had either run out of stock or were about to.

E. E. Hunt, the chief delegate for Antwerp, described what he saw. "The lack of proper clothing . . . was pitiable. For three months some of the children of Willebroek [lying nearly equidistant between Antwerp and Brussels] had stayed away from school, literally because they had no clothing to go in. In every household the brightest child was selected to wear what clothes were available. Little boys appeared in their sisters' dresses and little girls in boys' clothes. This situation was commonplace."

The problem had been building since the start of the war. Hunt explained, "Appeals for clothes came to Antwerp from all parts of the province. The war had come at harvest time [August 1914], when clothes are a secondary consideration, and people had never had an opportunity to provide themselves for the winter." The following year of German occupation had only seen the clothing situation get worse.

The Belgians had attempted to address the issue since the war began. Nearly every village, town, and city had already created places called *comptoirs* (literally "counters"), where those who had registered could come in, get material and instructions on what garments to make, work on them at home, then bring back the finished pieces and be paid a small amount for the work. The clothes would go to the destitute, whose numbers were growing every day and would reach approximately 3 million in Belgium (and 1 million in northern France) by the following year.

In Antwerp a group of citizens had come together in late 1914/early 1915 to form a committee under the leadership of three prominent women, Madame Alphonse

As the war continued, more than food was needed. The Belgians developed a huge system of clothing operations, including a major central clothing station in Antwerp. (Public domain; *War Bread,* E. E. Hunt, Holt & Co., 1916.)

de Montigny de Wael, Madame Robert Osterrieth-Lippens, and Countess van de Werve de Vorsselaere. The committee had purchased all the thread, fabric, and clothing it could still find in the city. It then secured the use of the *Folies Bergère* Theater, where a variety of singing and dancing acts had performed before the war. In this musical and theatrical hall, the group established not only a *comptoir,* where more than 3,000 women picked up material for work at home, they also began an *ouvroir* (work, or sewing, room) that employed 900 people to make and mend clothes.

Hunt, as Antwerp's CRB chief delegate, quickly become aware of these efforts and designated the theatrical hall a Commission station so that all American donations of clothes that arrived in Antwerp were automatically sent directly to the workshop.

The city had also recognized the efforts of these women by providing a monthly subsidy of 50,000 francs to the group. That was followed by recognition by the Comité National, which ultimately took charge of the organization's finances.

As the workshop grew, it expanded out of its original building and was moved to the *Société Royale d'Harmonie*'s majestic symphony hall, which sat on Rue d'Arenberg in a fashionable part of town near the zoological gardens, the *Theatre Royale,* and the offices of Edouard Bunge.

As Hunt described the refashioned hall, the stage was "piled with boxes of goods. Galleries and pit were spread with rows of sewing machines and work tables, and the cloak room was transformed into a steam and sulphur disinfecting bath, where all materials, new and old, were taken apart and thoroughly cleansed."

Much of the work was done by women—a lot of women. According to Hunt, "nine hundred girls and young women worked under supervision in the warm and well-lighted hall, while three thousand older women were given sewing to do at home [through the *comptoir*]. A group of cobblers in the hall made and repaired shoes."

All these people were paid for their services. The women were paid 3 francs a *day*, which was the equivalent of 60 U.S. cents (the average American factory worker made $2 a day). Even this sum helped the women in their individual lives as well as ultimately helped the faltering economy. Additionally, each Monday the women were allowed to work on their own garments, and on Tuesday the poor of the city could bring in anything they wanted to be darned, mended, or patched for free.

Those who worked in the hall also received educational and entertainment bonuses. Numerous classes were offered in various aspects of the work, from sewing and cutting material to repairing garments. Periodic lectures covered such topics as "personal hygiene, domestic economy and efficiency" and "the literature and the history of [Belgium]." Additionally, once a week a singing teacher came in and taught the women Belgian folk songs as they worked. With the Germans rarely stepping inside the grand music hall, they missed the opportunity to arrest hundreds of women as they sang such banned patriotic songs as "Lion of Flanders" and the national anthem, "La Brabançonne." On occasion, even the huge pipe organ, which lay hidden among mountains of boxes, would accompany them.

The result of all the hard work was finished garments that were shipped to all around the province. The clothes were sold to local communes, which sold them to those who could pay or, more and more frequently, gave them to those who could not. In addition, the Antwerp clothing workshop sent some raw materials to groups of seamstresses living in the province's villages and towns so they could make and sell whatever they produced.

The system of *comptoirs* and *ouvroirs* was brilliant in its simplicity—provide labor to the unemployed by creating garments that were needed by those who could pay and those who were destitute—but there was a critical ingredient missing, native raw material. With Belgium cut off from the rest of the world, existing stocks were nearly exhausted by the autumn of 1915.

While most if not all of the initial clothing efforts had been locally begun, each of the communes realized as the war dragged on and native stocks ran out that it would take a national effort to secure new stocks from outside Belgium. Over time, all the local efforts ultimately fell under the control of the one centralized group operating in Belgium that might have the power to do something about the clothing situation—the Comité National de Secours (charity) et d'Alimentation (provisioning). A clothing department, the Division du Vêtements, within the Secours portion of the CN was established with headquarters in Brussels. Besides handling the importation and distribution of any clothes and clothing material, the Division du Vêtements's job was to administratively and financially support and standardize the countrywide manufacture and distribution of clothes, primarily to the destitute.

In late 1915, with available local stocks rapidly diminishing, the CN asked the CRB to begin importing raw materials for clothes.

The CRB had run a clothing donation campaign in the winter of 1914/1915 that had brought in a tremendous amount of clothes, but there was no effort to import a constant or steady flow of clothing and raw materials into Belgium. Any clothing donations were passed through into Belgium with little thought as to what was needed or usable. The CRB didn't even have an official clothing department.

With the CN's request for a steady supply of clothing material, that would all change and add a whole new dimension to relief in the spring of 1916.

Antwerp Says Goodbye to a Special Delegate

Hugging the Scheldt River like a newborn to its mother, Antwerp's medieval Old Town was a picturesque maze of narrow cobblestone streets, crooked alleys, and open squares accentuated by buildings with magnificent facades, ornate gables, and graceful spires. A reminder of the ancient past remained in the more than 300 Madonnas that graced numerous street corners. Placed high above the heads of many who never glanced up, these statues of the Virgin Mary had held candles and lighted the way for nighttime pedestrians hundreds of years before.

The heart of Old Town was the large market square, the *grand place* (later known as *Grote Markt*). Ornate sixteenth- and seventeenth-century guild halls, owned by the associations of the major industries and professions that had built the city, stood proudly on two sides. The square's centerpiece was a fountain that depicted the legendary Silvius Brabo, who brandished the severed hand of a giant. Legend had it that the name Antwerp had come from "handwerpen," meaning "to throw a hand," which Brabo had done after cutting off the hand of the giant because he would not let him pass.

Dominating the square and its guild halls was the 1561 *hôtel de ville* (city hall), with its Renaissance style and center section rising an impressive 184 feet high. The main staircase was adorned with colored Belgian marble and rose up two stories to a galleria of large murals interspersed with polished marble columns. At the top of the stairs, two medieval boys in bronze were on a knee, one on either side, each holding up a large candelabra. Above it all was a delicate glass ceiling symbolically supported by carved wooden female figures that represented different branches of industry.

Within the *hôtel de ville* was *La Salle des Mariages* (The Marriage Hall), which was embellished with a massive sixteenth-century fireplace; a richly dark, wood-beamed ceiling; six massive chandeliers; and five frescoes that represented marriage scenes.

On Saturday, October 16, 1915, Edward Eyre Hunt walked through Antwerp's Old Town and up the stairs of the *hôtel de ville* to *La Salle des Mariages*. He was there to accept the farewell gratitude of an impressive array of people. Those in the room included the burgomaster Jan de Vos, along with the aldermen and members of Antwerp's city council. No doubt also in attendance were provincial committeemen such as J. G. Delannoy and Edouard Bunge, who had become good friends to Hunt, as well as the three Bunge sisters—Erica, Eva, and Hilda—and any of Hunt's fellow delegates who were free that day.

Burgomaster Jan de Vos spoke first, telling the assembled group how much the Belgian people, and especially the citizens of Antwerp, appreciated all that had been done by Hunt and the CRB. "Mr. Hunt has," he stated, "by his devotion at all times, carried out his beautiful humane task in an exemplary manner."

Hunt was presented with a gold medal of honor with a figure of King Albert. On the medal was inscribed, "The City of Antwerp to Mr. Edward Eyre Hunt, 16th October, 1915."

Then the city's municipal secretary stood up and read a proclamation that had been printed on Antwerp's famous Plantin's Press by master printers. "Today, October 16th, 1915, the City Council of Antwerp has assembled with the Burgomaster and Aldermen, to say farewell to Mr. Edward Eyre Hunt on the occasion of his departure from this City, and to thank him for the devotion and the skill shown by him in carrying out his mission as Delegate of the Commission for Relief in Belgium to the National Relief Committee in the province of Antwerp. The gathering thereby requested Mr. Hunt to express to his chiefs, and especially to his fellow-citizens in the United States, the deeply moved feelings of gratitude which Belgium, sorely tried, but so wonderfully upheld, feels for her kind and noble friends across the sea."

Because the secretary had read the proclamation in Flemish, he then told the group he would read it again in English so that Hunt could understand it.

Hunt interrupted him in Flemish and said that he had understood. He told the group that during the 10 months he had lived in Antwerp he had felt bound to learn the language of the people he was trying to serve.

After more speeches, Hunt rose in reply. As the newspaper account of the event related, he was "much moved, and thanked them for their praise, and assured them that he would long hold in warm remembrance his stay in Antwerp."

The article ended with a simple statement: "A noble American citizen here gave a fine example to many Belgians."

Hunt must have been torn in his decision to leave Belgium. No record of his thoughts has been found, but there were many factors that undoubtedly contributed to his decision.

It had to have affected him strongly that only a few months before, at the end of July, the CRB and CN had agreed to a different kind of CRB delegate. Hunt had been the epitome of an active, decision-making delegate who had forged a good working provincial office. But delegates were now supposed to advise, consult, and only take action with the guidance and approval of the CRB Brussels head office and the Belgian provincial committees. This would definitely have rubbed Hunt the wrong way.

And with such a delegate change, it was obvious there had been a shift in how many delegates worked in his province. During most of the time Hunt was the chief delegate of Antwerp Province he reported that the usual number of delegates helping him was four to fulfill the needs of supervising relief to 1 million provincial residents. But by the time he left on October 16, there was only his replacement, J. B. Van Schaick (who had been caught up in spy charges and would stay only until December), and a new delegate, Griffin Barry. All the other Antwerp delegates had left the CRB or moved to other positions and had not been replaced by the Brussels office.

Times had changed, and Hunt probably felt it was time for him to do the same. But he had one more place to visit before he left Belgium for good.

He drove out to Chateau Oude Gracht to say his farewells to his friend Edouard Bunge, who had done so much to help him in his job, including giving him office space in his bank building and loaning him and the other delegates his Antwerp townhouse.

Hunt also came to say goodbye to the three Bunge sisters—Erica, Eva, and Hilda. Erica had been the most interested in him romantically, but nothing had ever happened. In the spring, Erica had written in her diary numerous times of interactions or failed interactions between them or between him and her sisters, which Erica resented. She had written about him in her diary when he had helped her pick out a new dog and on numerous other occasions. She had described him as being very nice, but also "very sentimental, and so depressed!"

When he came out to say his final farewell, Erica knew he was not happy. She wrote simply in her diary, "Hunt left for the USA on Sunday, October 17. Quite upset and miserable. Best to have a thorough change."

He left a present that she recorded in her diary. It was a poem he had written (although the first four words of the first line were from British romantic poet William Wordsworth).

My heart leaps up like light
 Across the stormy sea
And the black wreck of night
 Seems golden now to me.
And the black waves like fire
 That laugh with lips of foam
Calling like my desire
 Back to your hearts______
 My home
 EEH

And so, E. E. Hunt—a sensitive, selfless man who had volunteered to take on a job no one could describe and had become an extraordinary CRB delegate in the bargain—ended his time in the country he had come to love and returned to America. He would write of his life in Belgium in the excellent book *War Bread: A Personal Narrative of the War and Relief in Belgium*, published in America in 1916. He would also continue to help the CRB from the New York office, assisting the PR department in many ways and interviewing many of the men who wanted to join the CRB.

He had made an indelible mark on the CRB and on Belgium.

Erica Bunge and the Dairy Farm

While Erica was saddened to see Hunt go, she had much to take her mind off such matters of the heart. The dairy farm was a huge undertaking that absorbed much of her time.

Besides overseeing the construction of the new buildings and the revamping of the three existing structures for the dairy's use, Erica and estate supervisor Verheyen had to contend with managing a full complement of workers. They included 12 milkers, each milking 10 to 12 cows a day; two managers who strictly controlled the hygienic cleaning and filling of the milk canisters and the maintenance of the cooling equipment; four transporters; two night guards; and one laundress. Their wages ranged from three francs up to more than four francs a day, which were all paid by Edouard Bunge and Georges Born.

Every detail mattered. When there was no straw available for bedding, it was decided to collect pine needles and fallen leaves from around the estate and use those for the stalls.

As promised, the fodder for the herd was provided mostly by the Antwerp committee, with the Bunges' other two farms contributing whatever they could spare. Additionally, the cows grazed on the pastures of Hoogboom estate. Even so, feeding such a herd was a continual and consistent concern and would impact the daily milk production.

The Bunge dairy farm was operated by Erica and the farm manager Verheyen. It provided daily milk for the children of Antwerp. (Public domain; Raymond Roelands, *Geschiedenis van Kasteeldomein "Oude Gracht" in Hoogboom,* Archief Hobonia, Kallellen, Belgium.)

Before the war, a good dairy cow was one that produced between 21 and 30 liters of milk a day. If after the birth of a calf, milk production dropped to less than eight liters a day, the cow was sold.

Erica knew that during the occupation pre-war milk-production standards could not be matched. She was proud that within a few months of startup, the dairy was producing 2,530 liters a day, or roughly 19 liters per cow per day.

Once the milk was collected and sealed in clean canisters, it had to be moved as quickly as possible to Antwerp. Four men were in charge of getting the canisters loaded onto horse- or oxen-drawn wagons that pulled them to the nearby tramline stop. There, the milk was secured in a locked baggage car for its 45-minute trip into Antwerp. In the city, the canisters were turned over to the Antwerp committee and distributed via carts to children's canteens around the city.

Erica and Verheyen continually strived to get more liters of milk from the cows. When they succeeded in doing so in 1916, however, they would face another problem—a lack of canisters.

26

London

The Bates Issue Can No Longer Be Ignored

On September 15, 1915, the *New York Times* ran the story that Lindon Bates had announced to the press he would be building a 115-foot tower that would be a reproduction of Pompey's Pillar in Egypt as a memorial to his dead son. It would crown the top of a mountain in upstate New York and be surrounded by searchlights so it would be visible, day or night, for miles around. (It was never built.)

This was the kind of personal publicity that Hoover abhorred and indicated to others in the CRB that Bates was no longer of totally sound mind. To add to this perception, the New York office continued to send out press sheets and generate publicity that Hoover considered wasteful, if not hurtful to the relief program.

Many of Hoover's friends and closest advisers were counseling that Bates had to go. He was hurting the CRB on multiple fronts. Edgar Rickard wondered to John Beaver White in a cable that the loss of Bates junior on the *Lusitania* might be affecting the father's judgment and leading him to his "belligerent defiance." He even went so far as to say that the New York office's publicity sheets were causing "serious trouble" inside Belgium and was even threatening the very existence of the organization. He gave no evidence of that, but it fed the fire that was building against Bates.

With continuing problems arising from Bates and the New York office, Hoover, in a fit of frustration, cabled an outright command on September 22: "For political reasons do not wish one more word publicly or public appeals to emanate from your office. Applies here as well and includes your news sheet."

On October 1, Hoover received a reply. Bates would comply, but only "temporarily." Acting like Hoover's equal, Bates added that he expected reciprocal respect—Hoover should not release anything regarding American issues from his office without consulting Bates first.

It was time for Hoover to take the situation in hand. He could not afford to lose control of the New York office and, by extension, the support of the American government and American public. He reluctantly followed the prompting of numerous advisers, including Ambassador Page and friend Melville E. Stone, the general manager of the Associated Press, and booked passage on the *St. Paul* from Liverpool for October 16, 1915. He would confront his old friend and see if anything could be salvaged from their relationship. Hoover knew, however, that whatever happened to him and his relationship with Bates, the CRB had to continue at all costs.

Only three days before he was to sail, Hoover felt the need to once again set down on paper his thoughts about publicity. Maybe it was with the thought of traversing the dangerous seas (heightened since the sinking of the *Lusitania*), or more likely it was simply as a way to clarify his own position and clear his brain for the business to come. Either way, it was a seven-page document that detailed his thoughts on publicity and laid out numerous policies.

To Hoover, the appearance of anything like self-aggrandizement of individuals or even the organization itself "gives a Barnum & Bailey aspect to this work which is undignified, and is beneath the ideals which have dominated the whole work." Individuality was not acceptable because, he said, "There is no man, including myself, who cannot be replaced in this work—or it would be the sign of bad organization." He reminded all those readers of the document that the CRB was an institution that would someday have a "small corner in history." For those who worked in the CRB, they must be satisfied that "it will be sufficient reward for any man's labor that he was associated with it and to be known as one whose self-sacrificing voluntary efforts helped to make it."

He then laid down the law. "For the future there is to be no publicity of any kind from the Commission for Relief in Belgium, except that which I have personally edited with due consideration of its political and human bearing."

He went on to explain why that was. "As I have the responsibility of maintaining the position and character of this working organization with the various belligerent governments I have simply got to control the statements for which I necessarily have the responsibility, and I cannot permit such statements unless I have personally canvassed them myself."

He concluded with a not-so-veiled toe-the-line-or-leave statement for those who thought otherwise. "If anyone in the Commission believes this is an attempt to stifle individuality, my only wish is that he should seek for fields where his publicity necessities can be exploited without reflecting on this work or jeopardizing the lives of millions of people."

A day before Hoover sailed for New York, he cabled Bates again. This time he stated that the CRB's patron ambassadors had ordered him to stop all publicity until Hoover had had a chance to reorganize all publicity coming from the CRB. Hoover's hope was that referencing higher authorities than himself might have the desired effect of curtailing Bates's publicity efforts.

Hoover would have, no doubt, neglected to mention to Bates that on the same day, Friday, October 15, British cabinet official Lord Curzon had stood up at a meeting of the CRB's British committee and given a speech heralding Hoover's great organization as "one of the most striking achievements which we can find anywhere on record. This is the first time in history that a whole people has been fed by a private organization."

The Chief would still be on the open sea on October 22, which was the anniversary of the first full year of CRB operations. In any other situation, it would have been a time of celebration, for it was probably a surprise to practically everyone that the Commission still existed, let alone had achieved all that it had in its first year.

The First Year's Summary

After the official organization of the CRB in London on October 22, 1914, Hoover had asked Francqui for an estimate of what was needed to save the country from starving. Francqui had cabled back from Brussels on October 26, 1914, that the monthly needs would be a minimum of 60,000 tons of wheat (for bread), 15,000 tons of maize, and 3,000 tons of rice and dried peas—nearly 80,000 tons total. A formable amount in peacetime; an incredible amount during a world war.

In the first year of operations, Hoover had stimulated the formation of an international network of charity support groups, created a buying and shipping organization to provide a steady stream of ships to Rotterdam and a fleet of canal barges to transport the food into Belgium and northern France, and developed a corps of volunteers to enter Belgium and northern France to supervise the relief until it reached the hands of recipients.

Behind it all were impressive statistics. According to Kittredge's CRB history, from October 22, 1914, to October 31, 1915, a total 988,852 tons of foodstuffs had arrived in Rotterdam from 186 full cargoes, averaging 4,637 tons each, and 308 partial cargos, averaging 209 tons each. After the startup first months, Rotterdam had witnessed an average of four full cargos arriving every week. The total expenditures of the CRB in the first year were a staggering £17,257,591 (nearly $2 billion in today's dollars), which included the cost of cargos on route to Rotterdam on October 31.

To achieve such success, the Commission's overhead had been only about three-quarters of 1 percent of expenditures. In a time when most companies had overhead that ran from 2.5 to 5 percent, this was an unheard-of small operating expense. "This low overhead charge was made possible," Kittredge stated, "by the volunteer direction of the Commission and by the great amount of volunteer assistance which it received in carrying out its work."

Underpinning all the efforts were the governmental subsidizes and charity that kept the relief alive. From the exiled Belgium government the CRB had received more than £14.5 million. Additionally, charitable giving from around the world had brought in food to the value of £1,270,416, and cash donations of more than £1,500,000.

As for the food getting from Rotterdam into Belgium and northern France, from the 988,852 tons of food delivered to Rotterdam in the first year, 906,875 tons had been transported into the occupied territories and delivered to the individual provinces in already-agreed-upon proportions and percentages.

Altogether, Hoover had somehow created in only a year what others might have called a nation of relief that boasted its own flag, a fleet of ships, international agreements, and a civil administration. One British official termed the CRB a "piratical state organized for benevolence." And the head of that state, Hoover, was probably the only man in the world who could travel freely across all warring lines from Berlin to London, Brussels to Paris.

Equaling Hoover's and the CRB's impressive efforts was the work of Francqui, the CN, and the CF (feeding northern France). They had forged a huge organization of provincial committees and developed systems of pricing, rationing, food preparation, and distribution that included approximately 40,000 workers—many volunteers—who fed nearly 10 million people every day in Belgium (more than 7 million) and northern France (more than two million).

The entire system, in and out of German-held territory, was set up with a profit margin built in to pay for those who could not pay their own way. As Kittredge stated, the prices for those who could pay "included also a margin of from 10 to 50 per cent profit, which the Comité National was allowed to take, in the sale of commodities to the comparatively well-to-do, to support its benevolent department."

But what did all those figures really mean? It meant that an entire nation did not descend into starvation, chaos, and death, and that those closest to the front lines in northern France knew they were not forgotten by the rest of the world.

It did not mean that conditions in Belgium and northern France were normal. Most people were receiving only the minimum amount of food necessary for staying alive. As delegate Robinson Smith suggested somewhat sarcastically, Americans who wanted to see what it felt like to be a Belgian needed only to skip dinner. "That will make him feel exactly as millions of Belgians are feeling at the present hour. They have each day something to eat, but it is not enough. They have their litre of soup and their half-pound of bread and some potatoes and rice, but when five o'clock comes, they are hungry; some of them very hungry."

Smith followed that up immediately by stating that skipping one dinner did not properly convey what Belgians were truly feeling. "It is only when you have come to know this people, that you can realize the terror of their plight. When you picture Belgium, think not only of the black lines before the soup-kitchens, of the black groups of men without work in the squares by day, of the villages pitch-black by night; think too of the tens of thousands of the once well-to-do, who now have lost or are losing all that they have hitherto enjoyed. Surely and with almost mathematical progress poverty is penetrating into every home of the land, and all that class who in America form the suburbs can now count the months that their little capital will hold out."

In the end, Smith said, "Belgium is like a man running from a mad bull, the mad bull of hunger; thanks to people with souls all over the world, Belgium has a lead on that mad bull—she has supplies for three weeks ahead—but she is still running for dear life."

The personal understanding of that, from seeing the situation firsthand, was what kept most of the CRB men working as the Commission moved into its second year.

And it's what drove Hoover relentlessly, even as he took the time to sail across the Atlantic to face the trivial—yet disruptive—actions of one man: Lindon Bates.

27

NYC and D.C.

Hoover Confronts His Old Friend Bates

On Sunday, October 24, 1915, the *St. Paul* docked at New York City. Waiting at Hoover's hotel was a cablegram from London. It was a strongly worded message from eight of his most trusted advisers who were also members of the CRB directorate.

They began by acknowledging the one-year anniversary of the CRB and their proud association with an organization that is "above all criticism in its integrity, efficiency and high purpose and realise that this is due to your unusual personality and unselfish devotion."

The cablegram quickly turned to the major problem at hand. "We have been grieved at the discordant attitude of the New York Office particularly because of repeated failure to carry out definite instructions coupled with the argumentative tone of cables, character of publicity and failure to accept your suggestions and urgent appeals on many questions of policy."

Stating that the entire operation depended upon being "co-ordinated, governed and presided over by one mind," the group then told Hoover what he already knew, "the refusal of the New York Office to accept this basis of organization imperils the entire work and the millions dependent upon it." They also reminded him that out of all branch offices of the CRB, only the New York office had failed to follow Hoover's leadership.

His friends and advisers urged him to put aside his loyalty to Bates for the sake of the CRB. In a surprisingly strong stand, the group stated firmly, "We cannot consent to a continued situation which threatens to disrupt the solidarity of our organization." To balance such a declaration, the group ended with this: "You will be gratified by the many messages of congratulations and published acknowledgements commemorating this anniversary day."

On a happier note, also waiting for Hoover was his wife, Lou, and their two boys. Lou had left England in late May, spoken at the Bates funeral in June, then gone on to California to meet up with the children. When she had heard Herbert was sailing for America, she brought them back East so they could see their father.

Hoover took his first day ashore—the Sabbath—to spend time with them and to talk over the entire situation with his most trusted adviser, Lou.

The next day, Hoover sat down in the New York office with Bates. They talked for a few hours and had lunch with John Beaver White and Alexander Hemphill, the office's treasurer and the chairman of the board of the Guaranty Trust Company. After lunch they returned to the office where Bates asked to see Hoover privately, without White. Hoover refused and the men proceeded into Bates's office. All thoughts of calming nerves, smoothing ruffled feathers, and finding solutions to the Hoover-Bates difficulties were quickly forgotten the moment Bates told the other men what he had done.

Charges of Treason Leveled against the Chief

When Bates had heard Hoover was coming to America, he was sure it was to try and remove him from office. So, without consulting anyone, he had secretly traveled to Washington, D.C., and visited the State Department, the Justice Department, and Senator Henry Cabot Lodge, who sat on the Committee of Foreign Affairs and was a fierce opponent of President Wilson. Bates brought with him a huge file on Hoover. It laid out accusations that Hoover was un-neutral and had committed treasonous acts by violating the Logan Act of 1793. He had listed specific incidents and situations, including Hoover's radical idea to create an "industrial section" of the CRB that would revitalize Belgian industry. Bates had done all this because he "felt that his duty as a patriotic American necessitated his intervention with the American government."

The Logan Act stated that any unauthorized American citizen who "directly or indirectly commences or carries on any correspondence or intercourse with any foreign government or any officer or agent thereof, with intent to influence the measures or conduct of any foreign government or of any officer or agent thereof, in relation to any disputes or controversies with the United States, or to defeat the measures of the United States, shall be fined under this title or imprisoned not more than three years, or both."

While a case might certainly be made that some of what Hoover had done to keep the relief flowing into Belgium applied to the Logan Act, this was not the time for a legal review of the facts.

Hoover was at first somewhat amused, but as he read much of the file in Bates's presence, he turned horrified, then angry. Hoover was particularly upset that Bates had quoted from their private correspondence and that he had not consulted with anyone before his trip to the capital. He was convinced that Bates was doing it for revenge against Hoover's moves to relegate him to a secondary position in the CRB, and for publicity—publicity that would destroy Hoover's image, tarnish the CRB, and elevate Bates in the public eye for rooting out such a scandal.

Hoover was sure Bates had lost his mind, noting, "Mr. Bates was so tense I immediately came to the conclusion that his mind was deranged." But Hoover was also profoundly rattled that he had been so mistaken about Bates and his loyalty.

More important, Hoover had to do something to stop whatever negative reactions were taking place in Washington from Bates's accusations. He spent the next couple of days consulting with numerous prominent men in the city, including presidential adviser Colonel House.

On the one hand, Hoover felt Bates was mentally unstable and had to be removed. On the other hand, he felt that if he did so immediately, Bates would automatically go to the newspapers with his accusations. He knew the newspapers would have a field day with Bates's file—nothing would be left of Hoover's reputation or the relief efforts he had worked so hard to maintain. He wanted to handle the situation with compassion for Bates, but with an eye toward saving the public image of both himself and the CRB.

On Thursday, October 28, Hoover took a train to Washington. He had requested a meeting with two senior officials at the State Department. One of the men greeted him "with a grin and asked if I were 'prepared to spend a thousand years in jail.'" The humor faded quickly when Hoover discovered the department was truly disturbed by Bates's accusations and that Secretary of State Robert Lansing had ordered on October 15 that Walter Page and Brand Whitlock, "its representatives acting as Honorary Chairmen of the Commission . . . shall withdraw immediately from the Commission if the industrial section is organized as reported."

The department was also concerned that the CRB was setting precedents that would later jeopardize America's campaign for neutral rights in wartime. Senator Lodge had joined in by telling the State Department that Hoover had clearly violated the Logan Act, saying that sending charity from American citizens was one thing, but distributing money supplied by belligerent governments was another.

Until Hoover visited the State Department, he had had no conception the charges would be taken seriously. He had dismissed the Logan Act accusations of treason "because our negotiations were not on behalf of the United States but on behalf of a private, neutral organization sponsored by neutral Ambassadors and Ministers. However, it seemed that Senator [Henry Cabot] Lodge, a violent critic of President Wilson and the State Department, was developing a sensational story."

But in Washington, people in power were taking Bates's file very seriously. The State Department requested that Hoover defend himself in writing. He responded with three separate letters of explanation. In them, he spoke of the "extraordinary esteem and privilege" that he and the other CRB personnel received from other countries. He flatly refused to accept the idea that the CRB had established any kind of precedents that would hurt America, saying the CRB was no different than the Red Cross and other humanitarian agencies. He declared that he and his associates were not guilty of a single "atom of moral turpitude."

He ended by holding up the CRB as one great bright spot in the war, a bright spot that counterbalanced the criticisms of America that it was only a nation of shopkeepers looking to make a profit on the war.

"Even in these days of fierce contentions and hatreds, which are at times directed even to our own countrymen, no criticism has been leveled at the Commission for Relief in Belgium. From the nature of things, our people are much engaged in commerce with some of the belligerents, and our country is subjected to much adverse criticism. But out of all this fishing for profit in this pool of blood, the one refutation that our people are without humanity and ideals is the Commission for Relief in Belgium and the other philanthropic efforts of the American people."

Hoover's words worked their magic. The State Department, according Hoover, determined that there was nothing to Bates's accusations and they had been made more for publicity than to elicit a government response.

Just as this was happening, however, Bates sent a new communication to the State Department, highlighting a letter and memorandum of Hoover's that was already in the accusations file. These items, Bates was sure, truly indicated Hoover had violated the Logan Act. According to Bates, the worst was that they showed Hoover had done an un-neutral act by preparing a memorandum at the request of a British cabinet "friend" regarding German attitudes and then had sent that to presidential adviser Colonel House.

Hoover's response was weak, as he told the State Department that he did not enjoy friendships with any British cabinet officials (yes, he did) and that the memorandum had been prepared for a neutral country's official (possibly true).

The State Department once again accepted Hoover's side of the story. But that didn't mean Hoover was out of the woods. He headed back to New York on Saturday night, October 30, sure that all he had left to do was deal with Bates and face any fallout from possible sensational publicity. The next day he met with his journalist friend Will Irwin and Mr. Cosgrave, the editor of the *New York World*, to get the journalist's and editor's "views on the whole question."

For the next few days, Hoover worked on ideas to have Bates quietly removed from his position. One stipulation of Hoover's was that Bates keep confidential any private correspondence they had had. Bates refused. On Tuesday, November 2, Hoover cabled the London office, stating that he was dealing with "a streak of insanity."

Rumors were circulating in Washington, however, that Hoover should resign to clear away the entire messy situation. It was time to marshal forces to finally put an end to the whole affair. British associate William Goode, who was then in New York, cabled directly to Ambassador Page, outlining the situation and asking for immediate help. "There is a movement Washington due damaging misrepresentations by Bates to get Hoover resign Chairmanship of Commission. Phillips [in the State Department] investigating but I understand he does not grasp how

Walter H. Page was U.S. ambassador to the United Kingdom and helped Hoover immensely, including sending a letter to the State Department that declared, "The Commission for Relief in Belgium is Hoover." (Public domain; multiple sources.)

implicitly British and other Governments rely on Hoover's personality and how impossible it would be to carry on this whole work if he threw it up. Matter is vital. If you could cable bringing home to American Government necessity Hoover remaining at helm it would be great service unfortunate people Belgium. Also if you would cable Hemphill, Guaranty Trust, Hoover has no right offer resign as he is the Commission itself."

Page jumped in as always. He cabled the State Department on November 2 his enthusiastic support for Hoover as the only one who could handle the job. "The Commission for Relief in Belgium is Hoover," he declared, "and absolutely depends on Hoover who has personally made agreements with the Governments concerned and has carried these delicate negotiations through only because of his high character and standing and unusual ability. If he is driven to resign the Commission will instantly fall to pieces. The governmental sources of money will dry up and the work will have to be abandoned. I believe that no other man in sight could have done this task and I know that no other can now carry it on."

The same day, Hoover received an unexpected invitation from President Wilson to visit the White House the next day. That night Hoover had dinner with Colonel House, who prepared him for his upcoming visit with Wilson. At the end of the meal, Hoover and John Beaver White took the overnight train to the capital.

Much to Hoover's great relief, the 10:30 a.m. meeting went better than expected. The president greeted him warmly and complimented him on the fine work he was doing to help the Belgians. He also said that Hoover's recent troubles had come to his attention but that the State Department had found no basis for the accusations.

Hoover brought up Bates and probably didn't even realize that what he said about Bates's mind being "upset by virtue of the great blow he had had" losing his son might resonate strongly with Wilson, a man who had lost his first wife two years before. Hoover went on to say that he was currently asking some prominent men in New York to join an executive committee, but they "were a little loath to come into a quarrel and suggested it would be of the greatest possible service to us if [Wilson] would add his personal request to my own urging."

Wilson agreed and went further by asking if it might be helpful for the administration to make a public statement "as to their unqualified approval of all the work of the Commission and of its actions." Hoover jumped at the offer, suggesting it be sent out immediately "as it would probably head off any attack" by Bates or others. "He spoke again in the warmest possible terms of all the members of the Commission and the appreciation in which they were and should be held in the minds of the American people."

Wilson was true to his word, and that day the administration's press release touting the CRB was picked up by numerous American newspapers. The administration stated it was "highly pleased" with the CRB and that its work had been done "to the entire satisfaction" of all belligerents. It had been the source of no "international complications" whatsoever but instead had produced "international good will and disinterested service."

The president also wrote letters to seven men asking that they help Hoover, and gave them to Hoover to deliver.

Hoover left Washington that day and arrived in New York that night, but did not stay. He caught a midnight train for Boston to face another potential detractor. The next day he sat down with Senator Lodge. He wanted to show the powerful politician that he was ready to address any charges. At the end of the meeting, Lodge's concerns were completely alleviated.

Senator Lodge sent a letter to the State Department detailing his meeting with Hoover and reporting that "he has satisfied me on the points which disturbed me when I wrote to you." As to the Logan Act, Lodge was frank: "They have undoubtedly violated the Logan Act, but that is a domestic matter, the violations are technical, and considering the nature of the work I cannot conceive that any point should be made in regard to it." He concluded with a strong statement: "I am very glad now to be in a position to defend the Commission if any point is raised in Congress, for their work has been the finest thing ever done by a neutral in war and I wanted to be able to sustain them to the limit. That was why the attack of Mr. Bates disturbed me so."

Like he had done with Lloyd George in early 1915, Hoover had once again convinced another powerful, skeptical man of the rightness of his cause.

On November 5, Hoover was back in New York and convened the first meeting of a newly installed New York executive committee from those who had heeded Wilson's letters. The group immediately disbanded the old New York executive committee (on which Bates and two of his loyalists had sat) and elected John Beaver White to run the New York office.

The new direction for the New York office would be to begin a clothing campaign in America to raise money and donations for clothes to be sent to Belgium and northern France. While the Allies had established steady funding to provide food, there was no money for clothing, which would become a critical necessity in the coming winter. The executive committee would quickly take this new directive and from it "an energetic campaign was made by the reorganized committees formed in the different states and cities of America."

The new committee put forth the idea of inviting Bates to be a member. Hoover agreed "out of consideration for his past services," but when he wrote and told the London CRB executives, five of them quickly cabled back, "Bates has forfeited all claim for consideration and has disclosed characteristics which should preclude his further inclusion in the Committee on any understanding whatever." Page wrote to one of the London executives, "I think you are dead right—no more of this troublesome man. I hope that this ends this foolish trouble once and for all. Upon my word, I never saw a malicious thing spring up in such a way as this." Even the Comité National wanted Bates removed from all CRB operations.

Finally, Bates himself informed the committee that his relationship with the CRB was over—he would retire from the field. No sensational articles appeared regarding Bates's accusations.

For Hoover, it had been an emotional rollercoaster. He and Lou had known the Bates family for decades and considered them some of their finest friends. And yet his friend had attacked the CRB and Hoover's reputation—two of the most important components of Hoover's professional life.

On November 9, 1915, Hoover, Lou, and the two boys sailed for England aboard the *New Amsterdam* with what must have been a tremendous sense of relief. Both Hoover's reputation and his beloved CRB had come out of the Bates battle relatively unscathed. "I was able to return to London without anxieties for the Commission, but in sorrow at the tragedy of my old friend." In the end, however, he felt that the entire episode "strengthened our organization."

At the time of sailing, the CRB had just entered the start of its second year of operations. Hoover finally felt comfortable enough to state there was "a climate of apparent calm all along the line—with guarantees, finance, ships, and food moving to the Belgians and French." He was realistic enough, however, to add a caveat: the "slender balance which we had to maintain between two powerful empires at war gave us no certainties of a placid war. And we had none."

Only a few days later, Hoover's rare sense of equilibrium was once again upset when he received an urgent communiqué from Gibson—"a tense demand that I come at once to Belgium because several of our Americans were about to be expelled for espionage."

Unfortunately, Hoover was still aboard the *New Amsterdam* sailing back from New York. He would not reach land for days.

Gibson's call for help would have to wait—and would have to take a seat with the other crises waiting for Hoover's return.

28

Brussels

Baucq, Cavell, and Others Stand Trial

The Brussels raids conducted by the Germans at the end of July and early August that had captured Baucq and Cavell had also ensnared multiple individuals, both Belgian and French, who were charged with numerous crimes against the German state. Most of those captured were taken to the military prison at St. Gilles, located a few miles south of the center of Brussels, to await trial. They would languish in jail for two months before they were put on trial.

Occupied Belgium had been allowed to retain its own court system, and most of the accused were Belgian citizens, so they should have been tried within those courts. The Germans, however, decided that all civilians apprehended would stand before a military court, or tribunal, just as any German soldier would if charged with the same crimes.

Fairness was not part of the process. The defense attorneys did not get to see or talk to the defendants before the trial and didn't know what crimes their clients had been charged with. The majority of the proceedings were conducted in German, a language many Belgians and French did not understand. And defenders were not given the right to speak although, at the whim of the presiding judges, they were sometimes given the privilege to address the court.

On Thursday and Friday, October 7 and 8, 1915, the German tribunal, with five presiding judges, was convened in what had been before the war the senate chambers of the Belgian parliament. Thirty-five people were tried at the same time, including Baucq and Cavell. Most of them did not speak or understand German but quickly came to hear repeatedly the word *todesstrafe*—death sentence. Cavell, Baucq, the Princess de Cröy, the Countess de Belleville, and others were accused of "treason in time of war."

The defense attorneys did have a chance to speak, but without having consulted their clients beforehand, and not knowing until the trial what the crimes were, they were there more for show than as true advocates. Edith Cavell's attorney spoke in humanitarian terms about how the nurse had been helping soldiers from all sides so she naturally wanted to aid those who wanted to flee Belgium.

One defendant who was allowed to address the tribunal because of her royal status was the Princess Marie de Cröy. She stood before the German judges and declared that it was she, her brother, and others who had started hiding wounded Allied soldiers and that they had convinced Edith Cavell to get involved.

One account recorded that she stated, "Everyone must be prepared to take the full responsibility for their acts, and I want to bear the full responsibility for mine. It has been said that Miss Cavell was the head of a conspiracy: that she organized the escape of British and the recruitment of French and Belgians. It is not true. She was forced into it by my brother and me. It was we who at the beginning sheltered and hid these men. When she told us that she could not lodge any more, that her institution would be endangered if we sent more to her, we still took her others, and so did our confederates. It was under the pressure of circumstances that Miss Cavell has done that of which she is now accused. Therefore, it is not on her, but on us, on my brother and me, that the greater part of the responsibility for these acts lies. For me, I repeat, I am ready to take responsibility."

Cavell did not recant her earlier confession and estimated she had helped approximately 200 men flee Belgium.

At the conclusion of the trial on October 8, the defendants were told they would be informed of their sentences at the prison.

The following day, the German judges gathered in a closed session and passed judgment. Edith Cavell, Philippe Baucq, French teacher Louise Thuliez, apothecary Louis Séverin, and Countess Jeanne de Belleville were sentenced to death. Twenty-two others received imprisonment or hard labor terms of two to 15 years (including Princess de Cröy). Eight were acquitted.

Two days later, on Monday, October 11, the prosecutor came to the prison and gathered the prisoners to pronounce the sentences. He did so in German. Four of those sentenced to death appealed for clemency, including Baucq, while Cavell did not, telling another prisoner, "No. I am English. It is useless. They want my life."

Before the appeals could be filed, the military governor of Belgium, General Traugott von Sauberzweig, ordered that Baucq and Cavell be executed at dawn the next day, Tuesday, October 12. Under German military law, he was allowed to do so and he later stated that he had wanted to set an example for all others who were not abiding by the German occupation.

The news of the sentences and imminent execution of Cavell and Baucq was smuggled out of the prison and reached the American Legation that evening.

Gibson and Villalobar Get Involved

It's not clear exactly when Brand Whitlock and Hugh Gibson found out about the arrest of Edith Cavell, although it couldn't have been too long after the fact because of the tremendous rumor network that flourished throughout Brussels.

Whitlock's published journal entries, which were usually so detailed and descriptive, jump from July 25, 1915, to August 6 (the day after the arrest), to August 20, to August 25, to September 2, without a word about Cavell.

One explanation is that since the occupation had begun, there had been continual German arrests, trials, and sentences carried out against Belgian and French civilians. To the Americans of the legation and the CRB, these were extremely sad and frightening affairs but the Americans were powerless to lodge official protests because, as representatives of a neutral country, they had to maintain their neutrality.

So when it came to Baucq and the other Belgians and French being held, they were simply more unfortunate civilian casualties of German brutality. Nothing could be done.

Edith Cavell was an entirely different matter. She was a British subject, a nurse, and, as Whitlock wrote, "a noble woman of our own blood and tongue." When the war had started, the British diplomats had left Belgium and asked Whitlock, as minister of the U.S. Legation, to represent any English civilian issues that might arise. He had agreed. While many were concerned about Cavell's arrest, however, it was inconceivable to most that any real harm could come to a British nurse. She had simply aided men to the border—others who had been accused of the same crime had received only jail time.

Officially, Whitlock finally wrote to von der Lancken on August 31, 1915—more than three weeks after her arrest—inquiring about Cavell and asking that the Germans allow the legation's Belgian lawyer, Gaston de Leval, to consult with her and provide for her defense. Von der Lancken did not reply. Ten days later, Whitlock wrote again, repeating his requests.

Two days later, von der Lancken wrote back informing Whitlock that Cavell had "admitted that she concealed in her house French and English soldiers, as well as Belgians of military age, all desirous of proceeding to the front. She has also admitted having furnished these soldiers with the money necessary for their journey to France, and having facilitated their departure from Belgium by providing guides who enabled them secretly to cross the Dutch border." He went on to state that her defense was being handled by Thomas Braun and that de Leval would not be able to see her.

Whitlock immediately forwarded the communications to Ambassador Page in London so that the British government could stay abreast of the situation.

During this time, Whitlock was becoming more and more depressed and had reportedly become ill. In his narrative account *Belgium*, he was unusually lax in providing dates around his first knowledge of the case and made it clear he was not able to physically do much because of his doctor's orders. It's telling that he started his "Edith Cavell" chapter with a long paragraph explaining how his depressed state had led to an ailment that had confined him to bed.

The Germans executed British nurse Edith Cavell on October 12, 1915, despite a late-night attempt by Hugh Gibson and Spanish Ambassador Villalobar to have it stopped. (Public domain; *A Journal from Our Legation in Belgium,* Hugh Gibson, Doubleday, Page & Co., 1917.)

"The long strain had told on all of us, and worse than the strain was the almost intolerable depression, one with the atmosphere all about, that settled down like a black cloud. October had come, with all the signs of the early autumn and the menace of another dark winter of war. The grey, dripping skies seemed but the reflection of the universal spirit of man. There were bitter rains and fogs that pinched the nose and clutched at the throat with cold fingers. Then, imprudently I went out one afternoon in the rain, and that evening the good Dr. Derscheid came with his little thermometer and bundled me off to bed . . . [Whitlock's ellipses]."

Gibson was another matter. He had always been the man of action compared with his boss's passivity. He was the person to always jump in when any emergency arose. In this instance, he, too, was vague about when he first heard of the case, but he was anything but passive when it came to the last night of Cavell's life.

The news of the inconceivable—the death sentence for Cavell, Baucq, and the three others—was smuggled out of the prison by a person who showed up at Gaston de Leval's home after 6:00 p.m. The execution was scheduled less than 12 hours away. De Leval raced to Whitlock and told him the news; a messenger was sent to find Gibson.

Gibson and de Leval left Whitlock's with two items from the ill minister—a note to von der Lancken and a letter to von Bissing requesting clemency. They first went to find Villalobar, whom they knew would be a strong diplomatic advocate and had a good relationship with von der Lancken. He would also add diplomatic weight to their efforts, considering Gibson was only the secretary of the U.S. Legation and Leval was a despised Belgian. They found him dining at Baron Lambert's home and he immediately agreed to join them.

When they reached the *Politische Abteilung* (Political Department) no one was there. They pounded on the door until a servant appeared. He said von der Lancken and the rest of the staff were out for the evening. He refused to say where they were, but he agreed to go in the U.S. Legation car to find him and request he return "at once to see us in regard to a matter of utmost urgency," according to Gibson's official report.

In that report, nothing was said of von der Lancken's whereabouts. Later, Gibson wrote a friend that the German and his staff had gone to a burlesque theatre and had "kept the minister's car waiting [in front of] the door of the place of 'amusement' for nearly three quarters of an hour—till the performance was finished."

When von der Lancken finally returned just after 10:00 p.m., he brought with him two young members of his staff, Count Harrach and Herr von Falkenhausen. Gibson gave the baron Whitlock's note and request for clemency. Von der Lancken read them aloud.

The German immediately told the delegation of three men that he could not believe the sentence had been passed and wanted to know where they had gotten such information. Gibson refused to say. Von der Lancken stated, "It was quite improbable that sentence had been pronounced, and that even so it would not be executed in so short a time, and that in any event it would be quite impossible to take any action before morning."

Gibson suggested he find out for himself. Von der Lancken left the room to make some phone calls. A short time later he came back and confirmed everything.

While de Leval sat quietly in the background (he was a Belgian whom the Germans barely acknowledged, let alone listened to), Gibson and Villalobar began to pressure von der Lancken to plea for a delay in the execution so von Bissing could have time to consider the request for clemency. Gibson even went so far as to point out "the fearful effect of a summary execution on this sort upon public opinion, both here and abroad, and, although I had no authority for doing so, called attention to the possibility that it might bring about reprisals."

Villalobar was as forceful, if not more so, in a plea for clemency.

Von der Lancken pointed out that the military governor, von Sauberzweig, who had ordered the immediate executions, was the supreme authority, and appeals could only come from the Kaiser. He said that von Bissing had no authority to step in.

The two diplomats then urged von der Lancken to contact General von Sauberzweig and request reconsideration. After continued heated discussion, von der Lancken agreed to contact the general. He left the room to do so.

A half an hour later he returned and said he had spoken with von Sauberzweig, and the man stated that he had made his decision "only after mature deliberation; that the circumstances in her case were of such a character that he considered the infliction of the death penalty imperative; and that in view of the circumstances of this case he must decline to accept your plea of clemency, or any representation in regard to the matter."

At that time, von der Lancken asked that Gibson officially take back the two missives from Whitlock. Gibson refused. Von der Lancken insisted, and finally Gibson took them back. The German stated strongly that there was no hope in the matter and that "even the Emperor himself could not intervene."

"We continued to appeal to every sentiment," Gibson reported, "to secure a delay." Villalobar even pulled von der Lancken into another room to press the case more forcibly regarding "a number of things which he would have felt hesitancy in saying in the presence of the younger officers and of M. de Leval, a Belgian subject."

As Gibson finally concluded, "Unfortunately, our efforts were unavailing." The three men left the *Politische Abteilung* after midnight, and Gibson reported back to Whitlock what had happened.

Later, Gibson related to a friend some inside information that was not in his official report. "To put the thing in plain words," Gibson wrote, "Lancken was furious that we had discovered their plan to execute Miss Cavell and had made an effort to save her instead of allowing her to be shot and finding ourselves face to face with a 'fait accompli.'"

Gibson felt that "the German Authorities here should be down on all fours in gratitude to us for the considerate tone of our report and for their escape from having everything written in plain language."

He went on to state that by not reading Cavell's sentence in court and doing it behind closed doors at the prison, the Germans had shown "this was a very evident attempt to prevent any appeal for mercy and after all these precautions the Germans are naturally somewhat surprised that we learned of the intended execution."

What galled Gibson most, however, was the attitude of von der Lancken and his two staff during the discussion. He wrote his friend, "I also avoided [in my report] all mention of the unspeakable cynical and callous attitude of everybody towards the execution. I would at any time prefer to present a plea of mercy to a marble statue and if some of the actual remarks made by them were put down on paper, it would make your blood run cold."

In a weak moment a few hours after arguing with von der Lancken, Gibson let slip a small but telling detail of the night. CRB delegate "Duke" Wellington lived near Gibson. He later related that he saw Gibson "the morning after he had spent the entire night pleading for the life of Edith Cavell. Of course he was an utter wreck. He told us how he and the Marquis de Villalobar, the Spanish Ambassador, had tried to save her life. . . . I remember him telling us the next morning, 'After all this, one of them walked over to a pitcher of beer, poured himself a drink and said, 'well, all of this talk certainly gives you a thirst.' [The German officer] was just as cold as he could be."

Belgian Philippe Baucq, who had been the major distributor for La Libre Belgique, *was executed alongside English nurse Edith Cavell.* (Public domain; *Histoire de* La Libre Belgique *Clandestine,* Pierre Goemaere, Bureaux de *La Libre Belgique,* Bruxelles, 1919.)

No record exists of what Baucq did or said the last night he was in his cell. Even though Whitlock had never met the man, he did give him a few kind words in his book. It served as a kind of eulogy. "It would have been too bald, too patent, even from the Prussian viewpoint, to hurry out a woman all alone and kill her. And so it was Baucq's sinister luck to be chosen for a fate that might have been no worse than that of Severin, or the others whose lives were saved. Poor Baucq has not been often mentioned in connection with this tragedy. He was no less illegally condemned, no less foully done to death, but his fate was swallowed up in the greater horror of the assassination of his companion of that tragic dawn at Etterbeek. He left a wife and two children. One of them was a little girl of twelve who, several days after, went to a neighbor's and asked if she might come in and be alone for a while.

"'I wish to weep for my father,' she said, 'but I do not like to do it before Mamma; I must be brave for her.'

"There were heroisms even among the Belgian children," Whitlock concluded.

Edith Cavell had spent the last night in her cell writing letters. She also met with the British chaplain in Brussels, Mr. Stirling Gahan, who reported that she had said, "I have seen death so often that it is not strange or fearful to me. . . . They have all been kind to me here. But this I would say, standing as I do in view of God and eternity: I realize that patriotism is not enough. I must have no hatred or bitterness towards anyone."

Before dawn on Tuesday, October 12, Edith Cavell and Philippe Baucq were driven from St. Gilles Prison across town to Tir National, the national shooting range that had been taken over by the Germans for executions. There, each of them had been blindfolded and tied to pole, then shot to death by a squad of German soldiers.

With a feeling of utter helplessness, Whitlock sent Gibson's report and a report by de Leval to the embassy in London. Independently, the news of Cavell's execution made it out of Belgium the same day and into Holland, where it quickly spread around the world. Not long after, Gibson's and de Leval's reports were published in Allied and American newspapers.

The world was horrified, and, as Whitlock wrote, "Even the Germans, who seemed always to do a deed and to consider its effect afterwards, knew that they had another Louvain, another *Lusitania*, for which to answer before the bar of civilisation."

The *New York Times* ran a front-page story declaring "Miss Cavell's Death Inflames England" and "Her Execution Is Denounced as 'the Most Damnable Crime of the War.'" The newspaper reported that on Thursday, October 21, in Trafalgar Square "all heads were bared to the memory of Miss Cavell. One speaker, holding in his hand a wreath to her memory, to be placed on the plinth of the Nelson Column exclaimed: 'Who will avenge the murder of this splendid Englishwoman?' In response to this appeal many new recruits came forward."

President Wilson and the king of Spain made appeals to the German government in Berlin on behalf of the Countess de Belleville and mademoiselle Thuliez. Those two and Severin had their death sentences reduced to imprisonment.

In the days to come, von der Lancken would have Whitlock and Gibson in his office angrily reviewing all the worldwide coverage generated by the Gibson and de Leval reports. As Whitlock and Gibson later explained, the Germans needed someone to blame for such negative press, and they chose the easy mark, the Belgian attorney Gaston de Leval.

With the German anger and opposition to de Leval over the Cavell case, Whitlock gained approval from the State Department and agreement from the Germans for the Belgian attorney and his family to leave Belgium. They did so and settled in London for the remainder of the war.

After the Cavell execution and the securing of de Leval's safe passage out of Belgium, Whitlock could not go on without a break. The State Department had offered him a leave of absence, and he quickly took it. He and his wife, along with their little lapdog Mieke and a mountain of luggage, left Brussels on Saturday, November 6. The departure was reported through Belgium's rumor mill and quickly spread across the country. There were even rumors that Whitlock was going home to be Wilson's vice president in the upcoming election (not true). Gibson would become chargé d'affaires until his boss returned.

While the Cavell case had an instant and significant negative impact on worldwide opinion about the Germans, its effect on the Belgians was merely more of what had been happening since the occupation began. One Belgian writer put it, "The world has heard with horror of the death of Miss Cavell. . . . But if England has lost one great martyr, Belgium has lost hundreds, who perished in the same way, sometimes for smaller offences, often for no offense at all. For the German judges are in a hurry, and they have no time to enquire too closely in such matters. The vengeance of a spy, the slightest suspicion of a policeman, sometimes even an anonymous letter, are enough to convince them of the guilt of the accused person. . . . Frightfulness must be kept up at any price. The reign of terror is the condition of the German regime."

Other effects from the Cavell execution would take longer to reveal themselves.

Nearly a year later, Hoover would have a personal confrontation with Cavell's executioner, General von Sauberzweig, while he was in Berlin on a mission about the CRB. Their emotionally charged meeting would have a tremendous impact on the future of the CRB.

La Libre Belgique Honors Baucq and Cavell

The loss of Philippe Baucq to van Doren was huge, not only personally but in the effort to continue producing the underground newspaper. With luck, though, the new central depot at St. Michel College worked out, and van Doren and the rest of group were able to put out each week's issue on time. By October the circulation had reached more than 20,000 and, as one history stated, "with every issue the tone of the paper was gaining in aggressiveness and virulence."

Even though Baucq had been a large part of the organization, his name was never mentioned in the paper. It was a hard and fast rule that helped to save lives. One history explained, "The object was not only to deprive the Germans of the satisfaction of registering a hit, but also to assist the arrested man in his defence. Unless absolute proof was brought against him he could safely deny participation in the affair, or at least claim that his role was a minor one. . . . Time and time again when the Germans believed they had at last laid hands on the 'brains' of the organisation, the immediate and continued appearance of the paper after his arrest constituted undeniable proof that the man they held was not the head of the enterprise."

When Baucq was executed, van Doren seriously considered putting out a special memorial issue in his honor. It was decided not to mention his name, but that didn't mean they could not acknowledge his death in another way. Van Doren had thousands of memorial cards printed up, and he arranged a memorial service that was attended by a large crowd.

In issue number 49, right after Baucq's death, an article on the front page titled "Our Heroes" gave a twist to the dreaded German *affiches* that continually announced the sentences of fellow citizens. "Freiherr von Bissing takes it upon himself to placard our walls with a roll of honour bearing the names of Belgian patriots who pay with their blood the services they render to their country. The population thank him, for without his lists we might long remain ignorant of those heroes who, suspected of 'espionage,' proudly brave torture and death. Honour and glory to them!"

That was followed by a long open letter to the governor general. Strong, provocative words stabbed at the German: "You can rob us, imprison us, shoot us even, but you will never silence us. . . . As for annihilating the *Libre Belgique,* don't hope for it, it is impossible. It will ever be beyond your grasp, because it is nowhere. It is a will-o'-the-wisp, rising from the graves of those whom your compatriots massacred at Louvain, at Tamines, at Dinant; and it haunts you. . . . It is the voice of all the mothers, the voice of all the widows and of all the orphans who weep for their lost ones. And every day that voice increases in intensity. It resounds throughout all our provinces and reaches far beyond our frontiers. And it will never be silent until the last of your soldiers and spies has left our land."

The following issue, number 50, had a dramatic front page that spoke directly to the Cavell and Baucq executions. Van Doren tried something unusual for the illustration. In the Wiertz Museum in Brussels hung a frightening painting that was titled "Napoleon in Hell." It depicted the dictator surrounded by spirits of those he had killed. Van Doren had an art student copy it and then another artist replace Napoleon's head with the head of the German Kaiser's image. Among the spirits haunting him was the image of Edith Cavell.

The created photo was a stunning visual and was heightened by the fact the issue came out on November 1, All Saints' Day. It became the talk of Belgium and infuriated every German who saw it—especially von Bissing.

Spies, Spies, Everywhere Spies

When Whitlock left Belgium, many Belgians were crestfallen since they perceived their hero, the figurehead of American food relief, was deserting them.

Gibson had a somewhat different opinion and was happy to see his boss go, describing Whitlock as "the man who can strut sitting down."

With the minister's departure, Gibson became the chargé d'affaires, or temporary minister, of the U.S. Legation in Brussels. It wasn't long before he had to face a CRB crisis. On Friday, November 12, 1915, Gibson sent Hoover an urgent, coded message through the American Embassy in London—a handful of CRB delegates had been charged with espionage; Hoover was needed at once in Brussels.

Baron von Bissing had received information from his extensive spy network in Belgium and Holland that certain CRB delegates were guilty of crimes against the German Empire. Gibson had been told by von der Lancken that four Americans and a Belgian (three in Belgium, two in Holland) were accused of espionage and that the three Americans working in Belgium were to be expelled immediately. Later, in an unrelated charge, von der Lancken told Gibson that William Poland, then assistant director in Brussels, was to be kicked out as well because a letter he had written to a German official was deemed offensive. Taken together, these transgressions were unacceptable, von der Lancken said, and were even causing von Bissing to consider throwing out the entire CRB.

Gibson knew this crisis demanded action at the highest level, so he quickly contacted Hoover, knowing he would probably be the only man who could resolve it. Unfortunately, on November 12 Hoover was aboard the *New Amsterdam* sailing from New York to England after spending a month in America resolving the Bates crisis. With a multitude of issues in London awaiting Hoover's arrival, it would be two weeks before the Chief could get himself to Brussels.

While von de Lancken's charges were the most significant accusations ever leveled against the CRB, they represented only a tiny percentage of the counterespionage activity generated by the vast and extensive German spy network thriving in Belgium.

According to Gibson, and to most others living in occupied Belgium, spying by the Germans was big business. Since Baron von Bissing had taken over a year before as governor general, he had developed a giant network of spies and informers who were considered by most Belgians to be stupid, unscrupulous, and underpaid. Estimates were as high as 5,000 German spies throughout the country.

Permeating all strata and walks of life, these spies looked and acted like ordinary citizens. They dressed like everyone else, strolled the boulevards, rode the trams, ate leisurely in restaurants and cafés, lingered in bars—all the while listening to every nearby conversation. They were even known to peek in windows, rummage through trash, and shyly talk to servants about the goings-on in households. "Altogether," Gibson remarked, they were "making life as disagreeable as it could possibly be."

What they were after was anyone's guess. The general goal was not so much to gain information as it was to simply denounce people to the German military court. The more people they denounced, the greater their job security. Those who did not provide adequate numbers of people to prosecute were declared incompetent and let go.

For Belgians, this meant literally thousands were punished for crimes they didn't commit. All it took was for one of von Bissing's minions to overhear a partial conversation that sounded like a plot to hurt the Germans or appeared to be praise for the Allies. The most innocent of comments, taken out of context, could be construed by a spy in a way that helped him or her maintain a respectable number of denouncements.

Many of these spy charges also stemmed from house searches—something every Belgian dreaded. As Gibson explained, "The method was to pounce upon a house, arrest everyone found inside and station men inside the door to arrest all callers, search the place from cellar to garret, breaking open drawers, breaking furniture, tearing up the floors and leaving the whole house more or less of a wreck."

If nothing was found, the Germans simply walked away without saying a word or paying for any damages. No Belgian felt safe enough to protest such treatment.

On the other hand, if any foreign newspapers, suspicious documents, or even personal letters from beyond Belgium's borders were found, all occupants in the house were immediately taken into custody. This could mean fines and/or prison time. In a few extreme cases, it meant death.

For the American Legation staff and the CRB delegates, the spies were normally not as intrusive or destructive as they were with the Belgians. Many of them were perceived as buffoons who became fodder for jokes and pranks, especially those assigned to follow specific Americans.

In Gibson's case, the German who was assigned to him was a "poor watery eyed individual who used to follow me about the streets and lean up against the front of my house and take the names of people who came to see me." Gibson felt so sorry for the "pathetic figure" that on cold and rainy nights—which were the norm for many months of the year in Belgium—Gibson would go outside and "tell him that I was expecting no callers and that he could be excused for the night. He always gratefully accepted the hint and went away."

Gibson's spy became such a fixture that the young men of the CRB couldn't resist becoming friendly with him. In fact, they would "send him on errands, leave messages with him for me now and then[, and] gave him little tips which were much appreciated."

Gibson's dry, sarcastic sense of the absurd took over when one time the poor man returned from a few days' unannounced absence. "When he returned I had him on the mat. I told him as fiercely as I could that he was about the poorest excuse for a spy that I had ever seen; that I was a long-suffering person and for that reason would let him off that time, but that if he ever again left me unprotected for such a long time I would report him to the Kommandantur and see that he lost his job."

The hapless German, confronted by such a thoroughly affronted Gibson, "was greatly alarmed, offered frightened excuses and never neglected me after that."

Gibson was not so flippant when he had to confront Baron von der Lancken's spy charges against the five CRB men.

Those Accused of Spying Are Revealed

Learning that Hoover would not be able to get to Brussels immediately, Gibson had a flurry of formal and informal meetings with anyone who he thought might be helpful in giving him insight into how to proceed. They were people such as the Spanish minister, Villalobar, who was the consummate diplomat, polished and sophisticated, yet brutal at times in his approach to negotiations and with a temper that was legendary. He had been by Gibson's side during the Cavell affair, and he was one person Gibson knew could be trusted to give wise advice.

"These are busy days," Gibson wrote about the last week of November, "and nobody can see just where they are leading but there are hopes of straightening out a very unsatisfactory situation. It has been a week of plain speaking to everybody and I think there is a general awakening and rubbing of eyes as to our position. All the cards are on the table and the next few days will develop a good deal as to the future of the C.R.B. and of other things besides."

Gibson also met with von der Lancken to try and get more information from him about the charges. Von der Lancken refused all requests for details of the accusations, stating there was no need to provide such details—his office had the right to name anyone as persona non grata for any reason and at any time. As neutrals, the CRB and the American Legation had to accept without question the occupying government's decision. Without any specifics, there wasn't much Gibson could do to counteract the German position on expulsion.

While Gibson failed to get specific information about the charges, he did, at least, find out who the men were. The three to-be-ousted American CRB delegates working in Belgium were Joe Green, Lewis Richards, and J. B. Van Schaick, and the two men in the Rotterdam office were American Carl Young and Belgian Jean van den Branden.

Joe Green, 28, was a new CRB delegate who had joined less than two months before at the end of September. Initially, he had been offered a position in Antwerp Province, but he declined because he had heard the relief work was so well organized in Antwerp (in large part due to E. E. Hunt's fine foundational work) that there wasn't much for CRB delegates to do. He requested something more challenging, and because of his fluency in French (he had been studying at a Paris university before the war) and his relative maturity, he was appointed chief delegate of Hainaut Province on October 15, 1915, and was stationed in the city of Mons.

Even though he had been with the CRB only a short time, Green was already gaining a reputation as a staunch supporter of fairness who never backed down from a fight when he thought he was in the right—which was most of the time. He was also a person who was not comfortable with idle chitchat and his temper could flair at times. A childhood friend and later CRB delegate who liked and respected him nevertheless described Green as a self-centered contrarian. "It is impossible to argue with him. . . . As a result of his living and thinking always in opposition to the world and to society he has but very few friends."

After only two months of service with the CRB, delegate Joe Green was accused by the Germans of spying and ordered out of Belgium. Hoover and Gibson fought to have him stay. (Author's archives.)

Overall, he was not an easy man to get to know, but an easy one to respect. Matching his personality was his generally stern look, which was heightened by thick dark hair and an imposing, substantial moustache. While slightly above average in height, his strong opinions and willingness to share them freely made him seem somehow taller than he was.

Because Green's talents and attributes were obvious, when Whitlock left for America Gibson immediately offered Green a job at the legation. The newly minted CRB delegate wanted to ultimately join the Foreign Service and saw Gibson's offer as a fast-track way in. He quickly agreed and the State Department cabled its approval. On the day Green came up from Hainaut Province to assume his new duties, however, Gibson had been informed of the accusations against Green and the four others. The new position was put on hold. (It would never materialize.)

Additionally, according to Green, who rarely minced words, the Brussels CRB director at the time, Vernon Kellogg, "was not noted for his strength in an emergency and I have never been able to forgive him for the spineless attitude he took in the matter. He told me to pack my trunks and leave. Fortunately, Gibson came to the rescue, and it was arranged that I should return to the Hainaut and resume my work there pending Mr. Hoover's arrival ten days later." Green returned to Mons and spent two "anxious weeks," as "spies, male and female were continually on my trail."

Another accused delegate was Lewis Richards. He was an independently wealthy concert pianist who lived prior to the war in Brussels with his Belgian wife and two children. He had been an early CRB delegate and had served in various provinces, but at the time of the German accusations he was moving back and forth between Brussels and London, where his ill wife and children had taken up residence. His wife's family owned Restaurant de la Monnaie in Brussels, which became a natural gathering place for many CRB delegates. He was a favorite of both Gibson and Hoover, and because he had lived among Belgian high society before the war, he acted as an unofficial counselor for both men to better understand the thinking of the Belgians in charge of the Comité National. Clean-shaven and well-dressed, Richards was a somewhat short and pudgy man who would probably have been overlooked in a crowd.

John Brodhead Van Schaick was rarely overlooked. The third delegate accused of spying was a tall, well-built man with a commanding presence. Van Schaick was a 50-year-old lawyer who had only a month before taken over as Antwerp's chief delegate from E. E. Hunt, who was finally heading back to America. When the war had broken out, Van Schaick had decided he would find a way to serve, despite his advanced age. He sailed for Europe in December 1914 and spent most of 1915 with the ambulance corps in France, driving wounded back from the front. Like Green, Van Schaick had joined the CRB in September.

The two Rotterdam men accused by the Germans were American Carl Young, the office director, and Jean van den Branden, a Belgian from the Comité National who had been allowed out of Belgium to work at the Rotterdam office as a liaison between the CN and CRB.

The five accused had little in common and had given no suspicions to their bosses of working against the Germans or for the Allies. They were sure—as was Gibson—that the charges against them were simply misinterpreted bits and pieces overheard by agents of the German counterespionage network.

Nonetheless, nothing Gibson could say or do would get von der Lancken to tell him what the charges were or to back down from his insistence that they leave the CRB.

Hoover arrived in Brussels on the evening of Saturday, November 27, and he and Gibson huddled together to determine the best strategy for approaching the situation. The next day began a whirlwind of activity. "There have been conferences day and night with all sorts of people and we keep them on the jump," Gibson wrote.

One such small conference was when Hoover met privately with Joe Green. As Green later recalled, Hoover asked him point-blank if he had gathered any military intelligence information and passed it on to the Rotterdam office. Green quickly stated he had not and that he had "made a promise when I came into Belgium that I would not engage in any such conduct and I have kept that promise."

"That's all I want to know," Hoover said, and he left the room without another word.

Even though the whole situation was a major crisis for the relief program, Gibson couldn't help but relish having such stimulating company as Hoover. "It is a joy to work with Hoover and I would give anything if he could stay on here for a month."

On Tuesday, November 30, Gibson had a long meeting alone with von der Lancken to get the latest feel for his attitude and to set the stage for a meeting with Hoover.

Hoover, Gibson, and Von Der Lancken Discuss the Spy Charges

The next day, December 1, Hoover, von der Lancken, and Gibson met at 2:30 p.m. in von der Lancken's office. Gibson wrote a memorandum dated the same day that recorded who said what to whom. While Gibson and von der Lancken were fluent in both French and German and could converse smoothly, Hoover could neither speak nor understand either language. Gibson probably acted as a translator between the two men, although von der Lancken did understand English.

When the three men sat down together, Hoover did not wait for any diplomatic preliminaries or for von der Lancken to start the meeting. Following his usual method of operations, Hoover came out swinging with a strong offense. He told the German that he and his CRB colleagues were "very much disheartened by the general attitude of the German officials in Belgium toward the Commission." Going a step further, he compared Belgium's supervision by the civilian German government to northern France's supervision by German General Staff officers. Hoover contended that the staff officers in northern France "realize the great importance of our work and . . . accord us sympathetic and helpful co-operation." That was not the case in Belgium under von Bissing's civil government.

Gibson interrupted to support Hoover's contention. Diplomatically, he said, the legation had not yet had to intervene even once in northern France because any issues had been resolved with the officers assigned to deal with food relief. That was definitely not the case in Belgium, where the legation was constantly involved in smoothing out difficulties between the German general government and the CRB/CN relief work.

After such softening blows, Hoover moved in to address specifically the men accused of spying. He didn't get far—von der Lancken interrupted by throwing down a personal gauntlet.

"I'm willing to stand upon the letter of the promise you made to me last year," he stated strongly. "You formally informed me that if any time a member of the Commission should become persona non grata to the German Authorities, he would be removed from the country."

Von der Lancken concluded firmly, "You placed no conditions on that promise, so you cannot now, as a matter of right, ask for any information about the accusations."

"That might be a technical interpretation of an isolated statement," Hoover admitted. But he shot back quickly, "It was made in connection with the general arrangement of the relief work and was, of course, based upon the assumption that no injustice should be done to any of the members of the Commission." Removal without valid reasons was just such an injustice, Hoover insisted.

The baron wasn't convinced and repeated that he and the government he represented had a right to "exact the removal of any of the Commission men without giving any proof of their unfitness to remain in Belgium." Von der Lancken steadfastly refused to reveal the specific charges.

Seeing they were at an impasse, Hoover took another tact, pivoting in hopes von der Lancken would see the bigger picture of the relief work as a whole and come to understand that the delegates were de facto representatives of the American people and its government.

German Baron von der Lancken was the head of the political bureau and met with Gibson and Hoover multiple times regarding spy charges leveled against three delegates. (Photo taken after WWI.) (Public domain; multiple sources.)

"Consider the broader point of view," Hoover said. "Eleven million [actually less than 10 million] people depend upon the continuance of the Commission work. The men engaged in the work are representative of our best type of Americans, [and] in view of the great popular interest in the work, they are truly representative of the American people and even, in a sense, of the American government. We cannot, therefore, tolerate any treatment of them which is incompatible with their dignity and self respect as representative Americans." Bringing it back to the men currently charged, he stated, "If the three accused persons were expelled from the country it would be a blot upon their reputations forever, and I could not permit such an injustice."

Hoover went on to declare that "upon the presentation of the slightest evidence against any one of the men of the Commission, I will unhesitatingly remove him."

He then stated directly, "Our whole usefulness depends upon our scrupulous honesty and upon the confidence of the various governments. I would be the last man to shelter any one being guilty of favoring any belligerent in any improper manner."

Hoover wrapped up his thought with a strong finish that had no hint of humor, "As far as strict neutrality is concerned, the Commission is more Catholic than the Pope."

The implication of Hoover's statements was that men of such stature would, of course, never do anything to negatively impact their promised neutrality. In an age where men still backed up deeds and agreements with their sacred word of honor as gentlemen—and most took that as a meaningful sign of fidelity to the truth—Hoover was speaking to von der Lancken more as a gentleman than as a military man.

Finally, after much back and forth between the American and the German, von der Lancken began to crack. He stated cryptically, "If you would investigate in Rotterdam, you would be able to unearth proof of the unfitness of the men in question."

Such ambiguous language normally drove Hoover crazy. This day was no different. "The commission," he declared strongly, "has been very frank and loyal with the German government. It deserves the same from the Germans." He would not be put off any longer. "I have the right to be furnished with the definite information against any men accused."

Finally, the German relented—to a point.

"I have proof," von der Lancken said grudgingly, "that there exists a system of some sort by which Green, Richards, and Van Schaick were gathering and forwarding, or perhaps causing to be forwarded to Holland, information hurtful to Germany's military interests."

"This information," von der Lancken added, "was received and made use of by Mr. Young, manager of the Rotterdam office of the CRB and Mr. van den Branden."

That was not the end of it. "I have positive proof," he declared, "that two English spies had called upon Mr. Young and had asked to be sent into Belgium to carry on their work under cover of the Commission. Mr. Young accepted the idea, but that another American in the office had protested to him saying that this would be in violation of our obligations to Germany."

There was a moment of silence in the room. Finally, after the drawn-out arguments and counter-arguments, Hoover and Gibson had something they could work with. Not much, but something.

Hoover turned to von der Lancken. "I cannot give credence to any such story, but I vow that I will personally institute an investigation on the grounds that every word said by you is absolutely true."

The baron acknowledged Hoover's personal commitment to giving the matter a full, serious investigation. He said he would await Hoover's findings.

The three men then turned to the thorny issue of the insulting letter written by William Poland (the CRB Brussels assistant director who had just been promoted to director) to Dr. Reith, one of the German civil administrators working with the CRB. Von der Lancken felt it necessary to read the entire letter out loud.

"I have," he stated, "shown the letter and talked the matter over with several German officers and they all considered it a very insulting letter. . . . Mister Poland must apologize for his attitude towards Dr. Reith or he must leave Belgium." He couldn't resist adding a point about German attention to detail. "You may be surprised to find [us] so punctilious about littler matters of this sort, but we are so and you must [abide]."

Hoover replied that Poland's words were more representative of a business letter than a diplomatic letter. Poland was a businessman, used to employing direct language, and was highly frustrated by the Germans reluctance to deal with critical CRB matters quickly. Hoover also brought up the fact that Dr. Reith had once called Poland to his office, where the American was "scolded by a clerk, which made him quite prepared to resign and leave the country."

This led to a long discussion that Hoover had little patience for. As usual, the American tried a straight approach that might end things quickly. "Will you consider the matter closed on my personal assurance that Mr. Poland intended no offense and, knowing that his letter has caused offense, no more letters of the same sort will be written?"

Von der Lancken "grudgingly agreed to this."

Now that Hoover felt he had gained some ground, he pressed his larger point again. He returned to reiterating how the Germans were not seeing the broader picture of saving millions of people from starvation. Instead they were hindering the work with petty issues and making it difficult for the CRB to gather and keep "the right kind of man to carry on the work." If this kind of hindrance remained, Hoover vowed that the CRB would not be able to continue—his well-used tactic.

Von der Lancken appeared unimpressed with the threat of CRB withdrawal. As Gibson summed up the meeting—which lasted all afternoon—von der Lancken "returned to the petty questions of the letter written by Mr. Poland and other things of relatively minor importance. While he said in a half hearted way that he admired many things about the work done, he added that the Commission was not at all necessary to the German authorities and that if we were to withdraw the Belgians need not starve. He seemed quite unable to rise above the minor questions which seemed to cause him much irritation."

As the meeting finally concluded, Gibson and Hoover knew what had to be done.

Gibson, for his part, had already done it. He wrote that evening, "In accord with Hoover I have precipitated "a kill or cure situation," which in this case meant Gibson officially told the German government, probably through von der Lancken, that he "threatened to withdraw" if the charges weren't dropped and relations improved between the CRB and the German general government in Belgium.

He wrote in a dispatch to the State Department that he had told von der Lancken "we might as well talk the matter over very frankly and that if the German Authorities in Belgium could not see their way to affording us the same helpful co-operation we received from the Military Authorities in Northern France, it would be much better to stop the work now than to invite complications and ultimate disaster by continuing the work in spite of German antagonism."

In the heat of the moment, Gibson might not have fully comprehended how big his threat was and how important the use of the words "we" and "us" were when they combined his role as representative of the United States and the private organization, the CRB. In diplomatic circles, and as the chargé d'affaires of the United States of America, his words had so much more impact than coming from someone such as the private citizen Herbert Hoover. While Hoover had become an important person in relief, he was still only a private citizen, so when he threatened to withdraw from the relief (which he did multiple times during the life of the CRB), it was seen and perceived in a different manner than when the threat came from an official of a world power. While it's hard to believe the highly intelligent and savvy Gibson did not know the full extent of his words, it's probably true he would not have guessed that those words would end up in a few months landing on his doorstep with devastating consequences.

Hoover Turns to the German Military for Help

As for what Hoover had to do after the von der Lancken meeting, he had to accomplish two goals: get the immediate spy charges dropped and somehow resolve the long-term issues with the German general government in Belgium. For that, he had already taken behind-the-scenes action that he hoped would solve the problem once and for all.

Even before the meeting with von der Lancken, Hoover had once again gone over von Bissing's head. The old Prussian was a nearly constant thorn in the sides of the CRB and CN, and Hoover was getting fed up. He knew that even if he did answer satisfactorily all current spy accusations, he would still be left with the problem of von Bissing's reluctance to fully comprehend, accept, and significantly assist the relief work.

Von Bissing's deficiencies in this regard were compounded by the fact that while he was the head of the general government within Belgium—which had been tasked with supervising the relief efforts in the civilian zone—he had little if anything to do with the everyday supervision of the CRB and CN. Initially, that overall task had fallen to Max von Sandt, who was the head of the civil administration of the general government. In June 1915, however, much of that responsibility had been transferred to the *Politische Abteilung*, or Political Department, which was run by von der Lancken. That had not helped matters, though, and as one CRB history noted, "For some time a rivalry between these two departments had been developing as to which should have the privilege of surveillance of the activities of the Commission and the Comité National." That rivalry was the cause of many headaches for the CRB and CN. In the current situation, it had been von der Lancken's department that had brought forth the spy charges.

For Hoover, supervision by these two departments was hindering the work and must be changed. He knew the only three authorities who could command von Bissing were the Berlin civilian government, the military's General Staff, and the Kaiser.

In this case, Hoover felt the Berlin government should not be approached so soon after the U.S. ambassador in Berlin, James Gerard, had gotten it to override von Bissing on another matter. The Kaiser was not an option because the issue was such a relatively small one. That left Hoover with the German General Staff as his possible savior.

Headquartered in Charleville, France, the German General Staff was a huge military bureaucracy that ran the entire war effort. At its head was Kaiser Wilhelm, who had a residence in the town. Because northern France was part of the Army Zone, the relief work there fell under the jurisdiction and supervision of the military. The CRB had its own office in the town so that it could be close to both the French people it was serving and those who were in charge of supervising its work.

With true German efficiency, the military had appointed two officers in the intelligence department to act as liaisons between the German military government and the CRB: Major von Kessler and Count Wengersky. Recently another officer, Captain Conrad Uhl, had joined them. All three understood and spoke English and probably French.

Because of these officers and their understanding of the scope and importance of the work, the relations between the General Staff and the CRB were excellent, so far. Any problems that had arisen had been dealt with immediately by these officers, who were generally sympathetic to the relief work. Hoover felt they understood the bigger picture of how humanitarian aid had to have significant support from the occupying forces to be fully efficient and effective.

After Hoover decided to go over von Bissing's head regarding the spy charges, he contacted the two main CRB men in Charleville, Vernon Kellogg (then outgoing CRB director in Brussels who was at the time in Charleville) and Caspar Whitney (CRB general representative to northern France) to come to Brussels and bring the three German officers—von Kessler, Wengersky, and Uhl. On the motorcar trip up, Kellogg had used his fluency in German and his relaxed style to find out more about the spy charges. Von Kessler confirmed that much of the information obtained by the Germans had come from the CRB's Rotterdam office.

The group from Charleville arrived in Brussels after Hoover and Gibson had met with von der Lancken. On Thursday, December 2, Hoover met with von Kessler, Wengersky, Uhl, and Kellogg and Whitney. Notably absent from this gathering was von Bissing, von der Lancken, and any other representative of the German general government in Belgium. Gibson was not there either, no doubt to officially distance the American government (as represented by Gibson) from what Hoover hoped to achieve.

Major von Kessler was one of the German liaison officers between the German General Staff and the CRB. He would help smooth over the problems the CRB was having with von Bissing. (Public domain; Herbert Hoover Presidential Library Archives, West Branch, Iowa.)

As to the meeting's agenda, Hoover, of course, wanted the three German military men to intervene with von Bissing and von der Lancken to dismiss the specific spy charges. But he also hoped that these three German officers, who were sympathetic to the relief work, could somehow expand their influence from just northern France to all of occupied Belgium—thus removing, or diminishing the role of, the German general government in the everyday operations of the CRB and the CN.

For the plan to work, Hoover had to get them to agree to such a move, then get them to present it to von Bissing. While von Bissing did have final say in anything that happened within his Belgian territory, he was—and would always be—first and foremost a military man. He'd had a distinguished career before the war and then had been brought out of retirement to lead the VII Army Corps from the invasion through to November 1914. He would listen—and no doubt follow—the advice of officers appointed by the General Staff.

Hoover opened the meeting by stating that "the relations of the Commission with the [General] Staff in the North of France had always been so cordial and the Staff engagements so justly and liberally carried out, the Staff attitude so open and frank, that he felt he could be frank even to brutality."

He then proceeded to be just that. Current conditions in Belgium were "intolerable," he said, adding that if the relief ended in Belgium it "must collapse" in northern France as well. He laid out the history of the CRB and—stretching the truth about von Bissing to better serve his purposes—said that von Bissing's attitude was "correct, if not cordial," but that he was surrounded by "an absolute pack of bureaucratic underlings" who's only desire was to gain the governor general's attention by using the CRB as a badminton "shuttlecock with which they beat each other over the head, hoping the Governor would notice their valiant conduct."

Hoover then went first into the issue of Poland and his reportedly insulting letter. He read the letter to the group. Von Kessler said its contents were "innocent and justified and that it was in text and character far different from that represented to him by the authorities."

Hoover was blunt, stating that if experienced businessmen like Poland were to be "jerked out of the country on the breath of an arrogant clerk," then "we would have to chuck the whole job at once." Once again, Hoover was threatening to pull the entire relief operations.

Seeing that von Kessler agreed with him, Hoover moved on to the matter of the spy charges. Von Kessler provided more details, saying that it was his understanding that the three delegates in Belgium (Green, Richards, and Van Schaick) had transmitted verbally to Young in Rotterdam details about the September German offensive on the Western Front.

Insulting business letters were one thing, but giving away military secrets was another. To an officer of the German General Staff, "such [military] matters as this transcended every food question." Von Kessler also brought up a Major Winchell who von Kessler had been told was an Allied agent approved by Young as a new CRB delegate.

Hoover could not yet answer all the charges, but he was able to dismiss the somewhat comical story of Winchell. Hoover had already learned that Major Winchell was, in fact, a major, but in the non-military Salvation Army. Supposedly, a bad joke made in the Rotterdam office was that the man was part of the Salvation Army's intelligence service. That joke had somehow reached the ears of a German agent who had passed it along as a serious matter. Once Hoover explained the situation, the issue was quickly dropped.

Regarding the other accusations, Hoover still didn't have all the facts, but he did know one critical piece of information. He told the General Staff officers that in the case of Green and Van Schaick, both had joined the CRB only after the Germans' September offensive, which made it impossible for them to have passed any military information to Young.

Von Kessler and the others were convinced in those two cases and said they would pass their opinions on to von Bissing.

As for the bigger picture and Hoover's desire for a new supervising agency, von Kessler did not fail. In fact, von Kessler had already talked with his superiors and had talked with von Bissing and had recommended to the governor general that a special department be created to supervise the CRB and CN. A handful of representatives from various departments would sit on the committee and would include a member of the General Staff. Von Bissing had agreed and Captain Uhl had been brought to Brussels to serve in that department. Uhl had been chosen, von Kessler said, because "he was a good American resident of Santa Barbara, California."

Hoover could not have been more pleased. And two days later, von der Lancken confirmed in a conversation he had with Hoover that von Bissing had, indeed, created a new committee, titled *Vermittlungsstelle* (literal translation, "exchange"), comprised of a representative of the political, finance, and civil departments, together with an officer of the General Staff (Captain Uhl). It would begin functioning in a week or two. Additionally, von der Lancken told Hoover he had met with Poland, and "the incident was now out of the way happily."

That still left a few of the spy charges. Hoover knew what he had to do.

A "Benedict" Is Uncovered

On Monday morning, December 6, Hoover headed for Rotterdam—he would face each man in the Rotterdam office, demand to know the true story, and find out who had instigated such nonsense.

While the trip from Brussels north to Rotterdam was less than 95 miles (150 km), it was a trip that could take all day, with countless harassing stops at German sentry posts throughout Belgium and tedious, time-consuming border crossing procedures set up by both the Germans and the Dutch. Even Hoover, with his numerous passes signed by the highest authorities, could still get stalled by an overly officious German.

When Hoover did get to Rotterdam, he went straight to work. He quickly got to the bottom of the story. He found that he had, as he later described, a "Benedict" in the Rotterdam office. He never named the man publicly "out of consideration to his fine family in the United States." According to Hoover, "He had set up an espionage job for himself with the German intelligence agents in that city. The youngster was a second-generation German, spoke German, and had seemed to us a perfect associate for handling our routine relations with the German authorities in Holland."

All indications are that it was Joseph Frank Brandon Erdlets Jr., a 32-year-old mining engineer acquaintance who had gone to work in the CRB Rotterdam office. Erdlets and his family had strong ties to Germany, and he could speak German very well. He had an overly inflated sense of himself and the work he was doing, and he was known to be a busybody. Whether or not he worked for German intelligence is unproven, but he was a talker who would inappropriately discuss with outsiders what he saw and heard in the office. Somewhere along the line, one of his listeners had obviously been a German espionage agent who had passed on whatever rumors Erdlets was touting as facts.

Regarding the three CRB delegates accused of spying, their charges had come from contact with Erdlets. As Hoover later wrote, Green, Richards, and Van Schaick "had come to the Rotterdam office in connection with their work and whose minds 'Benedict' [Erdlets] had probed for their opinions of the Germans, thereupon reporting their chatter to the German authorities."

One of Erdlets's misinterpretations was the comical story of Major Winchell. It was Erdlets who had overheard his boss, Carl Young, make the silly joke that Winchell was part of the Salvation Army's intelligence service. That bit of whimsy, in Erdlets's hands, had morphed into proof that Young was allowing Allied spies into German-occupied Belgium.

Within a very short time, Hoover had secured written statements from all parties disclaiming all the German charges, from sending Allied agents into Belgium to receiving and passing on military secrets from agents within Belgium. To add weight to these documents, Hoover also had Dr. Henry van Dyke, the U.S. minister to the Netherlands at The Hague, certify the statements so that the full honor and integrity of the American government was backing them up.

As for Erdlets, nothing was mentioned in official CRB documents, but Hoover had Erdlets pulled from the Rotterdam office and told him to head home to America, where Hoover hoped he would cause no more problems. Unfortunately, during Erdlets's layover in London waiting for the next ship to sail for America, he and his mouth went to work again. This time, the consequences—felt a few months later, in March 1916—would be even graver and have personal ramifications for Hoover.

At the time, however, with the documents safely in hand, a relieved Hoover rushed back to Brussels, making the entire roundtrip in only a day and a half—quite a feat for what he had accomplished and for getting in and out of the "ring of steel" so quickly. His packet of documents finally took care of all spy charges against the CRB men. Hoover later wrote that he sent the three CRB delegates "to work in our London office, as they were given to chatter," but this was not the case. Only Van Schaick was sent to London. Lewis Richards remained where he was in Brussels. Green left Mons on December 15, 1915, to begin work as a delegate for the Agglomération Bruxelloise (metropolitan Brussels), where he would continue to do good work that would raise the hackles of both the Germans and Émile Francqui and have long-term consequences.

Social Obligations Begin to Mend Fences

With the serious spy charges resolved, at least for the moment, and before leaving Brussels, Hoover had to face an even worse crisis, one that he found nearly unbearable—social obligations. While these events were trivial in Hoover's mind and had nothing to do directly with the relief work, they were for many Belgians and the diplomatic corps critical components to ensuring the smooth running of the massive relief work organization. Socializing was an important way to bridge the divides between the many strong, combative personalities involved.

Whitlock—whom Hoover perceived lacked the qualities of strong leadership and backbone needed for the wartime job—had been excellent at bridging divides, mending fences, smoothing ruffled egos, and building understanding (or at least acceptance) in the minds of the major players who did not trust or like one another. When Whitlock had left Brussels for his medical leave, many in the CRB had been happy and relieved, and yet Whitlock's diplomatic skills in dealing with the tremendous competing forces would be missed.

Gibson certainly knew all the social protocols and etiquette that Whitlock did, and when he was on his game, he was charming, knowledgeable, and adept at handling most social and diplomatic situations. But his sometimes hotheaded temper and his desire to bulldoze through frustrating problems could be a detriment to himself and his new position.

In Hoover's situation, Gibson was the perfect social counselor. He was trusted and respected by Hoover while also knowing the relief operation, the major players, and Hoover's deep-seated desire to avoid all such frivolous activities that were not directly related to relief.

Gibson was fully aware that Hoover had not respected Whitlock, that he did not like or trust Émile Francqui and many of the CN executives, and that he felt von Bissing and von der Lancken were more interested in protecting and expanding their own fiefdoms than saving people from starvation.

Gibson also knew that Hoover had little patience for the Spanish minister, Villalobar, one of the official patron ministers of the CRB. As Hoover later said dryly, about Villalobar, "He did not like Americans much," although he did admit that the Spaniard was "devoted to the Relief."

Villalobar was one of the most fascinating men the international diplomatic corps had ever seen. Born into a wealthy and prominent family, he was deformed with reportedly stumps for legs and one deformed hand, no hair, and a larger-than-normal-sized head. But he was also considered "extraordinarily brilliant" and had spent his childhood hidden away with special tutors.

In a time when such severely crippled people were routinely institutionalized, Villalobar was given every opportunity to overcome his handicaps. As a result, he became determined to make his mark in the world. After honing his mental skills and having the finest prostheses built, he carefully crafted a public image of himself that appeared nearly normal and was the only one he allowed to be photographed. He was able to walk, but with difficulty, always wore a military cap, had gloves and used a cape to hide his hands, and only allowed staged photographs of his upper body. Understandably, he held his life together with an iron will, strong ego, and steadfast adherence to duty, honor, and integrity. On his dark side, however, stood jealousies, bitterness, pettiness, and tremendous rage that would suddenly engulf unsuspecting servants and lower-echelon personnel. Few saw those sides of the minister, but when they did, they never forgot them.

Spanish Ambassador Villalobar was one of the three patrons of Belgium relief and was a highly complex, capable man. As Hoover remarked, however, "He did not like Americans much." (Author's archives.)

When Villalobar entered the diplomatic corps, he quickly quieted the skeptics with how sophisticated and deft he was at handling any situation. Multilingual, he was known to be quick-witted, able to think clearly in a crisis, and capable of coming up with creative solutions to what seemed to be irresolvable problems. As minister of one of the neutral powers in Belgium and an official patron of the relief work, he and his office held significant rank in the minds of the Germans. Additionally, he and Brand Whitlock had formed a strong friendship before Whitlock had left for his leave.

Hoover was not so enamored with Villalobar or the country he represented. He considered America to be the primary sponsor of the relief and believed the two other diplomatic patrons, Spain and Holland, had been added more to appease others than to actually contribute much to the work. His opinion was not helped in this matter when, in the early days of the CRB, Villalobar had created a significant fuss over not being properly listed on the letterhead of the new relief organization. In that event, the Spaniard's feathers had to be soothed before other issues could be addressed. Such perceived pettiness was not something Hoover suffered lightly.

Their relationship had not improved much since then. And because Hoover was nearly the antithesis of what an early 1900s diplomat should be, Villalobar had no better of an opinion of the American.

But Hoover's belief that Villalobar was peripheral was far from the truth. Villalobar's contributions were many and significant. He had also stood by Gibson through the long night as the two of them had fought to save the life of Edith

Cavell. A good relationship between Hoover and Villalobar could have an important positive impact on the relief work.

Gibson understood the importance of good relations between Hoover and Villalobar, and he knew that one of his important behind-the-scenes jobs was to improve those relations. He wrote to his mother on Saturday, December 4, 1915, and stated proudly, "For the past month I have been working hard on Villalobar to impress on him the need of a change of attitude toward Hoover. There has been a marked improvement."

In fact, on Friday, the day before, Villalobar had given a large luncheon with Hoover as the guest of honor. It would have been filled with all that Hoover disliked—idle conversation with those with whom he had little in common, a long, drawn-out meal when time was always of the essence, and plenty of lengthy speeches singing Hoover's praises, which embarrassed him immensely.

To build on that successful social event, Gibson had then hosted a dinner party on Sunday night, December 5, at the legation, the night before Hoover drove to Rotterdam to deal with the spy charges. The event was a formal affair with the table decked out in fine silverware and china, rock crystal glassware, and orchids. No doubt servants presented fine wines, multiple courses, fruits and cheeses, and after-dinner drinks.

Gibson relished the fact that it was the first such event where Belgians had been invited to dine at the legation since the war began. Whitlock would have loved to have presided over the evening. As it was, Gibson hosted 14 people besides Hoover and himself. On the Belgian side, the honored guests included Villalobar, Émile Francqui, Baron and Baroness Rothschild-Lambert (the baron was an influential member of the CN), Chevalier and Madame Edmond de Wouters (de Wouters was a Hoover friend who was the liaison between the CN and CRB in Brussels), and Madame Phillipson-Wiener (later to become the CN representative of the relief's clothing department). The Americans attending were Vernon Kellogg (who was leaving for America), Poland, Lewis Richards, Edward Curtis (the newly returned CRB courier), and Miss Caroline Larner, a staff member of the legation.

Gibson had a grand time and later referred to the evening as "the love feast I had for Hoover to smooth over some of the scars of battle." He happily reported to his mother, "I don't mind saying that it was a corking good dinner." Gibson did admit, however, that "it was a bore for Hoover who hates dinners but it was good politics and he played his part well."

While Hoover and Villalobar did not part as friends that night, they at least parted on speaking terms.

On Friday, December 10, Gibson said goodbye to Hoover, who headed back to London. Gibson couched Hoover's diplomatic successes in a hunting metaphor when he wrote that the CRB chief had left for London with a "good bag of game."

Soon, unfortunately, Gibson would become the game for German hunters.

A Routine Ride Turns Ugly

With the spy charges dropped, a new committee being formed that would liaison with the relief work, a successful dinner party completed at the legation, and Hoover preparing to head back to London the next day, Gibson took a much-needed break on Thursday, December 9. He left the office to do what he loved to do—ride a horse. It was one of the few pleasurable activities he was occasionally still able to do while serving as temporary head of the legation.

An avid horseman, Gibson had more chances to ride than time to do so. Open invitations came from wealthy Belgians lucky enough to have retained their stables under the occupation. When Gibson was able to get away from his diplomatic duties, he would either ride within the city and its parks or use his diplomatic privilege to motor out to stables on the edge of the city where he could give the horse its head. After such open-space riding, he would write his mother about the excitement of galloping across fields and forests, splashing through streams and—depending upon the horse—even taking a few low fences.

"It was snapping cold and the horses were full of ginger," Gibson wrote of one such ride. "We routed out roe-buck several times in riding through the woods and had some fine chases across country over fences, ditches and rough country generally. The nags are fine at jumping and that sort of ride bucks one up a lot."

At times, Gibson needed a solitary ride to clear his head and rejuvenate himself for the next set of diplomatic challenges to be faced. Other times, however, his naturally social side would need a fellow rider for companionship and maybe some unfettered conversations free of listening German ears. One of his favorite riding partners was Ynès Reyntiens, a young Belgian from a well-to-do family who was quick-witted, spirited, and never afraid to compete with men. Years after the war, she would marry Gibson.

Reyntiens joined him on that chilly Thursday, December 9, when they went riding not far from the legation. It was a ride they had done many times before.

Trouble began shortly into their ride.

Only a few blocks from the legation and its stables was a railroad crossing, which was supervised by a German Landsturmer. The country was filled with these Landsturm guards—older men used for noncombat duties. Most Belgians thought of them as rumpled, pretend soldiers who spent most of their time being tired, bored, ornery, or all three. At the railroad crossing near the legation, one stood beside the railroad tracks with the job of lowering and raising a heavy gate as trains rumbled through. That did not stop him from, at times, with no train in sight, lowering the gate on what seemed to be whims—most likely as a way to pass the time, amuse himself, or harass any Belgian pedestrians wanting to cross the tracks.

On this day, as Reyntiens approached the crossing the German suddenly dropped the gate.

Her horse reared and just missed being struck, while the gate came "within an ace" of killing Ynès, according to Gibson.

The old German yelled an insulting remark.

"Hold your tongue!" Reyntiens commanded in German, as she reined in her startled horse.

Gibson, knowing his riding partner could handle the matter, simply drew his horse closer and took the soldier's number as the German reluctantly began to raise the gate.

That might have been the end of it, but the Landsturmer couldn't let it go that he had been told off by a Belgian—and a woman to boot. He turned bold.

"You're under arrest for insulting the German army," he announced.

Gibson took up the challenge with gusto. "I am the chargé d'affaires of the United States Legation in Belgium," he stated loudly in flawless German. He added all his ranks and titles; this was no time to hang back. "I refuse to consider myself under arrest!"

The old German looked at him for a moment, didn't say a word, then simply unshouldered his rifle and began attaching his long steel bayonet.

Gibson pulled out his own big guns, drawing from his coat his papers and documents that stated he was not to be detained by anyone for any reason—signed by the governor general.

The two men argued—Gibson demanding the German look at the documents—the German steadfastly refusing to do so and repeating they were both under arrest. As the man continued to brandish his rifle with fixed bayonet, Gibson told him what was going to happen to him if he didn't let them go immediately. "We had some warm conversation," Gibson said dryly.

A crowd quickly gathered, wanting desperately to see someone get the better of a German. Gibson got a few onlookers to run to the legation so that someone there could send word of what was happening to German headquarters.

Suddenly a guard of four soldiers appeared. Gibson laid out his arguments and once again offered his papers, but still no one looked at them. It was decided the two offenders should be taken to the nearest sentry post at the Gare de Luxembourg, a few blocks away, where an officer of the German Army would decide their fate. As the soldiers escorted the two riders down the street, the entire crowd followed close behind.

Word of the affair had flown ahead of the parade, and as they approached the post, Gibson saw at the gate an officer who was "lashing himself into a fury and getting ready to eat us alive." The German ordered them inside, at once.

Gibson quickly dismounted and stormed into the room, Ynès hard on his heels. He didn't even give the German time to speak.

"If you don't change your tone and listen to what I have to say, you'll be spending a few days in jail next to your soldier!" He brandished his handful of papers like a sword pointed at the officer. "Now read these documents!"

It took a few more minutes of arguing, but finally the officer read Gibson's documents. He slowly looked up and grudgingly agreed that he did not, in fact, have the right to detain Gibson.

"You're free to go," he said somewhat painfully.

Without a word, Gibson and Ynès marched out victoriously and climbed back onto their horses. The crowd stood in silent awe as the two turned and rode away.

Vindicated, Gibson didn't leave it at that, though. He rode straight to the *Politische Abteilung* (Political Department), where he stormed into the building, went to those he already knew well, and "saw to it that the matter was acted upon without delay and that the solider was given what was coming to him on three counts: 1. for dropping the gate without warning. 2. for insulting a lady and 3. for refusing to look at my papers."

Even that wasn't enough for Gibson—whose temper and inflamed sense of justice sometimes created a need for retribution that exceeded what a situation called for. In a final act of sticking-it-to-the-soldier, he and Ynès rode back across the railroad crossing "so that there could be no doubt as to what had happened." It was important, Gibson felt, that the man be shown who was boss. Gibson would not be denied his proper amount of respect when it came to his position—especially when in public and accompanied by a woman.

The next day, the burgomaster of Brussels came by to congratulate Gibson on being the hero of the city for getting the best of the Germans. As reported by the mayor, the story that was flying around town was that the Landsturmer and a few of his friends had tried to pull Ynès off her horse. Gibson had courageously come to the rescue by riding them down and beating them off with his riding crop. The famous Belgian word-of-mouth telegraph—which served up facts and rumors with equal vigor—had done its job. Gibson later wrote his mother, "Stories never lose anything in the telling here."

At the time, Gibson believed the affair had come to a satisfactory conclusion and could be looked back on with much good humor. He told the story to many of his CRB and Belgian friends, and they all shared a laugh at the expense of the Landsturmer and German stupidity.

Less than two months later, however, the event would come back to haunt Gibson as it played a major role in an upheaval that would drastically impact his life and the relief operations.

29

London

Hoover Asks the British for More Imports

By December 1915, with the depletion of seasonal native supplies, it was obvious to Hoover, Francqui, and many others in the CRB and the CN that Belgium and northern France would need more imports if the goal of maintaining 1,800 calories per person per day (little more than half normal intake) was to be achieved.

Even as far back as March 2, 1915, Francqui had sent a letter to Hoover requesting more food for Belgium. "The monthly consignments," he wrote, "are hardly sufficient to satisfy the demands of our Provincial Committees. I therefore allow myself to suggest that you should make new efforts with a view to increasing the tonnage of the imports."

Over the course of 1915—and with only a few "arbitrary restrictions placed from time to time by the British Government on the import program"—items such as meats, potatoes, and fats (e.g., lard) were approved and began to supplement the principal imports of wheat, maize, rice, beans, and peas. Combining all those items, the CRB had a limit set by the British of 80,000 tons for Belgium per month before the harvest and a reduction to a "minimum supplement of native supplies after the harvest."

Maintaining such tonnage had been a formable task, especially because in April the CRB had received approval to begin importing 15,000 to 18,000 tons of foodstuffs to the more than 2 million civilians of northern France and had to gear up for that. (The northern France imports had risen to 35,000 tons per month by the end of the year.)

Even with such substantial numbers, however, by December Hoover knew it was time to ask the British Foreign Office for an increase in import tonnage. On December 21, 1915, Hoover wrote a letter and extensive memorandum to Lord Eustace Percy, the British liaison between the CRB and the Foreign Office. He dealt separately with Belgium and northern France, while outlining nearly 30 items and explaining why each was needed.

For the critical import, wheat, he wrote, "The available native wheat supply, which is under our control, affords us about 13,500 tons of wheat per month. It is therefore necessary for us to import about 54,000 tons per month, in order to give a 250 gram flour ration to the population. Owing to the lateness of the harvest all over the world, our stocks in Belgium have run down until we have, aside from stuff in transit, today only an average of two days' supply in our warehouses in Belgium, and it is therefore necessary for us to build up some stocks in the country, which implies larger importations in the immediate future, with, of course a slackening off towards the end."

For maize, or corn, he stated, "Maize is used partly for human food, in the form of a porridge product called cerealine, designed for children, while the refuse and the rest of the maize is used for fodder. The amount which we have set for ourselves for this purpose is 20,000 tons per month. This represents half the normal importation into Belgium and is used largely for poultry purposes and the feeding of municipal livestock."

In the Belgium portion of the memorandum, Hoover described the foodstuffs as "the imports desired by our friends in Belgium," while in the northern France section he explained that the items had been chosen by the district committees and CRB delegates who agreed "this is the absolute minimum supply with which health can be preserved in the population."

A smart negotiator, Hoover never actually asked for increases, he simply let the totals of the memorandum's charts show the increases and said this is what was needed. Why bring attention to numbers if his arguments for each item got him approval for the whole program? For Belgium, the increase reflected a more than 55 percent rise from 80,000 tons to 126,400 tons per month. He also asked for nonfood items—more medical supplies and clothing for the civilians, and more gasoline and motorcar supplies for the CRB staff to use in Belgium.

For northern France, he requested an increase from the current 35,000 tons to 48,000 tons per month, and he wrote to the French government asking that it support his proposal to the British Foreign Office, which it did.

Lord Percy, on receiving Hoover's request, passed it up to his boss, Foreign Secretary Sir Edward Grey. Hoover would have to wait more than two months before getting a direct answer. He would, however, get an indication of how the British were feeling about relief when Ambassador Page received a major letter from Grey on December 31.

Before Page received that letter, Hoover was sent other missives from the Foreign Office regarding supposed infractions by the German military of their nonrequisition guarantees. Once again, Hoover was sure they had all come from investigations initiated by the "Allied military authorities," which were dead set against the relief program. “Those agencies were violently opposed to us from the start and made life miserable not only for us but for those in the British Foreign Office who were our steadfast friends.”

Hoover always admitted, “In a country overrun by the German Army and with the added irritant of a sentry posted at every corner, there were bound to be many minor infractions of our food guarantees.” He was scrupulous in running down every accusation and then sending back a full report. One of his generic, and yet compelling, reasons why most allegations were false was that “the Belgian ration ran from sixteen hundred to eighteen hundred calories, often only 50 per cent of the British ration, and that people in such straits were not given to handing over generously the C.R.B. food to Germans.”

Most of these transgressions, Hoover said, were found to be committed by members of the thriving black market in Belgium, not the German military. Because of the tightly controlled rationing systems in Belgium, northern France, and Germany, any food and material outside those systems could command high prices. The black market was a multinational affair and smugglers included men and women from Belgium, France, Holland, Denmark, Sweden, Norway, and Britain.

Items for sale would come in the dead of night via the North Sea and along the lacework of Dutch and Belgian canals aboard small boats and barges. Sales were mostly to Germans and well-to-do Belgians—anyone who could afford the prices. Because of the British blockade against Germany, the German authorities never spent much time or energy cracking down on the black market; it was just one more pathway to getting food. The CRB's main focus was finding and reporting the smuggling that came in through Holland.

Besides the black market, there were other ways that the British believed the Germans were using the system for their benefit.

One example was an allegation on December 28 that revolved around the CRB's condensed milk shipments for Belgian and French children. More than 2.5 million children were fed in special canteens every day, and during the noon meal they were provided with a little milk, which mostly came from a “huge number of small tins of condensed milk.”

Word somehow got back to the Allies that the Germans were rounding up all the empty tins to use for various things—everything from repacking to melting down to become new tops to German grenades. Lord Percy qualified his government's concerns: “Our people are firm on the point about the return of the empty tins. The danger does not arise from the amount of metal in the tins but from the tins themselves. Germany is very short of tins, so much so that she is sending out empty tins to be refilled with preserved meat, etc., in neutral countries, and is collecting empties high and low.”

He acknowledged that the collection of empties would entail a substantial level of work and organization to get them back to Rotterdam, but he offered various ways of doing so and even added "You might get something from the resale of these empties in Holland or here."

In the end, the CRB initiated a deposit program for 10 francs per tin can with the communal authorities, and they would return the deposit once the empties were returned. "The burden of accounting by the canteens and the communes was exasperating, and the difficulty of transportation by trucks and barges was another burden, but we got the tins back and deposited them in Holland."

The nearly constant stream of accusations and the need to answer every one with tedious investigations and reports finally led Hoover to the realization that the problem needed to be confronted at the source. He was determined that the rapidly approaching New Year would see a reorganization for the better of the currently ineffective Inspection and Control Department within Belgium.

His decision would have a major impact on the CRB—and on Joe Green in particular.

On Friday, New Year's Eve, 10 days after Hoover's letter requesting an increase in imports, a reply of sorts finally came. Unfortunately, Hoover's request "evoked an explosion from the British."

Bypassing private citizen Herbert Hoover, Foreign Secretary Sir Edward Grey sent a long letter to U.S. Ambassador Walter Page "as patron, in your unofficial capacity, of the Commission for Relief in Belgium." He opened the letter by stating, "A very critical situation has now arisen regarding the affairs of that Commission, and I must therefore put before you briefly the views of His Majesty's Government."

Grey then went over the history of the food-relief agreements and detailed specific cases where the British government felt the Germans had taken advantage of or abused the system. While the Germans might have "observed in the letter" its agreement not to requisition food that would have to be replaced by the CRB, "it has never been observed in the spirit, and even the letter has frequently been violated." Grey also brought up the fact that Germany was still requiring Belgium to pay a war levy of 40 million francs a month.

Taken altogether, Grey continued, the result was that the CRB, "which had expected to be able to reduce its activities after the harvest, has increased them. It has made a series of new requests for import permits in respect of various fresh articles of food, and it has largely increased its importations of bacon and lard. It is planning to import large quantities of clothing for the destitute."

All of this was unacceptable to the British. "This gradual expansion cannot continue, and within the last few days, as Your Excellency is aware, His Majesty's Government have felt themselves obliged to suspend temporarily the importation of various articles into Belgium by the Commission."

Halfway through his long letter, Grey came to his point. "The time has therefore arrived when the whole work must be placed on a more clearly defined basis. . . . I must now inform Your Excellency that His Majesty's Government can no longer tolerate the present position."

Grey told Ambassador Page that his government would soon "lay down a programme of imports for the Commission which will be regarded as final. However long the German occupation of Belgium may continue, this programme will in no circumstances be expanded."

The foreign secretary went on to outline five stipulations that outlined the minimum that was necessary to "safeguard the livelihood of the Belgium people." The first two stated that nothing imported into Belgium would be allowed to be exported out of the country. The third stipulation reiterated the rule that the German Army must not be allowed to use or take anything that was imported by the CRB. The fourth item simply stated, "These prohibitions shall be rigorously maintained without exception of any kind." The fifth and final one would have been music to Hoover's ears because it stated that the CRB "shall be allowed to exercise any control over the stocks mentioned . . . which may be necessary in order to conserve them for the future, or make them available for the present needs of the population."

In Grey's last paragraph was the true heart of the British government's objections—that the efforts of the CRB, "through no fault of its own, [have become] a method of replacement instead of one of relief, and an encouragement to the Germans to deplete the resources of the country."

Hoover would have to wait until the New Year to find out exactly what the British government's new proposed program of imports would be. He knew, however, that "Sir Edward's action arose from pressures of the British and French military departments."

He also knew the fate of the people within occupied Belgium and northern France lay in the balance.

New Recruits Head for Belgium

As 1915 came to a close, a handful of men were preparing to sail for Belgium as new members of the CRB. They came from a wide variety of backgrounds, upbringings, and education. All had a strong desire to join the humanitarian efforts of Hoover's growing organization, which was gaining an international renown for what it was doing in Belgium and northern France. As the war news from the Western Front became more serious and shocking in its levels of intensity and bloodshed, the news of the CRB trying to save lives was inspiring and uplifting.

Two of the men who responded deeply to such positive action were Clare Morse Torrey of Berkeley, California, and Milton McIntyre Brown of Cincinnati, Ohio.

Clare Torrey had lived in the Bay Area of California all his life. His middle name, Morse, came from a San Francisco surgeon, Dr. Morse, who had amputated his father's leg after it had turned gangrenous from a wound received in the Alaskan gold fields. After the unsuccessful efforts in the gold fields, Torrey's father went on to try the grocery business before settling into a postal job for the rest of his career.

The family lived at 1158 Golden Gate Avenue close to Jefferson Square Park when the impressionable young man of 15 was rattled awake at 5:12 a.m., Wednesday, April 18, 1906, by the largest earthquake San Francisco had ever felt. When the initial quake and its hundreds of aftershocks subsided, fires raged throughout the city for days. In the end, approximately 3,000 people died, and 80 percent of the city was destroyed in an event that would be considered the worst natural disaster America had even seen.

Young Torrey and his family escaped unharmed, and the teenager was immediately caught up by the images of thousands of refugees fleeing the city. "The most pathetic sight I had ever seen was the march of the people who had been dispossessed by the fires," he said. By noon the sun was bloodred from all the smoke, while in nearby Golden Gate Park people gathered around as the U.S. Red Cross began relief efforts. Torrey was on the receiving end of relief when he was handed three cans of pineapple, the only remaining stock at the time. Soon after, he was on the other end of relief as a local shopkeeper put him to work. The merchant gave Torrey a wheelbarrow with a large chest attached that was filled with sundry items like cigars, tobacco, and candy. He told Torrey what the prices of each were and sent him two blocks over to Fillmore Street, which had become a major artery for people. "So I chose a spot and started to shout my wares."

Within the first few days after the quake, Torrey had seen firsthand what happened in times of great need and catastrophe, had been on the receiving end of relief, and had helped provide people with items they needed or wanted in the devastated city. He would never forget the experience.

The young man went on to graduate from the University of California, Berkeley in 1911 and earn a law degree in 1913. He then returned to the university and began multiple tasks—he taught freshman English; took on the prestigious job of personal secretary to the president of the school, Benjamin Ide Wheeler; and became an officer of the university.

By 1915, Torrey was an up-and-coming 25-year-old. He was partial to high, stiff collars, sophisticated ties, and well-appointed suits. He had a full head of dark hair that he kept swept back off his forehead, light eyes, and a neatly cropped moustache. His general countenance from working at the university was academic-serious, but he was quick to smile and his distinctive laugh could be heard through a crowded room.

In the fall, friend and fellow UC Berkeley graduate Tracy Kittredge had returned from nearly a year as a CRB delegate in Belgium. The stories he told Torrey

Clare Morse Torrey had survived the 1906 San Francisco earthquake and had experienced firsthand the importance of relief efforts. In December 1915 he followed his interest to serve others by joining the CRB. (Author's archives.)

were enthralling as he brought to life the indomitable spirit of the Belgian people, the camaraderie of the other delegates, the difficulties in dealing with the Germans, the scope and magnitude of the work, and the sense of awe most of the men felt for the CRB founder, Hoover—the man they affectionately called "the Chief."

Because the CRB was always looking for men, Kittredge had been asked to keep an eye open for those he thought could handle the job. He wrote Hoover recommending Torrey, along with two other men, John L. Simpson (from Torrey's suggestion) and Eddy (no first name). In an October 29, 1915, message to Hoover, Kittredge stated, "Mr. Clare Torrey was President of Associated Students of the University three years ago, having graduated [with a law degree] in 1913. He has been for the past year and a half Secretary to President Wheeler, and I think this speaks better than anything else of his character and ability in an administrative as well as in a diplomatic capacity." Hoover cabled back to send Simpson and either Torrey or Eddy, "whichever you think is best." Kittredge chose Torrey, who sailed on the SS *New York* on December 4.

Torrey had arranged for a six-month leave from the university. But he also had to deal with a more personal issue. He was engaged to be married to Miss Deborah Hathaway Dyer. They had met while students at UC Berkeley—she was a year behind him. They were both medal winners in school and had both been speakers at their commencements—he in 1913, she in 1914. While no date had been set for their marriage, it was planned to be held at her parents' home in Oakland. Seeing his determination to do such humanitarian work, she gracefully gave him permission to go serve in the CRB, knowing his job had given him a six-month leave.

When Clare arrived in London in mid-December, he knew he had to report to the CRB office, but he also knew he had to do another job he had agreed to take on for the university while in England. Before he had left America, he had agreed to act as the university's agent to examine a set of bells that were being bought for the new Sather Tower on campus. The bells were in a foundry in Loughborough, 115 miles north of London. Torrey was to inspect them before they would be shipped to the university. He had agreed to do so because he felt it was the least he could do for the university, which was giving him time off to join the CRB, and because he felt he could do the job in a relatively short time without holding up the CRB.

He was a little anxious and hesitant to mention his other obligation when he arrived at the CRB office. He was also nervous about meeting Hoover. "I was a little scared of him because he was a such a busy man and so brusque in his manner, yet he was very friendly."

But Torrey would quickly learn that Hoover had no patience for those not focused on what he felt was important—namely, the feeding of Belgium and northern France. Torrey began to tell him about the bells.

"You haven't time to go," the Chief stated. "You'll have to get somebody else to do it." He then moved on to other topics.

Caught off guard, Torrey quickly agreed, not knowing how he would do so. After a fast search through London, he found a member of the Society of Antiquaries who said he knew something about bells. Torrey sent him up to the bell foundry in Loughborough, where he duly examined the bells and pronounced them acceptable. They were shipped to the university and installed in the tower. The story didn't end there, however. As Torrey related later, apparently, the man's "ear wasn't at his best that day." One of the bells was out of key and "people blamed me for it." Every time it would chime, "They would say, 'That's Torrey's bell.'" When he finally heard the news months later while in Belgium, he felt a sense of embarrassment, even halfway around the world. (Eventually the bell was corrected.)

As the hastily hired bell examiner was making his poor inspection, Torrey was being sent into Belgium. Reaching Brussels in late December, he found he would be starting the New Year as a delegate in Namur Province, 70 miles southeast of Brussels.

By spring 1916, he and Hoover would have another memorable exchange that would cause Torrey much greater consternation than their first meeting.

Milton M. Brown had been born and raised in Glendale, the clifftop suburb of Cincinnati. The third child in a family of four boys and a girl, he was raised on a large dose of outdoor self-reliance that was fine-tuned every summer by a trip to the wilderness of the Georgian Bay of Lake Huron. There, among the wind-shaped pines, moss-covered rocks, and cold, clear water of the Canadian Shield, he roamed the islands, explored the bays, and fished the inlets with his brothers, sister, and friends. Ojibwa guides took care of the basics, as the family slept and ate on canvas-covered tent platforms. For children, it was an idyllic place of loon calls across still waters, bears gorging on blueberries, and sunsets that flamed across the sky.

Brown graduated from Princeton in 1913 and spent the first six months of 1914 exploring Rome, Naples, and the Amalfi Coast of Italy, doing research and taking photos in preparation to be a travel lecturer on the Chautauqua Circuit. In late July, he was on one of the last passenger steamers to leave Italy before the war broke out across Europe.

Back in America, he polished his text, organized his glass slides, then began speaking at universities and private institutions in the Midwest. In Asheville, North Carolina, the local paper, the *Citizen*, reported on April 30, 1915: "Milton McIntyre Brown, travel-lecturer, gave an unusually interesting talk last evening at the auditorium of the Young Men's Christian Association on 'Naples, Pompeii and Vesuvius.' The lecture was illustrated by a wealth of colored stereopticon slides. . . . All parts of the city were shown, the modern part with its splendid avenues and the older sections of the city with its narrow streets and picturesque natives."

Through a somewhat convoluted process (described later), Brown was accepted as a CRB delegate and arrangements were made for him to sail to Europe in January 1916.

As December came to a close, Brown was excited and nervous about this great humanitarian adventure. He was excited to be a part of the war in such a positive way and actually doing something rather than just sitting and reading about the conflict from thousands of miles away. He was nervous that he would somehow not live up to what would be expected of him in the CRB, but he was also looking forward to being a cog in the wheel of such massive food relief. He was certain of only two things: he would be back by the summer of 1916 and he was about to get involved in the largest food relief the world had ever seen.

He would be wrong on both counts.

30

Brussels

A German Agent Begins Hunting *La Libre Belgique*

When the underground newspaper first appeared in early 1915, von Bissing had instructed his Brussels secret police to find those responsible and shut down the publication. With every issue that was delivered, the governor general fumed more. By the end of the year there were three separate brigades of secret police in Brussels searching for the perpetrators.

Sometime during the year, a suggestion had been made that the newspaper might be published outside of Brussels in one of the provinces. It was then that the German police in Charleroi were told to take up the case. A German detective with the last name Grisenbrock, who was considered an expert at counterintelligence, was put in charge.

Working with him was a younger detective with the last name Haelen, who had been transferred from the staff of the Berlin Criminal Investigation Department to the Counter-Espionage Service in Occupied Territory. One history detailed that Haelen had been educated in Paris and spoke French "without a trace of that unfortunate accent which betrayed most members of the secret police."

He was also renowned for being handsome, refined, and highly successful at seducing young women and gaining valuable information.

During Haelen's work in various provinces, he had determined that the newspaper was most probably published in Brussels.

Grisenbrock assigned him to the *La Libre Belgique* case and sent him to the capital at the end of 1915. Haelen knew he would have to somehow become part of the contraband newspaper distribution chain to have any chance of discovering who was publishing the newspaper. He took on the persona of a disheveled, shabbily dressed, uncultured man and lingered long at the same small cafés frequented by newsvendors. He quickly learned that the sale of German newspapers or those approved and controlled by the Germans were merely fronts for the sale of the more profitable contraband Allied newspapers that were being smuggled from across the Dutch border.

One day, he discreetly followed one of the newsvendors and ended up finding the depot used by the border smugglers. It was a café on a narrow street lined with little cafés described picturesquely by *Underground News* as "where gentlemen of catholic tastes in extra-conjugal adventures could find divertissement with ladies abundant of charms and scanty of attire."

The raggedly dressed but handsome young Haelen was an immediate hit in such an atmosphere. Soon he became a vendor of contraband newspapers.

It was then that he made his first real progress. One of the other vendors he met was a young man, Emile, who sold newspapers for a living but also distributed *La Libre Belgique* as a patriotic aside. Haelen innocently offered to help him and asked where he could get copies on a regular basis. Emile said he got them from a girl and would be happy to bring Haelen some.

That evening Emile had no idea he was being followed when he went out to the suburbs and stopped in to see a girl at a newsagent's shop.

"The following day," one history stated, "the shop had a new customer, a handsome, well-dressed and wholly charming young man who had come to live in the neighborhood. At a time when attractive young men were few and money short it is not surprising that the pretty girl behind the counter found his attentions rather exciting."

Van Doren had no idea the secret police had just taken a huge step in its task of hunting him down.

SECTION III

CRISES, 1916

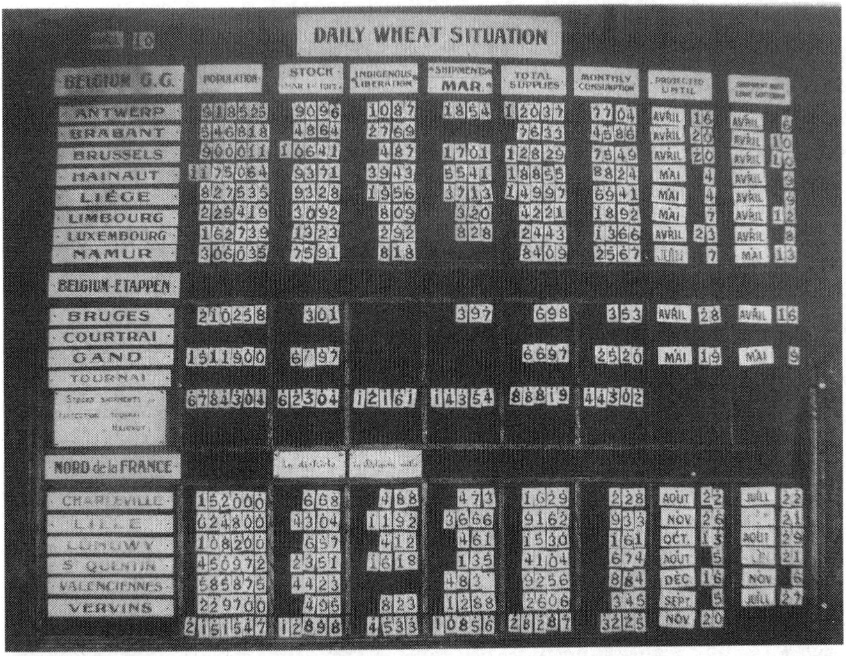

Top: The massive size of relief operations, and Hoover's insistence on detailed record-keeping, led to the creation of tote boards such as the "Daily Wheat Situation." Bottom: CRB executive William Honnold sits with Hoover in London discussing relief. (Both: Public domain; Herbert Hoover Presidential Library Archives, West Branch, Iowa.)

31

London

No Fresh Start

The New Year did not start well for Herbert Hoover.

He had received no direct answer from the British to his December request to increase imports.

The New Year's Eve letter from British Foreign Secretary Sir Edward Grey to Ambassador Page had been highly critical of German adherence to the food guarantees, detailed supposed abuses, and intimated that the entire relief program was on shaky ground.

That was followed by a January letter from Lord Percy to Hoover outlining serious infractions regarding imported rice. The British had learned—no doubt through its spy network—that supposedly some of the Belgian committees had sold portions of their CRB rice stocks to the Germans for shipment back to Germany. "I need not emphasise," Percy declared, "the serious nature of what has occurred, undermining as it must, our whole confidence in the watertightness of your system."

"I must therefore ask you for a statement of the full accounts of rice thus sold by the Committees, and we shall expect to hear within a month that the Germans have handed over an equivalent amount of rice to the Comité National from German stocks."

Percy demanded that the CRB stop importing rice immediately, and if his requests were not met by the allotted time, "we shall reconsider, not only the question of rice imports but the question of your imports as a whole, since it will then be evident that we cannot rely either upon the efficiency of your organization in Belgium nor upon the request of the Germans for their own pledges."

As if all that wasn't enough to the start of the New Year, Hoover was also facing a serious illness and had taken to his bed under doctors' orders. He had ear abscesses—an exceedingly painful and dangerous ailment normally seen in infants and children. Many times started by an untreated throat or ear infection, an ear abscess could lead to death in a world that did not yet have pharmaceutical antibiotics. Hoover, no doubt, had had his eardrum lanced to release the pressure and to drain the pus and had to have his ear soaked with hydrogen peroxide a few times a day. He was told by his London doctors that he should stop all work for three months at least.

On January 11, 1916, Hoover wrote to Gibson that he had been in bed for 10 days and that an assortment of doctors had told him, "I have not the ghost of a hope of getting out of the house for ten days and that I may consider myself lucky if I survive without having to go away for three months. According to them I have been burning the candle at both ends and in the middle too, but as I am infinitely better acquainted with my own mechanism than they are you can take it that I shall be in Belgium inside of ten days anyhow."

Hoover did not succeed in that claim, but he did send a telegram a week later saying why he still could not come. It wasn't his health—which remained poor—it was because "opposition to our work is growing" and he needed to stay in London because the situation looked "rather black."

From his sickbed and his office, Hoover maintained a tight grasp on all that was happening in the relief efforts. To fend off the continued problems with reported infractions of the food guarantees—and "to meet the British objections" in Grey's December 31, 1915, letter to Page—Hoover relayed to his new Brussels director, William Poland, the desire to restructure the Inspection and Control Department that already existed.

During the first year of operation, the CRB and CN had organized a Bureau of Inspection and Control that was operated jointly by Americans and Belgians. Any infractions that were uncovered involving Germans were reported to the local German authorities for action. Any cases that involved Belgians were turned over to the Comité National's provincial committees, and the accused were brought before Belgian courts. In theory, it was a sound foundation for success.

As Hoover related, however, that wasn't the case, at least in the minds of the Americans. "Our C.R.B. men soon found that they were having difficulty with the Belgians in this joint operation. The Belgians were naturally loath to expose their countrymen, especially in times when both privation and temptation were so great.

"In order that we should be able to cope with the flood of Allied complaints, I proposed, in January, 1916—and Francqui accepted—a separation of the C.R.B. inspection from joint operation with the C.N. Our men were to report their findings to the C.N. and to our American Director in Brussels."

It was time to see what William Poland and his men could do to pound out the details with Francqui and the CN to make a more efficient and effective Inspection and Control Department.

Hoover turned from that problem to the myriad of others that awaited his attention.

The serious accusation of rice being sold by the Belgians to the Germans for shipment back to Germany had to be faced quickly because of Percy's deadline. Hoover knew the charges were false and decided "it offered us an opportunity to discredit the British Intelligence with the Foreign Office." He ordered that all bills of lading for every canal barge and railway car used from Holland into Belgium be brought to London. He also had sent over all the receipts and accounts of the CRB warehouses, as well as the receipts from the thousands of Belgian communes. All of those were then audited by the CRB's public accountants—who were British.

From all that work came the good news that during the 14 months of relief operations, which had resulted in the importation of 1.2 million tons of food, only 400 tons were unaccounted for. That was way below the amounts of rice the British had accused of being bought by the Germans.

Hoover did admit that "smuggler allies of our Inspection staff informed us of a few communal committees which had sold rice at black-market prices and had bought potatoes, which had greater food value, from the same sources. Our informants insisted that they had sold the rice in Belgium. It amounted to a total of about ten tons." He included this in his report to the British. Faced with Hoover's impressive array of documents, receipts, and reports, the British quietly let the rice issue drop and moved on to other perceived problems.

When it came to Hoover's critical request to increase imports, there was still no word. He would have to wait until the end of February to receive an answer.

Ongoing Problems with Finding Good Delegates

Even with personal health issues and a nearly constant stream of international problems, Hoover would have said there was one key element to successfully maintaining neutrality and continuing relief within Belgium—the CRB delegates. Without honorable, trustworthy American delegates to uphold the many guarantees made with the Allies and the Germans, the relief would have been quickly shut down by one or the other of the warring nations.

Because good delegates were such a critical component, it followed that recruitment was also a wellspring of continual contention and constant struggle as CRB executives tried to find and retain the best people.

In the founding days of the CRB (October, November, and December 1914)—when Hoover was desperate to find neutral Americans who would drop everything, work for free, go into unknown German-occupied Belgium, and do a job that no one could adequately describe—his personnel standards had been relatively low. "We are badly in need of Americans to take charge of our work in various Relief Stations in Belgium," Hoover had written to Perrin Galpin, the Oxford student who ultimately would choose the first 25 CRB delegates from Oxford and would go himself. Hoover then gave a short description of the only criteria he had at the time: "We want people with some experience roughing it, who speak French, have tact, and can get on with the Germans." That was it—all the skills necessary for a position that had not yet been clearly defined.

Some accounts say that Hoover personally picked the first groups of Rhodes scholars who served as CRB delegates. Joe Green even said that Hoover had to personally approve everyone who became a CRB delegate in Belgium. In the case of the first Rhodes scholars, the evidence clearly shows that Hoover asked Perrin Galpin to choose the men. Practically speaking, Hoover simply didn't have the time to choose delegates as he dealt with much larger issues and crises. And while Hoover had a reputation for being a good judge of character and picking the right men for the right jobs, a later delegate who idolized the Chief wrote in his journal that the one "defect" Hoover had was his "inability of judging men accurately, and that he has made many mistakes in the misplacement of confidence in this man or that, and has been entirely in error in his belief in the capabilities of certain numbers of the Commission."

Regardless of Hoover's ability or inability to judge people, the American Legation staff and CRB executives in Brussels quickly discovered that some of the first student delegates were not up to the task. At least six of the first 25 Oxford students to enter Belgium were never officially listed by the CRB as having served as delegates. The assumption is that they either did not complete their agreed-upon service or they did so to such an unsatisfactory degree that the CRB did not want to include them in official records.

On a preliminary, unofficial roster, one of the unacknowledged six was an Oxford student with the last name Mechling. He was listed as entering Belgium on December 8, 1914, but under the column marked "Date of Departure," it simply stated "'Fired' at once." Another man on that preliminary roster, last name Fleming, was shown to have entered Belgium on December 14, 1914, and left February 20, 1915, with the handwritten notation "no good" beside his information.

Brand Whitlock and Hugh Gibson both saw the difficulties of using young, untested men who could be more impulsive than prudent, more combative than diplomatic. Whitlock, who publicly had only good things to say about the young American delegates, described some of them in private as "a lot of impulsive, ignorant young doctors of Philosophy." Gibson who could be impulsive as well—and would soon get into serious trouble for such behavior—became friends with some of the early CRB delegates and Oxford students but nevertheless wrote that many of the Rhodes scholars "are half-baked kids who ought not to be allowed to leave school."

Throughout 1915, personnel problems persisted as the New York CRB office sent over numerous recruits. Most were good, hard workers who fit into the relief program, while a few did not work out so well. A man named Dawson, showing no university degree, went into Belgium in June 1915 and left in August 1915. While he is acknowledged on official CRB membership lists, his personnel file contains a cable from the CRB London office asking the New York office to "secure for us necessary men, mature type, preferably University men, must have refinement of character as well as maturity and ability, do not want more Dawson, [or] Bradford type."

As CRB director in Brussels William Poland explained to new recruit John "Pink" Simpson, "You know, this is a delicate situation here. Some people come and don't get along very well and have to be sent home. You do get along, and we'd like you to stay."

Simpson—who turned out to be a well-respected delegate—had a simple description of what was needed: "The requirements were common sense, reasonable intelligence, and ability to get along with people."

Even so, some washed out. For those, there were numerous ways that their departure would be arranged. Some were simply invited to leave and given a ticket back to America. Others, who were not appropriate for behind-the-lines work but might be useful elsewhere, were transferred.

Hoover and CRB executives walked a fine line with the unacceptable delegates, primarily because all the men were volunteers who were giving their time and, in some cases, their own money to do the work. Hoover especially was averse to simply firing a person who couldn't do the work and on many occasions tried to save the feelings of those who were being removed.

Hoover felt no such compunction, however, when it came to those who wanted to cause a PR stir about what was "really" happening in Belgium or wanted to glorify their own participation. Hoover knew what negative publicity could do and did whatever he could to avoid, or at least minimize, it.

For those who deserved a little respect, a pathway for departure was created. As delegate Pink Simpson explained years later, those men were "promoted" to the CRB London office. "If a fellow in Belgium wasn't getting along very well, he would be 'promoted' to a position in the London office. [He would be told] there was a great gap there and they badly need somebody, and so he would receive that honor, and he'd go to London. And after he'd been in London for a couple of weeks with nothing whatsoever to do, he'd go home. . . . Those of us who were on the in, one of us would say, 'Did you hear that so-and-so has been promoted?' 'No, but I knew he would be pretty soon.'" Or they'd simply state, "so-and-so was needed in London."

No such respect was given to another delegate, last name Murdock, who worked for the CRB from early 1915 until late 1915. His name never made the official list of delegates, but he was the sole subject of a humorous five-page essay by Gilchrist Stockton titled "The Flock's Black Sheep." While probably not completely factually

Gilchrist Stockton, who did two tours as a CRB delegate, wrote a humorous essay titled "The Flock's Black Sheep," which touched on the relatively rare occurrence of unacceptable delegates. (Public domain; author's archives.)

accurate, the essay captured the feeling that Murdock was a flimflam man who had talked his way into the CRB.

"If he had been born in Blarney," the essay stated, "and had spent his childhood osculating the Blarney Stone he could hardly have been endowed with a power of persuasion more irresistible." The smooth talker was a Californian who had "pined to relieve the distress in Belgium, so he had interviewed Mrs. Hoover" (not the other way around). He supposedly told some that he could speak Flemish—all he had to do was speak German and clip his words.

"It has been claimed that gold cannot be gilded," Stockton continued, "but Murdock did it. According to his own true story he was . . . worth seventeen million dollars and had given three millions personally to Belgium Relief. He then decided to throw in his time to boot in order to oversee the spending of his own and other people's money. He was a brother-in-law of Brand Whitlock and when Hoover needed volunteers, Brand Whitlock had telegraphed Woodrow Wilson, 'Send Murdock.'" (No Whitlock relationship with Murdock has been found.)

According to the essay, once the CRB men caught on to Murdock, "It was officially decided that Murdock's services would be invaluable in Bechuanaland [a British protectorate that in 1966 became Botswana]."

Stockton finished, "Then came his departure thick with mystery, a confused mixture of threatened suicide . . . avoidance of international complications, consul's daughter, kidnapping, and other melodramatic phrases too fantastical even to weave into the 'Memoirs of Murdock.' If he would only tell his own true story."

Murdock left Belgium at the end of 1915.

While the Stockton essay was a greatly exaggerated piece of humor, the underlying premise of Murdock's personality seemed to be confirmed later. In early 1916, Vernon Kellogg, who had served as Brussels director and was then home in northern California, ran into Murdock. He wrote to John Beaver White, the director of the CRB New York office, on January 18, 1916, and reported, "Yesterday in San Francisco I met Murdock. He told me a number of extraordinary fairy tales about his doings since leaving Belgium, many of which I personally know to be lies and others of which I strongly suspect to being in the same category. He seems to be trying to connect again with the Commission work. . . . I have no doubt that he will soon be introducing himself as a member of the Commission. I think you had better send me a copy of the confession which is on file in your office (sent over by Hoover or Young from Rotterdam to you) so that I can be armed in case it is necessary to call Murdock down." Later, in another letter, Kellogg called Murdock a "disagreeable person."

Problems with some of the younger delegates made Hoover ask mature men such as 56-year-old Robert Arrowsmith to return to delegate work in Belgium. "Experience and maturity are so vital to us for certain positions," Hoover wrote. (Public domain; author's archives.)

Such delegate problems were relatively rare in the small organization that saw only approximately 185 Americans who ever participated as CRB delegates in Belgium and northern France. (A complete, accurate record has never been compiled). Ten unacceptable delegates have been identified (by this author), leading to a realistic estimate of between 5 to 10 percent that washed out during the life of the CRB. The stories of those who did not make it in the CRB are important, however, to gain a full understanding of the relief program and what Hoover had to deal with.

Delegate problems continued into 1916. In one cable from Hoover to the New York office, he declared, "We don't need more boys." In the same message, Hoover asked that previous delegate Robert Arrowsmith, 56 years old, be convinced to return to Belgium. His request showed what kind of men Hoover was hoping to recruit. "We are greatly in need of Arrowsmith's services for very important work [stop] Previous experience and maturity are so vital to us for certain positions that we beg of you to secure him if he can possibly come [stop] Should have two or three more men of maturity."

An example of the problems was a man named Gunn, 27, who came from San Rafael, California. He was a real estate dealer and could speak French. He came to Belgium in October 1915 and worked as a delegate in Liège. Never listed on any official membership rosters, he has the dubious distinction of being the only delegate to have his photo in a CRB file with the caption "Expelled from Belgium."

The only explanation came from a letter on January 16, 1916, that Gibson wrote to a counterpart in the American Embassy in London. Reporting that Gunn was being sent out of Belgium the next day, Gibson wrote that the CRB had "decided some time ago that it no longer needed his services—for reasons which you will probably understand when you see him—but he declined to leave and has been staying on and doing things which have made us decidedly uncomfortable. The situation got so bad that it was necessary to put heavy pressure to bear and unless something unexpected happens he will clear out with the Commission courier tomorrow morning. He now states that he intends to go to France. This is merely to tip you off that it would be well to be extra careful about helping him get there."

Actions by some delegates—even those who were older and considered good workers—could have serious consequences for all the remaining delegates, as illustrated by 44-year-old Reverend Charles N. Lathrop, who served in the CRB from September to December 1915. While considered a good delegate in the work he did, his departure from Belgium caused problems for those who remained.

CRB Brussels Director Poland explained the situation in a letter to Hugh Gibson on January 3, 1916. Poland first wrote that the evening before Lathrop had departed Brussels, he had had an "extended chat with [Lathrop] in regard to the obligation of C.R.B. representatives to observe strict neutrality and particularly to avoid carrying messages or documents out of the country, which might be of service or detriment to either belligerent, or in fact, concerning themselves with any affairs except the ravitaillement [relief] work of the C.R.B." Lathrop had agreed.

At the frontier, however, the German border guards—who had been generally honoring the agreement not to search CRB representatives—decided to do so with Lathrop. The car, passengers, and luggage were searched by two German officers and three civilian detectives. They quickly discovered a written account by Lathrop of a visit he had made to the villages of Dinant and Tamines, which contained "a record of houses destroyed, civilians shot, women and children ill-treated, etc." Carrying such a document out of Belgium was a direct violation of the CRB agreements with Germany.

Lucky for Lathrop, the Germans did not strip-search him, for they would have found additional notes and a detailed speech by the bishop of Liège concerning German atrocities.

After a half an hour of discussion, the Germans confiscated what they had found and let him and the CRB courier go.

Poland was furious at Lathrop and admitted to Gibson, "The whole occurrence is a serious reflextion [*sic*] upon the men of our organization and upon our undertaking to remain strictly neutral. It will for a considerable time to come, make the work of our men more difficult and the German Authorities more suspicious of our organization. I can find no excuse whatever for Mr. Lathrop and am more disturbed by his action on account of the high regard in which we all held him."

He went on to warn Gibson that he thought Lathrop's plan for the documents was to "publish certain data which he has collected in regard to alleged atrocities and other actions of the Germans, and it is my belief that radical steps should be taken by the London directory to insure that he publishes nothing whatever. I should have communicated it sooner, but was made aware of these last details yesterday evening only."

Gibson, as representative of a neutral country and one of the major patrons of the relief work, was also angry. A day later he wrote Hoover and enclosed a copy of Poland's letter in the diplomatic pouch. "The other members of the Commission," he wrote, "are now paying for the misdeeds of Mr. Lathrop." He told Hoover that, prior to the search, conditions at the frontier had "recently been much better and there had been no desire to search Commission men or cars as they crossed." But with the Lathrop incident, he said, "Naturally, the Germans were furious and since then every American going out or coming in, has had the charming experience of being searched. It simply means that suspicion is thrown upon the good faith of every American engaged in the work."

Even though Hoover was then bedridden with his ear abscesses, he met with Lathrop when the man reached London in early January 1916. They had a talk, and the reverend turned over all his notes and the speech by the bishop of Liège that he had smuggled out of Belgium. Hoover reported to Gibson, "There need be no fear whatever about Lathrop. I think the incident was considerably exaggerated, but he was obviously a darned idiot, and I think it is a good thing to have a scare among our people." Hoover wrote tongue-in-cheek that a large placard should be printed that stated in "big letters" that each delegate will be "searched to the skin and that the American Legation and the C.R.B. will absolutely refuse to interest themselves in his subsequent fate if the goods are found upon him."

Hoover acknowledged to Gibson the difficulty of finding good men. "I am full of apologies for failure to deliver new men, but to find men speaking French, of good character and position, who are willing to volunteer in an old story like this, is getting perfectly appalling. There is no longer the romance attached to it that there was in the early days, and I am simply having to beg men to go."

In a later letter to Gibson, Hoover indirectly referenced the delegate problems when he wrote, "Volunteers always get tired, they have other interests, things get delegated to minor staff, vigilance always relaxes, and sooner or later some explosion occurs."

One explosion would come from the person who had brought about the 1915 spy charges—Joseph Erdlets Jr. Before his 1915 departure from England, he had done something that in 1916 would call into question Hoover's personal integrity.

A Delegate's Journey to Acceptance Is Representative

For an organization that was justifiably proud of bringing sound business practices to food relief, the CRB never seemed to completely systemize the recruiting part of the operation. In many ways it would always remain at heart a who-you-know process built on delegate recommendations and periodically prodded into swift action by the simple need for bodies in Belgium.

Milton Brown's entry into the CRB was indicative of how haphazard the process was. He arrived in London in early January 1916 and quickly went into Belgium, but his application journey had started many months before and had finally, in a seemingly disorganized way, achieved acceptance.

In mid-1915, Brown was 24 and only two years out of Princeton. His childhood and college friend, Joe Green, had agreed to become a CRB delegate in late summer and had stimulated Brown's interest in applying. Additionally, in early September, Princeton's dean of the college, Howard McClenahan, followed through on a promise to the CRB New York office that he would look for appropriate men to recommend. He wrote, "I can recommend Mr. Brown very heartily. He is a young man of very fine ability, fine character, and of excellent judgment. I believe that he would do the work which a younger man can do in Belgium most admirably." He also noted that he was writing the letter without Brown's knowledge.

Nearly three weeks later, on September 23, the dean received a reply that politely brushed off Brown's chances. "At the present time . . . the Commission is well supplied with men of about Mr. Brown's age and the need is for men of more mature years, say at least thirty-five, who have in addition to the other qualifications a good business experience." The letter went on to give a standard rejection line that Brown's name would be kept on file if something came up.

More than a month later, on Tuesday, November 2, 1915, Brown, then living in Cincinnati, received a letter from Joe Green in Belgium telling Brown that he had recommended Brown to the New York office and that Dean McClenahan had done so as well.

The fact that Brown had not heard from the CRB did not deter the young man. He wrote the next day to the New York office, explaining that he had just learned of the recommendations and "had I known that anything was being done in the matter, and had I known to whom to address myself I would have most certainly applied for an appointment much earlier."

Brown described his current job as travel lecturer on the Chautauqua circuit and then rushed headlong into his rather thin qualifications, noting he would be turning 25 that month and had studied "a great deal of French and believe that in but a very short time I could speak and understand it without difficulty (some work in a Berlitz school before going over would be of great benefit to me). I can speak and understand Italian fairly well." Other than stating his position as a travel lecturer, Brown gave no business experience.

He did note that he had been on the long-distance cross-country team at Princeton. "I am in good health," he continued, "and my general condition is such that I am rarely indisposed in any way." He even mentioned his summers spent "in the rough life of a camp in the Canadian woods." He also declared that he would "welcome any amount of hard work to do what little I could to alleviate the suffering of the people of Belgium."

Brown finished by giving impressive references: from an editor of an engineering magazine; the president of Princeton, Mr. John Grier Hibben, who knew him personally and as a student; and the president of Procter & Gamble Company, William Cooper Procter, "to whom I have been a very near neighbor all my life." (Brown's father, Harry Whiting Brown, had been Procter & Gamble's first marketing director.)

Within a few days, the New York office had received a letter of recommendation from Princeton President Hibben. "Mr. Brown is a man of excellent ability and of thoroughly trustworthy character." Brown's father had even written a reference letter for his son.

The New York office was underwhelmed. Those who did the hiring had heard it all many times before and had later felt the displeasure of the CRB London office when some of those young men they had sent over were unacceptable. Still, a recommendation from the president of Princeton was not something to be taken too lightly. An internal message on November 8 reported that Director John Beaver White "thinks this party [Brown] will prove to be too young, but states that we can write to Mr. Hibben that we will be pleased to see [Brown] and give him every consideration."

Two days later Princeton's president received a note saying the CRB would be "very glad indeed to see Mr. Brown and talk over the situation with him, extending every consideration."

Five days later, on November 13, 1915, John Beaver White wrote to Brown. He immediately cautioned the young man that "at the present time we are sending over a few older and experienced business men for some of the first positions in Belgium. At a later date we shall need a number of younger men, and it is possible that you would be available to fill one of these positions."

Meantime, White continued, if Brown happened to be in New York he should come by and see them. The CRB director ended with another cautionary note. "It is essential that men going to Belgium should know fluently either French or German, preferably the former or both. From your letter we should judge that you have only a working knowledge of French, and consequently would not be able to converse fluently."

The day Brown received White's letter, he replied that he would "like to call on you at your New York office on Monday or Tuesday, November 22nd or 23rd, to discuss the matter of my application for an appointment to your staff in Belgium." He asked that he be cabled, at his expense, if either day worked because he would be leaving in a few days for New York. A cable arrived a couple of days later saying either day would work.

Brown was excited. He was in, or at least he had a personal interview where he hoped to impress someone with his maturity. Not thinking twice about the 650-mile journey, Brown jumped on a train and headed for New York.

On Tuesday, November 23, 1915, four days before his 25th birthday, Brown was interviewed in the New York office. He saw E. E. Hunt, who had recently returned from Belgium and was helping out wherever he could. He grilled Brown in French to see how his language skills were. He also talked about what it was like in Belgium and the kind of men they were looking for to do the work. Brown did the best he could to impress the older, wiser man. Brown was also introduced to Director White.

On November 26, White wrote to Edgar Rickard in the CRB London office about Brown and sent copies of Brown's initial letter and the two recommendations. Without giving any kind of endorsement, White stated simply, "Mr. Brown called on us on the 23rd, and if you can use any more young men, he is the type that will get along in Belgium." As for Brown's linguistic skills, White reported they were "not all that could be desired; on the other hand he reads French fluently and has considerable speaking knowledge, and as he intends to study over the next month, he will probably be as well equipped in this respect when he enters Belgium as some of the men who have been there for a period." White did add, "His business experience is confined to his lecture work, and therefore is very little."

White concluded by asking for a cable back about whether Brown should be sent. He never heard back (not unusual in the hectic activity within both offices).

Christmas came and went, and Brown did not hear if he had a position with the CRB. Finally, on December 28, 1915, he sent a handwritten letter to Director White saying that he had had several requests for his lecture but was holding off on committing to them in hopes of being accepted for delegate work in Belgium.

Unfortunately, White was out sick and did not reply immediately. Nearly two weeks later, on January 11, 1916, White finally cabled Brown, "If you have brushed up your French so that you can say that you really speak it fluently, we can arrange to have you sail on the eighteenth. Telegraph reply." Suddenly the recruiting process had become lightening quick.

The same day Brown telegraphed back: "All right on French can sail on eighteenth when shall I report at New York have you any advice or instructions regarding passport baggage clothing."

Surprisingly, after having been in operation for more than a year, the CRB New York office still had no formalized package of instructions or information on how a new delegate should prepare for such a long journey. White telegraphed back terse instructions.

White also cabled the London office on January 12 stating that Brown was coming and mentioned that "particulars regarding Mr. Brown, as well as letters of recommendation, were forwarded you on November 26th, in our Executive Letter No. 518, addressed to Mr. Rickard."

Milton M. Brown, 25, went through a drawn-out application process before suddenly being told he could go to Belgium. This was the photo used on his "emergency" passport. (Public domain; author's archives.)

In a whirlwind, Brown secured his passport and readied himself for the unknown. He boarded a train and left Cincinnati on a snowy Sunday, accompanied by his parents who wanted to see him off. The anticipated six-month separation would be the longest Brown had ever had from his three brothers, sister, and parents. The burden of that was heightened by a physical ailment he did not identify but wrote about in his journal: "I was leaving in a physical condition that some surgeons might have pronounced dangerous." (It was probably a digestive issue because he took olive oil every day while aboard ship, but never mentioned it again.)

On Wednesday, January 19, 1916, more than four months after the haphazard application process had begun, Brown finally boarded the *New Amsterdam* heading for Belgium. He realized how lucky he was to have been accepted, especially when he met six other CRB delegates traveling with him. The 25-year-old couldn't help but compare himself to those men, whom he described in a letter home: new recruit Henry Bradford, about 50, an engineer and railroad builder who had worked in South Africa and "his tongue is a bit rough"; new recruit professor Herbert Hamilton, about 35, had taught English at Amherst; returning delegate Francis Potter, about 33, had for five years been attached to the legation in Lisbon and Rome; returning delegate and Francis's brother, Phil Potter, about 30, was a Harvard graduate and had lived all over Europe; new recruit Fred Eckstein, 26, was a Yale graduate, had been with Doubleday in book advertising, and was "very brilliant on national and international matters. Hard to know, lived at least a year in France and Belgium"; and William Dunn, another Yale grad, who was "not as brilliant [as Eckstein] but more agreeable."

"The more I consider these men and their experience," Brown wrote, "the more fortunate I consider myself to be one of them. How I got my appointment I can't imagine, especially when I hear that many applicants are being turned away."

Brown's inner concerns would have only increased if he had known that Eckstein had written his mother while onboard that the newly met Brown "is a lightweight. He is a graduate of Princeton and nice enough, but—" (Later the two men would become friends as they each fell in love with a Bunge sister.)

Brown's concerns weren't only work related. During the crossing and the sailing through waters where German U-boats were known to hunt, Brown kept measuring to find the shortest distance from his stateroom to his assigned lifeboat #8. That did not deter him, however, from contemplating his decision to join the CRB and what he hoped to accomplish. "We all take chances, or life would be nothing but a rut; if the prospects are bright enough to shine beyond the darkness of the risks then are those chances well worth the taking. Here is a country suffering in the last extremity: what an opportunity to do something! Think of actually being able to put your finger upon the pulse of things in Europe to-day, even in so small a way as through the Commission for Relief in Belgium; to be at last a small cog in the great machine that is striving to alleviate some of the greatest distress the world has ever seen!"

When the group reached Rotterdam, the new delegates were given a quick orientation as to what to expect and how neutrality was critical to the entire relief program. Many of the new delegates were surprised to find that binoculars and cameras were not allowed into Belgium. As one new recruit later wrote, the men in the Rotterdam office had smiled when he "acknowledged the possession of binoculars and a camera. Of the binoculars I was particularly proud. They had been a parting present. 'Where do you think you are going! Through the Niagara Rapids in the Maid of the Mist, or down to Luna Park?' But my embarrassment disappeared, when, in turning over these possessions, I saw the [office] safe half full of other cameras and field glasses left for safe keeping by previous delegates."

Brown didn't have to give up his camera; he hadn't brought one. Before leaving the United States, he had asked if his camera skills as a travel lecturer might be utilized in Belgium for some kind of CRB work. E. E. Hunt had politely told him no camera would be allowed.

32

Brussels

New Year's Day at the American Legation in Brussels brought to the staff a renewed sense of purpose and a deep feeling of community as hundreds of Belgians came to pay their respects to those who were providing food relief. The Belgians also wanted to acknowledge that the Americans were constant reminders that Belgium had not been forgotten by the rest of the world. Belgians from all walks of life left calling cards, flowers, little notes—whatever they felt was appropriate or could afford—and signed the legation's register.

Gibson spent the first part of the day with high-level members of the Comité National, such as Ernest Solvay (the CN founder and internationally recognized scientist and philanthropist), Francqui, Lambert, and many others. They drank champagne and made long toasts and shared fine cigars. The fervent hope was that the war would end in the coming year, although after a year and a half of fighting, it did not seem probable. More realistic were the toasts that the food relief would keep on coming—although that, too, was always in doubt. In the end, the only surety lay in the fact that since the war's beginning, despite all obstacles, no mass starvation had taken place in Belgium or northern France. That was definitely something to toast.

Gibson said he then "donned my badge of servitude," meaning his formal clothes and top hat as chargé d'affaires of the legation and drove around Brussels honoring the long tradition of leaving his card at various homes, such as those of the remaining diplomatic corps, Belgian politicians and court officials, von Bissing, von der Lancken, other German officers, and a few personal friends.

In the early afternoon, Gibson returned to the legation to receive more callers. "Our punch and tea tables were well patronized," he remarked drily. More than a 150 dropped in, including many of the CRB delegates in from the provinces, as well as "all the nicest people I know in Brussels." As Gibson later wrote, "Ordinarily, Belgian functions are rather stiff but the admixture of Americans and some of the younger diplomats gave it quite a different tone and people really seemed to enjoy themselves."

After that, Gibson attended a formal dinner that took him late into the night. It was so late, in fact, that the next day he didn't even climb out of bed until close to lunch, and then stayed at home where he "rested hard all day."

New Delegates Arrive for the New Year

In January and February 1916, new delegates arrived in Brussels in a slow but steady fashion. Of particular note was Prentiss Gray. At 31 and with experience in shipping, "Prent" was not the usual fresh-faced recent college graduate who had symbolized the CRB in 1914 and 1915.

Born and raised in northern California, Prentiss Nathaniel Gray had two sisters, and his father owned and managed the Oregon Coast Steamship Company. Gray had attended the University of California, where he had been business manager of the yearbook and elected student body president. As a captain in the school's militia, he helped maintain civic order after the San Francisco earthquake in 1906. One month later he was a commencement speaker at his graduation, after which he joined his father in running the steamship company.

By 1915 he had nearly 10 years of business experience with the family's steamship company and had managed simultaneously a land development company. He also had become a family man, marrying Laura Sherman in 1908 and becoming a father with the birth of their first child, Barbara, six years later. In the autumn of 1915, Gray attended a football game, and an encounter on the way there would have a profound impact on the rest of his life.

A family story related how Gray ran into a college friend, John "Pink" Simpson, on the Telegraph Avenue streetcar in Oakland. They were both heading to a football game on the Berkeley campus. Simpson was in the process of applying to be a CRB delegate (he would leave in December 1915) and was full of excitement and stories about what he had learned of the Commission and the relief work in Belgium and northern France. He suggested that Gray consider applying, especially because of his shipping company experience.

Gray did so immediately, along with another college friend, A.C.B. Fletcher, and both were accepted. At a time when the CRB New York office was tightening requirements for delegates—most notably fluency in French, as evidenced by Milton Brown's application process—Gray had a real handicap: he couldn't speak French. In all probability, he was accepted primarily for his shipping experience, his age, and the fact that he came from Hoover's neck of the woods.

Leaving behind his wife and little baby, Gray and his friend Fletcher, along with a few other CRB delegates, sailed for Europe after a slightly rocky start. "We expected to leave on the steamer *Noordam* of the Holland-American line," Gray wrote in his diary on Wednesday, February 2, 1916, "but bad weather forced her to put into St. John's [Canada] for repairs. Then we were booked on the *Rojndam*. She struck a mine as she was leaving a British port. Finally our passage was changed to the *Rotterdam* which left the dock at 8:00 p.m. tonight."

At nearly six-feet two-inches tall, Gray stood out from most crowds. With a high forehead, thinning brown hair, and rimless glasses, he had a scholarly, serious look but was also quick with a big smile.

Prentiss Gray was married and had a young daughter when he headed for Belgium to become a delegate. While he could not speak French—which usually disqualified men—he had experience in shipping, which was vital to the CRB. (Public domain; author's archives.)

Gray's initial impression of Brussels was stark and depressing. "I have an overpowering feeling that the place has been dead a long time. Ghostlike silence reigns over everything. Now and then German troops swing through the city singing 'Die Wacht am Rhine.' Again the roar of the guns reverberates strongly on certain turns of the wind, bringing us up with a halt. Nothing, nobody, smiles not even the sun filtering through the ever-present mist in a watery way. Here and there throughout the city certain streets are forbidden thoroughfares upon which no Belgian may walk. Innumerable idlers and listless storekeepers bespeak the general feeling of oppression. Industrial disaster has settled down grimly over the land. Almost unconsciously we talk in whispers and look about to see that we are not being followed."

That depressing atmosphere had a strong impact on new delegates. Gray noted, "It seems as if all joy, had oozed out of our hearts. We are deluged with unending cautions by C.R.B. officials warning us against showing the slightest interest in German military movements. Their admonitions only increase and intensify this pall of depression which hangs over us. Professional neutrals, we must be without giving the slightest outward recognition that a great struggle is raging under our very eyes. It is for us to make good the word of neutrality of Herbert Hoover so that the feeding of these people by this American institution, the Commission for Relief in Belgium, shall be made possible."

As for relief work, Gray had little idea of what he was supposed to do. "I had rather pictured myself passing out loaves of bread to long lines of hungry people." He quickly realized that the American responsibility for feeding nearly 10 million people did not "permit the individual American delegate to distribute charity itself. He is but a part of this tremendous commercial enterprise which is financing, transporting, and distributing the foodstuffs of a nation."

And the need was great. "This land I have seen is industrially and mentally dead with thousands of idle people of haggard mien [look or manner]. The expected signs of starvation are not apparent, but evidences of insufficient nourishment and lack of employment are everywhere."

After nearly a week in Brussels—staying in an American pension on the *Place Stéphanie*, where many first-time delegates initially resided—Gray was assigned to be a delegate in Antwerp Province and immediately headed to his new post.

Van Doren Plays with Fire

While the overwhelming majority of Belgians were patriotic and anti-German, there were civilians who welcomed the Germans and aided them in the occupation. It was widely known that the German secret police would receive anonymous tips and letters from such sympathetic Belgians, who would report suspicious activities, expressions of anti-German sentiment, and the comings and goings of what the tipster thought were spies and smugglers. One history noted, "Even if the victim was innocent, as happened more often than not, he or she was lucky to escape with a week's imprisonment, while in all probability the house would be ransacked meanwhile."

Many times in these searches the Germans would come across some other contraband or offense that had not been mentioned in the anonymous letter. Because of that, the secret police diligently followed up on every tip in hopes of stumbling onto something illegal—especially something related to finding the editors of *La Libre Belgique*.

At the start of the New Year, Eugene van Doren decided to use the Germans' thoroughness for his readers' amusement and to harass the secret police. He carefully crafted two anonymous letters.

In the first, van Doren wrote as if he was confused or not sure of himself, but still wanted to tell his bit of news. He wrote of a Monsieur Vésale who was "an active member of the *Libre Belgique*." His home could be found around the *Place des Barricades*, but van Doren gave no specific address.

Within a day of receiving the letter, the secret police had numerous agents working around the square, inquiring quietly about where such a man could be found. The residents were wary, and most said they had no idea who the Germans were asking about. Finally, after a half a day of useless searching, the agents finally came across a helpful Belgian. He said of course he knew of Monsieur Vésale. He saw him every day and tipped his hat as he walked by.

Where does he live? the frustrated Germans asked.

Why right there, the man replied, and pointed to the large statue in the center of the square. Rushing over, they found written on the granite base the name of Belgian André Vésale, considered by many to be the greatest anatomist of the Renaissance.

Van Doren's second letter was much more serious. He wrote with firm conviction as if he knew what he was talking about and had intimate acquaintance with the facts. He gave specifics that could be checked out and verified; then he revealed the big prize—the address of the "automobile cellar" where *La Libre Belgique* could be found.

The secret police immediately confirmed as true the small facts provided in the letter—this must be a legitimate letter from a true Belgian sympathizer.

That night a detective and a squad of German police drove to the address—a rundown old building in a poor section of the city. It looked neglected and uninhabited. Just the place, the Germans thought, for the headquarters of the notorious underground newspaper.

Ordering some men around back to catch any who might try to escape, the detective and a handful of police approached the front. Breaking in the door, they rushed in with flashlights and revolvers at the ready. They cautiously went down a long passage and then crossed a yard to a shed in the back. They burst through the door ready to fire.

Standing quietly, not making a move, were piles of old and broken toilets and other sanitary equipment. The shed was used by the city for a storage depot.

Printing from his secret press in his own factory's backyard, van Doren was especially pleased with the next issue of *La Libre Belgique*. In it was an account of the Germans' heroic efforts in tracking down the information in van Doren's two letters. Adding insult to injury, van Doren sent the issue to the secret police with the article circled in blue pen.

Van Doren could be proud of how the newspaper had expanded since its beginning. By the start of 1916, the publication had a press run of 25,000 copies, distribution depots in every major city, and couriers to take each issue to practically every corner of the country (excluding the Army Zone). To do so, as *Underground News* reported, copies were "concealed in crates of 'returned empties,' between sheets of frosted glass labeled 'very fragile,' and even in parcels of fish marked 'perishable.'"

When it came to the issues traveling with fish, van Doren couldn't help himself when he wrote in one editorial, "Some of our readers have complained of the disagreeable smell of certain copies of the paper. We ask them to excuse us, but they must understand that in time of war one is not always able to choose one's traveling companions. Thus the *Libre Belgique* is sometimes obliged to travel with soused herring, Camembert cheese and carbide. We crave for the *Libre Belgique* the same indulgence our readers are obliged momentarily to show toward certain fellow-passengers in the tram. However, spring will soon be here, and we will do the impossible to have the *Libre Belgique* scented with rose or violet perfume."

On Thursday, January 20, 1916, the playfulness changed to tragedy. Gabrielle Petit, the young woman who worked for British Intelligence, helped ferry men to the border, and was a distributor for *La Libre Belgique,* was arrested by the secret police. Her fiancé had been killed only four months after they had said goodbye at the English ferry port of Folkestone.

According to one history, Petit was at home after returning from a clandestine trip to Charleroi and was expecting a courier from the Dutch border. He never showed up that night. The next night, however, a man did arrive at her door, giving her the prearranged signal and password. She was suspicious but let him in. The next day, January 20, she was arrested and sent to St. Gilles Prison, where Edith Cavell had been held.

Petit's story would play out a month later after 28 days in solitary confinement as the secret police tried to force her to reveal her contacts. During that time, she would turn 23 years old.

A few days after Petit's arrest, the Germans did go to the home of Petit's aunt and uncle, the Pilattes, and search it. They found copies of *La Libre Belgique* and took the two into custody. They left behind a German policeman to guard the couple's little girl and wait for anyone who might come by. The secret police had learned that they could catch other conspirators by staking out a raided house for a day or two.

That morning, van Doren approached the Pilattes house, unaware that Petit and her aunt and uncle had been arrested. A few houses from his destination he heard a whispered call. He turned and found the Pilattes child signaling him. She told him of the arrests and that she had only been able to get out of the house by telling the policeman that she had to go to school. She had not known where van Doren lived but knew he would come by, so she had waited for him.

That close call did nothing to dampen van Doren's enthusiasm for the work, but it did convince him that changes should be made for a higher level of protection. One history explained, "To avoid arousing suspicions of his servants van Doren had ceased having large quantities of the paper in his own house; he had also changed his tactics in supplying sub-distributors. Instead of going to their houses he met them at some prearranged place; in a store, in a tram shelter or a cafe, and never at the same place twice in succession."

One of his favorite choices of transfer was in the big elevators at the larger stores in Brussels. He and his distributor would meet at a prearranged time, when they would separately enter the same elevator. If everything looked good, van Doren would put his package of copies down between them, then walk out at the elevator's next stop.

NUMÉRO 62 — DEUXIÈME ANNÉE — FÉVRIER 1916

PRIX DU NUMÉRO — élastique, de zéro à l'infini (prière aux revendeurs de ne pas dépasser cette limite)

LA LIBRE BELGIQUE

FONDÉE

LE 1er FÉVRIER 1915

CHAGRIN D'AMOUR

Depuis un an déjà je te cherche nuit et jour,
Petite abhorrée, tu m'échappes toujours.

The front page of the one-year anniversary issue of La Libre Belgique *was filled with an illustration of German Governor General von Bissing despondent over his unsuccessful search for the creators of the underground newspaper. (Underground News: The Complete Story of the Secret Newspaper That Made War History,* Oscard E. Millard, Robert M. McBride and Co., 1938.)

Only a week after his close call at the Pilattes house, van Doren proudly printed issue number 62, which celebrated the one-year anniversary of the newspaper's start. It was an amazing and incredible achievement. To honor the occasion, the issue was filled with items that would rankle the Germans and make Belgians proud. Van Doren also added to the newspaper's title "Second Year."

The entire front page was filled with an illustration of a despondent von Bissing sitting at his desk overflowing with papers relating to his search for the underground newspaper. Roaring by above his head was a cartoon image of the "automobile cellar" where the paper was supposedly produced. Around him were images of the two hoaxes van Doren had recently played on the secret police. The title of the illustration was *Chagrin d'Amour* (grief of love, or headache). The caption read: "For one year now I seek you night and day, abhorrent little rag, you escape me always!" Even the illustration's credit lines mocked von Bissing. The layout was by "G. Lafrousse" (*j'ai la frousse*; I'm in a funk), while the drawing was by "E. Papeur" (*aie pas peur*; don't be afraid).

Victor Jourdain had written an editorial titled "Our Birthday." He thanked all those who had helped produce and distribute the publication, including the "driver of our phantom automobile." He also apologized to those who had been caught, tortured, and imprisoned for the paper: "We offer them our sincere apologies and count on their patriotism to forgive us for the trouble caused them by the clumsiness and incompetence of the German police."

Once again he finished with a defiant call of patriotism: "Even if its enemies succeeded in cutting it to pieces they would not destroy it. *And we defy our persecutors ever to silence us.* Truth will cry louder than their lies, and will always find a way to Belgian hearts and consciences. The encouragement we have received from all sides has lightened our task and proved to us that our efforts have not been in vain."

As Jourdain and van Doren were producing issues, the German espionage agent, Haelen, had been working two simultaneous jobs, one as the attentive suitor to Madeleine, the girl at the suburban news shop, and the other as a contraband newsvendor with Emile in the inner city.

In early 1916 he reported back to Grisenbrock, his boss in Charleroi, that he had a growing web of people that he felt certain were involved in the underground newspaper. Should he have them all brought in?

No, replied Grisenbrock. The Charleroi detective in charge of the search was not going to make the same mistake that the secret police in Brussels kept making—arresting small operators rather than letting them lead the police to the organizers.

The problem that Grisenbrock and Haelen had was that Haelen was only one person. He couldn't follow all those who he had come to know had a connection, no matter how slight, to *La Libre Belgique*. And Grisenbrock didn't have the men to send up to Brussels. That meant Haelen would have to ask the secret police in Brussels, with their three separate brigades, to help.

Such a request for manpower did not sit well with the Brussels brigades for numerous reasons, ranging from personal self-interest to professional rivalry. At the time, there was a 10,000-German-mark reward for the editors of the underground newspaper. That had stimulated the Germans to start acting in self-interest rather than to coordinate and work together as a team. Compounding the issue was that Grisenbrock and his Charleroi men had been placed in charge of the overall search for *La Libre Belgique*, which did not go over well with the Brussels secret police.

There was little if any cooperation between the groups. Arrests in Brussels were being made haphazardly and prematurely, as was the case of the Pilattes, who had been apprehended before they could be followed.

The Pilattes had unknowingly become part of the growing web being developed by Haelen, so when he and Grisenbrock found out about the arrests they were furious. Grisenbrock came down hard on the Brussels brigades and issued strict orders that no further arrests were to be made until he gave the order.

Part of the web of people that Haelen was building included a professor named Gheude, who provided Madeleine with a stack of *La Libre Belgique* each week.

Gheude worked closely with van Doren.

Whitlock Returns and Intrigues Follow

Less than two weeks into the New Year, on Monday evening, January 10, Brand Whitlock, his wife, their dog Mieke, and mounds of luggage came roaring back into the legation. Gibson was alerted at his residence by Eugene, one of the legation staff, and hurried over to greet his returning boss. He was relieved to see that "they both look infinitely better than when they left."

It must have been hard for Gibson to welcome back the boss he had never really respected, and who would, by returning, force him back into the secondary position he had definitely outgrown in his months as chargé d'affaires. To his credit, he showed or wrote of no animosity or reluctance in doing so—even in his unguarded letters to his mother. He did, however, make a few light comical jabs about the adulation the Whitlocks had received when in America and on returning to Belgium. To his mother, he wrote that they were "full of the ovation they had received everywhere. . . . The W's were evidently made a tremendous lot of while they were home. They are still bursting with it."

Being the ambitious person that he was, Gibson could not have helped being somewhat resentful of all the praise Brand Whitlock had received for many things that Gibson felt he, not Whitlock, had done in occupied Belgium. Gibson didn't mention it or seem to dwell on it.

Hugh Gibson had been chargé d'affaires *of the legation while his boss, Brand Whitlock, had been away in America. Once Whitlock returned, Gibson was back to being legation secretary, although that would not last long.* (Public domain; author's archives.)

On the other side of things, Whitlock came back bearing an important gift for Gibson. It was a way of repaying him for all the hard work and devotion to duty he had shown during Whitlock's absence. The State Department had granted Gibson personal leave, to be taken as soon as Whitlock had settled back into his position.

Gibson could definitely use it. After visits with his Belgian doctor, he wrote his mother that the doctor had said, "There is nothing the matter with me beyond the fact that I am very much run-down. Nothing that will not be remedied by rest. He says a month of hard loafing in the open air is the minimum but I know my own recuperative power and also just how much loafing I can stand. After 3 weeks or a month I shall be fit as T.R. [Teddy Roosevelt, a man Gibson greatly admired]."

Gibson immediately began thinking of where he might take his leave, from Switzerland to America. His wealthy Belgian friends offered him the use of their homes outside of the country, and he even hinted to his mother that King Albert had offered to have him "visit him for as long as I like."

Only a few days later, however, Gibson began rethinking time off. Hoover had been scheduled to come to Brussels during the first week of the Whitlocks' return, but had abruptly canceled because of his ear abscess. Then Hoover's message came saying how the situation in London "looks rather black."

Gibson immediately decided that he could not go on leave while things were in such a state, although he wrote his mother he was confident because, "we have pulled out of more black holes that I have been able to tell you of and perhaps we can keep on doing it."

It's interesting to note that throughout Gibson's writings he used "our" and "we" when talking about the relief work. Here was a man totally and wholeheartedly committed to the CRB and what it was trying to do. Officially, as a member of America's diplomatic corps, he was not supposed to be an active participant in the nongovernmental, private-citizen-run Commission work. His and Whitlock's role was supposed to be one of neutral patron—impartially sitting back and observing the work from afar. But the nature of the work, and the difficulties with handling all the various problems created by the other countries involved, forced the staff of the American Legation in Brussels and the American Embassy in London to do so much more than what the paper title stated. And Gibson became the embodiment of how the diplomatic corps in Belgium and Britain became fully vested in helping the CRB succeed. They knew they were personally part of the relief work, whether their government officially acknowledged that fact or not.

This went doubly for Gibson, who probably felt that he was nearly indispensable to the relief program in Belgium and was privy to most of what was happening among all the players. He would have especially thought that way after the return of his boss, whom he felt had never been up to the rigorous, confrontational challenges of being minister of the legation in Belgium and patron minister of the CRB.

Gibson would have been surprised to learn that only three days after Whitlock returned, he was the topic of negative conversation in a meeting between Whitlock and von der Lancken. The meeting took place in the German's office, covered numerous subjects, and lasted two hours. As Whitlock recorded in his journal, at the end of the meeting von der Lancken brought up "old objections to Gibson" and that the secretary had become in the Germans' eyes *persona non grata*. Whitlock wrote that Gibson didn't have the "slightest suspicion" of how the Germans felt. In response, Whitlock told von der Lancken he would "find a way," presumably to remove Gibson as painlessly as possible, but asked von der Lancken in the meantime "not to permit anything foolish to be done" by the Germans. It appears that Whitlock wanted to remove Gibson in his own way and at his own pace, but he was never good at confrontations and did much to avoid them.

Only a few weeks later, Whitlock would be pushed to confront Gibson, and he then became part of another intrigue that would try to eliminate the CRB from Belgium.

A Belgian/American Wedding Brings a Welcome Distraction

As Whitlock and Gibson attempted to settle back into their previous roles, Gibson tried to overcome the fatigue that had been plaguing him in the previous month. To help relax, Gibson took some time off on Friday, January 21, to take a drive with a CRB courier and friend, Edward Curtis, out to Louvain.

"The air was glorious and there was even sun—which is an event in Belgium," Gibson wrote to his mother. The drive in the countryside was helpful, most notably just to get Gibson out of the legation and out of Brussels, which was so overrun with German soldiers that no one could ever forget the war. Even in the countryside, though, the war intruded on Gibson and Curtis.

Charles Carstairs was a CRB delegate who fell in love with a Belgian woman. In late January 1916, they married at the Chateau Mariemont with Hugh Gibson as best man. (Public domain; author's archives.)

"As soon as we got into the country," he wrote later, "we ran into two Zeppelins flying low and circling around each other like a pair of love-lorn sausages. They have been scarce around here for some months and even in the old days they seldom played around in the daytime. We usually saw them slipping away to England in the dusk or creeping home from one of their trips."

Back in Brussels, to compound any job-related stress, Gibson also suffered through a few days of dental problems, having "strenuous times" during two sessions on one day and a long sitting on the following day. "I have never had such a siege with the tooth-puller," he wrote his mother, "and did not realize how it takes the tuck out of you."

That did not stop Gibson from performing an important diplomatic function. The second day of Gibson's dental problems was Thursday, January 27, which was a German day of celebration—the 57th birthday of Kaiser Wilhelm. With Whitlock not stirring from his bed chambers that morning, Gibson took it upon himself to travel about town doing the traditional duty of leaving his card at the home of the governor general, the military governor of Brussels, and von der Lancken as a sign of respect. He had some difficulty getting around town because of the various German reviews and receptions going on that shut down some streets. That evening a torchlight parade caused more traffic problems as it wound through the city.

The next day, with his teeth still aching, Gibson worked most of the day at the legation before roaring off in his motorcar heading south to Chateau Mariemont, in the Walloon province of Hainaut, where he was to be the best man at a CRB delegate's wedding.

The groom was Charles H. Carstairs, who had attended Yale and graduated from Ecole des Sciences Politiques in Paris. He had joined the CRB in February 1915 and had been assigned to Hainaut Province. While working there, he had fallen in love with a Belgian woman, Helen Guinotte, one of five daughters of the burgomaster of the little village of Bellecourt. They were to be married a few kilometers down the road from their village at the massive Chateau Mariemont, which was owned by Raoul Warocqué, a 45-year-old industrialist who had built on two generations of family fortune to become one of the richest men in Europe.

Before the war, Warcoqué had taken the money he had made from coal mines, gas and electric companies, railroads, and other international businesses and had opened schools, an orphanage, a maternity hospital, and a soup kitchen to feed the poor. When the war came, his business stature and charitable giving made him a natural for supporting Belgium relief through the Comité National, the provincial committee, and the CRB. Even though he was relatively young, Warocqué was not a healthy man. He was overweight and had "serious breathing problems." He would receive "special treatments every morning under the supervision of a physician." Even so, "he was an extremely jovial and friendly fellow . . . [with] quite a zest for life and many interests."

That enthusiasm for living fit naturally with hosting a joyous wedding, especially when the bride was the daughter of a local burgomaster and the groom was a CRB delegate who had worked in the province and grown to know Warocqué well.

When Gibson arrived after dark, he was delighted to find that the Belgian industrialist had opened up his entire chateau for the first time since the war and, it was "lighted up like Coney Island." That night there were 30 seated at the formal dinner, and all of them were staying the night in the large chateau. CRBers in attendance were Edward Curtis, William Poland, Hallam Tuck, L. C. "Duke" Wellington, Dorsey Stephens, Frederick Meert, and Rene Jensen. Foreign diplomats included Germàn Bulle, the Mexican chargé d'affaires considered by most to be a CRBer, and Sven Harald Pousette, the secretary to the Swedish Legation in Brussels. Whitlock was there, along with American Legation staffer Caroline Larner; Mrs. Whitlock had stayed home in Brussels because their dog, Mieke, was sick.

The festivities on Friday night and the ceremonies on Saturday were joyous ones that included events not only at the chateau but also in the village of Bellecourt. A civil service was first held at Bellecourt's *hôtel de ville* (the town hall) and then at the local Catholic church. Because Carstairs was Episcopalian and Helen was Catholic, Gibson had had to secure the intervention of the Apostolic Nuncio to Belgium in Brussels so that an abbreviated religious service could be performed. The shortened service, held in the local church, was followed by a sit-down lunch for 40 people.

While the entire wedding was a lively and happy affair, the war was still very much in the minds of many, including the bride's sister, Paula, who had planned on marrying around the same time but her fiancé was "sitting behind a machine-gun at the front and his chateau is occupied by the Governor-General." Absent ones made the affair that much more poignant and meaningful.

For Gibson, the wedding was a great distraction from work, but far too short. He was back in the legation the next day, Sunday, January 30, to do a little work.

When he got there, however, he found that there was "weeping and wailing and gnashing of teeth." The Whitlocks' beloved little Mieke had died in the night. "All the family quite broken up," Gibson reported to his mother. Later, he took a rousing horseback ride with Ynès and had a talk with his good friend Lewis Richards, who had just returned from London and reported that Hoover was still sick but "out of bed and fighting to keep our work going."

It appeared as if things were looking up.

The Reorganization of the Inspection and Control Department

William Poland had joined the CRB in Belgium in September as assistant director to Vernon Kellogg and became director in December 1915. An internationally known civil engineer, he would become a critical member of the CRB executive team. Delegate Pink Simpson would call him "one of the finest men that ever lived."

When Poland received word from Hoover in London that he and his men were to reorganize the Bureau of Inspection and Control to give the CRB greater freedom and control, he turned to a relatively new arrival to the CRB who had already proven himself in such matters—Joe Green.

From October 15, 1915, to December 15, 1915, Green had served as chief delegate to Hainaut Province. When he took over the province from Robinson Smith, he found the "commercial sides of the business, shipping, milling, and so forth," had already been "systematised" and were functioning smoothly. Distribution by the local committees, however, was not "properly supervised," in his opinion. He moved forward to get a better handle on the situation. "I had just begun to put the Inspection on a proper footing in the Hainaut when I was appointed to the Agglomération Bruxelloise [the greater Brussels section, created for the purpose of providing relief]."

At his new post, Green was charged with implementing a plan of inspection over the local warehouse. The plan had already been readied, but it had not been executed because there was a "three-cornered fight" between Francqui, CN member Max Hallet, and CRB delegate Pierre Humbert as to who would run the show. In short order, Green somehow managed to placate everyone while assuming joint control of the operation with Hallet, "which really left things in my hands, as Hallet had no time to attend to such matters."

Such success led Poland to appoint Green to be the CRB representative of the new jointly run Inspection and Control Department. In January there were a series of meetings between Francqui, CN Vice President Chevalier Emmanuel de Wouters d'Oplinter, Poland, and Green.

It was at these meetings that Green had his first real interactions with Francqui. He found out quickly that the Belgian was a force to be reckoned with.

Émile Francqui was as enigmatic as Hoover. He could also be a thorn in the side of both the CRB and Hoover. (Public domain; Herbert Hoover Presidential Library Archives, West Branch, Iowa.)

To many—especially the Americans—Francqui was as enigmatic as Hoover. Few of the Americans had spent any real time with him, beyond observing his dictatorial running of the CN meetings. Those who had spent time with him rarely, if ever, shared any personal insights about the Belgian that ended up in historical records.

Hoover was inordinately diplomatic in a short postwar description of Francqui: "Outstanding among all the Belgians of his time was Émile Francqui. He had a gruff personality, but with great loyalties, affections, and devoted friendships. He was a natural administrator. His quickness and adroitness of mind were equal to any sort of intellectual battle. He had a fine sense of humor and in his many narratives about our work showed a talent for both lucid expression and dramatization."

Green would get to know Francqui better than most CRBers through his work as head of the Inspection and Control Department. Green, who could be quite abrasive, abrupt, and brutal in his personal assessment of others, wrote an extensive, vividly revealing "portrait" of Francqui.

While it is one-sided and at times a harsh assessment—with only two positive-quality acknowledgments—it is representative of the feelings many Americans had toward the Belgian.

"It is a curious irony of fate," Green stated, "that the man at the head of what is undoubtedly the greatest social and charitable work ever organised, should be a man absolutely bereft of any finer feelings. He thinks in francs and centimes. He has absolutely no conception of the meanings of such words as patriotism, social duty, self-sacrifice etc.: He believes money to be all-powerful, and does not hesitate to express his ideas in the matter. He is utterly incapable of believing that any man can do anything except for his own personal advantage, and his own personal advantage considered in the financial sense."

Green's introduction of Francqui's two positive attributes starts off in an equally harsh tone: "I have never seen him display any feelings except hatred and anger, and the only good thing I know of his personal character, apart from his business ability, is that he likes to play with children and the children like to play with him. That must be a sign of some good characteristic of which we never saw any other evidence, but for which we must give him credit."

As for Francqui's dictatorial running of the CN and the other Belgians on the committee, Green gave credit to one important fact: "Some of them hate him, most of them fear him, and all of them agree that he is the one man who can hold the National Committee together, and keep Catholics and Liberals and Socialists from scratching each other's eyes out."

When it came to the CRB and the American side of the relief, Francqui, in Green's opinion, had no equal, but for the wrong reason: "His constant opposition to us and our work caused us more difficulty than all of our troubles with the Germans and with the Allied Governments put together. Not only did he oppose us at every step, but he added insult to injury, and often treated us in public with atrociously bad manners. . . . I remember that on one occasion he referred to us as '*ces gens de la C.R.B.*' ['these people of the CRB']."

"He constantly intrigued," Green continued, "against the Commission in Brussels, in Paris, at Le Havre and in London. When he found that he could not reduce us to a position of subordination his [unsuccessful] effort was to have us thrown out of the country and replaced by Spaniards or other neutrals, who would be easier to handle. He once told [CRB Brussels director] Dr. Kellogg that the Americans would one day leave Belgium 'dans un éclat de rire' ['in a burst of laughter'] on the part of the Belgians."

What made the entire situation tolerable, Green maintained, was that "his feelings and opinions were shared by only three or four of his colleagues. . . . The game which he was playing was as distasteful to most Belgians as it was to us. . . . One of the leaders of the [Liberal] party once told Mr. Francqui to his face that the systematic depreciation of the C.R.B. was a national disgrace, and that represents the attitude of all but half a dozen or so, some of whom unfortunately are men of considerable influence."

This was the man Green had to face across a negotiating table.

As Green met with Francqui, Poland, and de Wouters to pound out the details of reorganizing the Inspection and Control Department, he had no idea of what he was getting into, or with whom. But he learned quickly. When Poland read a draft of a final agreement, Green reported that Francqui erupted in anger. "He stormed for a while, and then agreed to take the draft home and redraft it to suit his idea." When Francqui came back the next day, however, the draft was little different in any important aspects and Poland agreed to it with only minor changes.

The new Inspection and Control Department would be run with Green as the CRB representative and a man named Van Gend as the CN representative, but there would be a better separation between the two groups than in the earlier bureau. The CRB would have greater freedom of action than before. Green was charged with ensuring the distribution of food was done fairly and justly throughout the country and investigating all accusations of abuse that happened within and outside the system. All findings and reports would be given to both the CN and the CRB.

Once the organizational paperwork was approved by Francqui and Poland, Green noted that he and Van Gend were "left to work out our own salvation." Within a few weeks they had worked out any differences they might have had and had organized the central office of the department. From there they branched out and started to get the provincial committees to understand how the new inspection and control would work.

"This was the important part of our work," Green explained. "Without the acceptance of the local and provincial groups to a centralized inspection and control department, nothing would be achieved."

A big hurdle was that Van Gend, as a Belgian, could not obtain an automobile pass, and as Green related, "he had no standing with the members of the Provincial Committees." To Green this meant additional lobbying activity. "I soon found that the only way to stiffen up the Provincial Inspection was to bring pressure through the American representatives. This I did by making constant visits to the Provinces, urging them on and making suggestions in one Province drawn from the experience in another, and by explaining minutely what was wanted time after time at the Thursday afternoon meetings of the Representatives in Brussels," he wrote.

Green also knew that another critical part of his job was investigating all the allegations of abuse that the British Foreign Office kept bringing to Hoover. He and his staff immediately began to recruit "trustworthy Belgians, whose names they never disclosed, to help them in their investigations."

Hoover was quickly impressed. "These energetic American youngsters, under the leadership of Joseph C. Green, at once undertook to get to the bottom of the black-market activities in and around Belgium. They established contacts with 'patriotic' Belgian black-marketeers and smugglers, whose code of morals forbade them to deprive their own countrymen of food. These men co-operated with our staff in locating actual or supposed leakages from Belgium and Northern France to outside countries."

This was critical to Hoover's fight against the British and French militarists, who kept going to the British Foreign Office with accusations of abuses taking place in Belgium. Many of their accusations "consisted of records of black-market operations and of canal-boat movements in and out of Belgium and Holland." With the newly energized department, Hoover declared, "We were able to meet head-on the deluge of accusations by the British and French espionage staffs concerning alleged violations of guarantees."

During this time of organization, Green knew that the new, stronger role of Americans in inspection and control did not sit well with Francqui. At first, the Belgian tried working his way into the American's good graces. He repeatedly called him "mon cher ami," slapped him on the back at every opportunity, and asked him to numerous dinners at his home. He would call Green to his private office for meetings, where he rarely talked business. Instead, according to Green, he often "told smutty stories which I was obligated to consider humorous, or else told me things obviously in the hope that I would repeat them to the Director or to Mr. Hoover."

All such staged camaraderie ended quickly the first time Francqui tried to give Green a direct order. The American told him as "politely as possible I was unable to execute." Francqui was not happy. In fact, "he flew into a terrible rage, shook his great double chin, pounded the table and literally tore his hair." Green calmly noted, "I had always thought up to that moment that this [tearing of hair] was only an expression used by playwrights and novelists."

That ended the "mon cher ami" and the dinner invitations for good. From then on, Francqui "never recognised me when he could avoid it, and he maligned me behind my back to Americans, Belgians and Germans alike. Some of the elaborate and detailed lies which he told about me were the most remarkable inventions."

Green simply put his head down and kept on working, trying hard to ignore Francqui.

33

Northern France

In the cold predawn of January 11, 1916, most of the residents of the French city of Lille were still fast asleep. Two predominant features of the industrial city were the rather drab multistoried textile factories that dominated entire neighborhoods and the rows of modest homes of the laborers who worked in them. With the war and German occupation, many of the factories had closed, and residents had struggled to survive under the harsh military rule in the Etape part of the Army Zone. This was especially true of the residents of Lille because the city was only 10 miles from the trenches and, consequently, was the major staging area and storage depot for the German military forces in Flanders.

The Germans controlled all aspects of civilian life. No resident was allowed to use a telephone, post a letter, congregate in the street, or leave his or her neighborhood without authorization. And the German order of lights-out-at-sunset left the city fearfully black and nearly invisible within the darkened countryside.

Even so, things were about to get worse.

At 3:30 a.m. the city was rocked by a gigantic explosion as a huge flash of yellow light pierced the night sky. Heard as far away as Holland, the explosion flung boulder-sized rubble and hot-metal debris more than a mile while shattering windows and busting in doors throughout the city and all the way to Roubaix, nearly 10 miles to the north. The Moulins District in the southeast quadrant of the city was nearly wiped off the map. Twenty-one factories and 738 homes were destroyed in the district. When daylight finally came, stunned residents found a crater nearly 500 feet wide and 100 feet deep on one side of the Boulevard de Belfort.

One small piece of good news: Lille's city center was more or less spared from great damage only because it had been shielded by a couple of textile factories built of concrete that took much of the direct force of the blast.

But the physical devastation the city endured was nothing compared to the human toll. One hundred and eight residents—mostly women and children—died, along with 30 German soldiers. Four hundred more people were injured, 116 severely. More than 1,200 families were suddenly homeless and more than 5,000 were instantly out of work.

The blast originated from, and annihilated, the Germans' munitions depot "18 Bridges," so named for the 18 arches that highlighted the old gunpowder storage areas of the facility. The city's proximity to the front led to the suspicion that the cause was Allied artillery, aviation attack, or sabotage. No cause was ever determined, even after the Germans offered a reward for information.

The blast's impact on the residents was devastating and was compounded by the fact that the city was cut off from the rest of France and the world. In the cold aftermath of the explosion, however, the people of Lille could take some comfort in knowing they weren't completely alone. The prior spring, in April 1915, the city and the rest of German-occupied northern France had come under the food-relief umbrella of the CRB and the Comité d'Alimentation du Nord de la France (CF).

That meant a CRB delegate was ready to help out.

The Delegates for Lille and Valenciennes

By the time of the Lille explosion, the district of Lille had seen a couple of delegates come and go (Lewis Richards and Bill Sperry). The current chief delegate was Laurence C. Wellington, better known as Duke or The Duke, to his fellow delegates (a joking reference to the Duke of Wellington, the 1815 commander of the Allied Army who, with the help of the Prussian Army, defeated Napoleon Bonaparte at the Battle of Waterloo in Belgium).

The American Duke was soon to turn 26 but looked younger with a slender build, average height, clean-shaven face, and blond hair that hosted an unruly cowlick in the front. He had been one of the first 10 Oxford students to go into Belgium in December 1914. (He was one of the few non-Rhodes scholars in the early groups.) He spoke German and French and was initially assigned to be chief delegate of Luxembourg Province.

Wellington took quickly to the work and chose to stay beyond his six weeks agreement. An only child from Amherst, Massachusetts, he stayed at his post until May 1915, when he reluctantly rushed home for his sick mother. But he couldn't stay away, and less than three months later he was back in Belgium in August 1915. It was then that he was given the tough assignment of chief delegate of Lille and inherited the German accompanying officer, or nurse, already there, Captain Bahr, who had a reputation for being drunk much of the time. Duke quickly learned to provide adequate liquor to accommodate the needs of his German officer.

Because the trenches were only 10 miles south, the city of Lille was occasionally shelled by the Allies, which meant Wellington and Bahr lived farther from the front in Valenciennes, a town on the banks of the Scheldt River that was in the Valenciennes District. They lived together, as did most of the northern France delegates and their German officers.

In the same house was the CRB chief delegate to the Valenciennes District, Gardner Richardson (who had written the extensive report for E. E. Hunt on the Antwerp unemployed), and Richardson's German officer, Lieutenant Paul Neuerbourg. Rounding out the menagerie was a German orderly for each officer, two German chauffeurs, and two older French ladies from Valenciennes who came in to cook and clean.

Laurence C. "Duke" Wellington was one of the first 10 Oxford students to become a CRB delegate, spoke French and German, and in 1916 became chief delegate for the district of Lille in northern France. (Public domain; author's archives.)

The house was unlike any either American had known before. This was especially true at night. After eating a meal together, the group would follow different pursuits. Lieutenant Neuerbourg would take his hangdog eyes and toothbrush moustache and settle into a chair in the living room to read a book. Captain Bahr would increase his drinking considerably from the day's steady consumption. In short order, he would be carted up the stairs by his orderly to sleep it off as Neuerbourg kept reading. Within a few hours, Captain Bahr would come shakily down the stairs dressed only in his nightshirt, spiked helmet, the fur neck piece from his greatcoat under his chin, and his belt with its shiny buckle proclaiming 'gott mit uns' [god with us] around his middle. "In this garb," Duke said, "he would sit down and have a few more before he retired for the night." Neuerbourg would keep reading.

Meanwhile, the two Americans would have quietly left and wandered down the street to a place where they could play billiards and drink beer. On the walk home, they would sing songs, sometimes attracting the attention of the German military police, who thought only drunk people sang in the street. The Americans chose not to argue otherwise, as their German nurses would later take care of any problems with the military police.

During the workday, the two CRB delegates shared an office in Valenciennes. They were there only when they weren't traveling around their individual districts making inspections and attending meetings of local communes and district committees.

Richardson had been at his post in Valenciennes for nearly six months, and Duke had been at his job three months when the Lille explosion happened.

They immediately wanted to go see the blast site to assess the damage and see what could be done for the residents. There was also the natural curiosity to see the full extent of the explosion. Both Germans quickly said no; there was no need to do so, and it had nothing to do with food relief. Wellington was allowed to go to Lille for his regular local commune and district meetings but nothing he or Richardson could say would get the German officers to say yes to an explosion site visit.

In one of the Lille committee meetings Wellington attended, he was asked to somehow help with the thousands of shattered windowpanes throughout the city. It was the dead of winter, and something had to be done to seal them, even if it was temporary.

In short order, Wellington came up with a creative solution. He discovered that there were tons of heavy paraffin paper lying idle in a warehouse in Brussels. Working through the Brussels office, he had a substantial supply shipped down to Lille so that windows could be sealed until glass replacements were found.

There was one slight glitch. When the boxes were opened, it was discovered all the paraffin paper was red. Duke later recalled, "When it was put in the windows of the city of Lille they all turned crimson."

Some of those red windows were probably still there less than four months after the blast when something new came to Lille. It would be an event far worse than the January explosion.

The German "Nurses" Get a Name Change

In early 1916, the German Begleitsoffiziers, or accompanying officers, in the Etape region of northern France and Belgium's East and West Flanders had their official title changed. The Begleitsoffizier would from then on be known as Verpflegungsoffizier, or officer dealing with food or matters of feeding.

The name change was an important reflection of the evolving relationship between German nurse and American delegate, and how each interacted with the food-relief process.

In Belgium, the CRB delegate was involved in both the administration and business sides of the shipping, supervising, and distribution of food. He had no German officer following him around; he could move about Belgium in relative freedom to supervise and inspect the operations of the CN relief committees, and he could investigate on his own initiative any complaints or accusations of abuse.

In northern France, the founding concept was that the German officer would be there only to accompany the CRB delegate, to help smooth his way, to act as protector from the local German authorities, and to observe his interactions with French residents to make sure they were always about the relief effort and nothing more.

The reality had become somewhat different. In northern France, the delegate's freedoms were severely curtailed, as his German "nurse" was required to be with him at all times, living with him in the same house and taking all meals together. The American wasn't able to inspect operations at will or conduct investigations without the permission of his German shadow. Such close quarters, with no regular opportunities for separation, created a great deal of personal pressure within the young Americans and caused many of them to last only a month or two in northern France.

It followed then that with the German officers remaining in their positions and many delegates coming and going, the officers naturally became more active participants in the relief program. They had institutional understanding, which included relationships with all the various local relief workers and committees, personal knowledge of what had been done, and an awareness of what needed to be done to keep the food coming. The successive new CRB delegates would come into the situation with little if any preparation and would have to rely heavily on the German officer to get a full grasp of what the job entailed.

All of that meant the German officer ended up in nearly full command of the situation.

That didn't mean the German nurses weren't doing a good job of following the relief's principles and guidelines, as defined by the military's agreements with the CRB. For the most part, the officers "took very seriously their obligation," Kittredge related. "It was their duty as soldiers to see that the other German authorities adhered to the convention approved by the supreme command, and the officers were very energetic in enforcing the assurances and guarantees given by the German army in these first conventions and in later supplementary agreements."

This left the CRB delegate in a somewhat paradoxical position. On one hand, because of the personal hardships attached to the job, it was acknowledged, "The [Brussels CRB] director sends only the best men to France." And yet, a "supreme insult" that was well-known inside the CRB stated, "North of France delegates are about as important as so many mosquitoes." Joe Green stated in his typically blunt way, the Germans in northern France "really did most of the work and our men became in reality mere accompanying representatives."

The truth of the importance and impact of the CRB delegate in northern France would lie somewhere in between. One northern France delegate put it, "Effort and accomplishment could not be gauged by ordinary standards."

Besides the personal tensions of living together, the CRB delegate and the German officer had to contend with international events that impacted them both. The German initiation of submarine warfare without warning vessels in February 1915 had been denounced around the world. This was especially true in America, where public opinion was strongly against the lack of warning. One delegate stated, the German nurses "realized that American public opinion had condemned them and they were bitter with rage."

The Germans responded to such criticism by bringing up the fact that American companies were supplying both munitions and food to the Allies while not selling the same to Germany. On these two subjects, they would make "the most violent and blustering protests" to their CRB delegate.

Such tensions and opposing positions on sensitive subjects easily transferred to the work, where it seemed to be a constant struggle between American and German as to who was calling the shots and controlling the situation. "It's trench warfare," an unnamed associate once told the delegates of northern France, "and you are losing, and you will lose. Only you must lose as slowly as possible."

It took a special man to lose very slowly while making sure the French civilians kept eating and the German officer didn't blow up.

Pink Simpson Takes On the Germans and Northern France

One delegate who beat the odds and lasted six months in northern France was John Lowery Simpson, better known as "Pink." (A childhood classmate already had the obvious red-headed name, so Simpson got stuck with Pink.) A 1913 graduate of the University of California, Simpson became a lawyer and took a job in the legal department of California's Immigration and Housing Commission after reviewing migrant worker cases stemming from a riot. In late 1915, he had just accepted, but not yet taken, a new position as an "economic expert" for the Federal Trade Commission (FTC) in Washington, D.C., when he was invited to join the CRB.

Simpson had received the CRB call to duty thanks to a process that had started with delegate and college friend Tracy Kittredge, who had returned to California and was helping recruit new delegates. Kittredge had cabled Hoover on October 29, 1915, and recommended Clare Torrey and Simpson, stating that Torrey could go in a couple of months while "Mr. Simpson is perhaps the best man available at the moment, whom I know." Kittredge also mentioned a third man, A. J. Eddy. On November 1, 1915, Hoover cabled Kittredge, "Send Simpson and Torrey or Eddy whichever you think is best." Kittredge's choice was Torrey and Simpson.

Simpson quickly asked for and received permission from the FTC to postpone starting his new job for six months so he could aid the CRB's humanitarian work.

He left America on November 20, before Torrey, and arrived in Belgium in early December 1915.

Upon arrival in Belgium, Simpson was immediately assigned to be a delegate in the Antwerp Province. He must have made a good strong impression with his language skills, business sense, and ability to learn the job quickly because only a month and a half later he was promoted to chief delegate in northern France's Vervins District. He took the place of Major Robert Dutton, who been working in the post since northern France relief had begun in April 1915 and had stayed on the job an incredible nine months before Pink's arrival.

CRB delegate John L. "Pink" Simpson had a flippant, many times facetious, sense of humor. As one of the northern France delegates who was tethered to a German "nurse," Pink lasted in the position longer than most. (Public domain; author's archives.)

Officially, Simpson became chief delegate on February 1, 1916, only two weeks before his 25th birthday. In his CRB portrait photo, he appears to be a serious young man with his head cocked just so, hair parted sharply on the left, and a mustache neatly trimmed to not curl around the edges of his lips. An altogether fastidious young man.

But looking a bit closer, there was an every-so-slight raised eyebrow that in Simpson's case hinted at his flippant, many times facetious, sense of humor. By all reports, his entire attitude was one of relaxed, perpetual wonder at what was happening around him. He loved to dance and had an easy, quick way of making friends with men and women. A fellow delegate later wrote tongue-in-cheek how Pink was known in Belgium for "founding Girls Friendly Societies, [and] is now giving dancing lessons to the young ladies of Liège." Erica Bunge and her sisters affectionately called him Pinkske and jokingly said of him, "You can't believe a word he says."

Simpson later wrote dramatically that while in Belgium and northern France he felt as if he were a Roman "legionnaire" waging war. He also said later that to the Belgians, "the Americans were tin gods. You'd think we were making a great sacrifice, and yet we enjoyed it all."

His unique sense of humor and dramatic bend made him see the opening up of northern France to the CRB as "the vistas of a new adventure for American youth."

He saw a major difference between occupied Belgium and occupied France. In Belgium, after the first few months of occupation, "there had been restored . . .

some kind of social structure. There were central offices, ministers, civil authorities, negotiations, dinners—even tennis occasionally."

That was not the case in France. There was only "one dominating fact, insistent like tunnel pressure against the ears; a state of war," Pink maintained. "In Northern France there was no normality; there was no code of action; there was no 'way of doing things.' There was a state of war."

Such conditions, Simpson suggested, were why northern France held a "fascination for the American youth: it was forbidden territory. Once past the line you stood where the army was supreme. Inhabitants walked outside their communes by courtesy of special permission. Civilians rode on trains only with thrice-special passports. When one penetrated farther south one caught the grey sheen of moving troops; or one descried long supply trains—even occasional smoke of artillery fire. On fine nights there was the 'line' to be detected by the distant flare of rockets and the dull glow of the guns."

When Simpson took over as chief delegate, he inherited from his predecessor, Major Dutton, the German nurse Captain Weber. It would be an interesting experience for both. Simpson described it as "not a mere relationship of two human beings—it was an institution. It was a composite of the Siamese twins, a Punch and Judy show, a parliamentary debate, and important quantities of high explosive."

Summing up in two sentences, he stated, "The American was sent into Northern France to watch the food. The German officer was sent to watch the American." Using a creative analogy, he said, "It was like an interminable camping trip where two individuals, confined to each other's society, find added to the general limitations of that life the lurking suspicion that 'the other fellow' is dipping secretly into the sugar stock. They may like each other, respect each other, desire the utmost good fortune—*but*, is he really making off with some of the sugar?"

Less than three weeks after arriving in Vervins, Pink found himself pushing back against Captain Weber. When some new communes were added to the relief list, Simpson had received instructions to visit those communes and report back to Brussels before food would be shipped.

Simpson admitted later, it was "not a matter of stupendous importance," but it became a big issue quickly. Pink told Weber that they needed to visit the communes before the food would be shipped; Weber immediately said it was not allowed. Pink insisted; Weber refused. A special meeting was called of officials in Vervins. Simpson forced Weber to take him to Charleville to German general headquarters to present his side of the case. All of that drove Weber into a frenzy so great that he "completely lost himself in rage."

In the end, the issue was resolved with compromise—a meeting with the civilian delegates of the new communes would be allowed, then the first shipments would arrive, and then Pink could go in to inspect the communes.

Such incidents did not happen often, but when they did the emotions they drew out could not be easily or quickly put back from where they had come. And the potential for explosive topics was always lying in wait, like a pasture sown with hidden land mines.

Most of the time, relations were at least civil. While the Americans called each German accompanying officer a "nurse," Simpson reported that "what the officer called the American is one of the secrets of the German Army into which we were never able to penetrate." Quickly, the two men began to understand each other's quirks and priorities.

One evening, another German officer came for a visit. He remarked to Simpson that it must be "taxing, and very unpleasant," to work on behalf of the French, who hated the Germans, and be surrounded by all the army restrictions.

Captain Weber flew into a rage. "Get out!" he commanded his fellow officer, knowing such a sympathetic comment would only encourage the American. "[Simpson] thinks he's very cute standing up against the German Army. He glories in it!"

Another major thorn in the side of the German nurses—and most other German soldiers—was America's selling of munitions to the Allies but not to the Germans. "A munitions discussion," Pink said, "may be counted as a disaster. No topic on earth seemed so pregnant of disagreeable possibilities as to American shipments of munitions to the Allies. President Wilson was always hauled into the discussion by some hook or crook."

German Captain Weber was Pink Simson's "nurse," or accompanying officer. Simpson described the relationship as "a composite of the Siamese twins, a Punch and Judy show, a parliamentary debate, and important qualities of high explosive." (Public domain; Herbert Hoover Presidential Library Archives, West Branch, Iowa.)

But even here, Simpson found a humorous perspective. "While my [German] companions were denouncing him as trying to precipitate war between Germany and the United States, I was usually trying to hide a grin. I could not but think of those at home who were criticizing the President's too-pacifist policy."

Normally, such discussions were avoided by the Americans at all costs. If they did take place, however, there was one universal retort that had been made by an anonymous CRB delegate and had become "perhaps the most famous in C.R.B. folklore: 'Well, anyway, Captain So-and-so, we elected our President, and you had your Kaiser wished on you.'"

Simpson noted that before the war, the German nurses were "considered very pleasant people to know and have relations with. The war had converted them into brutes." With that said, however, he was the first to admit that many times "one is perhaps a little too inclined to remember these officers' arrogant usurpation of power in the feeding work, and to forget that they did actually render some extremely valuable services. They dealt with railway officials and with local *Kommandants*. They arranged to have storehouses and offices put at the disposition of the committees. They ousted soldiers from the bakeries, demanded the passports which made district meetings possible, sent telegrams far and wide, escorted Representatives into villages well within the zone of artillery fire. They were the buffers between the Americans and French organizations on the one hand and the German Army on the other."

And then there were those small, but highly important moments of personal assistance, such as when Pink had been pulled aside by a Landsturmer "who was marching me off with fixed bayonet to a fate I dare not divine," when Weber came to the rescue.

The actual work of a CRB delegate was straightforward: make sure no imported food was appropriated by the army, and ensure that the food was distributed equally and fairly throughout the district.

The process to do so, however, was complicated. Shipments had to be recorded and tracked, distribution needed to be calculated and administrated, orders had to be transmitted back and forth between communal committees and the Brussels office, local meetings had to be attended and recorded, and some semblance of inspection had to be achieved to assure the delegate that no abuses of the system were taking place.

A CRB office was established in the district center that handled all documents, reports, and correspondence. Assisting were one or two secretaries who were either German soldiers or carefully selected Frenchmen. From there, the CRB delegate would send out "circular and special letters to the French committees transmitting instructions from Brussels, with additional measures added at his own initiative to suit the special features of his district. He wrote calling attention to irregularities, authorizing changes when necessary, and occasionally responding to requests for information or for the settlement of local disputes on the part of the French committees. He furthermore used his office communication system to assemble statistics and information from the different parts of the district at the behest of the Commission for Relief in Belgium or the Comité Francais in Brussels."

More important than the delegate's office work was his fieldwork. Because northern France was in the Army Zone, there was no CRB centralized Inspection and Control Department as there was in Belgium. As a result, this meant that each northern France delegate was "compelled to do an immense amount of traveling and inspecting." Pink and Weber would spend days on the road motoring through the district in the German's large Mercedes-Benz staff car. Wherever possible, Pink would push to visit not only the regional centers but the individual communes of the district—a difficult task considering there were 431 communes in the Vervins District. Pink would randomly choose communes in different corners of the district to try and get a sense of the entire district.

When he and Weber motored into a local commune, they would search out the communal representative and then begin the inspection. "A normal inspection," Simpson said, "consisted in looking over the books, viewing the storehouse for the food, ascertaining the quality of the protection from the army, inquiring into the manner of distribution, noticing the arrangements for baking, the quality of bread, etc."

And then there were the informal moments—some that became defining moments. Early on in their relationship, Pink and Captain Weber came to a commune where they found German soldiers sleeping in a room that had access to the warehouse where the CRB-imported flour was stored. Pink wrote in a detailed scene what happened next:

I was still new to the work. "This must of course be changed," I observed.

"Nothing of the sort," retorted the captain. "Your business is to see that no food is taken by the army. You have no proof that that has occurred here. I deny that you have the right to demand a change."

I finally closed a fruitless argument by stating that I intended to report the matter to Brussels.

"Very well," snorted the officer.

In the afternoon we passed by the place again. The officer absented himself for a few moments, and on returning announced: "On my own initiative I have ordered new arrangements made here. We shall examine them when next we pass in this vicinity. But you understand that it is I who have done this, that I deny absolutely your right to insist."

I grunted, and, still outraged, I privately recounted the whole incident to my Director at Brussels the following Saturday. "If such a principal is admitted," I protested, "the power of the Representative . . ."

"The power of the Representative!" The director smiled.

"By the way, Simpson," he added. "I believe you said the Captain ordered the place to be put in shape, didn't you?"

"Yes, he did."

"Well, I guess that's what you wanted, wasn't it?" remarked the Director. And I am sure that his eye twinkled.

Another incident showed how little most German soldiers in the trenches knew about the relief work and the CRB delegates. Captain Weber took Pink one night to dine at a German officers' mess not far from the front. Immediately, Pink noted a difference between the Germans he usually met and the men he was then sitting with to eat. "These chaps were men just off the line, quite a different lot from the various functionaries and officials one comes in contact with thirty miles 'inland' from the battle."

As he sat there in the mess tent, under the flickering light of candles, a young German lieutenant leaned over and asked courteously in perfect English, "But what in the world are you doing here?"

Pink explained who he was; the goal of the CRB, CN, and CF; the relationship with Captain Weber; and how the food was being distributed to the French civilians stuck in the Army Zone.

The man was attentive and surprised. He said he had never heard of such food relief.

"On the whole," Pink said, "he took a friendly and curious interest in me, nudged me when it was time to respond to a toast, told me about his work, yet could not refrain from glancing at me now and then as though to say, 'After all, my dear chap, it's deuced funny that you should be here.'"

The young officer said it was good of the German Army to give Pink a car and a German officer. Most of all, he hoped that Simpson would tell his friends when he went home to America that "not all Germans were 'brutes.'"

At one point, though, the lieutenant had shown a flare of anger. "America!" he declared, "You've never been neutral, you know." But then he added quickly, "You must pardon me; my brother was killed at my side a few weeks ago, and I am not quite myself."

Pink would never forget that moment in the German mess tent and would fight back with his German nurse as often as he dared, reminding himself of what another had told him, that the best he could ever do was to "lose as slowly as possible."

Some of the delegates working in northern France began to understand how their German nurses worked, what made them tick, and what made them do what they did. They would share that information with their fellow delegates at the Saturday meetings in Brussels. Some obvious truths emerged—the German nurses were practically slaves to authority and chain-of-command. They also felt that they were the ones in charge, not the Americans. Their thinking was that northern France was German-conquered territory; it was their government that allowed the Americans to bring in relief; therefore, they were in command.

This meant they found it offensive when a delegate tried to give orders, even if those orders were reasonable and/or justified. They especially disliked when a delegate made formal complaints to the CRB Brussels office or, worse, to the German High Command in Charleville, because that reflected badly on them as the officers in charge. With their great respect for authority, however, they did normally honor any requests or orders issued from the CRB office in Brussels "even though they would have indignantly refused to take any action had the delegate made any such request."

Those insights led to a devious delegate workaround. Kittredge in his CRB history noted, "Many of the representatives, therefore, gave up the useless procedure of arguing with their officer and accomplished what they wanted by the simple expedient of dictating letters to themselves while at Brussels over the week-end, giving themselves definite instructions that such and such classes of people should or should not be fed, that the reports should be handled in this or that manner, etc. They would then have these letters signed by the director of the Commission at Brussels. The following week the letter would be despatched [*sic*] to them through the German officers, as was the case with all mail. The German officer would receive the letter of instructions and, without saying anything to the delegate and often without handing him the letter, would proceed to carry the instructions into effect on his own initiative."

It was a case of American ingenuity outsmarting Prussian love of authority.

34

Elsewhere in Belgium

The Germans Put Pressure on the Belgians to Work

During the winter of 1915/1916—less than a year after the "strike of folded arms" and the German failure to break the railway strike in Malines—the Germans tried again to force Belgians to work in railway shops. They had developed a simple method around Belgium—cut off any local unemployment funds, offer a job to those cut off, and if they refused, arrest them and bring them before a German court, which would dole out prison sentences to those still refusing to work.

One target was the town of Rochefort, in the province of Namur. Situated 31 miles (50 km) southeast of the provincial capital of Namur, Rochefort lay along the Lomme River and was close to the forested rolling hills and stony ridges of the Ardennes. Before the war, the Walloon, or French-speaking, town of 3,000 people was known as a resort destination famous for its limestone caves, especially the one in town, the Grotte de Rochefort, which boasted the nearly 400-foot-high Sabbath Room.

On Monday, February, 7, 1916, the Germans made a move against a small group of 14 unemployed men, or *chômeurs*, living in Rochefort. As investigated and reported after the fact by CRB delegate Clare Torrey, three men—Josef Francau, Eugene Paquet, and Emile Delhaize—told him that they had been receiving a *chômeur* payment from the local committees of the CN's Secours Department of three francs (60 cents) a week. On February 7, however, the three men, along with 11 other men from Rochefort had received a summons from the German Kommandantur to appear at Jemelle, a village two kilometers away where a railway shop helped to maintain and construct the rolling stock.

Torrey reported that the 14 men had dutifully presented themselves at the railroad shop of Jemelle at 8:00 a.m. on the prescribed day. The German officer running the shop asked them all to work, saying it would be mainly repair work and would pay 3 marks and 60 pfennigs a day (less than $1 a day, but a good wage for German-occupied Belgium). Some of the men, after being questioned, were even offered higher wages for positions such as locomotive engineer, chief workman, and inspector of material.

All 14 immediately said no, having decided that work was either directly or indirectly related to the military. Torrey's report traced the harrowing journey the men then took: They were all detained at Jemelle until 10 p.m. that night. Then they were escorted to the Kommandantur's office at Rochefort, where they were interrogated and strip-searched. Next they were taken under guard to Namur, where they were thrown in prison for more than two weeks. On Friday, February 25, they were hauled before a German judge and their trial was quickly concluded with a sentence of one month in prison starting from February 8. On Friday, March 10, they were released from prison.

Meanwhile, the Germans had ordered the Secours Central Bureau in Namur to stop all payments to the workers who were refusing work. Torrey stated, "This order was complied with."

And the Germans had not given up. Torrey concluded his report by stating, "Further, the Namur agents of police, acting under orders of the military authorities, are now making visits to the houses of former railroad workmen, demanding of them to take up such work again, and noting any reasons given for refusal."

While the CRB officially had nothing to do with the conflict between the Germans and Belgians over employment, it was unavoidable that the CRB delegates were pulled into the situation and felt the need to investigate any reported cases of German coercion of Belgian workers. Clare Torrey's report would end up with Hoover, who would circulate it to many others. It was just one more piece of evidence regarding German coercion of Belgian *chômeurs*.

The 14 men at Rochefort might not have felt very lucky then, but they definitely were when compared with what happened later in the year to some of their countrymen.

35

Brussels

The Germans Seek Revenge on Gibson

On Monday, February 7, Whitlock was still saddened by his dog's death when he was disturbed during his morning shaving. His servant came in and told him he was requested by Baron von der Lancken to come at once to see him. He hurried through the rest of his morning rituals, anxiously trying to think of what von der Lancken wanted so urgently.

When he arrived at the German's office, Whitlock found out quickly: von der Lancken "wished to talk of Gibson; said he must leave at once, today or at latest tomorrow." Whitlock was taken aback. He had thought von der Lancken would wait for him to remove Gibson. Now here he was in von der Lancken's office being told Gibson was to leave immediately. Outwardly, Whitlock remained calm and got the German to talk at length about the situation. The baron put his demand in the context of the larger diplomatic picture. He talked about the strain in the relations between America and Germany, especially since the May 7, 1915, sinking of the *Lusitania*, which von der Lancken felt should have been dropped because 10 months had passed since the sinking. "We do not understand the President; why does he not let the affair die out? . . . We are not doing anything more!" The baron was referring to the fact that the Kaiser had bowed to worldwide condemnation and ended unrestricted submarine warfare.

Such frustration at the highest levels of government was bound to have its impact all the way down the line. It was now Gibson's turn to feel the impact. His perceived sins against the German Empire had been accumulating for far too long and could no longer go unpunished. Von der Lancken told Whitlock that Governor General von Bissing wanted him out. Whitlock asked von der Lancken to plead with von Bissing to reconsider. Before Whitlock left, the baron said he would once again talk with the governor general.

When Whitlock returned to the legation, he had a long talk with Gibson, who objected strenuously, explaining away all that von der Lancken had brought up.

Later, von der Lancken called to tell Whitlock he had spoken again to von Bissing, who was unmoved. He said he could not "restrain [von Bissing's] hand," Gibson had to go, and that he "cannot go too quickly, you understand."

Whitlock was a bit overwhelmed and dreaded the confrontation that he knew had to come. "The whole thing made me sick." By the time he was ready to retire for the evening, he wrote in his journal, "I am sick and tired tonight. It has been a hard day."

According to von der Lancken, it was not only von Bissing who objected to Gibson remaining in Belgium; it was the German military as well. To all of them, Gibson's crimes had commenced nearly as soon as the war began and had continued to the present. Their accusations could be distilled down to five items:

1. Gibson had demonstrated flagrant disregard for military protocols during the 1914 invasion as he continually traveled back and forth through the battle lines—ostensibly to relay diplomatic messages between the Brussels legation and the State Department back home (via cablegrams sent from Antwerp, before the city's surrender). The military was sure he had carried war-related information about the Germans through the lines to the Allied forces, despite Gibson's personal assurances as a gentleman and diplomat that he had not.

   In Gibson's published accounts and in his unpublished letters, he does mention numerous conversations with Belgian and Allied government officials while on the Allied side of the battle lines, but he never wrote exactly what was discussed. While he probably shared anecdotal bits and pieces of what he saw as he traveled through the German lines, there is no evidence that he participated in any concerted effort to transmit military information. The one exception was to help both sides—he carried a marked-up map of downtown Antwerp to the Germans so their artillery could purposefully avoid damaging culturally significant structures during their three days of bombardment in October 1914.
2. After Gibson's somewhat famous 1914 visit to Louvain as the city was still being torched by the Germans, he had been directly requested by von der Lancken to give an official account that stated he had seen Belgian *franc-tireurs* (civilian guerillas) firing upon the Germans. The Germans wanted to blame Belgian civilian fighters for the destruction of the university town and its renowned library, especially after the world's condemnation of their actions.

   Gibson had seen no such thing and he refused all demands to make an official statement saying that he had. Such refusal was seen as an affront to the German occupation government.
3. Gibson's strong stand against the execution of Edith Cavell was held against him. Once he discovered the German plan to execute Cavell before the sentence was known to anyone outside the court, he and Villalobar had spent a long night arguing with von der Lancken, who had refused

their demands to take the case to von Bissing and even the Kaiser. Later, Gibson's account of the event and the information about the trial that had leaked out to the rest of the world was a huge public relations nightmare for the Germans. Much of the blame for that was laid at Gibson's feet by the Germans.

Gibson would have proudly agreed to those charges against him involving Cavell, in the belief it had been his duty as a neutral American diplomat—and as a human being—to do whatever was necessary to try and stop the British nurse's execution.

4. Another negative in German eyes was the autumn 1915 CRB situation with Hoover, von der Lancken, and Gibson, in which Gibson, on the recommendation of Hoover, had unleashed a "kill or cure" threat to withdraw if the spy charges against CRB delegates were not dropped. Such brashness was not what von der Lancken and von Bissing wanted in an American diplomat. They could barely tolerate it in Hoover, the private citizen, but it would not be tolerated in a secretary of a legation.

   Gibson would have argued that he had every right to make such a threat and would do it again if he had half the chance. The relief work was much more valuable, he felt, than any diplomatic protocols.

5. Most recently, there was Gibson's horseback riding incident with Ynès Reyntiens and the German sentry at the railroad crossing. The Germans felt that Gibson had acted inappropriately and had used his diplomatic immunity to ridicule men of the German Army.

   In this case, Gibson would have argued that as a diplomat—and one who was working so hard to save a nation from starvation—he should be accorded due respect. The sentry had been wrong to do what he did and got what he deserved.

In all the matters that Whitlock lay before Gibson, the younger man made his defense with passion and strong words. But as Whitlock later pointed out in his journal, "I have tried to handle the Gibson affair so as not to injure him, for he is not wholly blameless; is young, romantic, and as a follower of Theodore Roosevelt, given to swashbuckling." Whitlock did admit that Gibson was an "excellent secretary in time of peace, but when the blast of war resounds in our ears, he imitates the action of the tiger."

As for the horseback riding incident, Whitlock was sharp in his criticism. "He might have avoided the arrest by the sentry. . . . He is so touchy on all points of honor, but honor cannot set a leg, or take away the grief of a wound, or feed the Belgians. One can't live according to the code duello [regulations for dueling], and I can't get him to be patient and await events and let old Nemesis take care of his enemies. He is truculent and impetuous, always wishes to rattle the sabre in the scabbard."

When the Germans announced they wanted Gibson removed from the legation, Brand Whitlock dreaded the confrontation with Gibson. "The whole thing made me sick," he wrote. (Public domain; multiple sources.)

Three days after Whitlock's meeting with von der Lancken, on a cold and snowy day, and with a "rotten headache" pounding in his skull, Whitlock had had enough of the entire affair. He had much on his mind—including an offer from President Wilson to become ambassador to Russia (which he turned down)—and the Gibson problem was one he could take care of immediately. He finally told Gibson definitively that he must leave Belgium and report to Le Havre, France, where the exiled Belgian government was located. Officially it would be a leave of absence for health reasons.

Gibson demanded that the entire situation be officially recorded. Whitlock dutifully sent a dispatch to the State Department outlining the situation and what he had decided to do. In the cable, Whitlock explained how this was the "dignified" thing to do to save official confrontation between America and Germany. He also recommended that Gibson be "advanced to the rank and remuneration of Chargé d'affaires."

Gibson said he felt nothing should be done until a reply was received (which could take a week or more). Whitlock laid down the law. He told his secretary, "rather sharply, indeed," that he, as minister of the U.S. Legation, "needed no instructions" when it came to this. The matter was settled—Gibson was to leave as soon as German passes could be arranged.

Gibson was furious and could not understand why Whitlock would not stand up for him and insist that he must stay. To a lesser degree he even felt von der Lancken should stand up for him to von Bissing. "I have had a devilish time," he wrote his mother later, "dirty attempts to hurt me by people from whom I had a right to expect better things. There is no question of honor involved." He called those against him the "black hand crowd" (the secret Serbian society that had planned the assassinations of the Austrian archduke and his wife, which had ignited the war).

Even though the Germans wanted him gone, it took eight days for all passes to be completed and for the border to be reopened after a prolonged closure. In the meantime, Gibson got his Belgian affairs in order, attended a few farewell parties, and tried to come to peace with his ouster.

On Friday, February 18, at 10 a.m., Gibson left Brussels "amid the restrained sadness there is in all parting," as Whitlock wrote in his journal. He then added rather insincerely that Gibson "abandoned us to a dull day of dreary rain." Gibson would have assuredly never used the word "abandon" with his leaving the legation; he had been kicked out. Either way, he headed for Rotterdam, accompanied by Americans Heineman and Hulse, who were sailing for home on the SS *Rotterdam*.

Because the State Department had agreed to the leave of absence and had instructed Gibson not to go to Le Havre, he went to London to await orders.

A Response Is Negotiated; A Plot Is Hatched

Close on Gibson's heels were Villalobar, Francqui, and CN executive Baron Lambert, who were heading to London officially as envoys carrying letters of guarantees from von Bissing to deal with the major crisis of the British threatening to shut down the entire relief operation. That was the threat Hoover had written to Gibson about in January and why Hoover was staying in London (apart from his ear abscess).

The situation began back on December 31, 1915, when Sir Edward Grey sent a long letter to Ambassador Page detailing German violations of the relief agreements and stating that the British government was intending to shut down all relief unless the Germans accepted certain stipulations.

Even with such a major crisis, transmission of any information was still largely dependent on the snail's pace of human couriers, diplomatic pouches, and borders that could be randomly opened or closed. Whitlock finally received Grey's letter, with a note from Page, two weeks later, on January 14, 1916.

The minister knew immediately this would take multiple meetings with von der Lancken, Villalobar, and Francqui, with occasional inclusion of the third patron of relief, Dutch Minister van Vollenhoven. Whitlock explained in his journal that "English Tories are seeking an excuse to stop the feeding of Belgium if the blame can be laid to the Germans. Since [the Germans] understand this we feel that we can secure from the Governor-General an assurance that any abuses—and there have been abuses, and infractions of the spirit though not of the letter of the assurances and the convention—will be discontinued and those responsible punished."

On such an important issue, Whitlock and his friends Francqui and Villalobar even bypassed protocol to speed up possible resolution. "We decided that Villalobar should commit an 'indiscretion' and let von der Lancken see Sir Edward's [Grey's] letter so that he might know the contents without our having to read it officially. Then we take steps, in communications, to arrange the whole matter."

Through the following month, the meetings, proposals, counterproposals, and hard bargaining went back and forth. Finally, by the middle of February, the group had come up with three letters from von Bissing that addressed the British concerns, accusations, and pending shutdown of the relief. It was decided—after von der Lancken agreed—that Villalobar, Francqui, and Lambert would travel to London to present the letters of guarantee. Whitlock pointed out in his journal that Hoover had already done the work, but the three would not be denied: "Villalobar formally, or von der Lancken on his nod, formally made request, as Villalobar had previously demanded, that Villalobar go to London to negotiate the business (which Hoover had already done) and Villalobar bowed, consented, and said he wished Francqui and Lambert to accompany him. And it was so ordered."

This insistence on going to London had other reasons than to deliver von Bissing's three letters. While that work was being done, other meetings were taking place about another topic. Francqui and Villalobar had worked—and no doubt consulted with Whitlock—on a plan to remove the CRB from the relief work. Even though Whitlock did not mention the plan in his journal, he must have known and participated in the discussions because as the U.S. minister in Belgium and major patron of the relief work, his approval would have been necessary for Villalobar and Francqui to proceed with any relief-related plans. Gibson was obviously not included in the plot because of his outspoken admiration and friendship with respect to Hoover.

Meanwhile, Hoover—nursing his ear and struggling to get the British to reconsider their current thinking about relief—was in London with no idea that he was about to be stabbed in the back.

36

London

Gibson arrived in London on Saturday, February 20, 1916, and found himself surrounded by friends who respected him and wanted him to stay active in the relief work. Hoover's opinion of Gibson did not waver over the removal from Brussels—if nothing else, it increased his esteem.

Hoover later wrote, "From the first moment, [Gibson] was a part of the C.R.B. He plunged into every problem with great sense; he provided real friendship and willing aid to all our American members. He had a superlative wit and was at all times a sunny soul, cheerful amid the greatest discouragement. We came to rely upon him for all our problems in Belgium, whether with the Belgians or the Germans."

Hoover pushed for Gibson to stay in London and lobbied for him to get a post at the American Embassy in London. Page was all for it. As Gibson waited for official word from the State Department, he ended up acting as an informal adviser to Hoover, Page, Colonel House (adviser to President Wilson, who was at that time in London), and even Lord Eustace Percy, the British government's liaison with the CRB who happened to be Gibson's old friend and "playmate of Washington days" before the war.

During the informal conferences Gibson had with these men, he talked through the thorny issues of food relief and gave his insights into the Belgian and German personalities in the game. There is no doubt, however, that he also talked disparagingly of Whitlock. Gibson believed his ex-boss had dishonored him and betrayed him and was incapable of properly standing up to the strong German and Belgian personalities he had to deal with nearly every day.

Writing his mother, he spoke of the situation without naming names, but to whom he was referring was obvious. "The bad one [Whitlock] was the gent who had more reason than anyone else to be boosting me because of the way I had served him. I think you can gather who it is. He lost his grip a long time ago and I kept his reputation more or less intact by dint of hard work and steady talk. He resented even the small amount of work I expected of him and lent himself to the intrigue of another [Francqui] who objected to our country getting any credit out of the situation."

Gibson found a fertile field for planting such thoughts in Hoover, who had never felt Whitlock was the right man for the wartime position of U.S. minister to Belgium. Together, Gibson and Hoover began to push whenever and wherever they could for Whitlock's removal.

It's a testament to Whitlock and the diplomatic strengths he did possess that he remained in his position throughout the war. In fact, Colonel House, who became acquainted with the minister while traveling on the same ship that brought the Whitlocks back to Belgium, wrote in his diary on January 5, 1916: "I can better understand now why Whitlock has made such a success in Belgium under difficulties. He has the kindly human instinct. He is not given to hate or recrimination. He can see the other man's point of view and he is not absorbed with his own ego. He knows literature and the fines arts. . . . He knows our political institutions and our people and their aspirations, and he is in every way a worthy representative of the United States during these troublous times. When peace comes I think the President should send him higher up." Such comments from a man who had the president's ear could have been why Whitlock was offered in late January the promotion to become ambassador to Russia (which he turned down).

Meanwhile, in London, Gibson worked on relief issues as if he was already employed by Page and waited to hear if he would be officially posted to the embassy. He wrote his mother that once he arrived in London, he realized that his detractors in Belgium "have done me no harm and on the contrary it may prove that in spite of themselves they have helped me greatly."

While he enjoyed the informal work with the embassy and the CRB, Gibson was also highly frustrated at the State Department's lack of decisiveness when it came to where he should be posted. He cabled on March 9 for instructions. The State Department in turn cabled Whitlock asking for his advice regarding Gibson's possible return to Brussels.

At the same time, Ambassador Page cabled the State Department saying he needed help and would "be particularly glad if [Gibson] could be assigned . . . to this Embassy where his ability and experience would be of the greatest value. He would also be most useful in connection with the negotiations concerning the Belgian Relief Commissions with which he is thoroughly familiar."

A few days later, on March 13, 1916, Whitlock cabled a reply to the State Department's question about Gibson's future in Brussels. It was short and to the point: "Gibson's return here so long as present situation lasts would create embarrassments that I am sure we all wish to avoid."

Gibson complained about Whitlock's answer but that didn't change anything. He sat in London and fumed, waiting for a new posting.

The British Finally Reply to Hoover's Request for Increased Imports

Ten days before Hoover finally heard from the British government about his import requests, he was in Paris fighting for his cause. He bluntly told a small group of French government officials and military officers that "it seemed absurd to us, an American body, that we should be at constant trench warfare with the French and British General Staffs over this work. That we were in constant battle over imports absolutely vital to preserve the life of French people and we were prepared to surrender and let them do the job if they could do it better. That we were always in an equal quarrel with the German Staff over native food—and we were getting very, very tired and worn."

He had noted with some satisfaction that his threat to leave the field had caused some concern.

After getting back to London, however, Hoover received on February 23, 1916, the British Foreign Office reply to his December 1915 increased-import requests. He might have thought when he first made his appeal that it couldn't hurt to ask. Sadly, in this case it did hurt to ask. The letter, which was from Lord Percy to Hoover, not only denied the increases but decreased imports to both Belgium and northern France. For Belgium, the allowable tonnage was decreased by 12,000 tons from the original 80,000 tons a month, and the CRB was limited to a small number of items.

	Tons
Wheat	54,000
Yeast	250
Bacon and lard	2,400
Peas and beans	3,000
Maize and meal	8,000
Condensed milk	500
Total	68,150

While some medical supplies were allowed, as well as gasoline and other items for the CRB cars, it was still a devastating blow to the CRB, CN, and the Belgians.

As for northern France—which was in much greater need than Belgium—it, too, was impacted. Hoover wrote, "The British Foreign Office, under pressure from the militarists in Britain and France, instead of approving our increased imports to Northern France, informed us of a reduction in our monthly supplies, by about 5,000 tons, to 30,000 tons per month."

Hoover stated the obvious when he said, "It was a great shock to us—and to the people of Northern France. The native ground crops were practically exhausted at this time of the year."

The Chief knew that the reductions to Belgium and northern France were "far below the level at which we could maintain public health. The effect was a program 50 per cent short of the minimum needs of fats and proteins."

Hoover had nearly reached his limit. "We had no taste for being an instrument of slow starvation, and by the end of February, 1916, we—who had, after all, taken on our heavy burdens voluntarily—became, to use a British expression, 'about fed up' with these obstructionist attitudes."

As this critical piece of humanitarian relief was seemingly crumbling away, Hoover had to put up with something nearly as distasteful.

Is the CRB Really Necessary for Relief to Continue?

On the heels of Gibson's arrival in London, others came who Hoover, with his classical bend, might have jokingly referred to as the three horsemen of the apocalypse: CN President Francqui, CN executive Baron Jean Lambert, and Spanish Minister Villalobar.

The three arrived in London about the same time Gibson did. Officially, they were there to present to the English letters of guarantees from von Bissing that had been pounded out in Brussels by von der Lancken, Whitlock, Villalobar, Francqui, and van Vollenhoven. There was no real need for such a presentation—Hoover had already transmitted the basics of the guarantees to the British.

The three men were there for two other reasons.

The first was a crazy scheme of peace that they hoped might lead to a Treaty of Brussels that would end the war. Nothing came of that idea.

The second reason was to implement the plan they had worked on in Brussels to eliminate the CRB from the relief work.

Most of those in executive positions in the CRB and CN knew there was no love lost between the two groups.

The Belgians—and Francqui in particular—felt they were fully capable of not only running the distribution (which they did exceedingly well) but also handling the CRB's major responsibilities: securing of financing for the massive relief; buying and shipping of goods; warehousing, processing, and release of supplies to local communes; supervising operations to catch abuses by Belgians and Germans; and handling multiple government relations and guarantees.

The Americans—and Hoover in particular—felt that there could be no sustained and substantial food relief without the continuing efforts and constant vigil of neutral Americans; that the Belgians could be too easily manipulated by the Germans because of their position as prisoners of the German Empire; that the Belgians did not have the unrestricted freedom of movement that the neutral

Americans had, which was essential for the relief to continue; and that the Belgians didn't fully understand the British attitude toward Belgian relief.

Such drastically different points of view made for constant friction, and as CRB delegate Kittredge stated, they were "the basis of most of the rather painful misunderstandings which occasionally arose between the Commission and the Comité National."

When Hoover wrote about the situation after the war, he framed much of the details in diplomatic terms that would have been far from his mind at the time. Hoover was not one to hold back or be concerned about how diplomatically he said something. British Lord Curzon stated that "Mr. Hoover is the bluntest man in Europe," while Gibson once commented, "Hoover does not often let his feelings get away with him but when he does it is worth coming miles to hear." Any such diplomatic wording after the war was, no doubt, done to show that the Americans and the CRB were taking the high moral road when retelling the story of relief. It can be easily argued that Hoover wanted nothing—no matter how small—to besmirch posterity's view of himself and the CRB.

As for the February 1916 London situation, it had begun a month or more before in Brussels. According to Hoover's postwar diplomatic phrasing, "There had developed a problem in human relations and emotion which involved the C.R.B. and the Comité National." In other words, the two groups were not getting along. From there, Hoover built a logical case.

First, he explained that from the beginning, the CRB had "gradually . . . built up the moral and physical strength of the C.R.B. and the Comité National. Through the efforts of the two organizations and their Minister Patrons [American, Spanish, and Dutch], many oppressions had been relaxed, economic life was greatly restored, and the people, until then, were being provided with enough food, medical supplies, and clothing to keep them alive."

He also stated that through Francqui's leadership the CN had lifted the Belgian spirits, as the Comité du Nord had bolstered the northern French. "It was a great satisfaction to us that we had contributed to building the forces which sustained the morale, the spiritual strength, and the courage of the Belgian and French peoples."

Anyone who knew Hoover well, however, would realize that such compliments about a group he did not trust should have been taken with a shipload of salt. In addition, in his kind words, he was actually reminding people that the CN's newfound strength was, in fact, a product of CRB efforts.

Hoover continued his fawning praise. "In Belgium, the Comité National had perfected their organizations to such a point that much less supervision by the C.R.B. was necessary. We in the C.R.B. rejoiced at any sort of relief of our responsibilities and fully supported a greater assumption of them by the Committees."

This was blatantly not true. At the time, no one in the CRB felt the CN had perfected its organization, no one agreed CRB responsibilities were lessening (let alone rejoicing about it), and certainly no one in the CRB supported turning over their jobs to the CN and its provincial committees.

Because it would appear unseemly, Hoover could not publicly disagree with points about CN autonomy and proclaim the CRB to be a necessity. Luckily, he had someone else who could and would—the English government in particular, and the Allied governments in general. So, in the same postwar writings, Hoover followed the CN compliments with a very big "however."

"However, the Allied Foreign Offices had a different view. Their view was that the Comité National and the Comité du Nord were prisoners of the Germans. As I have stated, the Allies insisted that the C.R.B. must administer, under its own name, the transportation, warehousing, processing, and district release of supplies from its warehouses to the communes. And since the C.R.B. was the repository of the Allied subsidies, they insisted that it must rigidly account for both food and expenditures, including the monies received from the sales of food and other supplies in Belgium, and that it must maintain a strong American inspection staff over the work of the Comité National and the Comité du Nord and make constant reports to the Allies."

To somewhat soften the point, Hoover tried to give the Belgians their due: "All of this could be nothing less than irksome, especially to the Belgians—that a wholly unimportant group of American youngsters should be imposing orders on the efficient and able local committees. The Belgians felt that they were not subjects of the Allied Governments and that they had made great sacrifices in the Allied cause and should be treated accordingly.

"The sympathies of our men—and my own—were entirely with the Belgians," Hoover continued, meaning the Belgian people, not the Belgians of the CN. "We in the C.R.B. felt that greater responsibility should be recognized by the Allied Governments and assigned to the Comité National."

All such comments led up to another big "however."

"However, in the latter part of February, 1916, some bright mind in the Comité [National] prepared an elaborate set of rules and regulations setting up our respective relations, the effect of which would considerably diminish the responsibilities of the C.R.B."

Because nothing got done in the CN without Francqui's input and/or approval, it was obvious who the "bright mind" probably was.

"We welcomed the idea," Hoover continued disingenuously. "However, I feared that the authorities in London and Paris would construe it as a limitation of their requirements of the C.R.B. We did not report it to the Allied Governments, hoping that we could work matters out ourselves and feeling that peace would soon come to the world again. Nevertheless, ignoring the difficulty did not quiet it."

If Hoover truly believed all of what he wrote above about the CRB/CN situation, he would have worked hard to develop true Belgian self-sufficiency and used his influence with all the governments to let the Belgians do it themselves. But he consistently did the exact opposite, working always to build and consolidate his and the CRB's power position, and when faced with opposition he couldn't directly overcome, he threatened to pull out as a way of forcing his opponents' hands.

Most documents support the idea that Hoover personally believed the Belgians should not be left on their own. He didn't feel they were able to, and didn't feel the Germans would allow them to if they were able. And he knew he could always hide behind the Allies "requirements" to keep the CRB in place.

As for a frank assessment of what Francqui was really doing in London, Green stated it clearly: "Francqui left for London with the Marquis de Villalobar, on his famous attempt to get rid of the C.R.B. entirely."

So, when Francqui, Lambert, and Villalobar came to London in mid-February 1916, Hoover surely knew they were up to something. They did not disappoint, as each of them quickly took actions or said things that undermined the CRB.

Reportedly, Lambert went around London telling everyone who would listen that the CRB was run by "nice young college boys who rode about Belgium in motor cars, lived well at chateaux, and generally had a fine time." That had to sting, especially because it did describe the short-lived experience of a few problem delegates who were quickly expelled by the CRB.

When Hoover got wind of what Lambert was saying, he summoned the Belgian to his London office. He told him in no uncertain terms that he was spreading falsehoods that could lead to the shutting down of relief. The Americans were the only ones the British accepted to supervise the humanitarian aid. Without British trust in the Americans' abilities to do so, there would be no food relief. In effect, Lambert was cutting off his nose to spite his face. Chastised, Lambert promised to correct the impressions he had left with others.

Villalobar did something far worse—at least in the eyes of the diplomatic corps and Hoover. He went and saw Sir Edward Grey directly, bypassing his own Spanish ambassador in London (Merry de Val) and snubbing U.S. Ambassador Walter Page, who was considered by the British to be the linchpin patron of the relief. Villalobar compounded the infraction by also having dinner with Prime Minister Asquith and his wife, Margot, where he "discoursed fully on the Comité National, saying it was a government within a government, and doing political work for the Allies in Belgium." His inference was that the CN could do the work without the CRB and was basically working for the Allies under the Germans' noses.

While it was true the CN was a Belgian organization, all sides believed that the CN needed to be as neutral in word and act as the CRB tried to be. Without such a total commitment to neutrality throughout the entire process of relief, the food would never be allowed in to feed the Belgians.

In a smart political move that kept Prime Minister Asquith officially out of Villalobar's quagmire, Mrs. Asquith sent word to Hoover of Villalobar's "amazing indiscretion."

Hoover was incensed and told the Spaniard what he thought of his actions not only to his face but in a letter of protest. Villalobar, in turn, was deeply offended by Hoover's words—continuing the mutual distrust and disrespect that was the hallmark of most of their relationship.

Not to be outdone, Francqui had brought with him the plan to remove the CRB from the entire operation. Luckily for Hoover, Gibson had gotten wind of it and told Hoover that the three were going to offer the English a plan whereby the exiled Belgian government in Le Havre would take over the purchasing and shipping of all food and the CN would take on the CRB's responsibilities inside Belgium.

Following the adage that the best defense is a good offense, Hoover took the battle to Francqui. Or maybe he was taking a lesson from French marshal Ferdinand Foche, who reportedly stated during the first battle of the Marne in September 1914: "My center is giving way, my right is in retreat; situation excellent. I shall attack!"

Hoover Gets Fed Up—The CRB Resigns

After suffering through recent multiple days in bed with his ear abscesses, the many months of problems and challenges that never seemed to get fully resolved, and the recent rejection of his request for import increases, Hoover took the invasion of the three envoys from Brussels as the last straw.

"By the end of February, 1916, the various embarrassments besetting the Commission were becoming wholly intolerable to my colleagues and to me." He wrote of how the work was taking its toll on the CRB delegates and staff and "required working twelve hours a day, seven days a week, and it brought many personal dangers, as well as constant, bitter, and unnecessary discouragements."

Before he took decisive action, and maybe to help him think through the situation, he wrote out nine points where events and/or individuals had become "intolerable." Some were major developments; others were personal situations.

The first two involved the refusal of the Belgian and French governments to allow their vessels to be used for shipping CRB food.

The third was Hoover's feeling that Whitlock was "not the type of man for the rough-stuff into which he had been precipitated. He was too sensitive a person to be American minister amidst such suffering and tragedy. He shrank from battles with von Bissing and resented the constant pressures for action applied by us and by his First Secretary, Hugh Gibson." Hoover was especially angry and frustrated at what he felt was Whitlock's recent decision to remove Gibson from his post in Brussels.

The fourth point was a major one—the Germans, through von Bissing, had not upheld their December 1915 agreement to not requisition Belgian native food. "Although the civil authorities in Berlin and their military authorities in Northern France were co-operative, in Belgium itself we were subjected to a great deal of Governor General von Bissing's arrogance and anti-Americanism."

That had led to point five, that the British, acting also for the French, had reduced the food imports allowed into Belgium and Northern France, just after Hoover had requested increases to better serve the needy civilians. "These cuts included the supplies for soup kitchens and even supplies for our canteen system which were vital to the lives of the children. We were thus being forced to become instruments of slow starvation, not only of adults, but also of children."

The sixth point was about the general conflicts between the CRB and the CN, which Hoover put diplomatically: "There was an inherent conflict between the responsibilities imposed upon the C.R.B. by the Allies and the very natural feelings of the Belgians in Belgium."

The seventh and eighth points involved the British military's continual harassment of the CRB in its efforts to discredit the organization and end relief.

Specifically, the seventh point, Hoover stated it, was that "the British Military Intelligence was constantly feeding the Foreign Office stories of trivial or mythical infractions or violations of the guarantees by the Germans, and we were constantly being hectored and harassed as if we had some evil intent."

The eighth point was personal. The chief of British Naval Intelligence, Captain Hall, whose boss was Winston Churchill, had called Hoover into his office a month before. He asked multiple questions about the German military operations in the areas served by the CRB. Hoover refused to answer on the grounds that he and the CRB must remain absolutely neutral. "He pressed me, arguing that inasmuch as the Relief was being supported by the British and French Governments, it was my duty to aid their interests." Hoover refused again, saying his duty was to the Belgians and Northern French who would starve without the CRB.

The harassment didn't stop there. Hoover included in his eighth point that a few weeks later a naval intelligence agent had begun calling on Hoover's friends and associates "making extensive inquiries about my private business, my character, and had even inquired about if it was possible that I could be a German spy." (This one issue would not go away and, in fact, would ultimately develop into a serious situation in the near future.)

The ninth and last point of Hoover's list was the fact that Francqui, Lambert, and Villalobar had come to London to undermine the CRB.

With all these issues fresh in mind, Hoover decided it was time to act decisively.

He wrote a long letter to Ambassador Page saying that he felt it was time the CRB resign and turn over the reins to the CN. He sent a copy of the letter to each of the patron ministers and, in a critical statement at the end of his letter, asked Page to pass it on to the "interested governments and ascertain whether they would be prepared to transfer the guarantees and responsibilities to the Comité National in such a manner as to ensure the continued feeding of and relief of the Belgian civil population."

Even though Hoover worked directly with the British nearly every day—most notably Lord Eustace Percy, the official liaison between the CRB and the British—he probably felt the impact of his letter would be stronger by having been forwarded to the British through Ambassador Page than sent by him, an American citizen with no official title.

Hoover's last statement of the letter regarding transference of all guarantees and responsibilities to the CN was his way of ensuring his resignation would not be accepted. He was sure the British, in particular, would not agree to turning over the CRB's operations to the CN. Additionally, most of those who knew Hoover well would never have thought he meant to follow through with the resignation. This threat was a tactic that he had used before. It was meant primarily to force a resolution of the multiple issues that were hobbling him and his organization. After nearly a year and a half of work, Hoover was simply too honorable and too committed to the relief to actually go through with full departure.

But few on the other side of the resignation letter would have tested Hoover on that. Especially those closest to the work, such as Francqui. Hoover had written his Page letter on Wednesday, February 24, 1916, and had presented a copy of it to Francqui on the following Thursday evening, February 25.

Francqui no doubt saw that any power position he might have had in presenting his plan to the British was suddenly undercut by Hoover's dramatic action. The proud Belgian was quick to respond with a letter that must have been difficult to write. The day after receiving Hoover's letter, he all but admitted defeat when he wrote to Ambassador Page on Friday, February 26, "You know . . . that without the active leadership of Mr. Hoover it would have been absolutely impossible for us to continue the provisioning and assistance of the Belgians; also you will not be astonished when I insist, not only in my own personal name, but also in the name of my colleagues and in that of all my fellow-countrymen, that Your Excellency should use your kind influence of Mr. Hoover that he should abandon the idea set out in his letter of the 24th."

The Belgian also showed he could be just as disingenuous as Hoover when he wrote to Page, "The harmony which has never ceased to exist between the C.R.B. and the organization that I direct in Belgium is today too intimate to allow of any blow being struck at either without the risk of destroying the whole organization of both. Also, I feel obliged to inform Your Excellency that it would be impossible for

Sir Edward Grey was the British foreign secretary. He responded to Hoover's February 1916 threat to resign and pull the CRB out of Belgium and northern France. (Public domain; multiple sources.)

me to continue for one moment without the co-operation of Mr. Hoover to carry on the work which he and I have assumed." The man who had come to London to get rid of Hoover and the CRB was now saying he couldn't do the work without them.

The British reacted just as swiftly. They first dealt with Villalobar. Sir Edward Grey, the foreign secretary, wrote to Villalobar stating strongly that Hoover was "the only person directly and personally responsible for the manner in which the whole work, both inside and outside Belgium is carried on." The 'inside and outside" qualifier was a huge statement of support for Hoover and one that would have galled Villalobar.

Grey didn't leave it at that, knowing full well how Villalobar felt about Hoover. He told the Spaniard in diplomatic terms that he and the others should play nice, understand just how heavy the burden was for Hoover and the CRB, and that Villalobar and the others should "in every possible way lighten that burden by making [the CRB's] responsibility as easy to discharge as possible."

It took Grey two weeks longer to officially reply to Page's forwarding of Hoover's resignation letter, but his response on March 13, 1916, was no less vehement than his letter to Villalobar. "I must state clearly that His Majesty's Government can only allow the work of relief to continue if the entire responsibility for it both inside and outside Belgium is borne by neutrals who, having complete freedom to come and go, and having no official position limiting their personal liability, can in fact be held responsible for the carrying out of the various conditions upon which His Majesty's Government has insisted. The American Commission is the only organization which fulfills these requirements, and His Majesty's Government therefore feel obliged to insist that either the whole work should cease or the American Commission shall continue to direct it as heretofore.

"I shall be glad if you will convey these observations to Mr. Hoover, and ask him to reconsider his views in the light of these contributions."

That was followed by another letter from Grey to Page restating the continued cooperation of the British government and the Commission. "I therefore beg that you will be so good as to make it clear to Mr. Hoover and those associated with him in this great humanitarian work that it is the desire and intention of His Majesty's Government that various public departments connected with the work should co-operate with the Commission in the closest way.

"I am happy to be able to say that the Commission continues to enjoy the complete confidence of His Majesty's Government, and I should like to add my own personal tribute to the admirable organisation which they have evolved, and to the tireless energy of all its members, who are so devotedly carrying out their difficult task."

The Germans were nearly as supportive. When Ambassador Gerard passed on Hoover's desire to resign and turn the whole operation over to the Belgians, the German minister of foreign affairs, Gottlieb von Jagow, reacted strongly, stating that his country would not agree to the Belgians controlling relief. Further, he expressed the complete confidence of the Berlin government and the military General Staff in Hoover and the CRB to run the humanitarian operation.

The Threat of Resignation Improves German Guarantees and Imports

As Ambassador Gerard was talking with von Jagow about Hoover's possible resignation, he also took a moment to bring up another issue. He informed von Jagow that von Bissing was not living up to the agreement of December 1915 about requisitioning Belgian native food. Von Jagow promised to look into it and a short time later there was a marked change in von Bissing's attitude.

Hoover took Gerard's information and pressed the issue by asking Whitlock to demand the Germans stop any exports of food from Belgium and any requisitioning of native food. He even supplied Whitlock with some of the accusations that the British military had brought against the CRB regarding those issues. Whitlock, joined by Villalobar, worked with von der Lancken to secure such an agreement. On April 14 Governor General von Bissing signed a long document that agreed to both terms. This gave many in the British Foreign Office greater confidence that the CRB was maintaining the integrity of relief.

Because of this document, it became a relatively easy task to get von Bissing to agree that the 1916 Belgian harvest would be solely for the use of Belgians. (He did so July 8, 1916. However, the harvest in the Army Zone, under the control of the German military, would be a totally different issue and would lead to a showdown in Berlin in late summer.)

After all the responses to Hoover's threatened resignation had come in, the Chief must have had a huge feeling of vindication. He simply summed up the situation by stating, "After prayerful conferences with my colleagues and after having received many promises of better co-operation, we agreed to carry on, with the hope that we had cleared the air."

Realizing, however, this advantage would not remain in place too long, Hoover decided to ask for an increase in imports, in the hope that the devastating decrease in imports that the British had imposed in February might be reversed. On April 5, Hoover asked Lord Percy to increase CRB imports from the February-established 68,150 tons per month to 75,500 tons per months—which was still below the 80,000 tons per month agreed to when relief had first started. He also asked that the northern France imports be increased from 29,700 tons a month to 36,800 tons.

Hoover's strategy and timing were pitch-perfect. On May 10, 1916, the British agreed to the 75,500 tons per month for Belgium and the 36,800 tons per month for northern France. On June 14 they also agreed to lift an embargo they had imposed on clothing imports.

This did not mean, however, that those who wanted to bring down the American and his relief operation were silenced.

Attacks Continue from the British Admiralty and Military Intelligence

Even as Hoover was receiving gratifying confirmations that all the governments wanted him and his organization to remain and renewed statements of cooperation from Francqui and von Bissing, British Intelligence kept bringing to the Foreign Office a steady stream of reports about supposed "leakages" of food from the system into German hands or into the black market. Hoover put it, "The requests that we continue and the promises of better co-operation did not include the British Admiralty, who now seemed to renew their determination to wipe us out."

In March, Lord Percy wrote Hoover with a list of small boat shipments from Belgium to Holland to Germany that reportedly contained numerous items of Belgian native stocks.

Green's Inspection and Control Department made quick work of the accusations, finding out through its contacts in the smuggler trade that the foodstuffs had come not from Belgium but from Holland, Denmark, and even Britain, and were all black-market deals.

The situation became worse, however, when Lord Percy confidentially told Hoover some highly disturbing news. Hoover explained, "British Naval Intelligence had sent the Foreign Office a long series of charges against the C.R.B. and against me personally and had demanded my removal." The accusations included "reflections on my personal integrity" and "asserted that I had large private holdings in Germany, was an undoubted German spy, and generally was delivering the Relief food to the Germans."

Percy told Hoover that his boss, Sir Edward Grey, was sure all the charges were false, but Grey was "concerned" that the accusations might have a negative impact on members of the cabinet. He suggested that Hoover "appear before some sort of inquiry at which Captain Hall would represent the Navy."

Hoover was incensed. "I stated that I would do no such thing, that I was not a British subject, that even if I were I would not stand for an inquisition by such a crooked bunch as the Admiralty Intelligence has so often proved to be."

Percy approached the inquiry from another direction—one that was assured of catching Hoover's attention. Percy said that if Hoover didn't stand before such an inquiry, the forces against him would take their arguments to the public and attack the CRB in the press. Bad publicity might be the least of the fallout from such an event.

Lord Eustace Percy advised Hoover how to best handle the attacks that came from the British admiralty and British military intelligence. Hoover considered him a good friend of the CRB. (Public domain; multiple sources.)

Hoover, an excellent manipulator of the press who understood the full power of newspapers and magazines, knew the press was the key to keeping public opinion on his side. And positive public opinion was necessary for the relief effort to have any chance of continuing. The relief effort could ill afford any negative press regarding him or CRB operations.

Even so, Hoover could not agree to stand before an inquiry at the time. He did tell Ambassador Page the entire story, "including the constant misrepresentations and complaints by Admiralty Intelligence and Captain Hall's bald attempt to question me on German military operations."

Hoover also told Page that even if he did agree to stand before a British judge, he could not do so right then because of more pressing relief problems. Since the British had decreased imports to Belgium and northern France in February, Hoover had been receiving distressing reports from northern France. He felt it was critical that he leave immediately for a personal inspection to see how bad things really were. Ambassador Page assured him that no action would be taken until his return. Hoover left at the end of March for a whirlwind tour of northern France.

In the meantime, Percy had asked Hoover for a memorandum that he would give to the presiding judge of the inquiry, a King's Bench judge, Justice Sir Sidney Rowlatt. Hoover's staff prepared it and sent it to the judge on April 5 (the same day Hoover asked the Foreign Office to increase imports).

After Hoover's return in early April, Page recommended that he see the judge. Hoover did so, but as he later wrote of the experience, "It was an unpalatable performance for an American who thought his service should be enough of an answer." Regardless of how he felt, Hoover was as forthright and open as he always was. He answered all the questions and went so far as to open all his files and accounts, including his private ones, and told the lawyer of his engineering firm to tell the judge "anything he would like to know about me personally or my private business."

Ambassador Page asked Hoover to write up what had happened. In the April 12, 1916, letter to Page, Hoover did not hold back. He started by admitting that a person in a position of "public responsibility as I hold . . . must be prepared at all times to submit to any open and competently conducted investigation."

But then, with that acknowledged, Hoover let loose. "On the other hand . . . I feel I have the right to demand a distinction between such investigation into the conduct of the work and a personal inquisition wherein I am summoned to answer anonymous attacks upon my private character. . . . The form of inquiry adopted bordered upon a presumption of guilt and necessity to prove innocence."

He admitted that even though he went of his own free will, and the judge was courteous, "the whole proceeding is one of deep humiliation." He ended his letter with a warning that if the findings of the judge were inconclusive, he would demand that "further steps be taken to produce the authors of this outrage and to call upon them to meet me, that the thing may be gone into to the very bottom."

Page did not sit back passively. He met with Sir Edward Grey and demanded to see the charges against Hoover. He met with the judge and, as Hoover related it, "He had used some vigorous language, including comment on the fact that the neutral Ambassadors should have been consulted before any such injustice was launched." He even secured copies of the charges and of the justice's report to show to Hoover.

As for the charges, many of them stemmed from allegations made by someone Hoover had dealt with before: "Benedict," Joseph Erdlets Jr., the man who had worked in the Rotterdam office and spread rumors that had led to the December 1915 spy charges against four CRB men (Joe Green, Lewis Richards, Carl Young, and John B. Van Schaick). Back in December 1915, once Hoover had uncovered Erdlets as the perpetrator of spy accusations, he had removed him from the Rotterdam office and sent him back to London to catch the next ship home to America. While in London, however, the ever-troublesome Erdlets had talked to the police as he was being escorted out of the country. His stories had ultimately reached British Intelligence.

Hoover explained that Erdlets had "related a strange story. One of his charges accused me of being a German spy. Another alleged that I had large financial interests in Germany and that I had employed a Captain Merton in our Brussels office who was an official in these 'interests.' The Justice found that I had no such interests but that before the war I had been merely a 'vendor' of minerals to German smelters."

The charges also included a long list of food "leakages," which Hoover and his Inspection and Control Department had already resolved.

The judge presented a long report to Sir Edward Grey that Lord Percy allowed Hoover to read. It "completely vindicated both the CRB and me."

To try and counteract any future challenges and accusations, Hoover began to flood the British Foreign Office with the CRB's detailed paperwork, including extensive reports and material from Joe Green's Inspection and Control Department. "I began sending them," he explained, "copies of every report of leakages discovered and investigated by our American inspectors, the details of the exact movements of every car or canal boat and its contents, from the Dutch ports to its destination, the receipts from warehouses, the record of issues from the warehouses to food processors, and the receipts of each commune." In an age without copy machines, this had to have been an impressive and exhaustive undertaking that surely must have overwhelmed the British Foreign Office.

The situation did not end there. Friends of Hoover wanted to give him a show of support after such unjust treatment. The Duke of Norfolk, who was a longtime supporter of the CRB and chairman of the CRB's British Empire Committee, organized a public meeting with the lord mayor of London that was held at the lord mayor's official residence, Mansion House. The main speaker was Lloyd George, then still chancellor of the exchequer but soon to be minister of munitions.

Whether the event was a result of a subtle Hoover comment or was a spontaneous act by the Duke of Norfolk, nothing could diminish the impact of Lloyd George's ringing endorsement. "A noble friend and colleague of mine, Lord Curzon," George stated, "has described Mr. Hoover's work as 'a miracle of scientific organisation.' That, I believe, is not an over-statement."

With a nod to the recent events, George said that the CRB's massive relief effort "naturally" brought the CRB "under the closest supervision of the Admiralty and the War Office here. I am glad to be in a position to say on behalf of those Departments of His Majesty's Government, that we are convinced that the relief food reached the Belgians and the French, and reached them alone." Cheers erupted from the assembled group, which, no doubt, did not include a CRB nemesis, Winston Churchill, who had lost his job as first lord of the admiralty after the disastrous Gallipoli campaign.

Lloyd George ended his speech by stating that the CRB was "one of the finest achievements in the history of human and philanthropic organisation."

Hoover had survived another crisis and was ready to turn back to the relief work.

The Sussex *was a French passenger ferry that was torpedoed by a German U-boat on March 24, 1916; some Americans were injured. President Wilson strongly condemned the attack. The Germans replied to worldwide condemnation by issuing what became known as the "Sussex Pledge," promising not to attack passenger vessels.* (Public domain; multiple sources.)

The *Sussex* Pledge Helps CRB shipping

As Hoover was battling accusations from British Intelligence, a German U-boat attack nearly brought America into the war. On March 24, 1916, a German submarine torpedoed a French passenger ferry, the *Sussex,* in the English Channel. Even with its bow blown away, the ship miraculously stayed afloat and was towed into a French port. There were approximately 80 casualties, including a few Americans.

Since the sinking of the *Lusitania* a year before, the Germans had been attempting to keep their submarine warfare confined to military vessels. The attack on a passenger vessel that included Americans was too much for President Wilson to ignore.

On Wednesday, April 19, the president addressed a joint session of congress. Two days later his speech was sent by cable from the State Department to the U.S. Embassy in London, which shared it with Hoover and the other CRB delegates in London and Brussels.

Wilson began by expressing his frustration that "again and again the Imperial Government has given this Government its solemn assurances that at least passenger vessels would not be thus dealt with and yet it has again and again permitted its undersea commanders to disregard those assurances with entire immunity."

The president strongly condemned the German naval attacks, citing the sinking of the *Lusitania* and the torpedoing of the *Sussex* as clear indications that the Germans could not conduct submarine warfare that conformed to the "sacred and indisputable rules of international law, and the universally recognized dictates of humanity."

Such actions, Wilson maintained, left America no choice but to state that "unless the Imperial German Government should now immediately declare and effect an abandonment of its present methods of warfare against passenger or freight carrying vessels, this Government can have no choice but to sever diplomatic relations with the Government of the German Empire altogether."

The time for patience and talk was over. Cutting diplomatic ties usually was the step prior to declaring war.

It did not take the Germans long to respond. Within a week, submarine activity had declined, and on Thursday, May 4, the German government issued what became known as the Sussex Pledge. The Germans promised not to attack passenger vessels and to only sink merchant vessels after they had been searched and contraband found.

CRB shipping gained an additional level of security that would last for nearly a year.

37

Elsewhere in Belgium and Northern France

The Bunges, Their Dairy Farm, and a CRB Delegate

The winter of 1915/1916 had not been too harsh, and spring had been relatively normal (cold, wet, and overcast), but it was still difficult to continually feed the Bunges' 130 dairy cows. When Edouard Bunge and his partner, Georges Born, had agreed to pay for the purchase and establishment of a dairy farm to provide milk to the city's children, it had been contingent on the Antwerp committee providing the fodder necessary to maintain the herd. Such a herd required a substantial amount of food.

In winter, a herd of 100 needed every day approximately 3,350 pounds (1,520 kg) of fodder that included corn cakes, cornstarch, brand, potato peelings, bran, and hay. In summer that nearly tripled to 9,125 pounds (4,148 kg) per day of clover, wheat grains, cornstarch, potato peelings, and bran. Depending on the season, the Bunge farms tried to give the dairy any available corn and rye, while also providing pastureland for grazing.

The Antwerp committee was hard-pressed at times to provide so much fodder. It shared that problem with many other locations around the country. Throughout Belgium the concern over fodder for all livestock was so large that the CN and CRB became involved, especially when it came to milk-producing cows.

Hoover explained, in the spring of 1915 "we had been trying for some time to build up special dairies to provide milk products for the children's services. Our organization had purchased hundreds of milch cows from Holland and had rescued some serviceable cows from the slaughterhouses."

Most probably the CRB took the idea of buying cows and creating dairies from independent operations such as that of the Bunges that had sprung up spontaneously in the early days of relief. The idea, however, would have little life—von Bissing would shortly put a stop to the CRB buying milk cows.

But with countrywide dairy operations and general livestock needs, the demand for fodder continued to grow. The CN and the CRB handled the problem by including fodder in its requests for imports of human food. The two—human

By the spring of 1916, the Bunge dairy farm was up and running and sending milk everyday into Antwerp. Note the sabots *(wooden shoes) on the workers.* (Both photos: Raymond Roelands, *Geschiedenis van Kasteeldomein "Oude Gracht" in Hoogboom*, Archief Hobonia, Kallellen, Belgium)

and livestock needs—would be tied together throughout the life of the relief, and become an important issue when discussion arose regarding who was to get the Belgian harvest each year. One CRB history noted, "It is obvious that since the maintenance of meat, fat, and milk supplies depended on fodder, the fodder question was closely related to that of local food supplies."

Feed for the dairy cows wasn't the only problem that Erica Bunge and her farm manager, Verheyen, faced in the spring of 1916. They had been able to get the cows to produce more milk, which they were justifiably proud of, but that meant they needed more containers to carry the milk, and they had none for the growing production. Additionally, with greater production, the dairy farm needed more skilled milkers.

A quick search of the area turned up no canisters.

After a more detailed investigation, however, a supply was located in an abandoned milk plant in the nearby town of Schoten. The shuttered dairy's owner, Eugene d'Arripe, was found, and a request from the Antwerp relief committee was sent to him for not only the use of the canisters but also to hire his out-of-work employees for the Bunge dairy farm. The man quickly said yes and the Bunge dairy received all it needed of both canisters and milkers.

During this time, Erica and the rest of the Bunge family continued to open the Chateau Oude Gracht to the numerous American delegates traveling about the country. A visit to the dairy farm was one of the first things that Erica would offer new delegates.

One new delegate who began appearing at Chateau Oude Gracht was Milton Brown. He had only arrived in Belgium in early February 1916 and in March was still unclear as to the exact job he would be doing for relief. This did not stop him from appreciating the Bunge family and what they were doing, not only for food relief but also for the morale of the American delegates.

In a later letter to his parents long after he had come to know the Bunges, he explained in detail who they were: "The whole family speaks English almost as well as any one of us does. Mr. Bunge is one of the most delightful, loveable old gentlemen I have ever met. . . . He is a very prominent man in Antwerp, loved and respected by everyone. He is an active, keen business man, with a big business before the war in wheat and in Congo rubber; the Bunge Co. being one of the best known colonial firms in Belgium."

He told his father and mother that Edouard had lost his wife in 1907, leaving him with five daughters, of whom two had married before the war and lived outside Belgium. He then went on to describe the three other Bunge daughters.

When it came to Hilda, the youngest at 21, he wrote, "She is a sweet, loveable little girl whom circumstances are fast developing into a noble womanly woman.

One cannot help but love her, not only for her charm and attractiveness but for her love for the weak, for her industry and occupation."

Eva, the 23-year-old middle sister, has a "nature that is a bit complex. . . . She, too, is doing much for the needy; her heart is true."

He wrote that Erica, 24 years old, possessed a "character that is something I have never seen the equal of, nor ever expect to." His admiration and interest in her was clear.

As for what Erica thought of Brown, no record exists because her diary ended before he arrived in Belgium, but Brown continued to visit Chateau Oude Gracht and found Erica more and more fascinating.

Von Bissing Takes Another Step toward Separation

Throughout 1915 and into early 1916, the German governor general kept up his support for a policy known as *Flamenpolitik,* or separation of the Flemings, who spoke Flemish, from the Walloons, who spoke French. One famous Belgian writer of the time, Émile Cammaerts, explained, Germany "suddenly espoused [the Flemings'] grievances . . . tried by every means at her disposal to conciliate Flemish sympathies and to stir up antagonism and jealousies by treating Flemings and Walloons differently, whether prisoners in Germany or in occupied Belgium."

Cammaerts articulated the German thought process behind the policy: "If we are unable to hold Belgium, any pro-German demonstrations in the Northern provinces may suggest the idea that it is the wish of the Flemings to be bound to the Empire and give a pretext for the annexation of Antwerp and Flanders. If even that is impossible and if we are obliged to give back his Kingdom to King Albert, we shall have sown so many germs of discontent in the country that it will be impossible for the Government to restore Belgium in her full unity and power. She will never become against us the strong bulwark of the Allies."

Von Bissing and the Germans chose to make education the wedge by which they hoped to divide the country. The University of Ghent became the most significant battleground.

Before the war, Belgium had had two state universities, one in Ghent within the Flemish north and one in Liège, within the Walloon south. The official language for both schools was French, although a few lectures at Ghent were given in Flemish. For many years the Flemish movement had hoped to make the University of Ghent the country's first Flemish institution, followed by the establishment of another Flemish university in Antwerp, which was the center of all things Flemish. In Belgium's parliament, the issue had been debated numerous times over the years, and a proposal had been on the table to slowly transform the Ghent school to an all Flemish institution when the war broke out.

At the moment of German invasion, however, the entire country had come together as one. Brand Whitlock wrote, "[T]he war came on and put an end to public discussion in Belgium, for the Flemish and Walloons closed their ranks and stood shoulder to shoulder against the invader." Additionally, once the occupation began, all Belgian schools of higher education had shut down in protest.

That did not stop von Bissing and the German government from their plans. The governor general had put in his 1915 budget some money to transform the University of Ghent into a Flemish institution, even though Ghent was not under his control because it lay in East Flanders within the area of the Army Zone referred to as the Etape, or Etappengebiet.

On March 25, 1916, von Bissing received the military support he needed. Prince Albrecht, the commander of the Fourth Army in charge of East Flanders, decreed that "[t]he courses in the University of Ghent will be given in the Flemish language. . . . [Von Bissing's civil administration] is charged with the publication of regulations destined to the execution of this order."

Brand Whitlock put into writing what most Belgians thought, but could not ask, when they read the decree: "Why this sudden concern for the education of youth in Belgium? Why this solicitude for the culture of a people who were being harried and harassed and imprisoned and put to death? What military necessity was it that required a German general to interfere in the curriculum of a university there in an occupied territory, in the midst of savage warfare, in a city under martial law, and in such abnormal conditions that the University, unable to continue its functions had been obliged to close its doors? What had the commander of an army in the field, there in the Étappengebiet, to do with education?"

The Belgian reaction was swift. An official protest letter to von Bissing came from Antwerp, signed by numerous influential Flemings. The first name, and probable author of the letter, was Louis Franck, a lawyer, Antwerp councilman, head of the provincial committee, member of the CN, and generally considered leader of the Flemish movement. Below his name were two presidents of Flemish federations and members of a pre-war commission for the establishment of a Flemish university.

The letter declared that issues between Belgians were just that, issues that were of no concern to outsiders. The Belgians would deal with such issues when the Germans left their country. Brand Whitlock noted, Franck also saw that the transformation of the Ghent university was "but the first maneuver of a Machiavellian design to divide the Belgian people, and to destroy the Belgian nation. It was not enough that the country be violated, invaded, ravished and despoiled . . . . The very soul of the nation must be destroyed."

Other protests came from professors at the university as well as influential people throughout Belgium. Two of the protesting professors who had taught at Ghent were historians known in Europe and America: Paul Frédéricq and Henri

Pirenne. Their protests became outspoken and stirred many others to action. When von Bissing ordered the school reopened and transformed into a Flemish university, the two historians led the rest of the faculty into refusing.

For their efforts, the two Belgian professors were deported to Germany.

The country's famous rumor mill—one CRB delegate said that Belgians had an "extraordinary ability to circulate groundless rumors"—came up with two good stories about the two men that were never verified but illustrated how many felt around the country.

In the first story, before Frédéricq and Pirenne were deported, von Bissing supposedly called Pirenne to Brussels and offered him numerous generous incentives to accept the role of university rector. The Belgian had said he would be pleased and honored to do so as long as the document naming him rector was signed by King Albert.

The second story said that von Bissing had the two men brought to him on their way to Germany. When Frédéricq entered the room, von Bissing had said in Flemish, "You see, Professor, I have learned Flemish since I have been here."

"And I," the professor said, "since you came, I have forgotten it."

Later, von Bissing denied ever having met either man.

Numerous difficulties would continue to plague von Bissing's dream that the University of Ghent reopen as the country's first Flemish institution of higher learning. By autumn, however, the plan would come together.

Pink under Pressure to Return to America

In the Army Zone's Vervins District of northern France, Pink Simpson continued to struggle with his German nurse, Captain Weber, to maintain some semblance of CRB control of the food relief. The personal pressures were enormous, but Pink used his sense of humor as mental armor that kept him focused more on feeding the people and less on what his personal life was like.

Regardless of how good Simpson was at handling the personal stresses, in April and May two American pressures forced him to nearly leave his post and the CRB. He reluctantly reported both to the director in Brussels, who relayed the information to Hoover in London.

The first was the commitment he had made to the Federal Trade Commission that he would return to America to take the position that was being held open to him since November 1915.

For Hoover, it was but a minor administrative problem. On April 25, 1916, he cabled his executive team in New York to handle the situation, explaining, "We are very keen to keep Simpson since he is one of the few men who can stand the strain in Northern France and we are in desperate straits to retain men in that territory."

When he didn't hear back within a couple of weeks, Hoover cabled his New York director, John Lucey, on May 10, "Imperative we hear result as Simpson must leave within three weeks if he meets his engagements but this will entirely disrupt our northern France organization." That same day the FTC replied that another six months would be acceptable. (Another extension of three more months, through March 1, 1917, would later be approved.)

The second American pressure Simpson was feeling revolved around his mother. He had been the sole financial provider for her for years and since joining the CRB—which was strictly voluntary and came with only a small monthly stipend for expenses—his income had dropped and it appeared that he would have to leave the CRB soon to return to America so he could provide for his mother.

It says a lot for Pink and the job he was doing in northern France that Hoover decided to personally step in. Hoover authorized payment of $100 dollars per month ($2,110 in 2018 dollars) in CRB funds to Pink's mother, Mrs. Gertrude Simpson, in Woodland, California. As explained on the instructions for payment, it was "to reimburse Mrs. Simpson for the loss of income incurred by her son remaining in the service of the Commission in Belgium, as a delegate." This arrangement was never publicized, but it is a small indication of Hoover's loyalty, heart, and compassion for those who had earned his respect.

Pink continued to earn Hoover's respect and was in northern France when a major crisis sprang from the weeds like a coiled snake. His German companion, Captain Weber, would play a crucial role in what happened.

Deportations Come to Northern France

The most congested and industrialized area of northern France under German rule was found in the tightly packed metropolitan area containing the three cities of Lille, Roubaix, and Tourcoing. Eighty percent of the working population was comprised of laborers, most of whom were employed in textile mills.

Many of those people had been very hungry a year before, in the spring of 1915, before the CRB had arranged with the German military and the Allies to import food into northern France. The first shipments of food had begun arriving in April 1915 and had continued since then.

The food supplied, however, was minimal compared to what had been consumed before the war, and hunger was a constant companion to many. In fact, in March 1916, an event occurred that shocked and alarmed the German military—approximately two hundred people had rioted in Roubaix, breaking into a few grocery stores and stealing whatever food was found.

That riot added fuel to a fire of articles in the German press calling for the Belgians and northern French to work for their occupiers. The feeling was that Germany had had to call up so many men for war service that the conquered should have to replace those lost laborers. By the spring of 1916, the concept had evolved—if inducements did not succeed, forced labor would be acceptable in the eyes of many Germans.

The German military formulated a plan. Approximately 50,000 out-of-work laborers in the industrialized cities of Lille, Roubaix, and Tourcoing would be relocated to the agricultural areas around Vervins and Charleville to put them to work in the fields. It would not only help the unemployment situation where they were taken from, but it would also help increase the agricultural productivity of the regions they were sent to. A small salary would be paid. Additionally, those deportees who did not work in the fields would be put to work in the German "saw-mills, roadways and other trench industries"—jobs that German soldiers and some Russian prisoners had been doing.

The CRB was officially notified of the German plan in mid-April 1916 by German Captain Count Wengersky of the German General Staff in Charleville. Wengersky, who was assigned to be a CRB liaison, told CRB Director William Poland that the General Staff's intention was to "evacuate" the 50,000 French to agricultural areas. Poland was assured that "volunteers would be asked for, whole families would be transported together when practicable, the main object was to obtain laborers, and, in general, laborers only would be selected."

Poland was in a tricky situation. He knew—and Hoover had drilled it into the heads of all CRB personnel—that the linchpin of the entire food relief program was that the CRB remain absolutely neutral, no matter what the situation. To protest the proposed deportations could be construed as an un-neutral act that could justify the Germans kicking the CRB out of northern France, if not Belgium as well. Was such a protest worth the loss of an entire program that was feeding nearly 10 million people daily?

Poland diplomatically replied that "while in principle we could not object to the moving of the population of these cities to points where they could support themselves, still we anticipated that such a movement could be carried out only with disturbance and suffering."

Part of the plan was that the deported people still needed to be fed by the CRB. Because most of them would be going into the Vervins District, Pink and Captain Weber became involved because they were in charge of that area. A conference was held among Captain Weber, Lille's French committee, and the CRB delegate for Lille, Duke Wellington. Weber was brought in not so much as representative for Vervins district but as the representative from the German general headquarters in Charleville.

As imagined, the Lille committee was stunned by the plan, especially after the city had experienced the horror of the huge German munitions explosion only three months before. The committee members objected vehemently to the proposed deportations, but their protests were ignored. Weber did request that those to be relocated should still receive any allotted military pensions or unemployment payments they were already collecting. The Lille committee refused, saying it would be impossible to do so. Weber then requested that the CRB transfer the appropriate amount of food relief to follow those workers being moved. That issue, as he was reminded, would have to be taken up with the Brussels office. He did so later, and it was ultimately approved.

When the time came to implement the plan, the Germans first tried calling for volunteers. The vast majority of workers in the area were urban dwellers who knew little, if anything, about working in the fields. They were also patriotic, and most felt that working in any capacity for the Germans was an insult to their native land. Out of the 50,000 workers the Germans hoped to relocate, they only received 35 to 40 volunteers.

On April 22, 1916—the day before Easter in a heavily Catholic country—the German High Command chose to give orders to begin forced deportations in Lille. Officially, only the unemployed, or *chômeurs,* were supposed to be taken.

The Lille military commander seemed to see it otherwise. He ordered all residents to be in their homes from 6:00 p.m. until 8:00 a.m., with "candles or other lights in the halls and with their luggage ready for transport. German troops would go through the house and select the people to be sent off."

Eyewitnesses to the deportations included Wellington and Gardner Richardson. Duke wrote an extensive report on the entire issue that was circulated heavily by Hoover. While the report was well written and mostly matter-of-fact in its presentation, Duke's personal feelings came through in expressions such as "the situation which ensued . . . is beyond description," "they were herded . . . like so many beasts," and "the order . . . was naturally carried out in a blunt, brutal, military way." He wrote that an entire regiment was deployed to a particular quarter of the city, and "machine guns were placed in the streets, and six, eight, or ten fully armed soldiers entered each house to remove all inhabitants capable of doing field labor."

Each officer, Duke reported, "had orders to deliver a given number of souls at a designated point, and they were herded through the streets on foot or in cars like so many beasts, being made to wait hours in the cold. Any reluctant attitude was treated with the bayonet point."

While the stated goal was to take only unemployed laborers, the reality was that boys of 15 and men as old as 65 were taken, regardless of their employment status. Worst of all, however, was that women and young girls were also taken. Duke's constrained writing could not completely hide his condemnation. "Girls of good family, women up to the age of fifty, and men up to the age of sixty-five were taken from all parts of the cities without any discrimination or consideration as to what class of society they were from. Girls who had known nothing but the protection of refined homes were thrown together with prostitutes or men of low life."

Every house and every family were touched in some way. Those who had loved ones taken were nearly inconsolable while those who had been spared were left fearful of the next time the Germans came to take people. "Every household, whether entered or not, was thrown into panic for fear that some of its members might be taken sooner or later."

Duke felt helpless to aid those in distress and took little comfort in the fact the CRB provided deportees with food for the two days it would probably take to move them to the agricultural areas. "The Commission has done all in its power to relieve this extreme distress by providing any extra clothing or food that has been available."

Acknowledging his personal desire to help, Wellington stated, "Naturally, the American representative wished to do all in his power to alleviate the situation in any way possible." The only thing he was able to do was report the inhumanity and brutality of the deportations to CRB Director Poland at the next Saturday meeting in Brussels. He did so on April 29.

Poland was horrified at what had taken place, which was contrary to what Count Wengersky had assured him would happen. The CRB director was determined to do something about it but wasn't sure what that would be. Neutrality was one thing, but as one CRB history related, the Lille deportations forced the CRB to get involved "in the maelstrom of the controversies of the war and compelled it to take a definite stand against action taken by the Germans toward the French population."

In a stroke of good luck and timing, during the staff meeting when Duke reported what he had seen, Poland received a phone call from the German Army headquarters in Charleville. He was told that U.S. Ambassador to Germany James Gerard was then in Charleville to talk with the Kaiser regarding the diplomatic crisis around the torpedoing of the *Sussex*. While in Charleville, Gerard had asked to see the CRB delegates of northern France, so Major-General Zoellner, on the staff of the quartermaster general in Charleville, had agreed to set up a meeting. Because the northern France delegates were then in Brussels, a special train was arranged to immediately take Poland, the delegates, and their German nurses down to Charleville.

A Bombshell Makes a Tea Party Memorable

On the train ride south, Poland made the huge decision to bring up the Lille deportations in front of both Ambassador Gerard and Major-General Zoellner. He even asked the German nurses who were on the train to support his opposition to how the deportations were being handled. According to Kittredge, the German officers "promised him that they would support his representations. They agreed with him, they said, that the deportations were brutal and unnecessary and should be stopped."

CRB Brussels Director William Poland transformed a German reception for U.S. Ambassador Gerard into a discussion about the German deportations in Lille. (Public domain; author's archives.)

As Kittredge reported, when they arrived in Charleville, the Americans discovered they were only there as "ornaments" at a tea party "in connection with the demonstration the Germans were giving to the Ambassador of how *they* cared for the [French] people." In attendance were Ambassador Gerard, Major-General Zoellner, German CRB liaisons in Charleville Count Wengersky and Captain Otto Karl zur Strassen, numerous German barons, lesser German officers, the northern France CRB delegates, and accompanying officers Captain Weber and Lieutenants (and brothers) Paul and Fritz Neuerbourg.

No matter how frivolous the event was meant to be, Poland did not let the opportunity pass, as his "sympathetic nature, revolting at the [Lille deportation] tale, impelled him to do something to stop the tragic happenings which had been reported."

In great understatement, Poland noted in his official report, "The proper opportunity occurring, I begged leave to call General Zoellner's attention to the distressing conditions which had arisen in Lille, as a result of the evacuation movement."

A much less constrained description—and probably a more accurate accounting—by CRB delegate and historian Kittredge puts it in a slightly different way. "A bombshell bursting in the room would have hardly produced more astonishment than the raising of this question in the midst of what was ostensibly a quiet social tea. Mr. Poland described to the Ambassador and to General Zoellner the distressing conditions which had arisen in Lille as a result of the evacuation and proceeded to protest most energetically against the whole proceedings."

Poland went on to refute what he felt were three major reasons the Germans were taking such action. He then turned to the two CRB delegates who had personal knowledge of the brutality of the deportations—Duke Wellington and Gardner Richardson (chief delegate in Charleville). They both confirmed what Poland had said.

Count Wengersky and Captain zur Strassen countered by maintaining that the deportations had been carried out in a "proper and satisfactory manner," and that "the French people were very happy to be taken from Lille to the quiet, peaceful, rural districts of the departments of the Aisne, Marne and the Ardennes."

This was the moment when Poland turned to the German officers he had talked to on the train, the ones who had promised to support his efforts to end the deportations. None spoke. Once again, Poland's account of what happened was minimalistic: "Oberleutnant Fritz Neuerbourg and Captain Weber were silent." It was left to Kittredge's history to provide a little stronger statement: "Of all the German officers who had promised to support Mr. Poland's representations, not one dared open his mouth in the presence of his superior officer."

Major-General Zoellner, Poland reported, "expressed himself as much surprised and stated that the condition described was not intended in his order."

It was then that Lieutenant Paul Neuerbourg spoke up. He had not been on the train and had not heard that Poland would be speaking out against the deportations. Kittredge stated that he "proved himself, however, to be a man in the best sense of the word. He confirmed everything Mr. Poland had said and agreed with Mr. Poland that it had been a very great mistake on the part of the German army to carry out the new deportation." It was a highly risky and courageous act by an obviously principled man.

Stunned silence must have followed such a statement from an officer far down the command chain. Ambassador Gerard, Poland said, "was much affected by the statements." Major-General Zoellner promised there would be an immediate investigation and that the commander of the Lille District would be ordered to appear in Charleville to explain what had happened and why the conditions had been so harsh.

After the tea party, action was swift. Orders were telegraphed to Lille halting the deportations immediately.

Nonetheless, in the eight days the deportations took place nearly 20,000 men, women, and children were taken. A month later, Wellington reported that around 300–400 people had returned because they were sick, but the fate of the rest remained a great unknown. He explained, "Any avowed attempt to make investigations of this sort would be met with a flat refusal from the German authorities who control the work of the C.R.B. and who keep its representatives under the closest surveillance [in the Army Zone]." (Most did return after the harvest season was done.)

Wellington was able to convince his German nurse, Captain Bahr, to visit the small village of Quéant south of Lille in the Valenciennes District, where approximately 40 deportees—the majority of whom were women—had been unloaded. The American was not allowed to talk to any of the deportees but was able to speak with the village's mayor, who asked him why the people had been sent there.

"To work in the fields," Wellington told him.

With a look of confusion on his face, the mayor replied, "But these are girls of nice families; they know nothing of field labor; and moreover, we have already more than enough Russian prisoners to do that kind of work. There is no place to put these new people. The town is choked with troops. They swallow everything and there is not even a bit of straw for our friends from Lille to sleep on, much less a roof to put over their heads. My wife and I are doing what we can, but there is very little left here."

Wellington ended his report by stating, "It is known that the unfortunates were carted about in motor trucks, unloaded, and reloaded like merchandise. In some cases the promised salaries were paid by the Germans either entirely or in part in food instead of cash. . . . A vivid imagination is not required to make conclusions as to the inevitable dangers to which particularly the women were exposed. Quartered in the same houses with troops, forced to work in the fields, to harvest the German crop, the story of the inhabitants of Lille, Roubaix, and Tourcoing is an 'Evangeline' [Henry Wadsworth Longfellow's famous 1847 poem that follows a woman searching for her husband after they were pulled apart by deportation] too horrible for poetical treatment."

What happened to the forthright Lieutenant Paul Neuerbourg, who had spoken up in front of his superiors against the deportations? He remained at his post and continued to work to make the relief program succeed.

Gardner Richardson was moved into the position of chief delegate to Charleville, which he held from the end of April to May. He was then named general delegate for all of northern France's six districts to take the place of the inept Caspar Whitney, who simply couldn't do the job, according to Kittredge. It would not be an easy position for Richardson, primarily because, Kittredge reported, "he was never forgiven by the officers at Charleville for the determined way in which he had stood to his guns in giving evidence of the conditions of the deportees who had arrived in Charleville."

Richardson would last in that position for three months before it was determined that two delegates in Charleville (the general delegate and the chief delegate) were not necessary. Richardson would be reassigned to be chief delegate of the Antwerp Province, returning to the province where he had first started and where he would serve the rest of his CRB days in Belgium.

Duke Wellington—who was the first to report the Lille deportations—left his position as chief delegate to Lille and was pulled back to Brussels to let the entire situation cool down. Later, while in London, he would be surprised by a job offer to take him away from the CRB.

The story of the Lille deportations became sensational news around the world once the details were smuggled out of northern France. The world was shocked by the Germans' plan and horrified by how it had been implemented. The British

Press Bureau released a dramatic eyewitness account by a Lille resident, while the French government published an official version of what happened. Most of the Allied press played on the more dramatic, sensational sides of how the Germans had taken young women and children and placed them in compromising, if not dangerous, situations. For many, it was just another indication of "German frightfulness."

In actuality, the Lille deportations showed how much power lay in the hands of local German commanders within the Army Zone. The German High Command had ordered what it felt was a reasonable solution to unemployment in one area and lack of field laborers in another. The details of implementation, however, were left to the local commanders, who, in this case, seemed to go beyond the bounds of human decency and the wishes of those who had created the orders.

The German military's complete control in the Army Zone, however, left the CRB in a difficult position. Kittredge put it, "The Commission and its representatives, realizing their helplessness to control the German army, could not forget their mission was one of humanity and their chief aim was to see that the civil population was kept alive and in health. The Commission, of course, used its influence to the greatest possible extent to secure modification of the harshness of the German rule toward the population, but with varying success."

To clarify the situation, the U.S. State Department asked Hoover to prepare a confidential report on the Lille deportations. Hoover, not usually a defender of the German High Command, was unequivocal in who was to blame for the brutality of the deportations. "It is our belief that the brutality of the operation was largely the fault of the local commandants and lack of adequate arrangements for the reception of and distribution of the evacuees. We do not believe that any such brutalities were committed with intent of the high authorities. We believe they honestly and expeditiously corrected the matter as far as they were able when it came to their attention, and we are informed that disciplinary measures were taken. We do not believe the stories of rape, concubinage, etc., spread in the propagandist press." In closing, Hoover couldn't resist making one more observation: "The incident is one of sufficiently terrible order, but as things go in this war it has resulted in less volume of human suffering than many other continuing barbarities in Europe."

In May 1916, the Germans made assurances to the nations of the world that such deportations would never be done again.

Before the year was out, they would renege on that promise in a way that would far surpass what had happened in Lille.

38

Brussels

Petit Is Tried; German Raids Take Their Toll

Gabrielle Petit—the young Belgian girl who was a distributor of *La Libre Belgique* and aided those trying to escape into Holland—was tried by a German military court not long after her January 20 arrest. She freely confessed to helping young men reach the Dutch border, spying on German troops for the British, and distributing the underground newspaper *La Libre Belgique*. Throughout the trial she was defiant, according to a later booklet that lionized her life. The prosecutor called for her execution, and the German judges gave her the death penalty.

In an unusual move, the Germans did not immediately carry out the sentence. The young woman was thrown into solitary confinement for 28 days, and the secret police pushed her to give up her contacts within British Intelligence and tell them who was publishing *La Libre Belgique*. She gave them no names, even when offered clemency. She did, however, scribble on the cell walls, according to the booklet, and wrote the inspiring words, "It's the humble ones that make unknown heroes."

On Saturday morning, April 1, 1916, the young Belgian woman who had turned 23 only a little more than a month before, was taken to the now-famous German execution grounds at Tir National and shot and buried.

It was less than six months since the execution of Edith Cavell and the worldwide condemnation that had followed. Sadly, Petit's execution elicited no such similar protests, and few people knew of or even acknowledged her death. She became one of only 11 women executed by the Germans during World War I.

Petit, however, would have her day of acknowledgment after the war was over.

Van Doren and the others who knew Petit mourned her death, but the publisher of *La Libre Belgique* was about to face his own biggest challenge.

The newspaper had by then succeeded beyond his wildest hopes. One history noted, "It is impossible to talk of the *Libre Belgique* in terms of ordinary newspapers published under normal conditions. Its circulation was governed not by the number of people who wanted to read it but by the limitations of those who produced and distributed it. Of the seven million inhabitants of occupied [Belgium] there was not one who had not heard of the paper and very few who would not have given much to receive a copy regularly."

Gabrielle Petit, a 23-year-old Belgian woman who had worked in the underground ferrying men to the border and distributing copies of La Libre Belgique, *was executed by the Germans on Saturday morning, April 1, 1916.* (Public domain; multiple sources.)

But warnings of the Germans closing in were on the wind. Two Belgian women traveling in a train on special passes from Brussels to Liège had overheard a conversation between two Germans in plainclothes who were obviously either military or police. The women had told a priest about what they had overhead, and the conversation, through roundabout channels, finally reached van Doren. The women had heard the Germans talk about "a certain Kreude who supplied the *Libre Belgique* to someone in a cafe who passed himself off as a newsvendor. There was also mention of the ten thousand marks reward [for the editors of *La Libre Belgique*] that someone was soon going to get."

Van Doren was sure the person named as "Kreude" was professor Gheude, one of his important distributors. Gheude did not know van Doren's real name and thought he was only a major distributor, not the publisher, but their association could be dangerous to both men. Van Doren immediately told Gheude the story, but the professor did not believe it could be him.

Taking no chances, van Doren decided to stay away from the man's house and to transfer copies only in the street. He also warned the printers, the Allard brothers, to be more cautious when giving copies to Gheude.

His cautions were prescient. A week later, when van Doren and Gheude met one of the Allards at a tram stop to receive copies of the new issue, van Doren noticed a man in a checkered hat watching them too closely. He quickly told the two other men to leave immediately. A few nights after that, van Doren recognized the same man following him. He quickly lost the man in the dark Brussels streets but knew the Germans were getting closer.

A few evenings later, Gheude was supposed to meet two sub-distributors in the *Place du Chatelain*, in a southern suburb of Brussels. It was very dark and one of the two sub-distributors, a woman, spotted Gheude as he strode confidently under a lone streetlight. Before the woman could go to him, the second sub-distributor made contact with Gheude and the professor gave him a bundle of papers. Just then, police swarmed out of the darkness and grabbed Gheude and the other man. Gheude was knocked to the ground, but the other man broke free and ran with his parcel. The woman pulled back into the shadows and hurried away to tell Gheude's wife.

When Madame Gheude heard the news, she knew she could do nothing to help her husband, but she could try and warn van Doren—a man she only knew as a major distributor. But she had no idea where he lived. Through multiple connections another woman, Marquerite Belot, ended up walking through the night to Louvain to wake Lily Maindiaux, who knew where van Doren lived. Maindiaux immediately walked to Brussels to warn van Doren, who had not yet heard about Gheude's arrest and had been planning to meet him that evening.

Van Doren had been saved from possible arrest by an incredibly extensive network of people, the same informal network that ensured little happened in Brussels that would ever remain secret.

As for Gheude's arrest, it was another blundering of the Brussels secret police into the careful investigation spearheaded by the undercover agent, Haelen, and led by his boss, Grisenbrock in Charleroi. Once Grisenbrock heard the news, he once again came down heavily on the Brussels group, informing them that they had jumped too soon and missed a great opportunity to catch the real leaders of *La Libre Belgique.*

Such reprimands were not taken well by the three brigades of Brussels secret police that were chafing under the distant leadership of Grisenbrock. The spy, Haelen, was sending all his reports directly to Grisenbrock, who was not sharing what he learned with the Brussels secret police. He gave them only enough information for them to aid in following various leads that Haelen provided.

The professional rivalry finally got to be too much for the Brussels contingent to contain. *Underground News* explained, they "determined to show the sleuths of Charleroi that they *did* know how a raid should be carried out." But where and whom to raid?

The limited bits of information the Brussels brigades were receiving from Grisenbrock simply confirmed the feeling that most in the units had had all along—the Jesuits were running *La Libre Belgique,* and the printing press must be hidden by them. The logical place for hiding such a large and loud item, the Brussels police reasoned, would be somewhere on the campus of St. Michel College.

The Roman Catholic secondary school had been built in 1905 to replace a previous Jesuit school that had become too small. Located in the southeastern suburb of Etterbeek, the school had become heavily involved in van Doren's underground paper. One of the masters, Father Dubar, had helped the Abbé de Moor on numerous occasions and had suggested the house of the school's barber as a place for the paper's composing room back in 1915. Father Dubar had also made contact with van Doren and had set up one of the distribution circles, which included numerous priests and students (many of whom did not know the others were involved).

An organized, coordinated raid on the school would have devastating results for those who were apprehended, as well as for the continued operation of the publication itself.

On an early morning in late March 1916, more than 150 German secret police, regular police, and soldiers with fixed bayonets, stormed the campus. In minutes all entrances and exits were covered, the priests and laypersons on campus were rounded up, and the Germans quickly began going room to room.

A squad of sappers (men who specialized in combat engineering and demolition) began to search the buildings for the hidden room that contained the newspaper's printing press. It was quickly determined that there was a difference in height between the front of the school's chapel and the back, which exposed part of the foundation walls. Someone decided the press must be behind that section of foundation. The sappers attacked the massive concrete wall with picks and sledge hammers.

Hours later, exhausted and out of sorts, they stopped.

That day, the Germans found nothing of consequence. The reason, according to one history, was that "the secret of the monster raid had been badly kept. There were too many people concerned in it. The Landsturm [older German soldiers for noncombat duties], many of whom were Bavarians who loathed their Prussian officers nearly as heartily as did the Belgians, did not enjoy these expeditions that periodically disturbed the even tenor of their existence in Brussels. And when the order went round that a platoon would be wanted for service at daybreak the grousing of those concerned reached interested ears."

Reportedly, the only item the Germans received from the raid was a stinging letter of protest from Grisenbrock's department to Governor General von Bissing.

The informal network of Belgian patriots who were ready at a moment's notice to pass on such intelligence to all who would listen had once again saved those involved with *La Libre Belgique*.

Through that network, van Doren also learned two valuable pieces of information that put him on high alert.

- The housekeeper for the departed Abbé de Moor had been pulled into the secret police headquarters on Rue de Berlaimont. She had been offered various incentives to tell the Germans what relationship had existed between de Moor and van Doren. After refusing, she had been severely questioned before being released.

- Madame Pilatte, the aunt of Gabrielle Petit, had been released from prison after being offered a large reward for any help she would give to finding the publisher of *La Libre Belgique.*

It was early April 1916, and van Doren knew the German net was closing in on him. He had to make some drastic changes to stay free and alive. The first thing he did was make some hollow cement blocks that he filled with all the documents and files relating to his work with the newspaper. He then stopped having meetings in the street and came up with a new way of making transfers of information and copies of the paper.

In a city where industry and commerce were basically dead, so was the residential real estate market. Van Doren found numerous empty houses and approached either the real estate agent or owner and asked to see each property. When he received a key, he would make copies, then go inspect the home and decide on a hiding place for materials. He would then send a key and a description of the hiding place to his printers and major distributors. These empty homes became effective dead drops for him and his associates.

Van Doren also cut back on his visits to see Father Dubar at St. Michel College and only went when he could take his children so he could blend in with all the other parents and children who were constantly coming and going from the school. And when he was out in public doing work for *La Libre Belgique* he would take on a disguise.

As he was making these alterations to operations, van Doren also had to contend with a broken gas engine that ran his secret press. It delayed the printing and delivery of issue number 69, which sent ripples of concern through Belgium's rumor mill. Had the leaders of the underground newspaper been caught?

Van Doren and his assistant, Plancade, who lived in the house in front of the cardboard manufacturing building where the press was hidden, struggled to get the engine repaired. They had to give issue number 70 to another printer, while they kept working on the engine. Finally the engine was fixed, and they began printing issue number 71.

It would be the last issue the two men would work on together.

Thursday evening, April 13, was a miserable night. A cold, heavy rain was falling hard, and van Doren was happy he was inside his home, upstairs with children and his wife, who was expecting another child. He was in his slippers and settling into the night after a fine supper when his daughter Mariette came in and asked what was happening out front.

He went to the window and looked down. There outside his front door were two civilians, looking like they were waiting for someone. He quickly looked

Four ways that Eugene van Doren appeared in public as a way of hiding his identity from the Germans. (*Underground News: The Complete Story of the Secret Newspaper That Made War History,* Oscard E. Millard, Robert M. McBride and Co., 1938.)

down the street. At the far end of the block he spied three cars that were spilling out with German police.

Underground News captured the scene that followed between van Doren and his wife:

> *"They're here," he said quietly. "Shall I stay or try to get away?"*
>
> *For a moment the room swam around her and the blood fled from her face. He clasped her to him gently and she looked up into his eyes.*
>
> *"Go!" she said tensely. "Go quickly!"*
>
> *He sprang to the door and down the stairs into the kitchen.*
>
> *"The Boches are here—don't open the front door till I'm away," he ordered.*
>
> *Before the bewildered maid could reply he was through the back door.*

From that quietly dramatic scene, van Doren rushed into the backyard, chased by the sounds of pounding and yelling at the front door. He managed after three attempts to scale his backyard wall and land in an empty building lot. He was about to climb over the lot's fence to a side street when he heard someone coming. Quickly dropping back down, he hid in a muddy hole as a German policeman and dog passed slowly by on the side street, the heavy rain probably hampering the dog's sense of smell.

When they were gone, he got over the fence and started down the street, his soaked felt slippers making comical squishing noises with every footfall. He raced to his mother-in-law's house nearby where Victor Jourdain's son Joseph lived. He told Joseph to run and warn Victor, and then borrowed a coat and hat and returned to the street.

In the dark, cold, and rainy night, van Doren had no idea where he could go. Leaving his neighborhood, he thought of going to warn the Allards, who were still printing some of the newspaper, or to other associates' houses. But walking around in slippers and an ill-fitting coat and hat would draw unwanted attention. He finally decided to go to a nearby monastery and seek sanctuary. Once he told his story, however, the monks turned him away.

It was then that he thought about another brother-in-law, Leon Winterbeek, who lived on the other side of Cinquantenaire Park, not far from where he was. Winterbeek was a man he rarely saw and had no inkling that van Doren was the ringleader of *La Libre Belgique*. The Germans would probably not even know of him and his relation to van Doren.

When he got to the house, he told Leon his story. Van Doren also asked him to go warn another man whom Leon did not know. As van Doren warmed himself by the fire, Winterbeek quickly went off on his errand. He found the house with no problem and told the man who answered the door all of what van Doren had told him. After listening intently to the whole tale, the man suddenly grabbed Winterbeek and dragged him into the house. Winterbeek had gotten there too late—he had told van Doren's story to a German secret policeman.

A short time later, the Germans were at Winterbeek's door, pounding on it and yelling to open up. The exhausted van Doren was up in a heartbeat and, after finding the ground-floor windows all barred, realized the only way out was the attic. Racing up the stairs he barged in on the sleeping cook, whom he warned that the Germans were coming and she should pretend to be asleep. He climbed out onto the roof and climbed over a small wall on to the next house's roof. There he found a space between two chimneys where he tried to make his tall, lean frame as small as possible.

Van Doren spent a miserable wet and cold night shivering on the rooftop. German flashlights had come within inches of revealing him. He thought of how thorough the Germans had been and was sure that the raids had not been organized by the Brussels secret police. Not a word had been whispered on the street of a major raid, unlike the raid on St. Michel College. Someone else, a brilliant strategist with a loyal force of men, had to have been the leader of such a well-executed and surprising raid. He wondered how many other associates of *La Libre Belgique* had been caught. Mostly, though, he agonized over what must have happened to his wife and children.

Near dawn he crept back into the house and found the Germans had left. The cook, maid, and Madame Winterbeek were awake and were shocked to see him alive and still free. He received a change of clothes and some food and hot coffee. Reinforced and revived, van Doren strode off down the street, barely acknowledging the continuing cold rain.

The night on the roof had made him think about what he should do. He had decided to ask for help from an old friend whom he had not seen in years. He was sure the Germans would not have come across the name in any of the associates who might have been apprehended.

Walking through the rain, he anguished over what might have happened to his wife and children.

Madame van Doren and the maid had stood by the front door ignoring as long as possible the pounding and shouting by the Germans to open up. At the last second, when the men were about to break it down, she calmly walked back up the stairs, turned, and told the maid to open the door. As a plainclothes detective and nine German police stormed in, she stood atop the stairs and demanded to know what was going on.

Without a word, the police scattered and began a thorough search of every room, closet, bureau, and cupboard, looking not only for van Doren but any for evidence of his involvement with *La Libre Belgique*. Most importantly, they found a recent photo of van Doren that they could circulate to police throughout Belgium.

They quickly came to realize that van Doren had escaped. The frustrated detective told Madame van Doren that she was under arrest. She was given a chance to pack a small suitcase and say goodbye to her children, the youngest of whom was only seven months old. As she walked out, she noticed that the policemen were settling down to a night of waiting for any unsuspecting associates of her husband who might show up.

Madame van Doren was surprised to find she was not being taken to the Brussels Kommandantur, or the secret police offices on Rue de Berlaimont, or St. Gilles Prison—the usual Brussels places where recently arrested Belgians were sent. Instead, the car pulled up to one of the city's main train stations, Gare du Midi. She was escorted by the detective to a waiting room that had been transformed into a kind of command post, with a long table in the middle where numerous policemen sat. As they walked in, the detective announced, "Frau van Doren—wife of the founder and head of the *Libre Belgique*." Everyone in the room stopped and stared. She was shown to a seat in front of one man—Charleroi Chief Detective Grisenbrock.

Grisenbrock had masterminded that night's raids, which had been conducted all over Brussels, netting hundreds of people. He had come from Charleroi to direct operations and to process all his prisoners before sending them immediately to Charleroi, where they would await trial at the military tribunal there.

"He did not intend," one history explained "to let the Brussels [secret police] steal any of his thunder; they had done nothing but blunder from beginning to end. It was their fault that the very man he most wanted, the man Haelen had run to earth and dogged for weeks, accumulating conclusive evidence that he was the head of the *Libre Belgique*, had not yet been brought in. Their bad organisation and half-hearted co-operation had nearly wrecked the grand coup he had so carefully planned. It was the man he wanted, not his wife. He began questioning her irritably."

Madame van Doren stood up stoically to Grisenbrock's questioning and was then allowed, because of her pregnancy, to sit on a padded bench in the warm waiting room as a long parade of Belgians were brought into the command post and questioned. She was horrified to see all who were brought in: the Allard brothers, Leon Winterbeek, and her brother-in-law, C. van Doren. She was heartened not to hear the name Jourdain or see her husband brought in. But her relief at that was instantly dashed when two Germans came in and recounted how they had found the secret press behind a cement wall in an abandoned cardboard manufacturing building. Later, the Germans brought in van Doren's enthusiastic young assistant, Theo Plancade, as well as St. Michel College's Father Dubar, and even the van Dorens' governess.

Just before dawn a train, loaded with all the processed prisoners, pulled out of the station and headed to Charleroi. When it arrived, the group was transported to the cavalry barracks, which had been converted to a makeshift prison.

Grisenbrock and Haelen had done well. More than 200 Belgians were taken into custody on the evening of Thursday, April 13, 1916. And even though they had failed to capture van Doren—the man they were certain was the leader of *Libre Belgique*—Grisenbrock and Haelen were just as certain they had cut off enough of the newspaper's "body" that it could not survive. They had found the secret press, they had apprehended the man who ran the press, and they had arrested the main distributors and many of their subordinates.

Von Bissing and all the German high command who had followed the manhunt for more than a year were overjoyed. One history stated, "Grisenbrock's coup had been a *coup de maître* [master stroke], and decorations and money rewards were showered upon him. In one night he had rounded up more than two hundred people, struck at the vitals of the clandestine organisation, probed the secret of the 'automobile cellar' and put the ringleader to flight."

He would have little time to celebrate.

Twelve days later, on Tuesday, April 25, Governor General von Bissing opened up an envelope in his morning mail. Inside was issue number 72 of *La Libre Belgique*, and signed "with the editor's compliments."

Von Bissing was furious. After the raids, the governor general had received a congratulatory message from the Kaiser.

Once the Kaiser heard about the new issue of the underground newspaper, he sent another message to von Bissing. This one insisted that the paper be stopped at all costs. New orders to the secret police went out from von Bissing to start another drive to find the leaders. These orders went out to the Brussels brigades because Grisenbrock was tied up with questioning those who had already been captured.

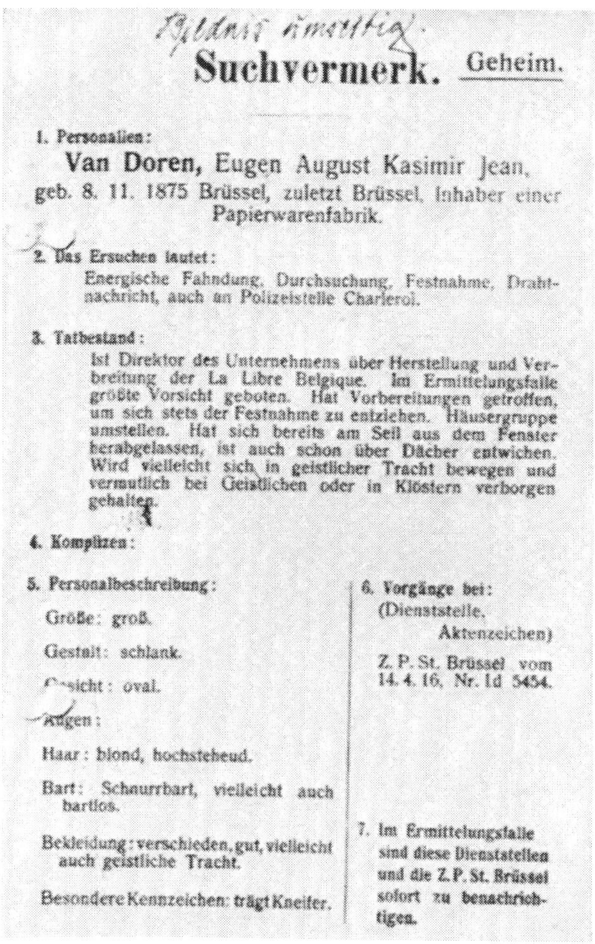

Suchvermerk. Geheim.

1. Personalien:

Van Doren, Eugen August Kasimir Jean,
geb. 8. 11. 1875 Brüssel, zuletzt Brüssel, Inhaber einer Papierwarenfabrik.

2. Das Ersuchen lautet:

Energische Fahndung, Durchsuchung, Festnahme, Drahtnachricht, auch an Polizeistelle Charleroi.

3. Tatbestand:

Ist Direktor des Unternehmens über Herstellung und Verbreitung der La Libre Belgique. Im Ermittelungsfalle größte Vorsicht geboten. Hat Vorbereitungen getroffen, um sich stets der Festnahme zu entziehen. Häusergruppe umstellen. Hat sich bereits am Seil aus dem Fenster herabgelassen, ist auch schon über Dächer entwichen. Wird vielleicht sich in geistlicher Tracht bewegen und vermutlich bei Geistlichen oder in Klöstern verborgen gehalten.

4. Komplizen:

5. Personalbeschreibung:

Größe: groß.

Gestalt: schlank.

Gesicht: oval.

Augen:

Haar: blond, hochsteheud.

Bart: Schnurrbart, vielleicht auch bartlos.

Bekleidung: verschieden, gut, vielleicht auch geistliche Tracht.

Besondere Kennzeichen: trägt Kneifer.

6. Vorgänge bei: (Dienststelle, Aktenzeichen)

Z. P. St. Brüssel vom 14. 4. 16, Nr. Id 5454.

7. Im Ermittelungsfalle sind diese Dienststellen und die Z. P. St. Brüssel sofort zu benachrichtigen.

The German secret police wanted poster for Eugene van Doren. (*Underground News: The Complete Story of the Secret Newspaper That Made War History,* Oscard E. Millard, Robert M. McBride and Co., 1938.)

The new issue of *La Libre Belgique* was not only a surprise to von Bissing; it was a surprise to van Doren, who had nothing to do with its publication.

On the desperate morning of Friday, April 14, van Doren had taken the huge chance of dropping in on an old friend, a man named Waegemaekers, whom he had not seen in years. The man took him in immediately, and it was agreed that the Germans would be hard-pressed to find any link that would lead them to Waegemaekers's door. It was soon decided, however, that the best place to hide would be at the home of Waegemaekers's father, a place van Doren had never visited.

When he found out the hideout was on the Rue de la Blanchisserie, van Doren laughed. The home was only a short walk from the German staff officers' headquarters and the Palace Hotel, which was overrun with German officers. In the weeks and months to come, the manhunt for van Doren was so great throughout Belgium that he would never again be involved in producing his beloved underground newspaper. Worse still, he would not see his wife and children again until just before the end of the war.

The hundreds who had been rounded up on April 13 would have to wait until June 1916 for their mass trial in Charleroi. Many of them were heartened when news filtered into the prison that *La Libre Belgique* was still alive, but most of them wondered, who was running the newspaper?

The Human Side of the Chief

Hoover's depth, breadth, and scope of understanding when it came to running a huge international organization were tremendous. But there were times when he was drawn into personal issues far removed from international business and food relief. Many of those situations originated within the ranks of the young American delegates, who looked upon Hoover not only as the Chief but also as somewhat of a father figure. Hoover rarely, if ever, failed to provide guidance and support to these men—albeit in the quiet, taciturn way that was his.

In April 1916, when Hoover was in Brussels, he was approached by Clare Torrey, the CRB delegate whom Hoover had talked out of rounding up bells for the University of California. The young Torrey had been working in Namur Province since December 1915. On one of the delegates' Thursday gatherings in Brussels, Hoover had been in attendance, and Torrey had pulled him aside. He reminded Hoover that he had only a six-month leave of absence from the university, meaning he would be reluctantly leaving in June or July. Hoover quickly pushed that aside with the surety that he could get the school to extend the leave. Torrey then reminded him of the fact he was engaged and supposed to get married after returning from Belgium.

"Bring the girl over," Hoover stated.

Torrey was astounded by the very generous offer. He immediately cabled Miss Dyer: "Will you come to Europe and marry me some time in May? You may take up relief work in Belgium if you wish."

"Yes. Deborah," she had replied. She immediately began making hasty plans for the strenuous, unusual trip. Her story was quickly picked up by local newspapers. *The Call,* one of San Francisco's daily newspapers, related the romantic tale of the "plucky college girl." It stated, "Traveling more than 3,500 miles unattended to marry the man she loves is another indication of the spirit which guides the work of those willing Americans who today are administrating to the wants of the destitute in Belgium and Northern France."

The bride-to-be, the newspaper explained, was to leave New York on the steamship *Philadelphia* on May 20 and arrive in London, where the marriage would take place. In a slightly ominous sentence, the article stated, "The thought of traveling across the continent, and of facing submarines and Zeppelin raids did not deter Miss Dyer."

By the time his fiancée was to leave San Francisco, Torrey had transferred from Namur to Brussels, where he became the secretary to the CRB office. He moved into a house occupied by other delegates and manned by a butler.

In a British-reserved sort of way, Torrey recounted what happened next.

I was dressing for a dinner that Mr. Hoover was giving for us when the butler came up and said, "There's an American monsieur downstairs who wants to see you."

"What's his name?"

"He didn't say."

So I went down, and Mr. Hoover was there. I'll never forget his words.

"Clare, that girl doesn't want to marry you."

"You don't mean it."

"Yes. I got a cable from her. She's not sailing after all."

"Well, that's quite a blow."

"I knew that you'd feel it deeply." He said, "I had a similar experience when I was young. It all worked out happily in the end." But, he said, "It's quite a knock, isn't it?"

"Yes, it is."

"Well, you go ahead now. We have confidence in you and I hope you'll stay along."

"Well, I'll have to think that over."

He said, "All right—good luck," and he left me.

It was a very fine interview.

So I went to the dinner feeling very downcast. He gave me permission to go out to Holland for the sake of better communication, but it wasn't very good at that. So I went out and nursed my wounds for two or three days at a seaside hotel there, and then came back. Before coming back I met Mr. Hoover in Holland and he said, "What are you going to do?"

"I'll stay longer."

"That's fine."

So that was a very wonderful experience, as you can imagine—his kindness and his fatherly attitude.

Green Gets to Work on Inspection and Control

Into the spring and early summer, Joe Green took command of the American side of the Inspection and Control Department and worked as best he could with his CN counterpart, Van Gend. He gave a simple, straightforward description of what his department was supposed to do in a letter to his parents: "We [Americans] have given guarantees to the Allied Governments that the foodstuffs imported shall be distributed equitably to the civil population, shall not become the object of trade and shall not fall into the hands of the Germans. To carry these out, minute regulations have been made which are not always observed by the various Committees.... Our department had to see that all of these guarantees were kept, and that the regulations made for that purpose were observed."

There was distrust from all sides, as Green explained. "Our Inspection work was naturally a delicate business. The Germans suspected us and some of our activities seemed to them hardly distinguishable from ordinary spying. The Belgians are naturally adverse to 'Regulations,' and as our Department personified 'Regulation', we had immense difficulties, especially at the beginning, with various persons, some of whom were very prominent and very influential."

Green felt his biggest job was getting a uniform approach of inspection and control instituted in each of the provinces. Each province already had some form of inspection and control, but some systems were better than others, and not much had been standardized. Resistance to Green and Van Gend's initial efforts came from some of the provincial committees, which were opposed to this centralized method, more so from what they felt was overreach by the Comité National than from American interference.

To help the provinces overcome their hesitancy, Green knew he needed strong CRB delegates at the local level to convince Belgian leaders how important such a system was to ensuring the continuation of food relief. Such help was not always forthcoming, as Green also had to contend with differing levels of competence among the CRB delegates.

Some provinces, such as Antwerp, were easy because an effective and efficient inspection service had already been implemented by the Belgians. All Green had to do was to get American participation, which came with little effort. The situation wasn't perfect, but as Green explained, "The American representatives there never took their place as real executive officers of the [inspection] Service, but as the thing was efficiently managed by the Belgians, and as no information was kept from them, we never thought it worth while to make any comment on the situation."

In Hainaut Province, William Hallam Tuck was a strong chief delegate and not only carried out Green's recommendations but came up with his own ideas.

In Limbourg Province, Green said he found the inspection "exceedingly rudimentary" and that the representative, Herbert F. Hamilton, "delayed all progress for several months." It was only after CRB delegate Robert Dutton replaced him that things were "put in good order."

In Liège Province, Robert Arrowsmith was "slow at getting his hand in, but after many visits and minute directions as to what was wanted, he succeeded in setting up an excellent service with the full cooperation of [the Belgians]."

Even so, success wasn't always easy or complete. When Prentiss Gray and Alfred Fletcher visited Liège in the spring to see how other provinces operated, they spent time "poking into the side streets." They also talked with Liège delegate Fred Chatfield, who, "from the moment of our arrival," Gray wrote, "has bragged about the wonderful control which he exercises over the bakers and which prevents any sale of the Commission's flour in the open market." Gray couldn't help but report that he and Fletcher had a good deal of fun with Chatfield when, "in our wandering about town, we happened to stumble across a street vendor selling, at a scandalously high price, bread which was unmistakably made from C.R.B. flour." Gray noted drily, "Chatfield is planning to discharge all his inspectors tomorrow."

A province that was particularly difficult was Luxembourg, where one of the Belgians in charge, Baron Evence Coppée, "detested interference on the part of the National Committee, and felt and expressed the greatest contempt for Van Gend. He opposed the whole scheme of organisation and only came around slowly after many discussions on the subject."

Adding to the problem was that the CRB's chief delegate in Luxembourg, Harry Dunn, "never could get a firm hand on things." Once Dunn left in June, Green personally took over the province for five weeks "and succeeded in establishing a proper cooperation between the American representative and the Provincial Committee."

In the all-important area that was equated to a province and known as Agglomération Bruxelloise (greater Brussels), the problems came from all directions. This was Francqui's backyard, and the Belgians were resistant to American supervision. But Green also had to face problems from his own side. In his frank assessment, Dr. David Barrows, the CRB delegate who had replaced him, "was more interested in Counts and Countesses than in the details of Inspection, and rather let things slide. In the period of chaos which followed his administration, [Milton] Brown kept things going until [Prentiss] Gray and [E. Coppée] Thurston took over the Province. They both suffered from 'Antwerp training' [Belgians running things efficiently] and naturally things did not go as well as they might have. Gray made serious but rather fruitless efforts to make the Belgians build up an efficient organisation of their own. It was not, however, until [Robert] Jackson took over the Province at the end of the summer that there was a really strong hand at the helm."

Each American provincial representative was instructed to send in a weekly report, from which Green compiled an extensive countrywide weekly report for the CRB Brussels director, Hoover, Whitlock, and Francqui.

For Green, the work was not all office time and lengthy reports. "My Belgian colleagues stayed at the office. I was there part of every week and the rest of the time on the road in my auto, inspecting our provincial offices, attending meetings of Provincial and Regional committees, and trying to arrange various matters with prominent Belgians and with the German authorities."

It was heady work for a 29-year-old who had dealt more with the dons of academia than the captains of industry and commerce. "I enjoyed the work thoroughly," Green later said, referring to the time from February through most of the summer. "You could see the results." He felt he had accomplished most of the establishing work by midsummer and proudly told his parents in a letter, "We built up out of existing elements a great uniform system of inspection throughout the country and made the whole machine more efficient. It was one of the proudest moments of my life when Mr. Hoover announced that my services had brought the efficiency of the organisation from 23% up to 63%, and that that was about as far as it could go under the circumstances."

During this time, Francqui—who was opposed to any and all American supervision over the work of the CN and the distribution of food and clothes—did nothing to seriously restrict Green's efforts.

In August, he would come out swinging.

Clothes Become an Important Part of Relief

Just as the CN was being obstinate about having the CRB as equal partner in food relief, so too the Comité National was resistant to the CRB intruding into the clothing (Division du Vêtements) area of the CN's charity (secours) department.

The issue had not arisen in the early days of relief, primarily because the CRB had focused on the immediate need for nutrition. It was obvious that clothes could wait. So it was relatively easy for the CRB's Brussels office to turn a somewhat blind eye to the CN's tight control and refusal to share much clothing information. Kittredge put it, "In the first year and a half of the work the Brussels office had not concerned itself particularly with the work of the Benevolent Department [secours], except to ask for occasional reports on the manner in which the relief moneys were being distributed."

By spring of 1916, however, as clothes and shoes had worn out and the requests for raw material and finished garments had increased across Belgium, clothes were becoming an important issue, although still not as important as food. Workshops, or *ouvroirs,* had sprung up in cities nationwide—the largest being in Antwerp and Brussels—and they employed thousands of women and men to mend old clothes and construct new garments from raw material. Many of the women seamstresses worked at the *ouvroirs,* while others, mostly older, worked from home through their local *comptoirs.*

The CN had centralized all the local clothing efforts into the Division du Vêtements, which was part of the CN's secours (charity) efforts for the destitute, which then numbered approximately 3 million in Belgium and 1 million in

Since the early days of Belgium relief, the Comité National's Division du Vêtements (Division of Clothing) had been solely organized and operated by the Belgians. (Public domain; Herbert Hoover Presidential Library Archives, West Branch, Iowa.)

northern France. In late 1915 the CN had asked for imports of clothes and clothing materials.

On following through with the CN's request, the CRB quickly discovered that the Allies were strongly opposed to the large-scale commercial importing of any textile raw materials because of their own need for such. Hoover explained, the CRB then "turned to imports of second-hand clothing, and later we added large amounts of manufactured materials."

The CRB placed large orders in the United Kingdom and the United States, which were "forwarded as fast as import permits were granted, and as war conditions in the trade and in transportation would allow," according to one delegate. Goods from those orders began to arrive in Belgium in February 1916.

Prior to that, in January, the CRB launched a major appeal to Americans for new clothes and raw materials. New clothes were preferable to used ones because of the multiple difficulties used clothes posed regarding cleanliness and transfer of pests (lice, bedbugs, etc.).

Before reaching Belgium, all the material—donated and ordered—had to be sorted, searched, and reviewed to ensure each item was appropriate, useful, and contained no contraband. Such was the case with the silk hats that were donated; they never reached Belgium because there was no need for them. Most items were accepted, however, because the Belgians were creative in taking garments apart and refashioning the pieces. That was the case with knitted items such as wool sweaters. Belgians and northern French women rarely wore sweaters, so when those items reached an *ouvroir* the women would laboriously unravel each sweater so they could knit more usable and acceptable shawls.

Donated items were also many times packed with something special from the giver, such as a few coins or dollars, or even a personal note. When found by sorters, the money was given to the CRB's general fund, and any written material was reluctantly confiscated because it was not allowed through the British blockade or the German border into Belgium.

Every item had its own unique origin story, but few ever became known. One exception was told by a CRB delegate, who related how one small box of items began its journey to Belgium. The delegate was Charlotte Kellogg, and she was the CRB's only officially recognized woman delegate. Wife of Vernon Kellogg (twice Brussels director), she would go to Belgium with her husband in June 1916 and earn the admiration and respect of most CRB delegates, one of whom later wrote, "everyone is crazy about her; she is a delightfully charming woman of tireless energy." Charlotte began working in the CRB bureau office in San Francisco and it was there that she learned the origin story of one box of donations.

She explained in her book, *Women in Belgium*, "When the C.R.B. sent out a call for new clothing materials in January, 1916, somehow it reached a weather-beaten schoolhouse on a lonely stretch of coast 30 miles south of San Francisco. The teacher hurriedly got together some wool, and began showing her eight pupils (they all happened to be boys), how to knit caps for other boys their own size. Their families gathered what they could, and on her first free Saturday, the teacher started in an open buggy in the rain for the C.R.B. Bureau in San Francisco. This meant 30 miles over wretched roads, uphill and down, with her precious box.

"When we opened it," Charlotte continued, "we found eight knitted caps, one small sack of rice, one pair of fur-lined gloves, a bag of beans, a lady's belt, plaid flannel for a blouse, and 40 cents for eight five-cent stamps for the letters the boys hoped to receive in answer to those they had carefully tucked inside the caps.

"They did not know," Charlotte noted, "that our orders were to remove all writing from all gifts, tho once in a while a line did slip in."

That thoughtful gift box gathered by eight boys, a teacher, and a small northern California community was added to the thousands of other generous gifts from the West and freighted by train to New York City. There they were combined with donations from all over the country and loaded onto a ship bound for Rotterdam. In Rotterdam, all the clothing donations were sent to a huge CRB warehouse that Charlotte described as "a corrugated zinc structure as big as a city block." There all the garments and materials were examined, sorted, valued, and painstakingly listed, then reloaded onto one of the canal barges bound for Belgium.

The CRB not only handled clothing donations; it also actively bought much-needed material to make clothes. Hoover explained, "Useful as these gifts of newly made and second-hand clothing were, they did not meet our problem. We were driven to importing cloth and material, needles, thread, buttons, shoes, and leather fittings. We started by buying 'mill-ends,' 'out-of-style goods,' and 'market gluts.' Soon we were obligated to give huge orders to manufacturers."

All these activities in and out of Belgium had not gone unnoticed by the British. They quickly added cloth and clothes items to their demands and guarantees that were necessary for the humanitarian aid to continue.

In April, when the British had found out the Germans were requisitioning clothes and wool from the Belgians, they had shut down all imports of cloth and clothing by the CRB. It took two months of negotiations for Hoover to get the clothing imports restarted on a limited basis. That June agreement had only been accomplished because the British were assured by Hoover that the CRB would have more direct supervision of that area of relief. The June 14 agreement letter from British Foreign Secretary Grey to Ambassador Page stated that the clothing imports would be allowed as long as they were "distributed under the strict system of control guaranteed by the Commission."

This meant, however, that the CRB needed more direct participation in the CN's clothing operations.

Brown Finds His Place—Just Not in Food Relief

As Joe Green battled in the spring and into summer to establish the Inspection and Control Department, he had relied, wherever possible, on men he knew he could trust. One of those was Milton Brown, an old friend from Glendale, Ohio, a fellow Princeton graduate, and the man he had talked into joining the CRB.

A slight man of five-foot eight-inches, Brown was, on first impression, someone who could easily get lost in a crowd. His passport description reported: medium forehead, medium mouth, medium chin, and medium complexion. With short brown hair kept tight to the head and a medium-looking brown moustache, there seemed to be nothing that stood out when it came to the new CRB delegate. But startling blue eyes, a nervous enthusiasm for practically everything, a desire to please, and a surface questioning of his own abilities that was counterbalanced by a deeply ingrained feeling he could do anything gave him a personality that attracted others to him.

When Brown had arrived in early February 1916, he had immediately become Green's assistant because Green had "spoken for him." He was put in charge of cataloguing various elements of inspection and control and lived with Green in a house that was a 10-minute walk from the CRB office at 66 Rue des Colonies. The office building, Brown wrote, was "one of the largest and most modern office buildings in Brussels with overflow offices in other buildings."

In a short time, Green called on Brown to help out in the Agglomération Bruxelloise (greater Brussels) to get a better handle on inspection and control methods. Brown was asked to do a report on the rations of flour and bread for Brussels and completed a 40-page report by the end of February.

In March, Brown finally met Hoover. The Chief had come to Brussels on Tuesday night, March 21, and the next day, as Brown was stepping out of the office elevator, he caught a glimpse of the man. It was only on Thursday morning, during the weekly Comité National meeting, that the young Brown witnessed the impact Hoover had on people.

Brown wrote in his journal what happened: "On Thursday morning the C.N. meeting was well under way, when the door quietly opened and a rather thick-set, boyish-looking man softly entered and, as if slightly embarrassed, looked about him for a place to sit down near the door. His neck was large, his jaw heavy, his chin firm and rather prominent—the whole head and profile that of a fighter, with the high forehead which we usually find on a man of great intelligence. That was Herbert C. Hoover, and the members of the Comité National in meeting assembled rose as one man—that action, and that fraction of a second of silence which followed, being the most spontaneous act of reverence and respect which I have ever seen. And then the room broke out into applause and Mr. Hoover was ushered around to the other side of the long table to sit at the right-hand of the presiding vice-president, M. Janssen."

After the regular business of the meeting was completed, Hoover rose and for five minutes addressed the group in English regarding shipping issues that were being faced. After he sat down, Louis Franck, a councilman from Antwerp, stood and "delivered Mr. Hoover's remarks in French, showing a splendid exhibition of memory by giving the talk almost word for word and omitting nothing."

The next night, Brown was invited along with a few other delegates to dine at director Poland's house with Hoover.

The impressionable Brown wrote dramatically to his father on Sunday night, "This one weekend will be an inspiration for me that will last me the rest of my life. These last few days alone would have more than made my trip over here worth while; and the memory of this meeting [Hoover] will be one of the most splendid recollections for me in the long years after the work here is done."

Overall, Brown was so affected by the work and by Hoover that he decided not to return to America after the completion of his six-month agreement. He wrote his father, "You told me when I left, to be my own judge of the wisdom of my return, and I have. And not only that but I have talked to several of the older men here who know the program I have laid out for my life and each has advised me that to do anything than stay would be very unwise."

Brown's father received a letter from a homeward-bound delegate, Earl Osborn, in late April that explained why Milton had decided to stay. Osborn explained that the reason he was writing was because "we are so restricted in what we can write from Belgium that it is unpleasant writing letters from there." As for Milt staying, Osborn wrote, "Finally comes a reason which it is hard for an outsider to fully appreciate. I mean our affection for the CRB, as an institution and our loyalty and admiration for Mr. Hoover as a man and as our Chief. Not only are we seeing history made but we are making it ourselves; feeding a war stricken nation and saving its poor from misery is a deed which stands out among the general sordidness of these times and we end up feeling that we are really doing something worth while."

In Belgium, Milton found meeting and getting to know men of many backgrounds and ages were surprising byproducts of the CRB experience. "That is one of the strange things," Brown wrote is mother, "about the life of the American delegates; men of all ages live together and go about together like a lot of college men, regardless of any distinction; there is no line drawn between the young and the old and we live in fraternity [type] houses at home. You see, while this is much like an enormous business concern in many respects, there are great differences. We are all in it for one great principle, and some of the youngest men here are way above those much older than they [because] the former may have been here much longer and so are better acquainted with the work."

Brown also discovered that the war was never too far away. The sound of the Western Front guns seemed omnipresent, lying low in the ambient noise of a day, ready at a moment's conscious thought to rise to awareness. This was especially true in the evening. One spring night in Brussels, Brown was walking home from dinner with delegate Alfred Fletcher when they stopped to listen to the murmur of the far-off guns.

"So distinct is it tonight that one can actually count the shots, if one counts rapidly enough; and as we stood and listened in one of the deserted streets, we tried to picture what was the cost of that threatening roar which came to us from perhaps a hundred miles away."

As the two Americans contemplated what was happening to those on the receiving end of the bombardment, something intruded on their thoughts. "A man and woman passed us just then and they were laughing as they went by. At any other time than this, in some other land perhaps, their soft laughter might have been music in the night, a serenade; but there, at that time when the very air seemed charged with the breath of dying men and that steady, low cadence of the guns was so audible, the sound of their mirth jarred the nerves and brought a curse to the lips. And yet I should not begrudge them their laugh. It is wrong in <u>me</u> I suppose, not in them. Poor people! They have suffered enough; perhaps I should be glad that there is any mirth left in Belgium."

Before long Brown was promoted. Hoover had established the new clothing division within the CRB and needed someone to head up the clothing department in Brussels and be the American representative on the clothing board that was run by the CN. That person would tackle the CN's refusal to allow greater involvement of the CRB in its clothing operations. Somewhat surprisingly, Brown—a newly minted delegate—was tapped for the difficult position, presumably because of what Brussels Director Poland had seen of him and the work he had done for Green. Or it could have simply been that Brown was the only available person at the time.

Either way, Brown was offered the job and gladly took it, even though he later admitted that "clothing was never considered as more than a side-issue of the work of the C.R.B. and so did not receive the proper attention which such complicated shipments demanded." Even Hoover's own 477-page book covering the CRB, *An American Epic,* devoted a mere five pages to the clothing situation, starting with this statement: "The provision of clothing was a secondary but essential operation throughout the history of the C.R.B."

No matter what the others thought of the clothing department, Brown, the young and serious new delegate, was determined to do the best he could at the job he had been given.

As for the work, Kittredge explained that Brown was "requested to check over the work of the Section de Vêtements [Division du Vêtements] of the Comité National and to remain in close touch with all its operations." Not an easy task when Francqui and his associates did not want the CRB to enter into the world of clothing relief that they controlled.

Before Brown got to work, however, he would first have to get to know the Belgians in charge of the clothing process. Brown's CN counterpart in the Division du Vêtements was a woman, Madame F. M. Philippson-Wiener, whose husband was a member of the board of directors of the Comité National. Her boss was Emmanuel Janssen, one of three vice presidents of the CN, an ally of Francqui's, and, according to Whitlock, "said to be strongly anti-American."

Brown knew that diplomacy and tact were needed for what he had to do. He determined that the most important first step would be to learn as much as he could about the current operations. Once he understood that, he could better determine how he would go about securing the detailed information the CRB needed to counteract British concerns about possible misuse and abuse in the clothing process.

In this regard, he found Madame Philippson-Wiener more than happy to show him what was being accomplished. Brown wrote his mother that Philippson-Wiener was "not a mere patron and director, but is the active business manager of it all, having built it up from nothing at all." What Brown learned surprised him.

Belgian Efficiency at Its Best

The Brussels clothing operation was much larger than Antwerp's and was organized in slightly different ways. There were four major components to the processing of clothing:

- The receiving center for all raw materials and imports, housed in an entertainment venue, Cirque Royal, a few blocks east of St. Gudula Church. It also served as the headquarters of the purchasing department of the Division du Vêtements.
- The central clothing warehouse in the Pôle Nord (North Pole), where clothes and materials were sorted and finished items were stored until shipped out for distribution. The facility was also the headquarters of Madame Philippson-Wiener and her many departmental assistants.
- The cutting shops, where bolts of cloth were cut into pieces for the making of specific garments.
- The *comptoirs,* where the workers would pick up their packages of cut pieces to take home and work on, before returning the finished items. Twenty such *comptoirs* were scattered throughout Brussels. All finished clothes were then sent to Pôle Nord for cataloguing and storage.

Brown was especially impressed when he visited Pôle Nord, which was also known as Palais d'Eté (Palace of Summer). Built in 1874, the structure had originally housed some of the indoor markets of the large, ornate Halles Centrales. By the end of the 1800s, that section of Halles Centrales had evolved into a winter ice-skating rink (Pôle Nord) and a summer musical/entertainment/exhibition hall (Palais d'Eté).

The huge hall had been taken over by the Division du Vêtements. Brown described the facility and its massive operation. "This vast open hall is alive and humming with busy men and women. An ice-skating rink in antebellum days, the seats have been taken out of the galleries which surround the rink, and the latter built over to provide space for sorting and inspecting of clothing—an area of perhaps some twenty thousand square feet. Where the tiers of seats in the balcony rise to the eaves of the roof innumerable long rows of shelving have been installed which hold their burdens of clothing neatly piled in classified order, of blankets, suits, underwear, hat, caps, waists, dresses, lingerie, and a hundred odd different kinds of garments."

Brown continued, "Underneath this balcony and encircling the rink, save for a narrow corridor left open for the circulation of small trucks, are other lines of shelving filled to the ceiling in the same way. And each row of shelves is placarded, 'Men's Suits, size 36 in.,' 'Boy's Overcoats, size 16,' 'Woolen Blankets,' etc., etc., etc.

"Outside the rink itself," Brown explained, "confusion appears to reign unrestrained, but not so: there is merely a great litter of bales, sacks, and baskets of

The huge central clothing supply station in Brussels. Delegate Milton Brown, who was appointed to head the CRB's clothing department, described the station as "humming with busy men and women." (Public domain; *Fighting Starvation in Belgium,* Vernon Kellogg, George H. Doran Co., 1918.)

newly-made clothing just returned from the comptoirs, which clerks and assistants are counting, checking, inspecting, measuring, to see that the cloth given out for their manufacture has not been cut down by the worker, and a smaller size garment returned than was ordered. Then, when all has been found to be in order, the packages are properly entered in the records of stock on hand, and are carried to the little conveyor, which hoists them from the rink up to the balcony where each package is distributed among the various shelves according to the style and size of the garments."

Watching over the entire operation were large American flags draped over the balcony railings. Inside rooms within the huge hall housed the shoe department and numerous spaces for bookkeepers, checkers, and clerks.

As for the organization of the process itself, that was just as impressive. A book of garment tables had the statistical specifications for each of the 125 different kinds of items manufactured by the division. Brown explained, "For each man's shirt, size 36, for example, in bolt cloth of 90 cm. width, so many centimetres of cloth are necessary, also so many large buttons, so many small buttons, and any other accessories that may be needed." For maximizing every inch of cloth, standard patterns had been created and were used by the cutting shops.

The entire process was set into motion by specific needs. For example, if 1,000 men's shirts were needed, an order would be made out for so many shirts at specific sizes and styles. The order would go out to both the purchasing department at Cirque Royal and a specific cutting house. The purchasing department would determine the amount of material needed, as well as how many accessories were required, such as buttons, hooks, and eyes. All of these items would be sent from Cirque Royal to the cutting house.

The cutting house would use its standard patterns to cut all the material and create individual bundles to make a set number of shirts per bundle. The bundles would then be sent to a *comptoir*, which would log in the received bundles and then hand them out to various workers to take home to assemble.

The 20 *comptoirs* in Brussels employed a total of approximately 15,000 workers, both men and women. Workers registered at a particular *comptoir* would be divided into 12 groups, with each group having a certain day every two weeks when its members would come in to receive their individual bundles of garments to assemble.

So, when the men's shirt bundles were ready at the *comptoir*, the women assigned to come in that day would arrive, return the finished pieces they had been working on for the past two weeks, get paid for their work, and then pick up the new bundle to assemble a certain number of men's shirts. Two weeks later, they would return the finished men's shirts, get paid, then pick up another bundle of something else to be assembled.

The *comptoir* would send the finished shirts to the Pôle Nord to be logged in and stored until sent out to the needy.

The statistics could be numbing. The Brussels operation in its first month of operation in September 1914 had only distributed 1,617 items, of which 1,065 were mattresses and blankets. By 1916, Brussels was distributing on average more than 400,000 garments a month. At one time, according to one delegate, there could be more than 3 million "pieces, yards and pairs" waiting to be dealt with. During the peak time of autumn, in preparation for winter, the facility could have hundreds of thousands of finished garments waiting for distribution. All items, as they went through the system, were carefully catalogued and listed by a large number of clerks and accountants.

The level of detail was so amazing that Hoover later wrote, "So efficient were [the Belgian women in the *ouvroirs*] that one could stop a small boy on the street and note the indelible number on the inside of the collar of his blouse. With no questions asked of him, but from the records these women made, one could know his name, his address, the members of his family, their monetary resources, the date the material had arrived at the work room, and the name of the woman who had made the blouse."

Brown was overwhelmed by Pôle Nord and the entire system, especially the *comptoirs*, which he considered "the most interesting feature of the Brussels organization, from the technological and the sociological point of view." He gained tremendous respect for Madame Philippson-Wiener when he discovered that she had been the one responsible for the "establishment of the *comptoir* system at Brussels." He admired that the system taught the workers a skill that could be used after the war because every item coming out of the *comptoirs* "looks as though it must have been machine-made—the product of a modern factory." And because the workers could assemble the garments at home, domestic life was not as disrupted as it would be if the workers had to spend all day in a workshop. Brown gave all the credit for the *comptoirs* to Madame Philippson-Wiener.

Overall, Brown readily acknowledged the incredible job the Belgians had done. "The whole organization is a demonstration of efficiency and practicality, the equal, if not the superior, of that to be found in the best managed commercial firm of this sort. . . . It is the splendid technical results, the business-like principles of operation which make one feel that one is studying a great manufacturing concern operating under keen competition, and in the centre of a business world which demands at all times the best, the most economical, the most practical."

"Determined Opposition" Stymies Brown

But merely observing the operations was completely different than gaining access to the critical statistical information needed by the CRB for the British. When Brown began requesting information from Madame Philippson-Wiener, she refused, on orders from CN Vice President Janssen, her boss. Janssen continually refused to give Brown any details about the clothes being handled by the Belgians.

Kittredge reported that Brown "encountered determined opposition from the Belgian head of the department [Janssen], who refused to give him the information he requested or to permit him to take any direct part in the work of the Section de Vêtements. This attitude was supported by the comité exécutif of the Comité National itself."

The Belgians were justifiably proud of their clothing operations, and it is easy to understand why they were reluctant to allow the young Americans into the system. The Belgians had conceived it, built it, knew that it worked—and worked well—so why did they need to let the Americans in and possibly gum up the works?

The Americans, and Hoover in particular, saw it simply as a necessity of the agreements the CRB had with the British. The CRB was ultimately responsible for guaranteeing the entire operation of food and clothing imported into Belgium. They, therefore, needed to have access to all areas of operation to determine if the agreements were being upheld.

In May, discussions between Hoover and Janssen over the issue went nowhere. Finally, with Whitlock's diplomatic help, an agreement was struck. The CRB won the concession that Brown would be allowed access to the information needed to file reports and confirm each part of the operations. The CRB conceded, however, that Brown would have no executive functions nor have the ability to dictate any changes or new regulations to any part of the operations. He could observe and collect information, nothing more.

Brown detailed the job's four primary functions, as outlined by the new agreement. The wording showed dutiful respect to the sensitive topic of Americans and executive control. His job, as it was told to him, was to:

1. "assist the executive of the Division du Vêtements of the Comité National in any matter connected with the [clothing] establishment";
2. "not exercise any administrative functions, nor give any instructions to the staff. Any suggestions he may have to offer should be conveyed to the above-mentioned executive or to the Director of the Commission in Brussels";
3. "learn the entire needs of the establishment as to raw materials, etc., so that through him Rotterdam, London, and the United States may be kept properly in accord as to shipments and future requirements"; and
4. prepare "statistical reports . . . showing the number of garments issued to various provinces month by month, and a monthly report presented on the whole working of the establishment."

The first two duties were obviously CN inspired (help the Belgians but don't order anyone around) while the second two were CRB inspired (learn all you can and make meaningful reports).

Even with the CN's promise that it would be more open about the clothing operations, Brown had his work cut out for him. And he later acknowledged, "It was not long before necessity expanded [the four duties] into a very much more detailed occupation."

One subset of clothing that fell under Brown's domain—and benefited greatly from CRB intervention—was the Belgian lace industry.

Belgian Lace Making Is Revitalized

Belgium was famous for both its fine needle lace and its fine bobbin lace. Various regions of the country were known for specific styles of handmade lace that had been developed in their locales over the centuries. Before the war, tourists traveling through practically any village or town on good-weather days would see women of all ages sitting in chairs beside their cottages, hands full of bobbins or plying their needles, weaving thin threads into delicate patterns. Many of the convent schools produced their own lace through educating and working their pupils. Approximately 50,000 women made their living, or helped support their families, by this delicate, traditional art form.

While the vast majority of the lace workers were women, some men were also involved in lace making. Most of the men were Flemish seasonal farm workers who lived in the north but went south in the summer to work the fields. When they came back home after harvest, many of them would spend their idle time making lace.

A few years prior to the war, Belgium's Bavarian-born Queen Elizabeth had taken the industry under her protective patronage after learning of the industry's widespread and systematic exploitation of its workers and the growing threat of machine-made lace. The queen established a committee of prominent women, "Amies de la Dentelle" (Friends of the Lace), who led the movement for better working conditions, improved education, and higher standards.

After the war broke out, lace makers were instantly cut off from their raw material (thread) and from markets outside of Belgium. Members of the queen's committee continued to work, but with the new effort of keeping the industry alive. Other lace committees sprang up around the country to help the workers. Efforts were ultimately centralized in a Brussels Lace Committee. Its honorary president was Mrs. Brand Whitlock, the wife of Brand Whitlock; patrons included Mrs. Lou Henry Hoover, wife of Herbert Hoover, and four Belgian women: Comtesse Elizabeth d'Oultremont, lady-in-waiting to Queen Elizabeth; American-born Vicomtesse de Beughem, married to a Belgian aristocrat; Madame Josse Allard, wife of a Belgian banker; and Madame Kefer-Mali, related to the Belgian consul general of New York.

When the CRB and CN began enrolling people to receive assistance, more than 43,000 lace workers applied for help. The entire industry was in crisis.

In early 1915, as Hoover reported, the Lace Committee requested that the CRB import linen thread and needles for the industry and then buy the pieces of lace produced for export back out of Belgium. The CRB would sell the lace and gain back its money while the lace workers would be paid for their services.

The simple, direct plan, which involved a nonmilitary item, was something most could understand and accept. Hoover was able to get the Allied governments to agree to import thread from England and Ireland and needles for lace making. Brown explained, "They agreed on condition that all lace made from this thread be exported for sale in some neutral country or country of the Allies."

On the other side, the Germans permitted the importation of thread into Belgium on the condition that all the moneys realized from the sale of the lace be turned back into the work in Belgium. That was fine with the CRB.

There were strict controls of the thread. For every kilo of lace thread imported, the CRB had to export an equivalent quantity of lace. According to Brown, the entire operation developed into a substantial enterprise. "Our exports for the Lace Committee amount to something between three hundred thousand and half a million francs worth of lace per month, which lace is sold in Holland, England, France, the United States or elsewhere." Any lace not sold was warehoused in Rotterdam.

As for the workers, with the stamp of approval of the Comité National, rules and regulations were established for the entire lace industry. No person was allowed to work more than 30 hours a week or collect more than 3 francs (60 cents) a week. This way, more workers were given something to do and a little money. According to Charlotte Kellogg, this meant 45,000 women had partial employment, of which "25,000 were skilled, 10,000 of average ability, and 10,000 beginners." Each lace worker had to pay for any thread received to guarantee it would not be sold to someone else. Additionally, all thread was weighed so that each lace worker was responsible for bringing back an equal weight in lace.

Designs in lace had always been important, but they took on new meaning during the German occupation. The Germans had outlawed any patriotic themes, so lace with images such as Allied flags or war slogans were carefully hidden from certain eyes. Or a subtler approach was used, such as using the symbolic animals of certain countries—the lion for Belgium, the unicorn for the United Kingdom, the cock for France, the bear for Russia, and the eagle for America. Some of these pieces of patriotic lace ended up being wrapped around the waists of some CRB delegates and smuggled out of Belgium (which was against all CRB regulations and agreements).

The work could be tremendously elaborate and delicate, and in many cases it could take a long time and multiple lace makers to produce. As an example, a large round needle-lace tablecloth was given to Lou Hoover in appreciation for her efforts on behalf of not only the lace makers but also the Belgian people. The piece was highly complex and was reported by one lace researcher, Evelyn McMillian, to have taken "as many as thirty women at least three months to make."

In a rare sign of détente between the CRB and the CN, disagreements over the Lace Committee and its operations were seldom recorded.

It might not be a coincidence that lace was one of the few areas of relief that was supervised mostly by women.

39

London

Francqui Starts Another Round

All of Joe Green's hard work in the Inspection and Control Department did not go unnoticed—especially by Émile Francqui. Green's command of the department and his American reach into the provincial committees became more than an annoyance to the Belgian.

The summer of 1916 saw another flare-up of Francqui's concern over who was really running the show—he and the CN or Hoover and the CRB. It would be the start of what Kittredge later stated was "one of the longest and most difficult and trying of the controversies in which the Commission was engaged."

In May Hoover had sent a letter to Francqui regarding changes in the accounting of certain aspects of the relief. It was a relatively minor issue, but it elicited a strong memorandum from Francqui in June 1916 that, according to Kittredge, "refused to admit that the Commission for Relief in Belgium possessed any independent existence or authority. . . . Francqui brought into question again the relationship between the Commission and the Comité National. [He] held to his own ideas, in spite of his experience in London in February [1916] and in spite of the agreement with Hoover in the previous July [1915]."

The Belgian insisted that "he, as the head of the joint organisation in Belgium, was alone responsible for the Belgian end of the work, and that the director of the Commission in Brussels and the Commission's American representatives were merely his assistants, able to render great service because of their neutrality but possessing no power of independent action."

Francqui refused to accept the role of the CRB as set forth in the July 1915 CRB/CN agreement and in Sir Edward Grey's March 1916 statement that relief could only continue if the CRB was the sole organization responsible both inside and outside Belgium. He also seemed to have forgotten his own letter of support for the CRB in February when Hoover had offered to pull out.

Kittredge summed up, "What M. Francqui really desired was that the Commission should continue to send food into Belgium and should maintain American representatives there to give weight and prestige to the position of the Comité National; but that these [CRB] representatives should restrict themselves to whatever functions the Comité National chose to assign them. Francqui contended that the whole work of food distribution should be done by the Belgian committees without interference from the Commission for Relief in Belgium, and that the Commission for Relief in Belgium should accept these assurances of the Comité National that all was well in Belgium and should transmit these assurances to the allied governments."

Hoover responded to Francqui's June memorandum with his only letter back to Francqui, once again explaining why he felt the CRB was the principal agent in charge—the Allied governments had allowed the food relief only because it was run by a neutral organization that could supervise the operations and guarantee the Germans upheld their promises.

To add to the situation, the British Foreign Office got wind of the discord between the CRB and CN and asked Hoover to comment.

Hoover was in a somewhat tough position. He couldn't come out and tell the British how discordant the relations had become between the CRB and CN for fear they might shut down the entire program. On the other hand, he desperately needed and wanted the support of the Allies to bring Francqui around to his way of thinking.

Walking that tightrope, Hoover replied to Lord Percy on June 30, 1916, giving his official reasoning behind the difficulties. "The Belgian people, having built up under most terrible difficulties a strong institution in the shape of the Comité National, have a natural desire that it should steadily and systematically be held up to the front as a rallying-point of Belgian sentiment and solidarity, and that its brilliance should not be diminished by a parallel and a too prominent foreign institution. The most extreme form of this desire would be the total elimination of the Americans from Belgium, which I do not believe is at all intended."

Hoover followed with what was becoming a typical roundabout approach to difficult situations with Francqui and the CN. He agreed with Francqui—shyly adding, of course, that it would be with the full acceptance of the British, knowing full well it would not be. "I am anxious to agree with M. Francqui in the desirability . . . of entirely subordinating the Commission for Relief in Belgium organization in Belgium to the Comité National and to do so with your full approval. Always bear in mind that this is not a business of personal *amour propre* [self-esteem], as we do not care an atom what position we occupy in the scheme as long as the Belgian people are fed."

Contrary to what he wrote, Hoover cared very deeply about what position he and the CRB held in Belgium and backed that up with strong actions on numerous occasions. It was one of his unshakable core beliefs that relief would never work unless the CRB was a free and independent body both inside and outside of Belgium. So, Hoover's seeming acquiescence to Francqui's point of view was given, no doubt, in the hope that the British would once again reject the Belgian's position.

Once again, the British did not fail Hoover. Lord Percy's reply to Hoover on July 15, 1916, reiterated the British government's position that the CRB had sole responsibility for relief. Percy brought up the July 20, 1915 agreement of understanding between the CRB and CN that all parties had signed, and he requested that the British government be informed of any opposition to that previous agreement. After detailing the major conditions by which relief was allowed by the British, Percy then gave Hoover a tremendous gift: "There would seem to be in Belgium a lack of real appreciation of the conditions which have been laid down by His Majesty's Government and of the constant vigilance which is necessary to carry them out. It may therefore be worth while to review these conditions with the suggestion that this communication should be forwarded not only to the Comité National, but to each of the provincial and other subsidiary committees for their information and guidance."

Hoover had just been told that he could bypass Francqui's possible censorship and send Lord Percy's letter directly to the provincial and local committees.

As Hoover sat in London pondering what he should do with Lord Percy's ringing endorsement, Joe Green was about to face a major assault by Francqui and his associates on his authority as chief of the Inspection and Control Department. It would ultimately lead to a major showdown between Hoover and Francqui.

40

Elsewhere in Belgium

Gray Experiences Different Sides of Belgium

Prentiss Gray took quickly to being a delegate of Antwerp Province. He lived very comfortably with a few other delegates and a full complement of servants in the large Antwerp townhouse provided by Edouard Bunge. He also spent occasional weekends at the Bunge estate and Chateau Oude Gracht. While he enjoyed the luxury and the time off, he worked hard at understanding how the occupation was impacting all Belgians, and he strove to learn as much as he could about the relief operations.

When it came to the work, Gray naturally gravitated to the shipping side because of his many years in the shipping business. He spent one rainy, cold Monday on the wharves with the CRB's dock man, "endeavoring to become familiar with intricacies involved in the discharge of lighters from Rotterdam and the handling of freight."

Before the war, the port of Antwerp had been one of the largest commercial ports in the world. Even though it had a metropolitan population of only 400,000, its port was the third-busiest in the world when it came to vessel tonnage in and out. (At the time, the busiest five, in order, were New York, Hamburg, Antwerp, Rotterdam, and London.) As the 1910 *Baedeker's Belgium and Holland* tour book related, Antwerp, "situated on the broad and deep Scheldt [River], 55 [miles] from the sea, is one of the greatest seaports of Europe, serving as an outlet for the commerce of Germany as well as of Belgium."

In the northern section of the city were six huge manmade *bassins* (basins) that handled the loading and unloading of everything from seagoing ships and canal barges to pleasure boats. The *bassins* were linked not only with one another but to the river Scheldt to the east and a large canal to the west. Once the war began, the activity within the basins instantly died. When the CRB began shipping food in canal barges from Rotterdam, it used only the Bassin Guillaume for operations.

As Gray walked along the waterfront, "I was struck with the absolute desolation and desertion. Twenty-five thousand dock workers are idle in this city alone, and

CRB delegate Prentiss Gray was joined in German-occupied Belgium by his wife, Laura, and their young daughter, Barbara. Pictured with the Belgian Baetens family, Gray is at far left, Laura is in the middle, and Barbara is in the middle front. (Public domain; *Prentiss N. Gray: Fifteen Months in Belgium, A C.R.B. Diary,* edited by his son, Sherman, and grandson, Prentiss, 2013.)

since Antwerp fell [in October 1914], none of the magnificent dock equipment has turned a wheel. Not a steamer or a barge discharges any of the wharves except the Bassin Guillaume, where our relief barges are unloaded. The entire water front is deserted."

In contrast, Bassin Guillaume "presented a scene of feverish activity," according to Gray. "The city of Antwerp has turned over to us four large floating elevators. These make it possible for the grain to be trans-shipped from the lighters coming from Rotterdam into smaller ones which are capable of navigating the inland waterways to all of the provinces of Belgium except one, the Luxembourg."

A few days later, Gray began to see a more personal side to Belgium's occupation and the impact it was having on residents. He was invited to dinner at the Belgian home of Monsieur Blaess, who worked in the ship-owning department of the CRB. Gray arrived at eight that night. The husband had not arrived home by the time the group sat down to eat at nine. "Madame Blaess and her three daughters, although exceedingly nervous, repressed their feelings in an effort to make us feel at home. As the evening progressed their growing fear that M. Blaess had been thrown into jail was perfectly evident. When he finally came in at ten-thirty, their joy simply carried them off their feet."

Later that night, Gray wrote a diary entry that reflected his empathetic nature. "What a terrible thing this dread must be! Imagine living in the constant fear that, when anyone dear to you is out of sight for more than a few hours, the news may eventually come that he had been transported to Germany for some minor offense, or is lying incommunicado in prison!"

Less than a month after arriving in Belgium, Gray was told he had become chief delegate to Antwerp Province as part of multiple moves of various delegates around the country. He was completely surprised because he felt he had not yet fully learned the job, but happily accepted the position.

Only a few weeks after his promotion, he was sitting in his office when suddenly a man came in whom Gray had only seen in photos—Herbert Hoover. On his way from Rotterdam to Brussels, the Chief had stopped in to introduce himself and see how Gray was getting along. Hoover asked Gray numerous detailed questions, which Gray struggled to answer and "showed quite plainly that [Hoover] knew more about my job than I did." In a few minutes, Hoover was gone and left Gray "trying to recover from my embarrassment."

As Gray grappled with the new job, he decided he needed to truly see how the Belgian poor in his province were living. He wanted to find out "what the people were actually getting from the revitaillement [relief] service, also what supplemental feeding they were able to purchase with their meager earnings."

He found more than he had expected when he visited the town of Boom, less than nine miles (15 km) south of Antwerp. Worthy of only a phrase in the Baedeker's tour book, "a town with 16,800 inhabitants and numerous brick-kilns," Boom was described by Gray simply as "a dirty little town supported before the war by its brick yards. The brick company absolutely controlled the town by owning all of the land and most of the houses of the workingmen."

The brick company's doctor had reported to Gray that all residents were in "exceedingly good health and doing very well under our system of feeding." Gray wanted to see for himself.

During the next four hours, the American chief delegate to Antwerp Province went door-to-door and visited 20 families who welcomed him into their homes. Even with his limited French skills and nonexistent knowledge of Flemish, he was able to ascertain the situation.

"All but three," Gray wrote later, "had been without meat, except for the bacon supplied by the Commission, since the beginning of the war. None had any stock of food in the house, and all were living from week to week on what they drew from the communal warehouse. This is not difficult to understand as the brick company pays only from fourteen to sixteen francs per week for an adult's labor, and from seven to eight francs for that of a child. Employees work from twelve to sixteen hours a day."

Those facts were nothing compared to what he saw, which overwhelmed him. "I have never seen people in a sadder state of health, nor living in more squalor and filthiness. Even in peace time, I understand Boom has been considered a poor town. Nevertheless, unless something is done to relieve this situation we shall have a death rate here that is perfectly appalling."

Such experiences led Gray to do something that few, if any of the other delegates, had ever attempted. He decided he would spend a week living on what was given to a Belgian living only on charity. He documented his experiment in his diary.

"I have always had a desire to discover what the poor people of Belgium really eat. Consequently, I have decided to live on three francs sixty per week, which is the allowance made by the Relief to the Chomeurs [unemployed], as those people are called who are out of work and living on public charity."

Living in Edouard Bunge's luxurious mansion with servants and all the food he wanted, Gray did a good job of sticking to his plan. "My diet began with breakfast this morning which consisted of fifty grams of bread, carefully weighed out and one cup of tea without sugar. Tea is most decidedly a luxury, but as I cannot drink the imitation coffee, I decided to spend a part of my weekly stipend on this extravagance."

Gray's lunch came not only with a little food but with a spot of humor. The food consisted of 150 grams of bread and three-quarters of a liter of soup; the humor came from the mansion's butler. "The butler obtained [the soup] at the communal soup kitchen for me, much to the merriment of the women who have charge of their kitchen." Gray added, "The butler is entirely disgusted with my idea, but I fancy he rather likes the notion of walking through the streets with soup for the American delegate."

Dinner was "a feast." Gray had 100 grams of bread, another quarter liter of soup, and half a can of corn. In his search for how to stretch his unemployed allowance, he had discovered an important fact—Belgians did not normally eat corn, which had been strictly for animals before the war. This meant that all the canned corn at the local "American Shop"—where certain one-off, or unique, items were sold directly to Belgians—could be bought at reduced prices. Gray stocked up so he could have half a can a day.

On the second day of Gray's self-imposed diet, he awoke "with an acute emptiness in the region of my belt." But he kept to his diet.

The third day he was quite excited to discover he was a little below on his spending, which meant he could get something extra. "I rushed out to purchase some potatoes. I find, however, that the few centimes I have left over will only buy three tiny ones about the size of large marbles. This gives me about one hundred grams of potatoes for the noon meal, but with three-quarters of a litre of soup, and bread, I think I will be able to get through week."

The fourth day he declared, "Starvation is splendid for your mathematics. I found this morning that I am still eighteen centimes ahead of the game, having expended only forty-five centimes per day up to date. On Friday I think I will blow this entire sum for a piece of meat, if it is not out of reach in price." He had quickly lost interest in soup. "I am nearly foundered with soup. I believe I can hear the bread splash every time I take a bite."

Friday, May 12, came, and with it the realization that "meat is out of the question. So I have squandered my entire surplus for seventy-five grams of rice which I substituted tonight for the sugar corn. At least it is a change, although a little dry going down, without sugar, milk or butter."

Gray's diet wasn't the only thing that had changed with the experiment. His fellow delegate Robert Withington had been "pleading with me for three days to give it up. He says my disposition is beyond description."

After five full days and nights, Gray ended his experiment. He had lost six and a half pounds in five days, but he had gained much greater insight into what the daily diet was for tens of thousands of the poorest Belgians. And how important the relief work was to the civilians. "Before I left America I had no conception of what it meant always to see starvation just a few days ahead. When I came here I began to realize the catastrophe of having a barge sink in a lock of the canal. If it is not cleared at once, a whole province will go without bread."

This empathy led Gray many times to frustration. "With it all, is that helpless, hopeless feeling that comes to you when you receive an appeal from the North of France, that they have had no meat for months. The best you can do is to send a few [train] cars of mussels until you are able to get a little dried fish off to them."

Such feelings and experiences helped to shape Gray's thinking about relief. "Recently I have been trying to analyze my feelings on this whole relief situation. I don't imagine for a moment that I have turned philanthropist. All of us must admit, however, that we owe some duty to humanity, so we are glad that we have been given this opportunity to play a small role with the man who has actually saved ten million people from starvation.

"It is a big thing," Gray continued, "to have worked for Herbert Hoover. Some day when the history of what we are going through now is told, every school child in America will know his name, just as every child in Belgium and France knows him now as the man who provides their daily bread."

Hoover also helped Gray maintain perspective and work ethic when it came to the imbalance between the luxury provided by wealthy Belgians and the work on behalf of most Belgians who were struggling to stay ahead of starvation. "Weekend parties and dinners are diplomatic necessities in our jobs," Gray acknowledged, "but Hoover puts the stuff in every American that sends him to his job before eight in the morning and keeps him there until seven-thirty at night, with lunch served in the office. There are a few for whom the pace is too fast and shortly they are 'needed in London' [removed from Belgium]. For most there are not hours enough to half-finish."

As for the Germans, Gray worked to maintain a public appearance of neutrality at all times, but he admitted freely that his "inner neutrality" had left him on the very first official motorcar ride as an Antwerp delegate. During the approximately 29-mile drive between Antwerp and Brussels, Gray and his car were stopped nine times by German sentries. At the village of Waelhem, Gray wrote that "my eyes 'popped out of my head' at sight of the ruin caused by the [1914 invasion] shell-fire.... The fort of Waelhem ... was terrifically battered by the German long range guns.... Shells which missed their mark and fell in the village have unroofed and destroyed nearly every house."

At a sentry stop on a bridge at Malines, Gray noted something else with horror as the sentry examined his papers. Absently looking around, Gray suddenly noticed the sentry's bayonet. "The back edge of it was serrated like a saw. Looking quickly at the bayonets of the other German soldiers standing about, I found that they had all been filed in this way. Cold shivers ran up my back as I inquired of my chauffeur the reason for such weapons, hoping he could give me some logical explanation. His answer was that the Germans had discovered it was easier to pull the bayonet out of human flesh if it was done with a sawing motion. Nicks cut in the back of the bayonet facilitated this."

Gray declared, "Here, on this bridge at Malines, all of my inward neutrality dropped away from me. The brutality of a system which would permit such unnecessary horrors has chilled me to the bone." (During WWI, serrated bayonets were manufactured by the Germans, not filed down by individual soldiers. Germany stopped making serrated bayonets because of worldwide condemnation.)

Despite his lack of inner neutrality, Gray would soon be promoted again.

The Mass Trial in Charleroi

At 6:00 a.m., Monday, June 19, 1916, a German military court was called to order in the drill hall of the city's cavalry barracks, where most of the more than 200 Belgians arrested in the April 13 raids tied to *La Libre Belgique* had been held. By the time of the trial, only 46 stood accused of the crime of high treason.

Deciding their fate were the president and judge advocate of the tribunal, as well as four German military officers. They sat at a long table covered in green baize. Nearby was another table stacked high with files, dossiers, and other forms of evidence against the accused.

The defendants had been allowed five Belgian counsels, but none of them had been able to review the evidence, speak to their clients, or prepare any kind of defense. Sentries stood behind them. A large gallery of spectators included the German police and detectives of the Brussels and Charleroi brigades who had helped in the raids. Detective Grisenbrock and his spy Haelen sat next to the prosecutors and were the star witnesses.

Lasting three days, the trial was never about justice; it was about seeking revenge against those who published an underground newspaper that continued to belittle and demean the German Empire and its representatives. In court, pieces of *La Libre Belgique* were read aloud, including passages that called the Kaiser "Attila II," von Bissing a "Bi-singe" (double monkey), and German soldiers barbarians. Much to the surprise of the defendants, the judge advocate read aloud one paragraph of an article from *La Libre Belgique* about spies that ended with the derogatory statement: "The German police like to think of themselves as the personification of Sherlock Holmes. But whereas the English detective resembles a graceful cat pouncing on a mouse, the German sleuth is like a mad bull in a china shop."

On the stand, Grisenbrock proudly described the discovery of van Doren's secret press, which, in fact, had been found only because Theo Plancade had left on a gas light in the hidden chamber. The flickering light had revealed a crack in the wall that the Germans had spotted. Grisenbrock wasn't so proud when an orderly came into the courtroom and handed him a sealed envelope. When he opened it, he found the most recent issue of *La Libre Belgique.*

While Grisenbrock's raids had been highly effective in rounding up many of the distributors and even a couple of printers, it had not captured any of the writers or columnists who created the newspaper's content. It was a glaring omission that frustrated the Germans.

The defendants repeated two relatively effective arguments that would be used by many others in future trials. The first was the fact that the underground newspaper was still appearing, which was a strong argument that the accused did not have much to do with the publication. The second argument was to place any blame on someone who had not been caught, or was known to have escaped to Holland. Because van Doren had eluded the Germans, he was credited by some of the defendants as having done much more than he actually had done.

After three days, 43 of the 46 accused of high treason were sentenced. What struck many was the seeming unevenness of sentences.

Gheude, who was heavily involved in the newspaper's operations, was sentenced to only nine months prison and a 2,000-mark fine, while a young barrister, René Paillot, who had little to do with the publication, was sent to prison for five years. Father Dubar, who was a close associate of van Doren's, had given a bracing and aggressive defense, but many were surprised he escaped with his life. He was sentenced to 12 years of hard labor.

Theo Plancade, the young and enthusiastic assistant to van Doren, had been treated badly from the start. Because he had been caught with the secret press, the Germans knew that he was a close associate of van Doren. As such, while awaiting trial he had been beaten and tortured for information. He had not given anything away. His sentence was two years and eight months of hard labor. As one history noted, the Germans "never abandoned their efforts to make him reveal van Doren's hiding place, and on the sworn testimony of his fellow prisoners he was treated diabolically. He died a slow and ghastly death in a concentration camp."

Madame van Doren had been kept in prison for more than two months. Every few days she had been escorted to Grisenbrock's office and questioned. She was never charged with a crime and was finally released before the trial and gave birth outside prison walls.

The last words regarding the Germans' travesty of justice were those of *La Libre Belgique*. In an article titled "Boche Justice," it sent out a warning: "Prussian squires, who sit behind those baize-covered tables at your courts-martial and under a cloak of legality condemn innocents, beware! Beware lest on the day of reckoning the Allies in their peace terms demand that you be delivered up to answer for your wrongs before a court of true Justice."

After the trial, the question that remained, however, was: How had the underground newspaper survived?

Gray Faces Promotion and Pain in June

On June 3, 1916, Gray received a telegram in Antwerp from Brussels Director Poland saying that he should pack his bag and come down to Brussels. He had been told in May that after only two months of serving as chief delegate to Antwerp Province he would be promoted. He was to become director of the Rotterdam office, replacing Carl Young, who was going home.

Gray assumed Poland's telegram was the first step in that promotion. The following night Gray dined with Hoover and Poland to discuss his immediate transfer to Rotterdam. "But after dinner," Gray said, "Mr. Hoover told me that, instead of going to Rotterdam, he would like to have me remain in Brussels as assistant director."

In the CRB's never-ending challenge to find and retain good staff, necessity seemed to be the mother of promotions. Poland would be leaving in July to become London director and Dr. Vernon Kellogg would be returning after time spent back in America. Kellogg would be Brussels director, managing all diplomatic and German issues, while Gray would be assistant director, handle all business and financial functions, and serve as the chief delegate of the Agglomération Bruxelloise.

Gray was doubtful he could manage it all and wrote to his wife that after being told that he would be the CRB's assistant director, Hoover and Poland had "also calmly saddled me with the title of Acting Chief Representative Agglomération Bruxelloise. Just how they expect me to run the Agglomeration and attend to the business management of the C.R.B. in Brussels is a bit of a mystery still."

On Friday, June 16, Gray arrived in Brussels to take on the new task of running the operations side of the CRB. That night he attended a farewell dinner for

A rare break from the relief work. A CRB baseball game during the summer of 1916. The delegates from northern France took on the delegates of Belgium at the Leopold Club located south of Brussels. Spectators were Belgians unfamiliar with the game. (Public domain; Herbert Hoover Presidential Library Archives, West Branch, Iowa.)

director Poland and delegate Lewis Richards, who were both leaving for London the next day. About 40 men were in attendance, including all the delegates from across Belgium and northern France.

The next day was Gray's official first day on the job. It did not turn out as he might have imagined. It was Saturday, and because all the CRB delegates were still in Brussels from the prior evening's dinner, a day of relaxation had been planned.

The big event of the day was to be a baseball game put on by the American delegates for the Belgians, who knew little of the game. The teams would be the CRB's Belgian delegates versus the CRB's northern France delegates. The athletic exhibition would be held at the Leopold Club (later renamed the Royal Leopold Club) south of Brussels. Highly anticipated by the young men, the ball game would take place in the afternoon following numerous smaller social events hosted by various delegates.

Gray attended a luncheon put on by Clare Torrey at the house he lived in on Rue Ducale. Gray felt right at home with fellow guests from Antwerp, who included Edouard Bunge; his daughters Erica, Eva, and Hilda; and two other young Belgian cousins of the Bunges, Hélène and Alice Karcher. Twelve CRB delegates were also there.

Gray noted that "after luncheon we drove out to the Leopold Club. There, before a curious crowd of Belgians, who doubtlessly thought we had gone entirely crazy, we started the baseball game."

In the fifth inning, Gray stepped up to the plate and got a good piece of the ball. He ran to first, then second, and then headed toward third before realizing he might not get there safely. He made a quick decision and slid toward third.

In the mayhem that ensued, Gray broke his right arm.

Milton Brown noted what happened next. "In order not to leave a bad impression upon the crowd who had gathered to see this strange American game, we packed him off to the hospital in one of our machines and finished our nine innings."

The first full day on his new job, Gray had just lost the use of his dominant hand.

By the end of June, Vernon Kellogg had returned to take over as Brussels director. Gray wrote, "I am sure I am going to like his way of doing things. He has turned over to me the financial and business interests [of the CRB], while he will handle the policy and diplomatic end."

On the Fourth of July, Gray and the rest of the American CRBers were invited by Brand Whitlock to a lunch at the Royal Golf Club. Earlier that day there had a been another baseball game at the Leopold Club. Gray, who was still wearing a cast, was given an important job: "to sit on the sidelines and keep the Belgians from cheering the fouls."

As for the lunch, Gray noted that it was followed by "the Minister's two-hour dissertation on what he had done for the Belgians." Having already determined, as most delegates had, that Whitlock was more puffery than substance, Gray reported that "we were all bored to death," as the minister "explained, 'How I saved Belgium.'"

A Weekend at Chateau Oude Gracht

Brown, who attended the Fourth of July festivities, also noted Whitlock's long speech, but he recorded something much more important. "The work has gotten clear into the depths of me now and to give it up would be to lose one of the biggest things that has ever come into my life—the very biggest. I should say, I have ceased to think of it as an opportunity; rather it has become a magnificent privilege, to lose which would forego one of the richest memories I shall ever have in the future years of my life."

As summer progressed, Brown settled into his job as chief of the CRB clothing department. "The work in general is going as well as ever," he wrote to his mother, "and I find myself getting deeper into it all the time, not only in my duties but in the spirit of the thing as well. It is something that will always be unique in the experiences of my life and while the letters from home telling of the summer plans and

On the Fourth of July 1916, the Americans took off time from their work to play a baseball game and then attend a luncheon put on by Brand Whitlock at the Royal Golf Club. Prentiss Gray noted that Whitlock gave a "two-hour dissertation on what he had done for the Belgians." Whitlock is the tall man in the middle of the photo. (Public domain; *A Journal from Our Legation in Belgium,* Hugh Gibson, Doubleday, Page & Co., 1917.)

of the intimate little affairs of the family always bring a bit of a lump into my throat, never the less I have never regretted my decision, and consider myself infinitely fortunate to be able to avail myself of this wonderful privilege."

While work was critical to Brown, so was his time away. Since spring he had periodically traveled to the Bunges' estate outside Antwerp for rest and relaxation. It had become like a second home, the Bunges had become like family, and Brown had developed a growing romantic interest in Erica. He was drawn to her passion in all that she did—from helping at the children's canteens to running the dairy farm on the Hoogboom estate. During any break in work that gave him a little time, Brown would head north to Chateau Oude Gracht.

His interest in visiting the Bunges was shared by fellow CRBer Fred Eckstein, who was already romantically interested in Eva Bunge. Eckstein had graduated from Yale and considered himself a well-read intellectual. Eva was a woman fascinated with international politics and was heavily involved with helping her country in any way possible. The two shared a love of books and stimulating, challenging conversations. They even looked a little alike, with each sporting wire-rimmed glasses and naturally wavy hair.

On Saturday, June 24, Brown and Joe Green motored from Brussels to the Bunge estate, arriving around five for "tea time." Eckstein was already there, along with four other American delegates from around Belgium. The Americans were entertained by Erica, Eva, and Hilda Bunge, and two other young Belgian women.

For a moment in time, the war seemed to disappear, and the weekend turned into what resembled a pre-war gathering of well-to-do young men and women simply enjoying life.

That evening, all 12 clambered into skiffs and rowed around the lake in front of the chateau singing songs. The Belgian women would sing a Belgian song, then the men would answer with an American tune or even one of their university songs.

One tune they all knew was the Yale "Whiffenpoof Song," which had become popular since its publication in 1909. Even the Belgian women knew the song and sang along. As dusk began to spread across the lake, it was chased by the young voices raised on high.

"We are poor little lambs
Who have lost our way.
Baa, Baa, Baa.
We are little black sheep,
Who have gone astray.
Baa, Baa, Baa.
Gentlemen songsters off on a spree,
Doomed from here to eternity.
Lord have mercy on such as we.
Baa, Baa, Baa."

Sunday, the group headed to the estate's clay tennis courts and spent the morning playing tennis. A lavish lunch in the chateau's formal dining room was complete with wines for each course and servants quickly answering every need. The statue-like Isidore, the chateau's *maître d'hôtel,* remained ramrod straight against one wall eying both guests and servants.

Adjourning to the wide terrace overlooking the lake, the group lounged about, talking and smoking. Later, Brown and another delegate went for a swim in the lake.

After "tea time," everyone took off for a long walk together into the woods and fields of the Hoogboom estate, "where we lolled around and fought mosquitoes. After that we tried lying in the hay piled in the fields, with slightly better success. We came in for dinner then, and that was followed, as on the previous evening by a skiff party on the lake."

At one moment during the leisurely day, Brown and Green shared a quiet private moment related to their families' summer cottages on Canada's Georgian Bay of Lake Huron. Brown later wrote, "There was one touch of homesickness in that view on the lake, for [the Bunges] have planted a tiny island with evergreens which stand up against the twilight much as some of the islands at camp [in Canada].

Relaxing at Chateau Oude Gracht

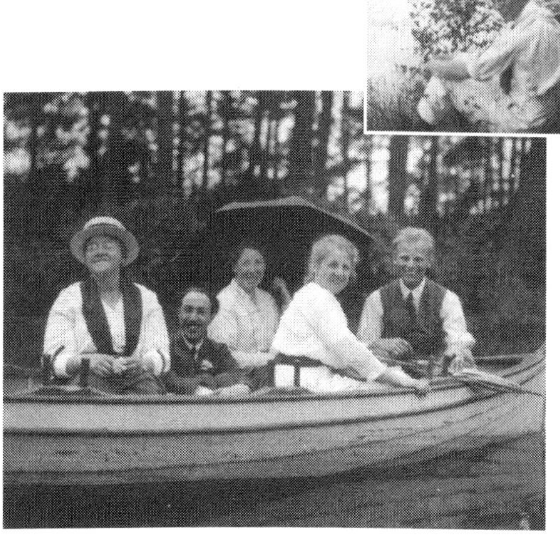

For a moment in time, the war seemed far away. On numerous weekends the Bunge sisters, along with their friends, entertained any American delegates who showed up. (Author's archives.)

And Joe turned to me and said, 'What does that remind you of?' And I said, 'Yes, I wondered if you would see that.'"

The party broke up by Monday morning as the delegates headed in separate directions to return to their posts. Brown went to Antwerp and did some work there before taking a train back to Brussels, where he arrived home late that night.

He admitted to his grandmother in a letter, "When these week-ends in the country are as strenuous and necessitate as late hours as this kind of trip usually does, in one sense of the word they are not such a very great rest. And yet in another they are, for after having pegged along working from ten to twelve hours a day, just the absolute freedom from every thought and worry of the office tends to relieve the nervous pressure tremendously, and tonight, while I do feel tired, I feel a great deal better than after an ordinary day at the office."

He neglected to tell his grandmother—or any other relative back home—that he was falling in love with Erica Bunge. His parents would find out later about the budding relationship, but not from their son.

A New Delegate Comes to Hainaut Province

In mid-July a tall, gangly American barely in his twenties came to live in the Belgian town of Tournai to take on the duties of a CRB delegate in Hainaut Province, the country's largest in area and population, with approximately 1.3 million people.

At 21, Maurice Pate was one of the youngest CRB delegates and his French was weak. It was a surprise to some that he was allowed in, considering the shift in 1915 and early 1916 by CRB executives to reject young, untested men who weren't fluent in French. His maturity must have impressed his interviewers.

From an early age, Pate had shown he was up to practically any task. He had spent much of his youth in Denver as the oldest of seven children. He attended East High School and was involved in numerous activities, including student "congress," advertising manager for the yearbook, participant in the senior class play, and author of the commencement essay. In the yearbook, each member of the senior class had a short quote that was supposed to capture who they were. Tellingly, Pate's was "a man not of words but of action."

He entered Princeton University in 1911 while still only 17 years old. He was as active there as he had been at East High School—working on a Red Cross committee, becoming business affairs manager of a school publication, and operating the launch for the school's rowing team. In an age when it was desirable to be part of a university club, Pate chose, as one history related, to take his "meals with a nonclub group who called themselves the Gargoyles." He graduated in 1915 with a bachelor of science degree in mathematics and physics with high honors.

Pate immediately took a job at the First National Bank in Hartley, Iowa, but the stories he read in the newspapers of Belgium and the relief efforts of the CRB led him to apply to become a delegate.

He wrote to the CRB office in New York asking to be considered and then traveled to the city from Denver in May 1916 for a series of interviews. He first talked with a man named Healey, the secretary of the CRB's New York office, after which he was interviewed in French by a Mr. Mali to determine his linguistic skills. Four days later he was called back in to speak with Captain Lucey, who had established the CRB Rotterdam office in 1914 and had temporarily been Brussels director before returning to America to become director of the CRB office in New York City.

In a time when some of the more experienced applicants were nearly instantaneously accepted and shipped off to Belgium, Pate was told to wait. He took a room at 23 West 125th Street and studied French for three weeks with a Mr. Jetteur.

Finally, nearly a month after his first interview, on Wednesday, June 13, Pate received his appointment to the CRB. Four days later he was on the Holland-American liner *Ryndam* heading for Rotterdam.

Onboard with him were four other new CRB recruits: Harry Dunn and William Gwynn, both from California; Ernest Liefeld, who was going to Brussels as a German translator and interpreter for the CRB; and William Hall from Connecticut, who was Pate's roommate for the voyage. Also traveling to Belgium was Charlotte Kellogg, the wife of Brussels Director Vernon Kellogg and sole woman CRB delegate.

The ship stopped at Falmouth in Britain (where Kellogg got off to visit Hoover in London) before going on to Rotterdam. By the time Pate and the other CRB delegates got off the ship on July 5, 1916, they had been onboard 18 days. The group waited again in Rotterdam before all paperwork and passports were prepared and approved by the Germans.

Pate spent the days waiting by traveling around Holland and learning more about the relief operations. He toured the huge CRB warehouses and went out into the harbor to watch the floating elevators unloading ships. He was mightily impressed and wrote his mother and father, "Three large boats were being unloaded. One was filled solidly with wheat and we saw the grain being sucked up by the elevators and carried over into the barges. Two elevators working steadily unload this ship's cargo of 100,000 bushels in 12 hours. Every minute is precious as the value of the service of the larger boats is figured at $1,000 to $1,500 per day, and even with its present fleet of over a hundred transatlantic ships every vessel has to be used day and night to bring the necessary supplies: wheat, flour, peas, beans, bacon, condensed milk."

On Saturday, July 15, 1916, Pate, along with Harry Dunn, Ernest Liefeld, and Lewis Richards, headed for Belgium. When they got to the Dutch town of Roosendaal they were taken by car to the Belgian frontier, where they had to get out and pass

Maurice Pate, 21, joined the CRB as one of the youngest delegates. While his French was poor, his presence and maturity impressed those who interviewed him. (Public domain; author's archives.)

through Dutch customs before walking over to the German side. As they did so, Pate noted, "The German and Dutch soldiers on opposite sides of the line were talking in a friendly way." One of the German border guards spoke to the German-speaking Liefeld and asked to see a U.S. coin. Pate gave him a Buffalo nickel, "which pleased him very much."

The group then got into another motorcar, which was waiting on the Belgian side. As they headed for Brussels, Pate noted that seven kilometers from the frontier "we saw the charged system of electric wires which surround Belgium and after presenting our passports were allowed to pass through the gate in the wire."

After arriving in Brussels, Pate was given his assignment to be a delegate in Hainaut Province. On Wednesday, July 19, he headed off by himself to the Brussels train station to catch the train to Mons, where he was to meet other CRB delegates before taking up his position in Tournai.

His first official outing as a CRB delegate didn't start off well—he missed his train.

After that rather inauspicious beginning, and finally arriving in Tournai, Pate settled quickly into his new life. Situated 56 miles (90 km) southwest of Brussels and 30 miles (49 km) northwest of Hainaut Province's capital, Mons, Tournai straddled both banks of the Scheldt River. Tournai was one of the most ancient towns in Belgium, and its fortification walls had long before been turned into promenades, while the cathedral, according to a contemporary tour book was "one of the noblest specimens of mediaeval architecture," with four massive towers rising 270 feet above the town. On the river, the tree-lined quays before the war had been bustling with a constant flow of barges, many of which carried coal from the nearby region of Le Borinage. Tournai was home to approximately 37,000 residents, many of whom worked from their homes as weavers of what was known as "Brussels carpets" (the loops of pile are uncut) and embroidery items.

A few miles from the town was Mont Saint-Aubert, with a small restaurant at the top run by Madame Pottiau. The hill was less than five miles from the

Belgian/French border and little more than 20 miles from the western front. Pate wrote that the hilltop "gives wonderful views of all the surrounding country."

Pate took a room in the home of Mr. Castaigne, a 50-year-old attorney and the president of the regional relief committee who had never married and had lived with his mother until she had died a few years before. "A fine character," Pate wrote about Castaigne, "and one of the most interesting men I ever met."

The two men began a daily routine of language lessons—Pate teaching Castaigne English as the other taught the American French. It would not be long before Pate became proficient in the language, due in large part to almost total immersion. He wrote his brother, "Would you actually believe it seems a little strange to be writing in English? Since my arrival in Tournai last week I have only seen two people who could speak English. Have resigned to the situation, however, and am undertaking to do everything—speaking and writing—in French." Pate even had brought from America a French New Testament Bible, which he read every morning before taking a cold shower and starting his workday.

His commute to the office wasn't far—across the street were the Tournai CRB and the CN offices, both housed in a well-furnished Belgian home that was owned by a Belgian officer who was away at the front. Pate's office space, which overlooked the garden, was shared with a Belgian secretary and, in another room, a stenographer. "All correspondence, etc," Pate wrote, "is carried on in French—whence the Belgian secretary. The work of the American delegates consists in a general supervision over milling, shipping, and distribution, and in keeping the Brussels office in touch with the local situation."

Because Hainaut Province was the largest in area and population, it had multiple delegates. When Pate arrived, the chief delegate was Hallam Tuck, who lived in Mons. He supervised the work of John Glenn and Edgar Williams, both of whom also lived in Mons; Charles Carstairs, who lived with his Belgian wife; and Pate and Philip Potter, who both lived in Tournai.

The Tournai District was divided into 83 communes, each of which had its own president and local relief committee. There were also two flour mills, one of which provided flour to nearby northern France and 110 CRB distributing stations. Pate and Potter had to maintain contact with all the groups and facilities by constantly traveling about the district in their motorcars.

While he was one of the youngest CRB delegates, Pate would quickly become known as a diligent worker and an astute observer who could turn good thoughts into action.

41

Brussels

The Paper Skips a Beat but Does Not Fail

By July 1916, the Belgian rumor mill had run through nearly every possible scenario and every possible question regarding *La Libre Belgique* since the German raids of April 13 and the Charleroi mass trial in June. How had the stout-hearted little newspaper survived?

The reality of what had happened to the newspaper was nearly as far fetched as what people imagined.

There was no doubt Grisenbrock and Haelen had done severe damage to *La Libre Belgique* with the massive raids on April 13. They had uncovered the secret press, driven van Doren into hiding, brought down two of the paper's major distribution depots, and caught two major distributors, Father Dubar and Gheude.

For the first few days after the raids, everyone associated with the newspaper who had not been arrested sat back in stunned surprise, waiting for his or her turn to come. But like survivors from a natural disaster, after a few days they began to emerge from the rubble to assess the situation and start the cleanup.

Victor Jourdain, the editorial force behind the publication, had been warned by his son Joseph. Together with his assistant and live-in daughter, Julie, they had secreted away all incriminating materials and then waited for the Germans to show up. They never did. While the Germans did search Joseph Jourdain's house, they had not followed the lead to his father's home, which they had searched a long time before and found nothing. The Germans also failed to make a connection between van Doren and the Jourdains (besides the family relationship), which proved van Doren's earlier decision to stay completely away from Victor Jourdain's home had been a wise one.

Father Paquet—one of the original five members of the inner circle (which included Abbé de Moor, van Doren, and Victor and Julie Jourdain)—had escaped another German raid on the Jesuit residence. He decided to wait at least a few days before going to see how Victor and Julie had fared.

When the reduced inner circle (now composed of Father Paquet, and the three Jourdains—Victor, Julie, and Joseph) did meet again a few days after the raid, they realized that without van Doren they were completely separated from the rest of the organization—most notably the printers and distributors. Father Paquet knew that two editorial contributors and most of his sub-distributor priests were still free, but that was all that he knew.

Father Paquet was one of La Libre Belgique*'s inner circle who had to pick up the pieces after the Germans' huge raid of April 1916, which had driven van Doren into hiding.* (Public domain; *Histoire de* La Libre Belgique *Clandestine,* Pierre Goemaere, Bureaux de *La Libre Belgique,* Bruxelles, 1919.)

The group would basically have to start from scratch again, but this time without the creative, enthusiastic van Doren as the connecting thread between all the pieces.

Editorially, they had plenty of material that was backlogged from previous issues. Victor and Julie would work on developing a new issue. Father Paquet, along with the two editorial contributors he knew and a few trusted priests, would attempt to collect as many threads as possible from van Doren's organization. Joseph would go and see Madame Massardo, who had helped van Doren in the early days by finding a printer and might be helpful again. She and her daughter ran the stationery and newspaper shop in the fashionable arcade, Galerie Saint Hubert, which had been raided before but nothing had ever been found. (The husband, though, had had to escape over the border into Holland.)

When Joseph went to the shop, he was surprised to discover that Lucie Massardo knew of "Mr. Willem" (van Doren's alias). She also knew about the raids and had heard that Mr. Willem had been driven into hiding. Assuring her that he was only an intermediary for the "committee" that led *La Libre Belgique,* Joseph asked if she could find a printer for them. She laughed and told him that she had been so sure Willem was the leader of the newspaper that she had prepared an issue of her own.

She then told Joseph, "My son was to meet the printer this afternoon. If Monsieur will only bring me the copy, it shall go at once. Also, if my children can assist in the distribution . . . we ask nothing better than to do our share."

The Jourdains couldn't believe their luck, which continued in another surprising way.

That same day, only a half an hour after Joseph had delivered the editorial copy for issue number 72 to Madame Massardo, the shopkeeper had another visitor. This one was a short, well-groomed, well-dressed man who looked quickly around the shop and then hesitantly approached her. As the *Underground News* described the scene:

"Madame," he announced abruptly, "the Libre Belgique *has been discovered. At all costs the next issue must be got out." He tapped his breast pocket. "I have the copy. Can you find a printer?"*

Madame Massardo burst out laughing. "And to think I was afraid the Libre *was dead!" she exclaimed, clapping her hands together delightedly.*

"I'm afraid, Madame . . ." interposed [the man] with a puzzled frown.

"Pardon me, Monsieur. It is because you are the second person today who comes with copy for No. 72.

The man who had brought the copy was Gustave Snoeck, the manager of the Crédit Anversois (Antwerp Credit) bank. He ran the underground paper's principal depot for Antwerp. He had been alerted to the April 13 raids by his courier, who had barely escaped when he had tried to collect issue number 71 at a Brussels depot. Snoeck had immediately headed for Brussels and found that all his associates had been arrested. He knew, however, that Madame Massardo dealt in contraband newspapers—maybe she would know how to find a printer for his version of *La Libre Belgique*.

In a few days, Madame Massardo had arranged a meeting between Snoeck and Joseph Jourdain, which led to an immediate reconnection between Brussels and Antwerp and the bringing back of previous editorial contributors to the Jourdain group.

The network was regrowing itself by reconnecting the severed pieces. In doing so, it was confirming earlier printed statements of bravado that had declared the publication was more than just one person or one group of people.

But one more piece had to be added before the organization was fully back in business—a ringleader, or coordinator, who could successfully manage all the pieces.

Albert Le Roux had been a major distributor with a vast network of subdistributors. He and his wife owned a stationery store in Brussels. The April raids had cut him off from any of the other newspaper survivors. After weeks of furtive searching for new connections to the editorial side of the paper, he had found no one, even when the new issues had come out. In desperation, he put out his own issue, number 74, as a way of signaling to Victor Jourdain's group that someone was out there looking for them. Within a few days, Father Paquet was able to find Le Roux and he was brought into the new fold.

Le Roux, who worked under the alias of Mr. Pauwel (Flemish for "peacock"), would play an important role in *La Libre Belgique.* Only a week or so before the June mass trial in Charleroi, the Germans had made another, much smaller set of raids, most notably on Victor and Julie's home/office. The Jourdains had had enough time to hide everything, but a decision was made that Albert Le Roux should take over the editorial side of the paper for a few weeks to let things cool down.

During Le Roux's short time as editor, he came up with an idea that would help to stir the nation. He spent weeks planning the July 21, 1916 issue, which would commemorate Belgium's independence day.

Governor General von Bissing had already issued *affiches* outlawing any celebration of the day in any shape or form. On Wednesday, July 19, he issued a last-minute order that forbade even the use or display of the national colors (black, yellow, and red), with a fine of 20,000 marks and six months in prison for those who did so.

Von Bissing's last order had been issued as Le Roux's issue was being printed. The new editor couldn't be prouder because the issue's front page had a thick border of black, yellow, and red. He had also worked for weeks to coordinate a distribution of the issue to as many parts of Belgium as possible. One history detailed his efforts: "Le Roux had asked all the provincial distributors with whom he was in contact to make special arrangements to collect their bundles and get them away to the provinces the same afternoon. Packed in boxes labelled 'conserves,' a bundle of copies was dispatched by [others] to Liège; Victor Félix, with a forged *Reiseschein* [German travel pass] in his pocket and five hundred copies of the *Libre Belgique* in a suitcase, calmly took the train to Antwerp, and another courier, similarly equipped, set out by train for Namur." Le Roux even had a copy smuggled into each of the German prison camps were Belgians were being kept.

Those distribution feats would have been impressive during peacetime. It was nearly unthinkable that they were feasible during an occupation in which the Germans were specifically hunting for the publication.

Albert Le Roux had no way of knowing that his special edition of *La Libre Belgique* would add a final accent to a special event that was about to take place in Brussels.

Cardinal Mercier Stirs Up Patriotism

On July 21, 1831, Leopold of Saxe-Coburg, a German nobleman, had sworn allegiance to the Belgian constitution and became the new country's first king. This was the official start of the independent nation of Belgium under a constitutional

To many Belgians, Cardinal Désiré Félicien François Joseph Mercier was the moral voice of the country. The cardinal spoke at Brussel's famous Church of St. Gudula in July 1916 and inspired his fellow citizens. (Public domain; *A Journal from Our Legation in Belgium,* Hugh Gibson, Doubleday, Page & Co., 1917.)

monarchy and parliament. Starting in 1890, the date of July 21 had become Belgium's national day and was celebrated with joyous religious, governmental, and social events throughout the country.

Knowing the importance of such a day, the military governor of Brussels, Lieutenant General Hurt, added to von Bissing's proclamations. Hurt issued his own *affiche* that outlawed any "demonstration on the occasion; such as public meetings, processions, speeches, addresses, school treats, the floral decoration of certain statues, beflagging of buildings, public or private, early closing of shops, restaurants, etc." The penalties for participating in such activities included six months in jail and a fine of 20,000 German marks.

On the day before July 21, Hurt once again posted a warning. This one advised that the general public should "have nothing to do with a certain section of irresponsible people who, it was rumored, were endeavoring to influence the population against the observance of the decree and that penalties for infraction of the order would be applied ruthlessly and without mercy."

To back up such threats, the Germans noticeably increased their Brussels street patrols and brought out armored cars to drive up and down major thoroughfares.

The Belgians couldn't resist such a challenge—especially in Brussels. Brand Whitlock described in his journal, "The Belgians have been celebrating [the day] as well as they could, considering the heavy and brutal hand of the occupation that rests upon them. . . . The city wears a holiday air, not gay, of course, but there are many abroad, most of them in Sunday best, and the upper class wearing high hats and the eternal redingote [a woman's long coat with a cutaway or contrasting front]."

With the country's national colors outlawed, somehow word had spread that the color to wear that day was green, so most had little ribbons or spots of green somewhere on their outfits. "Even the dogs," Whitlock wrote, "wore the green ribbon, though they are, as I understand it, wisely international."

Word had also spread that Cardinal Mercier would be giving a public address in Brussels at the famous Church of St. Gudula. Long before the cardinal appeared, the large gothic church was filled to overflowing. Hundreds more stood outside in the square in front of the church, which sat on a hill overlooking the lower town. When the cardinal made his way to the pulpit, the tension and excitement were palpable. His first words were of caution.

"Before beginning I want you to do an act of self-restraint; should any of you feel overcome by strong emotions, kindly refrain from showing it. The hour for expressing adequately the intensity of your feelings has not yet struck."

Mercier than proceeded to give a speech that seemed to test the audience's restraint. Snippets included:

- "Today, the hymn of joy dies on our lips."
- "There is courage in leaping to the attack; there is no less in holding back from it; there is even more virtue at times in suffering than in action."
- "The hour of our deliverance draws near, but has not yet struck. Let us remain patient. Let not our courage falter. Let us leave to divine Providence the care of perfecting our national education."

He subtly addressed the German attempts to divide Flemish and Walloon by saying that Belgians needed to "turn away and continue, without deigning to reply, to remain faithful to the pact of union, friendship."

Looking into the future, the cardinal offered, "When in 1930 we remember the dark years of 1914–1916, they will appear to us brighter, more majestic and . . . will prove the happiest and most fruitful of our national history."

As Mercier concluded his service, the organ struck up the banned national anthem, "La Brabançonne." The crowd listened in restrained silence but were so overwhelmed as the last organ notes died away that they shouted, "Long live Belgium!" "Long live the king!" As the beloved cardinal was escorted away, the chant continued with "Long live the cardinal!" "Long live liberty!"

Adding to the day, Le Roux's special issue of *La Libre Belgique* hit the streets in the late afternoon with its patriotic front cover in full color. Copies were secretly passed from person to person. Others risked jail to paste them on top of the German *affiches* around the city.

Later that night, the cardinal's motorcar was spotted at the gate of a catholic boys school, Saint Louis Institute. A crowd quickly gathered. When Mercier came out and got into his car for the drive back to Malines, the crowd erupted in cheers and chants. A German officer with a detachment of soldiers appeared, and violence broke out, with several civilians injured.

The incident did not go unnoticed by Military Governor Hurt. The next issue of *La Libre Belgique* published Hurt's letter to the *burgomaster* of Brussels, which stated, "When the Cardinal in the evening passed through the city in his motorcar, a demonstration hostile to the German authorities took place of such a nature as to rouse the population to resistance and ill-considered acts. . . . In consequence I have suggested to the Governor General that he should inflict a fine upon the entire population of Brussels. The Governor General has agreed to my proposal and has inflicted a fine of a million marks."

Cardinal Mercier had an exchange of letters with von Bissing, but nothing would sway the governor general from imposing the fine.

Hoover's Quick Stop in Brussels

In late July after the cardinal's speech in St. Gudula, Hoover stopped in Brussels on a trip that would take him to German military headquarters in Charleville and on to Berlin as part of his negotiations with the Germans over who would get what portion of the 1916 harvest within the two areas of the Army Zone (the Operations area and the Etape area, both containing part of northern France and a few small pieces of Belgium).

While in Brussels, Hoover attempted to resolve the Francqui conflict over whose group was in charge in Belgium. He held the important weapon of Lord Percy's July 15, 1916, endorsement letter that he was free to send to the provincial and local committees. But Hoover was reluctant to use it, preferring to first try to reach an amiable agreement with Francqui.

As he explained to Brand Whitlock, he faced one side where the British were upset by news from "Belgian sources" that the CRB efforts were being undermined by Francqui and his associates. Just as important, though, on the other side, "I am certain that at least some of the Belgians have a growing sense that we are becoming a hard taskmaster, and if we can possibly accomplish our responsibilities without giving any appearance of undue interference I want it done." He did acknowledge, however, that if all else failed, the Percy letter could be sent.

Whitlock wrote of the Percy letter in his journal on July 28, which also included an account of the continuing battle between Hoover and Francqui. "Hoover in; a long talk; the old feeling against Francqui, somewhat justified, no doubt, for Francqui has written him a letter asking that the American representation be diminished and that he, Hoover, stay out of Belgium! [Francqui's June memorandum to Hoover.] Hoover had sent this letter to the British Foreign Office, with a warm endorsement, but the Foreign Office refused, and sent a long letter [Percy's July letter to Hoover] recognizing only the Americans. Hoover very big about it, will not even let Francqui know of the letter, so generous is he."

The toll that such continued conflict was taking on Hoover was obvious even to the CRB delegates who rarely saw him. Maurice Pate, the new delegate in Tournai, came to Brussels on Thursday, July 27, 1916, to attend the weekly meeting of delegates. He wrote in his journal that night, "Mr. Hoover, just arrived from London, gave a short talk. He is a man of very few words. Perhaps no man at the present time has more on his mind than Mr. Hoover—and he shows it—giving the impression of one near a breakdown."

When Hoover sat down with Francqui, much of their talk revolved around the Inspection and Control Department and Green's role as CRB representative. Hoover "insisted firmly that [Green] must be allowed to exercise independent control over the activities of the department."

As Hoover left Brussels for a trip to German military headquarters in Charleville and ultimately on to Berlin, he thought Francqui had agreed with him on the independent nature of the Inspection and Control Department.

Brown's Heart in Two Places

By August, Milton Brown had settled into his job as head of the clothing department, which was headquartered in the Brussels CRB main office at 66 Rue des Colonies. He shared an office with William Sperry, who was then head of the CRB's milling department. Brown had been given a Belgian stenographer and clerk to assist him. Even with those two helping, "I find that my work is not lessened any," he wrote to his brother Bruce. "My assistants merely relieve me of certain work in order that I may take up other work which heretofore I have not been able to touch. But there are still the office days that keep me at my desk until 7 p.m. or have me chasing about the city on rush business where minutes count."

Brown's additional work with the Agglomération Bruxelloise had ended in mid-July so he could concentrate solely on clothing. He wrote his father, "In one way I do not like the idea of this [focusing solely on clothing] for I am afraid it will mean getting out of all contact with the great machinery of the feeding of these countries, yet it will give me an opportunity to specialize in the clothing of them—a job which up to the present no other delegate has had. For that reason it will be very interesting: pioneering in a fresh field."

Brown moved forward in his new position to gain all the information from the CN that the CRB needed to ensure the British guarantees were being met. He still faced CN resistance at times, but it was nothing like the spring conflict that Hoover had had to resolve with the CN's clothing director Emmanuel Janssen.

Brown respected and worked well with Madame F. M. Philippson-Wiener, his Belgian counterpart in the CN's clothing department. Together they tried to increase imports of used and new clothing, as well as clothing materials. They also worked to streamline the American end so that any items coming into Belgium would not have to go through a long and involved inventory process. At every Thursday delegate meeting in Brussels, Brown gave a report on his progress and tried to instill in his fellow delegates the same passion he felt for providing clothing that they felt for providing food.

"Each day," Brown wrote to his brother Harry, "the work wraps itself about my heart a little more and I begrudge the hours I have to spend in sleeping when I might be doing something better."

Brown neglected to say that there was one exception to that statement: visits to the Bunges at Chateau Oude Gracht. While his heart was definitely in his work, it was also starting to find a home elsewhere.

On Friday, August 18, he and Fred Eckstein took the 2:00 p.m. tram from Antwerp and arrived at Chateau Oude Gracht at 3:15 p.m. for a weekend of relaxation. Brown was looking forward to spending more time with Erica, while Eckstein was interested in seeing Eva.

"As for the [Bunge] girls," Brown wrote his brother, "there is a trio which would stand up against a world of girls; their father a Belgian Carnegie, they lead the life of simple, earnest, big hearted women, though they are all three younger than I. . . . One runs the house [Eva]; another the farm [Erica]; and another something else [Hilda]."

The weekend went quickly. Saturday was tennis and walking in the woods, then the traditional billiards game to end the evening; Sunday was more tennis and a swim in the lake, another walk, and billiards after dinner. The three Bunge sisters had, Brown wrote, "an unlimited amount of energy and are always doing something, tiring out the poor American delegate before they get fairly started."

The Bunge sisters' energy did not stop with a leisurely weekend. Brown told his brother, "All three have their duties in [Antwerp]: this [Monday] morning, after that strenuous week-end two of them [Erica and Hilda] were up at six-thirty and off to town at eight to serve at one of the 'soups' or to weigh babies at the baby-cantine."

In the same letter to his brother, Brown also brought up a troubling situation—to him at least. Joe Green, the old friend from Cincinnati who had helped him join the CRB and lived with him in a townhouse in Brussels, had written to Brown's parents. "Green, my present 'wife,'" Milton wrote his brother, "tells me that he wrote home to the folks asking how they would like a continental marriage for their son." Green had not mentioned names.

Brown was quick to deny. "I don't know how much else he said but whatever he said is a ---- lie! Tell the little Mother not to worry, and that when I come home I shall come alone. Remember Joe's propensity for exaggeration and believe me."

His repudiation of any romance would be repeated in other letters to his family. No matter how strident the denials, however, they all sounded a bit hollow, especially when many were immediately followed by enthusiastic descriptions of weekends spent with the Bunges.

42

Berlin

In the month of August, Berlin saw a somewhat strange coincidence. Both Governor General von Bissing and Herbert Hoover visited the city. They each came for different reasons but faced consequences from the same thing—a shift in power within the German government.

Since the start of the war, the Berlin civilian government, led by Chancellor Theobald von Bethmann-Hollweg, had been able to rein in the more aggressive German militarists in many policies and strategies. But in August 1916, as the war dragged on much longer than expected, Field Marshal Paul von Hindenburg became chief of the General Staff. A successful commander who wanted to end the war decisively by using more aggressive strategies, von Hindenburg was very popular with the German public. The Kaiser, no doubt feeling as if von Hindenburg could succeed, relinquished more of his wartime powers to von Hindenburg. Von Hindenburg, along with his deputy, Erich Ludendorff, ended up leading a de facto military dictatorship. Over time, Bethmann-Hollweg and his moderate policies would be pushed aside by the aggressive military leadership.

Within a short period of time, the CRB and the Belgians would feel the direct impact of the new military regime and its major decisions.

The civilian-to-military power shift was why von Bissing had been called to Berlin. He came for an important meeting about all the occupied territories, but in a move that would have surprised most Belgians and CRB delegates, the governor general was reprimanded by von Hindenburg as having been too easy on the Belgians.

The Northern France Harvest Leads to Crisis

The path that brought Hoover to Berlin in August had been a long and difficult one that revolved around northern France and who would get what percentage of the 1916 harvest. In many ways the northern France harvest was more important than the Belgian harvest because the civilians of northern France were in the

Operations and Etape areas of the Army Zone, where life was much more controlled and harsh than in Belgium.

Hoover had seen firsthand how difficult life was when he had had a whirlwind tour of northern France at the end of March. Accompanied by several German officers and some of the delegates, he found communities where meat and potatoes had all but disappeared, grocery stores where shelves were bare or stocked with empty boxes and tins, and restaurants where only bread and coffee were offered. Inevitably, the group found that any food that was available was from CRB imports, and Hoover knew that the current amount of imports was woefully inadequate to meet the needs of the millions of northern French trapped inside the German Army Zone.

In Lille, Hoover learned from local community leaders that general mortality had increased by 30 percent over the year before, births in 1915 were only 40 percent of what they had been in 1914, and elderly mortality had increased by 30 percent. The Lille committee's general secretary had written a plea for help that stated, "Salvation can only come to us through the Commission for Relief in Belgium."

Hoover returned to London with the renewed desire to get more for the northern French. In relatively rapid succession, events took place that at first improved the situation but then threatened it:

- April 1, Hoover wrote German Major von Kessler explaining the conditions in northern France and stating that without German guarantees to not requisition native food, the Allies might decide the CRB was "degenerating into a replacement by importation" operation and would end the relief.
- April 5, Hoover wrote the British outlining the situation in northern France and asked for an increase in imports.
- During April, the Germans agreed to provide the northern French with a ration of potatoes.
- April 11, the British agreed to increase northern France imports from 29,700 tons a month to 36,800 tons a month.
- May 10, the Germans agreed to allow dairy cows into northern France to provide milk for children.
- June 13, the French insisted that the Germans turn over to civilians the entire 1916 harvest in northern France.
- July 7, the British backed up the French and insisted the whole harvest must go to the people, or imports would not be allowed.
- In July, the Germans refused to commit to giving all of the 1916 harvest to the northern French.

In an effort to resolve the issue, Hoover wrote to the CRB's director in Paris, Louis Chevrillon, and visited the city to try and convince the French government that its demand regarding the 1916 harvest was unrealistic. He explained that the harvest in northern France was completely different than the harvest in Belgium. In northern France there was no civilian government to make or enforce any guarantees. And while the entire two subzones of the Army Zone (Operations and Etape) were run by the military, any German headquarters recommendations were interpreted by each of the different army groups that commanded the various sections within the two subzones—creating a variety of policies and regulations.

Hoover also pointed out there was the issue of wheat and who cultivated it. He identified four separate "classes" that showed the complexity of the situation:

1. Land planted by, and harvested by, the Germans.
2. Abandoned land that the Germans hired French laborers to cultivate.
3. Land the Germans ploughed and seeded but the French either helped work or owned.
4. Land exclusively cultivated by the French.

Much of the farming area, Hoover pointed out, was so close to the front that it was impractical and unrealistic to expect civilians to put themselves in harm's way to harvest the crops. It would be more practical to have the Germans collect the entire crop and then get them to remit a percentage to the CRB for distribution.

By early August, with no resolution in sight, Hoover headed to German military headquarters in Charleville, France, to take up the issue in person. He joined Vernon Kellogg who was already there in negotiations as the CRB's Brussels director. They had multiple conferences with both the German liaison officers to the CRB, Major von Kessler and Count Wengersky, and with German Quartermaster General Traugott von Sauberzweig. According to Kellogg, the quartermaster general was second only in the military hierarchy to the chief of staff of the armies. Von Sauberzweig had another distinction as well—he had been the military governor of Brussels who many considered responsible for the 1915 execution of British nurse Edith Cavell.

According to Hoover, in the meetings "the Germans insisted that the only practical base of organizing the matter was for them to requisition all the crops produced by the peasants themselves and to add to this quantity the amounts to which the peasants were entitled from working their partnership farms with the Germans and then give a per diem ration to the civilian population."

To prove the impracticality of any other way, the Germans offered to take Hoover and Kellogg on a tour of the land in question. As they motored about not far behind the trenches, the Germans asked if the Americans wanted to see the Battle of Somme (a British- and French-initiated battle from July 1 to November 18 that was one of the bloodiest of the war, with 1 million men wounded or killed for no discernible advantage won by either side). Hoover recorded his immediate impressions as the group stood on a hillside observation post not far from the battlefield:

"At the post the constant rumble of artillery seemed to pulverize the air. Seen through powerful glasses, in the distant view lay the unending blur of trenches, of volcanic explosions of dust which filled the air where over a length of sixty miles a million and a half men were fighting and dying. Once in awhile, like ants, the lines of men seemed to show through the clouds of dust. Here under the thunder and belching volcanoes of 10,000 guns . . . the lives of Germans and Englishmen were thrown away. On the nearby road unending lines of Germans plodded along the right side to the front, not with drums and bands, but in the silence of sodden resignation. Down the left side came the unending lines of wounded men, the 'walking classes,' staggering among cavalcades of ambulances. . . . The horror of it all did not in the least affect the German officers in the post. To them it was pure mechanics. The battle had already been raging for days. Not one of the Germans showed the slightest anxiety. They said that the British were losing two to one—butting their heads against a stone wall. And that was true. It was all a horrible, devastating reality, no romance, no glory."

In typical Hoover understatement, he wrote, "It was obvious that in the midst of such operations it was only the Germans who could collect the crops."

The question remained, however, what percentage of the crop would be given to the northern French and Belgians within the Army Zone?

Hoover had already collected an estimate of what the French felt was fair, what the Americans thought was needed, and what the Germans were prepared to give.

"They differed widely," Hoover commented drily.

The French estimate was basically what normal production would have been, which was totally unrealistic. The CRB estimate was for an increase of critical bread grains over the year before, but it "exceeded the German estimate by more than a thirty-million-dollar value based on import costs."

In the Charleville conferences, one major sticking point had been a rival relief effort into northern France. Against the objections of the CRB, the French government had approved a French company to import a small amount of food through Switzerland into northern France and sell it, according to Hoover, "at high prices to individuals and communes." The Germans had not objected. While the amounts totaled less than 2 percent of the need, it "disturbed our whole rationing system," Hoover said.

While Major von Kessler was "inclined to settle on our estimate," according to Hoover, Quartermaster General von Sauberzweig had different ideas. He liked the concept of the French company and its imports coming through Switzerland. He seized on the idea and felt that such a commercial effort could be increased to the point where the CRB would no longer be needed. No doubt in his mind it was the perfect way to get rid of the pesky CRB delegates and all their inspections, complaints, reports, and demands.

Von Sauberzweig, Hoover stated, "was obstinate, arrogant, and generally overbearing." The group had come to an impasse, and no amount of talking or haggling seemed ready to break it. Hoover then suggested a course of action that he probably hoped would take the quartermaster general out of the discussions. He suggested that because Ambassador Gerard had "initiated the matter with high authorities in Berlin, von Kessler, representing the German General Staff, should accompany Dr. Kellogg and myself and discuss the problem in Berlin."

Unfortunately, von Sauberzweig, who was no friend to the CRB, was already going to Berlin to attend an important meeting.

Hoover Fights for the Life of the CRB

When the group arrived in Berlin, events happened differently than Hoover and Kellogg had hoped. In the morning, Major von Kessler and von Sauberzweig met the two Americans at their hotel and told them they would not be allowed to attend a high-level conference that had been previously arranged. Kellogg explained, "The conference was one of important representatives of the General Staff, the General Government of Belgium, the Foreign Office, the Department of Interior, and of all other departments immediately interested in the handling of the civil populations in all occupied territories."

Von Sauberzweig would be the highest-ranking military man at the conference, and because the military was in the process of usurping the civilian government's power, that meant those in attendance would look to the quartermaster general for what would be done.

Hoover was not happy about being excluded. "We were disappointed not to be allowed to present our cases ourselves."

At 4:00 p.m., during a break in the meeting, Major von Kessler and the quartermaster general returned to the hotel lobby to meet Hoover and Kellogg. Both Germans were upset. Von Sauberzweig immediately ordered a whisky and soda and downed it while Major von Kessler related in English what had happened during that day's meeting before the break (later recorded by Kellogg). As a supporter of the CRB, von Kessler was upset because the meeting had not gone well. He said it looked bad for the future of the CRB, especially in light of a British Foreign Office dispatch that had been recently published in all the German newspapers. The British government had demanded that the Germans turn over to civilians not only the entire 1916 northern France harvest but also all the harvests in other occupied territories as well, just as it had agreed to do with the Belgian harvest.

"Extremely violent speeches" about the CRB's relief work had been made by numerous people, most notably the military men, von Kessler said. There were demands that the entire humanitarian aid be stopped completely and alerts be sent to the worldwide press laying the blame for the cessation on the English blockade. The speakers reportedly stated it was "no worse for Belgians and French to starve than for Germans to starve."

Kellogg elaborated that the "bellicose speakers . . . declared that Germany could not for one moment dictate its attitude and action toward the occupied territories, and that the only position Germany could take henceforth was to throw the population on the shoulders of England, which could open its blockade or let the Belgians and French starve, just as it was trying to let the Germans starve.

"The feeling all over Germany was high," Kellogg continued, "and the conference seemed likely to end the commission's work then and there."

Hoover probably couldn't help but think about his pivotal January 1915 meeting with Lloyd George when he had walked in thinking the discussion would be only about a financial aspect of relief and had found himself facing the possible end of relief. Here in Berlin, he and Kellogg had felt any discussions would merely determine the percentage of 1916 northern French crops the locals would receive, but suddenly they were facing the possible demise of the entire CRB operation.

At this point, with such bad news hanging in the air, Hoover's and Kellogg's retellings of the event diverge, but ultimately they reached the same conclusion.

Kellogg's account, which included Count Wengersky in the hotel meeting, stated that "just one ray of light came to us in this dark hour." That opening was that one of the Germans (probably von Kessler) made the remark that "if the request for a larger allocation of the native products to the civilian population had come simply from the Commission, something might have been done, but with England demanding it—'No, a thousand times No.'"

Kellogg stated, "This was our cue. We repudiated England! What England demanded was its affair. Let the Germans fight it out with England. What the Commission pleaded for was its own affair—the affair of saving the lives of human beings; of keeping body and soul together for ten million people, known to the world as Belgians and French, but known to the Commission as human beings, men, women, and children, especially children, crying for help!"

Hoover's account is even more dramatic. He stated that at the worst moment, "there came one of those unforgettable episodes" that would change the course of millions of lives.

According to Hoover, during von Kessler's retelling of what had happened in the meeting earlier that day, the quartermaster general had been conspicuously quiet, downing multiple whisky and sodas. Hoover knew that the German was opposed to the CRB, so why was he upset?

It was then that von Kessler explained. He "apologetically mentioned that the General was greatly broken up by the news he had just received that his son had been permanently blinded in a gas attack on the Western Front."

Hoover and Kellogg expressed their sympathy.

Taking another drink, von Sauberzweig then began a discourse on the war, as Kellogg and von Kessler translated for Hoover. "He said that civilians were messing into it too much and that it was no longer a soldier's war with manly weapons. Civilians had made these poison gases. They were engaged in many activities which they should keep out of."

At a critical moment, when Hoover needed someone to translate his exact words into German, Major von Kessler agreed to do so. (Public domain; Herbert Hoover Presidential Library Archives, West Branch, Iowa.)

The general veered off to angrily describe how women and children in Germany were starving because of the British blockade. At one point, he made what seemed an offhanded remark, "and then, there was the case of that Cavell woman."

Reference to such a highly charged topic was a surprise. Hoover felt the German wanted to talk about the execution of the British nurse, so he and Kellogg subtly urged him on by expressing interest in hearing what he had meant by his remark.

"He said," Hoover wrote, "she had organized an espionage group of a thousand Belgian women. He said he had warned them. He had punished some of them mildly. They would not stop. He was compelled as a soldier to make an example and stop it. He had her tried, she confessed, and as a soldier he was compelled to execute her to protect the German army."

In fulfilling his duty by signing her execution orders, though, "he had been 'painted as a monster all over the world.' He said he was 'called a murderer; a second Duke of Alva.' The neutral peoples think 'I am the most infamous of men.' "

Hoover saw an opening. He recognized someone who "obviously did not like the kind of publicity he had received in the neutral world."

This was a problem that matched Hoover's strength and knowledge—public opinion. He was a master of realizing how important PR was to any endeavor, whether it be relief or redemption.

Feeling as if there was little left to lose, Hoover turned to Kellogg and told him to translate exactly what he was about to say. Kellogg agreed.

"I said that the conclusion of the Germans authorities [to get rid of the CRB] would mean death for millions of people, mostly children; that as he was the responsible officer he would be portrayed to the world as a monster infinitely bigger and blacker than the picture they drew of him after the Cavell incident."

Hoover started to pick up steam, probably sensing he was on the right track with this troubled man. He pushed the point so strongly that Kellogg stopped translating and said it was too much.

Von Kessler jumped in, saying he would translate. "He did so with no reservations." Hoover continued to pound the point home, that to kill the CRB would be far worse in the eyes of the world than executing Cavell. Would von Sauberzweig want that on his conscience?

The general, who had been silent, but listening, suddenly remarked that Hoover might be on to something.

Both stories could have been, and probably were, true. Kellogg, with his sense of propriety, could have chosen to refrain from telling the von Sauberzweig story because it was too personal; Hoover, with his strong feelings toward the British, might have decided to not relate how the CRB publicly rejected the British to the Germans.

The end of Hoover's von Sauberzweig story stated, "Whether it was the threat, the whisky, or his grief, or the human appeal that had moved him, I do not know. He directed von Kessler to inform Minister Lewald [the interior minister] that he thought the negotiation ought to continue. He would be obliged if the Minister would take the matter in hand and settle it."

According to Hoover, the hotel meeting then broke up and Hoover, Kellogg, and von Kessler went directly to Lewald's office, where they quickly established a statement of agreement and wrote it up. "The draft was everything I could have wished," Hoover reported, "except that one-third of the text was devoted to the inhuman effect of the blockade on German women and children and was obviously intended for publication. I requested him to change a line which implied the Commission's commendation of his views—as it would make my job more difficult with the British. He returned in a few moments and said approximately, 'Let us cut out that whole part anyway—we will answer the British with bullets.'"

Hoover and Kellogg took the letter to Ambassador Gerard, who told them they should take the document and get out of Berlin immediately, "within the hour, lest the generals reverse the civilians again."

Kellogg's account explains that because the Americans were not allowed in the conference, they worked before resumption of the meeting on individuals representing the Foreign Office, Department of the Interior, and von Bissing's Belgian government. Kellogg described, "We argued here and pleaded there. And it all had to be done before that fateful conference of the day's length should dissolve.

"The long story must be cut short," Kellogg concluded. "We succeeded! The Commission was allowed to continue its work."

No matter the tale told, the end result was the same—a statement of agreement was reached, and Hoover went back to London to sell it to the British (they accepted it), while Kellogg went back to Charleville to "hasten the formulation and the agreements."

As Kellogg stated simply, "The crisis was past."

By the end of August, the Germans had agreed to provide twice the proportion of the harvest as had been provided in 1915. Kittredge explained, von Kessler estimated that it would amount to four-fifths of the 1916 harvest "as the year was a bad one and the harvest had been poor." Kellogg would estimate the same amount to be only approximately one-half—rather than four-fifths—of the French crop in northern France.

Either way, the northern French and the Belgian civilians living in the Army Zone were going to get something.

By September the agreements had been formalized, and the Germans, British, and French had put their stamp of approval on them. The French had also agreed to shut down the commercial importation of food through Switzerland.

One critical behind-the-scenes condition had been added to help the Germans save face from the earlier British demands about the harvest in the worldwide press. Hoover referred to it in a letter to his CRB director in Paris, Chevrillon. "One important condition of this arrangement is . . . that there shall be no attempt to put it over the Germans by the Allied Governments in this matter. The British Government is willing enough to suppress any exultation. . . . It is certain enough that the agreement is the result of pressure and it is undesirable at this stage to rub it in."

A sad footnote to the event, and to the history of the CRB, was what happened to Major von Kessler. He had been a strong supporter of the CRB, a major broker in the deal, and the official German signer of the 1916 harvest agreement. In September, he was suddenly transferred (another name for demoted) from his liaison position in Charleville to Romania, and, as Kittredge stated, "consequently the Commission lost his powerful and intelligent support."

With von Hindenburg and Ludendorff settling into their increasing military power position in government, von Kessler's transfer was probably retribution for what the generals perceived to be a bad deal for Germany.

Ultimately, the Germans never did live up fully to the agreement, citing the bad harvest and destruction of crops from the Battle of the Somme as reasons for providing only a portion of food they had promised. Kittredge concluded, "The Commission made repeated efforts to induce the Germans to live up to their promises, but those efforts were more or less resultless."

The northern French and Belgians in the Army Zone would have to make do with what little they received from the Germans and the steady contributions from the CRB. The CRB did its best to increase imports to account for lack of German food delivered from the harvest.

43

Brussels

When Hoover returned to Brussels from Berlin on Sunday, August 6, he had to have felt good about saving the CRB and getting a tentative agreement with the Germans for the 1916 northern France harvest.

The good feelings didn't last too long. He found that in only a week away from Brussels a disagreeable Francqui had once again replaced the seemingly agreeable Francqui he had seen before leaving for Charleville and Berlin. The Belgian still wanted the CRB out and the CN to control all relief operations. Whitlock recorded in his journal that night, "Hoover very bitter, as always, against Francqui, and the Comité National generally, and with much reason. There is without a doubt a constant effort on Francqui's part to depreciate the work of the Americans. It is of course very disturbing."

It had taken Hoover a week to find out Francqui's true feelings about the current negotiations; it would take Green even less time to do so.

Green Feels the Heavy Hand of Francqui

Only a day after Hoover's July departure for Charleville and Berlin—and through August and into fall—Green was continually confronted by Francqui on multiple fronts:

- Green was told no letters from him or his staff could be sent out without being first countersigned by Francqui. Later, he was notified that a stamp would be placed on his outgoing mail that instructed all replies should be sent to the Comité National—cutting him out of the communications loop.
- Francqui actually tore up one Green letter that requested an investigation by the Greater Brussels inspection service about a German violation of the relief agreements. Francqui told Green's CN counterpart, Van Gend, to inform Green that no such letters should be written in the future.

- The normal flow of reports to Green's department regarding all food regulation violations brought before the Belgian courts was suddenly funneled through Francqui's office, which suppressed some reports and altered others to remove certain facts Francqui did not want Green to see.
- Other official agencies in Belgium were instructed to reduce, if not completely cut off, information to Green.
- The professional investigators utilized by Green were told that all reports normally sent to Green and his department were to be sent only to the Comité National.

Green argued every point and fought every battle he felt he should. But there was no letup. Francqui and his associates kept trying to cut him out of the entire inspection and control operations. Hoover, having returned to London in August, kept up with all that was going on with Francqui and the Inspection and Control Department. As he heard more and more, he was, Kittredge stated with uncharacteristically restraint, "naturally very indignant." Still, Hoover wanted to try and work things out with Francqui before involving the British.

In mid-September, the Chief was back in Brussels to try and work things out with Francqui. Charlotte Kellogg had come with Hoover to join her husband, Vernon Kellogg, who had just returned to once again become CRB Brussels director. The Kelloggs decided to host a luncheon for Hoover, Francqui, Whitlock, several other delegates, and Prentiss Gray, the new CRB Brussels assistant director. The Kelloggs were aware of the personal animosity between Hoover and Francqui and the current policy disagreement between them, but hoped a relaxing social lunch might be helpful to negotiations.

Unfortunately the reverse was true. "The meal nearly broke up in a fight," Gray reported, "because Hoover and Francqui had a discussion over certain policies of the Commission for Relief in Belgium." Neither man was going to back down. "It was a tense moment," Gray noted, "but it passed over when Mr. Hoover firmly nailed down his ultimatum and walked quietly away."

Little was accomplished and Hoover returned to London once again frustrated.

In the first week of October, Hoover returned to Brussels and had numerous meetings with Francqui and others, to no avail. Kittredge termed them "rather inconclusive meetings" and summed up the situation: "The difficulties with the Comité National became more and more irritating. They reached their climax, perhaps, when by the order of M. Francqui the Commission's representative for the Department of Inspection and Control [Green] was practically ejected from the office of that department and informed that he was no longer to have any direct participation in its administration."

Leaving Brussels once again frustrated, Hoover decided it was finally time to bring in the British.

44

London

The British Get Involved in the CRB/CN Conflicts

Upon returning from Brussels in early October, Hoover realized there was no convincing Francqui that the CRB needed to be an independent entity inside Belgium to fulfill the agreements made with the Allied governments.

Whitlock had given Hoover an idea when he had suggested during the last visit to Brussels that if worse came to worse, Whitlock could ask the British government to define the responsibilities of both the CRB and CN. The impatient Hoover knew that asking Whitlock to do that would have added days or weeks to the process, so he simply took the idea and wrote a letter to Ambassador Walter Page on October 16, 1916, outlining the situation, referencing Whitlock's idea, and asking that the Allied governments define exactly the functions of the CRB and CN. Hoover had had it with Francqui and wanted a detailed document that would reiterate as clearly as possible all the previous documents—that the CRB was the sole neutral entity responsible for the supervision of the humanitarian program, in and out of Belgium.

Only two days later, on Wednesday, October 18, the situation took a dramatic turn and multiple actions were taken.

It all began when Hoover received new information from Brussels that infuriated him. He sat down and wrote another letter, this one to Lord Eustace Percy. He began by stating that he felt compelled to tell all only because the British had requested earlier that he report any problems the CRB encountered in executing its duties.

Hoover then went straight to the point. "I am this morning informed from Brussels that the head Bureau [of Inspection and Control] in Brussels has ceased operations, in consequence of the removal of the files and documents from the C.R.B. office and instructions given to the Belgian Staff to no longer report to the American Representative in joint charge of the Bureau [Joe Green]. I am also informed that in the Agglomeration of Brussels instructions have been given likewise that Belgian Officials of the Bureau shall no longer report to the

American representative in that province. Furthermore, I am informed that instructions [from the CN] have been given to the Procureur General . . . to no longer co-operate with the American representatives in the prosecution of [relief] irregularities throughout the country."

This was no passive resistance from the CN—which had been going on since the beginning of relief. This was an outright coup in which Joe Green had had all his department files removed and his Belgian staff told not to listen to him.

Only Francqui could have issued such orders, although Hoover did not name any instigators.

Hoover knew Francqui's action was potential dynamite, especially because at the moment he was facing a bigger problem than Francqui. He was in negotiations with the British government to increase imports and subsidies for the relief. Without those, people would starve. Would his letter to Percy bring about a disastrous negative decision about imports and subsidies?

Hoover decided to consult with Page before sending the letter. On the same day he wrote the Percy letter, he sent a copy to the ambassador. In his cover letter he was blunt: "During the whole of the last nine months, there has been a systematic attempt on the part of a small group of Belgians to relegate the American participation in relief work in Belgium to a purely ornamental position, and this [recent action] represents the final act of such a systematic campaign."

In all probability Hoover's correspondence with Page was sent after either a phone call or personal meeting with Page or Gibson (although none was recorded). The men were in the same city, they had become respected friends, and such dramatic action from Francqui would not have been left to a letter (which shows an embassy stamp as being received the next day, October 19).

Further proof that they talked is evidenced by what Page did on that day of October 18. A day before he officially received Hoover's letter, Page and the other relief patron, the Spanish Minister Merry del Val, met with Lord Grey. "Without going too much into detail and without reference to the incidents in Mr. Hoover's letter, we asked Lord Grey to outline to us in precise terms what [the CRB and CN] responsibilities and relations are."

The ambassador also told Hoover what he probably already knew—the mood of the British government was such that his Percy letter might either hurt the imports/subsidies negotiations or get the British to demand Francqui's removal, a move Hoover did not want.

Hoover knew that even though Francqui was difficult to deal with, he was the only Belgian who had the strength of character to keep all of Belgium's religious and political factions working together on distribution. Just like many thought that without Hoover the relief would collapse, Hoover felt that without Francqui the Belgian side of relief would collapse. Despite their immense dislike of each other, Hoover and Francqui knew deep down that they actually needed each other. Even

Francqui's current maneuvering was *not* to remove the CRB completely from relief; it was merely to make it a non-decision-making assistant to Francqui and the CN.

Still, on October 18, Page wrote a long letter to Whitlock. He sent a copy of Hoover's letter, told of his meeting with Lord Grey, and that he had advised Hoover not to send the letter. Regarding Francqui's recent actions, he wrote, "It seems to me that as a matter of the dignity of our people, the time has now arrived when you and I must take such a stand with the Belgian Committees as will protect us and the Americans engaged in this work from such incidents as these in the future." Francqui, Page explained, did not have high standing with the British government and "while I sympathise with Mr. Hoover's earnest representations that he is an invaluable man in the position which he occupies and that every support must be given him, that support will be withdrawn by myself if we are to meet with any more such incidents as these."

Page concluded with a strong call for Whitlock to act. "I am trusting to the measures which you will adopt during Mr. Hoover's forthcoming visit, to settle these relations once and for all. I do feel that he deserves our personal shelter and that we should not expect him to take personally on his back the entire brunt of these matters."

Hoover did decide to postpone sending his letter to Lord Percy. He hoped behind-the-scenes efforts such as Page's could resolve the issue without airing such dirty laundry to the British. Leaks, however, were everywhere, and the stories of Francqui's actions were circulating throughout certain London circles.

On October 20, 1916, Lord Edward Grey (previously Sir Edward Grey), the foreign secretary, replied to Page's and Hoover's requests for exact definitions of the CRB and the CN functions and their relation to the relief work. Addressed to Page, the long, detailed letter was everything Hoover could have asked for. A few short quotes illustrate how strongly the British government felt that the CRB must be the sole entity responsible for relief in and out of Belgium:

- "His Majesty's Government cannot therefore accept any substitution of the Comité National for the Commission for Relief in Belgium in such agreements."
- The CN and its committees "must act as the agent of and on behalf of the Commission."
- "The bureau of inspection and control should independently satisfy itself that the whole relief organisation was functioning properly and that this bureau should be maintained, either solely under the control of the Commission for Relief in Belgium or, preferably, in co-operation with the Comité National."
- "I must again repeat that on no other conditions than those laid down above can His Majesty's Government permit food importations into Belgium."

That letter was followed on the same day by a powerful note to Page from Lord Robert Cecil, writing for Lord Grey. He never mentioned what had happened to Green in Brussels, but he implied such knowledge when he wrote, "I must explain confidentially to you, the vital importance attached by us to the Bureau of Inspection and Control in Belgium. It is not too much to say that it is on our knowledge of the detailed working of this Bureau that our whole confidence in the efficiency of the organisation in Belgium is based.

"Without this knowledge I should feel wholly unable to recommend to His Majesty's Government any increase in the importations of the Commission or in the subsidies granted to it by the Allied Governments, and any doubt as to its smooth working places me in the gravest position at this moment when increased funds and increased importations are being asked for. I could not in these circumstances even guarantee the continuance of present importations, since my confidence in the absence of leakages of foodstuffs to the Germans would be wholly destroyed."

The message was clear: Without a properly functioning, independent Inspection and Control Department, there would be no relief.

Three days later—and no doubt after numerous discussions with Hoover, Gibson, and others—Page wrote another strongly worded letter to Whitlock. Page was not officially Whitlock's boss, but he was an ambassador of a prestigious U.S. Embassy while Whitlock was a step down as minister of a legation, so in the State Department hierarchy, Page's words took on great import.

The ambassador gave his opinions about the CRB and the CN, and he protested the CN challenges to the CRB's authority. It also appeared to be a call to both stiffen Whitlock's spine and ask for his help to diplomatically resolve the issue with Francqui. The general feeling about Whitlock in London—bolstered continually by Gibson, Hoover, and others—was that he disliked conflict and confrontation, lacked the strength of character to stand up to Francqui and the Germans, and was sometimes more on the side of the Belgians than the Americans.

Page wrote that the harsh German rule over the Belgians made it necessary for the neutral CRB to be in control of relief or "the whole thing would break down." He added that the CRB was functioning in compliance with the initial agreements made with the British government, and "any action taken by the Belgians which tends to controvert this will, if it ever gets known, would be the death knell of the entire relief."

Recently, Page continued, "reports coming out of Belgium through various channels have disclosed to the British Government an attitude of determined independence and assumption of domination by the Belgian committees and the subjection of the Americans." Page maintained it was Hoover who had kept the situation from turning into a crisis a long time ago by minimizing the conflicts between the CRB and the CN so as not to alarm the Allies.

But the situation had now changed. Page showed his deep knowledge of what was going on (probably provided by Gibson and Hoover) when he wrote, "The action of the Belgian committees in replacing the name of the Commission for Relief in Belgium by that of the Comité National on distributing stations in Belgium, and the tendency of the Comité National to set itself up in agreements with the German authorities as the responsible agency of the work with occasional references to the C.R.B. as an importing body, and its reports which scarcely acknowledge the existence of the C.R.B. or give it studied omission, are all indicative of a set policy."

This was totally unacceptable in Page's mind. Coming strongly to the point midway through the letter, he declared to Whitlock, "The Comité National is not the pivot on which the relief revolves in Belgium."

Page then professed his confusion over the Belgians' feelings in the matter. "I do not see why the co-operation and participation of the American gentlemen in the work should be offensive to the *amour propre* [self-esteem] of the Belgians, or why they should hesitate to fully and loyally recognize and welcome such participation."

Acknowledging Whitlock's role and personal sacrifices he had made in the relief effort, Page went on to state, "It seems unfair that you should be called upon to straighten out such a situation as this; and especially that, when all is said and done, this American effort should be represented as a minor contribution."

Hoover, no doubt, had a role in Page's letter, although he would probably have been the first to say he thought Whitlock had no chance of getting Francqui to change his attitude to the Commission.

As if this wasn't enough, by early November Belgian officials in London had become aware of the growing conflict in Belgium, how strongly the British felt about the CRB's position in Belgium, and how firmly the U.S. ambassador stood by the CRB. Ambassador Page surely played a major role in making them aware of what was going on. According to Kittredge, because of all this information, Belgian officials sent confidential messages to a select group of provincial committee leaders, telling them that the relief work "would be impossible without friendly co-operation between the Commission and the Comité National and without the Commission enjoying independent control over all operations of food distribution."

After marshalling such forces, Hoover felt it was time to once again face Francqui. He headed to Brussels.

Francqui waited in Brussels holding his trump card.

Hoover Again Requests an Increase in Imports

At times it seemed as if Belgium relief took a backseat to the infighting taking place between Hoover and Francqui. But as the two men waged their personal battles, they always were able to continue their more important duties and tasks regarding relief.

In the midst of his current troubles with Francqui, Hoover had decided in September to once again ask for increased imports. He had received reports from the CRB delegates that showed native food was less than the year before and that the current 75,500 tons of food per month to Belgium "remained heartbreakingly below the need."

Another report he received was from Dr. William Palmer Lucas, a professor of pediatrics, a child specialist and head of the department of children's diseases in the medical college of the University of California. Earlier in the year, Hoover had asked the doctor to come to Belgium as a delegate to study how nearly two years of rationing had impacted Belgians, most notably the more than 2.5 million children. The doctor was in Belgium from May to August 1916. He consulted with Belgian physicians; visited hospitals, clinics, and schools; and observed the operations of the soup kitchens. From all that, he wrote an extensive report that Hoover called "impressive."

As covered by a publication in Britain titled *Field,* Dr. Lucas began his report with a quick overview. Thirty-five percent of the overall population was made up of the "well-to-do" classes and agricultural classes, both of which had not suffered too much due to lack of food. As the publication noted, however, "when one turns to the remaining 65 per cent, the effects of two years' captivity on short rations become apparent. Dr. Lucas is convinced that the vitality and resistance to disease of the majority have been lowered and that this is mainly due to 'underfeeding.' " One large Antwerp dispensary showed Dr. Lucas figures that indicated the weight of adults had dropped on average 10 to 12 pounds since the occupation began.

"The adolescent children," Dr. Lucas wrote, "are probably suffering more than any group. . . . Many cases of tuberculosis that were supposed to be cured are reappearing." He went on to quantify the situation. "The increase in attendance at tuberculosis clinics was in some cases over 100 per cent more than it was before the war. Every tuberculosis sanatorium in Belgium is crowded, the waiting lists of all the sanatoria have increased, and the waiting cases are more acute than formerly."

By extension, those who could not get into a sanatorium remained out in public, where they might likely spread the deadly disease, contributing to a spiraling effect of a greater and greater number of cases.

As for nutrition, Dr. Lucas pointed to the milk supply, which he termed "insufficient for the needs of the children and the sick, and this is especially true of the larger cities. Milk, as at present sold, is not only very expensive, but it is also of very poor quality, being diluted or skimmed."

Hoover wrote about Dr. Lucas, "With the aid of the Belgian physicians, he quickly found that there was a growing spread of rickets, certain glandular diseases, and tuberculosis, all of which originated or were stimulated by insufficient special fats, protein, and certain salts. In practical terms, the children needed more meat, condensed milk, sugar, and certain salts. He recommended cocoa as adding flavor as well as nourishment."

The report would bolster Hoover's feelings about the need to increase imports. He began his efforts by first sending a letter to the two patron ministers in Brussels, Whitlock and Villalobar, about the situation. Dated September 15, it was short and to the point, detailing five pieces of critical information:

- The potato crop, which had been insufficient for needs last year, was estimated to be 30 percent lower for 1916.
- The grains for making bread would come in at 20 percent lower than in 1915.
- Meat would be less than before, "and as there is no systematic distribution except through the soup [as an ingredient], it will in any event benefit but a small class of the better-to-do."
- Indigenous fats had no system of distribution, which meant they mostly fell into "the hands of the well-to-do."
- "The industrial classes already show greater decreased vitality, increased tuberculosis, and other bad signs."

Hoover concluded by stating, "The imports of food must during the winter rise to much larger quantities than anything we have hitherto contemplated, and this in the face of the highest prices the world has ever known."

He followed this letter by sending a request to the British Foreign Office on October 7 for an increase of imports to Belgium from the currently approved 75,500 tons a month to 86,986 tons. He included in his request Dr. Lucas's report and an extensive report on the current situation in Belgium. He included information not only on necessities but also on luxuries. One of them was coffee: "Coffee is now wholly exhausted in Belgium and the people are using roasted cereals—which would answer if a small amount of real coffee could be mixed therein." The import request included 1,100 tons of coffee per month. Northern France was also included, but separately, in Hoover's request.

In a somewhat surprisingly quick decision, the British Foreign Office determined the Belgians and northern French should have the proposed increases (less only 400 tons). As detailed by Lord Percy in a memorandum sent November 11, 1916, the items and monthly tons for Belgium and northern France were:

Belgium	*Metric tons*	*Northern France*	*Metric tons*
Wheat	59,000	Flour	19,300*
Maize	8,000	Cerealine (maize)	2,200
Rice	5,000	Rice	4,400
Peas and beans	3,000	Peas and beans	1,650
Meat	500	Meat	1,800
Fish	850	Fish	500
Bacon and lard	5,686	Bacon and lard	3,200
Cheese	500	Cheese	720
Condensed milk	1,000	Butter	360
Cocoa	1,100	Condensed milk	1,650
Coffee	1,100	Cocoa	350
Yeast materials	1,000	Coffee	1,100
Soap	1,000	Sugar	1,320
		Soap	1,000
Clothing and clothing materials			
Medical supplies (*not including rubber goods*)		*(equivalent of 23,500 tons of wheat)	

For the Commission's Staff	
Petrol	20,000 liters (plus 650 more for the U.S. Consulate)
Lubricating oil	1,000 liters
Mineral transmission grease and motor car accessories	100 kilos

Hoover's request for an imports increase was sent before he left London for Brussels to confront Francqui. The November 11, 1916, happy news that the British had approved his request would be there when he got back.

Gibson Finds a Home and Makes a Move

After what seemed like an agonizingly long wait, Gibson finally had heard on May 16, 1916, that he had been "temporarily" assigned to the U.S. Embassy in London. That posting was made permanent two months later on July 15. He could finally return to the work officially, although he had been consulting and doing whatever was asked of him since he had arrived in London in February. He couldn't have been happier and quickly fell into his new role.

Gibson reported that the embassy was then in a building in Grosvenor Gardens. Officially his title was secretary of the embassy, but he told his mother he was the newly appointed chief of staff, and that was closer to reality. He wrote, "A good part of the staff is of course untrained and consequently there is a good deal of confusion and duplication. I am supposed to tear it all to pieces and fit it together again as a smooth-running machine."

After only a few days on the job, he wrote, "The tearing to pieces is going on apace and the fitting together will soon have to begin. . . . As soon as some of the more radical changes are accomplished my job will be that of a chief of staff to run this big shop and coordinate the work of the 3 outside divisions. It will be most interesting and I only hope I can get it running smoothly before I am moved off somewhere else."

In another letter to his mother, he wrote, "Among other things I am the official untangler of the Embassy—if you know what that means—and all the messes that develop are brought to me to be straightened out. After my experience here I could take on the job of puzzle editor of a newspaper without any apprehension."

Gibson was so committed to the job that he took a room in a house right around the corner from the office. That way he could "keep a closer eye on my patient until she gets well or gives up the ghost."

As he became immersed in the new job of covering all of American interests in the United Kingdom and warring Europe, his focus on the CRB naturally lessened to a degree. But it could never be put too far out of his mind—his love of the Belgian people, the relief work, and the Americans involved was simply too great to let him stray too far from the center of action.

If he couldn't be in Belgium, being in London and stationed at the U.S. Embassy in the same office as Ambassador Page was in many ways as good, if not better. In London he could remain in nearly constant contact with Hoover (when he was in London) and the CRB office. He could aid the cause by his good relationship with Eustace Percy, whom he had known when they were young diplomats in Washington, D.C. And Hoover knew Gibson was available at a moment's notice—day or night—to pay him a visit, whether at his office or at his London home, Red House on Hornton Street, London West, and talk through whatever problem presented itself at the time. Gibson also naturally fell into the role of everyday liaison between Page's embassy and the CRB. But most important to Hoover, Gibson was simply a well-placed U.S. government official who knew, understood, and appreciated the CRB for what it was doing.

Gibson also stayed in touch with numerous CRB delegates in Belgium who had become good friends. Whenever one of them was in London, it was a must to meet up with Gibson for lively conversation that many of them termed "bicker sessions." It was during these times that Gibson received news of Belgian friends, strategic tidbits about what Francqui and the CN were up to, and gossip about his old boss, Brand Whitlock, and the rest of the legation staff. It was through such conversations that Gibson kept current on the Belgian situation, which helped him retain his value as an inside consultant to Hoover and the CRB.

In the fall of 1916, Gibson played an important role in the lives of two CRB delegates—Clare Torrey and Duke Wellington.

Torrey had decided in September 1916 that he needed to get back to his job at the University of California, Berkeley (UCB) because the university president,

Wheeler, had not extended his leave of absence any further. But his heart wasn't into returning and turning his back on Belgium and the CRB. Nevertheless, he reluctantly said goodbye to Belgium and headed to England to catch a steamer home. While in London, however, he got together with Gibson and told his friend about his reluctance to head home after such an exciting nine months.

Gibson surprised Torrey by offering him a job as attaché at the London embassy. Clare knew that his replacement at UCB was doing a good job, so he took the job. He received his official certificate of appointment from Secretary of State Robert Lansing on Tuesday, October 17, 1916. His position was as "special assistant to the American Ambassador in London," and because it was made during the war, it was "not for any stated period." He salary would be $3,000 a year (when the average U.S. factory worker made $2 a day, or $730 a year).

Part of his job was working with the CRB. This meant more contact with Hoover than he had ever known in Belgium. "I went to the [CRB] office of Mr. Hoover very frequently and was always invited to lunch. The Chief was usually there so I got to know him pretty well—much better—and of course I got to like him enormously because he was very, very friendly and generous in every way."

Torrey would remain with the U.S. Embassy in London approximately six months when, in May 1917, he left to join the French Army. A couple of months before leaving his post, Torrey received high praise from Page, who wrote to the State Department about Torrey's "excellent work" on a "troublesome Transatlantic case. One of the best papers that I have seen for many a long day was the full statement of the case prepared by Torrey. It was a voluminous piece of work, most admirably done."

As for Duke Wellington, in late August/early September 1916 he had come back to Europe after his three months at home with his sick mother. While home he had gotten engaged to be married, but he still felt the CRB was important enough to return. He arrived back in London at the end of August. Into September he waited to be assigned to a position in Belgium. While waiting, he spent time with Gibson, who told him the embassy was still understaffed and asked whether he would consider becoming an attaché at the embassy.

Wellington took the job, knowing he would still have contact with the CRB, would be paid better than some diplomats (the same as Torrey), and, therefore, could afford to get married. He cabled his fiancée, and she began plans to come to London. He, too, became more acquainted with Hoover as he acted as a liaison between the U.S. Embassy and the CRB office in London. His admiration for the Chief included Hoover's ability to cut to the heart of any matter. "No one whom I have ever known," Wellington said, "had his gift for coming immediately to the heart of any problem. He had no liking for useless verbiage, or extraneous detail."

As for Gibson, it would not be long before he—the self-described "untangler" of the embassy—became entangled himself in a December situation far removed from official embassy and CRB affairs.

45

Elsewhere in Belgium

The All-Flemish University of Ghent Opens

Through the summer and early autumn, von Bissing continued to face Belgian protests regarding his plan to open a Flemish institution of higher learning in Ghent. Most Belgian teachers refused to participate. Students refused to enroll.

Von Bissing and his *Politische Abteilung* (political bureau), run by Baron von der Lancken, had to finally import teachers from Holland and Germany. Students were found within the Flemish prisoners in Germany and recruited from young Flemings threatened with deportation.

When the school was officially opened in October 1916, von Bissing had prepared a speech to celebrate the event. According to contemporary Belgian writer Émile Cammaerts, the governor general's remarks included the lines: "The God of War, with his drawn sword, has held the new institution at the font [a baptismal receptacle]. May the God of Peace be gracious to her for long years to come."

Cammaerts commented, "With one hand General von Bissing was baptizing the baby—rather a difficult operation—with the other he brandished his fiery sword over the heads of all the true Flemings who refused to adopt it."

Differing accounts have the number of initial students as low as 12 and has high as 80—still pathetic for a university. Whitlock wrote, "I was told by our Consul at Ghent that there were twelve students in attendance." Dr. Vernon Kellogg, CRB Brussels director and a renowned professor himself, reported, "Von Bissing had arranged for fifty professors, some German, some Dutch, and a few renegade and bribable Flemish, to accept chairs at Ghent. . . . With a grand flourish—but an all-German flourish—the reestablished Flemish university at Ghent opened with fifty professors—and forty students!"

Life for the students was not easy, with most of the country considering them traitors. Cammaerts wrote of the students that they "are obliged to wear a special cap and are under the ban of the whole population. No true 'Gantois' [resident of Ghent] passes them in the street without whispering 'Vive l'Armée." This is the pitiful medley of cranks, traitors and unwilling students which General von Bissing is pleased to a call a 'University.'"

If nothing else, the starting of the all-Flemish university helped to solidify the feelings of most Belgians against such division. A Belgian military man, Commandant de Gerlache de Gomery, wrote that "in spite of a duality of language, common aspirations and common destinies have given them one single soul. When the vital interests of the country are at stake, all hearts beat in union, and then, according to the happy expression of a national poet, 'Fleming and Walloon are only baptismal names: Belgian is our family name.'"

Less than a year later, von Bissing would take a much more drastic countrywide step in his efforts to divide Belgium and Belgians.

Delegate Pate Doesn't Want to Leave

By autumn 1916, Maurice Pate had become well acquainted with his job and the Tournai District of Hainaut Province. In August he had completed touring 45 of the 82 communes within his district. His traveling was so extensive that one week in September he and his Belgian chauffeur, Julian van Mohl, logged more than 600 miles in the motorcar. He was also getting better at French. "I have acquired enough French," he wrote his mother, "to comprehend all that is said at the meetings. In fact everything I do in the province—interviews, written reports and all office work is carried on in the native language. About the only times I hear English is on the occasion of visits at Brussels, but this has proved a very good thing from the standpoint of being obliged to learn French."

Most days he worked from 7:00 a.m. until 7:00 p.m. and took work home with him. He felt he was constantly on the move and never doing the same task in the same day. He inspected warehouses and flour mills, attended countless provincial and communal meetings, argued with German officials over reports of infractions of agreements, tried to adjudicate Belgian claims against German relief abuses, and attempted wherever possible to streamline or improve the processes of bringing relief to individual Belgians.

Pate also had to put up with numerous German sentry stops whenever traveling by car. One stop in late summer was indicative of what happened many times, even though he had all the proper passes and approvals. "Started for Mons and Brussels by auto at 9:30 a.m. Held up by two German soldiers as we were about to leave town, and taken to authorities headquarters in Tournai. The auto thoroughly searched. All tires taken off, cushions, engine, and all carefully gone over in a two hour examination. The authorities were very courteous but thorough. I was asked to present everything in my pockets and the chauffeur was searched down to his shoes. We were released at 11:39 and make a flying trip to Mons."

There were, however, moments of respite that took him quite by surprise. An experienced CRBer had warned him when he first arrived in Rotterdam that the Americans "if anything are treated too well. They are given the finest of everything—over-wined and dined." Chateaux and servants were at their disposal and large lunches and dinners were the norm to conclude any business.

For Pate—the austere, hardworking teetotaler—it was something that did not interest him. He wrote his mother and father, "This side does not appeal to me. What I want and have looked forward to is to be able to accomplish something and be part of this undertaking."

He admitted, however, that he knew he would have to "enter the social activities and one of the first things I will probably have to do is to have a dress suit made." He had even bought in Rotterdam a tennis racquet and some tennis balls to take into Belgium because "tennis is very popular there."

"It may seem strange," he wrote his parents before he had entered Belgium, "to reconcile all this with the present seriousness of things for the people in Belgium—America cannot appreciate the situation here (and I am just beginning to)—but the recreation is probably necessary along with the work."

As for eating and drinking, Pate wrote his brother, "At nearly all Belgian dinners wine forms one of the principal parts—and folks joke a good deal over my passing it up." He was glad a previous delegate to the region had also shunned alcohol, which made it slightly easier for hosts to accept Pate's refusal to drink. "Fortunate for me to have had Robinson Smith as predecessor in the Hainaut, and at the same time Temperance Champion—he had broken the ice everywhere."

He quickly discovered, however, how important to morale any break from the work was—from lunches, dinners, and social evenings to walks, tennis, golf, and baseball. For Pate, a major outlet, when he found the time, was walking the few miles to Mont Saint-Aubert and climbing to the top, where he could view the countryside, which he considered "the most fertile in Belgium—green and indescribably beautiful." Atop the hill, however, on clear nights he could see the flash of the cannons at the front and would think, "It seems impossible to realize the devastation going on 20 miles away."

At work, he was constantly impressed and inspired by the Belgians, who gave tirelessly in the process of relief. He detailed this in many entries of his diary. "Spent morning visiting communes," he wrote in late summer 1916. "At each place, I see the secretary [of the local committee], inspect the local food-distributing station, and examine the account-books. The spirit of self-sacrifice shown by the workers in many communes is laudable—out of 82 communes in this district we pay no rent for the stores; in the majority of the communes the farmers [haul] the food without charge and volunteers do the distributing and keep records. This has been going on for two years and yet the original interest and sacrifice show. We have two chemists working at Tournai (railroad men temporarily out of work) who spend 10 hours per day at the laboratory—examining specimens of grain, flour, milk—without remuneration. In many places the books are kept by young ladies."

He was equally impressed with the Germans and their occupation of Belgium and northern France. Throughout his diary and letters home, there are no recriminations regarding German policies or actions, individually or collectively. In fact, his writings show little emotion and are mostly straightforward accounts of daily events.

In this regard, he was quite different from the majority of young American delegates, who freely expressed in their personal writings their anger and frustrations at most German actions.

"The present occupation of Belgium," Pate wrote in his diary, "in spite of stories we have heard in the U.S. is undoubtedly the lightest-military occupation in the world's history. . . . Naturally where one party is in power, without opportunity of repeal, injustice exists. There are many Belgians—a number probably innocent, and a number too patriotic to perform some mission favorable to the occupying authority—now imprisoned in Germany. On the whole, however, the military government is fairly lenient—movement of Belgians within the country is now nearly unrestricted, and 'first-hand' stories of clear German injustice are rare. There have probably been invented and 'expanded' more stories about the occupation of Belgium than any other event in history. The fundamental mistake was the occupation itself—but the after-events should be judged fairly."

Such remarks would have elicited strong negative reactions from many Belgians and delegates if they had been heard. And yet, Pate seemed well-liked and enjoyed a good reputation with not only CRB delegates but also CRB executives, including Hoover. No doubt Pate was careful with sharing such thoughts about the Germans. Or he could have been so neutral-minded—as Hoover wished all the delegates to be—that anger, hatred, and frustration were simply not part of his personality.

His feelings about the Germans did not seem to change even when his district of Tournai became part of the Etape area of the Army Zone in October 1916 and a German "nurse" was imposed upon him. Nor did his diary entries change when mass deportations began soon after.

What did change were his feelings about returning home. By October Pate had become so immersed in the work that he wrote his parents that he wanted to change his homeward-bound plans. His initial commitment to the CRB was for six months, which would end in January 1917. In his letter, he said he wanted to stay at least to see his district through the full winter of 1916/1917. "I do not believe I should quit the post before the end of the winter, that is the last of March."

His reasoning was clear; he felt as he learned the job he had become a valuable resource for the CRB and the Belgians. "During three and one-half months here I have been able to get every department of the work and every nook in the region at my finger tips. The experience thus gained will be an important aid in carrying the work through what will very likely be a difficult winter."

Pate had no way of knowing that by staying through the entire season, he would witness the worst winter in 25 years.

46

Brussels

The CRB and *La Libre Belgique* Must Stay Apart

The members of the American Commission were just as interested and fascinated by the underground newspaper as most Belgians. But they had to remain as far from it as possible. Any hint that they read or owned a copy would be grounds for the Germans to declare the delegate unfit for service in Belgium.

Charlotte Kellogg knew the power of the little publication.

"Throughout the entire war," she wrote, "nothing so delighted and braced the [Belgian] people as the appearance, from time to time, of the now world-famous tiny newspaper, *La Libre Belgique—Free Belgium*. And nothing more infuriated the Germans than the persistent victory of this secret press."

But she also knew the consequences of being caught with a copy. "Frequently individuals were caught reading or trying to pass it on, and for them the punishment was ruthless."

As a member of an organization that promised to be completely neutral, Kellogg knew that "we had to be careful to have no connection with it, but we could not help, from time to time, seeing an issue."

The day before she was to leave Belgium for Holland, she had a direct run-in with the newspaper. Her reaction illustrated how cautious and anxious people were when it came to possession of a copy of *La Libre Belgique*.

"Laure, my faithful Belgian maid and friend," she explained, "brought up from the letter box at the door a handful of farewell notes and cards, and with them a packet, which, as she passed it to me, loosened, revealing several copies of *Free Belgium*. Laure's face turned suddenly white. I thought she would fall, until I said quickly, 'Pull yourself together; get a match! You and I alone have seen these; we'll burn them at once here in the fire-place—no one can possibly know."

As the maid ran to get matches, Kellogg could not help but look at the publication. "I glanced hurriedly down the forbidden columns. There I found a heartbreaking appeal to the workmen of the world to rise up against the deportation of Belgian workmen. Poor people! Some one had hoped that I might, despite my agreements, attempt to carry this message across the death barrier [the Germans' electric fence on the Belgian/Dutch border]. But even had my conscience consented, I should have tried in vain, for neutral though I was, I was searched to the skin at the frontier."

Autumn Falls Heavy on *La Libre Belgique*

The entire organization of the underground paper continued to be assaulted by the Germans through the summer and autumn of 1916. There were no more large, coordinated raids, but smaller ones took their toll.

Madame Massardo, who had been arrested in June but released five weeks later without being charged, continued her critical role of ferrying editorial copy to the printer and distributing copies. But she and her daughter, also named Lucie, had become much more careful, knowing they were being watched all the time. She kept all incriminating materials in a space behind the skirting board along the wall behind the counter.

In October, both Massardo women were arrested, despite the fact that no incriminating materials had been found in the shop. But customers who had been apprehended by the Germans had said they had received their copies of the underground paper at the Massardo shop. Besides the women, the 13-year-old and 17-year-old sons of Madame Massardo were also taken in custody. The family would have to sit in St. Gilles Prison until they were tried in early 1917.

Compounding the situation was the fact that the secret police had been following the Massardo women and had uncovered other parts of the organization. In quick succession the printer was arrested and Le Roux's distribution depot was raided, catching numerous people but not Le Roux. Outside of Brussels, the secret police grabbed bank manager Gustave Snoeck and numerous employees, shutting down the main Antwerp depot. They were also successful at closing down the Liège depot.

In less than two months, by December 1916, 52 members of the organization had been arrested. Le Roux had lost his top lieutenant, the paper's only printer, and numerous distributors and sub-distributors. One history noted, "This slow process of attrition threatened to be more disastrous than the big coup of April the 13th."

During that time, Le Roux was constantly on the alert, trying to outthink the Germans in what they might know and when the threads of people they were following would bring the police to his door. He felt confident he had some time left because he had always tried to insulate himself from as many distribution circles as possible and had used his lieutenant, who only knew him as Mr. Pauwel, as a go-between with the printer.

However, after losing his second-in-command and finding no printer who would take on the risky job of printing the paper, Le Roux reached out to the two people he thought he could trust and might be able to help: Father Paquet, who was part of the inner circle and living at the Jesuit residence, and Father Delehaye, who was a Jesuit at St. Michel and had taken over Father Dubar's distribution group. Neither man had any immediate ideas, but they said they would work on finding a new printer and new recruits as soon as possible.

Shortly, through their help, Le Roux had his second-in-command. Jules Donnez was a strong, powerfully built man who was direct and effective. He would quickly make an important contribution when he found a new printer who would take on the risky job.

As all these difficulties were being dealt with, no one reading *La Libre Belgique's* defiant and bold editorial content would have guessed that such challenges were being constantly hurled at the group.

The 98th issue, on November 13, 1916, had a front-page story about the deportation of Belgian workers titled "Man-Hunters."

The 100th issue had an editorial to von Bissing and the German occupiers that proudly declared, "The Belgian people are not subjected and never will be subjected. . . . The enemy has not disarmed; as we write these lines he is driving our brothers into slavery, his brutes are raiding our homes and terrorising the population. Until the hour of deliverance, WE SWEAR IT [in large black type], we will not disarm either! Our hundredth shot is fired. To arms again, and let's aim true and strike hard!"

Those strikes, however, were not recommended by the newspaper to be physical blows, and that was an important distinction. *La Libre Belgique* never once advocated for physical violence or revolt against the German oppressors. The lessons learned during the 1914 German invasion had not been forgotten. The paper's leaders knew how the Germans responded to physical violence from civilians—returning it with far greater brutal force.

As one history noted, while the editorial contributors never "missed an opportunity for making von Bissing or his Emperor the butt of their caustic wit, incitement to revolt or revenge was rigidly banned from the paper. Repeatedly, when the Governor-General enforced deliberately provocative measures with the aim of goading the population into providing him with an excuse for the 'ruthless repression' with which he loved to menace them, the *Libre Belgique* preached patience and calm." But, as the history book stated, the newspaper "also preached resistance . . . passive resistance."

Such a message, combined with the fact the publication continued to appear despite the best efforts of von Bissing and his secret police, was not lost on the outside world. Issues were continually smuggled out of Belgium and into Holland, where the paper's old friend, the Abbé de Moor, would reprint it and circulate copies to the world press.

By the end of 1916, Albert Le Roux had become the new hub of La Libre Belgique. (Public domain; *Histoire de* La Libre Belgique *Clandestine,* Pierre Goemaere, Bureaux de *La Libre Belgique,* Bruxelles, 1919.)

Earlier in the year the paper was the subject of a large article in the *New York Times,* which headlined the Germans' $10,000 reward for the publishers and that the "Editors Counsel the Belgians to be Patient Under Their Wrongs and Await Day of Vengeance."

On Friday, November 24, 1916, the *London Times* acknowledged the underground newspaper and what it cost those who were caught in its association. "The daring little journal La Libre Belgique still appears periodically, and is a thorn in the flesh of the Governor-General, who has failed to discover the elusive printer. A search was made at Ghent last month, and half-a-dozen printers of the town were arrested. One was sent off to prison in Germany for three years, but the paper came out again. The Abbé Munk, suspected of being a contributor, is in Charleroi gaol, condemned after a mock trial to 12 years' imprisonment. To be found in possession of a copy of this newspaper is a penal offense, so it is read in secret and destroyed afterwards."

By the end of 1916, Albert Le Roux was the new hub of the paper, taking the place of van Doren. Jourdain's editorial content was delivered by Father Paquet, while other articles by regular contributors came through Father Delehaye at St. Michel. Le Roux would then decide what went into which issue, correct the final proofs before printing, and pay the printer (through his own pocket, contributions, and sales, whenever possible, to readers).

Despite all the raids and arrests that had started with Madame Massardo and had continued through the summer and autumn, the paper never once failed to show up. It was a feat that made a world of difference to the Belgians under the German yoke.

Hugh Gibson said in a later speech to a large group of Americans back home, "The paper contains news from the foreign press, refutations of the official German proclamations and well written articles calculated to maintain the morale of the Belgians and turn the Germans to contempt and ridicule."

"It is difficult for us," Gibson continued, "to understand the influence of these [underground] papers. The messages of confidence and patriotism they contain are widely discussed among the people and do a lot toward keeping up the courage that is so necessary. And to every Belgian that reads them they give the comforting feeling that he is outwitting the tyrant—and there is a great deal of comfort to be derived from that feeling."

The new year would bring another mass trial, a surprisingly audacious outing by one of *La Libre Belgique's* columnists, and a German raid that would strike at the heart of the paper's inner circle.

Brown Finds Points of Trouble within the Clothing Operations

Since early summer, when the CRB/CN agreement allowing Brown access to the Belgian clothing operations went into effect, he had worked diligently to understand the entire operation and see where breakdowns in the system might be slowing down the process or allowing possible abuse. He found there was one major stumbling block that seemed, at times, to gum up the entire operation.

To his surprise, the party responsible was the CRB.

Through the help of Madame Philippson-Wiener, the CN's clothing department operations manager, Brown had come to understand and greatly appreciate the efficiency of the Belgian processing of clothes. The largest delays were usually encountered in the receiving of imported materials. What Brown found was that the shipments of clothes and clothing materials were rarely, if ever, properly handled before coming into Belgium. He started looking into the shipping side of the equation and discovered how differently the food shipments were handled from the clothing shipments.

A shipment of grain, for example, was surprisingly easy and straightforward to handle. Brown explained, "A cargo of grain arrives at Rotterdam and the ship comes up alongside the great [grain] elevators; the hold is opened up and sucked empty of its contents within a few hours; the wheat being weighed automatically as it leaves the vessel. There is only the recording of these weights to be done, and the grain can be sent off into Belgium."

In significant contrast was a shipment of clothing, which was "vastly more complicated." Every "bale of goods" had to be opened up and each garment or bolt of cloth had to be identified as to its class, texture, weight, and length. If a bolt of cloth was found to be short or long from what the seller's tag stated, then that figure had to be changed, not only in Rotterdam, but in the files of New York, London, and Brussels. Donation bundles also had to be opened and every item inspected, identified, and assigned a monetary value. Every crate of shoes had to be opened and inventoried in the same way.

Brown summed up, "Such were a few of the difficulties met with by the Commission in regard to shipments of clothing and clothing materials. . . . It is difficult to imagine a more troublesome undertaking than this kind of shipping in war time and under the conditions surrounding the work of the organisation."

Brown found that because of inadequate or incomplete handling in New York and/or Rotterdam, when a shipment arrived in Brussels, the process of inventorying had to be done over so that "weeks elapsed before the goods in them were available for distribution to the people or to the workshops."

Additional problems Brown found:

- No standardized identification system upon initial receipt of the goods in America.
- No periodic tracking of clothing shipments (as was done with food), so that the Brussels Division du Vêtements would know "what is going forward to them, what has already been shipped and what they may expect and the dates." Such advance notice "was never done . . . and the inconvenience caused the Brussels Organization cannot be imagined."
- A "great many bolts of cloth," not having been packaged correctly, were damaged by the hooks of the stevedores in their loading or unloading.
- The seller tickets identifying the length of each bolt of cloth were "never in exact accord" so that "a bolt was always a few yards over or short."
- Shipments were many times broken up and sent piecemeal but with no consideration for usage, so cloth might show up for men's coats, but the accessories necessary to assemble the coats would have been held back in another shipment, so the cloth could not be used until the accessories showed up—slowing down the entire process.

Shipping and receiving weren't the only issues Brown had to deal with. There was still internal conflict with the CN. The Belgians had reluctantly agreed to allow the CRB to understand the clothing operations only because the British had forced the issue. The British would not allow imports without a full understanding of the operations and the Belgian safeguards put in place to guarantee the Germans could not get any clothes or clothing materials.

Brown had been chosen to study the organization and report how it functioned, down to the smallest details.

The CN was reluctant to give Brown the information he needed. He later wrote, "For months and months I endeavored to get this [information] but each time I did so I came up against a stone wall in Mr. Janssen. It was discouraging work and I sometimes felt almost sick over it—that he, whom, really, I like very much in spite of it all, could not see the value of such a move to his own people."

Emmanuel Janssen was the director of the CN's Division du Vêtements (clothing division). He not only refused to give Brown all the information he needed, but he also ordered Madame Philippson-Wiener to do the same and to limit her time with Brown.

Regardless of Brown's frustrations, he still admired the Belgians creative and inspired use of materials, especially in the case of used clothes. The American related, after the garments were "beaten and brushed, then disinfected," they were then handed over to the "menders or remodellers—to a veritable hospital for old clothes, where were performed marvellous feats of cure and regeneration. The lining of a baby's bonnet may once have been the necktie of a Fifth Avenue dandy; a little girl's dress came out of a ball gown that was once worn in Australia. . . . Practically everything received was utilisable, either in the exact state in which it arrived, or with some little mending and patching here and there, or else complete knock-down and remaking into other articles. Old collars and silk robes, fur coats and shoe laces—nearly everything was welcome."

In trying to aid the Belgians, Brown began to tell the clothing story to any CRB delegates who would listen, and he wrote up reports on what needed to be done to improve the shipping and handling so the Belgian system could become even more efficient. He also gave weekly reports at the Thursday delegate meetings. Most of the delegates, however, were more focused on the food relief than on the clothing operations.

While Brown was unable to get most delegates to share his passion for the clothing part of relief, he did share with them the unique life of a neutral American delegate in Belgium during time of war. That included experiencing the air raids that the Allies conducted periodically on Brussels, Antwerp, and other Belgian cities.

One autumn night, Joe Green and Brown were entertaining 10 other delegates in their Brussels townhouse. They had long ago finished a meal and were lounging around one of the rooms smoking, drinking, and discussing numerous topics in what they referred to as "bicker sessions." At 1:00 a.m. one of the men suddenly shouted for quiet: "Wait a minute! There they go!" It was the German defense guns firing at some perceived threat from the sky. In a heartbeat the young delegates raced to the roof to see the action. In spite of a quarter moon, the men couldn't spot the aircraft.

"We could only hear it buzzing away up there in the sky and could tell that it was coming nearer. Suddenly it seemed fairly to jump out of the darkness and went whizzing by just overhead so close it seemed that we could have touched it with a 10-foot pole, and a great yell of delight went up from the people gathered in the boulevard below—and all this to the tune of the guns all around the city and the crack! crack! crack! of the machine gun."

Bits of shell tapped "gently on the roofs around us" as the plane shot back into the dark. The Americans could follow the plane by the sound of its engine. In a minute or two they could tell it was heading back toward them. Just before it roared by again, "a light-rocket went up and burst at the very tail of his machine, lighting up the whole plane perfectly, whereas the guns redoubled their efforts and roared away furiously."

The plane made another low pass before it "wandered off and was gone. The battle, perhaps 30 minutes, was off and we all came below to our 'bicker session' again."

The autumn also saw Brown visit Chateau Oude Gracht and Erica Bunge as often as possible. He wrote his parents that the Bunges were "the dearest friends I have in Belgium."

Nowhere did Brown mention his special interest in Erica.

Hoover Tries One Last Time with Francqui

On October 26, two days before Hoover arrived in Brussels, Brand Whitlock wrote in his diary, "Hoover comes tomorrow, with his faithful companion, trouble."

Two days after Hoover appeared, Whitlock wrote, "Hoover, by his lack of tact, his tone of severity, has caused much of this trouble [with Francqui]. Our Americans do not recognize that the position of the recipient of charity is so delicate that the donor should not add to the embarrassment by criticism and by intimidations that there is lack of appreciation. Hoover would drive everybody with a bull whip; he is a strong man with a good heart, but lacks diplomacy in his dealings with Francqui. He is expected this afternoon and then the storm breaks! A plague on both your houses!"

Three days after Hoover arrived, Whitlock wrote that his American colleague was "full of fight, and determined, doggedly determined to force the issue with Francqui." Hoover gave Whitlock a French translation of Lord Grey's October 20 letter detailing the functions of both the CRB and CN and asked that Whitlock give it to Francqui. Hoover then had numerous meetings with Francqui, as well as with members of the CN's executive committee over the next week.

Francqui was just as adamant as before. The CN was boss in Belgium, just as the CRB was boss outside Belgium. According to Kittredge, Francqui's attitude was "defiant and unyielding. . . . He declared that there could no co-operation between the Comité National and the Commission. . . . All control in Belgium must be by the Comité National."

Francqui was taking such a tough, intractable stance because he had what he felt was a trump card. He had finally made a deal with the exiled Belgian government. Whitlock explained, "It appears . . . that Francqui and the Comité National have made their peace with the Belgian Government at Havre [France]. The Belgian Government recognizes Francqui and Company as its representatives in Belgium, and in return the Francqui and Company, who were becoming dangerous revolutionary rivals, agree to abdicate when the King comes back. Meanwhile Francqui assumes the powers and rank of a dictator, and has even told Hoover that the Comité National must be shown the respect due a government! The man indeed is quite blown with pride, and this morning told Hoover that the Belgians wished no more charity from America!"

Besides having the Belgian government on his side, Francqui also felt the Germans would support his push for control. He knew very well that Baron von Bissing and his civil government in Belgium resented the American presence—especially an American presence that kept trying to dictate terms, conditions, and agreements. Von Bissing would surely welcome a demoting of the Americans to the status of assistants to the CN.

Each of the players seemed to be orbiting around a different belief—Francqui was confident he could control and manipulate the Germans; the Germans equally believed they could control and manipulate the Belgians; the Allies were sure the Belgians would definitely be controlled and manipulated by the Germans. In the middle of it all stood Hoover—the one man few, if any, felt could be controlled or manipulated by anyone.

Still, Francqui's perception of Belgian government support led him to refuse to meet Hoover anywhere in the middle for any agreement between the CRB and the CN.

Reflecting some of Hoover's frustration, Kittredge declared, "It is useless and unnecessary at this point to run through all the details of the conferences that were held. So far as practical results are concerned, nothing was accomplished."

Hoover was as direct with the American delegates as he had been with Francqui. Milton Brown recorded a Hoover speech about the topic that he gave in a Thursday delegate meeting, noting the speech was as close to verbatim as possible from notes taken during the meeting.

"We are not here in the service of any government," Hoover told them as preamble, "neither of the Belgian Government, the British Government, nor our own government, nor are we in here in the service of the Comité National, or of any other organization or individuals. We are in here purely and solely in the service of the . . . destitute people of Belgium."

The Chief then stretched the truth to indicate the CRB had been around before the CN (not true): "Just to show you our position before the C.N., we were founded September 5th of that first year; the C.N. was not organized until October 29th." (An early version of the CN began in September 1914; the CRB was officially formed in London on October 22, 1914.)

Hoover made the point that the British would not have approved imports if the CRB had "been linked up with any government or any Belgian organization; they only permitted it because there was a neutral organization in here to handle these foodstuffs."

He spoke of how the delegates had to remain absolutely neutral, even when it came to the Belgians. "To do this, we must keep ourselves from personal difficulties. The keynote of our work is collaboration, cooperation. We want only to cooperate with the C.N. If the C.N. puts us into a subjective position—that we cannot and will not allow; we are servitors of none but the destitute of this country; we stand before the Allied Governments and before the world as their protectors and we can never permit ourselves to come in here and work as the subjects of any organization. If the C.N. does not accept this position into which we have been thrust and refuse to accept this work as cooperation then we shall have to get out, and the responsibility of our going will rest upon their shoulders."

Brown also wrote that Hoover told them about how the CN had weeks before taken the CRB name off all foodstuffs and had made up posters announcing the food belonged to the CN. Hoover told the delegates, "the danger of that is if the Germans begin seizing all food, they won't respect the CN food, but they would respect the property of the CRB."

After talking with the delegates, Hoover continued to take the fight to Francqui in numerous meetings, but with no success. Whitlock's journal has small comments such as "Hoover was worn and haggard after a hard morning with Francqui," and "the arrival of Hoover, gloomy, sad, discouraged."

Whitlock did give the Lord Grey letter to Francqui in a private moment at the legation over tea. Before he saw the letter, Francqui began talking about his meetings with Hoover and went into "a rage, banging the tea-table with his hand, shouting to me—to me! of the Americans." At one point, to Whitlock's surprise, Francqui even used an insulting expression "since the American invasion." When Whitlock handed Francqui the Grey letter, the Belgian read the French translation "with a black visage." When he finished, he declared, "It is Hoover who wrote that. I know his style. . . . That is the limit!"

After the whirlwind days of Hoover and Francqui, Whitlock admitted, "The more one sees of Francqui, while admiring his brilliant mind, the less one respects him; the more one sees of Hoover, the more one respects and likes him."

Hoover left Brussels once again frustrated but determined to somehow resolve the issue completely.

47

Coercion Turns to Mass Deportations, Autumn/Winter 1916

The Process Evolved in Stages

As Hoover and Francqui grappled for control of the relief, a much bigger issue faced Belgium and northern France—the German handling of the unemployed, or *chômeurs*. It had been an evolving process ever since the occupation began and ultimately would fall generally into three stages.

STAGE ONE, SPRING 1916: The Germans attempted to coerce unemployed Belgian workers to return to work with a contract and respectable wages. These efforts had been focused mainly on railroad workers and had caused events such as the earlier April 1915 "strike of folded arms" in the small town of Luttre, the larger May/June 1915 strike in the city of Malines, and the February 1916 demands placed on a small group of men in the village of Rochefort.

STAGE TWO, SUMMER 1916: The Germans announced that anyone who rejected the work contract and wages being offered would be forced to work beyond their homes, but still within occupied Belgium or northern France. The Germans' major effort in this regard had been the 1916 Lille deportation of urban workers to work the fields within agricultural areas of occupied northern France.

While these two stages were mostly harsh and brutal in their implementation, each had kept deportees within the occupied territories and had initially offered respectable wages. And in some cases, a cash bonus was offered to any who signed the work contracts. If such incentives could be considered at all humane—and many believed they contained no such humanity—an argument could be made that they were because of the German civilian government in Berlin. That government, led by Bethmann-Hollweg, was generally concerned with how the world perceived such actions, and it had been a moderating force in countering the German military's desire to be more aggressive with the unemployed within occupied territories.

Despite the German enticements to work, most Belgians and French had refused and many had raised their voices in a chorus of "we will not sign!"

By the summer of 1916, these sporadic attempts at coercing the unemployed were becoming a serious concern for the CRB and the CN. In July, after conferences with the Germans to extract the relief program from the issue, Hoover and Whitlock had helped Villalobar write a letter to von der Lancken that had stated what had been verbally agreed to: "That the German authorities will at no time employ the Comité National or the C.R.B. as a means to force the population of working people, against their will and against their conscience, to employment either directly or indirectly benefitting the German Imperial Army."

A little more than a week later, von der Lancken had confirmed the understanding "that the Governor-General will at no time make use of the Comité National to force the Belgian working population to employment for the benefit of the German army, contrary to the stipulations of The Hague Conventions."

The Americans were, however, in a tough position regarding the coercion of workers and deportations. The Germans were officially breaking no guarantees that had been made regarding relief when they tried to force the unemployed to work, or even to deport them. But the moral issue still remained that the Germans' actions were barbaric and inhumane. As Hoover explained, there were "no technical violations of relief guarantees," but this didn't mean complaints by the CRB weren't filed and arguments weren't made to try and stop the Germans. The points Hoover made were twofold, that the coercion of workers would have "disastrous effects . . . not only on neutral opinion, but on the conduct of relief."

Complicating the issue was the fact that the emotional appeal by Brussels Director William Poland and delegates Wellington and Richardson at the tea party in Charleville had been successful in stopping the spring 1916 Lille deportations of urban workers to field work. Regardless of the positive outcome that was achieved, their efforts had been highly unneutral and could have led to the shutting down of the entire relief program.

Hoover knew the CRB could not afford to make such a direct, moral challenge again, so he worked the edges of the issue, trying to convince the Germans that coercion and deportation were not in the true interests of Germany, but never stating they were not legally allowed to do so.

To a certain extent, the arguments did find their mark. Hoover even acknowledged in one history that German "civil officials and even the Governor-General [von Bissing] recognized the soundness of these arguments, and disapproved the policy, but affairs in Germany had reached a stage where the opinions of civil officials carried but little weight. Recognition, at the [Military] Great Headquarters . . . of the inferiority of man power of the Central Powers led to drastic action."

What Hoover was referring to was the major power shift in Germany that had happened in August. The relatively moderate civilian leadership of Theobald Bethmann-Hollweg had been replaced by the more aggressive military leadership of Hindenburg and Ludendorff. An early result of that shift was Governor General von Bissing's trip to Berlin, where he had been reprimanded for being too lenient on his Belgian subjects.

In early September another larger change began when Hindenburg demanded of his own country the full mobilization of Germany, which meant implementing conscription. Many Germans did not like the idea of conscription and there were calls in the German press for complete utilization of manpower in the occupied territories of Belgium and Poland before full conscription should be enacted in Germany.

When conscription and forced labor were brought before the German Reichstag (parliament), debate raged for months. Two deputies of the minority Independent Socialist Democratic Party, Haase and Dittmann, protested any forced labor, but were ultimately unsuccessful in stopping legislation. On December 2, 1916, the Auxiliary Service Act was passed. It not only addressed forced labor in the occupied territories but also made all Germans from 16 to 50 subject to compulsory service. Regarding forced labor, Germany Secretary of the Interior Dr. Karl Helfferich asserted on the day of the act's passage that "setting the Belgian unemployed to work is thoroughly consonant with international law. We therefore take our stand, formally and in practice, on international law, making use of our undoubted rights."

Even before the Auxiliary Service Act was passed in Germany, the policy toward Belgian unemployed changed because of the military's new power position. On Tuesday, October 3, 1916, the German General Headquarters issued a decree that ushered in the last and most brutal stage.

STAGE THREE, AUTUMN/WINTER 1916: The Germans announced mass deportations with no destination given, no work identified, and little or no regard for employment status. The decree, which was initially just for the Army Zone, stated that the "voluntary or involuntary" unemployed "may be compelled to work even outside the place where they are living." Anyone who resisted could face up to three years in prison and a fine of 10,000 marks. "The German authorities and the Military Courts have the right to enforce the proper execution of this regulation." It was signed by Quartermaster General von Sauberzweig, the officer directly responsible for the execution of Edith Cavell.

Within the Army Zone, Bruges was the first town from which men were taken, followed in quick succession by Alost, Termonde, Ghent, and Courtrai. Thousands were taken.

Three weeks later, on October 24, the decree was expanded to include occupied Belgium under von Bissing's civil government control. This was a major shift from von Bissing's strategic attempts to coerce railroad men to work, and many thought it was because of the power shift that had happened in Berlin.

A CRB history confirmed the reason for von Bissing's change, stating the German military's "Great Headquarters had not overlooked the manpower of Belgium and [occupied] Poland and it was determined to make use of it. Belgian deportations, it was clear, would serve the double purpose of releasing more Germans for military service and of meeting one form of political opposition to an extension of German conscription. At any rate the Supreme Command 're-quested' the Governor-General in Brussels [von Bissing] to make up the shortage of labor in German industries by more extensive deportations from Belgium. The Governor-General acquiesced and wholesale deportations followed."

This was no sporadic effort in a specific place to get the unemployed to work for the Germans, as had been in most cases before. This was mass deportations of all men on a countrywide scale.

At stake were approximately 1.6 million Belgian men—employed and unemployed—between the ages of 17 and 55. Reportedly, the German General Staff had prepared a deportation plan for all the occupied territories within the German Empire. For Belgium, the plan called for 350,000 to 400,000 men to be deported, which meant almost one in four would be taken.

And with the deportations came a concerted effort by the Germans to secure the local *chômeur* lists. These extensive, detailed lists of the unemployed had been created by local communes not long after the occupation had begun. They were used to provide fair and equitable distribution of food and clothes. In many cases, the lists had also been provided to the CRB to aid in its inspection and control of relief.

As the Germans developed the concept of deporting the unemployed, they had also begun demanding the lists. They had approached the CRB to secure the lists, but CRB officials had quickly convinced the Germans that such an avenue was a dead end. The Belgians, however, were an entirely different story. They were under direct rule by the Germans, and multiple coercions could be used to get the lists from them.

But the Belgians knew the lists would make the Germans' job that much easier in determining who should be deported, so numerous burgomasters (mayors) and commune officials refused to give up their lists. Many of them ended up being jailed and/or fined. The refusals became so pronounced that the Germans felt the need to address the issue in an official statement.

General Hurt, the military governor of Brussels and the province of Brabant, sent out a letter to all the burgomasters that declared, "Where the Communes will not furnish the lists (of unemployed) the German administration will itself designate the men to be deported to Germany. If then . . . errors are committed, the burgomasters will only have themselves to blame, for the German administration has no time and no means for making an inquiry concerning the personal status of each person."

With or without the *chômeur* lists, the mass deportations began in late October in the provinces of Hainaut and Luxembourg, then quickly spread like a contagious disease through much of the country.

The CRB was drawn deeper into the issue as the Germans in many cases deported Belgians who were employed as critical support staff for the relief. One CRB general report on the topic explained, that the CRB had to "turn its attention most seriously to this expatriation of men, because included among the so-called chomeurs are a large number of its employees." The report acknowledged, "It is not within the realm of the duties of the C.R.B. to protest against the seizure of Belgians, but when it finds that the ravitaillement [relief] of Belgium is endangered by the fact of the requisition of its own personnel, it then feels that it should make vigorous protestation."

After numerous discussions about the issue, the Brussels *Vermittlungsstelle* (Political Department) under von der Lancken agreed to allow the CRB to print up white cards that it distributed to its Belgian employees stating the holder was employed by the American organization. The hope was that the Germans would keep their word to take only *chômeurs*—something the local commanders in charge had not consistently done.

The Americans Bear Witness

It was during this highly volatile time in the autumn of 1916 that Joe Green watched and reported in restrained anger the brutal taking of men from the small town of Virton, in Luxembourg Province. Fellow CRB delegates were seeing and experiencing the same thing, as they stood helplessly on the frontlines of the deportations. All they could do was file reports and hope the brutal "slave raids," as many called them, were somehow stopped.

Brand Whitlock wrote, "The delegates were instructed to be present [at the deportations] and to render any service they could, and Mr. [Hallam] Tuck and Mr. [John A.] Gade, delegates of the C.R.B. in the province of Hainaut, went over to the commune of St. Ghislain on the morning of October twenty-ninth to witness the selections, to prevent the seizure of the employees of the C.N. and the C.R.B., and to distribute food to those who were deported."

St. Ghislain was a small commune just west of Mons. It had once been the seat of a wealthy Bernardine abbey but had since then become a center for the coal industry. On the day prescribed by the Germans to appear, 2,000 men from the surrounding communes gathered in the small town. The scene was becoming all too familiar, as it was played out in many villages, towns, and cities. Whitlock described the painful event at St. Ghislain, "The women had followed [the men] in tears, and at the point where the selections were made lines of soldiers kept the women back by their bayonets."

When it came to choosing who would go and who would stay, no effort was made to find out who was employed and who was a *chômeur*. "Indeed," Whitlock noted, "the Germans did quite the reverse, showing a decided preference for men then employed as carpenters and blacksmiths." Then came the dreaded one-word command in German: *links* (left) or *rechts* (right)—freedom to the left, a cattle car to Germany to the right.

In late 1916, John A. Gade was a CRB delegate in Hainaut Province when the German deportations of Belgian men began. His report of what he saw would be circulated widely. (Public domain; author's archives.)

Once the ultimate decision had been made, Whitlock wrote, those who were to be deported were "not allowed even to speak to their wives or waiting families, only a despairing glance of farewell, a wave of the hand to the women sobbing and wringing their hands there in the cold, while the indifferent soldiers in grey kept them back with their bayonets."

The men were then "marched off to the long line of freight cars waiting on the siding." The rough-hewn cattle cars were supposed to hold only eight horses or 40 men, but the Germans usually forced up to 60 men into each car.

Whitlock reported that when Gade and Tuck came back from observing the deportation they were "sick with horror and full of rage."

The two men, however, would have to watch many such events. Gade explained that they had to keep "rushing back and forth to whatever place in [the] province a deportation was to take place, in order to protect and intercede as far as possible for . . . the Belgian employees and office force of the Relief Commission."

In short order, the deportations were scheduled to begin in the provincial capital of Mons, where the two Americans had their office and residence.

A week before the Mons deportations were to begin, the Germans covered the city with placards detailing what the Belgians had to do. Gade reported, "Ever-swelling, anxious groups" gathered and the "men read the French and German versions on the huge placards as if they were reading their own death-warrant." Men between 18 and 55 were to report on the morning of Thursday, November 16, 1916, in the suburb of Nimy, which had seen heavy fighting in 1914 during the first battle of Mons. According to Gade, the location, just outside of Mons proper, had been chosen purposefully so that the city's "mob could easily be kept away and there would be no danger of a riot."

Tuck and Gade had decided to be proactive in protecting their employees. They had sent a sample of the CRB employment card to the president of the German civil administration, and the day before the deportations they went to the office of the local German Kreischef (commissioner of police), where they gave card samples to a Captain Brande. The German captain told them to bring all their men in one group for processing at the start of the day. The total of the group was 175 men, which included those who worked with "the Regional and Local Committees of Secours and Alimentation . . . [and] the employees busied with distributing bread, busied in our mills, and on our docks."

Following the instructions they had been given, Gade reported, "Mr. Tuck and I marched our men to Nimy, and . . . presented them, cards in hand, in a unit for early inspection."

The German military officers in charge were not impressed. They immediately took 16 men who held CRB employment cards. Tuck and Gade objected "vigorously, especially when six dock hands badly needed at the moment were taken from us." Nothing worked.

The officers in charge kept repeating that they could not allow so many men to be excused. Tuck and Gade replied that "every man provided with one of our cards was essential to the work, and the number had most scrupulously been cut down to the smallest possible working force for the head office."

Even two Belgians who held CRB cards and sat on the important provincial committee were taken, despite the argument that they were essential to the CRB and the relief work.

No matter how hard the Americans tried, they could not get the German officers in charge to return the men who had been taken. Tuck and Gade were even able to gain the support of some German civil administrators who pleaded their case to the military officers in charge. Gade reported, "The officers of the civil government did much to assist us, but were repeatedly overruled by the officers of the military government."

In utter frustration, Gade asked a German officer if the white CRB employment cards offered *any* protection at all from deportation.

None, the man replied.

When all the CRB employed were processed, Tuck and Gade turned to head home and took in the whole scene around them. Gade wrote, "Down the many cobbled lanes of the city built upon the hill flowed endless arteries of men—the students under their professors, clerks behind their chiefs, and workmen behind their superintendents."

To control the Belgians were German soldiers, "endless rows of gray, with glistening bayonets [that] lined the roads and barred all approaches. Here and there a mitrailleuse [machine gun] had been set up. Distracted, desperate women, followed by howling children, ran up and down the fields beyond, pleading—aye, praying on their knees—to be permitted to give their men the bundles of clothing just purchased by the sale of the last household articles. But they might as well have prayed to images of stone."

Such scenes did not escape the notice of the outside world.

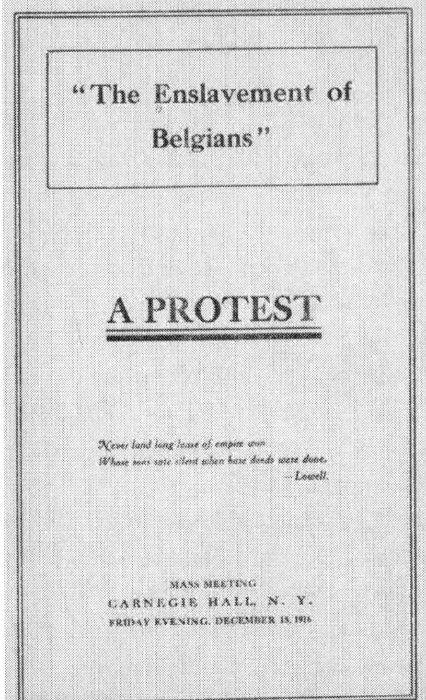

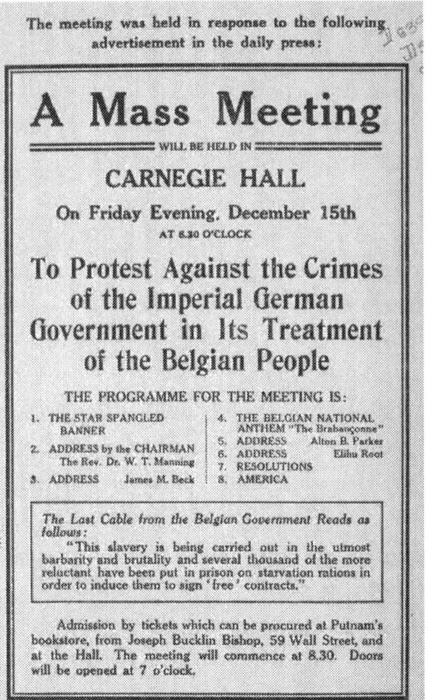

The German deportation of Belgians for work in Germany was condemned by the nations of the world. In America, protests were held in multiple cities, including one in New York on December 15, 1916. (Public domain; The Library of Congress.)

The World and Britain React

Shortly after the deportations began, the first reports filtered out of the occupied territories to the rest of the world. People around the globe were horrified at the stories of families ripped apart and cattle cars crammed with defiant men yelling, "We will not sign!" or singing the Belgian and French national anthems. To the rest of the world, the deportations quickly became known as "slave raids." Worldwide condemnation filled nearly every newspaper and magazine, while protest rallies were held.

In America, protests were held in multiple cities, including Boston and New York City. The *New York Times* reported that on Friday evening, December 15, 1916, Carnegie Hall was "packed to capacity" with more than 3,000 people there to protest "against the crimes of the Imperial German Government in its treatment of the Belgian people." A letter from Teddy Roosevelt was read to loud applause, especially when it came to the statement that "as long as neutrals keep silent, or speak apologetically, or take refuge in the futilities of the professional pacifists, there will be no cessation in these brutalities."

The main speaker was Elihu Root, former U.S. senator, secretary of state, and secretary of war. He called on the Wilson government to act and join in the worldwide protests. "The question is not what Germany is doing," he declared, "but what the rest of the world proposes to do, and, above all, what the United States, as the greatest of the neutral powers, proposes to do. . . . It is in the power of the United States, without recourse to arms, to bring this system of oppression to an end." He said that all the U.S. government had to do was to tell the German government to stop or it would send the German ambassador home. Germany, he contended, needed America "to save it from the wrath to come."

In Britain, an editorial in the *Daily News* declared, "The manhood of Belgium is being driven from its soil at the point of the sword, conscripted at once for slavery and for involuntary treason.

"This crowning infamy," the editorial continued, "is no sudden plunge into barbarism. It has, there is strong reason to know, been long and carefully considered as an ultimate phase of that law of 'necessity' to which Germany has sacrificed every bond and covenant to which it has set its seal."

In a strong nod to America and the implied wish for the country to join the fight, the editorial also stated, "This development of 'frightfulness' cannot fail to make a profound impression on the neutral world. It is not conceivable that it can be permitted to pass without some great word being uttered by those who stand outside this dreadful theatre of war but who cannot claim to stand outside the considerations of humanity."

Another editorial in the *Daily Telegram* was indicative of how many people felt. The deportations, the newspaper stated, were "no sudden or haphazard development, but stand as the outcome of a long and most deliberately calculated progress. . . . Gradually and steadily the country has been reduced to a condition of general unemployment, and the stage thus prepared for the next act of the drama."

By the end of the year, multiple countries had lodged official protests with the German government against the inhumanity of the deportations.

Despite the worldwide outcry and official government protests, the German military refused to change its policy. It even turned its back on the objections of its own people. In the German Reichstag, on December 2, 1916, deputies of the minority Independent Socialist Democratic Party stood in the great chamber and protested the deportations. Nothing swayed the German military. Ludendorff stated that the outcry from the rest of the world showed only a "very childish judgment of the war."

While the Allied and neutral press reports were strongly sympathetic to the Belgians and northern French having to endure such treatment, they were not all sympathetic to the balancing act America and the CRB were trying to maintain.

One editorial, titled "Slave Raiding in Belgium," published in the British *Birmingham Daily Post* must have garnered Hoover's attention and frustration.

It asked the question: "Have the neutrals any concern in the matter other than their natural solicitude for 'those principles of humanity?" Quickly answering its own question, the editorial declared, "They have. . . . They have become responsible for the administrative work of the neutral Commission of Relief in Belgium. They have taken pride—and with justice—in the magnitude of their efforts on behalf of the suffering of non-combatants of that unhappy country."

However, the editorial went on, "As matters stand, the Commission of Relief is being abused by the German Government in two ways." Those two ways were "by its very presence in the country, [the CRB] enables the German authorities to seize or destroy Belgian resources; by the assistance it gives to the helpless it facilitates the German process of deporting the able-bodied."

The newspaper concluded the editorial with a statement directed at those neutral countries that supported the CRB: "We suppose the neutrals will contend themselves with protests [against the deportations]. But if their protests be disregarded in the usual manner, it will clearly be incumbent on them to consider how far the continuance of their relief work is compatible with their neutrality."

Hoover knew this was the old argument that Winston Churchill and the other British militarists opposed to relief had been using since the beginning. Now, though, those arguments were being wrapped around the German deportations.

On October 20, 1916, he had received a letter from Lord Percy at the British Foreign Office. "In effect," Hoover recalled, the letter "was a proposal that the C.R.B. should use food pressures to stop [labor] coercion."

Lord Percy referred to a statement that Lord Robert Cecil had made recently in the House of Commons about the CRB and its relation to forced labor. Lord Cecil had outlined three British stipulations to allowing relief:

1. The CRB provide no relief to German civilians (something everyone had already agreed to).
2. The CRB provide "nothing, except bread, to any Belgian who earns enough to feed himself from native supplies."
3. Any Belgian coerced into working for the Germans must be feed by the Germans "entirely, without any assistance whatever from the CRB."

Lord Percy stated, "You should take this as a direction to the Commission on which they should model their action."

In effect, this meant that any forced labor was no longer the responsibility of the CRB and if the deportations began on a large scale, the British would decrease the amount of imports allowed by the CRB into Belgium.

Lord Percy went on to detail how Germany's forced labor policy was predicated on "the criterion that men who fall under your relief owing to unemployment are liable to be coerced. . . . This is clearly equivalent to the use of your relief as a means of coercing workmen against their conscience, and therefore constitutes a clear and deliberate violation of the German guarantees."

Hoover felt strongly that the British stipulations involving the issue of forced labor were "impossible to impose." "We could not discriminate," he wrote, "among 7,500,000 Belgians on just who was to receive relief and who not. If these workers lived at home, this idea was futile, since we could not starve their women and children. I was certain that Percy did not want to jeopardize our neutrality by any such action but was merely making a record for consumption among British officials. We, however, could not permit the use of food in such a manner."

Hoover Pushes for an Official Protest

That did not mean Hoover would do nothing regarding forced labor. He remembered von Bissing's agreement earlier that "food should not be used to coerce workers to work for them contrary to The Hague Conventions."

Hoover pressured Whitlock about formally objecting to von Bissing. Hoover knew an official protest from an American government official—Whitlock—would carry more weight than a protest from the CRB, and it would reinforce Hoover's earlier contention to the Germans that deportations would turn neutral countries against them.

Whitlock initially declined, and, as Hoover stated, "at this time was unwilling to take vigorous action."

Realizing how important this issue had become, Hoover turned to the CRB Brussels director, Dr. Vernon Kellogg. Kellogg had studied in Germany, spoke the language fluently, and was well respected by many German officers and officials. Kellogg wrote von Bissing on October 20, 1916, and minced no words: "It is common knowledge that demands are being made upon unemployed, and even employed men, to work for the German Army." Kellogg gave examples within von Bissing's civil government as well as in the Belgian Etape [one of the Army subzones]. And he went on to declare that if the CRB "should accept this situation without protest, they would be permitting an indirect infraction of the undertaking between the General Governor and the Protecting Ministers, and would even be a party to the punishment, by a limitation of the food rations, of these Belgian men."

Kellogg got nothing more than von Bissing's standard reply to all those who objected to the deportations: The old Prussian general answered that the English blockade had created Belgian unemployed, the unemployed were an overwhelming charitable burden, and Germany was simply providing labor to demoralized out-of-work men.

In an article in the *New York Times,* von Bissing was quoted as saying, "England has reduced nearly 500,000 Belgian labourers to a chronic state of demoralising idleness. It is in order to remedy these increasingly intolerable conditions, harmful alike to the Belgian nation and the individual, that I have ordered measures to encourage the voluntary migration of unemployed Belgian labourers to Germany and to evacuate the congenitally idle who refuse suitable work at good wages."

The governor general had also posted his reasoning in the German-controlled Brussels newspaper, *La Belgique*. After explaining again that the entire situation was the fault of the British blockade, he then went on to state, "Hundreds of people being without work in Belgium, and work abounding in Germany, the occupation of Belgian workmen in Germany has therefore become an economic and social necessity."

Von Bissing neglected to mention that the Germans had denuded Belgium of most of its industrial production and manufacturing ability, and that the CRB and the CN were providing adequate relief to all Belgians—employed and unemployed.

At the end of October, Hoover returned to Brussels. On Monday, October 30, he went to the *Vermittlungstelle* (Political Department) and saw Dr. Reith. With Hoover was Prentiss Gray and the new CRB Brussels director, Warren Gregory, a lawyer from San Francisco who was replacing Kellogg so he could do other CRB work.

As Gray noted, because the three Americans were there as representatives of a neutral organization "we had not come to argue the moral or political side of this question, but only to insist that the 55,000 [Belgian] employees of the Commission for Relief in Belgium should receive some [protection from the deportations] . . . they were not unemployed and, therefore were not deteriorating either mentally or physically."

Dr. Reith was as firm and unyielding as von Bissing. He refused to agree to protect the CRB Belgian employees from possible deportation, stating "these men who were issuing food rations could work much more efficiently at their former trades and, consequently, should be forced to employ their hands or minds to the highest point of efficiency by working for the German Government at the trade which they knew best."

The meeting lasted for four hours, during which time Hoover mostly "sat in the corner and jingled some English coins [in his pocket; a habit he was known for], as Gregory and Gray "wasted our breath arguing in circles."

In total frustration, Hoover finally ended things. Gray reported that "at the end of the four hours' discussion, the Chief, who had hardly spoken a word during the entire time, stood up and said, 'Hell, logic is useless. Let's go.' He walked out with Gregory and myself at his heels."

Having no success with the Germans, Hoover once again pushed Whitlock to make an official protest over the deportations. As Hoover remembered, Whitlock was "loath to act, so I sent him a strongly worded letter." Dated November 8, 1916, the short letter laid out the case for protest:

"Reports this morning from all over the country show seizure of men right and left regardless of employment, including members of our local committees and employees. I fear it is the beginning of the end.

"It is worth your considering uttering a full and strong protest with all the vigor of which you are so capable.

"This is a greater issue to the Belgian people than anything since the invasion and they look to you as to America for some strong action.

"It may result in nothing, but it will have put the American stamp on it in indelible terms, and if we do nothing else in Belgium we will go down in a blaze of indignation at this, its worst of any trials since the first agony."

The deportations—and the personal pressures such as Hoover's to file a protest—had a severe impact on the legation minister. Whitlock became more and more agitated and, as Charlotte Kellogg reported, "was positively ill." Still, he refused to officially protest to the Germans.

Besides Whitlock's usual aversion to any kind of conflict, his argument in this case was that making an official protest as a representative of neutral America would, in fact, show a lack of neutrality by the questioning of the Germans' handling of their own occupied territory. And that might push von Bissing to end all relief. His argument was basically the same as Hoover's to the British for why the CRB could not push too hard against the deportations.

In this regard, Whitlock might have been more attuned than Hoover to President Wilson and his desire not to take sides, even with such a deplorable act as mass deportations. The State Department issued a press statement on Wednesday, November 15, 1916, that was not an official protest but did convey deep concern. The two critical statements in the press release were:

- "Such deportations cannot but have a most unfortunate effect on neutral opinion, particularly in the United States, which has the welfare of the Belgian civilian population very much at heart."
- "The deportations are viewed here not only as a violation of international law [The Hague Conventions], but in a certain degree as a violation of Germany's assurances made to Mr. Gerard in June, which, though relating to the deportations of French women from Lille, Roubaix, and Turcoing, are felt to be applicable to the present case."

By sending out the press release, Wilson was communicating a strong message to Germany that official condemnation was not far off.

In Brussels, on Monday, November 20, Director Gregory wrote a long memorandum on the forced labor that included reports by delegates Gardner Richardson, Robert Jackson, and Frank Brackett. Figures, when known, were substantial. Richardson reported that every day during the Antwerp deportations, 4,000 men were told to report to the train station, and within only a few days 5,856 had been taken to Germany.

An issue of critical importance was whether the Germans were honoring the white employment cards the CRB handed out to its Belgian employees. "Thus far our cards have been respected," Gregory wrote, "with one exception noted below. Indeed, in Antwerp, one of our representatives [probably Richardson] succeeded in getting on the train and taking back two men who had already been passed, to the great admiration and gratitude of the Belgian people." The one exception had been in Mons, where nine CRB-employed men had been taken.

On the same day, November 20, Gregory also protested the deportation of CRB and CN employees at Mons to the German political department in Brussels and gave the names of the nine Belgian CRB employees who had been taken.

Only two days later, Lord Grey of the British Foreign Office wrote to U.S. Ambassador Page requesting that America apply pressure to the Germans to stop the deportations. As he stated, the forced labor "cut at the root of the guarantees on which the whole relief work in Belgium is based. . . . It may at any moment become materially impossible to continue a work the basic of guarantees of which have been destroyed."

Through such promoting, the United States officially protested to Berlin on November 29, 1916, declaring that it was "constrained to protest in a friendly spirit but most solemnly against this action, which is in contravention of all precedent and of those humane principles of international practice which have long been accepted and followed by civilized nations in their treatment of noncombatants in conquered territory."

The statement even mentioned the humanitarian aid to Belgium, declaring that if the deportations continued, they would "in all probability be fatal to the Belgian relief work, so humanely planned and so successfully carried out."

Meanwhile, the Belgians were fighting back as best they could.

A Belgian Moral Voice Rings to the Rafters

The Belgians had not taken the deportations quietly, despite the fact they lived under the harsh German rule. Towns and cities across the country had officially protested with letters to von Bissing that were written and signed by numerous local dignitaries. Countless burgomasters and committee members had refused to hand over the *chômeur* lists. And some, deciding not to chance a cattle car to Germany, had attempted the dangerous clandestine border crossing into Holland so they could join the free Belgians holding the little sliver of free Belgium with King Albert.

Besides the individual Belgian efforts to thwart the Germans in their deportations, there was one mighty voice that could not, and would not, be silenced.

It was the moral voice of the country, and it sprang from the tall, willow-reed-thin man of the red cloth—Cardinal Mercier.

Ever since penning the December 1914 pastoral letter, the cardinal had shown no reluctance to reacting strongly over any perceived German injustices against the Belgians, such as when von Bissing had tried to break the strike of the Malines railroad workers.

Nearly everything Mercier did either frustrated or angered the German governor general. Von Bissing used house arrest as a way of keeping Mercier contained, and he tried hard to stop the circulation of any letters or statements from the cardinal, but they always seemed to find their way out to the rest of the country and the world.

The solution of full imprisonment or even execution (such as what others suffered for lesser crimes) was unthinkable to the German. He knew his primary job as governor general was maintaining civilian order, and he believed wholeheartedly in the importance of the Catholic Church in helping to keep that order. "Any German statesman," von Bissing wrote, "who is appointed to control the German administration in Belgium must realise that Catholicism is, and will remain, a strong and living force in Belgium, and that among the most important requirements for successful German work is an intelligent regard for the Catholic Church and its disciples."

That belief would be sorely tested when Cardinal Mercier began protesting the deportations.

CRB delegate Charlotte Kellogg stated, "If the Cardinal had felt it his duty to speak out before, he felt a hundred fold his duty to speak in the fall of 1916. For then the Invader was initiating the most cruel of all the infamous occupation policies—the deportations of Belgians into Germany for forced labor in factories or for work behind the lines."

Mercier's first letter of protest to von Bissing came on October 19, 1916. He appealed to the governor general's sense of humanity, ending the letter: "In the name of the Belgian citizen's right to choose his residence and work; in the name of the inviolability of family life; in the name of those moral interests so gravely compromised by the practice of deportation . . . I respectfully beg you to withdraw the orders regarding forced labor and deportation issued to the working-men of Belgium, and also to send back to their homes such of them as have already been carried away in this manner." Realizing the gravity of the situation, the Cardinal sent a copy of his letter to the pope and to the three major neutral countries: America, Spain, and Holland.

On the same day, Mercier also wrote von der Lancken, asking that he use his influence on von Bissing to stop the deportations. Unlike his restrained letter to von Bissing, Mercier's letter to von der Lancken held little back when it came to discounting the pat German reasons for the forced labor. "Do not talk to us, I beg you, of the need of protecting domestic order or alleviating the burdens of public charity. Spare us that bitter irony. You know well that public order is not threatened, and that all the moral and civilian influences would lend you spontaneously their aid if it were in danger. The unemployed are not a burden on official charity, and it is not your money that aids them."

Baron von Bissing's reply once again brought up what he felt was the root cause of all of Belgium's woes—the British blockade. If not for the blockade, Germany would allow Belgium to trade with the rest of the world, and the unemployed would not be an issue. As the situation stood, however, the unemployed were a drain on public charity and could cause serious problems to "familial virtues." He wrote, "The working classes run the great risk of completely losing all ideals if the present state of affairs, which can but become worse, continues. For laziness is the family's worst enemy. Surely the man who works far away from his folk—a state of affairs which has existed always for the Belgian workman—contributes much more to the welfare of his family than by remaining at home in idleness."

Finding no help from the Germans, Mercier turned elsewhere. Charlotte Kellogg explained, "Knowing that fear was eating every day deeper into the heart of a desperate people, Cardinal Mercier determined to break through the prison wall and reach the conscience of the world outside."

On November 7, 1916, as described in his later book, *Cardinal Mercier's Own Story*, the prelate appealed, "in the name of the Belgian bishops" to the "public opinion of the whole world." Charlotte Kellogg termed the missive "An Appeal to Neutrals," but it was a plea to anyone who read it. The letter outlined what had led up to the deportations and declared simply, "The unvarnished truth is that every deported workman is an additional solider for the Germany Army. He will take the place of a German workman who will straightway join the army."

Mercier concluded with a heartfelt appeal from himself and the other Belgian bishops to anyone in any country, regardless of religious faith: "We, shepherds of these sheep snatched from us by brute force, harassed as we are at the idea of the moral and religious isolation which they will have to endure, impotent witnesses of the sorrows and dismay of so many homes broken up or threatened with this calamity, we turn toward those souls whether believing or unbelieving, who, in the allied or neutral countries, or even in enemy lands, entertain respect for the dignity of man."

His appeal was widely circulated around the world and helped stimulate unofficial and official condemnation of the deportations. While the pope and countries around the globe did stand up and protest, nothing shook the German military's resolve to deport Belgian workers.

Back in Belgium, letters of disagreement and outright argument continued back and forth between the cardinal, von der Lancken, and the governor general through the rest of the year. Hundreds, if not thousands, continued to be taken every day.

A particularly detailed eyewitness account by a Belgian was smuggled out of Belgium and published by the *New York Times*. The unnamed man detailed the day of deportation, Thursday, November 9, 1916, for the town of Nivelles and surrounding area, just southwest of Brussels. At the end of the long piece, the man stated that at 5:30 p.m. the train was full of deportees. "It consisted of thirty-two carriages, including no less than 1,000 men from the little town of Nivelles itself, taken haphazard, employed and unemployed."

As he watched the train pull slowly out of the station, he was startled by "a thundering chorus coming from the train. 'Long live the king! Long live Belgium!' and out of all the carriages there rose with wonderful suddenness the chant of the Brabançonne and the Marseillaise [the Belgian and French national anthems]. Along the railway tracks stood the women and children, screaming and lamenting and waving in despair their last farewell to the deported men."

The eyewitness couldn't watch the painful scene any longer and turned and walked back into town. He found no solace there. "I found myself in the midst of a group of soldiers singing as loudly as their throats would allow the 'Gloria Vittoria.' It was the song their comrades sang at the battle of the Yser [and reportedly played on a phonograph during the burning of Louvain], when they were being mowed down by the fire of the Belgian guns. This time, of course, they had to celebrate a great victory—one trainful more of slaves had been dispatched."

As the world press was circulating this and similar stories that highlighted the inhuman treatment during the deportations, German civilians back home were being told a somewhat different version of events. On Thursday, November 9, one of Germany's major newspapers from Cologne, *Kölnische Zeitung*, published an article about "the transport of Belgian *chomeurs* to Germany," which, the paper reported, "has taken its course quietly." There was no use of the word "deportation" nor any mention of disruptions or protests. In fact, the paper reported many of the workmen "state that after all considering the long time that they have done nothing and have earned nothing, that the prospect of taking up paying work is welcome, and that they have expected such a condition for a long time." As for the unheated, overcrowded cattle cars filled with desperate men yelling patriotic slogans and singing banned anthems, the newspaper neglected to give such details and only noted "the good care that is taken of the transferred chomeurs on the trains seems to work favorably on their spirits."

While the Belgians mainly stayed calm, that wasn't always the case, especially on meaningful, patriotic days. On Wednesday, November 15, Prentiss Gray in his journal described an important event, the Belgians' reaction to it, and the aftermath.

"Today was the King's Fete Day. It was rumored on the streets early this morning that Cardinal Mercier was coming to Brussels to say Mass in St. Gudula. Laura and I

[Gray's wife Laura and their young daughter, Barbara, had arrived October 24 to be with Prentiss] . . . *went down quite early in order to get seats near the altar.*

"By eleven o'clock, however, it became know that the Governor General had forbidden Cardinal Mercier's trip to Brussels and that Mass would be celebrated by the parish priest. The church was packed to the doors. After the service a choir boy began singing the Brabanconne [national anthem] *and as he finished the crowd took up the [song] and at the close was in an uproar, shouting, 'vive le Roi'* [long live the King].

"This was the most impressive demonstration I have seen. The people fairly went mad with excitement. They swarmed into the street still crying 'Vive le Roi!" and although the German sentries made some arrests on the outskirts they deemed discretion the better part of valor and did not attempt to disperse the crowd.

"At the King's Church on the Place Royale, a German officer stood up to the crowd and told them he would show them who their king was now. Somebody tripped him, and before it was over he was carried off in an ambulance."

"November 18. The Governor General has fined the City of Brussels a million marks, and closed up the town for a week on account of the demonstration on the King's Fete Day. No one is allowed on the streets after seven in the evening, except German soldiers and friendly neutrals."

By mid-December 1916 Cardinal Mercier, frustrated by the horror of the continual slave raids, wrote to his parish priests, "In spite of the protests addressed to Germany by the Sovereign Pontiff and several neutral states, the deportation of our civil population still continues. It is our duty to lessen to the best of our ability an evil we are powerless to prevent."

The cardinal laid out instructions for dealing with the deportations and for comforting those left behind, but he also stated, "We must leave no stone unturned to effect the repatriation of those who, according to the German Government's declarations, ought to be immune from deportation." He wrote that he had established a committee to handle all the cases of those who felt unjustly deported so they could be collected and combined before approaching the governor general.

Hoover's Deadly Dilemma

As Cardinal Mercier was instructing his priests on how to deal with the deportations, Hoover was struggling with his moral quandary. As a neutral providing food to belligerents behind the lines, he had no legal right to question the forced labor of civilians. As a Quaker and a man of integrity, honesty, and conscience, he could not ignore the situation.

The Germans made it even harder for him to stay clear of the issue as they took more than 1,000 Belgian CRB employees during their slave raids. CRB Brussels director Gregory wrote in a December general report about the deportations: "The Commission for Relief in Belgium has been obliged to turn its attention most seriously to this expatriation of men, because included among the so-called chomeurs are a large number of its employees. It is not within the realm of the duties of the C.R.B. to protest against the general seizure of Belgians, but when it finds that the ravitaillement [relief] of Belgium is endangered by the fact of the requisition of its own personnel, it then feels that it should make vigorous protestation."

On Tuesday, December 5, the British, French, Russian, and Italian governments joined the chorus of protests. A strongly worded joint press release spoke directly about the CRB and the possibility of the relief being shut down. "The Allies must warn the world of what is about to take place. As their own situation grows more desperate, the Central Empires intend to tear up every guarantee on which the work of the Relief Commission rests. They intend to cast aside all their promises, and to use Belgian foodstuffs and Belgian labor to support their own failing strength. The work of the relief which neutrals have built up for two years is about to lose its foundation, and is in danger of falling."

Outlining what the Allies had done to support the relief efforts, the press release then stated, "The Allies have only stipulated that the Germans should equally draw no advantage from the operations of the Commission; that they should not seize either imported or native supplies, and that the distribution of relief should not be used for the purpose of coercing Belgian workmen against their conscience."

After identifying the agreed-upon guarantees, and stating that without them "it will be impossible for the relief to continue," the Allies ended their press release with an "appeal to the civilized world, not on their own behalf, but on that of the innocent civilians who cannot protect themselves, to see that this great work of international benevolence and cooperation which has grown up in the midst of the war, and for which the Allies have advanced the money, shall not be endangered by treachery or destroyed by violence."

It was at this time, in early December, that Hoover faced one of his toughest decisions as the head of the CRB. "Should we risk the lives of ten million people with a declaration to the Germans that we would terminate the Relief if the deportations were not stopped? We had tried every measure of persuasion and every measure of pressure of neutral opinion. Nothing less than such an absolute declaration on our part would stand any chance of success, but what if it failed?"

It was a nearly unbearable decision—morally stand against the inhumane slave raids and possibly leave the Belgians without any further help from the CRB, or accept the unacceptable so that the Belgians could continue to be fed.

Threatening to pull the CRB out of Belgium had become a Hoover maneuver that had worked successfully multiple times in multiple situations. Each time he had used such a threat, he had not felt it necessary to ask the opinions of others outside his inner circle. At each event he had read the situation and players, determined that the desire to keep relief going was bigger than whatever his opponent at the time was trying to secure, and then threatened to pull out of relief. Each time he had read the situation correctly, and each time he had been rewarded with the request to stay.

This time, however, Hoover saw how steadfast the Germans were against tremendous worldwide pressures. As a result, he did something he rarely did—ask for advice from outside his inner circle.

"It seemed to me," Hoover wrote later, "that in these difficulties we had need of advice and assurance from higher authority before we took any irretrievable steps."

He put the issue—should the CRB threaten to pull out if the deportations did not stop?—before the two patron ministers in London, U.S. Ambassador Walter Page and Spanish Ambassador Don Alfonso Merry del Val y Zulueta.

They both were against any such demand and suggested that Hoover talk with Lord Grey, the British foreign secretary.

Grey had always been a stout supporter of the CRB and Hoover sat down with him in early December to lay out his possible course of action. The men took stock of the overall situation and the current numerous positive elements:

- The Germans were generally living up to their agreements not to requisition imported food.
- The 1916 harvest had been protected for use by the Belgians and French.
- The taking of native foods happened in "isolated instances, comparatively trivial in view of the larger quantities we were handling."
- Hoover and the CRB had survived the numerous accusations of abuse leveled by the British Admiralty, showing that relief was being handled with scrupulous care and oversight.

Lord Grey counseled Hoover that he should not make any threat to pull out of relief. The foreign secretary added, as Hoover noted, "that he thought the Admiralty had exhausted their pinpricks, expressed his admiration for the way we had conducted the Relief, and assured us of his continued support."

That support was lost only a few days later, however, when Lord Grey resigned as part of the overturning of the Asquith ministry on December 5. But the CRB was assured of continued support because one of its strongest supporters, David Lloyd George, took over as prime minister on Wednesday, December 6, 1916.

Hoover finally made his choice and decided not to tell the Germans he would pull relief if the deportations did not stop. He was still committed, however, to strive to "bring pressure on the German Government indirectly and to hold the German authorities to the terms of their guarantees."

Hoover's decision was a tough pill for the young, idealistic CRB delegates to swallow. For at least one, such a course of action was unacceptable. Hallam Tuck could not accept what he had seen of the deportations and still remain neutral in the company of those who had brought on such inhumanity. Brand Whitlock later wrote, "after what he saw Mr. Tuck resigned from the Commission, left Belgium, and entered the British Army to fight against such cruelty and oppression."

After witnessing the German deportations of Belgians, William Hallam Tuck could not remain neutral, as the CRB required. Following his conscience, he left the CRB and went to Britain to enlist. (Public domain; author's archives.)

Charlotte Kellogg confirmed the emotional toll the deportations were having on the delegates, and wrote of Tuck's individual action: "Our C.R.B. men were all but breaking under the strain [of the deportations]. Mr. Tuck, stationed at Mons, where some of the worst outrages occurred, left everything, and rushed out and across Holland and the Channel to England to join the British Army and fight his way back to Mons to put an end in the one way possible to the horrors he had witnessed. And it was all that Mr. Hoover and the Director in Brussels could do to keep others from following Tuck."

Tuck did leave the CRB. On Thursday, December 21, 1916, he departed for England to join the British Army. He had been torn about leaving, but he knew he could no longer maintain his neutrality. Still, he believed firmly in the CRB and stated what was probably on the minds of the other delegates: "The experience was one that no delegate will ever forget . . . best of all we were associated with Mr. Hoover and with a work which will get its full desserts when this war is over. We feel that it is one of the real things that an American has done during this war."

As for the Allied governments, once Hoover laid out the situation to them, they did not follow through on any threats they had made about pulling relief if the deportations didn't stop.

Back in America, the deportations were still raising questions and concerns. On Friday, December 29, Secretary of State Robert Lansing telegraphed the American Embassy in London with one sentence: "Department would be glad to have Hoover's opinion for its confidential information regarding continuance of Belgian deportations, whether there has been any change in the policy of the German authorities since the protest of this Government on November 29."

Hoover's long answer would come on the second day of the New Year.

48

London

Francqui and Hoover Play Their Final Cards

When Hoover returned to London from Brussels on Monday, November 20, 1916, he had the relief of knowing that the Foreign Office had approved his request for increased imports to Belgium and northern France.

This did not lessen his resolve to deal with the Francqui conflict. While in Brussels, during the numerous meetings and conferences he had attended, he had gathered an extensive collection of correspondence and memorandums that detailed each person's position and what had taken place. He immediately sent copies of correspondence between himself and Francqui to the British Foreign Office, the Belgian minister in London, and the relief's two patron ministers in London, Page and Merry del Val (the Spanish minister). His attached letter basically said that the Allied governments should decide the issue.

From mid-November to mid-December there was a blizzard of letters back and forth between and among the Allied governments, the CRB, the American government, and the Belgian government. The British and French were firm in their position that the CRB was to be sole controlling entity in and out of Belgium; that without the CRB there would be no relief. Whitlock was getting tired of the whole thing, writing in his journal on December 20, 1916, "As to that quarrel between Francqui and Hoover—I wash my hands of it."

Not surprisingly after Francqui's strong stand, the Belgian government initially stood behind its man and his view of how and who should control the relief in Belgium.

In the midst of this turmoil, Lord Eustace Percy took an extraordinary step. He wrote Hoover a letter marked "Private and Confidential" on November 25 that was never recorded in the official documents of the CRB nor reported on in Hoover's own history of the CRB, *An American Epic.*

Percy began by stating he was writing "first for the purpose of arriving at a clear understanding between us." This, in and of itself, was nothing extraordinary—correspondence was used routinely for such purpose. It was what followed that stood out: "secondly because I promised Dr. Kellogg to write down something which could be communicated privately to the Americans in Belgium in order to encourage them to go on with the work."

Such a statement indicated that Percy knew morale within the CRB delegates was low due to the continuing struggles between the CRB and the CN. It was also surprising that Percy would, for a moment, step out of his official role as a high-level officer in the British Foreign Office and speak man-to-man directly to Hoover and his cadre of young volunteers. The Englishman even admitted that his own government was "responsible for many of the sacrifices you have made in the past and even indignities put upon you, personally, during the early months of this year."

Percy acknowledged the current conflict between the CRB and the CN, the new, stronger Belgian-government position, and Hoover's role in all of it. "You came in to rescue the Belgian people at a time of apparent absolute collapse, when the Belgian Government was practically in flight and the whole internal life of Belgium was disorganised by three months of horror. The fact that after two years the Belgian Government has regained a measure of independent self-consciousness and policy, and that the people of Belgium have reestablished their national life on a basis which enables them to claim (however shortsightedly) an independent status, is to be regarded in one light as the most striking possible testimony to your work."

In a move that was reminiscent of Hoover's 1914 argument to Prime Minister Asquith that Britain should take the moral high ground when it came to helping Belgium, Percy then asked Hoover and the delegates to sacrifice even more, for the greater good of saving lives.

"We have got to negotiate, compromise, respect feelings with which we do not agree or which we even consider absurd, and put up with a great deal of that class of seeming ingratitude which arises from the strained nerves of the weaker belligerents. I make no sort of apology for asking you and every American connected with this work to put up with these things, and to bear constantly in mind that the need for neutral intervention and neutral self-denial becomes greater and not less as the situation approaches a crisis."

To reassure all those associated with the CRB, Percy stated "On my honour . . . neither you nor any other American will be asked by us to continue work, either in Belgium, or outside in the administration of the relief work, except on terms which will fully satisfy your dignity as Americans and your sense of responsibility as the originator and guarantors of the work."

He ended by writing that the legacy of the CRB would be safe with him. "I regard myself as responsible for seeing that this and the whole history of America's share in saving Belgium is fully cleared up and put in its true light before the world when peace comes and our tongues are again free."

While never officially recorded, a copy of this remarkable letter was found in the papers of Milton Brown, indicating it was probably circulated to at least a few, if not all, CRB delegates within Belgium.

It also appears to have been read by Francqui. In a letter marked personal from Brand Whitlock to Ambassador Page only four days later, on November 29, 1916, Whitlock wrote, "We have received the message of Lord Eustace Percy, and I am glad to say that it has produced the most favorable impression. . . . I took it immediately to Mr. Francqui in person. Mr. Francqui does not always read English with exactness and I translated much of it for him. We had a long conversation, at the end of which he had a conference with Mr. Gregory [CRB Brussels director], and they came to such terms of excellent understanding."

Whitlock then pronounced, "Since then relations between the C.N. and the C.R.B. seem to be on a perfectly satisfactory basis, and I think that we have at least obtained, what for some time seemed to be lacking, a spirit of friendly cooperation."

The U.S. minister went on to explain, "An important factor in this result is due to the splendid sympathy displayed by the men of the C.R.B. in those distressing local scenes of deportations all over the country, where they have rendered such wonderful service. The Belgians were deeply touched by this, Mr. Francqui not the least of any."

Whitlock concluded by stating, "I send you this little personal note, in order to express my sense of personal gratitude to Lord Eustace Percy. The appeal he made [to the Americans to put aside personal differences for the greater good of feeding the Belgians] produced its effect and Mr. Francqui rose generously and nobly to the occasion."

A handwritten note on the letter in the files of the U.S. Embassy in London (the files are now located in the National Archives in Washington, D.C.) states, "This was shown to Mr. Hoover 16-12-16 who advised that no action be taken. ES"

As for the impact of Percy's letter on Hoover, outwardly it appears as if it had little effect. When the Belgian government's position to stand behind Francqui came out in December, Hoover once again played his we-will-leave card and proposed that the exiled government could take over the entire relief work by establishing its own buying and transport organization to work with the CN in Belgium. This idea was flatly rejected by the French for its northern France territory. Hoover responded by saying that he and the CRB could continue to provision northern France and leave Belgium to the Belgians.

In the end, the pressures of the British and French, and the possibility of falling out of the good graces of neutral America, led the Belgian government to acquiesce to the belief that the neutral agency of the CRB, in an equal partnership with the CN, should have control of the distribution within Belgium. A tentative agreement to that effect was drawn up for approval by all parties.

Back in Belgium, when Francqui heard the news of the Belgian government's shift and the agreement that had been drawn up, he immediately secured permission from the Germans to leave Belgium and go to Paris. There he spoke with leaders of the Belgian government. It must not have been a very calm or quiet meeting. Ultimately, though, Francqui had to face the fact that his own government had come around to accepting the conditions dictated by the British Foreign Office and would not support his stand on the issue regarding control of the relief program.

On Thursday, December 28, 1916, Hoover was informed that Francqui had agreed to sign the document. That same day the two men met, even though Francqui's German pass had only been for the trip to Paris. According to Whitlock, Francqui "made a secret trip to London to see Hoover—was there four hours, Savoy Hotel, incognito, mysterious."

Tracy Kittredge, in his unofficial, unpublished history of the CRB, described the twists and turns that took place in that important meeting at the Savoy Hotel. Hoover added his own details in a letter to Whitlock the next day that appeared, in part, to be almost a stream-of-consciousness release of his frustration and anger. One sentence that explained a particularly thorny moment in the meeting went on for 160 words.

In the clandestine sit-down at the Savoy Hotel between Hoover and Francqui, the Belgian agreed to accept the document, which defined "the neutral and independent status of the Commission for Relief in Belgium and its relations to the Comité National." He did say there were certain "changes in form" that he and the Belgian government wanted to make. "Hoover immediately accepted the whole of the alterations and told Francqui that the intent in drafting the whole contract was to restore the relations between the two organisations to their original basis."

Francqui said he had been prepared to do that all along. "If this contract had been proposed any time," the Belgian reportedly stated, he would have been "glad to have accepted it, and there [would have] been no occasion for all the difficulties during the last three months."

Hoover was taken aback. Knowing he had gotten what he needed and wanted, Hoover chose *not* to take the moral high ground and let the statement go, as Whitlock and Percy would have counseled. He flatly rejected Francqui's remark (stimulating his later 160-word sentence to Whitlock) and told the Belgian that his "attitude in Brussels in October and November had shown that he wished to exclude the Commission for Relief in Belgium from any real co-operation in the work in Belgium; that his whole attitude totally ignored the fundamental fact that the relief was founded and was permitted to continue by the Governments concerned only as an organisation under the control of independent neutrals."

After that release of pent-up frustration, Hoover stated more calmly that "I did not wish to go into history and therefore, as we were now in accord, the matter ended with the execution of this memorandum."

To Francqui it wasn't that simple. He made a surprise move—he said he was resigning from the CN.

Hoover—finding himself on the other side of what had become *his* special maneuver—"protested vigorously to this, stating that since [Francqui] was entirely in accord with the contract there could be no reason for his withdrawal, that Hoover and the whole Commission were convinced that he was indispensable to the Belgian people in his position at the head of the Comité National."

Francqui insisted he was resigning.

Hoover insisted on knowing why.

According to Hoover, the Belgian finally said, "The reason was that he had found himself out of tune with myself during the past three months . . . that the American interest and my own connection had to be maintained at any cost; and that he did not wish to jeopardise the relief by remaining in a position where there was such possibility of breakage."

Not to be outdone, Hoover said Francqui's resignation "made my own position untenable, for, if he resigned because we disagreed on important policy and I could not come to his view that was one thing, and understandable, but to agree on policy and resign because he could not get on with me was another and a reflection on me."

If Francqui insisted on resigning, so would Hoover.

In any other situation—and with no lives hanging in the balance—the scene would have been laughable.

Francqui stared at the American for a long moment. He told Hoover, you use a "sledge hammer to kill gnats."

"I would use a pile-driver to kill a malarial mosquito," Hoover replied.

Another long moment.

"We thereupon agreed to go on," Hoover wrote Whitlock, "both of us to continue as before as the heads of our respective organisations, and that the entire matter would be considered as a bad dream and excised from our recollections."

In a parting shot, Francqui "expressed the fear that a document of this kind being circulated amongst the junior members of the C.R.B. might lead them into arrogance towards the local Belgians and the production of disagreeable incidents." He requested that the agreement not be widely circulated.

Hoover agreed and assured him, "We had no intention of handing clubs to irresponsible men." And, he reminded him, the earlier agreements of October 1914, July 1915, and February 1916 had never been in "common circulation."

The extensive document, officially dated December 30, 1916, was signed by Hoover on that day and by Francqui in early January and approved by the British, French, and Belgian governments.

After the fact, each man was magnanimous in his appraisal of the other.

Francqui wrote to Hoover on January 1, 1917, "None better than I know the tireless devotion which you have brought to bear on the accomplishment of the so difficult task which you have taken upon yourself. Like a veritable apostle you have for more than two years been making your voice of authority heard everywhere in the world in favour of my unhappy fellow-countrymen. You may be very sure that they are aware of your beneficent work and that they will cherish an eternal gratitude toward you. . . . We must go to the very end of the effort which we have undertaken in common and for that it is sufficient that we should both will that it should be so."

In Hoover's letter to Whitlock about the situation he stated, "The admiration which I have for M. Francqui's abilities and his devotion to the Belgian people is in no sense diminished and I hope we shall be able to demonstrate to him that while we will not accept the position of servants, we are the most advantageous of partners."

He couldn't help adding, however, "If I were to let myself down into pettiness for a moment, I might point out that this contract is identical in all its contents with the conditions of Lord Grey's of October 20, 1916, which was in itself but a review of pre-existing relations."

It was true that the December 30, 1916 agreement, which had been so difficult to forge, was very close in content and spirit to agreements dating to the beginning of 1916 and even earlier.

Additionally, a large section of the new document detailed the Inspection and Control Department, showing how critical this department was to ensuring relief would continue.

Joe Green was pleased but would not be there in Brussels to see the agreement fully implemented. His removal as chief of the Inspection and Control Department appears to have been a token gesture to Francqui as evidenced by Green's own description of what happened.

Green wrote to his family, "I was only a pawn in the game, but I occupied the position which was under fire, and finally I became the object of the most bitter personal attacks. . . . Mr. Hoover stood by me through thick and thin, and of course I had the support of my American colleagues. However we have come to the conclusion that my temporary absence from Belgium at this time will tend to clear the atmosphere."

In a decades later oral history, Green added, "Mr. Hoover decided that my difficulties with Émile Francqui, though they were not my fault, were causing so much friction that I had better be recalled."

Green left Belgium knowing he had done a great service for the CRB and the relief work. He would continue with the CRB in the London office.

There is very little about the nearly year-long CN/CRB conflict in any official CRB or Hoover-penned books. Many of the most important letters and documents relating to the issue, including the Hoover-to-Whitlock letter dated December 29, 1916, are not in the otherwise comprehensive, document-heavy *Public Relations of The Commission for Relief in Belgium, Documents.* Without Tracy B. Kittredge's generally comprehensive unofficial, unpublished history of the CRB (*The History of the Commission for Relief in Belgium, 1914–1917*), the entire story of Hoover and Francqui's most confrontational issue would be barely known.

Hugh Gibson, the friend and confidant of Hoover working in the American Embassy in London, hinted of the pressures Hoover must have gone through when he described Hoover during that trying time: "He is pretty tired and is having a very discouraging time but never says DIE. . . . I don't know how long human endurance can stand up under the strain that man has been subjected to all these months."

Kittredge, in his retelling of the situation, did give Francqui and the Belgians their due. "It was, of course, quite impossible for anyone in Belgium to realise the conditions which the Commission had to face outside of Belgium, and therefore the attitude of Francqui is better explained. It was no more than natural, too, that the leaders of the Belgian committees should want to keep as much of the relief work as possible in their own hands, and should be jealous of the part played by any outsider, even if the intentions and purposes of the latter were as altruistic and straightforward as those of Hoover and his associates."

The CRB and CN were finally on agreed-upon solid ground. The work could proceed in a more harmonious fashion, and the Belgian people would be better for it.

An End-of-the-Year Review

Overall, the end of 1916 saw a feeling of guarded optimism within the CRB as to how the work was progressing and how it would proceed in the future. Important pieces had fallen—or been forced—into place.

- The British had agreed in November to increase the imports up to what Hoover had asked for in October.
- The Germans were generally honoring their agreements and allowing the CRB delegates to do their jobs.
- Francqui and the CN—through the December 30 agreement—were finally in accord with the CRB on the roles and functions of both organizations.
- In a tight U.S. presidential race where many had thought Supreme Court Justice Charles Evans Hughes would win, Woodrow Wilson had been reelected on the pledge to keep America out of the war.

- Continued neutrality was the linchpin to allowing Americans to stay in Belgium.
- Worldwide public opinion acknowledged and supported the importance of the massive relief to Belgium and northern France.

This did not mean all was well in Belgium and northern France. The amount of food per person allowed to be imported was barely enough to stave off starvation. The war was dragging on as the Germans continued their deportations—leading many Belgian and French civilians to lose their hope and defiant spirit. On the German side, resentment was building toward the Americans not only for supplying food to the Belgians (as hunger was gaining ground in their homeland) but also for supplying the Allies with war materials.

One of the CRB's remaining major challenges was shipping, a critical component of relief. By 1916, the CRB either owned or leased 50 to 60 ships at any one time. Even with each ship protected by large CRB banners and flags, electric lighting, and German assurances of safe passage, 11 ships were either sunk or badly damaged by German submarines or mines in the North Sea or English Channel during 1916. Representing more than one-fifth of the CRB fleet, these vessel losses led to a growing hesitation by shipowners to put their valuable property in harm's way. Additionally, the Allies had greater and greater need for wartime supplies from around the world, which demanded more and more ships.

Greater demand for a diminishing supply of ships was not a good equation for the CRB, creating much higher prices for leasing of ships. To lease a ship prewar, the usual cost in 1914 had been about $2.25 per ton or less from New York to Rotterdam; by 1916 the CRB was paying $35 per ton and higher.

But far worse than having to pay high leasing costs was about to happen.

49

Elsewhere in Belgium

December Moments at Chateau Oude Gracht

December had been a tough month for many of the American delegates as they struggled to maintain the relief against growing hostility from the Germans and from some of the Belgians within the CN and provincial committees.

The need for moments of rest grew greater as they seemed harder to come by. Some of the delegates found occasional respite with the Bunges at Chateau Oude Gracht.

Early in the month, Maurice Pate had come up from Hainaut Province and spent the morning of Saturday, December 2, in the Brussels office. In the afternoon he drove up to Antwerp and then out to stay at Chateau Oude Gracht, which he had heard about but had not yet visited.

When he got there, he found fellow CRB delegate Dr. Charles Leach already there. Pate also met Edouard Bunge and the three Bunge sisters. He wrote in his diary, "The Bunges keep steady open house for the Americans—they have a beautiful country home with elevator and plentiful accommodations. The house overlooks a beautiful little lake and is surrounded by 160 acres of woods and farming lands. The property is near the Dutch frontier and one side is completely occupied by trenches constructed at the beginning of the war and now occupied by the Germans."

The group, Pate described, "spent a quiet and interesting evening together. The family, though of the wealthiest in Belgium are the most simple and hospitable people you would want to meet." They played a few parlor games followed by joining Edouard and Erica in their usual billiards game. Leach and Edouard were paired against Pate and Erica, who won the match.

The next day, Sunday, Pate joined Leach and the Bunge sisters on a walk from the chateau to the Bunges' other home, Calixberghe, a little over seven miles (12 km) away. "We made part of the way on foot," he wrote, "the rest on tram—passing Mr. B's famous stables of the 100 cows imported from Holland. These were brought in by Mr. Bunge to furnish free milk for the poor children and for the hospitals of Antwerp."

Pate was impressed with the dairy farm and the entire Hoogboom estate, which he later wrote "is a model for order and beauty of arrangement." He added, "One of the interesting customs that struck me particularly was the manner in which the horse stables were kept. Every stall was decorated with thatched straw held in place by interwoven red white and blue ribbons. In front of the stalls and through the carriage rooms the most elaborate designs were carried out in multicolored sands on the floors—which had to be renewed every two or three days."

When the group got to Calixberghe, they had lunch, and then Edouard Bunge showed Pate and Leach through the house, including a room "filled with collections from the Belgian Congo where he had large rubber holdings."

For Pate, the time spent with the Bunges was a short respite from the difficulties of relief work. It ended when he arose at 6:00 a.m. Monday morning and motored off with Edouard Bunge, who was heading down to Brussels that day. Once the two men reached Antwerp, they changed to the train and traveled a little differently than Pate was used to. As he noted later in his journal, Bunge was a "millionaire many times over," and yet he followed the Belgian custom of riding "in a stuffy, packed 3rd class car," which forced Pate, who was accompanying him, to do the same.

A few weeks later, the Bunges sent invitations to numerous delegates to come and spend Christmas Eve at Chateau Oude Gracht.

Prentiss Gray and his family (wife, Laura, and young daughter, Barbara) gratefully received and accepted the Bunge invitation. Gray needed the time off because he had spent much of December as the delegate of the northern French district of Valenciennes so that Phil Potter could get time off in London. The experience of seeing northern France and living with a German nurse had been highly stressful.

"Here," Gray noted on the first full day in northern France, "the appearance of the people is even more depressing than it is in Belgium. At first sight even, it is apparent that they are not only more emaciated, but are lacking in most of the things which, in Belgium, we still consider absolutely essential to life. When I talked to them they told me that they had had no meat except the Commission ration of bacon for more than six months. Occasionally a horse meets with an accident and the meat is sold readily for ten francs a kilo to a favored few."

Gray's living conditions were outwardly fine, in a house with two French servants, a German orderly named Ebben, and Gray's German officer, or nurse, Paul Neuerbourg, who had been the German who had stood up and confirmed the treatment of deportees at the April 1916 tea party in Charleroi. While the German officer had proved himself to be an honest man, he could also be cruel to subordinates, which was difficult for Gray to observe. In one incident, when their chauffeur turned down the wrong road, Neuerbourg "took out his riding whip and beat the fellow over the head for his supposed stupidity."

After one dinner, four other German officers came by, and Gray noted, "The evening party started." A few hours later, things had gotten somewhat out of hand, and Gray retired for the night. "By eleven o'clock they had the orderly, Ebben, sans [without] clothing, running around the table on all fours, busily eluding their kicks and barking like a dog for their edification."

Besides inviting the Gray family to spend Christmas with them, the Bunges also invited Milton Brown, Fred Eckstein, Gardner Richardson, and Pink Simpson—all of whom were favorites of the three Bunge sisters.

For Brown, it would be the first Christmas he had spent away from his family. He left Brussels after the usual weekly delegate meeting on Thursday afternoon, December 21, catching a ride with Richardson, who was the Antwerp delegate. From Antwerp, Brown went by himself and caught the tram out to Cappellen, then enjoyed the 15-minute walk from the station to the chateau. He especially loved the walk along the final long lane, which was guarded on both sides by ramrod-straight old trees and ended at the circular drive in front of the chateau. Isidore was there at the door to take his hat and coat and tell him he would inform the family of Brown's arrival. Isidore had another servant take Brown's small valise to an upstairs room and then showed him to the salon.

That evening, Brown enjoyed a quiet evening with just Edouard Bunge, Erica, Eva, and Hilda. Afterward, he followed an evening routine that he had come to love—he played billiards up in the billiard room with Edouard and Erica.

The following day, before the other delegates showed up, Brown went with two of the Bunge sisters to their other chateau at nearly Calixberghe. On the way there the three made a planned stopped at a school canteen in a village to watch the children get their daily bowl of soup and bread. They then went to Calixberghe and, as Brown wrote, "ate luncheon before a roaring big fire in the great hall." After that it was back to the school to hand out little gifts and listen to them recite and sing. "All in Flemish, of course, with the exception of a little sketch which four boys had learned in French (expressly for the benefit of the American visitor)."

On Friday evening Richardson arrived, and Brown wrote, "we had the usual evening of billiards, music (each of the girls is a finished musician either on the piano or vocally), fireside talk, etc."

The next morning, Brown worked all morning in his room while the three Bunge sisters were busy with their own work. Erica had numerous things to attend to, Brown noted, regarding the "direction of the farms." When Brown was finally done with his work, he joined the others. Soon, Pink Simpson and Fred Eckstein arrived. Prentiss, Laura, and Barbara Gray pulled up in their motorcar just before dinner, as did three young women cousins of the Bunges. On Saturday they had a boisterous dinner in the formal dining room.

On the morning of Christmas Eve, Sunday, the group of young Americans and Belgians had a game of field hockey out on the front lawn, which reminded Brown of his family's pickup games of baseball with the neighborhood kids in Glendale, Ohio.

That night, the cousins left for home, and the Bunges rode away in horse-drawn carriages to spend part of their Christmas Eve night with their grandmother in town. The Americans, cared for by the servants, were alone in the chateau. They had assumed it would be a quiet, simple dinner, but the Bunge sisters had had other plans. As Brown wrote his parents, "With their usual thoughtfulness and energy, busy as they had been, they had thought that perhaps we might be a bit blue on Christmas Eve, so far from all our loved ones."

When Isidore called them to dinner, they were completely surprised. Tiny evergreen trees were at each place setting, decorated with paper bonbons, tinsel, ornaments, and "countless little jokes and tricks for each of us and a few fireworks." A special Christmas tree had also been prepared for the Grays' daughter, Barbara.

The Americans were touched, but as Brown explained, "It didn't have the desired effect: Instead of making us gay, for the moment, at least, there was a bit of the blues around the table, and the glasses were often up [in toasts] to those dear ones so far, far away."

The toasts, it seemed, got a bit out of hand. Prentiss Gray added, "It was the first time that champagne had been served in the Bunge home since the beginning of the war and I am afraid we made up for lost time."

As the champagne and the Christmas spirit took over, the Americans repaid the Bunges as best they could. After dinner they all brought down from their rooms the small gifts they had each brought for the Belgians and arranged them around the Christmas tree the Bunges had prepared for Barbara.

When the Americans heard the carriages coming up the drive, they quickly lit candles and rushed out to greet the Bunges with Christmas carols. "It was something unexpected," Brown wrote, "and therefore I believe it pleased them immensely. Each [Bunge] had five or six presents, and as it was the only thing they had in the nature of a Christmas, its effect upon them made us very, very happy."

They all stayed up late, not wanting the moment to end. "It was far into Christmas morning before we retired," Gray noted.

Later, at a more reasonable hour on Christmas morning, the Bunges unwrapped the little gifts the Americans had brought. The delegates had gone in together to give a humidor to Edouard Bunge. "For the girls," Brown wrote his parents, "most of us had books, for that is the kind of girl each of them is: fond of the finer things of life, and the kind with whom we can frankly exchange ideas and opinions, and with whom we all have so much in common."

The Christmas tree in Chateau Oude Gracht. On Christmas Eve 1916, the American delegates and the Bunges stayed up late, not wanting the evening to end. Prentiss Gray said, "It was far into Christmas morning before we retired." (Author's archives.)

Even with a cold, rainy day, most of the group took a walk or visited the Bunge summer and winter farms and Erica's dairy. After dinner there was, according to Brown, another "splendid fireside evening of music—vocal, violin, cello, and piano."

Just before midnight on Christmas night, Brown was back in his room, writing a long letter to his family. He told them that he was spending Christmas weekend "with the dearest friends anyone of us has over here—a father whom we all admire as a splendid old gentleman, lovable and noble minded, and three perfectly delightful girls of wonderful character and accomplishment and energy. Thus, you see, being over here I could not possibly be happier."

He acknowledged that this Christmas was his "first away from you all, and the longing that is in my heart for each one of the dear ones is raging at its highest just now. But specifically, today of all days when the spirit of giving should be uppermost in our hearts I should have no regrets, should feel no unhappiness! It is the only time in the world I have had the opportunity of giving anything that cost me something, and whatever price I pay in my longing for home only reacts as a great pleasure to me, since it gives me the feeling of some sacrifice—however small—for what I am trying to give—the best that is in me!"

Brown did not mention that his love for Erica was growing and they had begun to talk in roundabout ways about a long-term future. Brown was very conscious of the fact that he had no real career prospects at the time and, therefore, could not ask Erica's father for her hand in marriage. But that did not stop the couple from talking about their future.

Brown also shared his thoughts with his friend Fred Eckstein, who was having similar feelings and thoughts about Eva Bunge.

Eckstein would be the first of the two Americans to take action in the new year.

Winter Rains Turn Severe

By late December, across much of Belgium and northern France, the weather turned foul. The normal winter rains came not with their soothing, gentle touch but with a vengeance that took many by surprise. It was as if the clouds were sick of the war and wanted to flush it all away. In the south the deluge was so bad that trains from Brussels to Tournai stopped running on a few days because parts of the line were underwater. CRB delegate Maurice Pate reported, "on account of heavy rains the country is under water in many places."

The new year would see it get worse.

And then a killer cold would come.

50

Brussels

The CRB Loses a Member Who Was "True as Steel"

On Christmas Eve, as some of the Americans celebrated with too much champagne at Chateau Oude Gracht, Baron Lambert, one of the CN executives, was hosting a dinner party in Brussels. In attendance was the jolly and festive Germàn Bulle, the Mexican chargé d'affaires who had been handling the securing of German passes for the CRB and the CN. The Americans truly loved the always-friendly Bulle and had even written a song about him:

When Bulle is the King of Mexico,
We'll have good positions,
And live on requisitions,
When Bulle is the King of Mexico.

At the end of the Lambert dinner, Bulle decided to walk home in the cold night air, accompanied by Count van der Straten-Ponthos of the Belgian foreign office. Part way home, the count suddenly realized Bulle was slurring his words; then it all turned to gibberish. He helped Bulle home, put him to bed, and sent for a doctor.

On Wednesday, December 27, 1916, Bulle passed away from the stroke he had suffered.

The British newspaper *Pall Mall Gazette* reported that he had been one of the CRB's "chief secretaries," whose father was a Norwegian who had moved to Mexico, become a citizen, and then married a Mexican woman. At the time of his son's death, the father was living in London with his two daughters, who both had homes in England. As for Germàn Bulle, the paper also speculated that "the breakdown of his health, which resulted in his death, may be traced to the devotion with which he worked for the commission of officials."

Whitlock, who had been a good friend, wrote, "There seemed to be nothing he could not do. Many a delicate mission he accomplished with me, many a little tangle he unravelled, many a little miracle he wrought."

Germàn Bulle, the Mexican chargé d'affaires, was considered a CRB delegate and loved by all the Americans. He died of a stroke on December 27, 1916. (Public domain; author's archives.)

On Saturday, December 30, at 1:00 p.m., all the CRB delegates from across Belgium and northern France came to Brussels for Bulle's funeral. Delegate Maurice Pate noted, "It was a very impressive ceremony attended by all the diplomats at Brussels as well as by the high German officers—since Bulle had been connected with the Mexican Embassy. Good-natured and kindly, he was one of the most beloved members of the CRB. The apoplectic stroke which caused his death—the first misfortune in Belgium to occur to a CRB man—was a great shock to us all."

Milton Brown wrote his family that Bulle "was one of the best liked men in the C.R.B.—a most intimate friend of mine—and one of the most popular men in Brussels. He was a Mexican of open, friendly nature, gentle and kind and of unbounded unselfishness. We shall miss him greatly around the office!"

Whitlock was more poetic and detailed in his description. "We buried him on a cold, dark winter morning, the last but one in the old year. In his little house in the Rue Joseph II he lay under flowers and the Mexican flag, in a room all black, amid the bewildering crackling of candles, with the concierge's two little children behind a curtain in the hall, broken-heartedly sobbing over the friend they had lost."

In the streets outside was a large crowd that Whitlock wrote included "every one I knew in Brussels; members of the Belgian Government who were left in the town, the remnants of the diplomatic corps, representatives of the C.N. and the C.R.B., and a half dozen German officers."

The international makeup of the crowd was not lost on Whitlock. "For one morning the war and its divisions were laid aside; for one morning even Belgians and Germans could meet in the community of affection and respect that one simple, modest, obscure life could inspire, and in the commonalty of sorrow that that kindly nature had left this earth."

"A great crowd in black," Whitlock noted, "followed the hearse on foot to the church of St.-Josse at the bottom of the Rue des Deux Eglises."

Whitlock, in his poetic rendering, neglected to mention there had nearly been an international incident that was so contradictory to how the man had lived his life. Prentiss Gray wrote, "During all his life, in a quiet, good humored way, [Bulle] has been smoothing out trouble. His funeral caused an outbreak of feeling that threatened disaster. As we all gathered in the Mexican Legation to pay our last respects, a discussion arose as to who should have precedence in walking behind the hearse."

According to Gray, two parties could not agree on how the procession should be. The Germans "bedecked in silver helmets and full regalia, insisted that, as the conquerors, they should precede Bulle's Belgian friends." The Belgians refused to be behind the Germans.

As the crowd waited outside to proceed, a compromise was finally struck. Two designated Belgians, one American, and one German would walk directly behind the hearse. Following them in exact order would be the diplomatic corps, the rest of the Germans, the rest of the Belgians, and the Americans of the CRB taking up the rear.

At the gravesite, everyone was asked to throw in a shovelful of dirt. "As we stood about the grave in the cold, drizzly rain," Gray wrote, "and listened to the sodden clods fall on the casket, I prayed that I should be allowed to escape alive from this land where they strode to make the last rites as harrowing as possible."

Hugh Gibson, a good friend of Bulle, heard the news at the American Embassy in London via the diplomatic pouch. Gibson summed up his strong feelings in a letter to his mother. "He was one of those rare people who was true as steel all the way through and it hurts to lose him."

SECTION IV

FAREWELL, JANUARY TO MAY 1917

In the first few months of 1917, Herbert Hoover was determined to ensure that food relief would continue even if America entered the war. Belgian children were the most affected by the war and the relief program. Not far behind were the destitute, who had little before the war and had practically nothing during the German occupation. (Both photos: public domain, children, Herbert Hoover Presidential Library Archives, West Branch, Iowa; adults, *The Millers' Belgian Relief Movement,* William C. Edgar, Northwestern Millers, 1915.)

51

London

Gibson Gets Entangled in More Than Relief

Back in December 1916, Ambassador Page's able-bodied secretary, Hugh Gibson, had done wonders with the reorganization of the embassy staff. He was a trusted adviser to Page, Hoover, and Britain's Foreign Office liaison Lord Eustace Percy. He had also become personal friends with Prime Minister Asquith, his wife, and their young daughter, Elizabeth.

During a British political crisis in December 1916, when Asquith was replaced as prime minister by Lloyd George, stories began to circulate in the press that 33-year-old Gibson and 19-year-old Elizabeth Asquith were having an affair or were planning to marry. It created a firestorm of negative press and gossip that brought unappreciated attention to Gibson and the Asquiths.

Gibson wrote his mother that he liked Elizabeth "very much—we are very congenial and get on extremely well together. Our friendship has not been affected by the rotten gossip, save for the fact that it makes it impossible for me to see anything of her without creating an awkward situation for her and starting the tongues wagging again. So *Gott strafe* [German for "God punish"] whoever started the stories." There was no talk of an engagement.

In a later book written by Elizabeth's mother, Margot Asquith, a footnote about Gibson stated, "Elizabeth Asquith announced her engagement to him during the political crisis of Dec. 1916; but they never married."

Regardless of whether or not there was an official engagement, the publicity was definitely unwanted and probably contributed to Gibson's taking to his bed with a bad case of the flu. Under doctor's orders he was bedridden for many days in late December. It was then that he received word that his friend, Germàn Bulle had had some kind of stroke in Brussels on the evening of December 23 and had died on December 27. Gibson's convalescence was aided by many friends who came by to see him, including Mrs. Asquith, who brought a potted plant and showed, by her appearance, that the family was not blaming Gibson for the bad press.

By Monday, New Year's Day, Gibson felt good enough to walk to his nearby office "to see if my legs still had hinges at the knee." He found the building empty except for Ambassador Page. The two men sat and caught up on all the news since Gibson's illness. But that little bit of exercise did him in and he had to decline an invitation from the Hoovers to come to a dinner that night to meet the fiancée of CRB delegate Duke Wellington; she had recently arrived from America.

A few days later, ex-Prime Minister Asquith came by to see Gibson. He noted that Asquith's "freedom from responsibility and the stay in the country have done him a world of good and he was in great form." After a little chit-chat, Asquith came to the point of his visit. He thanked Gibson for his "handsome and dignified behavior while the papers and the gossips were at work." Gibson reassured Asquith that he would "not appear in their vicinity for the present." Asquith said that "when things had blown over a bit I was to consider myself as welcome as ever at their house."

On Saturday, January 6, the no-longer-engaged Gibson attended Duke Wellington's wedding in St. Peter's Church in Eaton Square. The bride was Miss Dorothy Hancock Stiles, a 1914 graduate of Wellesley College who had sailed with her mother from America weeks before. Because her father had not come, Stiles was walked down the aisle by Ambassador Page. In attendance were many of the embassy staff and any of the CRB delegates who happened to be in London that day.

Only two days later, Gibson would take action that would alter the course of his life. Whether it was because of the December Asquith "scandal," his recent illness, his six-year absence from America, or a bit of all three, Gibson requested a leave of absence. On Monday, January 8, Page sent a telegram to the State Department: "Gibson's health requires immediate rest and change and as he has not been able to visit his home since 1911. I respectfully request he be granted short leave of absence with permission to visit the United States forthwith. May I have immediate reply in order that he may have the opportunity of sailing next Saturday with Hoover."

Two days later the request was granted. Gibson was going home and would sail on the SS *Philadelphia* with Hoover.

He would never return to his London embassy job, and his long European involvement with the CRB, including his influence on critical moments in the early stages, was over.

Hoover's Take on the Deportations

Two days before the end of 1916 Hoover had received from the State Department a request for his opinion regarding the issue of forced labor. Four days later, on Tuesday, January 2, 1917, Hoover replied with a statement that held mostly bad news.

"There has been no apparent change in German policy since the President's protest, deportation continuing on a large scale—now apparently three to five thousand per week." Hundreds of those, he said, were Belgian CRB employees. Reports from multiple sources had the Germans forcing men to do work in trench construction and, in some cases, they were so close to the front that some deportees had "recently returned wounded by shellfire." Those who refused work "met with refusal of food and other brutal acts."

Hoover stressed that "the assurances given to President [Wilson] that only unemployed were taken, and that they are not employed on military work or brutally treated, are absolutely untrue, not only before but since the assurances were given."

He did give von Bissing and his German civil government a bit of acknowledgment in the face of the military's overall control. "It does appear that the civil government in Brussels has made some efforts to prevent brutality in selection, to confine selections to unemployed, and to protect the employees of the Commission, and they have even solicited complaints, but they appear unable to control the military press gangs or effect any remedies."

After his meeting with Lord Grey in early December, Hoover was able to write the State Department about one relatively positive situation. "I am now convinced that the . . . [Allied] Governments will take no action against the Relief as a consequence of these deportations, as they are convinced that stoppage of relief would be no remedy, and, they generally recognize, would only accentuate the misery."

Hoover was still, however, worried about the Belgians and northern French, who were "now in a state of complete terror." He was also concerned about his young, idealistic staff of CRB delegates, who had to watch the deportations of people they had grown to love and respect. "It is difficult for us to control the natural feeling of our staff and we can only hope that no untoward incident may occur." Hoover was probably thinking of Hallam Tuck, one of the best of his delegates, who had left in December 1916 to join the British Army because he could not contain his anger and frustration, nor remain neutral, after seeing multiple deportations.

Acknowledging to the State Department that at the time any further U.S. protests against the deportations would only "produce irritation and the usual denials," Hoover recommended that President Wilson send a "personal and private" letter to the Emperor appealing to his humanity to stop the forced labor. He also spelled out the point Wilson might make: "If Germany is genuinely anxious for peace she can scarcely hope for sympathetic sentiment to grow abroad . . . with these acts, and that a total cessation of the deportations and forced labor and the return of the deported Belgians and French to their homes would be not only an act of great magnanimity but also of the greatest assistance in the promotion of peace sentiment."

In a later letter on the deportations, this one addressed directly to Secretary of State Lansing, Hoover not only covered the same issues but brought up another related one that "I do not think has been generally understood."

"The Belgian people," Hoover explained, "are entirely seized with the fact that labour of any kind which they perform for the Germans is of assistance to their enemies. In consequence, great numbers of them are resolute to the point of death in refusal to perform such labour. The Deportees are regarded as martyrs and are not expected to ever return. The reflex of this is a state of terror in the population beyond anything which has been known during the last hundred years."

Hoover's extreme frustration and anger was evident in his concluding paragraph. "It is useless for me to emphasize these points to you, despite my deep feeling in the matter. Its premeditation and dimensions make it the greatest crime against human liberty which the world has witnessed since the war began."

Nothing seemed to work against the German military's determination that the deportations continue. Hoover summed up the situation later: "Although the deportations continued despite diplomatic protests and a hostile world opinion, the Allies did not carry out their threat to put a stop to relief. They recognized, as did the members of the Commission, that while the responsibility might be placed on the Germans, it was the Belgians and French who would suffer the consequences. The Commission did what it could to mitigate the suffering caused by this policy, and to secure the return to Belgium of relief employees who had been deported."

Following Hoover's State Department message on January 2, Whitlock finally made a formal protest to von der Lancken on Wednesday, January 10. It had no discernible impact.

On Saturday, January 20, the deportations would finally come to Brussels.

Between those two events, Hoover would sail for America on Saturday, January 13, aboard the SS *Philadelphia* with Gibson. The ship's list of first-class passengers records a Harold Hoover and identifies his profession as "traveller." (No evidence was found to indicate Hoover was trying to travel incognito; the errors were probably made by the recorder.) The list also shows that Hoover's friend and confidant Hugh Gibson was aboard.

Hoover would be frustratingly far away from London when the biggest crisis in the life of the relief program struck.

52

Brussels

The Deportations Come to Brussels

On Wednesday, January 10, 1917, when legation Minister Whitlock finally made a formal protest to the Germans, he addressed it to Baron von der Lancken of the political department and asked that it be forwarded to von Bissing. It was not a blanket condemnation of the entire deportation program. Whitlock, as one of the three Minister Protectors of the CRB and CN relief efforts, lodged the protest strictly in regard to the CRB and CN Belgian employees who had been taken, particularly since they had been taken even though the men had held the white employment cards approved by the German civil government.

Whitlock reminded von der Lancken of the governor general's promise of July 1915 that the CRB and CN would be allowed the freedom to do the work of relief, and he stated that taking protected employees had put that work in jeopardy. Acknowledging that in some places the employment cards had been honored, he also detailed places where "not only has no account been taken of them but the military authorities have torn them up, saying that they were without value."

No matter how von der Lancken and von Bissing personally felt about the deportations—and indications were that they were not fully supportive of the policy—they had no say in the matter since Hindenburg, Ludendorff, and the military had taken control of the German government.

After Whitlock's protest, it was only 10 days before the deportations came to Brussels. When the Germans brought these slave raids (as many referred to them) to the Belgian capital, they did not introduce them in the same way they had done in countless villages and small towns across the country. No bold *affiches* were posted declaring that men of certain ages had to appear at the train station on a specific day and time.

The reason was obvious. Residents of Brussels were known to gather around and collectively read posted *affiches*, remarking and reacting to whatever was written. In such an atmosphere, and in such a large metropolitan area, deportation posters might channel and amplify individual anger, fear, and frustration into group action. The Germans had no interest in facing mass protests or riots, so public announcement of the deportations was out.

Instead, the Germans worked behind the scenes. They first developed lists of the unemployed throughout the city and then printed thousands of yellow cards. Each card told the recipient to be at the Gare du Midi train station on the morning of Saturday, January 20. In a classic carrot-and-stick approach, each card had an offer of employment and a threat of a fine for those who did not appear. During the week before January 20, the police began laboriously handing out the cards to those on the German-developed unemployed lists.

The change from *affiches* to individual cards had the desired result. Brand Whitlock wrote, "The effect was not that instantaneous sensation which the posting of an *affiche* produced in a village, but the news percolated gradually and created its horror."

As the cards were being distributed, the Germans added insult to injury two days before the event by releasing a long statement justifying the deportations as beneficial to the Belgian people. Signed by Governor Lieutenant General Hurt (von Bissing was sick and recuperating in Germany), it did not shy away from acknowledging what the world had thought of the deportations.

"Protestations full of phraseology are raised against this measure, as much in the occupied territory of Belgium as in the countries of neutrals or enemies. Big words serving as a ground for these protestations are principally: 'Violation of international law,' 'Assault on the dignity and on the liberty of Belgian working men,' 'Crime on humanity and on the family life,' 'Slavery and forced labour as for criminals.' . . . Up to the present time this design has failed because of the good sense of the population. However, under the effect of excitations without measure a certain number of working men sent away continue to esteem that the 'honour' and 'patriotism' demand that they refuse to go to work."

Hurt followed by reminding readers that for years there had been "several hundreds of thousands of unemployed seeking occupation in vain." For those, "public charity is not sufficient," and many of them "have left the straight path . . . [and] the love of gambling and of idleness have increased in large measures."

The Germans, Hurt wrote, were trying to correct these problems. Addressing each of the charges he had listed against the deportations, he then asked rhetorically: "Is it to the advantage of working men's families that many fathers, sons, and brothers acquire the habit of laziness or become thieves and criminals and finish as wrecks in prisons? Is it not more human to compel the unemployed to work to gain the necessary bread for their families?"

In a surprising admission at the end of the statement, Hurt did confirm that "some errors and mistakes were committed" in earlier deportations when employed men were taken. But Hurt blamed that on the local communes that did not furnish lists of their unemployed. Even so, Hurt stated that von Bissing had looked into those cases and "brought about the return of those persons who were wrongly sent away."

The day the Brussels deportations began, the weather seemed to signal its own objection. The early morning hours had seen a quick snowstorm whip through the city, followed by a frigid, arctic sunrise. Out of the winter darkness came the men trudging down the ancient cobbled streets. Small groups of 10 and 20 walked together, some of the men heavily bundled against the cold, others shivering without overcoats against the biting wind. Accompanying them were women and children, clinging, holding, grasping to say one last goodbye.

Taking no chances on whether or not the people of Brussels had accepted Hurt's reasoning for the deportations, the military was out in full force. The streets around the train station were blocked off by a squadron (more than 150) of the dreaded *uhlan* cavalry. The horsemen—carrying long pikes with razor-sharp steel tips—brutally rode continually through the growing crowd, never letting the people stand in one place for any length of time and restricting all but those with yellow cards from passing through to the train station. Inside, German officers waited to pass judgment as to left or right, freedom or deportation. Cattle cars waited on the tracks for the unlucky.

CRB Director Warren Gregory had obtained permission for delegates to be there as observers and for CN personnel to hand out a loaf of bread to each who was chosen. For the unlucky Belgians told to go right, the CRB and CN men at the station were the last stop—the last small piece of kindness and normalcy—before they stepped into the cattle cars bound for Germany.

That first day 750 men appeared at the station and more than 300 were taken. The deportations continued for several days, but the weather grew increasingly worse, as an arctic cold front bore down on the Belgian capital. Whitlock wrote, "At last even the Germans were moved; they announced on Thursday [January 25] that the deportations would be suspended."

By then hundreds more had been taken. Whitlock did admit, however, that Brussels "did not suffer in comparison with other places." He meant that generally the Germans had honored the CRB's and CN's white employment cards and had treated the Belgians with restraint. This was no doubt due to German concerns that the world was probably watching much closer in Brussels than it had in lesser-known hamlets, towns, and villages.

In the end, the deportations across Belgium and northern France stimulated more than anger or resignation. Whitlock concluded in his official State Department report, the German deportations had "lighted a fire of hatred that will never go out; they have brought home to every heart in the land, in a way that will impress its horror indelibly on the memory of three generations, a realisation of what German methods mean—not, as with the early atrocities, in the heat of passion and the first lust of war, but by one of those deeds that make one despair of the future of the human race, a deed coldly planned, studiously matured, and deliberately and systematically executed, a deed so cruel that German soldiers are said to have wept in its execution, and so monstrous that even German officers are now said to be ashamed."

The deportations also had the unfortunate result of turning some Belgians against the previously loved Americans. The Belgians remembered how the Americans had been able to stop the deportations from Lille in April 1916. Why couldn't they do so again? And if they couldn't stop them, why didn't their government declare war against the inhuman Huns? Whitlock wrote in his journal the night after the first Brussels deportations, "Saddest of all is the fact that Belgians now detest the Americans as much as anybody, because the United States does not go to war over the deportations!"

Peace Feelers Have Little Impact

The newly developed Belgian anti-American feeling was softened slightly a few days later when President Wilson's January 22 speech to the U.S. Senate was partially published in the German-controlled Belgian press. The president's speech outlined what he and America felt was needed for a lasting peace, including a "League for Peace." This concept of peace-with-purpose heartened some while frustrating others. Earlier, the Germans had put out general feelers regarding peace but the Allied governments had come back with numerous conditions unacceptable to the Germans.

The Germans were not happy with how their peace overture had been taken. Whitlock received confirmation of this with two firsthand accounts. Dr. Vernon Kellogg had recently returned from Charleville, where he had spent time with top German generals. He reported to Whitlock that "the generals down there are in a blind rage over the failure of the peace plans, and were furiously determined to pull down the pillars of the world." Affirming such dark sentiments was Baron von der Lancken, who was just back from Berlin and told Whitlock that "the military party was in the saddle." All of which meant, Whitlock wrote, "The Germans felt that the war was nearing its end, and that they could not win, and that, maddened by the response the Allies had made to the peace overtures, they would make war more frightful than ever."

In the midst of such German frustrations, Brussels had to endure the celebration of the Kaiser's 58th birthday on Saturday, January 27. A major part of the festivities was the firing of a string of cannons that CRB delegate Hunt said "frowned down upon the city" from the heights beside the "Acropolis of Brussels"—the majestic *palais de justice*, a half mile south of the *grand place*.

While the firing of the cannons must have been grating for residents to hear, the loud salutes did bring some unexpected joy—Whitlock related: "To the delight of the Belgians the [Germans'] horses reared and injured eight soldiers."

A touch of the surreal was added to the day when in the *grand place* the Germans, according to Whitlock, "acted a comedy! German officers mounted to the portico of the Hotel de Ville [city hall] and the Maison du Roi [house of the king], waving handkerchiefs to the crowds below—crowds composed of the horde of German civilians at Brussels summoned to impersonate the Brussels populace before the cinematographic machines that were industriously grinding in the corners of the beautiful square, taking pictures to be reproduced later as proof of the love the Belgians bore the invaders of their land, their homes, their liberties and their honour."

Even with such moments of inadvertent levity, the end of January felt nearly hopeless to Whitlock. "These days, the last in that dark month of January . . . were so cold, so still and so highly charged with foreboding."

On Wednesday night, January 31, Whitlock received word that Baron von der Lancken wanted to see him the next morning. As he wrote in his journal, it was "on very urgent business. What can it be? I have grown so nervous that apprehension is my companion, living in the midst of alarms. What can it be that is so very urgent?"

Everything would change with what von der Lancken had to tell him.

Brown's Clothing Efforts Finally Get a Break

As the deportations continued and signs were beginning to point to a possible American break with Germany, all the CRB delegates wondered what would happen to them and to the Belgians in their care. For most, it was a time of extreme anxiety but also one filled with the desire to somehow ensure the work would go on.

Milton Brown had been focusing on studying and reporting on the CN's clothing operations. That mission had been stymied in large part by the CN's clothing director, Emmanuel Janssen, who had refused to give Brown information he needed to make complete reports of how the Belgian system was set up. Even Brown's Belgian counterpart, Madame Philippson-Wiener, who he sensed liked and respected him, seemed to avoid him and arbitrarily refused to meet with him at various times.

By early 1917, that had changed. Brown explained, "The British Government sent word into Brussels that no more [clothing] stuffs could be imported until they received some sort of report on the control system in force and on the needs of the country." That had had the desired effect on Janssen. "He finally came to," Brown wrote, "the cause of the difficulties being so plainly brought home to him" by the British demands.

Janssen would finally allow Brown access to most of the information he needed to provide the British with a complete understanding of the Belgian clothing processes and what the country needed. Brown couldn't help but let slip a few notes of resentment when he wrote, "And then—after I had been asking the permission to do just that thing for months and months passed—[Janssen] sat there in a meeting of the [Division] du Vêtements and begged me to go to London and make a report upon these things. And not only that but he covertly blamed me and blamed the CRB for the situation in which the country found itself as regards clothing!"

At that critical stage, however, Brown was suddenly given an added duty due to a shortage of American men. In mid-January, CRB Director Warren Gregory asked him to take on temporarily the job of chief delegate to Namur Province from Francis Wickes, who would be absent. Brown began spending half a week in Brussels compiling critical information on the clothing situation and half a week down in Namur Province supervising a new delegate, 60-year-old Carlos H. Stone.

Even with the added duty, Brown found time for meetings with Madame Philippson-Wiener in which they discussed what might happen and what they might be able to do right away to help the clothing situation. They both realized, as did many others involved in the clothing department, that "very drastic action must be taken to provide the destitute with clothing, bedding, shoes, for the succeeding winter." A determination was made that the Division du Vêtements would compile lists of all materials that were considered necessary for the coming year and give them to the CRB in hopes that somehow the items on all the lists could be supplied.

When it came to his fellow CRB delegates, Brown mostly found apathy regarding the clothing issue. He knew the men were focused on the food relief and viewed clothing as a secondary priority. Brown began to believe it was his personal duty to focus on the clothing needs and promised Madame Philippson-Wiener that he would somehow get those needs met.

He also knew the task would be an uphill battle. Even if he could somehow bring together a huge clothing order and convince Hoover that it needed to be filled, he believed the British would probably never approve it. That was because Brown was aware, more than most, of two critical pieces of information—there were still native stocks related to the making of clothing left in Belgium (albeit small amounts) and the Germans had requisitioned "very considerable quantities from the country," and continued to do so.

The British had known for some time that the Germans were requisitioning raw materials for clothes making and had protested strongly to Hoover and the CRB back in early 1916. While there had been "a very energetic attempt" to get the Germans to guarantee to not requisition such materials, it "finally was abandoned." The primary reason why the British allowed clothing shipments to resume was because of Hoover's establishment of the Inspection and Control Department and the clothing department. These two departments had given the British confidence that no *imported* materials would be requisitioned. They could then turn a relative blind eye to the small amounts of native stocks being taken.

Because both departments would have questionable futures if the CRB delegates had to leave Belgium because America entered the war, Brown was doubtful the British would allow a big order of clothes and clothing material into Belgium.

That did not stop him, however, from working toward that goal.

The Belgians Continue Their Passive Resistance

In the early days of 1917, it was obvious to many that the occupation was getting harsher and harsher. Each day the war dragged on, German frustrations seemed to rise and actions against Belgian civilians increased.

From the American delegates' perspective, the occupation was in many cases a matter of freedom of their speech. "We had not dared speak of subjects nearest our hearts," delegate William Percy explained. "We knew we were being watched and ears were everywhere. We were not anxious to say things, but we were choked by the things we were forbidden to say. Americans at home cannot possibly know what that feeling is, and so they cannot possibly appreciate the freedom so abundantly theirs."

The Belgians understood. They knew the consequences of what was said, worn, or done that could mean fines, prison, or in the extreme, execution by firing squad. Nevertheless, they took the chance whenever and wherever they could to show their oppressors they were not completely vanquished.

One cold winter's night, Percy saw and heard the courage of the Belgians in one small patriotic act. He was walking along a wide Brussels boulevard. "Ice glinted from the trees, snow was deep and dry on the ground, pedestrians were hurrying home for supper through the crunchy silence."

Suddenly, there came a whistling, sharp and clear, cutting through the cold air. It was a tune that Percy quickly realized was the French national anthem, "La Marseillaise." The Germans had outlawed any singing, playing, or whistling of the tune and anyone caught doing so could be sentenced to prison.

"I looked around for the dare-devil whistler and saw instead the other passers-by becoming aware of what was happening." They all knew the consequences of such an act. "Everyone stopped or looked over his shoulder or into the eyes of those near him; everyone straightened up, quickened his step, and smiled. One after another we located the brash offender and were filled with warmth and excitement."

The man who was snubbing his nose at the Germans was "a hulking young driver of a van pulled by two magnificent Percherons. Slouched over the reins, devil-may-care, in his workman's corduroys and broad red sash, without lifting his eyes or looking right or left, he whistled piercingly and accurately from end to end the forbidden thrilling music."

For a brief moment in time, all those within earshot regained a sense of dignity, pride, and independence that was rarely felt anymore in German-occupied

Fidelis (Latin for "faithful") was the pen name for Albert van de Kerckhove, who wrote scathing articles about von Bissing. He also brazenly broke into the governor general's office. (Public domain; *Histoire de* La Libre Belgique *Clandestine*, Pierre Goemaere, Bureaux de *La Libre Belgique*, Bruxelles, 1919.)

Belgium. It was a quiet, subtle scene of courageous patriotism that Percy would never forget.

Nowhere was Belgium's passive resistance better illustrated than in the existence of *La Libre Belgique*, which always seemed to appear once a week. And the regular columnists voiced that resistance. All known by pen names, one of the most popular was Fidelis (Latin for "faithful"). He was a man named Albert van de Kerckhove and he had coined the nickname "B-singe" ("double monkey") for von Bissing. He also wrote scathing editorials about the editor of the German-controlled *Bruxellois* newspaper, which he called part of the "bochified" press.

In early 1917, *La Libre Belgique* was going strong, even though 52 people had been arrested in various raids during the last few months of 1916. The paper was still a thorn in the side of the governor general and was about to become even more so with two different events that would personally impact von Bissing. One was from a spontaneous moment; the other came from extensive planning. They both happened in January 1917 as the governor general was recuperating from an illness.

The first involved his staff officers, who became unwitting accessories. The men had wanted to curry favor with von Bissing, so after he was awarded a medal from the Kaiser, they decided to give a small gift to his wife, Baroness von Bissing, as a souvenir of the occasion. They chose a small bronze ornament. At the time, because the baroness was in Berlin, an officer wrapped up the gift and sent it off by post. When von Bissing's wife opened the package, she found the gift wrapped in a copy of *La Libre Belgique*. One history explained that some of the Belgian staff at the central post office were sub-distributors of the newspaper. One of them must have acted spontaneously after seeing the addressee.

The second event was much more serious and potentially dangerous. When von Bissing had become governor general of Belgium, he had requisitioned a chateau in a village on the outskirts of Brussels for his private use. He also took over a mansion in the city, which became his office and personal command center.

The ground floor held offices of his military staff while upstairs was his office and the office of his aide-de-camp.

According to a retelling by *Underground News*, during the lunch hour on a day in January when von Bissing was at his country home, two men approached the mansion in the city. One was dressed as a high-ranking German officer "complete with monocle and medals." The other was a tall, distinguished gentleman, impeccably dressed and carrying a briefcase. They confidently walked in and strode past a startled orderly stationed in the hall who quickly leaped to attention. The two intruders barely acknowledged him as they turned a corner and made for the staff offices.

With most personnel at lunch, the two intruders quickly made their way to a door at the end of the hall. The civilian knew his way around, and the two quickly took the back stairs to von Bissing's office. They spent a half an hour riffling through his papers and documents, taking what they wanted. Before they departed, they left a copy of the recent issue of *La Libre Belgique*.

Underground News concluded the story with a nod to the identity of the civilian leading the way: "That evening the officer, no longer an officer, was well on his way to the frontier with a wad of interesting documents concealed on his person. In his study [the civilian] Fidelis was chuckling as he visualised von Bissing's face when he discovered a copy of the *Libre Belgique* among his rifled papers."

With such brazen actions, and the continual barrage of defiant articles in the newspaper that could not be stopped, it wouldn't be surprising to believe what many Belgians thought—that von Bissing's illness was due in part to the frustration he must have felt toward that hated *La Libre Belgique*.

53

Elsewhere in Belgium

Flooding Followed by Arctic Cold

By January 1917, the heavy rains that had soaked Belgium from mid-December to late December were taking their toll.

On New Year's Day, in the city of Tournai in the western part of Belgium near the French border, delegate Maurice Pate went out to inspect the areas of the city flooded by the Scheldt River. Accompanied by a Belgian engineer, the two men went "in a rowboat and made a tour in our Venetian gondola through the streets where the water was 2 to 4 feet deep. All the inhabitants of the quarter were living in their second stories." When Pate and his companion came across an older woman alone in her house, they offered her some bread and fresh water. She gladly accepted and used a rope to hoist up the supplies to her second-floor window.

Within a few days the water in Tournai had subsided, but then a bitter cold swept across Belgium and Holland. Soon, daytime temperatures were hovering between 0 and 10 degrees Fahrenheit, and the vital canals—the primary roadways of relief from Rotterdam—began to freeze.

On Friday, January 26, Prentiss Gray wrote in his journal, "The weather has been gradually getting colder for the past week. This morning it was eighteen below zero, centigrade [–4 degrees Fahrenheit]. Before nightfall, reports began coming in that the canals had frozen in a great many places. We still hope to keep them open with ice breakers, without undue disturbance to our water transport."

Pate declared, "The most important question of the moment is the freezing of the canals. Water transport is now stopped and all CRB goods must be brought in by rail." This necessitated the creation of "an entirely new system of making food shipments by rail, and with the present demand for rolling stock every place in Europe this was a rather difficult task."

The approximately 100,000 tons of foodstuffs brought into Belgium monthly were in serious jeopardy.

As the transportation crisis continued to grow, a larger one suddenly appeared.

In late January and early February 1917, arctic weather froze Rotterdam harbor and most of the Belgian canals, which were the primary roadways of food relief. This photo shows men in Rotterdam harbor trying to break up the ice. (Public domain; Herbert Hoover Presidential Library Archives, West Branch, Iowa.)

54

Brussels

A New Devastating German Policy Is Announced

Arriving diplomatically early for his 10:00 a.m. appointment on Thursday, February 1, legation Minister Whitlock was shown into von der Lancken's "yellow salon, the scene of so many anxious, so many difficult, so many painful hours during those years." Choosing to not yet take his usual chair at the marble-topped table in the center of the room, Whitlock stood at a window staring out onto the bleak, snow-covered park and the Rue Ducale. He noted how the winter had been so harsh that the seagulls, which usually stayed closer to the North Sea, had been driven inland and were everywhere in the city, begging for food. The Belgians, he wrote, were seen many times "standing in the cold and flinging [the seagulls] the crumbs they could hardly spare."

Whitlock was pulled from his thoughts by Spanish Minister Marquis de Villalobar, who entered the room and came to stand beside him. He turned to Whitlock and in an effort to once again show his insider knowledge of situations, confidentially stated what the news would be from von der Lancken. The American was a bit taken aback: "Somehow for a second I was glad that the moment at last had come, glad that a situation so long impossible was at last made clear, above all that neutrality was at an end."

It was then that Dutch Minister Mynheer van Vollenhoven joined them. The group was complete—the three patron ministers of relief for Belgium and northern France were assembled to hear what von der Lancken had to say.

A short time later, Baron von der Lancken swept into the room in his gray uniform and well-worn leather leggings, obviously just in from a brisk morning's horseback ride in the city's park. Whitlock had learned to read the German's face. This time, von der Lancken "was pale, with those black circles under his eyes that always showed there when he was troubled or concerned." As the men settled into their usual chairs at the table, three more Germans they knew well (known only as Bucher, Dr. Reith, and Dr. Brohn) joined them.

Von der Lancken became formal and addressed the three ministers solemnly, confirming what Villalobar had just told Whitlock. "Gentlemen, I have an important communication to make to you, one concerning the submarine war. I address you in your capacity as protecting Ministers. The question concerns the revictualing [relief]."

Von der Lancken explained that the day before, on January 31, 1917, German Foreign Secretary Arthur Zimmermann had informed U.S. Ambassador Gerard of Germany's establishment of a war zone and blockade along the coasts of England, France, Spain, and Italy. Any ships—neutral or belligerent—caught in the war zone would be sunk without prior warning. Germany's unrestricted submarine warfare had begun again (after being halted by the Kaiser in 1915 after the sinking of the *Lusitania*).

Baron von der Lancken declared that the Germans still wanted the relief to continue. A statement was read that "the Imperial Government has not the slightest intention of hindering the work of the *ravitaillement* of Belgium." But the Germans demanded that the CRB keep its ships outside the war zone and strongly recommended that the CRB "divert by an immediate notice all ships *en route* toward those waters situated outside the forbidden zone. The ships that do not give heed to such a notice will do so at their own risk and peril." Von der Lancken passed out copies of the various documents and little maps that showed the war zone around Great Britain, France, Spain, and Italy.

Villalobar, after reviewing the lines around Spain, turned to von der Lancken and declared, "You haven't left us room enough even to go in bathing!"

Whitlock studied the war zone lines and felt "those dead lines across which—incredible insolence!—American ships were not to pass. . . . I knew what America would say, and yet just then, studying for the moment those charts, we did not discuss that question." Whitlock knew that unrestricted submarine warfare would be totally unacceptable to America. He was sure the Germans' renewed military strategy would draw America into the war.

The assembled group discussed the situation, which Whitlock acknowledged "was so far beyond any decision of ours, or any hope of change, since it represented the will of the military party, whose steady rise to autocratic power in Germany had been revealed by the successive measures of the deportations." He also noted that von Bissing was in the process of dying and "was no longer the depository of sovereign power in Belgium but a mere figurehead in whose name the General Staff governed Belgium, as it governed the *etape* and the north of France."

Shortly, the group decided to send for Émile Francqui and CRB Director Warren Gregory, who came quickly. Discussion ranged across numerous topics and side topics. Whitlock was glad that Gregory was there because "his legal mind, his clear conceptions, his logical thought, always pertinent and to the point, helped us to a decision that meant much for Belgium."

The group decided that Gregory and Francqui would go immediately to Holland. Gregory was to communicate with Hoover and the London CRB; Francqui was to telegraph King Albert, contact the exiled Belgian government in Le Havre, and meet with the French minister in The Hague—all to convince them to pressure the British to continue the relief. Van Vollenhoven would follow shortly so he could consult with the Dutch government.

As a way of getting the CRB ships to avoid the war zone completely, telegrams would be sent to each government to suggest that the British allow CRB ships to be checked for contraband in either New York or Rotterdam so they would not have to stop in English ports as they had been doing. The question remained whether or not the British would allow the relief ships to continue without stopping at British ports.

It was understood implicitly that the German military was renewing unrestricted submarine warfare in a belief that the action would end the war quickly. And even if the strategy did draw the Americans into the war, few Germans felt America could arm and engage in the conflict with any significance before the war would be over.

One of the Germans in the room, Dr. Brohn, commented in English on the submarine strategy: "It is hard, but in the end it is kind, for we must end [the war]. It is like a surgical operation."

"Yes, it must be finished," von der Lancken added in French.

When the meeting broke up, Whitlock noted, "Villalobar remaining as he always does, for his secret talk afterwards."

Returning to the legation, Whitlock worked all afternoon on a telegram to President Wilson, sent it off, then waited. He knew it could be days, if not longer, before a reply came. "And yet," he wrote, "I was perfectly certain of the answer; it would be war, inevitable from that moment in August, 1914, when the two old systems clashed once more in a world that . . . had grown too small for both to live in it any longer together."

In his journal, the minister wrote, "What madness, what stupidity, this war! I am too tired, too worried to think, or to write."

Another Mass Trial—Le Roux's Time Is Up

On Tuesday, February 13, 1917, another German mass trial of Belgians accused of aiding *La Libre Belgique* was held. This time the military tribunal was in Brussels, within the ornate senate chambers of Belgium's parliament building.

Presiding over the trial was a panel of German officers, each with his spiked helmet and leather gloves set perfectly beside him. The judge advocate was Dr. Stoeber, a ruthless interrogator known for securing hefty prison sentences. Four Belgian lawyers were present for the defendants, but once again they were not allowed to see or talk with their clients or review any files before the trial. They weren't even allowed to wear their usual robes and were instead dressed in street clothes.

From the 52 people who had been initially apprehended, 41 were accused of crimes and were brought in as a group. They sat together on benches before each one had to stand alone and face the judges and Dr. Stoeber's questions. The youngest was 13-year-old Jacques Massardo.

From the start, it was obvious the prosecution wasn't as prepared or as efficient as the one in Charleroi. The judge advocate did not have the benefit of a German detective like Grisenbrock to aid in the preparation or interrogations, and didn't even seem to understand the "relative importance of the accused."

Benefiting the defendants—and much like the previous Charleroi mass trial—was the fact that the underground paper had continued to come out and was filled with all the usual columnists. This seemed to mean that the ringleader of the paper and the regular contributors had not been captured, therefore diminishing the importance of those standing trial.

Nevertheless, the prosecution had to show to the judges that the accused were relevant. Early on it was obvious to those watching that Gustave Snoeck, the Antwerp bank manager who had run the city's major distribution depot, was seen as the most important person captured. He was questioned repeatedly about his position in the organization and who was further up the chain of command. Through his captivity and questioning, he never revealed more than what the Germans already knew.

His sentence reflected the Germans' perception of his level of importance. He was given nine years of hard labor and a fine of 3,000 marks.

Madame Massardo pleaded with the court to let her children go. They had been sitting in St. Gilles Prison since October. In the end, the mother received a two-year prison sentence, her daughter and 17-year-old son were given six months each, and her 13-year-old son received three months.

One of the accused, Albert Dankelman, was the only one who knew Le Roux and could have given him up, but he didn't. He admitted to distributing 10,000 copies of the paper, but nothing more. He was given a three-year sentence. One person was acquitted while six, who were simply relatives of those accused, were let go.

The *Underground News* concluded the description of the trial on a humorous note. "While Doktor Stoeber was making his final speech to the Tribunal, exhorting the judges to show no mercy to 'these traitors,' a [German] *Polizei* outside was unwittingly acting as sandwichman for the *Libre Belgique*, patrolling up and down before the Senate with a copy of the latest issue, No. 111, hanging from the tail of his tunic, to which it had been pinned by a nimble urchin."

The day the Germans finally came for Le Roux, the sun never appeared, at least not in Brussels. Friday, February 16, 1917, began as a cloud-filled, miserable morning of cold rain and sleet that pounded against windowpanes with a depressing insistence. A good day to sleep in. Le Roux had wanted to, but knew he was expected at a funeral of a Belgian soldier who had finally died from wounds suffered years before, during the invasion. He reluctantly dragged himself out of bed.

If he had not done so, he would have been with his wife in the shop at 11:30 a.m., when two German secret police walked in.

Even though husband and wife had planned for that day and had expected it for many months, Madame Le Roux was still taken aback for a moment. They asked for her husband. She said he was in town on business as she hurriedly began thinking of what she could do to warn him of the danger. She knew there was no escape for her, but she had to do something to try and save her husband.

The men told her she was under arrest for aiding her husband in publishing *La Libre Belgique*. They demanded to know where the copies of the paper were. When she refused, they began to search the shop, tearing apart displays, pulling out drawers, emptying them on the floor, and clearing off countertops with the swipe of an arm.

As she stared at them working, she finally remembered what she and her husband had decided. If there was ever any trouble, the person in the shop should put up the "closed" sign, if possible. But how to do that?

It was then that the men, frustrated at not finding anything incriminating, demanded to be shown the basement. *Underground News* described what happened next:

> *"One moment," she said. And, picking up the notice she had been tentatively fingering, she walked to the door.*
>
> *"What are you doing?" demanded the man suspiciously.*
>
> *"Nothing wrong, I suppose," retorted Madame Le Roux. "I can't leave the shop open and unattended, especially in this state. If you want me in the cellar . . ."*
>
> *"So . . . I will see to that." He took the notice from her.*
>
> *"As you like," she replied, watching the man with feigned indifference, as he hung the card on the door. Almost jubilant now she led the way downstairs.*

And with that small gesture from the secret policeman, Le Roux was saved. Walking back from the funeral, he had actually put his hand on the shop's doorknob when he spotted the closed sign and the disarray inside. He hurried away as his wife continued to show the Germans the cellar.

The irony of the entire situation was that the arrest was not facilitated by one of Le Roux's extensive connections he had built up as the hub of the newspaper. It was from his earliest days of working for the newspaper, when he was merely a sub-distributor with only 50 clients. For sentimental reasons, he had always kept those 50 clients and had personally still delivered every issue to them. One of those 50 had been caught with the contraband newspaper and had told the Germans who had given it to her.

If the Germans had believed for a moment that Le Roux could be the ringleader of the newspaper, they would have sent an entire squad of men to apprehend him. Instead, two secret police had torn apart his store and arrested Madame Le Roux.

Le Roux was certain that he had been given up by one of his more recent contacts and, therefore, the network was once again in grave jeopardy. He knew he had little time to spare, so he hurried off to alert his second-in-command, a man with the last name of Donnez. Not knowing Donnez's address and not having another meeting scheduled for two more days, Le Roux was left with going to the Catholic University of St. Louis and asking for a Father Demaret, who knew them both. The priest wasn't in, so Le Roux left the message that Mr. Pauwel (his alias) was leaving town immediately. He then hurried to St. Michel and told Father Delehaye what had happened. He gave Delehaye the names of Father Demaret and Donnez, wished him well, and left.

Le Roux headed for Liège on foot. It would be more than a month of hiding and an eventful clandestine trip to the border, but Le Roux, who had confidently steered *La Libre Belgique* for nearly 10 months, successfully crossed into Holland late Saturday night, March 31, 1917.

Madame Le Roux was held for weeks by the Germans before being released for lack of evidence. She was forbidden, however, to reopen the shop. Nearly a year later, in early 1918, she successfully got through the electric wire between Belgium and Holland and was reunited with her husband.

A New Man Helms the Underground Newspaper

Once again, *La Libre Belgique* was without a leader. But the organization was nothing if not resourceful and resilient, and there always seemed to be someone willing to step into the fight.

In this case it was a young man who had only five months before been ordained. The Abbé Rene van den Hout lived in what was called the "Old College" at the Catholic University of St. Louis in Brussels. He was above average in height and had a muscular frame. But there was more to him that just that.

According to one history, "There was a cold, implacable energy. He oozed authority. With half a glance he would have created an inferiority complex in an American heavyweight or an English Public School Man. His deep-set metallic grey eyes bored steadily into one until one could almost feel the holes pierced in one's self-esteem. There was a challenge in the set of his head, and his angular, high cheek-boned face gave an impression of rather grim determination. . . . His voice ranged in modulation from harsh imperiousness to suave persuasion, but the note of authority was never absent." He was 30 years old, but with his serious countenance and thinning black hair, he looked older.

One evening in late February 1917, van den Hout was in his room when Father Demaret stopped by. He came quickly to the point. He told of Le Roux's role in *La*

Abbé Rene van den Hout became the highly capable leader of La Libre Belgique *after the previous editor, Le Roux, had to flee Belgium.* (Public domain; *Histoire de* La Libre Belgique *Clandestine,* Pierre Goemaere, Bureaux de *La Libre Belgique,* Bruxelles, 1919.)

Libre Belgique and recent flight to Holland, and how he, Father Demaret, had stumbled through producing the last two issues of the newspaper. Editorial content had come from Father Delehaye at St. Michel, who was in contact with all the regular contributors, including Victor Jourdain (known only by an alias). Printing was arranged by the go-between services of Donnez, Le Roux's second-in-command who had still not been arrested but knew his time was running out.

Father Demaret told van den Hout the whole story because he had to flee—someone in the chain who knew him had been apprehended, and the Germans would soon be coming for him. Would the young abbé take charge of the underground newspaper?

With little hesitation, van den Hout took the job, but with the important stipulation that Father Demaret tell no one in Belgium or in Holland that he was involved with the publication. Father Demaret agreed and gave van den Hout a note for Donnez and the name of Father Delehaye at St. Michel. With that he was gone.

Abbé van den Hout had taken on the helm of *La Libre Belgique* without saying a word to Father Demaret about how he was already providing intelligence reports to Allied agents in Antwerp and had been ferrying thousands of copies of the underground newspaper to Antwerp distributors for months. He would immediately instigate new procedures for the newspaper's production and distribution that would separate him from everyday operations and countless rank-and-file distributors. As he liked to explain, generals don't fight in the trenches.

That strategy paid off quickly when Donnez came to van den Hout soon after and said he had to flee, but because there were no links to van den Hout, the abbé was safe. Van den Hout quickly replaced Donnez with a fellow priest and together they began to build a better, tighter organization.

Van den Hout's first issue, number 114, was so similar in style, tone, and content to previous issues that few readers would have guessed a change in management had occurred. An editorial the abbé wrote, "Que Faire?" ("What to Do?"), was a strongly worded piece about the recent German decree that the people of Brussels turn in all their copper. The abbé told readers to categorically refuse to do so, with the thought that not a gram of metal should go to the enemy.

The defiant *La Libre Belgique* was still standing strong and in good hands.

55

Hoover in America

Trying to Keep Relief Afloat

Hoover had returned to America primarily to secure a $150 million loan from American banks that would be guaranteed by the British, French, and Belgian governments. All had gone well with the negotiations, and on Wednesday, January 31, he had even met with President Wilson, who had "expressed his great interest in our work and his good wishes on the success of our loan." At the request of the bankers providing the loan, Hoover gave a speech to a meeting of the New York Chamber of Commerce on February 1.

But once the news circulated about the German U-boat announcement—followed by the action President Wilson took a few days later—the loan was suspended and never reinstituted.

The president had not been able to ignore the German U-boat provocation. On Saturday, February 3, 1917, Wilson went before congress and spoke at length, announcing that America was breaking diplomatic ties with Germany. He told the assembled group that the renewal of unrestricted submarine warfare gave the United States no choice but to do so to preserve its honor and dignity. He reiterated that he did not want to go to war with Germany but cautioned that any sinking of American vessels without warning would lead to such an outcome.

Within hours of Wilson's speech, the American steamship *Housatonic*, on a voyage from Galveston to Liverpool, was sunk as it approached the British Isles. The German U-boat commander had allowed the ship's crew to board lifeboats before sinking the vessel, and even had towed the lifeboats to where they were spotted by another freighter. All of that meant that the event did not conform to Wilson's threat regarding the sinking of U.S. vessels without warning, but it did heighten American sentiment against Germany.

Hoover knew that Germany's decision to unleash its U-boats and establish a naval war zone would probably have a devastating impact on relief shipping. He was painfully aware that during the year before—even without such a brutal strategy in place and despite safe-conduct passes and pronounced CRB vessel signage—11 ships of the CRB had been damaged or sunk by torpedoes or mines. This represented approximately one-fifth of the CRB's 50 to 60-vessel fleet.

For Hoover and the CRB, the immediate effects of the Germans' action were quick and crippling to relief shipping:

- Shipping owned by neutral countries (which made up a large portion of CRB vessels) pulled out of CRB operations and sat in safe harbors to see what would happen.
- Of 17 CRB vessels at sea, two were sunk by U-boats, two made it to Rotterdam, and 13 ended up stuck in English ports.
- Hoover ordered an immediate stop to all CRB buying, loading, and shipping relief supplies until safe passage could be secured for all CRB ships.

Compounding the CRB problems were two facts: One, Hoover was trapped in America because all passenger services were halted across the North Sea—"I could not reach Europe, which I urgently needed to do."

Two, Hoover was at the mercy of a single communications system that was breaking down more and more. If Hoover wanted to contact Brussels, in many cases that meant first sending a cable to London, which then relayed it via cable to Rotterdam, which then sent the message by courier service through the border into Belgium. Censors between each leg could slow down a message while the Germans could—and did—close the border on a whim or hold up any cables they wanted to. Even in the best of scenarios, a message could take days to reach its destination and by then be long out of touch with how events had changed in the meantime.

Like a field general separated from the battlefield and his commanders, Hoover struggled to maintain an understanding of what was happening in London, Rotterdam, and Belgium so he could send critical instructions that were relevant and useful.

Initially, Hoover quickly sent a message to Brussels CRB Director Gregory requesting a count of the quantity of food stocks on hand and instructing the delegates to stay at their posts for as long as possible. He cabled London Director William Poland to consult with the relief's patron ministers in London, Page and Merry del Val, and with the British Foreign Office, and then to send to Hoover and to the Rotterdam office any "conclusions reached."

Hoover also maintained strong contact with all his U.S. government contacts to ensure he was consulted about any relief-related decisions and communications. Those contacts, in return, kept in close contact with Hoover because he was the expert on relief, and the government wanted to somehow continue relief even though the move toward war was escalating.

On February 3, Hoover showed how strong those connections were when he was able to arrange for a cable from U.S. Secretary of State Lansing to Ambassador

Page that, according to Hoover, gave "the Secretary's view and my view at that moment and my instructions to our staff." The cable carried a clear and powerful message that Page should "express to the British Government the strong feeling of this country and of the Government that the relief of the Belgian and occupied French population must in any event continue, for this country will wish to show no less interest in this great work of humanity than has been shown during the last two years by the British and French Governments, [even] should it become impossible for the Americans to remain in Belgium and in control."

It also stated that Hoover felt it would be best, if necessary, that the Dutch take over the CRB's duties. (This cut out completely the Spanish and Villalobar. Such a replacement plan had been developed by Hoover years before, in May 1915, during the crisis created by the sinking of the *Lusitania*.) The cable then included direct instructions from Hoover to Poland and Kellogg (ignoring CRB Brussels Director Gregory) that began with the following: "Think it extremely desirable for all members in Belgium to remain at their posts even after the departure of diplomatic and consular staff, if Germans will guarantee their freedom to depart if situation becomes entirely untenable."

In a few days, Hoover knew that food stocks in Belgium totaled 227,000 tons of grain, 9,000 tons of meats and fats, and 12 tons of sundries, while Rotterdam was holding 64,000 tons of supplies, and northern France had warehoused 33,000 tons of grain, 8,200 tons of meats and fats, and 5,000 tons of sundries. That meant the CRB and CN had enough supplies to continue operations for 60 days, which, it was hoped, would get the relief through the immediate crisis.

When it came to the safety of the ships, a major concern sprang from the British agreements that required all CRB ships to stop at British ports for inspection. In the past, that had not been a problem, and in fact, it gave the ships the opportunity to re-coal with British coal for the return voyage rather than doing so in Rotterdam where the coal was less efficient.

With the new German war zone, however, if the British maintained that requirement, then all CRB shipping would have to travel at least twice through the war zone—something no captains or ship owners wanted to do.

On February 3, the CRB ship *Euphrates* was torpedoed and sunk without warning *outside* the war zone, even though it had illuminated signage declaring "Belgium Relief." Only one crew member survived. Hoover wrote, "The wickedness of this sinking added to my sleepless nights. It was days before I could shake off the harrowing scenes of those courageous sailors who had trusted the Germans' guarantees of immunity from attack." Two days later, another CRB ship was torpedoed outside the war zone; the crew escaped in lifeboats.

Into this confusing world where America was shifting ever closer from neutral to belligerent, the obstacles and uncertainties facing relief were tremendous. Hoover had four major issues to resolve simultaneously:

1. Get the British to drop the requirement that all CRB ships had to stop at British ports.
2. Get the Germans to assure the safety of all properly marked CRB ships.
3. Get the CRB ships in British ports safely to Rotterdam.
4. Find a way to continue the relief with or without American delegates.

With U.S. diplomatic ties cut and Hoover trapped in America, he had to rely on others for much of the negotiations with the Germans. He turned to one of his least favorite people, the Spanish minister in Brussels, Villalobar, and asked him to take up the issues with the Germans. Villalobar quickly agreed and headed for Berlin. Hoover also maintained contact with Brand Whitlock in hopes the minister could help as well, despite the severed diplomatic relations and Whitlock's personality that Hoover felt "shrank from the rough stuff of dealing with the Germans."

In a few weeks, after confusing and sometimes contradictory communications, the problems began to be resolved.

On the negative side, the more than 100,000 tons of food inside the holds of the CRB ships trapped in British ports never did get to Rotterdam. Because of the difficulty and unreliability of communications, a solution to the problem only reached London after the British had forced the unloading of the food. The supplies were ultimately sold in Britain, and while the sale made a profit for the CRB, most of the CRB men would have preferred seeing the food reach its destination.

On the positive side, the British did agree to let ships be inspected in other British ports, such as Halifax, rather than in the British Isles. The Germans agreed to a new safe route for CRB ships that traveled north of the Shetland Islands, along the Norwegian coast, then south in a narrow lane in the North Sea to Rotterdam.

Both decisions were problematic, however, because the stop in Halifax and the new route took up more time and burned more coal than before. Because the ships would not be able to re-coal in Britain anymore, this forced them to take on enough coal in America for a roundtrip journey, making for less cargo space for relief supplies. All of that meant, according to one CRB history, that "the Commission was in worse straits than ever as the few vessels left in its service were necessarily less effective in delivering the required program."

Overall, though, the result was that relief could continue. On February 24, Hoover instructed CRB ships in America to begin sailing again for Rotterdam. Sadly, on March 8, a German U-boat sunk another CRB ship, the *Storstad*, which resulted in the loss of two crew members. It was only on March 13 that the Germans officially issued orders to their submarine commanders regarding the CRB and the new route. The loss of CRB ships would become an all-too-frequent event in the coming months.

Out of the four major problems Hoover had been forced to face in early February, the last one still remained—find a way to continue the relief with or without American delegates if America entered the war.

Von Bissing and Von Der Lancken Create a Crisis

With America and Germany officially not speaking, any communications between the two had to formally go through intermediaries, such as neutral countries' representatives. When it came to CRB-related matters, communications between the two countries were handled primarily through the CRB's Spanish patron ministers—Merry del Val in London and Villalobar in Brussels—and, at times, those communications could have great difficulty getting in and out of Belgium.

On Sunday, February 11, Hoover received an urgent message through the newly necessary convoluted route (cable from Rotterdam, courier-delivered through the border from CRB Brussels director Gregory, from a Villalobar and Francqui message). Hoover learned that Villalobar had been informed by von der Lancken that the German government "could no longer authorize American subjects to continue in the service of the C.R.B. in the North of France and in the provinces of Belgium." The Germans would agree to allow only five or six delegates to remain in Brussels to keep the relief administration going—all the rest had to leave.

Walter Page in London, also hearing the news from Gregory, sent a cable the next day to Secretary of State Lansing stating his belief that all the delegates should leave immediately and "close the Commission's business immediately in Belgium and France and liquidate it as soon as possible." To his way of thinking, this was the end, and "America can now retire with clean record and make dignified exit without parley, leaving the onus on the German Government." He told the secretary of state, "I await Department's instructions to me to retire as Patron of Commission, which I hope will be given." He also counseled Lansing that Hoover should "announce retirement under German order emphatically and immediately. Further discussion may lose the present tactical advantage."

Page should have known, however, that no one was going to retire Hoover except Hoover. "I did not agree with Page's recommendation," Hoover wrote, "because not only did I feel that von Bissing was bluffing, but I also believed that through our negotiations we could restore our ship immunities."

Hoover, anxiously sitting in America, was certain the statement from von der Lancken was the work of von Bissing alone, without the consent or authority from the German Foreign Office in Berlin or the German General Staff in Charleville. He shot off a telegram the next day, February 12, that was sent to the Rotterdam office. It said to pass along the following to Whitlock, Gregory, and Villalobar, who should pass it along to von der Lancken and von Bissing: "The American members of the Commission can no longer carry out their responsibilities and undertakings with the other interested governments and toward the peoples of France and Belgium, the American members officially withdraw from participation in the work of the Commission for Relief in Belgium and from the relief work in France."

While Hoover's pullout instruction might have sounded like what Page had proposed, it was totally different.

Page wanted the U.S. government to officially and publicly announce the immediate withdrawal of the CRB and its delegates from the relief work.

Hoover's statement of withdrawal was in private and only to von der Lancken and von Bissing through the CRB's neutral patron ministers.

In other words, Page called for a fait accompli; Hoover called for a bluff in hopes of staying in the game.

While Hoover was not in London to mitigate Villalobar's and Francqui's news and to talk Page down from his stance, he was in the next best place—America. He met with Lansing on February 14 and 15 and explained why he disagreed with Page. Hoover even met with President Wilson.

A few days later, Hoover received confirmation that he had been right in believing von der Lancken's statement did not go higher than von Bissing. Merry del Val had queried the German Foreign Office, which replied to the Spaniard on February 18 with a strong statement of support for the CRB and its American delegates. "The Imperial Government had no intention of forcing the members of the Commission to suspend their work and to leave the occupied territories. They think on the contrary, that it would be useful if these gentlemen remained provisionally at their posts, even while considering the possibility of their replacement, in case of need, by other neutral agents suitable to the work. Further, nothing will prevent that certain of the American members remain in Brussels for the management of the Commission."

Before receiving Merry del Val's confirmation of the German position, a telegram was sent from Rotterdam on February 15 that told Hoover of a meeting between von der Lancken, two German associates, Villalobar, Whitlock, Francqui, and Gregory. At that meeting, Hoover's pullout telegram was discussed and von der Lancken had suddenly changed his mind and "agreed that our delegates may remain as heretofore and with the same privileges."

The same day, Hoover sent a reply to Rotterdam with instructions for Brussels that the CRB delegates should remain. Once again, he had topped von Bissing. In this case, Hoover had also bested Page's desire to retire from the field of relief.

Unfortunately, a variety of problems caused by Hoover being in America, errors in following instructions, and the lack of quick and smooth communications resulted in a few days of major confusion. Hoover later explained, when it came to his pullout declaration, "I had not wanted any publicity because I expected that von Bissing would be ordered to retreat and I had instructed our London office to send my reply to von Bissing only to our Spanish Patrons in the hope that their action would stop him. However, our London office had sent it to all our Patron Ministers and the British Foreign Office. It was immediately leaked to the press." That basically turned Hoover's negotiating strategy into Page's fait accompli.

The press came looking for Hoover and found him in Boston. He had not yet received the cable saying von Bissing had given in, so all he could do was confirm he had sent the pullout order. "Thus," Hoover said, "the confusion was compounded."

In the few days before the confusion was cleared up, the following happened:

- The French released a statement blaming the Germans for the end of relief.
- The English released a statement blaming the Germans for the end of relief.
- Merry del Val took the opportunity to declare magnanimously that "in my capacity of founder and President of the Commission, that it will be carried on under the administration of their Spanish colleagues."
- The British ambassador in Washington wrote to Secretary of State Lansing to express his government's "warm appreciation" for the relief work and "deeply regret their enforced withdrawal."

By the time the confusion was cleared up, Hoover had checked with all of his CRB directors (Gregory, Poland, Kellogg, Chevrillon, Honnold, Brown, and White) and found they all, with the exception of one, wanted the CRB to stay in Belgium. The exception was Gregory, who wanted to leave, along with a handful of delegates. Hoover told the rest that "we would go on until something else happened, such as a declaration of war by the United States.... I informed our Patron Ambassadors and the British Foreign Office that we would continue until something else happened which might necessitate our retirement."

On Tuesday, March 13, Hoover finally fulfilled his wish to leave the United States when he stepped aboard "an ancient Spanish cargo jalopy" bound for Cadiz, Spain. It had been the only ship he could find to get him close to London.

Hoover would have plenty of time to think, and he had much more than the CRB to think about. Once the Germans had reinstituted unrestricted submarine warfare and Wilson had broken diplomatic ties with Germany, it was obvious to Hoover that war was inevitable. That would mean the CRB, if it somehow still existed, would take a back seat to American interests in the minds of his countrymen. Because of his years of experience with the CRB, Hoover firmly believed in the need for centralization of food management (not only in America but worldwide) *and* that he was the best person for any position that oversaw such a program. He had spent weeks in and out of the nation's capital talking not only about the CRB but about the future food situation to anyone who would listen. To the American public, he had also laid the PR groundwork for his worthiness to handle such a position by conducting numerous newspaper interviews. Most notably, an article in the *New York Times* on April 12 had him promoting what Americans needed to do to start conserving the precious resource of food.

In a way, his returning to London was not only to continue to support the CRB but also to find ways of tying up the loose ends of the CRB so that he would be free to accept any important, higher-level position that might be offered.

But as Hoover's oceangoing jalopy took its time chugging across the Atlantic, those in Brussels were still struggling to make sense of what was happening because of their completely different view of events.

56

Brussels

"The Best Diplomat of All of Us!"

In the first week of February, when Whitlock heard the big news that America had severed diplomatic ties with Germany, he was not surprised. Nor was he surprised when Wilson's speech led to the immediate ousting of all German diplomats in America and the instructions to James Gerard and his embassy staff in Germany to leave Berlin. He waited for news of what he was supposed to do.

Initially, however, all communications with the American government and the outside world were suspended by the Germans, and the cablegrams Whitlock tried to send out were denied. He did receive indirect information that indicated the State Department wanted him to stay if the Germans allowed it.

A short time later, much to Whitlock's relief, one of the German generals in Belgium, Count von Moltke, sent over a packet of U.S.-coded telegrams, which Whitlock's staff immediately began to decipher. Unfortunately, the messages were incomplete and inconclusive as to what to do. Hoover had sent word, however, that the CRB delegates should stay at their posts. Count von Moltke continued to send over U.S. cablegrams as a gesture of respect and goodwill, while von Bissing, who had returned from Germany but was still sick, sent word that he hoped Whitlock and the CRB would stay.

During the next few weeks, discussions raged back and forth—principally among and between Whitlock, von der Lancken, Villalobar, and the American CRB principals, Gregory and Kellogg (who went back and forth from Brussels to Rotterdam). Francqui, for the most part, stood anxiously in the wings, at times consulting, demanding, and pleading with the various diplomatic principals in the hope that relief would somehow continue.

Making matters far worse was the fact that communications with Washington and with the CRB London office were spotty in frequency and completeness, and in some cases they were contradictory. Such uncertainty was unnerving to Whitlock, who wrote in his journal on Wednesday, February 7, 1917, "I am in a difficult position. I should like to remain, if by so doing the revictualing can continue.

Warren Gregory was a CRB Brussels director who had little patience for the timid uncertainty of Brand Whitlock. (Public domain; author's archives.)

I am ready to make any sort of sacrifice for the Belgians, but in what quality am I to remain? As a distinguished hostage, or what?" The Whitlocks did pack most of their belongings so they could depart at a moment's notice.

The CRB executives—most notably Director Gregory and Assistant Director Prentiss Gray—had little patience for Whitlock's timid uncertainty and lack of decisive action.

At one point, Gray reported that a message came from the legation that everyone was packing and that "the minister is in a panic and has gone to bed with a sick headache." After one meeting with von der Lancken that had included Whitlock and CRB Brussels Director Gregory, Gray wrote, "I never saw Gregory in a worse temper than when he returned from this meeting with von der Lancken. He stormed about the inaction of Whitlock and swore he had never seen 'the white livered fool do a thing to save a single man during the deportations and that the only time he had stirred himself at all was to save a stallion belonging to his friend, Baron Lambert.'"

Because it was still unclear how America could sever diplomatic ties with Germany and still maintain support for the CRB, positions shifted nearly daily: Should Whitlock take down the U.S. flag at the legation and remove it from his car? (he did both immediately without being ordered to do so); would the State Department change its mind again and order Whitlock home?; and, if Whitlock and the CRB delegates did stay, in what capacity would the Germans allow it?

On the last point, von der Lancken had stated clearly that Whitlock and the CRB could stay, but the minister would have no official diplomatic standing—which had previously included unfettered courier service, coded communications, and travel—and that the CRB delegates would have no motorcar privileges and be drastically limited in what they could and could not do. The idea of replacing them with other neutral nationalities was floated, with Villalobar pushing hard for any replacements to be Spanish—not Dutch or Swiss, as had been proposed.

Gregory, anticipating trouble, especially for CRB delegates in northern France because of their proximity to the battlefront, held those men back in Brussels after February 1. Unfortunately, without Americans in northern France, the

Germans, according to Kittredge's history, "took advantage of this immediately by beginning to exercise a direct control over the food distribution." That stimulated Gregory and the CRB to strongly support the idea of neutral replacements as soon as possible.

Von der Lancken pressed Whitlock for a decision on whether he would stay or go. Whitlock delayed giving his answer, still not having clear communications with the State Department or with Hoover.

After one meeting with von der Lancken, Whitlock finally revealed in his journal how he truly felt about the German and the situation: "Listening to him, watching that face, so false, so insidious, the peculiarly slithery, snaky impression this man always produces in me came over me; he said he would . . . take responsibility for my treatment on himself! And so, a long futile talk, and I went away sick at heart, telling von der Lancken to get it all in writing."

Francqui came by the legation and Whitlock reported that the head of the CN was "terribly blue." As a Belgian living in German-occupied Belgium, he knew he had no real say in any German, American, or British actions, but as the driving force behind the CN, he had much at stake and a good strategic understanding of the situation. With Whitlock, he once again wondered what would come of the relief and said that he wished Whitlock and a few of the CRB delegates would stay. Gone, according to Whitlock, were Francqui's "jokes, those flashes of wit that had once enlivened us and kept up our spirits."

With such uncertainty hanging over all aspects of his life in Belgium, Whitlock did the one thing in his spare time that he always did during trying times—he began rereading Sherlock Holmes. "I have read those stories over a score of times and forgotten them; they are always new and fascinating." And he kept working on his novel, which he had never forsaken throughout the years of relief work.

On Monday, February 12, Prentiss Gray returned from a trip to Holland and brought with him an important message from Secretary of State Lansing to Whitlock, instructing him to remain in Belgium until further instructions so he could protect the CRB delegates. Gray noted, "It was perfectly evident from the phraseology that Hoover had written the message to Whitlock. When I delivered the telegram to the Minister, all he said was: 'Damn it! I wish Hoover would stop writing my dispatches.'"

On Valentine's Day, Wednesday, February 14, Whitlock received a message from Hoover (his pullout cable sent February 12) that had been smuggled in from Rotterdam. Definitely not a love note, it said that because von der Lancken would be removing most privileges from the CRB delegates, the CRB would pull out at once from Belgium. Whitlock had a feeling it was a bluff and hoped it would bring about the desired changes in the German position.

Later that day, another meeting was convened in von der Lancken's salon with Whitlock, Francqui, Villalobar, CRB Director Gregory, von der Lancken, and two of his associates. Gregory and Whitlock were prepared to show the Germans Hoover's telegram, but the Germans already had it. Von der Lancken was not happy and wondered how Hoover had heard about his insistence that the CRB delegates would have no more freedom or privileges. Gregory explained that he had sent word to Hoover of von der Lancken's position in a telegram that Prentiss Gray had carried to Holland and then sent on to Hoover.

Whitlock reported, "It was plain that [the Germans, and von der Lancken in particular,] did not wish to be held responsible for the retirement of the Americans. . . . Von der Lancken announced then a complete change of position; in a word, he gave in; he said that the delegates could do as before."

Once again, Hoover's maneuver had accomplished its desired effect. Whitlock wrote, "It is sure that his bluff—if it was a bluff, and it wasn't altogether—wrought a great effect on the Germans."

Outside the building, the two Americans, the Spaniard, and the Belgian stood in the cold winter afternoon and marveled at what Hoover had once again pulled off. Whitlock noted that Francqui leaned against the wall and laughed, as Villalobar declared, "Hoover is the best diplomat of all of us!"

But things weren't entirely cleared up—primarily because of the confusion when Hoover's pullout message had been leaked to the press. Within a few days, other telegrams filtered into Belgium with contradictory orders. More meetings were held. The Germans would not allow all diplomatic and delegate privileges. The CRB was going to leave. Whitlock would go. At one meeting, Whitlock declared in frustration that there had been "many changing varying dispatches we had received—go, stay, don't go, don't stay, take our courier, keep the courier."

He blamed such vacillation on Hoover, who he felt was the puppeteer when it came to many of the State Department's orders. He knew Hoover was still back in America and was confident Hoover was trying to follow the Belgian situation as closely as possible—and trying to influence every governmental action related to relief. Whitlock told Gregory and Kellogg, "The [U.S.] Government has no ideas on the revictualing that Hoover doesn't give it."

This didn't mean, however, that Whitlock was sure of his own decisive powers. He lamented in his journal, "I wonder if I have acted wisely! One is so weak—and I am so tired—tired beyond any rest!"

There was much truth in Whitlock's statement about Hoover's influence, but many would have said justifiably so. Hoover had not only founded and operated the largest relief program the world had ever seen, he also knew well all the international cast of characters. If anyone should be counseling the U.S. government on the current situation as it related to Belgium and relief, a strong case could be made for Hoover being that adviser.

On Monday, February 24, Whitlock once again met with von der Lancken and von Moltke. When asked what his position was, to go or stay, Whitlock stated he would be leaving. Von der Lancken returned to assuring the American minister that the CRB delegates would have full privileges and that, while the Germans could not allow Whitlock to have courier service, he could send secure mail through Villalobar's courier. Whitlock wrote that von der Lancken continued by stating that "they greatly desired the revictualing to continue, that they wished the Americans to remain, that it was purely an American work, and that he had no faith in the ability of any others to carry it on. . . . In case of war—a word he did not like to utter . . . he hoped the organization of the C.R.B. at New York, London, and Rotterdam would continue undisturbed, as it is now, and that if others had to come in, they should gradually replace American delegates. But above all, they wanted me to stay."

On February 28, Whitlock received through Villalobar's diplomatic pouch four telegrams. One in particular from the State Department told him to remain in Belgium until all Americans had gone and stated that if the CRB left, it would be replaced by the Dutch not the Spanish. Whitlock could tell who had stimulated such an order. "The larger part of the telegram was, of course, of Hoover's inspiration, showing his hatred of Villalobar and of Francqui, and proposing that the whole C.R.B. be turned over to the Dutch Government." Overall, Whitlock was still uncertain as to what to do and wrote that the telegrams "are wobbly—instructions impossible to carry out, and rather weak, save that they are so drawn that, no matter what I may do, I may be put in the wrong."

The next day, Whitlock went to see Villalobar and told him, "We must begin to get in some understudies for the C.R.B. delegates." He was worried about bringing up Hoover's plan for the Dutch to take over completely, so he gingerly recommended that bringing in some Dutch delegates might be a good idea. Villalobar agreed, but also stated that he had already selected Spaniards to replace the Americans.

The question of who would replace and control the new delegates was still very much up in the air.

57

Elsewhere in Belgium, Rotterdam, and Northern France

The Deep Freeze Breaks but Hunger Persists

Between the canals freezing in mid-January and the February 1 announcement that the Germans were reinstituting unrestricted submarine warfare, the monthly allotment of CRB imported foodstuffs was severely decreased. For Belgium, the monthly imports of food, which had totaled 64,873 tons in December 1916 and 60,794 tons in January 1917, plummeted to less than half that, at 29,502 tons in February and to 27,651 tons in March. For northern France the statistics were just as bad: December and January had seen respectable tonnages of 34,115 and 27,803 tons, respectively, reaching civilians, but February and March were less than half that, at 11,246 and 14,548 tons.

While Hoover worked behind the scenes to get renewed protections for the international CRB ships so they could begin sailing again, local efforts were happening all across Belgium to free up barges stuck in frozen canals.

On Sunday, February 4, 1917, Maurice Pate and a Belgian associate walked from Tournai to where the Mons-Condé Canal met a larger river. The canal had frozen over to a depth of a foot, while the river still flowed. Pate watched as 60 Belgian men labored to free several trapped CRB canal barges that were filled with much-needed wheat. The men cut a path through the ice 20 feet wide and a mile long to get the barges back from the frozen canal to the river so they could return to Mons for unloading and distribution.

The situation was critical in Holland as well. Prentiss Gray reported, "The Rotterdam office is humming like a hive of bees. . . . The difficulties which Rotterdam has overcome are tremendous. These include cutting barges out of the ice in the harbor to enable them to come alongside the loading wharfs or elevators, rearranging the gear of the elevators so that the grain will flow down the spouts into the cars and—where this could not be done—rigging basket cranes for [transferring wheat from ships to barges]. The shipping organization, which has taken more than two years to build up, has been disrupted and disorganized in a day."

The cargo ships and canal barges in Rotterdam harbor became ice-bound in early February 1917. That created major problems for shipping food into Belgium. (Public domain; Herbert Hoover Presidential Library Archives, West Branch, Iowa.)

Replacing the ice-bound barges were railcars, or at least that had been the contingency plan for frozen canals drawn up in 1916. "The plan which we had laid out last fall," Gray said, "called for the loading and dispatch of 200 railroad cars per day from Rotterdam with a gradual increase to 300 cars per day."

Reality had put a wrench in the works. The weather had not disrupted the plan; the British had. "This [railcar] program has not been fulfilled to the letter because the British have been unkind enough to attack just at this moment, and the Germans have withdrawn many of our cars in order that supplies may be rushed to the front." (Gray was probably referring to attacks by the British along the Somme front that started on January 11 and continued into March.)

Even so, the food found its way into Belgium. Gray noted, "Still, we are moving about 2,500 tons a day and are carrying on the feeding without interruption."

By late February the arctic cold broke. "A thaw set in a few days ago," Gray reported on March 1. "Today we were able to begin picking up the lighters which had been frozen in and to dispatch newly-loaded barges from Rotterdam. We shall, however, maintain rail shipments to distant points long enough to keep their stocks of food on a parity with points nearer Rotterdam."

Nevertheless, CRB imports would take longer to regain their previous levels and were inadequate for the needs of the poorer civilians.

While the statistics of decreased tonnage of imported food were difficult for all relief workers to read, they paled in comparison to seeing the results such reductions created. The poorer residents in small villages and towns seemed to be hardest hit by the lack of food. In late February/early March, Pate visited numerous families in Hainaut Province and wrote an extensive report detailing the food situation of three of them. His full description of one of the families illustrates the kind of life many poor Belgians had to endure:

Family A: There are 7 persons in the family. The father and eldest son work 4 days per week in a mine at Quaregnon [5 miles southwest of Mons], earning Frs. 4.40 a day.

At home are the mother, 2 young children and a third adopted infant, a child of a lost relative.

The resources for the family of 7 are thus Frs. 35 a week or Frs. 5 per day. The food consumed by the family is exclusively that obtained at the C.R.B. magasin [warehouse] viz: the following quantities per day:

300 grams of bread.
8 grams of rice.
12 grams of lard and bacon.
10 grams of cerealine and other foodstuffs by occasion.
The 2 miners receive a supplementary ration of 100 grams of bread a day.

This particular region is almost entirely lacking in native foodstuffs [known, instead, as a coal mining area]. There are no more potatoes to be found and the cattle beet at 50 francs a hundred kilos is, with its little nutritional value, regarded as a luxury for the small purse.

In the case of the family in question, for breakfast, they eat one small slice of bread together with a cup of black brew made of burnt grain. During the day, the father and son, who leave the house at 4:30 in the morning, are at their work in the coalmine. Each takes with him 350 grams of bread, or 3 large slices. This, spread with white sour milk cheese, form their sole [nutrition] during the day's work. The men return home at 4 in the afternoon. The family, after their light breakfast, eat nothing during the day, because of the fact that the mother and children must sacrifice their ration to the men to give them the necessary strength to go to work. At 4:30 the family eat together a bowl of rice with a quantity of bread. To save themselves from the pains of hunger, they all go to bed about 6 o'clock.

On examination of the pantry it was found that there remained none of the lard which was distributed 4 days ago, and of which there will not be another distribution for one month. There were no other foodstuffs of any kind in the house except a small quantity of rice and 1 [kilogram] loaf of Holland bread. Were it not for this latter, which is distributed from time to time in the commune, the family would have been entirely without bread.

As I was about to leave the house, a woman of very respectable and neat appearance, a miner's wife, came in to borrow from her neighbor a small amount of bread, which she promised to return upon receiving a ration tomorrow. She had been obliged to give to her husband, when he descended the mine the same morning, what little was left in the house. The 2 children, both under three years of age, had been without bread during the entire day. The woman, distracted between furnishing the food which is absolutely necessary to her husband, as the family's 'bread winner' and in answering the cries of the children, had sacrificed herself to an extent which was very apparent in her physical appearance. She was depressed and morally exhausted. She said that she could not keep much longer under the present strain, and even had a great difficulty to keep [from throwing] herself into the canal.

The family of 7 persons above mentioned, never eats meat, except for an occasional Sunday, when a small quantity is purchased for the men.

In the examination of the house, a fact which struck me very forcibly, was the insanitory [sic] *condition due to lack of soap because of the present price of this article. They told me there was not a gram in the house. The fact of not being able to keep themselves clean, it is evident, has a very deteriorating and discouraging moral affect.*

Many of those people, and tens of thousands more, had lived like that for more than two years.

Brown, Eckstein, and the Bunges

The bitter cold had been felt all across Belgium. And food was not the only item that had been impacted by the frozen canals. In many places, rationed coal was cut even more to make dwindling supplies last longer. Everyone struggled to mitigate the effects of the subzero temperatures.

Erica Bunge, her farm manager Verheyen, and the staff of the dairy farm had struggled to keep the cows warm and fed while dealing with freezing metal milk canisters and frigid temperatures during the daily trips from the farm to the tram station drop-off for Antwerp.

Neither the Belgians nor the CRB delegates knew whether the food relief could survive the double punch of frozen canals and the Germans' U-boat offensive. But with the breaking of the arctic cold, there was slightly more hope that the food relief would continue.

During February, with numerous manmade and natural crises at hand, Brown and Eckstein faced the strong probability that their time in Belgium was rapidly coming to an end. While they hurried to do as much relief work as possible, they also took any spare moment they could find to visit Chateau Oude Gracht and the two Bunge sisters they had come to love.

Brown's feelings toward all of the Bunges had grown. The father, Edouard Bunge, had gained Brown's great respect. "I believe I admire him as much as any man I have ever known."

During this time, Brown and Erica spent as much time alone as possible, talking about their feelings and what they hoped to accomplish when the war came to an end. They expressed their love for each other and their wish to someday be together forever. But Brown purposefully did not ask her to marry him. He felt he was in no position to do so because his future was so uncertain. He loved the relief work he was doing but was sure he could not make that his career. Such uncertainty made him realize that he could not ask Erica to marry him or ask Edouard for his daughter's hand in marriage.

CRB delegate Fred Eckstein (who would change his last name to the less Germanic sounding Exton) became engaged to Eva Bunge in 1917. She would break it off after changing her mind. (Author's archives.)

But uncertainty seemed, in this case, to be the mother of commitment. Erica and Milton both privately declared their love for each other and committed to wait for each other, no matter how long the war took to resolve.

The same weekend they did so, Fred and Eva officially announced to the family their engagement. Brown wrote, "She is one of my dearest friends and naturally I am very much delighted, since I have come to like him so much." He also noted, "They are a couple admirably suited to one another and I'm sure will be happy together. Eva's nature is a bit complex but Fred understands her perfectly. She, too, is doing much for the needy; her heart is true and she will make a good wife for Fred. I have come to have a very strong affection for these two and am looking forward to seeing much of them in America if all goes well."

It was during this time that Brown wrote a long letter to his mother and father. Since the summer, when Joe Green had hinted at his relationship by asking Brown's parents how they would like a "continental marriage," Milton had denied such a situation in his letters home. It was finally time to come clean and tell his parents how he truly felt.

He began by describing the Bunges as "the dearest friends I have in the world over here."

When it came to the three Bunge daughters, he declared, "I could never begin to give you any idea of their wonderful characters and of the way in which they are standing this test." He gave a quick sketch of Eva and Hilda and then launched into a longer description of Erica, not yet telling them she was the one he loved.

Sitting on the terrace steps of Chateau Oude Gracht were: front row, left to right, Milton Brown, Erica Bunge, Duke Wellington, Alice Karcher, and Gardner Richardson; in the back, from left to right, Hallam Tuck, Eva Bunge, Hilda Bunge, and Hélène Karcher. (Author's archives.)

"As for the eldest of the sisters, who is a year younger than I, [her birthday] on November 9th—Erica, my description fails entirely." He did not start his description as Erica might have liked. "She is not pretty; but that is about all that can be said of her in the negative." He quickly moved on to the positives. "Her character is something I have never seen the equal of, nor ever expect to. She has a heart that never fails, and what she does for others could never, never be measured. She stands out so, head and shoulders above everyone else, that all the Americans who have visited here—and there have been many of them, young men and old—have put her down as one of the noblest women they have ever known."

Having set the scene, and having written three pages, it was time for Brown to get to the point of the letter: "You may know then, Mother and Father, that I am prouder than I can ever express, to be able to say that she is waiting for me here until this frightful war is over and I can come back to her and ask her to marry me."

He quickly acknowledged his mother's feelings. "I know perfectly how this is going to strike you Mother—especially you, who never wanted an international alliance in our family, but let me tell you more about her.

"She is not Catholic," the Protestant Brown wrote reassuringly, "but a protestant liberal. She is tremendously strong physically, far more so than I—one of those persons capable of bearing untold burdens, and of whom you are always certain in a crisis to meet it squarely and with unfailing judgment and common sense. She is very musical and plays beautifully."

Erica Bunge was described by Milton Brown as "one of the noblest women" any of the CRB delegates had ever met. In early 1917, she agreed to wait for Brown, who promised to return after the war and marry her. (Author's archives.)

With the Brown family's grounding in self-reliance and a strong work ethic, Milton knew his parents might have concerns over the Bunge family's wealth and whether Erica would fit into their summers roughing it at the Georgian Bay of Lake Huron. He tried to put their minds at ease. "She is not fond of society, and would make a wonderful camper. Her tastes are, above all things else, not frivolous. . . . Mr. Bunge is a very wealthy man, but the temptation to idleness which very well might result from it, finds no response in these girls. They forego absolutely all such things and their money means nothing whatever to them except as they can use it for the poor."

Brown then wrote of all that Erica did to better the world. "These days Erica is very, very busy with many charities in town. . . . Besides her work at the free clinic, at the cheap lunches for the poor, and a dozen other things, she manages her father's enormous model dairy (all of the milk from which goes in town daily to the poor) and the culinary department of the house. Then, having nothing else to do, she is studying, seriously, stenography and music, putting many hours a week on both! Besides all this she is a great reader and well up in all current events. In this latter connection she has always been her father's business 'pal' and always enters into the discussions with the men."

He acknowledged the economic divide between the Brown family and the Bunges when he declared, "You may appreciate then how proud I am that she loves me—I who came to her out of absolutely nothing whatever. She never knew that I existed, or my family, and yet she accepts me for what she finds me to be. That surely is the greatest compliment a man can have paid to him! I have talked to her—as, indeed, to all of them—about you all; I have shown your pictures so that she knows you all already, and I have told her much of our life at home and at camp, and of our great family love."

As for officially asking Erica to marry him, Brown explained, "I have never asked her that question yet—we agreed between us that I should not." There were three reasons for this. The first was that "when Eck [Eckstein] and Eva became engaged it came as a terrific shock to Mr. Bunge who already had so much to worry about in regard to Belgium, her present trouble and her future; and the loss of one of his three daughters [to Eckstein and a probable home in America] was almost too much for him." The second was that "we both feel that we have work to do for those who are suffering far more than we, and that it is scarcely fair to go too far with this, our own happiness, when there is so much of unhappiness about us." And finally, Brown's own lack of career prospects "will not permit me to plan to marry and that worries me not a little. But we are willing to wait and are prepared for a period of years, if necessary."

With a clear conscience that he had finally told his family the truth of his feelings for Erica, Brown headed back to Brussels to face an uncertain future, but knowing he had the love of the woman he loved.

Brown would not see her again before leaving Belgium.

A Planned German Withdrawal Brings a Flood of Refugees

From February 9 until March 20, 1917, the Germans made a strategic move along the Western Front that impacted the CRB and northern France. The Battle of the Somme in 1916 had created two salients, or bulges, in the lines that the Germans decided to eliminate by falling back to a shorter, easier-to-defend position known as the Hindenburg Line. The British later called the maneuver the retreat to the Hindenburg Line, but the Germans had planned Operation Alberich for a long time and it was a sound military decision.

Hoover wrote, "The result was the recovery by France of some 50 communes [small administrative districts] out of the 1,200 occupied by the German Army."

That was the good news for the CRB—fewer communes and fewer people to feed.

The bad news was that the Germans, in their preparations and establishment of a new trench line, forced approximately 50,000 northern French refugees to flood into Belgium's Hainaut Province. The trench movement also resulted in changing some areas of Belgium from the Occupation Zone, controlled by von Bissing's civil government, to the Etape subzone in the Army Zone, controlled by the military.

In the end, there were fewer northern French to feed, but the upheaval and influx of refugees created by the move was significant and took months for the Belgians, the northern French, the CN, and the CRB to absorb.

58

Brussels

A Final Blow Decides the Issues

Because of the poor and sporadic communications with the outside world, it was a few days into March before Whitlock heard the monumental news of what later would become known in America as the Zimmermann telegram.

Sent on January 16, the secret telegram was decoded by the British soon after and made public by the American government on Wednesday, February 28. The message was from German Foreign Secretary Zimmermann to the German ambassador to Mexico. Sent before the Germans had announced the restarting of unrestricted submarine warfare, it was an incredibly audacious proposal. The telegram read:

> *We intend to begin on the first of February unrestricted submarine warfare. We shall endeavor in spite of this to keep the United States of America neutral. In the event of this not succeeding, we make Mexico a proposal of alliance on the following basis: make war together, make peace together, generous financial support and an understanding on our part that Mexico is to reconquer the lost territory in Texas, New Mexico, and Arizona. The settlement in detail is left to you. You will inform the President [of Mexico] of the above most secretly as soon as the outbreak of war with the United States of America is certain and add the suggestion that he should, on his own initiative, invite Japan to immediate adherence and at the same time mediate between Japan and ourselves. Please call the President's attention to the fact that the ruthless employment of our submarines now offers the prospect of compelling England in a few months to make peace.*
>
> *Signed, Zimmermann*

The American public was outraged. Whitlock wrote later that he was told, "The country is aflame, all parties standing solidly by the President, even [peace advocate, William Jennings] Bryan, ready for war!"

The feeling was different in Belgium. Whitlock recorded, "Everybody laughing at the frightful blunder the Germans made in proposing to Mexico to become an ally."

As a diplomat, Whitlock was surprised at the Germans' stupidity but relieved it would finally reveal to all the Germans' true character. "The annals of diplomacy, I suppose, contain no filthier offer; but it is not without its compensations, since it must reveal the Germans to Americans and to all the world—if there is any one stupid enough not to know them by this time—in their true light, that of a people without morals, or honour, or even common politeness, barbarians through and through, pariahs among the nations, to be treated as such!"

The first week of March came in like a lion, according to Whitlock, who reported that Monday, March 5, was "cold again, winter, like the war, unending; deep snow." Not helping matters, Whitlock also wrote, Villalobar had a terrible cold, and Francqui was "very blue, very much downcast, silent, sombre." The American wondered if the Belgian's mood was due to the world situation or "the prospect of his approaching marriage" to his much younger niece (his previous wife had died in the early days of the war).

By this time, most of the international diplomats in Brussels now agreed that war between America and Germany was practically inevitable. Once again there were countless meetings, spotty communications, contradictory instructions, and fearful uncertainty.

In a gathering at Gregory's home, Whitlock and his wife, Nell, sat with Gregory and Kellogg discussing what needed to be done. "We decided to obtain, if possible, the guarantees from the Germans that the [American] men can [leave Belgium], but I had no hope, and so told them, and still have no hope, that the Germans will give any such guarantees. They talk about it, and von der Lancken and Brohn promise it . . . but I have no idea that we shall ever secure such assurances, and little they would respect them even if they were given."

For Gregory, at least, there was no indecision on his part as to what to do if America declared war. He announced in early March that if that happened, he felt that all Americans should leave immediately. "I know that I shall," Gregory told Whitlock. "In war a civilian's place is in his own country, or at least not in the enemy's country—if he can avoid it."

In this regard, Gregory, the CRB Brussels director, was at direct odds with Hoover's sentiment and the strong feelings of most of the CRB delegates. Prentiss Gray, the CRB's assistant director in Brussels, send a telegram to Hoover via the U.S. chargé d'affaires in Holland that stated, "The members of the Commission are nearly unanimous in the wish to stay with the work under any conditions and they are willing to accept any terms whereby the continuation of the work will be ensured."

Throughout this highly volatile and confusing time, the border between Belgium and Holland was periodically shut down. Whitlock described one case in which Rene Jensen, the Dane who had been with the CRB as a courier since January 1915, was not permitted to cross into Holland but was allowed to speak across the border to a CRB delegate—as long as they spoke German and in front of German officers.

Rene Jensen, a Dane, was a critical courier for the CRB between Brussels and Rotterdam. When the border shut down in early 1917, he was only allowed to speak across the border to a CRB delegate if he spoke German in front of a German officer. (Author's archives.)

Back in Washington, decisions had still not been made regarding whether the CRB Americans delegates were going and who would replace them. Whitlock, after recommending that men of other nationalities immediately begin replacing the Americans, was losing his patience and blaming the situation more and more on Hoover. On March 13 he wrote, "I gave this advice [of replacing the Americans immediately with other nationalities] as strongly as I knew how to state it. Very well. I have done my duty, and the Department has again allowed itself to be dominated by Hoover, who, despite all this vacillation he has shown in the last month, still clings obstinately to his stubborn purpose to have those [American] men remain in here, exposed to dangers that, with the Germans in their present frame of mind, are easily imagined. . . . Hoover, though three thousand miles away, thinks he knows more than Gregory, or Kellogg, or I, or any one who is here, and seems able to impose his brutal will on the Department [of State]. If any horror occurs, I shall have only the melancholy satisfaction of being on record—and have to take the blame anyhow!"

Whitlock would have been happy to hear that on the day he wrote that journal entry Hoover had sailed from America, ending what Whitlock considered to be Hoover's in-person stranglehold on the State Department.

Two days later, on Thursday, March 15, 1917, the talk of Brussels was not only about America's possible entry into the war but also about a new international development—the Russian revolution and the overthrow of the czar. Whitlock noted, "It is a splendid thing, sublime in its way, to see a people able, in the midst of the greatest war in history, to throw off the yoke of a wicked despotism, and quietly, in a few days, establish a constitutional government."

A much smaller upheaval occurred a few days later, when Villalobar presented four Spaniards (one of Cuban descent) as the initial neutral delegates to take the place of Americans. He introduced them to Gregory for approval. Whitlock reported (without giving details) that Gregory felt they were "impossible" and would not agree to their appointments as delegates. Shortly thereafter, Dutch delegates began to arrive.

In the meantime, in early March Gregory and Kellogg had requested passes out of Belgium for seven delegates. Four of them—Alfred Fletcher, Tracy Kittredge, Robert Maverick, and Philip K. Potter—had served in northern France up to February 1 and had been held back in Brussels ever since. According to Kittredge's history, because Gregory knew the Germans would never allow those four men back to their posts so close to the front, he went ahead and requested their safe passage out of Belgium. He also requested the same for two other delegates, William Percy and Arthur B. Maurice, who had been in Belgium only a few short months (since December 1916 and January 1917, respectively).

No reason was given for the early departure of these delegates, but in a later memoir Percy detailed the situation for himself and the other six (which has never been corroborated).

He wrote that when America severed diplomatic ties with Germany and war seemed inevitable, "I at once applied for permission to return home. The Commission did not relish my request and pointed out the indispensable humane service we were rendering. I listened but did not hear. I insisted on the safe conduct out which had been promised me when I came in. Six other kindred spirits joined in my revolt: we were intractable and eloquent rebels. So the anxious Commission requested of the Germans a safe conduct for us through Germany into Switzerland."

For a week no passes were received and Gregory, according to Whitlock, "doubted if they ever would, if any of the C.R.B. would be allowed to go even if I would." On March 19, however, Gregory finally received the passports for the seven CRB delegates to leave Belgium via Germany to Switzerland.

A lot would happen before the seven would make it to the train station.

The Confusion Stimulates Delegate Plans and Decisions

During this chaotic time of conflicting communications and lack of current, useful information, uncertainty reigned in all quarters. None of those in positions of power and authority—from the Germans and the relief patron ministers to the Belgians, the CRB executives, and the State Department—seemed to know what was happening or what should be done.

Low men on this teetering totem pole were the American delegates, who grabbed at every word and rumor and spent long hours huddled together discussing each new international development and what might happen to them. They argued over the best strategies and options and what precautions they should be taking. They knew they were in a precarious situation: At any moment they could officially become belligerents to those with whom they had worked since the beginning.

A critical question was how the Germans would react to American neutrals suddenly becoming enemies?

Most of the delegates had seen the effects of German institutionalized subjugation of an entire civilian population, while many others had personally witnessed the individual brutality of German officers and soldiers in following instructions—most notably during the deportations. The attitude of the Germans seemed to be that practically anything was acceptable if authorized. Milton Brown explained, "When you speak to a German officer about 'atrocities' he says, 'Atrocities? Why there never were any atrocities! What we did to Belgium in the first days of the war was all ordered by our military—it was military operations, therefore it was not an atrocity.'"

Mindful of such beliefs, the delegates could easily imagine that the Germans could just as likely throw them in jail, or even execute them, as they could allow them to leave the occupied territory peacefully.

The majority of delegates were young, idealistic, committed Americans who, regardless of their initial promise to remain absolutely neutral while behind German lines, had become strongly anti-German and pro-Allies. They had come to know and love the Belgians and northern French whom they had served, and they had clandestinely followed and admired the Belgian underground newspaper *La Libre Belgique.*

If prison, or worse, seemed to be in the near future, some of the Americans vowed not to quietly accept such a fate.

One of those was Brown. Throughout the month of March, while he was still striving to run the clothing department, he was also hastily preparing for the worst and planning an escape with others if the Germans came to arrest them.

He began by documenting much of what he had seen and done while in Belgium in multiple letters to numerous people, including a handwritten "Final Word to My Family," which was nearly 30 legal-sized pages long. He collected copies of the most important documents involving the work. He had started a diary when he first arrived in Belgium and had understood even then that such a written record would never leave Belgium while the war was still going on. Brown also had many mementos, including medals he had received from grateful Belgians, books he had bought, photos of Belgian friends, gifts for those back home, and numerous pieces of lace, many of which depicted outlawed patriotic themes and images.

Arranging all of what were his worldly possessions, he began "taking many precautions," he wrote his family, "that they be not discovered by the Germans."

Most notable to be hidden were pieces of his writing that freely expressed his hatred for the Germans. He explained multiple times in numerous documents, "When I came into Belgium on February 3, 1916, I was as neutral as anyone could be. I had not been able to believe any of the stories of Belgian atrocities and I knew nothing of the real spirit of Germany, of her civilization."

That changed within three weeks, a time span he stated was "even longer than most delegates." He noted, "It used to be my boast that I did not know the feeling of hatred, that I hated no one in the world nor any thing nor any force."

The change came in two stages. "For the first six months of my life under the German military rule, I found that I hated the Germans for what they had done to Belgium, for the brutal tyranny of their administration, for their lies and shams."

At that point, Brown's attitude toward the Germans went from a localized, individual perspective to a much larger international view that represented more of the Germans as a culture than as persons; from the individual to the collective mentality. During the second half of the year in Belgium, he realized the Germans were "a people totally destitute, at least collectively, of any sense of honor; to them the end always justifies the means, and that end is 'Deutschland uber alles' ['Germany over all']; even that might be excusable in another country, but never in 'Deutschland'—a state that is founded on principles which threaten the world. I hate them for their brutality, which is cold and calculating and relentless. I hate them for their damnable system which glorifies the military, which gives almost limitless powers to its officers and officials yet leaves them with no responsibility for their acts so that before them the individual has no defense.

"Often when walking home quietly from the office," Brown continued, "I found myself cursing, cursing, cursing them! In fact I have only learned to curse since coming to Belgium."

Seeing Belgium through these new-found lenses, Brown gained a completely different perspective on war and suffering. He wrote to his family, "We in America, for almost two generations, have been living without the sufferings of a real war, and some of us have perhaps come to look upon many of its rigors as romances, as things that belong to yesterday and are impossible today.

"From my Belgian year," he continued, "I have drawn the appreciation of the sufferings of war, and I have come to feel that the greatest horrors of war are not the brute struggles between the men on the firing lines, but the thousands of little dramas—domestic and military—which are enacted behind the Front, and especially in territory occupied by the enemy. Remember that men and women of all classes are constantly running risks of life and death, and are paying the penalty with their lives for acts of patriotism!"

Brown knew that such free expressions of his feelings, if found by the Germans, could have serious repercussions. He separated all the items he wanted to hide into four groups:

1. An envelope of work-related papers with forwarding instructions for after the war was prepared. The packet was included with the papers of other delegates and secured in a large sealed tin box located in the U.S. Legation. The packet would be put under the protection of still-neutral Spain and Minister Villalobar in the event that America entered the war.

2. Books and various small items were left with Belgian Fernand Baetens, who had since the beginning of relief run the CRB's Brussels shipping department and had become a good friend of Brown.
3. The lace he had collected and a list of how he wanted the pieces to be distributed was given to Erica Bunge, who was keeping it in the safe at Chateau Oude Gracht.
4. The large group of personal letters, documents, and diaries he had written were put in a box. He had had the box made in sheet lead and it was 32 inches long by 24 inches wide and six inches high. This he also gave to Erica for burial somewhere on the Bunges' estate.

An explanation of all that he had done was in Brown's "A Final Word to My Family," which he left with Erica. She was to mail the long letter to America two weeks after his departure in hopes it would get through the censors and back to Glendale, Ohio.

Regarding escape plans, the possibility of the Germans coming to arrest the American delegates was something that Brown discussed on multiple occasions with a group of delegates who had become good friends. He stated, "Those weeks of February and March were somewhat of a strain on us, for at one stage of the game we were wondering if the Germans would permit us to choose the prison camp to which we were to be sent. . . . Realizing that we might be arrested any minute, six or eight of us congenial spirits formed a close corporation based on the principle that the Germans were going to have to get up pretty early in the morning to catch us."

The others in the group were never identified, but they had all agreed that in the case of America entering the war, "we would be more useful on the [Allied] side of the lines than in a prison camp in Germany, and that therefore to be led off into captivity like a flock of sheep would not be at all in accordance with our desires."

Even though many of the Americans could speak French fluently and had numerous Belgians who would have hidden them, there seemed to be no discussion of staying inside Belgium to fight a rearguard action as *franc-tireurs* (guerrilla fighters). This was probably due to numerous reasons. There was no countrywide organized military-style civilian resistance due to the Germans' swift and brutal responses to such actions in the opening days of the war. All the Belgians still in authority, officially and unofficially—from Cardinal Mercier and local burgomasters to the writers of *La Libre Belgique*—publicly advocated that civilians remain just that through the duration of the war. The young Americans would never have wanted to put their Belgian friends in harm's way by staying to fight as *franc-tireurs*. And, quite probably, many of the men, despite the strong indications America would soon enter the war, still felt honor-bound to uphold their promise given when first entering Belgium, to remain neutral while in the country.

What was discussed was escaping to Holland. Brown personally took charge of investigating what it would take and how it would be done. What he discovered from talking secretly with many people was "not my idea of summer evening's sport." It entailed "insulating yourself and climbing over a barbed-wired fence then through a highly electrified fence, then over another barbed-wire to liberty on Dutch soil while the bullets from a sentinel's gun make the night silence hum with their music!"

Despite the obstacles, he "laid the plans before our little 'corporation' and we were ready to get under way upon the first signs of any monkey business on the part of the Boches [Germans]."

Altogether, he was ready to face the future, whatever it might hold. For three months he had not received a single letter from home—which had always been his wellspring of strength and self-confidence—but he did not feel alone. He was surrounded by a small, close-knit group of men committed to a shared goal and to one another. Most importantly, he felt strong knowing that Erica Bunge loved him and would wait for his return. He knew he was in the right place, at the right time, doing the right thing. He wrote his mother and father during this time, "God grant us the reunion we look forward to, but if not that, then may he give us the strength to do our duty nobly, to take chances with courage, and to meet Death prepared, at peace with the world and unafraid."

A German Decree Divides Belgium

In early March 1917, as the issue of Americans and relief in Belgium remained uncertain, German newspapers began to report on the subject of the German administration in Belgium. There was mention of a Belgian "Flemish Council," comprising reportedly Flemish leaders who had visited Berlin petitioning the government to divide the administration of Belgium into Flemish and French regions.

As reported by the German-controlled newspapers, the group was met by German Chancellor von Bethmann-Hollweg, who made a speech that welcomed the "delegates" in their capacity as "representatives of a people so closely united to the German people by political, economical and intellectual ties." He went on to declare they were united in a struggle together. "In the midst of a blood struggle Germans and Flemish might remember that the bitter fight against the encroachments of the Latin race should lead them to the same end."

The chancellor continued by stating, "We have still before us many struggles and much labor, but that does not prevent me from extending to you my hand, that we may combat together our common enemy."

The "unanimity of the Flemish people" would guarantee success, he said, and he vowed that "when peace shall have been established, the German Empire will do all in its power to encourage and to insure the development of the Flemish nation."

Most in Belgium would have said the group and its petition were not reflective of how the majority of the country truly felt, and that the group was artificially created in a staged event to justify German action.

La Libre Belgique minced no words when it came to the Flemish/French topic. Since the earliest issues, van Doren and Victor Jourdain had warned against the dangers of the Flemish separatist movement, stating that during a time of war it was important to stand united against a common foe. Conversely, von Bissing had exploited the issue by encouraging the extreme separatists, who began calling themselves Aktivists. The latest development had been the Aktivists' establishment of the Council of Flanders, which called for a Flemish independent government.

When the new leader of *La Libre Belgique,* Abbé van den Hout, learned about the council and its visit to Germany he was incensed. He secured a photo of the group and put it on the front page of the underground newspaper. The title of the photo was written large and bold: "Treason!"

Von Bissing's heavy-handed efforts to separate French- and Flemish-speaking Belgians, such as the creation of his highly unpopular Flemish university in Ghent, were all part of a long-term goal to create two Belgiums. From his sickbed, the old Prussian finally took major official action.

On Wednesday March 21, 1917, a small *affiche* signed by the governor general appeared throughout the country. It announced that Belgium would immediately become two administration regions. The Flemish region would comprise the provinces of Antwerp, Limbourg, East and West Flanders, as well as the districts of Brussels and Louvain. The French region would be made up of the provinces of Hainaut, Liège, Luxembourg, and Namur, as well as the district of Nivelles. The headquarters of the Flemish region would be in Brussels, and the French region would be directed from Namur.

Throughout Belgium, the protests against this action were universal. *La Libre Belgique* immediately attacked the plan point for point and ran the "Treason!" photo. Cardinal Mercier also termed the group "traitorous." The political leaders in Brussels met secretly on numerous occasions and unanimously agreed to resist the plan to divide their country.

A protest letter from the city council of the Flemish capital of Antwerp was indicative of how most Flemings felt. "We consider this measure as pernicious to the existence of our country and as favourable to our enemies. It is in contradiction with all our traditions and with our most important interests . . . and this patriotism embraces in the same affection the Flemish and the Walloons. Blind is he who does not see that a people has other interests to safeguard than those which concern simply linguistic questions, however respectable those may be."

Brand Whitlock, who had come to love Belgium, felt it was the worst action of the war. "The atrocities, the deportations and the rest destroyed the body; this was an attempt to destroy the soul; they murdered men; this would assassinate a nation."

The main protest would take place after the Americans had left Belgium (see the epilogue for details).

Evacuation Orders Finally Come from Washington

Outside Belgium, events were transpiring that would move America closer to war. By the last weeks of March, four more American merchant ships had been sunk by the Germans, pushing Wilson closer to following through on the threat he had made to Germany. According to Kittredge, on March 23 the State Department, "in view of the increasing tension in the relations with Germany, decided to order the immediate withdrawal of the Minister and the Commission's staff from Belgium."

The message reached Belgium on Sunday, March 25, 1917, via Villalobar, who brought it to Whitlock. Gregory was also at the legation as the dispatch, which had been in Spanish, was translated and read. It contained a cablegram from the U.S. Secretary of State to Whitlock. It read in part, "At the request of the President I transmit instructions to you to leave Belgium immediately accompanied by the personnel of the Legation, by the American consular officers and by the American members of the Commission for Relief in Belgium stop The Department begs you to telegraph the probable date of your departure from Belgium as well as the route and your plans stop Your official residence should be in Havre [France] with the personnel of the Legation stop."

The direct, explicit instructions were a "distinct relief" to both Whitlock and Gregory. Gregory said he would immediately send the Spanish and Dutch delegates he had met to the provinces and recall all the Americans to Brussels. Gone were his earlier objections to the Spanish delegates.

The seven CRB delegates who already had their safe passes were told they would be leaving by train on the evening of Thursday, March 29, accompanied by a German "nurse," Oberlieutenant Lüdert. Kittredge—reporting not only as the CRB historian but as one of the seven—stated, "The farewell dinner of the party and the scene of their departure will probably remain long in memory of those who took part. They were the first of the Americans definitively to leave Belgium. The others were to follow in a few days, but the departure of the first group marked the beginning of the end. The nature of the party that assembled to bid them farewell illustrates something of the character of the Commission. There were a number of the [German] officers who had worked with the departing delegates in France, many of the other American delegates, of the new Spanish and Dutch delegates and many Belgian friends."

As for the farewell dinner that Kittredge wrote would long be remembered, Percy provided some descriptive flairs to explain why it was such a memorable event. The evening of departure, the seven young delegates decided to have a final dinner at the restaurant in the Palace Hotel across from the train station. They took a table in the "brilliant crowded dining-room," feeling "flat and full of foreboding. We were leaving these wretched civilians to the mercy of the German army; they were afraid and we were afraid for them. . . . We were very sad."

William Percy gave a colorful account of the final evening in Belgium of seven CRB delegates before they left on March 29, 1917. (Author's archives.)

They ordered a cocktail, dinner, and a bottle of wine. Dressed in their civilian clothes and conversing in English, they quickly became the talk of the room, for the hotel and restaurant had been taken over by German officers since the beginning of the occupation, and few other than Germans frequented the place. "We soon realized we were creating something of a sensation."

The group then began to pick up strays like an old man in a park with leftover steak. An attaché came over and "asked us to drink with him one last solemn toast in champagne." A Portuguese man "rushed over and greeted us as long-lost allies; another bottle was opened." Two of the young German "nurses" who had accompanied the delegates while in northern France suddenly appeared and "drew their seats up to our table and began fraternal lamentations." One of them said, "To think that in a few months we shall be at the front line together, you on one side, we on the other, trying to kill each other! Waiter, a bottle of champagne."

"We all wept," Percy noted, "and our spirits rose."

The dinner turned into a rousing, noisy celebration. Others joined them, described by an inebriated Percy only as "vague individuals." The mood grew happier with each new toast. "Everybody felt better and better. We all loved one another and said so and pledged our devotion in glass after glass of magnificent champagne."

At one point, finally, someone "thought to look squarely and honestly into the face of a watch and discovered we had ten minutes in which to collect ourselves, pay the check, get across the street to the station and into the train."

Chairs were thrown back, coats and hats grabbed, and a confused rush for the door leading outside and to the ice-covered street. The men ran as best their liquor-legs could carry them, bolting up the stairs "into the waiting-room of the station in superb spirits, giddy with love and optimism, teeming with becks and calls and wreathed smiles."

When Philip Potter left Belgium, he was last seen "leaning out of the [train] car window knocking off the [German] sentries' helmets with his golf club." (Author's archives.)

The gay group was pulled up short by the scene that greeted them.

There before them was "the whole staff of the C.R.B. and half the Brussels population jamming the waiting-room, in tears, anxiously and solemnly waiting to bid us adieu."

"It was something of a set-back," Percy noted drily. The sad crowd had "brought hampers of food, cases of wine, and bouquets of flowers, and only our tardiness had kept the weeping burgomaster from delivering an oraison funèbre [funeral oration] of incomparable poignancy."

To cap off the tumultuous evening, "as the train pulled out we were boosted into it through the windows amid the sobs and cheers of our sorrowing friends."

Standing on the platform to say goodbye was Prentiss Gray, who noted, "Our last glimpse of them showed Phil Potter leaning out of the car window knocking off the sentries' helmets with his golf club."

Aboard the train, Percy finished his account by saying that as the men had dove through the train windows they had "landed in different compartments and it took hours to collect us. Our poor [German] nurse was a nervous wreck. United at last, we settled down to headaches."

No wonder Kittredge never forgot the evening.

As for the rest of the CRB delegates and Whitlock and his staff, the Germans did agree to allow them out of Belgium and arranged a special train that would take them to Switzerland. It would leave a few days later in the late afternoon of April 2, 1917.

Whitlock's Last Impressions of Brussels

The ensuing days, Whitlock wrote in his journal, were filled with packing and farewells, as the news of the Americans leaving "flew at once over the town, in that mysterious way it always had in Brussels."

Whitlock also took the time to walk and drive around the city he had come to love. By this time, the snow had gone, and the weather had returned to its usual early spring rains and "pale, melancholy days." No matter the weather, Whitlock realized just how much Brussels had changed since he had first seen it back in early 1914. "The town, once so gay and blithe and charming, had grown gradually sadder; now it seemed morose."

Visiting the *grand place*, he sought out the flower woman he and Nell had patronized for years and suddenly saw with fresh eyes how much she had changed. "She used to be so buxom, so lively, so gay, so full of instant repartee! . . . Now she was gay no more, but sad, depressed, and her hollow cough echoed all over the Square."

The entire city seemed to have changed much like the flower woman. "The shops were closed, the people were in rags, the lines at the soup kitchens trailed their squalid miseries farther and farther down the street; the doors of the *ouvroirs*, those posts of charity where sewing was given out, were besieged by throngs of pale and patient women."

And the Germans were everywhere, having "left their mark on everything in the city; its physical grace and beauty had been marred by the signs in German which they had put up. . . . Only German newspapers and German books were sold. . . . And there were [German] officers, pink and fat, racing by in motors, or insolently swaggering along the boulevard with an arrogance that had all the vulgarity of the parvenu [upstarts]."

Such visual affronts were not as bad as the periodic requisitioning of certain items that the Germans demanded as the occupation and the war had lingered on. In late March, as Whitlock had wandered through the streets of Brussels, the Germans had ordered all copper items to be turned in. On the Gare du Luxembourg, Whitlock noted sadly the "daily long lines of women surrendering up to the Germans their copper batteries, those pots and kettles which they had polished through so many years, which had been furbished and polished by their mothers and grandmothers before them, to make shining masses of gold in Flemish kitchens, taken from them now to be made into munitions of war with which to kill the husbands and brothers of those women." The Germans also went door-to-door to make sure all copper was collected.

The copper requisition touched the CRB delegates as well, but in a slightly different way. Arthur Maurice, who had entered Belgium only in January, faced the situation head-on. One night in March, he was at the Brussels house he was living in with other delegates when there was a knock at the door. Louis, one of the Belgian chauffeurs, had a message from an experienced delegate, William Sperry, who had hurriedly written a frantic note that the Germans would be "coming to go through the house for brass and copper. For the Love of Mike make sure that every man's room is safe. Destroy all French and English newspapers. Particularly see that those copies of *Punch* [an English magazine] with the pictures of [the Kaiser] are all before the war numbers. Go through every man's correspondence. It's no

During the last few days of the Americans in Belgium, Brand Whitlock noticed how the war had changed the city he had come to love. (Public domain; Robert Arrowsmith papers, Hoover Institution Archives, Stanford University, Stanford, California.)

time to be squeamish. I would do it myself only I am not coming to the house!" (Nothing is known about whether or not the search happened.)

Whitlock's continued wanderings through Brussels also saw him noting that in the city's *parc,* or major park, which sprawled out in front of the King's palace, "where the bright new greens were stealing, there were . . . no ladies and gentlemen riding spirited horses, and no lovers courting there; only ragged men in broken sabots [wooden shoes], and children, their fingers blue with cold, picking up twigs to make a little fire at home."

Even worse than the transformation the city had gone through was the transformation seen in the small number of Belgian deportees sent back from the work camps in Germany. Whitlock reported, "They were pitiable objects of German brutality; they were, for the most part, pale, emaciated men whose physical condition made them useless as workers, broken, maimed, helpless, hopeless; a few weeks in the slave compounds in Germany had so reduced [them] by sickness, exposure and starvation that they were hauled back to Belgium and flung down in their villages to die."

"Some of the returned *chômeurs* who were brought to Brussels and taken to hospitals had their feet frozen from exposure, or were in such a state of gangrene from maltreatment that it was necessary to amputate their legs. Those at Antwerp were returned at night to avoid notice, for their physical condition was so pitiable that the Germans seemed to be afraid or ashamed to exhibit them as examples of their work."

On Thursday, March 29, Cardinal Mercier came to see Whitlock, who described the prelate as "tall, majestic, with the simplicity of the truly great—such blue eyes of virtue and lofty courage!" Whitlock noted, "His Eminence expressed sorrow, and showed sorrow, at our going. He spoke with beautiful appreciation of America and what America had done for Belgium and said that Belgium had lost her 'stay and support.'"

That same day was the usual weekly meeting of the CN, which was normally attended by at least a handful of CRB delegates. Gregory attended, knowing it would be the last time he could address the full body of prominent Belgians. He had written out a farewell letter and read it to the group. He expressed his and the CRB's deep regret that they had to leave and extended his great appreciation for all the kindness and consideration they had received in the two and a half years they had been in Belgium. He ended by humbly stating, "If we have been of some slight service to you and to the Belgium people, the knowledge of that fact will be for us a sufficient reward and will be ever held by us in grateful remembrance."

Francqui then rose and, with all the pomp and ceremony he could muster, he read a letter from the CN to Gregory and the CRB that expressed the Belgians' sorrow at the departure of the Americans. "For the more than two years that we have laboured in common to serve our country," Francqui read, "you have laboured with all the warmth of your devotion to help a country that is not yours, but which your sentiments of human fellowship and respect for the right has made you love.

"The sadness we feel at the temporary separation," Francqui continued, "is nevertheless tempered by the joy we feel in learning that, in spite of your departure, you and your fellow-workers will continue on the outside to lavish on us your labour and devotion, under the skillful and wise management of Mr. Hoover.

"As you leave us," Francqui read, "you and your fellow-workers may take with you the assurance that Belgians will never forget the great work that has been realised through you. Each day the bread they eat, the food they enjoy, will recall them to the colossal work still carried beyond our frontiers by our American friends, a work on which the feeding and existence of the country absolutely depend."

The Belgian came to a strong conclusion as he read loudly, "In the history of mankind there is no example of a generosity so noble, and the sorrowful history of Belgium will show that your action has resulted in helping us, not only to live, but also to preserve our faith in the greatness of humanity and in the possible beauty of the future."

On Saturday, March 31, only two days before the special train was to take the Americans away, Belgians continued to flood the legation to say farewell. Cards and letters filled with great emotion were left for later reading.

That morning, Émile Francqui and the Comité National held a *grand déjeuner*, or great breakfast, at the Taverne Royale for the departing CRB delegates. There was an abundance of food, drink, and toasts and the putting aside of petty infighting to celebrate what the two great organizations had achieved in a time of war. Francqui made what Whitlock reported was a "touching speech," after which the U.S. minister returned the favor. "With much genuine regret and sorrow," Whitlock later wrote, "we bade adieu to the dear friends with whom we had laboured so long."

That evening, word came from Liège that Albert Heingartner, the U.S. Consul there, had suddenly died from heart failure, "falling thus," Whitlock noted, "at his post at the very moment in which his services ended. His death cast its shadow over the Legation. He had been long in the Consular Service; he came from my own state of Ohio. I could only send Cruger to close the Consulate and to render what aid he could to the stricken family in such an hour." (Mrs. Heingartner and her daughter decided not to take the special train on April 2 and instead waited for the arrival of the son from Vienna.)

Whitlock Has a Final Moment with Von Bissing

When the day of departure dawned in Brussels on Monday, April 2, Whitlock had no idea that later on the same day President Wilson would stand before a joint session of congress and ask for a declaration of war against Germany, stating, "The world must be made safe for democracy." (Wilson would get a declaration of war on April 6.) To the minister, the day was filled with final packing, organizing, and two special events—one spontaneous, one planned.

In the morning, a German motorcyclist came roaring up to the legation. He had an unexpected invitation from Baron von Bissing for Whitlock to attend a 1:00 p.m. lunch at the governor general's home at Trois Fontaines in the village of Vilvorde, 7.5 miles (12 km) outside Brussels. The American minister accepted, knowing he also had to attend a major farewell luncheon hosted by the burgomaster of Brussels, Baron Charles Lemonnier. Both were to start at the same time, but as he wrote, "I can not decline either!"

His dilemma was somewhat resolved when he remembered that the German invitation was on German time (an hour before Belgian time), while the other was on Belgian time. That meant if he hurried—and if his driver, Eugene, was speedy—he could see von Bissing at noon Belgian time and still catch most of the Belgian gathering. He told his wife, Nell, to go to the Belgian lunch and inform the group that he had been called away to see von Bissing and would be there as soon as possible.

Personally, Whitlock could not resist the German's invitation, knowing it would be the first time to see von Bissing since the governor general had recently returned from sick leave in Germany, and it would probably be the last time he would ever see the old Prussian.

Because Whitlock's German passport for local travel had expired a few days before, he hastily organized a new one and was off in his motorcar by 11:30 a.m. A minor glitch occurred at the bridge leading to Trois Fontaines when a German sentry, "an ass, placed himself across the roadway, and wouldn't budge." He was quickly dispatched, Whitlock noted, by "three peasants, laughing," who "carried him off in their strong arms."

As Whitlock's motorcar pulled up to the gate of the governor general's palatial residence, a squad of mounted German Imperial Guard greeted him, resplendent in their crisp white and red uniforms. Ushered into the formal salon, he found numerous General Staff officers. Soon after, they all bowed respectfully as Madame von Bissing and the governor general appeared. Whitlock reported that the

German was "feeble and haggard and looked much older; he walked stiffly and with difficulty."

Whitlock was seated next to Madame von Bissing, who spoke with him in English and French. It was a simple meal of three courses: eggs, meat, and a final course of cheese, coffee, and cigarettes. The governor general was seated across the table and for most of the meal did not speak of the American's imminent departure from Belgium. At one point, however, Baron von Bissing did raise his glass to Whitlock and after they had drunk, he stated in French, "You are going, then?"

Much to Whitlock's surprise, the German "in a kind of fury" then "boomed out across the table a great 'why?' . . . He said they would miss me, that the revictualing would not go on as well without me, and so on. Then, raising his glass of wine, he said, 'Bon voyage!'"

Whitlock laughed and replied without thinking, "And quick return?"

To the American's great relief, the German laughed at what Whitlock admitted was a comment "in rather questionable taste."

Shortly after, von Bissing acknowledged that Whitlock had to leave, and the group stood from the table. In the salon they said their goodbyes, with both Madame von Bissing and her husband thanking Whitlock for his kindness through the years.

Whitlock never saw von Bissing again. Within a few short days von Bissing would resign as governor general and would die a few days later at Trois Fontaines on April 18, 1917, at the age of 73, replaced by Ludwig von Falkenhausen. Vernon Kellogg gave a philosophical reason for his death: "Governor-general von Bissing died from too much telling the Belgians to do things—some important, many trivial—and too much trying to make them do them. He fumed and worried and suffered because they would not behave properly. Why would they not? Why should not Belgians be managed as Germans are managed? Why would they not? He died unenlightened. . . . I almost believe no German could."

With his farewell to von Bissing completed, Whitlock rushed to his car and had Eugene race back to Brussels and the other luncheon. He arrived at 1:30 p.m. Belgian time to find everyone already seated at the table but understanding of his tardiness. Villalobar was there, as were all the city aldermen and their wives.

Brown's Last Two Days in the Office

Brussels had been muted and muzzled for more than two years by the German occupation. In the last days of March, the city became even quieter and more morose as it mourned the upcoming departure of the CRB on the train dubbed the American Special.

In contrast, the youthful delegates were whirlwinds of activity as they tried to finish up any outstanding business and say their farewells to Belgian friends and co-

Milton Brown spent the last two days in Brussels at the CRB office at 66 Rue des Colonies trying to wrap up work for the clothing department. (Public domain; *In Occupied Belgium,* Robert Withington, The Cornill Co., 1921.)

workers. They knew the clock was ticking, and they were determined to do as much as possible before showing up at the train station.

Brown was no exception. On Sunday, April 1, the day before the train's departure, he worked at the office until 6:30 p.m. He then rushed home for a quick break before returning and working from 9:30 p.m. until 2:30 a.m. Monday. He once again raced home, this time to pack, which he had not even started. By 6 a.m. he had finished packing and grabbed a quick 45-minute nap before hurrying back to the office. Before leaving the house for the last time, he left instructions with one of the servants to get his bags to the train station as soon as possible.

That morning at the office he received what he had been longing to get for months—an order from the CN for clothing materials that totaled a staggering 25 million francs. His plan was to take that order, go to London, and then prepare a report for the British that would get them to accept and place the order. "This has been the ambition of my work for the past nine months—to obtain for the C.N. full permission to import whatever they needed." He felt that "if the entire situation could be laid before the Allied Governments and a complete report on the operations of the Division du Vêtements be given them, all opposition to such imports would cease." It was a bold plan for a big order, and Brown was determined to make it happen.

For the young American delegate, that last day, Monday, April 2, "was perfectly frightful with work—one long strain of nerves and energy up to the very last minute to finish my work. We had been told to leave the office at 4:30 in the afternoon, at twenty-five minutes to five I finished dictating my last letter. I rushed upstairs to say goodbye to the stenographers and clerks; all the Americans had left; it was a gloomy place! I went down again and signed my last letters. In saying goodbye to my three stenographers tears were in the eyes of each of them and one of them broke down completely."

It was a highly emotional moment, but Brown had been through "so much work and nervous strain during those last few days that my nerves were taut to the point where they could not give way." He wouldn't dare let himself feel what he knew was inside.

He walked out of the CRB office at 66 Rue des Colonies, which he had called home for more than a year, and started slowly making his way toward the train station. "I was no longer 'a member of the C.R.B. in Brussels.' Even my passport had expired and I could not ride in an automobile."

He would be overwhelmed at the station by a moment of apology he never expected.

The American Special

After Brand Whitlock finished his second luncheon of the day, he hurried back to the legation. Villalobar, "very sad and solemn," came to take the Whitlocks in his motorcar to the Gare du Nord train station. Following close behind were various vehicles carrying the Whitlocks' 15 trunks, which were surpassed only by the 20 trunks of legation secretary Ruddock, his wife, and their two children. Also part of the legation staff's luggage were two huge diplomatic pouches that contained the legation's complete records and, as Whitlock noted, "most precious of all, the sacred Code [for encrypted communications], to say nothing of the manuscript of my novel."

The *Place Rogier*, the square at the front of the train station, was packed with a huge crowd that had flowed into the station and filled it to capacity, despite a German proclamation prohibiting any demonstrations regarding the American departure. The Belgians' underground communications system had worked once again. Whitlock noted, "There had been, of course, no public announcement of our going, the hour was not known, yet the word had gone about in Brussels."

Partially out of respect and partially because of the fear of German reaction to any outbursts or public displays, which had been outlawed, the large crowd was silent. Whitlock and the others got out of their cars and made their way through the crowd to the station. The men pulled off their hats, and many women were in tears. "It was very still," Whitlock said. "There was not a word, not a sound. I went through the crowd; now and then a child was held out to me, its little hand outstretched, and low voices beside said: 'Au revoir—et bientôt' ['Goodbye—and see you soon']."

Inside, Whitlock noted, "All our friends were there, come to bid us good-bye, and friends of the members of the C.R.B., all the remaining members of the diplomatic corps, the city officials, representatives of the Comité National." The three giants of the CN—Solvay, Francqui, and Janssen—stood together to say goodbye. When Whitlock saw them, "I nearly broke down; the only time my nerve failed. Somehow they represented to me all I was leaving, all it meant."

With German guards and officers prominently watching the proceedings, there was little in the way of emotional outbursts. Whitlock recorded that the Belgians "were all silent, many in tears, and all knowing that any manifestation would be severely repressed. . . . It was all most touching."

Brown mingled with the other CRB delegates on the platform as they all said goodbye to their friends. "It was one of the hardest things I have ever had to go through in my life." He felt, as most of the others did, that he was deserting the beloved Belgians in their greatest hour of need. He felt guilty that he was going to reenter a world where freedom was a given and food was plentiful.

Most importantly, he thought of Erica. He had not written about his final moments with her, which had happened weeks before at Chateau Oude Gracht, but on the platform about to leave Belgium and not knowing if he'd ever be back or even survive the war, "I longed for one more glimpse of you and I knew I had had my last."

It was then that Madame Philippson-Wiener approached him. His counterpart and operations manager of the CN's clothing department asked to have a moment alone with him. They moved away as best they could from the crowd.

"Mr. Brown, there is something I want you to know before you go." Speaking in French, she leaned toward him to make sure no one else heard. "I have had to play a very disagreeable game with you and I have always been very, very sorry about it."

Brown believed he knew what she was about to say. This had to do, he was sure, with the resistance he had encountered, especially in the early days, when trying to gain the information about the clothing operations that he had needed.

"I did not want to do what I did but I was acting under orders and had to," she said with great feeling. "I regret very much indeed that I could not have seen more of you and have had more of your friendship but my position prevented that. . . . But I wanted you to know all this before you went and I don't want you to judge me too harshly."

It had been Janssen who had ordered her not to give him the information he wanted and not to spend too much time with him. Her apology "made me feel very fine indeed, especially in what she said to me. . . . I was always certain that she was not acting as she wanted to but only as her orders and her position forced her."

The Whitlocks had brought with them two staff, Marie and Eugene, and their two Pekingese dogs, Kin Kung and Tai Tai, while the Ruddocks had brought a German nurse and maid as well as their chef François and his wife and daughter, and a man servant, Alphonse. According to Whitlock, approximately 90 people boarded the special train:

- 20 legation staff
- 15 from the U.S. consuls who had been stationed across Belgium
- 18 members of the Chinese legation
- Approximately 40 members of the CRB—including Director Gregory and his 19-year-old son, Don, who had been serving as a delegate
- A few accompanying German officers

Staying behind with the approval of the German civil government were Prentiss Gray (along with his wife and child), who had volunteered to aid the transition to Dutch and Spanish delegates; six American delegates who had to be "quarantined" in Brussels for a few weeks because they had recently been close to the front; and American accountant Francis Neville with two associates (all from the accounting firm Deloitte, Plender, Griffiths & Company) to close up the CRB American accounting books.

Villalobar was the last to say his farewells to the Whitlocks. He gave a bouquet of forget-me-nots to Nell and then suddenly embraced Whitlock.

As the train pulled out of the station, Whitlock looked out the window of his coach. "Far across the expanse of rails, at the end of a street which came down to the edge of the wide way, at the barrier of a grade crossing in Schaerbeek, a great crowd was gathered, and as the train passed, above the mass of faces blurred by distance, there burst a white cloud of fluttered handkerchiefs."

Like many other delegates, Brown had been holding his emotions in check during the last few days in Brussels and especially on the train station platform. But that all changed as the American Special pulled away.

"I shall never, never forget the sight as that train began to pull out," Brown wrote later to Erica Bunge. "Nor shall I ever forget the feeling of utter despair that rushed through me as I realized that we were actually leaving Belgium. I stood it until, passing a side street a half a kilometer or so out from the station I saw a street crowd massed against the fence to see us pass, their hats and handkerchiefs waving frantically. That last real view of the Belgians for whom we had been giving the little we could to help, that final farewell was too much and I broke down and sobbed like a child; and the two men beside me did the same. I felt as though my heart were breaking—to be going out like that and leaving you and your countrymen to God-knows-what! I think it was the bitterest moment of my life."

"We waved our last farewell," said Prentiss Gray, the CRB director who was staying along with his family and six other delegates to wrap up American affairs and aid the transition to the Dutch and Spanish delegates. "A sense of oppression rushed over us and we turned sadly, and with heavy hearts passed out through the throngs of Belgians, themselves none too dry-eyed, who had been allowed to enter the station; we walked along the iron fence surrounding the train yard, where thousands more pressed their faces against the metal palings, in the eager hope of catching a last glimpse of the Americans whom they looked upon as protectors from the oppressor and the sole source of what little food they had."

Gray kept hearing the last words from Edward Curtis, one of the first to have joined the CRB in 1914. Curtis had been standing on the train's rear platform, and as it had begun to pull away, he had called out to Gray and the remaining delegates, "You lucky beggars to draw leftover tickets; Austria will sue for peace before we get to the border."

The Americans picked their way through the emotional crowd outside the station. "As we entered our motor car, which was flying the only C.R.B. flag left in Belgium, a cheer broke from the crowd."

Fearful of German reprisals for such a demonstration, Gray urged the chauffeur to hurry them away. It was a long, lonely ride back to their residence through mostly dark and deserted streets as the "awful oppression of Prison settled down into our souls."

Long after the train left Brussels, Whitlock was still tense. He worried that, despite German orders, many of his fellow passengers were carrying contraband photos, letters, or journals. He took it upon himself, as the titular head of the group, to destroy anything he felt could be construed as contraband. He confiscated a small boy's postcards, a woman's photo of her son in an English uniform, as well as "patriot souvenirs" and photographs collected from some of the CRB delegates. "I tore them all up and threw them out the window onto the clean German landscape."

Midmorning the train pulled into a station near the border with Switzerland. On the tracks nearby was a Swiss train, ready to take the group from Germany into neutral Switzerland.

The Germans' final inspection of the mounds of luggage and the approximately 90 people was, Whitlock wrote, "not severe" with one glaring exception. For some reason that was never given, Don Gregory, the 19-year-old son of CRB Director Gregory, was strip-searched "to the skin." Nothing was found, and the group was allowed on its way.

By afternoon, the train had pulled into Schaffhausen, Switzerland, and was greeted by three officers and two lines of smartly dressed Swiss soldiers.

After years of personal, internal struggle, doubts, and conflicting feelings, Brand Whitlock had finally escaped the post that had nearly broken him physically and mentally.

59

Elsewhere in Belgium and Northern France

Belgium's Moral Voice Rises Again

Through the first few months of 1917, Cardinal Mercier had never let up from the battle he had waged for his deported countrymen. In December 1916 the cardinal had established a committee to collect appeals for those who felt they had been unjustly taken. Even with numerous eyewitness accounts to the contrary, the German government maintained that only those who were unemployed and receiving charity were taken. The committee was swamped with appeals.

On January 24, 1917, the cardinal made his first official appeal for 698 men to the interim governor general, Baron von Huene (von Bissing had taken ill and was recuperating in Germany). That was quickly followed in the next month by six more letters that included appeals for reparations from more than 2,500 men.

As the cardinal was doing all that he could to get back at least some of the deported, he was visited on Sunday, February 11, 1917, by the Marquis de Villalobar and the Belgian minister of state, Monsieur Levie. They had a plan to gather the most notable men in Belgium to sign an appeal that would be taken directly to the Kaiser. It would be taken to Berlin by von der Lancken. Mercier agreed immediately not only to sign the document but also to write it.

The appeal stated that the undersigned "with heavy hearts have seen and still see every day thousands of their brethren torn from their families and dragged forcibly into exile, where they are compelled to choose between starvation and work which offends their dignity as patriots."

Mercier wielded as his sword what he knew best, religion. "Your Imperial Majesty prides yourself on your loyalty to your faith. May we not then be allowed to remind you of the simple and yet striking words of the Gospel, 'Do unto others that which you would have done to yourself'? . . . We venture to hope that your Majesty will be guided by but one sentiment—that of humanity."

The letter ended by stating that "the undersigned, representing the religious, political and judicial, economic and social authorities of the Belgian people, hope

American artist George Bellows captured the desperate, haunted feeling that shadowed the returning Belgian deportees. Many of the broken men died while in transit. (Public domain; multiple sources.)

that your Majesty will give the necessary orders to cease deporting Belgian workmen and to repatriate those who have been driven into exile."

The first signer was Cardinal Mercier. Under the title of "Relief and Victualing Committee" was Ernest Solvay as "president." He was actually the chairman of the CN, while the president was Émile Francqui, whose name, for some unknown reason, was not on the list.

Dated February 14, 1917, the document was delivered soon after not only to the Emperor but also to von Bissing, who had returned to Belgium and must have been furious at the audacity of those who went over his head to petition the Kaiser. However, that anger might have been mitigated by von Bissing's reportedly less-than-enthusiastic support for the deportations.

On Friday, March 9, 1917, Baron von der Lancken verbally told the president of the Belgian senate, Baron de Favereau, the Emperor's answer. No doubt contrary to what his generals wanted, the Kaiser ordered that all those who had been mistakenly deported as unemployed be returned and that the deportations would be suspended until further orders.

On March 14, the imperial degree was officially announced in Brussels publications. The short statement began, "Certain Belgian notables belonging to various parties have recently addressed H.M. the Emperor urging him to put an end to the forced deportations of Belgian workmen to Germany, and to have returned to their homes those Belgians who have been sent away."

The Kaiser had sent the petition on to Governor General von Bissing for "careful examination," while reserving the right to making his own decision after the review was complete.

In the meantime, the announcement continued, the Emperor had "given orders to have returned immediately to Belgium . . . those Belgians sent to Germany by mistake, and to suspend until further order the forced deportation to Germany of unemployed Belgians."

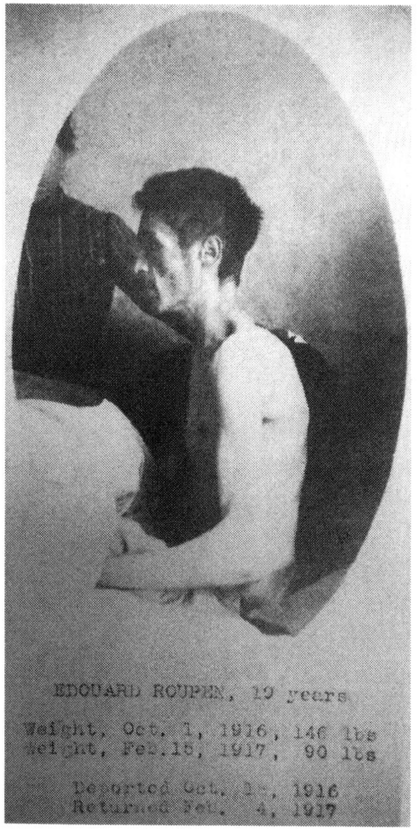

Deported by the Germans on October 1, 1916, 19-year-old Edouard Roupen weighed a healthy 146 pounds. When he was shipped back home in early February 1917, he weighed 90 pounds. (Public domain; Herbert Hoover Presidential Library, West Branch, Iowa.)

It was a great, but not complete, victory. Only those who had been taken by mistake—meaning men who had jobs when the deportations were supposedly taking just the unemployed—would be returned. Nothing had been said about the vast majority who were unemployed and had been taken forcibly or of the reported 10,000 to 13,000 who had signed contracts to work for the Germans (whether because they wanted to or because they felt signing would get their families better treatment).

Still, it was a significant victory. After more than a year, and after more than 120,000 had been ripped from their families (no official count was ever made)—the slave raids were over. And some of the men were coming home. Cardinal Mercier wrote in his book, "The deportations ceased after this and little by little the unhappy men, who had been taken away by force to Germany, were able to return to their country. The lamentable condition in which they were found on their return proved to the hilt what privations and sufferings they had gone through.

A large number, exhausted by the hardships inflicted on them in forcing them to work, had to be looked after in the hospitals."

One CRB delegate, William Percy, confirmed in March how physically poor the returning men were. "I saw trainloads of them arriving in the Antwerp station. They were creatures imagined by El Greco—skeletons, with blue flesh clinging to their bones, too weak to stand alone, too ill to be hungry any longer." Writing much later, during World War II, Percy commented, "This was only a miniature venture into slavery, a preliminary to the epic conquest and enslavement of whole peoples in 1940, but it seemed hideous and unprecedented to us in 1917."

Prentiss Gray gave more details when he wrote on Thursday, March 1, "Today a trainload of returned Deportees pulled into Antwerp from Aix la Chapelle. They had been *en route* twenty-four hours and during that time fifty-two had died. Every man was carried from the train on a stretcher to the hospital, broken wrecks of humanity for which the Germans could find no more use. Therefore they were being returned to Belgium so as not to use up hospital space or burial crews."

Gray followed the ambulances to the hospital and spoke to some of the men. "They told stories of their daily ration of a bowl of fish-head soup and a morsel of black bread no larger than your fist: stories of standing in the snow for hours without covering, guarded by a feldwebel [sergeant] who struck them across their freezing fingers when they tried to put their hands in their pockets: stories of standing in icy water till their feet were frost bitten: stories of starvation, of floggings and inhuman treatment."

Admitting some of the stories might be "overdrawn," Gray stated strongly, though, that "there were unmistakable signs in their physical condition of suffering beyond human endurance. Evidence there was plenty in frozen feet and hands, great red welts on their emaciated bodies, pneumonia and tuberculosis ran riot among them."

CRB delegate Robert Arrowsmith witnessed a trainload that came into Liège and later told Gray about what he saw. "Among them was a young man so weak that when his arm slipped over the side of the stretcher he did not have strength to lift it back. One of the Doctors gently took hold of his hand to replace it on his chest. The young fellow misunderstood the movement and resisting said with his last breath, 'Je ne signe pas' ['I will not sign,' referring to the document agreeing to work for the Germans]. He was dead before he reached the hospital."

Gray was tremendously moved by what he saw and wrote about the Belgian deportees and of this young man's resistance to the end. "It spoke volumes for his steadfastness of purpose in refusing to the very end to sign the voluntary agreement to work for the Germans despite the release from torture and starvation which it would have meant to him. It is sad that he should have passed away misinterpreting the first kindly act in many months."

Many of the deported would not get back to Belgium until the war was over, and others never made it back home.

60

London

Hoover Arrives Back in London

Nearly three weeks after the Chief had left America—and after an eventful time traveling from Cadiz, Spain, through France and across the English Channel—Hoover finally reached London on Tuesday, April 3, a day after the American Special train had left Brussels. Events had been moving much faster than he had.

- The State Department had told Whitlock at the end of March that he and the CRB men in Belgium were to get out.
- The Germans had agreed to allow a handful of American delegates to stay in an attempt to keep the relief alive.
- The Germans had arranged a special train to carry the Americans out of Belgium that left Brussels on April 2.
- The same day, April 2, President Wilson had addressed a special session of congress asking for a declaration of war.

A day after Hoover returned to London, he and the members of the CRB responded to Wilson's call for war with a cable to the president. The message spoke of their years of struggle to maintain neutrality in the face of the harsh German rule. "For two and a half years, we have been obliged to remain silent witnesses to the character of the forces dominating this war, but we now are at liberty to say that although we break, with great regret, our association with many German individuals who have given sympathetic support to our work, yet your message enunciates our conviction, born of our intimate experience and contact, that there is no hope for democracy or liberalism and consequently for real peace or the safety of our country unless the system which has brought the world into this unfathomable misery can be stamped out once and for all."

On Friday, April 6, Wilson got his declaration of war from congress. The Allies celebrated, the Belgians cheered silently, and the Germans probably cursed.

Hoover still worried about what would happen to the relief. Various plans were floated to see what would be acceptable to the Germans and the Allies now that

America was no longer neutral. Because of the admirable job Hoover and his men had done in all aspects of relief outside of Belgium—purchasing, transportation, financing, and accounting—both sides agreed to allow Hoover and his American associates to continue running those parts of the program. It was also agreed that the CRB would maintain a shipping and accounting office in Brussels but would employ Belgians to do the work.

The biggest issue still not resolved was who would replace the American CRB delegates in Belgium and northern France. Hoover stated the job "proved troublesome and long drawn out." Would it be the Dutch? The Spanish? The Danes? The Swiss? Everyone had a strong opinion and expressed it. Hoover's frustration at the players and the lack of a quick solution were obvious when he said, "There were international jealousies which I cannot attempt to explain."

After long and difficult negotiations, an agreement was struck that a joint committee of Spanish and Dutch, the Comité Hispano-Hollandais, would manage the relief and the new delegates stationed in Belgium. Final resolution of the arrangement, however, would not be fully completed for three more months. Regardless, the relief continued throughout the negotiations and would continue through the end of the war (see the epilogue for details).

Another major problem Hoover faced when he arrived back in London was the sinking of CRB vessels. This was "our most urgent problem during my stay in London."

The statistics regarding all shipping, Allied and neutral, told a shocking tale. Since the Germans had resumed unrestricted submarine warfare, the Allies and neutral countries had lost in gross tonnage from all causes: January 1917, 365,000 tons; February 1917, 537,000 tons; March 1917, 591,000 tons; April 1917, 867,000 tons.

Within those figures, the CRB had lost seven ships to torpedoes, two to mines, and five more were stranded or lost from the failure of the Germans to issue clear directions regarding the open channels. According to Hoover, all the CRB ships had official safe conduct passes, had appropriate signage (both printed and illuminated), and were outside the war zone when damaged or sunk. The statistics regarding the CRB's food deliveries to Rotterdam were frightening:

Deliveries Three Months Prior to German U-boat Campaign	
November 1916	65,494 tons
December 1916	70,458 tons
January 1917	90,019 tons
Deliveries after the Start of the German U-boat Campaign	
February 1917	24,294 tons
March 1917	10,116 tons
April 1917	61,719 tons
May 1917	19,742 tons

Two days after arriving back in London, Hoover was protesting the sinkings to Spanish ministers Merry del Val in London and Villalobar in Brussels, hoping they, representing the then-major neutral patron of the relief work, would officially protest to the Germans. In a telegram to Villalobar, Hoover stated, "Unless we can get some definite and believable assurance we cannot induce a single ship, much less the crews, to pursue this work and I have serious doubts whether the Allied Governments will allow us to go on sacrificing ship after ship in constant violation of every sacred undertaking made by the German authorities." He followed with a longer message identifying all the circumstances of each incident.

Both Spaniards promised the strongest support and Villalobar actively pushed the issue with both von der Lancken and von Bissing.

This was the start of weeks of back and forth between accusations issued by the British, French, Americans, and Spanish and denials declared by the German military, von Bissing, and von der Lancken. One comment from von der Lancken summed up the German position: "The accidents which have happened to the ships of the C.R.B. seem in general and at first sight imputable, either to fortuitous circumstances, to acts of imprudence on the part of the Captains of these ships, or to insufficient instructions having been given them by the Commission for Relief. What is certain is that in no case has an error or fault yet been proved against the ships of the Imperial Marine."

The British weighed in with a message to Hoover suggesting unrealistically that the CRB demand the Germans replace the foodstuffs destroyed as well as provide their own merchant fleet for CRB use.

Ever the pragmatist, Hoover wrote, "While I was no less indignant than the [British] Foreign Office, I had no faith that demanding the replacement of stores and ships would have any effect on the German mind. And to make the demand and have it refused would have put us in the practical position of having to quit the Relief. The terrible consequences of this would have fallen on the Belgians and French and not on the Germans."

To Hoover, the ship attacks indicated an issue within Germany. "Strange as it may seem," he said, "I believe that the civilian government in Berlin was sincere in wanting our ships protected but so far could not control their militarists."

In the end, the Germans never accepted culpability, but Hoover felt it was the Spanish who finally made somewhat of a difference. "Discouraging as all this was and as terrible as its consequences were, we still hoped that the energetic action of our Spanish Patrons might save the Relief. Our hopes were confirmed by the subsequent slowing down of sinkings."

61

Brussels

Von Bissing Leaves the Stage

When von Bissing died on Wednesday, April 18, 1917, *La Libre Belgique*'s editor, van den Hout, was quick to salute his death with "unconcealed satisfaction." To the paper, the general had died "worn out and embittered, his twin ambitions, the annexation of Belgium and the suppression of the *Libre Belgique*, unfulfilled."

As if the secret police's efforts were somehow tied to the strength of von Bissing, the first three months of van den Hout's management of the underground newspaper were uneventful. The largest struggle was continuing to find paper for printing. After much searching, van den Hout found a large stock that would keep the presses going for years, but he had no money to buy it and few ways of getting it from an Antwerp warehouse to Brussels. He solved the lack of funds with a discreet visit to Cardinal Mercier, during which time the newspaper was never officially mentioned, but as van den Hout was leaving, the cardinal gave him an envelope with a large sum of money and reportedly said, "Take this. My brother, I know, is interested in many worthy charitable works. This little donation will, I am sure, not come amiss."

Von Bissing's replacement, Governor General von Falkenhausen, would take on the hunt for the clandestine newspaper with aggressive dedication that would have made von Bissing proud (see the epilogue for details).

The Final Days of the Americans in Belgium

In early April, after the special train had carried away Whitlock and most of the CRB delegates, Prentiss Gray and his small band of American delegates had hunkered down to help the Dutch and Spanish delegates understand the job and continue the relief as best they could.

Still remaining and working in the office were delegates Francis Wickes, Maurice Pate, James Dangerfield Jr., Carlos H. Stone, Charles H. Carstairs, and Julius Van Hee (a U.S. Deputy Consul in Ghent who had become a delegate in January 1915).

Also remaining were the three U.S. accountants/auditors who had been serving in Brussels: Francis D. Neville, Oliver W. De Gruchy, and James A. St. Amour. As employees of the accounting firm of Deloitte, Plender, Griffiths & Company (which had volunteered its services to the CRB), the three men were never considered members of the CRB—despite their diligent and good work side-by-side with the CRB men. They should have been.

Belgian Fernand Baetens was in charge of the CRB's Brussels shipping department and was "the esteemed and indispensable adviser of all the American directors of the Commission." (Author's archives.)

There were three non-American men in the Brussels office considered members of the CRB: Rene Jensen, a Dane who had served mainly as a courier since early 1915 but was then secretary to the office; Belgian Armand Dulait, who had run the automobile department since its inception; and Fernand Baetens, who had been in charge of the critical shipping department since the beginning. Rounding out the office personnel were numerous Belgian clerks, stenographers, and assistants.

As the Brussels CRB office continued to function and strove to keep the relief going, negotiations in Brussels, Berlin, London, and Washington led to the belligerents agreeing that the Americans under Hoover's direction could continue relief efforts outside of Belgium (financing, purchasing, shipping). The CRB offices in New York, London, and Rotterdam would remain and function as they always had.

Hoover, who had returned to America to organize the country's food resources, retained the title of CRB chairman, but had given London Director William Poland the new title of director for Europe. Poland took on the everyday supervision of the Commission that Hoover had previously done. Kittredge related, "Following Hoover's traditions, [Poland] kept in close touch and personal contact with the problems of the various offices of the Commission."

As for the Brussels CRB office, that was another matter. It was decided that when Gray and the other Americans left, Belgians would take their place and the CRB director would be Fernand Baetens. While Baetens had run the shipping department, he was much more than that. Kittredge noted that Baetens "had been far more than shipping director; he had been the esteemed and indispensable adviser of all the American directors of the Commission."

On April 23, Gray sent a detailed letter explaining the reorganization and Baetens's promotion. The letter went to the three primary people of relief in Brussels—Francqui, Villalobar, and the Dutch minister, van Vollenhoven. They quickly responded with their enthusiastic approval and went on to once again thank the Americans of the CRB for what they had done.

By May 1, 1917, the situation had settled into relative calm. Seven Dutch and five Spanish delegates were in place and more would arrive in the coming weeks. Kittredge stated, "Delegates had gone to the districts of Northern France and the period of transition from the old regime, that of the Commission for Relief in Belgium, to the new, that of the Comité Hispano-Hollandais, was over."

It was time for Gray and his small group to leave Belgium. Earlier, though, Gray himself had become an issue of contention. He was such a positive, strong, and well-liked presence in Belgium that the exiled Belgian government asked that he be allowed to stay for an indefinite period of time. Hoover, however, insisted otherwise, knowing that despite the new Dutch/Spanish committee, one American still in Belgium would leave the United States open to blame for whatever might happen in Belgium. Hoover would not accept responsibility without an equal degree of power; he ordered Gray and the handful of American delegates out.

Baron von der Lancken arranged for a special train car to take them to Bern, Switzerland. Permitted to travel in the car were Gray; his wife, Laura; their child, Barbara; and an English nurse, May Cass, who had been trapped in Belgium at the beginning of the war and was ecstatic when she received her passport to go only hours before their departure. Besides Gray's group, the train car would carry delegates Wickes, Pate, Dangerfield, Stone, and Carstairs—with Carstairs's Belgian wife, child, and nurse. Accompanying the group would be Captain Schroeder, one of the German nurses who had served in northern France alongside the American delegates.

Leaving Belgium through Holland would be Julius Van Hee, who would be rejoining the consular service, and the accountants Neville, De Gruchy, and St. Amour, who would take up the same work in the CRB Rotterdam office.

The train was to leave the Brussels station at 9:30 p.m. on Tuesday, May 1. The group showed up early and found the station filled with Germans—some bearing flowers and candy—and Belgians wanting to say their last farewells.

The Americans knew what their leaving meant, which made departure that much harder. "The struggle which is theirs," Gray said, "has become our sorrow, marks of which we shall carry in our souls to the grave. The departure of our American friends a month before was hard but now we were leaving behind us friends who are just as close to us, and from whom we can hear no word till Belgium shall be evacuated, friends whose homes are threatened by the breaking of the lines on the Western Front, which cannot hold forever, and whose lives are hanging only by the thin thread of our food imports, which lately we have seen all but severed."

Gray hoped the Dutch and Spanish delegates would do a good job but was certain they could not replace the Americans in one aspect. The Belgians, he felt, "need the moral support that they have learned to lean upon; they need visible evidence that America is still behind them, trying to lift them out of their tribulations.... The presence of Americans in occupied Belgium, in a measure, has turned their thoughts away from the horrors of the war and emphasized the fact that there still exists in some people the milk of human kindness."

Gray believed that the work the CRB had done, and was still attempting to do, was "the only piece of constructive work in the war. All else is bent on destruction. Because the Belgians have found refuge in the sympathy of the Relief, they are very loath to see the last representatives of a friendly nation go."

At 10:20 p.m. the train pulled out of the station. During the trip to Bern, Gray noted two conflicting things: the passing Belgian scenes of destruction brought on during the invasion and German officer Schroeder's little kindnesses and concern for their comfort. "Here, in this individual," Gray wrote, "is the answer to the great question: How can the German people, whom all the world has characterized as kindly, sympathetic and cultured, have perpetrated the crimes connected with the ravages of Belgium? ... It is something more than military obedience that made them carry out the sack of Louvain, of Dinant and Aerschot, with the attendant rape and wanton murder; something more than discipline that instigated and continued the slave-raids in Belgium."

Gray's curiosity could not resist—"The moment we had passed the border [into Switzerland], I asked Schroeder how he reconciled these two divergent characteristics in himself. His answer was so typically German that it has become bromidic: 'Individual morality must be subservient to the good of the State.'"

Gray's last note on the trip was one of relief. "And so we have come to Switzerland where we can breathe free air, and where people smile."

Tracy B. Kittredge, the CRB delegate who had taken over the writing of the group's history from Joe Green, wrote a fine insider's look at the relief program titled *The History of the Commission for Relief in Belgium, 1914–1917*. While Hoover rejected it as the official history of the CRB (probably because it included details of the internal problems and squabbles that Hoover hated to air publicly), and although it was never officially published, the book stands as a significant contribution to the written record of the largest food and relief drive the world had ever seen.

Kittredge ended a section he termed "the final parting" by writing, "So came to an end the American occupation of Belgium. The romance and uniqueness of the experiences of the delegates cannot be adequately portrayed here. In the history of the world no group of men had probably ever held a similar position. They had

Tracy B. Kittredge took over the writing of the CRB history from Joe Green and created an intimate portrait of the relief program. Hoover rejected it as the official history, probably because it included details of the internal problems with Émile Francqui and the Comité National. (Author's archives.)

served the people of Belgium loyally and well and had succeeded in mitigating the harshness of the German regime. Now that they were no longer neutral they turned their work over to the new delegates of Dutch and Spanish nationality and withdrew with the consciousness of having lived up to their obligations—and with the knowledge that though they had left the scene of their endeavours, their work would be continued, and that the American participation in the relief would still go on outside Belgium. Some of the delegates went into the London, Rotterdam and New York offices and thus remained in the service of the Commission. These offices continued throughout 1917 and 1918 to keep the stream of supplies flowing into Belgium in the face of ever-increasing difficulties."

Milton Brown summed up many of the delegates' feelings about their CRB experience when he wrote that it was "the greatest thing that ever has, or ever can, come into my life and I am very, very glad that this wonderful privilege has been mine." He explained to Erica Bunge—and told to Hoover on April 21, 1917—the year he spent as a CRB delegate in Belgium was a "tremendous privilege rather than an experience—a privilege of doing something for others, of working hard uncommercially, of giving something for which we were not paid in money; a privilege I never hope to have duplicated."

62

London

Brown Begins Work in London

The American Special had arrived in Bern, Switzerland, on April 3 at 3:00 p.m. Immediately the CRB delegates heeded individual calls, some leaving to try and join up in one of the Allied armies, others searching for a quick way back to America, others waiting for orders from Hoover, and others taking a few days to sort through what had just happened.

Milton Brown, Fred Eckstein, and Robert Arrowsmith went to visit friends in another area of Switzerland, but when Eckstein and Arrowsmith got word that there might be opportunities for them in Paris, they turned around and headed back to Bern. Brown, knowing that he had a job with the CRB waiting for him in London, stayed and traveled by himself for a few days.

"When the biggest thing in your life suddenly comes to an end," Brown wrote Erica Bunge, "you must have a breathing spell in which to look about you and take stock of the memories of this part of your life. And, my own dear girl, during this time I had found you and had won your love, which is above all things else to me now, and I wanted a few days in which to think quietly of you as the last few days of my work in Belgium had not permitted me."

Brown also had time to reflect on his feelings about the Germans. The time alone had strengthened his attitude, and he had had a chance to read American writer Owen Wister's *Pentecost of Calamity*, which had helped him better understand the larger picture. He urged his parents to read the book.

"To me there seem to be two great principles at stake, that of Prussia and that of the other countries of the world. The former is that the individual exists only for the benefit of aggrandizement of the state; the latter is that the state only exists by the consent of and for the benefit of the individual. These two principles are at war, and the Prussian conception of civilization must be crushed!"

He had also come to a monumental decision. "I could not be true to the convictions I hold if I were not ready to die for them, to fight and die for a principle which must be made to survive in the world. And having come to this conclusion,

I feel that few men feel more strongly than I on this—and so I am ready to do my part against Germany or to die for what I believe is right."

Brown also realized he was prepared not only to die for the cause but to kill for it—something he had struggled with the entire time he was in Belgium.

By Thursday, April 12, he had arrived in Paris after traveling on three trains from Switzerland. At the CRB office in Paris he, along with the other delegates, read a telegram from Hoover that stated the U.S. Government had appointed him to the "National Defense Committee" with special oversight over food conditions in America and the Allied countries. The first step, the telegram read, was the immediate study of the food situation in the Allied countries. Tracy Kittredge, Alfred Fletcher, and Pink Simpson were appointed to start in France; Frederick Thwaits was to go to Italy; and Brown was called to London to help out Joe Green.

With English Channel service suspended because of German submarine activity, Brown did not get to London until Wednesday, April 18. There he was overjoyed to find waiting for him three months of personal mail from friends and loved ones in America. He also discovered he was not to work with Green on the food situation but was to do the clothing report he had wanted to do. CRB executives, however, had differing opinions about his proposed report.

Brown was surprised to find that William Poland, who had become the CRB's London director, "has a rather high opinion of me and of my ability—where he got it I can't imagine, having so far failed in doing the one big thing I wanted to do in my work [the clothing report]."

Poland told him to move forward with the report, as well as a shorter statistical report that would be added to the CRB's annual report.

But Hoover didn't agree. Brown sat down with him immediately after arriving in London. The delegate poured out to the Chief the whole story of his struggles with Janssen and what he hoped to do in preparing a clothing report and a substantial raw materials order that the British would approve.

"Brown, it's too late," Hoover told him. "The Governments of all the countries out here on this side have taken over all woolen, and some other, cloth factories, and to put through such an order is absolutely impossible."

He punctuated his thoughts with a final remark: "You don't realize in what a dangerous situation we are out here!"

"That frightened me," Brown wrote, "especially when he outlined a very dubious situation throughout the world as regards foodstuffs."

It was fortuitous for Brown that Hoover was leaving soon for America. After Hoover's talk, Brown, with the quiet support of Poland, proceeded to write up his report and the purchase order. His hope was dwindling, however, that it might someday reach the British Foreign Office for possible approval.

Brown took a small room in London. "I am living very modestly," he wrote his mother, "in a small top-floor room with a sloping ceiling, in a very pleasant typical

London family hotel. After the splendid house put at our disposition in Brussels I am entirely ready to forego luxury for a bit of plainness for which I am better fitted. I am perfectly comfortable and happy as I could be under the circumstances."

In his garret, Brown kept in a prominent place the one photo he had of Erica Bunge. He had not carried any photos on the American Special train for fear of them being confiscated. In Paris, however, Fred Eckstein had given Brown a copy of a photo Fred had smuggled out.

Every time Brown looked at the photo, he was reminded of one thought that "gives me infinite comfort: Whatever else may happen, you and I have established one eternal fact in the world. We may pass away—and shall in time—all memory of our ever having lived may fade and die; even every tangible record of our existence may be wiped out of Time; but the fact, the one bare fact that we have loved each other can never, never perish. The very world itself may disappear but that can never alter this one imperishable fact—our love!"

The photo Fred had given him was of Eva and Erica sitting against an outside wall and holding three dogs. Brown loved the photo, not knowing it was of a moment in 1914 when Erica had been interested in CRB delegate E. E. Hunt and he had helped her pick out a new dog.

By the end of May, Brown had not yet completed his report and was frustrated he was not in a more active war role. But he knew he had to see his project through to give the Belgians a chance for the raw materials they desperately needed.

Hoover Heads Home for a New Challenge

After arriving back in London from America on April 3, Hoover remained in London only three weeks. Not unexpectedly, he received a job offer from America that he quickly accepted, as long as he could remain as head of the CRB. The offer came from the Council of National Defense. President Wilson had established the organization in the summer of 1916 to coordinate the country's resources and industry because, he stated, "The country is best prepared for war when thoroughly prepared for peace." The group offered Hoover the position of chairman of its food committee.

They knew—and most of the world knew—that he was the perfect man to mobilize America's food resources for the coming struggle. While he would have preferred a position with more direct power and authority, he accepted in the hope, no doubt, that something even better would show itself.

On Thursday, April 19, two days before Hoover was to leave London for Liverpool to catch a boat back home, one of the founding members of the CRB and a London director, Colonel Millard Hunsiker, put on a farewell dinner for the Chief at the fashionable Savoy Hotel. Most of the Commission members in London attended, including Clare Torrey, Tracy Kittredge, Edward Curtis, and

Brown. Brown wrote to his brother Harry about the evening and ended by stating, "You people in America do not know Herbert C. Hoover or his true worth. I would almost venture the statement that he is better known in the higher diplomatic and governmental circles over here than any other American."

Also in attendance were two of the original Rhodes scholar delegates, John L. Glenn and David T. Nelson, who had left the CRB in October 1916 and October 1915, respectively, to return to Oxford. With America's entry into the war, they had suddenly decided to go home to enlist. They had arrived in London that day, and after going to the American Embassy to secure an emergency passport for Glenn, they had received a message from Torrey, who was working at the embassy, to join the group at the Savoy.

Nelson wrote in his journal that the evening was "marked by enthusiasm and much good feeling." At one point during the night, Glenn rose and presented Hoover with a silver cigar case on behalf of the CRB.

Hoover had never been one to appreciate or enjoy any kind of formal honoring of himself, but this event was something different. It was an evening of old friends and coworkers—the only ones who truly knew what the Commission for Relief in Belgium was all about. If Nelson's journal is to be believed, Hoover actually enjoyed himself and appreciated the sentiments that were shared that night.

The next day, Friday, April 20, was proclaimed "America Day" throughout Britain. In London the U.S. flag was flown with the British Union Jack from the Victoria Tower of the houses of parliament and over the prime minister's official residence at 10 Downing Street. For the first time in history, both flags were flown from the same mast above the Palace of Westminster.

Most, if not all, of the CRB delegates in London attended a much-anticipated event that day, a service at St. Paul's Cathedral titled "A Solemn Service to Almighty God on the Occasion of the Entry of the United States of America into the Great War for Freedom." Gilchrist Stockton, a fellow delegate who had joined the American Embassy staff in 1916, secured tickets for the sudden arrivals, Glenn and Nelson. They walked with Curtis and Brown over to the cathedral and got seats in time to see the guests of honor, the American Embassy staff, enter, "walking at an easy pace up the main aisle," according to Nelson. A few minutes later in came London's lord mayor and attendants, resplendent in "gorgeous robes." Then the king of England entered, dressed in "army uniform, red-faced and bald-headed, with several members of the royal family and attendants." Brown added, "The King and Queen marched up the central aisle, very near to where we were sitting; the service was most impressive."

The Right Reverend Charles Henry Brent, bishop of the Philippine Islands and a man who would later become chaplain general of the American Expeditionary Forces, preached the sermon. After the sermon, the congregation sang verses from the "Star-Spangled Banner," "The Battle Hymn of the Republic," and Britain's national anthem. Altogether, Nelson declared, the service was "simple and impressive."

The next day, Saturday, April 21, Hoover said goodbye to a small group of CRB men at London's busy Euston Station and boarded a train to Liverpool, where he had booked passage back to America on the SS *Philadelphia*.

Joining him on the voyage—and at his dining table—were his two close friends and advisers: Vernon Kellogg, the previous CRB Brussels director, and Ben Allen, a journalist with the Associated Press who had helped implement the CRB's publicity plans. Also on the voyage and at the dining table were the Bishop Brent, who had preached the St. Paul's sermon; former CRB delegates Richard H. Simpson, Thomas B. Dawson, John L. Glenn, and David T. Nelson; and a Miss Gertrude Davidson, a 27-year-old nurse.

Nelson documented in his journal that the ship was held up in port three and a half days "owing to a new nest of mines which had been dropped by U-boats." As the passengers waited anxiously to get underway, Hoover playfully suggested at lunch one day that the table's occupants jointly write a novel, with each person writing a separate chapter. Nelson recorded that Hoover ultimately "balked" when Ben Allen told Hoover he would have to write the first and last chapters, which would make the other chapters "merely descriptive passages."

That same day, after dinner, many of the diners retired to the smoking lounge and were enthralled by an informal discussion of the war, politics, and travel by Hoover, Reverend Brent, Kellogg, and Allen. Nelson wrote, "An attentive audience gathered round to listen." Hoover stated he would be "glad to see the U.S. abandon the Monroe Doctrine for it committed us to a burdensome, costly, and dangerous policy." Speaking of the recent sinkings of CRB ships, Hoover concluded that it was "impossible to place a limit on the outrages of which the Germans were capable judging by past experiences."

Ben Allen talked of his interview with the famous Belgian King Albert. He declared that the monarch was "the shyest man he had ever met." Hoover added, "Yes, shyness is a disease with him." He probably said that with no sense of irony, even though Hoover himself exhibited many traits of shyness—reticence to speak publicly, reluctance to socialize, and downright aversion to receiving public acknowledgment for personal achievement.

And yet, just like King Albert had somehow overcome the "disease" of shyness to bravely command a small force that had slowed down the German Army juggernaut enough to save France, Hoover had taken control of his shyness to launch and maintain the largest food and relief program the world had ever seen. In the process, Hoover had negotiated with multiple European governments, gone toe-to-toe with battle-hardened military commanders, and outplayed internal rivals within the relief program. Throughout it all, he had persevered and risen to overcome all obstacles, objections, and challengers.

A lesser man might have let such accomplishments go to his head and might have developed an insufferable sense of self-importance.

Hoover was not such a man. He remained an unassuming and generally humble man—the kind of man who could quietly sit in a ship's smoking room and entertain and educate an appreciative group via a conversation with friends.

Far ahead, beyond the cold Atlantic waters and dark sky, Hoover's future waited for him in America. With the delayed departure and longer route to avoid U-boats, the ship would take nearly two weeks to reach New York.

The unexpectedly extended stay aboard must have tried the patience of the impatient man-of-action Hoover. His thoughts were already on how he could marshal America's food resources for the coming battle. There was little, if any, regard for his fortune or mining operations. A whole new chapter of his life was about to begin, a chapter that he hoped would play out on an even bigger stage than the one he had acted upon for the past two and half years.

Even with such high aspirations, Hoover was still, for the most part, simply a private citizen once again selflessly heeding the call to public service.

Epilogue

Wrapping Up the Major Stories

A Short Summary of America's Entry into the War

For more than two and a half years, U.S. President Woodrow Wilson had kept America out of war, believing neutrality was the best path to take. Generally, American sentiment had initially been with the president. Public opinion began shifting toward war, however, after major events. A few of those included German "atrocities" (real and alleged) during the invasion (1914); the sinking of the *Lusitania* and the attack on the *Sussex* (1915 and 1916, respectively); America's selling of war supplies to the Allies; the Germans' reinstitution of unrestricted submarine warfare (February 1, 1917); and the release of the Zimmermann telegram (February 28, 1917).

Additionally, America's shift toward war was inadvertently aided in part by the Commission for Relief in Belgium.

Hoover's firm belief that public opinion was critical to the survival of the CRB led him and the CRB to provide newspapers and magazines with a constant stream of news about the relief efforts in Belgium and northern France. The resulting nearly continuous press coverage kept the dual stories of civilian suffering and the Germans' harsh occupation in the minds of many Americans.

Hoover also understood that a fully engaged public was best in supporting a cause. To convert Americans from merely readers of relief to active participants, he had created two pathways. The first was periodic national and international calls for donations—money, foodstuffs, and clothes. The second path was to establish U.S. state and local CRB committees that actively engaged communities in their own backyards. Hoover knew that a person who gave to a cause and/or worked for that cause would naturally follow its progress closely.

By the very nature of the relief coverage and how it changed over time—reflecting greater civilian suffering and a harsher German regime—"neutral" Americans who were fully engaged in the topic of food relief couldn't help but be pulled away from strict neutrality.

It's also quite probable that the horrific deportation of Belgian and northern French might not have been so widely exposed and reported on if the CRB delegates had not been actively engaged in the occupied territories and had not witnessed the "slave raids." Certainly, knowledge of general civilian suffering—which the Germans actively worked to suppress from the world—would not have filtered out of Belgium and northern France as much as it did. Numerous magazine articles by delegates (some approved by Hoover, others not) and E. E. Hunt's 1916 book, *War Bread*, did their small part in swaying public opinion toward the Allied side.

Even with such coverage, Americans were still divided for years, as simply illustrated by two song titles that were popular in 1915 and 1916, respectively: "I Didn't Raise My Boy to Be a Soldier" and "You'd Better Raise Your Boy to Be a Soldier."

Long before America entered the war, many citizens were already thinking the country's entry was inevitable. Since 1915, a preparedness movement, led by prominent Americans such as former president Teddy Roosevelt, had been growing, especially after the sinking of the *Lusitania*. The movement began to fund and to operate privately run camps in Plattsburgh, New York, and in other locations. These camps trained young men in marching, shooting, and general military procedures. The goal was to ultimately provide a huge pool of potential wartime officers. Tens of thousands of American men enrolled in these "Plattsburgh camps."

When America finally did enter the war on April 6, 1917, many people around the world, including the Germans, did not think the United States could mobilize fast enough to have a significant impact on the war before German U-boats forced the Allies to the peace table.

America surprised everyone, organizing faster than most would have guessed. Everything went into high gear, from a military draft to boot camps to the manufacturing of war material to the preservation of food in a Hoover-directed organization.

The American Expeditionary Forces (AEF) was established on July 5, 1917, in France under the command of General John J. "Black Jack" Pershing. American forces fought alongside the British, French, Canadian, and Australian armies on the Western Front. The most notable campaigns in which Americans fought included the Aisne campaign at the July 18, 1918, Battle of Chateau-Thierry; the Battle of Belleau Wood in the summer of 1918; and the Battle of Saint-Mihiel and the Meuse-Argonne Offensive toward the end of 1918.

The Great War—also known as the "war to end all wars" (from an expression coined by British writer H. G. Wells)—concluded when the guns finally fell silent on the eleventh hour of the eleventh day of the eleventh month of 1918. Estimates vary, but the total causality count from all sides is that there were approximately 9 million soldiers killed and 21 million wounded. Civilian deaths during the war and in its immediate aftermath likely exceeded 10 million. American casualties were approximately 320,000, of which 53,000 died in battle. An additional 204,000 were wounded.

No accurate death toll was ever made of how many Belgians and northern French died behind German lines during the war.

The Relief Continues through the War and Beyond

On May 1, 1917, Prentiss Gray, his family, and the remaining American delegates had taken a train out of Belgium. Three major food-relief problems still remained—securing ships for the CRB, getting the Germans to guarantee the 1917 harvest would go to the Belgians and northern French, and financing.

Regarding shipping, by May the CRB was able to ship approximately 60,000 tons of foodstuffs a month but needed ships to handle an additional 40,000 tons.

Even with the renewed unrestricted German U-boat campaign, available worldwide shipping from neutral countries was still substantial. According to Hoover, besides the neutrals' own shipping needs and their charters to the Allies, there were approximately 4 million tons of shipping available for commercial use all over the world. The CRB needed only a fraction of that to fulfill its needs, but because of U-boats torpedoing CRB ships, "the neutrals avoided charters with us."

In his new position as U.S. food administrator, Hoover had problems at home—most notably a drought that had impacted the 1917 harvest and decreased food supplies—but was determined to put pressure on the neutrals to provide the small amount of shipping the CRB needed.

On May 26, Hoover wrote to Secretary of State Lansing about the problem. He proposed an idea: "It seems to me the time has arrived when we might consider some definite service from these . . . [neutrals] of a character which does not jeopardize their ships but which leads them into the path of a little humanity. . . . That we should say to them that they should undertake to provide the transport of 100,000 tons of foodstuffs for the Belgian Relief . . . and that unless they are prepared to enter upon this path of decent dealing we shall reserve the questions of the export of foodstuffs from this country to . . . [them] until further notice."

Hoover continued, "It seems to me that if this hint were given at the present moment it probably would be as effective as direct action under embargo legislation."

The "hint" seemed to be a downright threat: Provide shipping, and we'll provide food; don't provide shipping, and we'll withhold food.

It wasn't long before Hoover followed through on the threat. "As soon as we received the embargo powers from the Congress, we halted the shipment of this food [to the neutrals]. As Food Administrator, I notified the neutrals that I was prepared to obtain export permits for them, provided that they delivered part of their accumulated food to Rotterdam for the Relief and provided also that they chartered us additional ships."

By August, with a bit of prompting and negotiating, the neutral countries of Norway, Sweden, and the Netherlands had agreed.

By 1918, however, another shipping crisis was caused by war events and strategies. On March 3, 1918, the new Russian Bolshevik government signed the Treaty of Brest-Litovsk with Germany and the other Central Powers, which ended its participation in World War I. That freed up German soldiers to join the Western

Front. As a result, Germany staged multiple attacks on the Western Front from March to July. While those attacks were ultimately checked by the Allies, they did speed up the demand for shipping to carry huge amounts of war material and troops from America to the Allies.

Between that increased need for ships and the Germans' continued U-boat success at sinking or damaging transports, the CRB's ability to charter ships was severely cut. But the Allied increased requisition of neutral ships for its purposes actually worked to the advantage of the CRB. According to Hoover, the Allied requisition program "drove the neutrals to charter to the C.R.B. as a lesser of perils." That secured adequate shipping for the CRB through the remainder of the war.

Regarding the 1917 harvest, it took a bit of time to resolve, as each previous harvest negotiation had. In the end, the Dutch and Spanish, along with the CRB Brussels office director, Belgian Fernand Baetens, were able to secure a guarantee from the Germans regarding the Occupation Zone, and they were able to secure an agreement that was similar to the 1916 harvest agreement arranged by Dr. Vernon Kellogg and Major von Kessler for northern France. In 1918, Villalobar and his Dutch counterpart in Brussels were once again able to secure the same arrangement for the 1918 harvest.

Continued financing would be much more of a struggle since the British and French had hoped that America's entry into the war would decrease their financial commitments to the CRB. America and Hoover did step up. Hoover explained, "I obtained an allotment of American 'loans' to Belgium and France for the C.R.B. amounting to $75,000,000." But there was an important requirement: "By Congressional stipulation, all American loans had to be spent in the United States." Hoover was able to increase congressional appropriations in November 1917, but the spending stipulation remained.

That still left money needed to handle the CRB's sterling and franc expenditures outside the United States. With some prodding, the British and French continued their subsidies to cover those expenses, but at a reduced rate.

When it came to operations within Belgium and northern France, from the founding of the new Spanish-Dutch committee through to the German surrender on November 11, 1918, the group did the best they could. The Dutch and Spanish committee "performed with devotion and skill the duties which devolved upon it in respect to belligerent guarantees and negotiations with the Germans," according to an early history of the CRB.

Outside of Belgium, the CRB continued as it always had with financing, purchasing, and shipping, with the only difference being that its chairman was in Washington, D.C. This was, in fact, fortuitous for the relief because, according to the early history, "In the face of a world shortage of ships and food and the increasing demands growing out of America's military effort, there were repeated insistent suggestions that in order to save the cause of the Allies from disaster the program of relief should be curtailed. Thanks to Hoover's position and influence in the councils of the Allies and the American Government these suggestions were never carried out, and Belgian and French relief received equal priority with war requirements."

An added benefit of the relief organization—one Hoover never would have mentioned before America entered the war but was one he stated clearly in a later book—was behind-the-lines intelligence. In his book *An American Epic*, he wrote, "We had constant insight into what was going on in Belgium and Northern France from our staff in Belgium through our Rotterdam office. That information was of daily value to us in Washington because it revealed the increasing failure of German food and raw-materials supplies." Luckily for the Belgians and northern French, the Germans, Hoover continued, "held fairly well to their guarantees concerning the native food supplies and our imports."

Germany's honoring of its agreements did not lessen the fact that Hoover, and by extension the American government and military, was receiving important intelligence regarding Germany's ability to continue waging war.

After the war, Belgium and many other countries received food relief as part of the American Relief Administration (ARA) until internal conditions were stabilized.

The State of the Belgians and Northern French

With the American entry into the war, the civilians in occupied territories had a cause for celebration, but they also faced the possibility that relief might end altogether or continue in some abbreviated form. As the months progressed, those who were fed and clothed by the CRB and CN came to be painfully aware that relief was decreasing, as overall living conditions were getting worse.

The average daily caloric intake per capita for the Belgians and northern French were a meager 1,522, which was less than half the prewar normal. And for many, according to Hoover, that average fell far short because "those who did heavy work had to have a minimum of 2,500 calories a day or there would have been no economic life; thus the rations for others fell far below 1,500 calories." Additionally, the calorie average was "totally inadequate in fats and proteins."

In October 1917, Belgian King Albert wrote to President Wilson outlining what was happening to his people and asking for renewed help and support of the relief efforts. Alluding to the big impact the German U-boat campaign was having on food reaching his country, he stated, "Since several months the imports of foodstuffs have been inadequate. . . . The Belgian population is confronted not only with hardship and suffering but with actual famine, the death rate is steadily increasing. Infantile mortality is appalling. Tuberculosis is spreading and threatening the future of the race."

Francqui, writing from Brussels back on July 2, 1917, told Hoover, "Since your departure, the situation has grown increasingly worse. The winter [1916/1917] was exceptionally long and severe and exhausted our last reserves in indigenous products. In the spring, the production of indigenous foods of general consumption was very restricted; for this reason and also because of the diminution in the importations, the demand made by the well-to-do classes was so heavy that the prices far surpassed the resources of the rest of the population."

He outlined in detail the changes, stating that 45 percent of the people were currently living "exclusively on the food imported by the C.R.B." and that the soup kitchens had gone from serving 2,100,000 at the end of 1916 to feeding 2,687,000. An additional 30 percent of civilians lived "*almost* [Francqui's emphasis] exclusively on the imported foodstuffs, being still in a position to procure for themselves a small addition in the foodstuffs sold by the communal or intercommunal stores, or on the open market."

"The remainder," Francqui continued, "that is about 25%, live on their own produce; this is the case with farmers living on their farms (20%) or for a great part depending on purchases in the open market, these are the rich classes (5%)."

Such conditions, Francqui contended, had led to an increase in mortality, and "in certain comparative graphs, the curve of mortality rises on the same proportion as the curve of the importations descends!"

Doctor reports were coming in from all parts of the country, Francqui wrote, that showed "the terrifying progress of morbidity; principally through tuberculosis and various diseases caused by mal-nutrition."

What this was doing to the general population was significant. The people were "beginning to lose the patience and proud stoicism which you at one time so much admired. They send us petitions, sometimes imploring, sometimes threatening. In between times, they give most disquieting demonstrations at the markets and before the foodshops. We are perhaps on the eve of more serious outbreaks."

A month later, on August 6, 1917, Francqui wrote again, using stronger language. "The situation is becoming more alarming. The last vital resources of the great majority of the population—reduced for over seven months to scarcely half a food ration capable of sustaining life—are on the eve of becoming exhausted. For many, life is nothing but slow death; now already many people are commencing to die of inanition.

"We look with terror," Francqui continued, "upon what the approaching winter will be if a sufficient ravitaillement is not assured, owing to lack of ships."

Hoover felt the Belgian's frustration, but could not return the communication with encouraging words or explanations of how many CRB ships had been sunk with full cargo holds of food, for fear it might provide a wartime advantage to the Germans. "The distracted Francqui could not know of the shortage of food faced by all of the Allied world or of the lack of transportation as a consequence of the unlimited submarine war. And I could not advise him of all this lest this revelation of trying times among the Allies fall into German hands."

By November and December of 1917, the CRB was able to get the minimum monthly needs to Rotterdam, but then things got worse again. Francqui's letters and the reports out of Belgium and northern France continued in their desperate tone through the early part of 1918.

Despite incredible challenges, Hoover, Francqui, and their organizations were able to successfully feed and clothe the Belgians and northern French throughout the war. (Public domain; E. E. Hunt, *War Bread,* Henry Holt and Company, 1916.)

Francqui informed Hoover in early April 1918 that the bread ration had been reduced from 330 grams to 250 grams. "This is all the more painful because this reduction of the ration had to be made at a period of the year when resources of native foodstuffs are at their lowest."

But with the resolution of shipping in mid-1918 and the bountiful American harvest that year, Hoover wrote that "Francqui's anguish was soon to be relieved. With our greatly increased fleet and our abundant harvest, I was able, in July, to transmit cheer and assurance that ample supplies were at last assured."

Throughout this time, small bright spots within Belgium were the still-productive places such as the Bunge dairy farm. It continued to produce and transport milk every day to the children of Antwerp. After the war, Edouard and Erica Bunge and George and Hélène Born received a commendation from the Belgian government for providing 1 million liters of free milk during the occupation.

As the war wound down in October 1918, a potential final crisis to relief efforts developed when the German Army began retreating back through northern France and southern Belgium. Hoover explained, "There now arose the problem of how to provision the population of Northern France and that of Southern Belgium behind the retreating Germans, since transport of supplies from Rotterdam was cut off."

William Poland, director of the CRB's London office, came up with a creative solution. He bought 20 million military rations from the British Army that were valued at approximately $4.5 million and distributed those to the civilians cut off from Rotterdam supplies.

And with that, Hoover wrote, "The Germans made speedy retreat under President Wilson's ultimatums, and the C.R.B.'s troubles with them were over."

The Fate of *La Libre Belgique*

The little underground newspaper with the lion's heart survived to the end of the war and proudly ceased operations the day King Albert (later known as King Albert I) marched back into Brussels. After the war there were numerous accounts of the paper's history, including newspaper and magazine articles, books, and even movies. No source, however, tells the story better than the book *Underground News: The Complete Story of the Secret Newspaper That Made War History* by Oscar E. Millard.

While the newspaper did survive through the entire war, its survival was never assured, and it was many times under great hardship. After May 1917, critical events in the life of the newspaper included the following:

"The Man They Want Murdered!": That was the headline in June 1917 above a photo of Belgium's King Albert working at his desk. Shortly after von Bissing's death, a document was printed in Germany that was reportedly von Bissing's political testament. The document focused on the annexation of Belgium and, according to *Underground News*, "suggested that the only way to achieve this end and secure Belgium for Germany was to murder King Albert." The new governor general, von Falkenhausen, had tried to suppress the document in Belgium, but editor van den Hout received a copy and published it. In the same issue, the editorial contributor Fidelis (Albert van de Kerckhove) wrote a long article attacking von Falkenhausen, stating he was a "bird of prey sent to live on the palpitating flesh of Belgium."

Von Falkenhausen had not been amused. The German governor general became as determined as von Bissing had been to kill the underground newspaper. He posted a 10,000-mark reward for the arrest of Fidelis. More importantly, he turned to Berlin to help hunt down the newspaper. Thirty men and four women who represented the best of the German counterintelligence service were called to Berlin from all over Europe to be trained and ultimately go undercover into Belgium.

A Priceless Photo: By the end of the summer of 1917, the counterespionage group of 34 highly trained men and women was ready to disperse throughout Belgium and track down the leaders of *La Libre Belgique.*

In an incredible stroke of luck for the newspaper—and an incredible stroke of stupidity on the part of the Germans—van den Hout received a photograph that had been taken of the group before its members left Berlin. The caption read, "Taken before their departure from Berlin on their special mission against the clandestine press in Belgium. Strictly forbidden to publish."

With great glee, the leader of the hunted newspaper published the photo on the front page of issue 131, dated September 23, 1917, only a few days after the group had arrived in Brussels; the heading read, "Could one be more obliging!"

Underground News reported in an accompanying long caption that there was a huge, new 100,000-mark reward to any of the agents who found the "automobile cellar of *La Libre Belgique*." The caption went on to state, "Berlin has decided to have finished at all costs with this clandestine propaganda, and, sportsmen as ever, our masters felt constrained to give us fair warning. The people entrusted with this sleuthing were photographed, so that no one should be taken by surprise."

Father Paquet of the Inner Circle Is Taken: In late summer 1917, Father Paquet, who lived at the Jesuit residence, was arrested. Because he was directly connected to Victor Jourdain, his arrest ended the long relationship between the paper and its cofounder, Jourdain. Numerous raids at the Jourdain home/office led to Julie Jourdain going into hiding with van Doren, Joseph Jourdain fleeing Brussels, and Victor retiring to his country home, where he died at age 77 on October 15, 1918, less than a month before the armistice. Father Paquet received a sentence of two years in prison, which was so difficult that he died shortly after his release.

Van den Hout Disappears but Goes Nowhere: Regardless of Abbé van den Hout's meticulous precautions, it was inevitable that someday the Germans would come for him. That day was Friday, November 9, 1917. They stormed the campus of St. Louis University, searching the classrooms and going to his room. He was nowhere to be found and everyone simply said he was out on business. A fellow priest, Abbé Beer, who had the room next to his, immediately realized van den Hout had to be warned. Beer and another priest used an unguarded exit from campus and raced to the two tram stations where they thought van den Hout might show up. Beer chose correctly and was able to alert van den Hout before he reached St. Louis.

The hunted man found sanctuary for the evening at a nearby church. Later that night Beer brought him some civilian clothes. Van den Hout knew that his photo and description would be telegraphed around Belgium and he had to either go into permanent hiding or escape to Holland.

He did neither. As the Abbé van den Hout was reported by many to be heading for the Dutch border, he was actually hiding in Brussels with a friend and letting his beard grow. Within a week or so he had become Monsieur Courtade, a fully documented, well-groomed, well-dressed barrister who had suddenly appeared and was taking command of *La Libre Belgique*.

He was at the helm of the publication as issue number 140 hit the streets on New Year's Day, 1918. The editorial began, "For the third and last time we wish our faithful readers a Happy New Year. In 1918 history will inscribe the date forever glorious of the triumph of Right and Justice; this year that begins will see the complete restoration of our dear country. 1918 will mark the return of our beloved sovereign and our heroic army. Let us prepare to receive them worthily; let us hold fast in spite of everything, uncompromising as ever towards the enemy and united as Belgians to the bitter end."

The newly created Courtade recruited Abbé Beer to be his intermediary with Father Delehaye at St. Michel, who was still providing the editorial content from many of the regular contributors.

The surprising smooth sailing during the last month of 1917 and the opening of 1918 was about to encounter a major storm.

The January 29, 1918 Raids; Von Falkenhausen's Celebration: With many failures behind them, the Germans went back to an old method used by Charleroi's Detective Grisenbrock. They didn't immediately arrest those they knew were involved, but rather they began following them in hopes of catching bigger fish.

At the end of January 1918, they felt they had identified the leaders of the whole organization. They struck on the night of Tuesday, January 29. The raids were scattered throughout Brussels and corralled a surprising number of high-level participants. For the first time, the Germans were able to apprehend editorial contributors, including Fidelis (Albert van de Kerckhove), as well as Father Delehaye and the primary printer. Nearly all the main distribution depots in Brussels were raided, and many distributors were taken into custody. All those rounded up were sent immediately to St. Gilles Prison to await questioning and trial.

To make matters worse, the issue confiscated in the raids was the one that celebrated the paper's third anniversary.

The capture of the leaders of *La Libre Belgique* was front-page news in Germany, and the secret police and the German military were overjoyed. In Brussels, as one history stated, "The rumoured death of the beloved and invincible *Libre* was received at first with incredulity which changed to stupefaction and dismay when the truth became known." Even Belgians thought the paper was dead.

Only two days after the raids, von Falkenhausen hosted a banquet for his staff officers, important officials, and a group of detectives from the city's three secret police brigades. When a telegram of congratulations from the Kaiser was read, the rowdy group cheered, stomped the floor, and pounded the tables with excitement. Abundant were the champagne toasts to the death of *La Libre Belgique*. *Underground News* recorded what happened next:

As the dinner was drawing to a close amidst hearty, bibulous felicitations, an orderly strode in, saluted, and handed to von Falkenhausen a sealed envelope marked "urgent." Negligently the Governor-General tore it open—and withdrew a copy of the Libre Belgique No. 143.

"Some of the men, in an advanced state of alcoholic exuberance, imagined that this was all part of the fun—a little hoax arranged for their entertainment. And they burst into a chorus of ribald jeers. But the jeers were cut short by a violent oath from von Falkenhausen and a harsh command for silence. White and trembling with anger he

crushed the paper in his hands, flung it on the table and strode from the room. His guests, sobered by this outburst, sprang unsteadily to attention as he swept out. Then one of them smoothed out the crumpled paper and they gathered around to see what had provoked the Governor's sudden outburst of rage.

On the front page was an autographed photograph of von Falkenhausen, with the message in his own hand: "My sincere congratulations, but do treat the animals kindly." The portrait was headed: "An Unexpected Honor," and below was the caption: On the occasion of our Birthday our amiable Governor has deigned to send us his autographed portrait. And to think some people dare to maintain that the Germans are never sports!

The editorial was, as usual, highly inflammatory and defiant. It spoke of how the Germans had tried everything to shut down the publication and had failed every time. It ended with patriotic fervor (and sounds like the genesis of the famous "I'll be there" speech by Tom Joad in *The Grapes of Wrath* written 21 years later by John Steinbeck): "So long as a German remains on our soil we will be there to oppose and defy him; so long as Right and Justice are violated we will be there to protest; so long as a base and vile press continues to pour out its torrents of lies and calumnies, we will be there to rectify; so long as they try to conceal the Truth, raising ever higher the walls of our prison, we will be there to fling the Truth in the face of our gaolers. . . . We will hold out to the bitter end."

With incredible effort, Courtade had nearly single-handedly done the impossible—republish the rounded-up issue before it was past due. And to infuriate the Germans further, all the articles were signed with the pseudonyms of the men who had been arrested.

The mass trial of those rounded up in January took place May 15, 1918. Sixty-one were accused of high crimes. Father Delehaye and van de Kerckhove both received the maximum sentence of 15 years. Surprisingly, van de Kerckhove continued to contribute Fidelis articles to *La Libre Belgique* through the food baskets that his wife sent him in prison.

Courtade's Final Days: Through the remaining months of the war, Courtade/van den Hout kept the publication alive, many times nearly by himself, as his second-in-command, Abbé Beer, had to flee in March. Courtade was an irrepressible force who came close to capture many times but somehow always escaped.

In September 1918 the long-anticipated Allied offensive on the Western Front began. By early October, Courtade was able to publish an issue with the large headline "COLLAPSE!"—which proclaimed the coming Allied victory. But with his excited announcement that the end was near, Courtade also preached another message: "Now, Belgians, calm! Keep your heads and your dignity to the end. Let them go as they came. Let us obey the directions of our legitimate authorities; let us beware, above all, of *agents-provocateurs* and those who would fish in troubled

LA FORCE AU SERVICE DU DROIT!

Ce que nous tenons, nous le tenons bien!...

Nº 171 et dernier NUMÉRO GRATUIT 12 Novembre 1918

LA LIBRE BELGIQUE

The front and back pages of the last issue of La Libre Belgique. *In a final jab at the enemy, the last page ended with the often-used German expression about the occupation of Belgium: "What we hold, we hold tight!"* (Public domain; Oscar E. Millard, *Underground News,* Robert M. McBride and Company, 1938.)

waters. Only another few weeks. . . . And as for the traitors, of all breeds, one simple word of advice: Go, while the going's good."

The German government in Belgium continued to hound the publication until the very end. On November 8, 1918, only three days before the armistice, the secret police made one last desperate attempt to shut down the press. By that time, however, regular German soldiers saw the war was practically over and warnings were given before the raids happened.

A day after the armistice, Tuesday, November 12, 1918, the little underground newspaper was freely circulated for the first time and had a huge pressrun of 100,000 copies.

The last issue, number 171, had a photo of King Albert, and inside was the final editorial from Abbé van den Hout that declared, "Our Last Issue!" He wrote simply but powerfully, "Our mission fulfilled, we can pass away. We swore that the German would find us facing him until the very last day, cost what it might. We have kept our promise faithfully. It was difficult, very difficult sometimes. . . . Our little sheet was hunted day and night. At first the Boches thought they would easily silence our importunate voice. . . . But the persecution only quadrupled the influence of the *Libre*. . . . Rapidly it became the heart of a resistance that will live in our annals as a worthy pendant of the exploits of our army. . . . On the question of those iniquitous requisitions, those barbarous deportations and that infamous attempt at administrative separation, the word was given by the *Libre Belgique*. And Belgians, *en masse,* followed it. . . . Sometimes everything seemed lost. They held everything: contributors, printer, depots, distributors. On hearing the news, one [German] Judge-Advocate exclaimed lyrically in court: 'This time it is finished! We have it at last!' And the next day it reappeared!"

Van den Hout also wrote: "What can we reply to that oft-repeated question 'Who is the *Libre?*' The *Libre Belgique* is a lineage, a tradition." He even admitted in his editorial that he did not know the names of previous editors, organizers, or most of the writers.

The abbé-turned-editor humbly signed his last editorial simply *La Libre Belgique*. And on the back page of the last issue was a final shot at the Germans. It was an expression used many times by Germans when describing their occupation of Belgium: "What we hold, we hold tight!"

Eugene van Doren: The cofounder (with Victor Jourdain) of *La Libre Belgique* came out of hiding and reunited with his wife and children after the armistice. He died in Brussels on March 27, 1951, at the age of 76.

Gabrielle Petit: The little-known patriotic young woman who had been executed by the Germans in April 1916 would not remain obscure for long. After the war, her story began to be told and retold, and in May 1919 a state funeral for her and two other patriots was attended by Belgium's Queen Elisabeth, Cardinal Mercier, and numerous other city, regional, and national officials. In her hometown of Tournai, a square was named in her honor. Books and movies were made about her life (with varying degrees of accuracy). In Brussels a large statue of her standing with left hand over her heart was erected in the *Place Saint-Jean*. A translation of the inscription reads: "To Gabrielle Petit, Shot by the Germans, 1 April 1916, and to the memory of all Belgian women who died for the country. I have just been condemned to death. I will be shot tomorrow. Long live the King. Long live Belgium . . . and I will show them that a Belgian woman knows how to die."

The Deportations

One history of the CRB stated, "By 1918 the Germans had gone beyond deportations to Germany, and were compelling Belgian and French beneficiaries of relief to labor on military construction. The Commission no longer had American representatives in Belgium, and it could do nothing except request the CRB representative in Brussels to raise the question with the C.N., the C.F., and the Spanish-Dutch Committee for such action as they deemed advisable under the circumstances."

Without giving a source, Hoover later reported, "The number of deportees who returned to Belgium and France after the German surrender in November, 1918, exceeded 700,000. This was not the total deported, however, because many had died in Germany." (Most experts now discount Hoover's estimate.)

European historian Jens Thiel, in a March 24, 2014, speech titled "Slave Raids during the First World War? Deportations and Forced Labour in Occupied Belgium," stated, "Between October 26, 1916, and February 10, 1917, approximately 60,000 Belgians were deported to Germany for forced labor" from the portion of Belgium controlled by Governor General von Bissing, and another 60,000 were Belgian and northern French who had been deported to other parts of both countries.

No matter what the final count, the deportations were psychologically devastating to the entire civilian population behind the German lines and played a role in shifting American thought and politics away from neutrality.

The Flemish/French Issue

When Baron von Bissing died on Wednesday, April 18, 1917, it had been less than a month since his *affiche* declaring the country would be divided into two administrations—the Flemish headquartered out of Brussels and the French from Namur.

Baron von Falkenhausen was appointed to succeed von Bissing as governor general in Belgium and continued the effort to separate the country into two.

Shortly after von Bissing's *affiche* was posted, Belgian government officials across Belgium met secretly to discuss what could be done passively to resist the new edict. Cardinal Mercier, the spiritual conscience of the country, wrote that in the end it was unanimously agreed that only the "highest officials of the central administration should resign and that lower officials should be free either to resign or remain at their posts."

The German response was in typical rigid fashion so that it would adhere to the perception that it was following the law. Before the Germans could take direct action against those who had resigned, the Germans had to correct something that had been done two years before. At that time, the Germans had issued an order allowing Belgian functionaries to resign without repercussions. That meant that those in 1917 who had just resigned over the Flemish separatist issue were within their legal rights. So, on Saturday, May 19, 1917, von Falkenhausen issued an order to revoke that promise.

With the past brought into alignment with current German needs, the Germans immediately arrested all those who had resigned over the Flemish issue. Those who did not agree to return to work were shipped off to German prisons.

Cardinal Mercier protested those arrests in a strongly worded letter to von Falkenhausen on June 6, 1917. The missive defended the rights of the men to refuse to work under international law and The Hague Conventions. He ended with a declaration of the Belgian spirit: "I beg of you to hearken to the voice of those who know intimately the Belgian people and their history, when they affirm that no violence will ever triumph over their patriotism."

The new governor general replied by stating he refused to discuss with the cardinal any questions that were not religious in nature.

It would be only after the end of the war that Belgium would return to being ruled by one administrative, governing body.

The CRB Clothing Department and the Belgian Lace Industry

Milton Brown labored in London for months. Finally, on Monday, August 6, 1917, he turned in his bound 190-page clothing report and a $12 million purchase order. Working with CRB London Director Poland, Brown presented it to the British Foreign Office. His "biggest ambition," as he had once described it, was completed.

In the covering memorandum to the Foreign Office, Brown was brutally honest about what the Germans were doing in Belgium. "The present situation is that unhappily we must admit very extensive seizures of goods within Belgium." That did not matter, as far as Brown was concerned, because "the fact remains, that the country suffered greatly last winter, is suffering now, and will suffer very much more severely in the future, until the end of the occupation, if large stocks of raw materials are not imported at once to be made up within the country."

Brown wanted the British to understand that the benefits of approving his huge clothing order were not only to provide Belgians and northern French with much-needed clothes. "It must be realized," he wrote, "that the benefits of this work are not only the provision of clothing for the destitute but that they include, as well, a very valuable employment for from 60,000 to 75,000 unemployed, the moral and economic results of which cannot be too highly appreciated."

He also acknowledged that the British had never known the details of the Belgian clothing system, which he was explaining for the first time in his report. "The very efficient system of control set up within Belgium to ensure such supplies reaching their proper destination has not been known." The Belgian system, Brown assured the British, "guarantees practically every single unit going to its proper destination."

In a section titled "Recommendations on the Purchase of the Accompanying Order," Brown went into minute detail as to how the order should be organized, if the British approved it.

As an example, regarding bolts of cloth, he stated, "All cloths should be from cloth measurements and a commission ticket attached to each bolt in place of the original, giving the class indication, the yardage, the unit price per yard, and the total value, as found by our agents. Then we must be responsible for all these records. Further, as a great many bolts of cloth in the past have been found to have been damaged by the hooks of the men handling them, I would advise that no attempt be made to have the manufacturers pack them for trans-oceanic shipment but only in light containers which could be substituted in this warehouse for heavy, serviceable cases, sufficiently strong to stand the hard wear demanded of them."

Not long after submission, the report and purchase order were approved by the British. Hoover explained that Brown's report, along with a report by Belgian doctors on the need for children to have adequate clothing, was enough for the British. "These reports and our own urgings finally secured approval of the Foreign Office for one of the largest single textile orders in the world up to that time."

In the end, the statistics on the clothing department were impressive, as related by Hoover: "Of the 24,384 tons of clothing that we handled, 10,571 tons were gifts and 13,313 tons were purchased. Of this total, 15,870 tons went to Belgium and 6,639 tons to Northern France. After the Armistice, we sold 1,375 tons of second-hand clothing to the American Relief Administration for its use in other parts of Europe."

Regarding the lace industry, by the end of the war a substantial amount of lace that had been produced with CRB-provided thread was warehoused. Such overstock was not left to waste, however. Hoover proudly reported, "Mrs. Hoover organized committees of American women in England and the United States who promoted the sales during and after the war. In the end, these indefatigable women sold all the lace, and the Belgian women's committee divided more than $1,000,000 net proceeds among the individual producers, each according to the value of her product."

Epilogue

What Happened to Them?

Herbert C. Hoover

(A short summary of this famous man.) As director of the U.S. Food Administration from August 10, 1917, until July 1, 1919, Hoover was America's "food czar" and instituted a voluntary program of food conservation that became known as "Hooverizing." Homemakers across America embraced the austerity measures to show support for the war and for the man known to many as the Great Humanitarian.

After the war, he led the American Relief Administration (ARA), which provided food and relief supplies to much of Central and Eastern Europe. The ARA had been formed on February 24, 1919, by an act of congress and was funded by $100 million in federal funds and $100 million in donations. The organization ultimately provided more than 4 million tons of relief supplies to more than 20 countries, including Russia during its famine in 1921, when more than 10 million people were fed daily. The ARA ended operations outside Russia in 1922 and inside Russia a year later.

On the American political scene, Hoover was considered by many a progressive and went through a short-lived candidacy for president in 1920. When Republican Warren G. Harding won the 1920 presidential election, he appointed Hoover to be his Secretary of Commerce. Hoover served in that position from 1921 to 1928.

In 1928, Hoover—having never held elective office—was elected president in a landslide over Democrat Al Smith.

After his presidency, he and his wife, Lou Henry Hoover, lived in northern California until 1940. In December 1940, they moved into New York City's Waldorf Astoria Towers, which was their home for the rest of their lives. After Lou's death in 1944, Hoover gave their California home to Stanford University and it became the official residency of the university's president.

After World War II, on March 1, 1946, President Harry S. Truman established the Famine Emergency Committee to aid in the fight against worldwide famine. Hoover was named honorary chairman, with St. Louis banker Chester Davis named chairman.

By the end of the war, Herbert C. Hoover had become known to some as the Great Humanitarian. (Public domain; Herbert Hoover Presidential Library Archives, West Branch, Iowa.)

When announcing the committee's formation during a radio broadcast, Truman stated, "It is my duty to join my voice with the voices of humanity everywhere in behalf of the starving millions of human beings all over the world. We have a high responsibility, as Americans, to go to their rescue. . . . We would not be Americans if we did not wish to share our comparative plenty with suffering people. I am sure I speak for every American when I say that the United States is determined to do everything in its power to relieve the famine of half the world."

In combination with the Department of Agriculture, the committee sponsored worldwide food missions that sent Hoover to 38 countries and states around the world. Hoover met with heads of state and government officials to enlist and coordinate their help in a global approach to fighting famine. Traveling with Hoover on these missions were numerous people, including many from the CRB days—Hugh Gibson, Perrin Galpin, Maurice Pate, and William Hallam Tuck.

From Hoover's reports, other findings of the committee, and work by other governmental agencies, America ended up exporting millions of tons of food to Asia and Europe, depleting its own reserves, but helping a starving world.

In 1947, Truman appointed Hoover to be chairman of the Commission on Organization of the Executive Branch of Government—unofficially known as the Hoover Commission—to recommend administrative changes to improve the efficiency of the federal government. The Commission provided congress with 273 recommendations and the result was the Reorganization Act of 1949, which was passed by congress in June 1949.

In 1953, when Hoover was nearly 80 years old, he was once again appointed—this time by President Dwight D. Eisenhower to chair the Second Hoover Commission. The Commission's final report was sent to congress in 1955.

Another lasting impact Hoover had on the world came from the official financial wrap-up of the CRB in August 1919. Hoover explained in a speech delivered in Belgium in July 1958, "At that time [1919] we found ourselves with about $39,000,000 in a special fund built up from the residues of world charity and from our trading with other nations." Hoover stated that $5 million, which was the French side of the money, was given to various charities in northern of France.

Hoover and Émile Francqui worked together to determine what to do with the remaining $34 million. A large part of it, according to Hoover, "replenished the endowments of the Belgian universities. And, in 1920, with . . . large sums remaining in the Belgian fund we established in Belgium the *Fondation Universitaire,* a center of academic and scientific cooperation, and in the United States the Belgian American Educational Foundation, to carry on intellectual exchanges between our two countries. We later established the Foundation Francqui. The C.R.B. and C.N. survivors still participate in the management of these foundations. These organizations have contributed greatly to the advancement of science, education and public welfare."

In 2018, the Belgian American Educational Foundation (BAEF) is the leading independent philanthropic organization in the support of exchanging university students, scientists, and scholars between the United States and Belgium. Headed since 1977 by Belgian (and Yale professor) Emile Boulpaep, the BAEF has provided more than 3,000 Belgians and more than 900 Americans with the opportunity for a period of advanced study or research in the partner country.

Hoover would be proud of how the CRB's residue funds from 1919 have kept working through the generations.

Hoover died on October 20, 1964, at age 90.

Milton M. Brown

After Brown's massive clothing order was approved by the British, Brown thought it best that he go back to the CRB New York City office to oversee the purchase order and its shipment. London Director Poland and CRB executive Millard Shaler convinced him not to go and instead suggested he write up extensive recommendations for the order. That's what he did, and he finished all the paperwork on Saturday, August 11, 1917.

Brown immediately hopped a boat to France. He went to Paris and joined the Press Censorship Bureau that was run by war-correspondent-turned-U.S.-military-man Major Frederick Palmer. He worked there until September, when he was recalled to the CRB London office to aid in organizing the clothing department for the upcoming clothing order.

In December 1917, Brown headed back to America for a brief visit home. While in America, Brown was told that, for various reasons, the raw materials that the CRB would be allowed to import into Belgium had been cut to 40 percent of the original order. So, instead of returning to London, he joined the CRB New York office and worked there from January to March 1918.

Finally, in April 1918, Brown did what he had wanted to do for a long time—enlist. He became part of the U.S. Army's Battery B, 324th Field Artillery, 83rd Division and served on the Western Front from September 1918 until the armistice.

(Left) Erica Bunge Brown and Milton Brown were married July 24, 1919. (Right) Milton Brown and Erica Bunge Brown in their late 70s while on the Brown family island in the Georgian Bay of Lake Huron. (Both photos: Author's archives.)

By May 1919 he had become a sergeant and was demobilized at Saint Aignan, France. He returned to America, only to sail July 8, 1919, on the SS *New Amsterdam* back to Europe so he could go to Belgium and see Erica Bunge.

On Wednesday, July 24, 1919, Erica and Milton married at Chateau Oude Gracht. The young couple sailed back to America on August 1, 1919, so that Erica could meet the Brown family and visit the island in the Georgian Bay of Lake Huron where the Browns had spent most of their summers.

The couple would go on to have three children: Erica Sophie Lucy Brown, Elizabeth Bunge Brown, and Milton McIntyre Brown Jr.

For the first years of their marriage, the Browns lived on Hoogboom estate in a home named Oud Eikelenberg. After Edouard Bunge died, Erica inherited the Chateau Oude Gracht and the south farm. She, Milton, and the children moved into Chateau Oude Gracht and lived there until September 1939, when World War II began.

The Browns returned to America and lived in Connecticut during the war. Immediately after the war, they returned to Belgium and reportedly found that Chateau Oude Gracht had been used at various times as a headquarters by six different armies (Belgian, French, British, German, Canadian, and American). While the chateau still stood, it was determined not to be worth restoring and was razed. Before that happened, however, Milton and Erica had two rooms, the library and study, taken apart piece by piece and reassembled and attached to their new American home on Whitehall Farm on the Eastern Shore of Maryland.

Throughout their lives, Milton and Erica gave to many charities and were great lovers of nature and wildlife. Their 850-acre Whitehall Farm became known as a wildlife preserve.

After surviving two world wars, they both had strong anti-German feelings that never went away.

Milton died on April 18, 1979, at age 88. Erica died on February 5, 1986, at 94.

They would have both been saddened to learn that Whitehall Farm was sold to a wealthy German who reportedly kept it as a hunting reserve that he rarely visited.

The Bunges

Edouard Bunge returned to running and expanding the Bunge company, which was also known as Bunge and Born (today Bunge Limited, an agribusiness and food company with more than 30,000 employees in over 40 countries). He died on November 18, 1927, at 76 years old. After his death, his four surviving daughters (one daughter, Dora, had died of the great influenza in 1919) peaceably divided up the Hoogboom estate and the family business.

Daughter Eva did not marry Fred Eckstein. She suddenly changed her mind and called off the engagement in 1917. After the war, she would marry Englishman Andrew James Widderson and they would move to Buenos Aires, Argentina, to help run the family company. They had four children: Leslie Andrew Widderson, Eva Marie Widderson, Ivy Louise Widderson, and Edward Andrew Widderson. Eva Marie Bunge Widderson died in 1987, at the age of 92.

In 1920, Hilda Bunge married William Hallam Tuck—the delegate who had left the CRB after witnessing the German deportations. They would live in a chateau in Switzerland and on an estate on the Eastern Shore of Maryland, not far from Milton and Erica. The Tucks would have three children: Emily Snowden Hallam Tuck, Dorothea "Dorita" Margaret Hallam Tuck, and Edward Hallam Tuck. Hilda died on August 21, 1980, at age 84.

William Hallam Tuck

After leaving the CRB in December 1916, Tuck joined the British Army, where he served until 1918 and reached the rank of captain Royal Artillery, British Expeditionary Force, attached to the 36th Brigade, Royal Australian Artillery. When America entered the war, Tuck joined the U.S. Army, where he served as a major in the 314th Field Artillery, 80th Division.

After the war he returned to the CRB. Tuck became good friends with Hoover and worked with the Chief in the American Relief Administration (ARA) and on Hoover's presidential campaigns. He also traveled with Hoover on the food missions of the Famine Emergency Committee. Tuck spent much of his life involved in various ways and with various groups regarding food relief and the welfare of humanity.

He was director general of the International Refugee Organization from 1947 to 1949, served as executive director of the Second Hoover Commission from 1953 to 1955, and was vice president of the Belgian American Educational Foundation from 1936 to 1966. Tuck continued a strong and active association with Hoover throughout the rest of Hoover's life.

On April 20, 1920, Tuck married Hilda Bunge at the Chateau Oude Gracht. On August 28, 1966, Tuck died at their summer home in Rougemont, Switzerland. He was 76 years old.

Hugh S. Gibson

Arriving back in America on January 21, 1917, Gibson was quickly reassigned to "special duty" for the State Department in Washington. That included being attached to two different official visits to the United States from the British Foreign Office and from a Belgian war mission. By August 24, 1917, he had been promoted to "class one" and by March 1918 he had reported for duty as first secretary to the U.S. Embassy in Paris. That was followed by special duty with Hoover from November 1918 to April 1919, after which he was a member of an inter-Allied mission to countries of the former Austro-Hungarian Empire (December 1918 to January 1919).

Finally, Gibson was given his own post as U.S. minister plenipotentiary to Poland in April 1919. He served there until 1924 before moving on to become U.S. minister to Switzerland. In February 1927, he was appointed as minister to both Belgium and Luxembourg and served until June 1933. He then headed off to be minister to Brazil before returning to be minister of Belgium and Luxembourg from July 1937 until June 1938. He resigned then after deciding his personal financial situation could not support accepting President Roosevelt's offer to be ambassador to Germany.

Gibson did much in his career to help America and the world. He became the assistant to Hoover in the Famine Emergency Committee and traveled with the Chief around the world assessing the world's food resources to avoid a possible global famine. He even graced the cover of *Time* magazine three times.

Gibson married Belgian Ynès Reyntiens, his friend and fellow riding partner from World War I Belgium, in February 1922. They lost a daughter at childbirth but had a son Michael who was born in 1929. Gibson died in Geneva on December 12, 1954, at 71, a man well loved, well respected, and greatly admired, not only for what he had done but for his tremendous sense of humor while doing it.

Prentiss Gray

After CRB Brussels Director Gray, his family, and the last American delegates left Belgium on May 1, 1917, Gray became the assistant director of the CRB's

New York office. He took on the significant tasks of purchasing and shipping. He stayed there until February 1918, when he went to Washington, D.C., to represent the Food Administration and the Commission for Relief in Belgium on its shipping board. He was chief of the marine transport administration for the U.S. Food Administration before becoming the director of the American Relief Administration (ARA) from 1918 to 1919.

In March 1919, Gray went back to Belgium and visited his good friend Edouard Bunge at Chateau Oude Gracht. Gray was wondering what he could do once the ARA work was done. The answer came in an unexpected way. He wrote in his dairy on March 21, 1919, "I left [Chateau Oude Gracht] early this morning with Mr. Bunge for Brussels for a meeting with the Minister of Ravitaillement [relief] to whom I elucidated the fact that the C.R.B. proposed to get out of the business [of importing food] at the earliest possible moment. Greatly to my surprise he thought that the business of importing foodstuffs should be put into the hands of the pre-war importers in such a way that they could begin to re-establish themselves. He asked [Edouard] Bunge [who had before the war imported grain to Belgium] if he would undertake to import the grain and fats formerly brought in by the C.R.B. and Bunge allowed he would if I would handle the business in America. After the proper amount of hesitation to recover from my surprise, I accepted and was turned over to a small committee to work out the details."

With Bunge's help and support, Gray formed the P.N. Gray & Company and entered the grain export business. He quickly expanded operations to include much more than just Belgium, taking the company into multiple European countries and even into Latin America. As he did so, he enlisted the help of numerous ex-CRB delegates who had become friends and now were employees of P.N. Gray & Company, including Edgar Rickard, A.C.B. Fletcher, Pink Simpson, Clare Torrey, Dorsey Stephens, Duke Wellington, Francis Wickes, and Philip Potter.

By 1923, however, the grain export business was not doing well, and Gray and a number of P.N. Gray & Company employees transitioned into the banking business. Gray became the president of the J. Henry Schroder Banking Corporation in New York City.

Gray and the firm expanded during the prosperous 1920s, survived the initial stock market crash of 1929, and had successfully retrenched by 1935, when tragedy struck.

The published introduction of Gray's diary—written by his son, Sherman Gray—reported that Prentiss had made plans in January 1935 "to hunt jaguar in the Florida Everglades with Mr. Ruly Carpenter of the E.I. du Pont Company. He was on his way to Mr. Carpenter's yacht 'Harmony,' at the mouth of the Shark River when the boat that had been sent for him exploded, killing both [Prentiss] and the driver instantly." Gray was 51 years old.

Joseph C. Green

Tracy Kittredge noted, "J. C. Green began the compilation of the official history [of the CRB] but left in May [1917] to take a commission in the army."

Green went on to work with Hoover as director for Romania and later in the Near East as part of the American Relief Administration (ARA). In 1920 he became the chairman of the Ohio committee for the election of Herbert Hoover (a short-lived candidacy by the Chief), as well as assistant professor of history at his alma mater, Princeton. Green would continue to teach as assistant professor until 1924, when he became associate professor. He stayed at Princeton teaching history until 1930.

From then on, Green worked at various jobs in the State Department including assistant of the division of western European affairs (1930–1935), chairman of the committee to revise foreign service examinations (1931–1942), chief of the office of arms and munitions control (1935–1939), chief of the division of controls (1939–1941), executive secretary of the national munitions control board (1935–1946), special assistant to the secretary of state (1941–1944), adviser on arms and munitions controls (1944–1946), and chairman of the advisory committee on foreign service examinations (1946–1952). In 1952 Green became U.S. ambassador to Jordan and served until 1953.

Green's personal life as an adult had started with a tragedy. Before the war and the CRB, Green had married Harriet Stearns on June 15, 1912, but she had died while on their honeymoon. After the war, Green married Gertrude Henshaw Norris, and they had two daughters and a son and lived in Washington, D.C.

Green would remain fast friends with his childhood friend and fellow CRB delegate, Milton Brown, throughout their lives. In the summer of 1969, he would be a guest of honor at Milton and Erica's 50th wedding anniversary, which was held on an island in the Georgian Bay of Lake Huron, where both Green and Brown had spent practically every summer of their youth.

Joe Green died on August 2, 1978, in Parry Sound, Ontario, on the shores of Lake Huron. He was 91.

Edward Eyre Hunt

After World War I, E. E. Hunt did relief work with the Red Cross in France and Italy and then worked as an economist. During the presidency of his friend Herbert Hoover, Hunt served on several presidential commissions. However, in 1933, following Hoover's failure to win a second term, Hunt retired temporarily from public life in order to write and publish a novel, *Greathouse* (1937). With the outbreak of World War II, Hunt returned to public service as chief industrial economist of the War Protection Board. From 1943 on he worked for the State Department, first in the Office of Foreign Relief and Rehabilitation and then in a series of other positions including director of the Italian Division. In 1947 he was made chief of protective services in the State Department and held that position until his death.

Hunt married Virginia Lloyd Fox shortly after World War I. She was an artist and author and had worked with wounded soldiers in France during the war. They had two children, Edward Eyre Hunt Jr. and Virginia Hunt. Edward Eyre Hunt died in Washington, D.C., on March 5, 1953, at the age of 67.

David T. Nelson

After leaving the CRB in October 1915, Nelson returned to Oxford and then joined an American ambulance volunteer organization at the Allied front in France in 1915–1916. When America entered the war, he served as an intelligence officer in the U.S. Army. After the war, Nelson earned a BA from Oxford (1919) and later an MA (1950). Returning to America in 1919, he worked at a Wall Street investment firm in New York before continuing his graduate studies in English at the University of Chicago.

In 1921 Nelson joined the faculty of Luther College in Decorah, Iowa. For the next 42 years he taught English, literature, headed the English department, coached various teams from tennis to debate, and participated in practically every policy-making committee.

He was also a strong community leader who was proud of his Norwegian heritage and wrote several books. Nelson married Esther C. Torrison on September 5, 1924, and they had four children: H. Elizabeth Nelson, David T. Nelson Jr., Robert K. Nelson, and John P. Nelson.

Dr. David T. Nelson died on October 9, 1969, at age 78.

Walter H. Page

In the autumn of 1918, Page became ill and resigned his post as U.S. ambassador to Britain. He returned to his home in Pinehurst, North Carolina, where he died on December 21, 1918, at age 63. Hoover wrote, "The C.R.B. would have failed had it not been for him. The personal affection our staff held for him was unbounded."

Clare M. Torrey

In May 1917, Torrey left his U.S. embassy job in London and joined the French Army. When his request for a combat position was refused, he quit and joined the American Army, where he saw combat in the Toul sector of France and was gassed. (It was not lethal, but he sustained permanent lung damage.)

Immediately after the war, in December 1918, while still in the service, Torrey was reassigned to Hoover in Paris during the peace conference to assist with European relief work. He lived with Hoover at 19 Rue de Lubeck and they had breakfast and dinner nearly every day. The man who had been told by Hoover in Belgium that his American fiancée was not coming to marry him finally had his day.

On April 29, 1919, Torrey married another American, Marion Steere Haley, whom he had met in Paris. Hoover hosted and paid for the bachelor dinner, held the wedding at his Paris house, and gave the bride away. Hoover then ordered Torrey and his new bride to Vienna, where Torrey opened and operated a child-feeding program in Austria that fed more than 250,000 children.

After he demobilized in September 1919, Torrey and his college and CRB friend Pink Simpson formed a partnership and, working with Prentiss Gray's shipping company, assisted the newly formed countries in Central Europe with their importation of food. The two ex-CRB men dealt with the governments of Austria, Hungary, Poland, and eventually Russia.

In 1923, Torrey joined an investment firm and opened its office in London. He returned to New York just before the crash of 1929. For the rest of Torrey's long career, he was in the investment banking business.

A second marriage to Susan P. Conroy on October 3, 1933, led to six children: Peter Torrey, Katherine Torrey, twins John and Michael Torrey, Susan Eyre Torrey, and James Alexander Torrey IV.

Clare Torrey died on September 25, 1977, just before his 87th birthday.

Brand Whitlock

When World War I ended, Whitlock returned to Belgium as the U.S. minister. During 1919, when he and his wife were back in America for a visit, the U.S. position in Belgium was raised to the rank of embassy—Whitlock returned to Belgium as its first U.S. ambassador. He would serve in that position through 1921.

In 1919, his two-volume *Belgium: A Personal Narrative,* which detailed his time in Belgium during the war, was released. Whitlock's early years had been spent as a journalist, and he was a prolific writer throughout his life, producing works of fiction, nonfiction, and poetry. He wrote 18 books on various topics, including a few novels.

He died in Cannes, France, in 1934, shortly after turning 65.

Émile Francqui

After the war, Francqui helped Hoover in determining what to do with the millions left over from the food-relief work. In 1920, Francqui founded the University Foundation, which would work with the Belgian American Education Foundation.

In April 1924, as one of Belgium's most prominent financial men, Francqui participated in the creation of the Dawes Plan, which was tasked with finding a solution for the collection of the German reparations debt following World War I.

Later, Leopold III, son of King Albert and the future king of Belgium, asked Francqui to find ways of improving the health of the people living in the Belgian Congo, where Francqui had served decades before as a 21-year-old military officer. In 1931, Francqui's work on this issue led to the establishment of the Prince Leopold Institute of Tropical Medicine, and he served as its first president.

A year later, Hoover and Francqui created the Francqui Foundation. Its mission was to "further the development of higher education and scientific research in Belgium."

In 1934, Francqui became Belgium's secretary of state. A year later, on November 1, 1935, Francqui died at age 72.

Marquis de Villalobar

After the war, Villalobar stayed at his Belgian post and was elevated to ambassador in 1921. The Belgians had a strong affection for the Spaniard, whose name graces Brussels's Avenue Marquis de Villalobar, which is near the Royal Golf Club of Belgium. He remained ambassador to Belgium until his death in 1926. Brand Whitlock wrote of him after his death, "He could treat people on occasions with a withering contempt, as from the cold heights of a cynical hauteur, and yet he was ever so kind to the misfortunate and would take infinite pains to help people out of trouble."

Baron Oscar von der Lancken

Little information is available about von der Lancken's life after the war. One surprising report listed the German as being on a non-German commission studying German war atrocities. He died on October 23, 1939, in Germany.

Maurice Pate

He devoted nearly his entire life to improving the lives of children around the world. After leaving the CRB, he was part of Hoover's American Relief Administration (ARA), serving in the Child Feeding Operations (1919–1921) and the European Children's Fund (1919–1922); he served as president of the Commission for Polish Relief (CPR, 1919–1922); and he was part of the ARA's Russian famine relief program (1922–1923).

Between the two world wars, Pate worked in the business world as a salesman and investment banker. From World War II on, he returned to relief efforts. He served as director of the Relief to American and Allied Prisoners of War for the American Red Cross (1941–1946) and was a member of Hoover's global missions with the Famine Emergency Committee.

On returning from those missions, Hoover recommended the establishment of the United Nations International Children's Emergency Fund (UNICEF; later changed to the permanent United Nations Children's Fund, but the acronym stuck). Pate became its first executive director. He served in that position until 1965.

Pate was nominated for a Nobel Peace Prize in 1960 for his work with UNICEF but turned down the nomination because he felt it would be more appropriate if the nomination was for the organization, not himself.

In 1927 Pate married Jadwiga Monkowska of Poland. They divorced 10 years later. In 1961 he married Martha B. Lucas. The man who worked nearly his entire life for the betterment of children, never had any of his own.

Maurice Pate died on January 19, 1965, at 70 years old. Nine months later, in October 1965, his beloved UNICEF won the Nobel Peace Prize.

Once, at a UNICEF dinner, Herbert Hoover described Pate as "the most effective human angel I know."

A Final Note about the CRB Delegates

During the life of the CRB, approximately 165 to 185 men (and one woman, Charlotte Kellogg) served as delegates in Belgium or northern France from 1914 until April 1917, when America entered the war. With multiple lists having numerous errors and omissions, and no lists attaching photos with names, an accurate accounting is difficult. (For the most accurate, up-to-date photo/name list, visit WWICrusaders.com.)

The majority of CRB delegates were young, idealistic university students in their twenties who embodied a spirit of giving and self-sacrifice. They dropped everything in their own lives to travel thousands of miles, enter the prison that was German-occupied Belgium, tackle a job that had never been done before, and rein in their personal feelings regarding the German occupation to work hard for the benefit of civilians in Belgium and northern France. Many of them did so unreservedly, with no great expectation of anything in return.

And in the end, the result of their labors—and the work of many others, including the thousands of Belgians volunteering in the relief efforts—was the largest food and relief program the world had ever seen. They had accomplished something that no one had ever thought possible—the feeding of an entire nation trapped in the midst of a world war.

Many of the young CRB delegates went on to lifetimes of public service in government agencies, political appointments, elected office, and nonprofit and charitable institutions. Two notables were Maurice Pate, who was the first director of UNICEF, and Hallam Tuck, who, as the director general of the International Refugee Organization from 1947 to 1949, was charged with helping millions of World War II refugees.

Unfortunately, most of the CRB delegate stories have been long forgotten, innocent victims swept away by the tidal wave of negative public opinion surrounding Hoover's later efforts as president. Because Hoover is perceived as having been a bad president, much of his great humanitarian work and the work of those associated with the relief have been neglected.

Their stories deserve to be told and remembered.

Acknowledgments

No book is a one-person project. I've been fortunate to have a team of professionals and multiple friends and family members who have helped me make this book the best possible.

But the story of how this book came about—and those who helped me along the way—starts with my grandparents.

As a young man, I was interested in the stories that my grandfather, Milton M. Brown, told about his time in German-occupied Belgium as one of Herbert Hoover's CRB delegates. My grandmother, Erica Bunge Brown, rarely spoke of that time, although I'm not sure, because I was a teenager then and had the attention span of a gnat. In the end, most of the stories I remember came not from my grandparents but from my mother, Erica Sophie Lucy Brown Miller, who had heard them from her parents.

After graduating from the University of Denver with a BA degree in history, I became a freelance writer, magazine editor, and book author.

In the early 1980s, I received an inheritance of CRB-related letters, journals, and photos of my grandfather and the edited diary and photos of my grandmother. (Before I received the material, my mother edited Erica Bunge's diary and then destroyed the original. As her son, I completely understand my mother's actions; as a historian, I'm saddened by what she did.)

Armed with my grandparents' material and with a passion for historical novels, I decided to write a historical novel about my grandparents and the CRB. Because I wanted the book to cover much more than just my family, I researched Herbert Hoover, the CRB, three delegates (Joe Green, Maurice Pate, and Fred Eckstein), and two U.S. diplomats (Brand Whitlock and Hugh Gibson). I also read a number of books written by other delegates about their service in the CRB.

After two full-time years of work, I produced an 850-page historical novel, *Honor Bound*. It was never published; fiction, it seemed, was not my strength.

Traditional book publishers did accept and publish a history book about another topic and a medical health book for men that I cowrote with Dr. Gordon Ehlers. The health book was included in *Publishers Weekly*'s Best Books of 2002.

From these books, I learned that my strength as a writer lay in writing nonfiction.

In 2009, I was diagnosed with stage 4 throat cancer and began a year I'd prefer to forget. By December 2012, I was ready for a big project, and I committed to writing a nonfiction book about the CRB and German-occupied Belgium. Out of that came *Behind the Lines,* which detailed the complex and chaotic beginnings of those stories (see the Author's Note). It was published in 2014 (the 100th anniversary of the start of World War I). The prestigious *Kirkus Reviews* gave it a Starred Review and included the book in its list of Best Books of 2014.

In 2015, I decided to write one volume that would tell the complete story of the CRB and Belgium through the eyes of multiple American CRB volunteers, individual Belgians, and those responsible for the underground newspaper, *La Libre Belgique.* I felt it was necessary for the book to be published in 2018 (the 100-year anniversary of the end of World War I). I researched and studied Belgium, the war, and the journals, diaries, and correspondence of approximately 50 CRB delegates.

The result is this book, *WWI Crusaders.*

Which brings me back to those I want to acknowledge.

In the research stage, I am grateful for the warm, welcoming, and helpful assistance of Matthew T. Schaefer, archivist at the Herbert Hoover Presidential Library Archives, West Branch, Iowa; Carol A. Leadenham, assistant archivist for reference (now retired); and David Jacobs, archival specialist at the Hoover Institution Archives at Stanford University, Stanford, California. I was also assisted in research at Stanford by PhD candidate in history, Michelle Mengsu Chang, and in Iowa by professional researcher Wesley Beck. Evelyn McMillan—a writer, researcher about World War I Belgian lace, and a librarian at Stanford University—was very helpful in providing information and proofing the book's sections about the Belgian lace industry. Amy Reytar was especially helpful in navigating the State Department records at the National Archives in College Park, Maryland.

In Belgium I was aided in research by three men who live northeast of Antwerp and have become friends: Raymond Roelands, Roger Van den Bleeken, and Marc Brans. They have studied for years the history of their area, especially during World War I. Roelands is the author of *Geschiedenis van Kasteeldomein "Oude Gracht" in Hoogboom* (*History of the Castle Domain "Oude Gracht" in Hoogboom*); Van den Bleeken and Brans are two of the authors of *Cappellen in den Grooten Oorlog* (*Cappellen in the Great War*).

In 2011, I was fortunate to have a chance meeting at the Herbert Hoover Presidential Library Archives with history professor Dr. Branden Little, who teaches at Weber State University in Ogden, Utah. He has been studying the CRB and many other humanitarian relief efforts for more than a decade. In the highly competitive world of academic research and writing, Dr. Little is unusual in his friendly openness to give of his time and historical sources. I'm proud to say that he has become a friend who has aided me in countless ways, big and small.

I must also thank the ever-gracious George Nash, scholar and biographer of Herbert Hoover. An extremely accessible and friendly man, he has been constantly supportive since I first began working on this project. He read pieces of this book and gave me valuable input, and when my efforts to find a critical document were fruitless, he was kind enough to send me a copy from his own files.

During the years that this project has been my life, I have been fortunate to come into contact with a number of descendants of CRB delegates. They were tremendously helpful and willing to share any information they had about their relatives and gave me permission to use that information to help tell the CRB story. They include Dr. Erskine Carmichael, nephew of delegate Oliver C. Carmichael; John P. Nelson, son of delegate David T. Nelson; Sherman and Prentiss Gray, son and grandson, respectively, of delegate Prentiss Gray; Margaret Hunt, granddaughter of delegate E. E. Hunt; Mariette and George Wickes, daughter and son, respectively, of Francis Wickes; Andy Hoover and Margaret Hoover, grandson and great granddaughter, respectively, of Herbert C. Hoover; Jim Torrey, son of delegate Clare Torrey; and Jessica Tuck, granddaughter of William Hallam Tuck (who married Hilda Bunge).

For help in the writing, editing, and proofing stages, I am thankful to some general readers—my siblings Carolyn, Leslie, Buck, and Eric; brother-in-law Gene Zimmerman; my cousins Evie Newell and Eric Karcher; and Larry Yoder. Three readers who worked their way through the entire book as it was being written and were tremendously helpful in improving the manuscript were David Hiller, Rod Manuel, and cousin David Newell.

I am indebted to professional editor Tom Locke, who ably handled the heavy lifting of editing and standardizing the text to conform to *The Chicago Manual of Style*. I'm thankful for the sharp eye of proofreader Laura Furney and for the highly specialized talents of freelance book indexer Doug Easton.

The book's front cover concept and design and an infographic used in marketing were beautifully developed by professional graphic designer—and friend—Laurie Shields of Laurie Shields Design. The interior pages, back cover, and spine were created by the talented team of Dan and Jim Pratt of Pratt Brothers Composition. The book's website, www.WWICrusaders.com, was created by the business-savvy team led by friends Mike Bren and Seth Daire of Crown Point Solutions.

Overall, this book would not have been written and published without the friendship and financial assistance of a small group of people who have believed in me and this project beyond all reasonable expectations. The group includes Jim Torrey, Evie Newell, Tina Miller, David Newell, Susan Burdick, and one person who wishes to remain anonymous. Thank you all—your commitment has truly overwhelmed me.

Finally, I must again thank my grandparents and my wife, Susan Burdick. The story came about because of my grandparents, but I would never be the writer I am today without Susan's unwavering love and support. I owe her all that I am—and more.

Notes

Abbreviations

HIA	Hoover Institution Archives, Stanford University, Stanford, California.
HHPLA	Herbert Hoover Presidential Library Archives, West Branch, Iowa.
NARA	National Archives and Records Administration, Washington, D.C., and College Park, MD.
RG 59	Record Group 59: General Records of the State Department.
RG 84	Record Group 84: Records of the Foreign Service Posts of the State Department.

Note: I use the first three words of a quote, a sentence, or a paragraph to identify what my attribution is referring to.

1. Left or Right 1–5

"No One Slept throughout the Night" 1–5

Virton details: Karl Baedeker, *Baedeker's Belgium and Holland* (Baedeker, 1910), 235.

When the war: 218 killed on Aug. 23 in the village of Ethe next to Virton; John Horne and Alan Kramer, *German Atrocities 1914*, Appendix 1, 437; Joseph Green essay, no title, Jan. 10, 1917, Joseph C. Green papers, box 19, Princeton Mudd Library.

"slave raids": a term used to describe the forced deportations of Belgian workers that began in 1916 and continued into 1917. The term was used many times in multiple sources; one example, "Slave Raids in Belgium," *London Times*, Nov. 8, 1916.

Virton, its *affiche,* and all details and quotes regarding the deportation not otherwise attributed: Joseph Green essay, no title, Jan. 10, 1917, Green papers, box 19, Princeton Mudd Library.

Virton deportations not otherwise attributed: Joseph Green essay, no title, Jan. 10, 1917; in a letter to his father and mother, Jan. 14, 1917, he writes that he was in Virton and did see the deportations; Green papers, boxes 19 and 37, Princeton Mudd Library.

Those who did: Arnold Toynbee, *The Belgian Deportations* (T. Fisher Unwin, Ltd., London, no date).

Description of *uhlan* crowd control: Milton M. Brown, from *Gloria Victis* by Brown (grandfather of the author) on the deportations at Malines, author's archives.

"left" or "right": Most accounts of the deportations include those two words, but not always to indicate the same thing. Left-to-freedom and right-to-deportation are in the accounts of Joe Green; Robert Jackson, handwritten relief memoir, part 3, pp. 4–5, HIA; Prentiss Gray's diary, 208, author's archives. Left-to-deportation and right-to-freedom is in the eye-witness account at Wavre in Britain's *Daily Telegraph*, (Dec. 1916); Toynbee, *The Belgian Deportations*; Brand Whitlock's *Belgium: A Personal Narrative* (D. Appleton and Co., 1919), vol. II, 628 and 645.

Recommended capacity of cattle cars: "The Agony of Belgium," *London Times*, Nov. 21, 1916.

Singing Belgian and French national anthems: Toynbee, *The Belgian Deportations*, 14, 95; Robert Withington, *In Occupied Belgium*, 111; Jules Van Den Heuvel, *Slave Raids in Belgium: Facts about the*

Deportations (T. Fisher Unwin, London), 1917, 34; "Slave Raids in Belgium," *London Times*, Nov. 8, 1916; Whitlock, *Belgium*, vol. II, 625.

hastily scribbled notes: "Slave Raids in Belgium," *London Times*, Nov. 8, 1916; Toynbee, *The Belgian Deportations*, 15; Whitlock, *Belgium*, vol. II, 625.

"They are carried": Green, letter to parents, Green papers, box 37, Princeton Mudd Library.

More than 120,000 deportees: Toynbee, *The Belgian Deportations*, 14, 69, states, "The latest accounts of all place the number already deported at 100,000"; Belgian historian, Jens Thiel, in a speech titled "Slave Raids during the First World War? Deportations and Forced Labor in Occupied Belgium" on March 24, 2014, stated, "between Oct. 26, 1916 and Feb. 10, 1917, approximately 60,000 Belgians were deported to Germany for forced labor" from the portion of Belgium controlled by Governor General von Bissing, but also states that approximately 60,000 more Belgians and French were taken from northern France, making the total 120,000 deportees or forced workers; Hoover, *American Epic*, footnote no. 1, 281, states, "The number of deportees who returned to Belgium and France after the German surrender in November, 1918, exceeded 700,000. This was not the total deported, however, because many had died in Germany." Most scholars today discount Hoover's figures; Britain's *Daily Telegraph*, Feb. 6, 1917, states 350,000 were deported, clip books, HHPLA.

"now the fear": "Enslavement of a Nation," *The Scotsman*, Nov. 24, 1916.

"Appalling stories have": Brand Whitlock's official report as recorded in "One of the Foulest Deeds in History," *London Times*, May 18, 1919.

Section I: Beginnings, 1914

2. Setting the Stage 9–24

Major Events of the War 9–10

54 fortresses: Edouard Bunge, "What I Saw of the Bombardment and Surrender of Antwerp," Oct. 1914, unpublished document, author's archives.

The subsequent flooding: Marshall, *American Heritage History*, 77.

During December 1914: Thomas Löwer, "Demystifying the Christmas Truce," The Heritage of the Great War website.

German-Occupied Belgium 10–12

Belgian nationalism and all quotes in the section not otherwise attributed: Hugh Gibson, "German Rule in Belgium" speech, Gibson papers, box 73, HIA.

Reflective of this: "One Belgian story," Émile Cammaerts, *Through the Iron Bars* (John Lane, The Bodley Head, London, 1917), 65–66.

Belgium compared to Maryland: 1910 editor of *Baedeker's Belgium and Holland* states Belgium to be 11,378 square miles; 2016 U.S. statistics, Maryland is 12,407 square miles.

People per square mile and population densities: Tracy B. Kittredge, *The History of the Commission for Relief in Belgium, 1914–1917* (unpublished), 8.

"To the Belgian": Arthur Humphreys, four articles that ran in the *London Times* and later compiled into a 46-page pamphlet, *The Heart of Belgium*.

"Famine sweeps over": Robinson Smith, "Hoover—The Man in Action," Smith papers, HIA.

The Genesis of Belgium Food Relief 12–14

"The whole machinery"; quotes not otherwise noted: Kittredge, *History of CRB*, 10, 11, 17, 13, 34.

"Waves of refugees": Hunt, *War Bread*, 189.

Americans Get Involved in Belgium Relief 15–20

The Comité Central gave: Kittredge, *History of CRB*, 12.

The reason was: Ibid., 35.

"his dress never varies": Smith, "Hoover," Robinson Smith papers, HIA.

In August 1914, and Hoover's work in London: Smith, *An Uncommon Man*, 80.

"He didn't want": John L. Simpson, "Activities in a Troubled World: War Relief, Banking, and Business," an interview conducted by Suzanne B. Riess, 1978, Regional Oral History Office, The Bancroft Library, University of California, Berkeley, California.

"immediately impressed": George I. Gay and H. H. Fisher, *Public Relations of the Commission for Relief in Belgium: Documents,* 2 vols. (Stanford University, Stanford University of Press, 1929), vol. I, 3.
"promised to help": Kittredge, *History of CRB,* 37.
"At this point": George H. Nash, *The Life of Herbert Hoover, The Humanitarian, 1914–1917* (W. W. Norton and Co., 1988), 19.
"It was an": Ibid., 19.
"the idea of": Kittredge, *History of CRB,* 37–38.
"approved heartily of": Ibid., 38.
"let the fortune": Will Irwin, *Herbert Hoover—a Reminiscent Biography* (Grosset and Dunlap, 128), 135.
Dannie Heineman to be offered vice-chairman: Kittredge, *History of CRB,* 38.
"The greatest hope": Hunt, *War Bread,* 319–320.
"a comprehensive": *New York Times,* Oct. 18, 1814; Kittredge, *History of CRB,* 40–41.

The CRB and the CN Are Born 20–22

As the concept: Kittredge, *History of CRB,* 43.
Expand the program nationwide: Nash, *The Life of Herbert Hoover,* 23.
"What!": Joe Green, "Some Portraits: Emile Francqui," Feb. 15, 1917, Green papers, Princeton Mudd Library. Green was not there when Francqui learned of Hoover's participation in Belgium relief, but this sounds very much like something Francqui would have said.
Whitlock, who was: Whitlock, *Belgium,* vol. I, 398–399.
But how much; totals on food; "considerably less": Gay and Fisher, *Public Relations,* vol. I, doc. 20.

CRB Delegates—A Necessary Prerequisite 22–24

Details of the early delegates in this section: multiple sources reviewed by author including multiple CRB lists; Kittredge, *History of CRB;* Gay and Fisher, *Public Relations,* vols. I and II; Delegate work list, Robert Arrowsmith papers, HIA.
One student; Galpin as student organizer: In my previous book, *Behind the Lines,* I stated incorrectly that Hoover or one of the CRB executives had approached Galpin asking for help in recruiting delegates at Oxford. In later research, I found a series of letters from Galpin that shows he approached the CRB after reading about its need for delegates, and that he suggested the Oxford students could use their six-week school break to go into Belgium. The letters, starting from Nov. 23, 1914, are in the Executive Alphabetical Files, 1912–1942, Perrin Galpin papers, box 15, Galpin, HIA.
Edgar Rickard wrote: Galpin papers, box 1, HIA.
"When this war": Ben Allen, "Feeding Seven Million Belgians: The Work of the American Commission for Relief," *The World's Work,* April 1915, Ben Allen papers, HIA.
"You must forget": Ibid.

3. The Students Head into Belgium 25–35

"What we were": Emil Holman papers, folder 1, HIA.
They had more: Galpin to CRB, Nov. 29, 1914, Galpin papers, box 1, HIA.
"will see that": Britain's *Daily Telegraph,* Nov. 7, 1914, clip books, HHPLA.
The 10 newly: Galpin to CRB, Dec. 2, 1914, Galpin papers, box 1, HIA.
"We propose to": Hoover to Galpin, Nov. 30, 1914, Galpin papers, box 1, HIA.
What is known; official records: The six delegates recorded by Galpin as having gone into Belgium as part of the second wave of Oxford students but not listed on any official CRB lists are: George B. Noble, Francis L. Patton, William H. Mechling, Clyde Eagleton, Alexander R. Wheeler, and Clarence A. Castle. Galpin to CRB London office, Dec. 4, 1914, Galpin papers, box 1, HIA.
Hoover had immediately: Kellogg, *Fighting Starvation* (New York: Doubleday, Page and Co., 1918), 27; Gay and Fisher, *Public Relations,* vol. I, 27–29.
All following Lucey biographical details and quotes in section not otherwise noted: Biographical sketch, *Mining and Oil Bulletin,* July 1921, 7.
By November Lucey; office and guarantees details: Kittredge, *History of CRB,* 68, 70, 72.
A substantial clerical: Ibid., 68.
"Consigned to"; details and quotes of first shipment: Britain's *Daily Citizen,* Nov. 14, 1914, clip books, HHPLA; Kittredge, *History of CRB,* 70.

Rotterdam office details: Gay and Fisher, *Public Relations*, vol. I, 27–29; Kellogg, *Fighting Starvation*, 27; Kittredge, *History of CRB*, 68.
"nervous, big": Hunt, *War Bread*, 200.
"You will be"; Nelson quotes in section: Nelson, *Letters and Diaries of David T. Nelson*, 34–37, 39, 42.

Nelson's Difficult Entry into Belgium 29–31

All quotes from Nelson in this section not otherwise noted: Nelson, *Letters and Diaries*, 43–44.

The Second Wave Hits 31–32

Galpin decision to join CRB: Perrin C. Galpin, "Reminiscences," oral history, Perrin Galpin papers, Research Office, Columbia University, 1957, 2.
"Since tomorrow"; "The amazing size": Galpin letter to Harry, Dec. 10, 1914, Galpin papers, HIA.
"My job will": Ibid.
"a new and"; "high-class restaurant": Baedeker, *Belgium*, 89.
"In those first": Kittredge, *History of CRB*, 92–93.

Nelson's Perspective on the Germans 32–34

"It was a": Nelson, *Letters and Diaries*, 43–44.
Details of Nelson's entry into Belgium: Ibid.
Nelson would find: Delegate work list, Robert Arrowsmith papers, HIA.
Liège statistics, quotes, and descriptions: Baedeker, *Belgium*, 247–248.
"When I entered"; all remaining quotes in section: Nelson, *Letters and Diaries*, 43–44.

A German Christmas in Belgium 34–35

All details and quotes in section: Nelson, *Letters and Diaries*, 46–48.

4. Brussels 36–50

War Settles Heavily on the City 36–43

"proud Paris of": Hunt, *War Bread*, 164.
"one of the finest"; Begun in 1402: Baedeker, *Belgium*, 128.
The city boasted: Ibid., 89–144.
"all telephone and": Hugh Gibson, "German Rule in Belgium" speech, Gibson papers, box 73, HIA.
Gibson had been; "delicate child"; other facts of Gibson's life: Gibson papers, HIA, and Wikipedia.
"After years of"; "For the last": Gibson, *A Diplomatic Diary* (Hodder and Stoughton, London, 1917), 1.
"longing for something"; "ready whenever there": Ibid.
"his wit and": Hunt, *War Bread*, 186.
He was nothing: Ibid.
"This is undoubtedly": Gibson to mother, Aug. 7, 1914, Gibson papers, box 1, HHPLA.
"tense look of": Hunt, *War Bread*, 186.
The post was known: Allan Nevins, ed., *The Letters and Journal of Brand Whitlock* (Appleton-Century Co., 1936); Letter to Rutger B. Jewett, April 9, 1914, 179.
"the dim, familiar": Whitlock, "Before the Storm," *Everybody's Magazine*, Feb. 1918.
"All our patience": Ibid.
"It was forbidden": Hugh Gibson, "German Rule in Belgium" speech, Gibson papers, box 73, HIA.
"We go to bed": "A City in Sadness," *Scotsman* newspaper, Nov. 23, 1914, clip books, HHPLA.
"We began to": Whitlock, "Before the Storm," *Everybody's Magazine*, Feb. 1918.
"Women holding young"; "proudly turned their"; "rather than sip": Hunt, *War Bread*, 166.
"besieged the [German] Pass": Ibid., 165.
"echoed to soldiers'": Ibid.
Cammaerts quotes: Cammaerts, *Through the Iron Bars*, 8–9.
"Oh, I see"; "I felt inclined": Gibson, *A Journal from Our Legation in Belgium* (Doubleday, Page and Co., 1917), 244.
"played as large": Whitlock, "Under the German Heel," *Everybody's Magazine*, issue #6, June 1918, Fifth installment.
"Resistance and disobedience": Hugh Gibson, "German Rule in Belgium" speech, Gibson papers, box 73, HIA.

"facing the wall": Jean Massart, *The Secret Press in Belgium* (E. P. Dutton and Co., New York, 1918), 51–52.
"Above the prostrate": Hunt, *War Bread*, 166.

Von Bissing Becomes Governor General 43–46

"His Majesty, the": Gibson, *A Journal*, 321.
"justly or unjustly": Whitlock, *Belgium*, vol. I, 393.
"old, and thin": Ibid.
"scrupulously clean"; "there gleamed": Ibid.
"A great heavy": Ibid., 393–394.
While von Bissing; all quotes in this paragraph: Ibid.
"carried with it": Hunt, *War Bread*, 171.
"Times had changed": Oscar E. Millard, *Underground News: The Complete Story of the Secret Newspaper that Made War History* (Robert M. McBride and Co., 1938), 37.
This meant that: Ibid., 37–38.
"Bissing's prime objective": Johan den Hertog, "The Commission for Relief in Belgium and the Political Diplomatic History of the First World War," *Diplomacy & Statescraft*, 21: 593–613, 2010, Taylor & Francis Group, LLC, Routledge. His source for this: "Bissing to Bethmann-Hollweg Letters & Journals of Whitlock Vol. 2, p. 165," but actually it's on page 173 and it is not that strongly stated.
"As the work": Gay and Fisher, *Public Relations*, vol. I, 18.
"contribution of war": Whitlock, *Belgium*, vol. I, 395–396.
$96 million; budget: Hunt, *War Bread*, 349.

Francqui Builds His Network 46–50

The CN was: Hunt, *War Bread*, 348–349.
"main rival in": History of the Francqui Foundation on its website.
"iron man of": John Hamill, *The Strange Career of Mr. Hoover under Two Flags* (Faro, Inc., 1931), 316.
Francqui descriptions; "a type familiar": Hunt, *War Bread*, 272–273.
"It is a"; Flemish issue: Ibid., 337.
"It takes quite": Earl Osborn journal, Jan. 27, 1916, Osborn and Dodge Family papers, Princeton Mudd Library.
In the beginning; nutrition and Dr. Hindhede: Hunt, *War Bread*, 280; Wikipedia.
"was one of": Hunt, *War Bread*, 280.
"a merry, rosy": Scott Paradise quoted by Edwin W. Morse in *The Vanguard of American Volunteers* (Charles Scribner's Sons, 1919), part V.
"extraordinarily low": Hunt, *War Bread*, 280.
Bread totals: Ibid.
As for the: Gay and Fisher, *Public Relations*, vol. I, 119.
Food totals: Ibid., doc. 20.
November had seen: Kittredge, *History of CRB*, 73.

5. Antwerp and Environs 51–63

The CRB's Chief Delegate in Antwerp Finds His Way 51–54

Description of Hunt: from photographs, recollections from his granddaughter, Margaret Hunt, and diary entries of the author's grandmother, Erica Bunge, in the author's archives.
Hunt's journey from America to Belgium and his following experiences and quotes: Hunt, *War Bread*.
"My fiancée's death": Letter from Hunt to Mr. Forman, Nov. 14, 1914, E. E. Hunt papers, box 1, HHPLA. Given the time it took letters to get back—usually three weeks at minimum—this meant the death occurred probably sometime in October.
"I could write": Hunt to Miss Holly, Nov. 23, 1914, E. E. Hunt papers, box 1, HHPLA.
"On the same": Ibid., Hunt to Mr. Forman.
"As an American"; remaining quotes in section: Hunt, *War Bread*, 201, 158, 202.

E. E. Hunt and Belgian Politics 54–56

All Hunt quotes in this section: Hunt, *War Bread*, 243–252, 261.

A Belgian Family Welcomes the Delegates 57–61

This section and all Bunge material: Author's archives, which include an edited diary and photos from Erica Bunge (the author's grandmother), papers from Edouard Bunge, and letters and documents from Milton M. Brown, CRB delegate and the author's grandfather. Also, family oral history.

Bunge's role on provincial committee and CN; his personal details: Hunt, *War Bread*, 262; oral history of the Bunge, Brown, and Miller families.

The Bunges' experiences during the siege of Antwerp: Edouard Bunge, "What I Saw of the Bombardment and Surrender of Antwerp," author's archives.

Pink story and quotes: John L. "Pink" Simpson, oral history for HHPLA and HIA, Sept. 20, 1967, John L. Simpson papers, box 21, HIA.

"If the Allies": Erica Bunge's diary, Jan. 3, 1915, author's archives.

The Belgian-Dutch Border Tightens 61–63

But the roads: Hunt, *War Bread*, 120.

"The Netherlands": Translation by Roger Van den Bleeken of the chapter by Jan Ingelbrecht, "Elektrische draadversperring te Putte," 213–232, in *Capellen in den Grooten Oorlog* (1914, Heemkring Hoghescote, B 2950 Kapellen, Belgium).

"The access of": Ibid.

"The sentinels": Jean Massart, *The Secret Press*, 4.

"Few could run": Hunt, *War Bread*, 292.

"The old Landsturmers": Scott Paradise in *Yale Alumni Weekly*, as quoted in *Vanguard of American Volunteers* by Edwin W. Morse (Charles Scribner's Sons, 1919), 187.

German Governor General: Commandant A. (Adrien) de Gerlache de Gomery, *Belgium in War Time*, translated from the French edition by Bernard Miall (George H. Doran Co.), 1915, 178–179.

"moorland"; "monotonous": Baedeker, *Belgium*, 205.

6. Brussels 64–75

Hoover Sees the Belgian Situation Firsthand 64–68

"had been engaged": Kittredge, *History of CRB*, 86.

"see for himself": Ibid., 90.

"had already": Whitlock, *Belgium*, vol. I, 402.

Hoover strip-searched: Smith, *An Uncommon Man*, 82.

"possibly the rather": Hoover, *Years of Adventure*, 159.

"German soldiers": Ibid.

"more impressed": Kittredge, *History of CRB*, 91–92.

"agreed that": Nevins, *Journal*, 70.

"At the Central": Britain's *Morning Post*, Nov. 9, 1914, clip books, HHPLA.

"dismal rain": Whitlock, *Belgium*, vol. I, 402.

On the morning; who accompanied Hoover: Nevins, *The Journal*, 70.

The soup itself: Britain's *Daily Graphic*, Nov. 9, 1914, clip books, HHPLA.

"They stood with": Whitlock, *Belgium*, vol. I, 403.

"somehow stabbed one": Ibid.

When Francqui and: Kittredge, *History of CRB*, 16.

"was very much": Whitlock, *Belgium*, vol. I, 403.

A Chance Meeting Leads to Clandestine Activities 68–71

"huge red posters": Hugh Gibson, "German Rule in Belgium" speech, Gibson papers, box 73, HIA.

vicar of Saint Albert: Charlotte Kellogg, *Mercier, the Fighting Cardinal of Belgium* (D. Appleton and Co., 1920), 68.

But the story; On August 20: Millard, *Underground News*, 23.

Description of Eugene van Doren; "mild and thoughtful": Ibid., 7.

Description of Vincent de Moor and all quotes: Ibid., 23.

Van Doren's initiation: Ibid., 23–24.

As van Doren: Ibid., 24.

duplicating machine; "ironical little sheets": Millard, *Underground News*, 24. A jelly press transfers images and text to a master sheet that is laid onto a flat bed of firm chemical jelly, which absorbs the image. Multiple copies can be made by pressing paper on the imaged jelly.
"Day by day": Massart, *The Secret Press*, 7.
Victor Jourdain details: Millard, *Underground News*, 19–20.
But Jourdan was: Ibid., 19–20.
At his home: Ibid., 42–43.
For Jourdain, van: Ibid., 35.
To transfer Jourdain's: Ibid., 33.

German Action Stimulates Greater Underground Efforts 71–74

In Namur it: Massart, *The Secret Press*, 87.
Von Bissing's control of the French-language press: Millard, *Underground News*, 54.
"proud of being": Whitlock, *Belgium*, vol. I, 420.
"entered, advanced, tall": Ibid.
"thin, scholarly, ascetic": Hunt, *War Bread*, 237.
von der Goltz agreement: Cardinal D. J. Mercier, *Cardinal Mercier's Own Story*. (George H. Doran Co., 1920), 3–24.
Correspondence with von Bissing: Ibid.
"abstain from hostile"; "no lawful authority": Ibid., 45.
"the result was": Millard, *Underground News*, 26.
"a dozen editions": Massart, *The Secret Press*, 29.

An Underground Newspaper Is Born 74–75

All quotes in this section: Millard, *Underground News*, 19, 36–39.

7. London 76–86

"The Supreme Test of the Man" 76–78

"Of a population"; "I can imagine": Britain's *Daily News & Ledger*, Dec. 7, 1914, clip books, HHPLA.
"The clock has"; "practically every Belgian": Ibid.
"It is difficult": Ibid.
three-dimensional chess: Hoover, in all probability, would have read or heard about Raumschach, the three-dimensional chess game invented by German doctor Ferdinand Maack in 1907.
"By December 1"; The Germans had: Kittredge, *History of CRB*, 100.
"The supreme test": Smith, "The Man of Action."
"The chief significance": Kittredge, *History of CRB*, 105.
"In carrying on": Ibid., 106.

British Opposition to the CRB 78–80

"the British posture": Nash, *The Life of Herbert Hoover*, 71.
"Kitchener had made": Nevins, *Journal*, 77.
Hoover and Asquith meeting: Nash, *The Life of Herbert Hoover*, 69.
"hold this until": Nevins, *Journal*, 77–78.
"You have America's"; "I will send": Ibid.
"You told me": Ibid.
"It did not": Nash, *The Life of Herbert Hoover*, 70.

CRB Publicity Helps to Drive World Opinion 80–82

"I employed myself": Hoover to Oscar T. Crosby, June 30, 1915, Gilchrist Stockton papers, HIA.
"The following letter": Britain's *Daily Telegraph*, Dec. 3, 1914, clip books, HHPLA.
"With a few": Ibid.
"One Huge Cemetery"; following quotes: London *Sunday Times*, Dec. 6, 1914, clip books, HHPLA.
Four days after; Allen trip to interview Belgian King: Victoria Allen, *The Outside Man*, unpublished, 167–200, Ben Allen papers, HIA. Victoria was the wife of Ben Allen, a journalist, a friend of Hoover, and a member of the founding group of the CRB.
"The Commission had": Britain's *Bristol Times Mirror*, Dec. 21, 1914, clip books, HHPLA.

"Large as these": Ibid.
"I wish to": Ibid.
"Each morning, between": Britain's *Morning Advertiser,* Dec. 22, 1914, clip books, HHPLA.
"a few": Ibid.
"If this sort": Ibid.

FINANCING BELGIUM RELIEF BECOMES CRITICAL 83–85

The key to: Gay and Fisher, *Public Relations,* vol. I, doc. 119, 222.
"formally authorize exchange": Ibid., 227–228.
"contribution of war": Whitlock, *Belgium,* vol. I, 395–396.
"was to be"; remaining quotes in section: Kittredge, *History of CRB,* 110.

HOOVER TURNS AGAIN TO DEAL WITH BRUSSELS 85–86

"By some sad": Whitlock to Walter Page, Dec. 19, 1914; Nash, *The Life of Herbert Hoover,* 77.
"During the month": Kittredge, *History of CRB,* 95.
"The provincial [CRB]": Ibid., 97.
"new administrative difficulties": Gay and Fisher, *Public Relations,* vol. I, 15.
"Everywhere that he": Kittredge, *History of CRB,* 97.
"We have had": Letter from Hoover to Will Irwin, Jan. 18, 1915, CRB correspondence, box 1, HIA.

8. Brussels 87–88

FRANCQUI RUNS THE CN SHOW 87–88

Description of the parlor room: Hunt, *War Bread,* 269.
"There is a": Ibid., 269–270.
The 40 men: Robinson Smith papers, Article 7, HIA; Hunt, *War Bread,* 270.
All following short descriptions and quotes not otherwise noted: Hunt, *War Bread,* 270–273.
"dominant over all": Arthur Bartlett Maurice, *Bottled Up in Belgium: The Last Delegate's Informal Story* (Moffat, Yard and Co., 1917), 65.

9. Elsewhere in Belgium 89–90

HARASSMENT BY GERMAN SENTRIES LEADS TO TROUBLE 89–90

"German love of"; "It is a": Hugh Gibson, "German Rule in Belgium" speech, Gibson papers, box 73, HIA.
The two students and stenographer story and all related quotes: Gibson to mother, Christmas 1914, Gibson papers, box 1, HHPLA.

SECTION II: CONFLICTS, 1915

10. The Mechanics of Relief 93–107

SHIPPING—A FUNDAMENTAL PROBLEM TO FIND AND PROTECT 93–96

The first two: Kittredge, *History of CRB,* 56.
"His fine idealism": Hoover, *American Epic,* 46.
Percy was able: Kittredge, *History of CRB,* 56.
The number of: Ibid.
As the CRB: Ibid.
"I told him": Hoover, *American Epic,* 130–131.
Meanwhile, it was: Kittredge, *History of CRB,* 57.
On board, each: Ibid.; Hoover, *American Epic,* 131.
Another stumbling block: Kittredge, *History of CRB,* 57.
Once that was: Ibid.

TRANSPORTATION—FOLLOWING THE WHEAT 96–102

The importation goal: Gay and Fisher, *Public Relations,* vol. I, doc. 20.
Wheat was the: The wheat shipping and distribution process from ship to breadline consumer was detailed by Robinson Smith in a series of articles he wrote that were compiled into a document titled "The Feeding of Belgium," Maurice Pate collection, box 13, folder 11, Princeton Mudd Library.

"Two weeks ago"; "Three months ago"; all quotes by Smith in this section: Smith, "The Feeding of Belgium," Princeton Mudd Library.

Belgium, like Holland; all following canal network details: Kittredge, *History of CRB*, 69–70.

"Thefts by the"; "Lightermen were also": Joe Green, Dock Office, Green papers, Princeton Mudd Library.

The flour was; all details about bakers: Smith, "The Feeding of Belgium," Princeton Mudd Library.

Distribution—Following a Recipient of Relief 102–104

"It is not"; all quotes in section: Smith, "The Feeding of Belgium," Princeton Mudd Library.

The CRB Relief Difference 104–105

"Relief means the"; all quotes: Smith, "The Feeding of Belgium," Princeton Mudd Library.

The Belgian Unemployed 105–107

"A great part": Hunt, *War Bread*, 180.

Bunge estate, employment, and the canal project: Material from Kapellen historians Roger Van den Bleeken and Raymond Roelands, and the author's family oral history.

Those lists of; the statistics: Hunt, *War Bread*, 304–305.

In fact, one: Hoover, *American Epic*, 255.

"At least ten": Léon Van der Essen, "Germany's Latest Crime," *Fortnightly Review*, no. 602 New Series, Feb. 1, 1917, 202.

One of those; "Young men need": Cammaerts, *Through the Iron Bars*, 48.

A few weeks: Ibid.; Cardinal Mercier letter to Baron von Bissing, October 19, 1916.

11. London 108–117

Northern France Becomes an Issue 108–111

All details and quotes from Gerard cable: Cable from Gerard to Hoover, Jan. 2, 1915; Gay and Fisher, *Public Relations*, vol. I, doc. 263, 394–395.

Hoover and the: Gay and Fisher, *Public Relations*, vol. I, 393–394; Kittredge, *History of CRB*, 136–137.

Émile Francqui's objection to feeding Givet-Fumay: Kittredge, *History of CRB*, 137.

King as U.S. Consul in Lille: He served from 1902–1911; no one is listed in the position until 1920.

Hoover letter to Chevrillon, March 10, 1915; all related quotes: Kittredge, *History of CRB*, 140–141.

"we have had"; "extra labor entailed"; "make a substantial"; "we are already": Gay and Fisher, *Public Relations*, vol. I, 395–396.

All following details and quotes regarding zones: Gay and Fisher, *Public Relations*, vol. I, 391–393.

Details of Etape; "Later on, this": Kittredge, *History of CRB*, 134.

Hoover's Financial Showdown with Lloyd George 111–115

In a January; all Kittredge quotes in this section: Kittredge, *History of CRB*, 111–113.

"the question of": Gay and Fisher, *Public Relations*, vol. I, doc. 129.

"A routine appointment": Nash, *The Life of Herbert Hoover*, 84.

"any transfer of"; all quotes in this section: Gay and Fisher, *Public Relations*, vol. I, doc. 129, 232–235.

The CRB's Military Opponents 115–117

"the first day"; "periodically demanded its": Hoover, *American Epic*, 21.

On the other; "called upon to"; "argued that the": Hoover, *American Epic*, 21–22.

"with some show"; "The allies are": Gibson, *A Journal*, 272.

"also violent in"; all remaining quotes in section: Hoover, *American Epic*, 22.

12. Brussels 118–134

German Sentries Still Cause Problems 118–120

"being stopped at": Hugh Gibson, "German Rule in Belgium" speech, Gibson papers, box 73, HIA.

"Our monthly passes": Hunt, *War Bread*, 309.

"complained rather bitterly": Gibson to mother, Jan. 26, 1915, box 31, HIA.

"laughed to scorn": Hugh Gibson, speech "German Rule in Belgium," Gibson papers, box 73, HIA.

"us that such": Ibid.

The Beutner story and all related quotes: Gibson to mother, Jan. 26, 1915, box 31, HIA; Hugh Gibson, speech "German Rule in Belgium," Gibson papers, box 73, HIA.
"While we were": Gibson to mother, Jan. 26, 1915, box 31, HIA.
Spaulding and Lowdermilk story and quotes: CRB personnel documents, Arrowsmith document, and Galpin documents, HIA.

Friction Grows between the CRB and CN 121–123

"At first there"; all quotes in this section: Kittredge, *History of CRB*, 196–197, 94, 96–97, 104.

Van Doren's Game Becomes Dangerously Real 123–125

"haphazard letterbox"; all quotes not otherwise noted: Millard, *Underground News*, 40–41, 32–34, 43.
Details of the first issue and following quotes: Multiple sources but primary is Millard, *Underground News*, 32–34.
Two quotes just: Multiple sources but primary is Millard, *Underground News*, 32–34.
With a heart: Ibid.

A Belgian Gauntlet Is Thrown Down 126–127

"smartly dressed"; quotes in section; scene of delivery: Millard, *Underground News*, 44, 34, 43, 53–54.

Von Bissing Cracks Down on the CRB 127–134

CRB passport: Hoover, *American Epic*, 26.
It was less: Gay and Fisher, *Public Relations*, vol. I, 46–47.
"The Germans naturally": Kittredge, *History of CRB*, 128.
What made it: Ibid.
"It was undoubtedly": Ibid.
To most Belgians: Ibid.
"came to express": Whitlock, 16-page memorandum to the State Dept., Aug. 10, 1917, RG 84, Diplomatic Posts, Belgium, Legation correspondence, Belgium, 1917, vol. 191, file 703.
8,000 American flags: Whitlock to Connett, April 3, 1915, in Gilchrist Stockton papers, HIA.
"We had flown": Hunt, *War Bread*, 310–311.
"there was but": Ibid., 310.
In meetings with: Ibid., 311.
Whitlock letter to Connett and all quotes from it: letter dated April 3, 1915, Gilchrist Stockton papers, HIA.
The German and; partial quotes in sentence: Kittredge, *History of CRB*, 197.
Besides the flag; "The Comité National": Ibid., 197–198.
"this was the": Ibid., 198.
"soon became aware"; In the German: Ibid., 129.
"discharge its obligations": Ibid., 128.
Whitlock going with Hoover to von Bissing meeting: Hoover, *American Epic*, 141.
Whitlock not being at the meeting; "For days I": Nevins, *The Journal*, 97–99.
"Von Bissing was": Hoover, *American Epic*, 141.
"I fully trusted": Allen, *The Outside Man*, 144, HIA.
Hoover meeting with von Bissing; von Bissing's statements to Hoover: Kittredge, *History of CRB*, 130.
"The Commission": Ibid., 129–130.
Hoover pointed out: Ibid.
"We did not": Hoover, *American Epic*, 141.
"boiling with rage"; "What do you": Nevins, *The Journal*, 98–99.
Hoover was furious: Ibid.
"It is absolutely": Ibid.
"misused"; all following quotes: Gay and Fisher, *Public Relations*, vol. I, doc. 31.
Von der Lancken: Kittredge, *History of CRB*, 130.

13. London 135–140

Hoover Stands Up for Northern France 135–138

Upon arriving back: Gay and Fisher, *Public Relations*, vol. I, 397.
Gifford Pinchot well-known in France: Kittredge, *History of CRB*, 142.

On February 17; Hoover letter to Poincaré and all details and quotes: Gay and Fisher, *Public Relations*, vol. I, doc. 266, 397–399

Hoover telegram to Pinchot and all details and quotes: Ibid., doc. 267, 399–400.

Pinchot memorandum and all details and quotes: Ibid., doc. 268, 400–401.

Hoover moving forward in two areas: Ibid., 403.

"charitable institutions which"; "fiction"; "because of the": Ibid., doc. 271, 403.

"wet nurse"; "to indicate jokingly": Kittredge, *History of CRB*, 324.

HOOVER TAKES DRASTIC DIPLOMATIC ACTION AGAINST VON BISSING 138–140

Von Bissing's letter and Heineman: Kittredge, *History of CRB*, 131; Gay and Fisher, *Public Relations*, vol. I, doc. 32, 50–51.

"reiterating a number": Hoover, *American Epic*, 143.

He and the rest: Kittredge, *History of CRB*, 131.

British military and civilian government attitude toward CRB: Hoover letter to Whitlock, March 6, 1915; Hoover, *American Epic*, 143–144; Gay and Fisher, *Public Relations*, vol. I, doc. 35, 54–55.

"The British Foreign": Hoover, *American Epic*, 143.

"I have had": Gay and Fisher, *Public Relations*, vol. I, doc. 33, 52–53.

Connett position; "unfavorably impressed with": Kittredge, *History of CRB*, 175–176.

When Hoover wrote; Connett's letter; "However," he then: Kittredge, *History of CRB*, 176.

"We have been": Gay and Fisher, *Public Relations*, vol. I, doc. 34, 53–54.

"Fundamental fact is": Ibid.

14. Antwerp and Environs 141–153

Delegate movements: CRB lists; Delegate work list, Robert Arrowsmith papers, HIA.

Stratton letter to Hunt, dated Feb. 3, 1915: Gilchrist Stockton's papers, HIA.

THE ANTWERP CRB DELEGATES DEAL WITH BREAD 142–145

"see that the"; all other quotes in section: Hunt, *War Bread*, 280, 285, 286, 291, 287, 288, 253, 289–290.

THE THREAT OF EPIDEMICS BECOMES REAL 145–146

"Belgium needed far"; all quotes in section: Hunt, *War Bread*, 296–298.

Four typhoid shots: Milton Brown to his mother, April 19, 1916, author's archives.

THE BUNGES OFFER RESPITE TO THE DELEGATES 146–148

As Hunt's respites: Hunt, *War Bread*, 265.

There, he and; all quotes in section: Erica Bunge's diary, author's archives and family oral history.

A DAIRY FARM IS STARTED ON HOOGBOOM ESTATE 148–153

Edouard Bunge's positions and his purchase of coffee: Hunt, *War Bread*, 262, 347.

As for Erica; wounded soldiers information: Erica Bunge's diary, Jan. 3, 1915, author's archives and oral history of the Bunge, Brown, and Miller families.

Even with such: Ibid.

A plan for a dairy farm: Oral history and a large three-panel presentation that was awarded to Edward Bunge, Erica Bunge, George Born, and Hélène Born after the war for providing 1 million liters of milk to the children of Antwerp; Robert Withington, *In Occupied Belgium* (Cornhill Co., 1921), 34; Raymond Roelands, *Geschiedenis van Kasteeldomein "Oude Gracht" in Hoogboom* (*History of the Castle Domain "Oude Gracht" in Hoogboom*) (hereinafter: Roelands, *Oude Gracht*).

Edouard Bunge had: Purchase documents, author's archives. Calixberghe still exists and is now known as Kasteel van Schoten (Castle of Schoten).

300 hectares: Roger Van den Bleeken, *Cappellen in den Grooten Oorlog* (*Cappellen in the Great War*), Heemkring Hoghescote vzw, 2014 (hereinafter: Van den Bleeken, *Cappellen*).

Details of the Bunge estate: Roelands, *Oude Gracht*.

"took a walk": Roelands, *Oude Gracht*.

The estate produced: Ibid.; oral history of the Bunge, Brown, and Miller families.

Major tubers and taproots: from http://www.xpats.com/5-forgotten-winter-vegetables-and-what-do-them.

Bunge bringing staff to Hoogboom estate: Roelands, *Oude Gracht*.

"I went to Hoogboom"; all Erica quotes: Erica Bunge's diary, Aug. 10, 1914, author's archives.
The war-preparation: Roelands, *Oude Gracht.*
On Wednesday, March; all details in section not otherwise noted: Van den Bleeken, *Cappellen.*
Erica was more: Author's family oral history.

15. Elsewhere in Belgium 154–163

Getting Down to Work 154–157

"is fine—just "; all other quotes in section: Nelson, *Letters and Diaries.*

The Christmas Ship Arrives 157–158

Details of 1914 Christmas ship: Kieran Corcoran, *Daily Mail* online, Dec. 26, 2014.
Details of the Sunday, Feb. 7, 1915, event; quotes in section: Nelson, *Letters and Diaries,* 55–56.

Belgian Patriotism 158–160

"Indefatigable industry": Baedeker, *Belgium,* 250.
"trying to blow"; all other quotes in section: Nelson, *Letters and Diaries,* 50–60.

A Motorcar Tale Leads to Chauffeurs for All 160–163

Initially, maintenance; all quotes in section: Kittredge, *History of CRB,* 178–179.

16. Northern France 164–170

The Army Zone Creates a Unique Situation 164–168

"Major von Kessler": Kittredge, *History of CRB,* 158.
In dramatic and; all quotes of the story: Ibid., 141–142.
Details of the northern France organization: Gay and Fisher, *Public Relations,* vol. I, 411–412.
Another major difference: Ibid., vol. I, 411–412.
A group photo: HHPLA, box 13, 1916:26–50, 1917: 76–99.
"a favorite of": Hoover, *American Epic,* 43.

No Job for the Faint of Heart 168–170

"These [accompanying officers]: Nevins, *Journal,* 245.
"In general it": Kittredge, *History of CRB,* 152.
"nurses"; "my man Friday": told by a purposefully misnamed delegate to Madame Saint-Rene Taillandier in her book, *The Soul of the CRB* (1919), 145–146.
"in the French": Ibid.
These meetings became; "The nervous strain": Kittredge, *History of CRB,* 153.
Dutton's CRB record: Arrowsmith member list, Arrowsmith papers, HIA.
Dutton dying of tuberculosis: Dutton's CRB personnel file, box 314, folder 17, HIA; obituary, *Washington Post,* Feb. 20, 1918.
"I was offered"; "behind the German": Nelson, *Letters and Diaries.*

17. Brussels and Environs 171–177

Whitlock Reluctantly Deals with CRB Passes 171–172

"Von Bissing is"; Whitlock quotes in section: Nevins, *Journal,* 107, 99.
Whitlock's feelings about the Germans: multiple entries in Nevins, *Journal.*
"Gerard at once"; "At the same": Hoover, *American Epic,* 144.
"It was exceedingly": Kittredge, *History of CRB,* 132.
Germàn Bulle and the pass department: Ibid., 132–133.
While passes would: Ibid.
Von Bissing turning to the CN: Hoover, *American Epic,* 144.

La Libre Belgique Becomes a Target 172–177

Sometimes the paper; "It appears without"; "My copy reaches": Gibson, *A Journal,* 337; Hugh Gibson, speech "German Rule in Belgium," Gibson papers, box 73, HIA.
"The exasperating": Millard, *Underground News,* 54.

"the messages of": Hugh Gibson, speech "German Rule in Belgium," Gibson papers, box 73, HIA.
"the Germans rage": Gibson, *A Journal*, 337.
Von Bissing quickly: Millard, *Underground News*, 54.
"The response": Ibid., 45.
Numbers of copies: Ibid.
"for each copy": Ibid., 49.
"Within a month": Ibid., 50.
Details of Galerie Saint Hubert: Baedeker, *Belgium*, 92, 126–127.
The first raid on Massardo's; all remaining quotes in section: Millard, *Underground News*, 45–50, 60.

18. London 178–186

The Dog Attacks 178–179

Back in February; all quotes in section: Hoover, *American Epic*, 130–133.

The Dog Bites Again—with Much Greater Consequences 179–183

In less than: Lusitania deaths changed to 1,197 after four survivors later died, and includes stowaways: The *Lusitania* Resource website, http://www.rmslusitania.info/people/statistics/.
Onboard the doomed: Lindon Bates Jr. collection, HIA.
Bates's activities onboard: The *Lusitania* Resource website.
Through the long: Lindon Bates Jr. collection, HIA.
Lou Hoover's eulogy for Bates: Blog post May 10, 2017, by Matthew Schaefer, archivist at HHPLA.
King Albert of: Lindon Bates Jr. collection, HIA.
Antwerp as third busiest port: *Statistical Abstract of the United States, 1913*, 704.
At the time; "leading New York": Kittredge, *History of CRB*, 62.
a strong publicity campaign: Gay and Fisher, *Public Relations*, vol. II, 246.
"You can always": Hoover to Bates, Feb. 9, 1915, CRB correspondence, box 2, HIA.
"daily and weekly": Gay and Fisher, *Public Relations*, vol. II, 245–246.
One of the: Ibid.
before Rox's death; Captain Lucey joining New York office: Kittredge, *History of CRB*, 210; Hoover, "The Episode of Mr. Lindon Bates," CRB Executive Chronological File, 1912–1919, Bates, Lindon W., box 9, folder 6, HIA (hereinafter: Hoover, "Bates Episode," HIA).
"encountered difficulty through": Kittredge, *History of CRB*, 211; Hoover, "Bates Episode," HIA.
By the end: Cablegram to Hoover, Oct. 24, 1915, Hunt papers, box 15, HIA; Hoover, "Bates Episode," HIA.

CRB Financing Leads to Misunderstandings in America 183–186

By the late; all quotes in section: Gay and Fisher, *Public Relations*, vol. II, 265–266, footnote 35 on 265, 574.

19. Elsewhere in Belgium 187–196

A Delegate Is Steamrolled into Oblivion 187–192

Warren story; related quotes: Robert Warren, "A Statement of Circumstances Leading Up to and Attending My Arrest at Esschen on Saturday, April 24th, 1915," Stockton papers, box 9, HIA.

The "Strike of Folded Arms" 192–195

"Every effort was": Kittredge, *History of CRB*, 318.
"strike of folded": Cammaerts, *Through the Iron Bars*, 44.
"It became more": Ibid.
Even in Germany: Kittredge, *History of CRB*, 317.
40,000–45,000: Van der Essen, "Germany's Latest Crime," 189.
"things went badly"; "Ignorant of the": Ibid.
In April and: Toynbee, *The Belgian Deportations*, 32. Additionally, the Luttre railway workers' situation, along with other worker events, is detailed in the Belgian Commission Reports, xviii and xix.
All details of the Luttre incident: Ibid.
Malines details; oldest rail line: Baedeker, *Belgium*, 159–169.
Details of Malines workers' protest: Cammaerts, *Through the Iron Bars*, 50.
"The patriotic duty": Ibid.

"forbade anyone to"; "the whole population": Toynbee, *The Belgian Deportations*, 33.
"The town of": Cammaerts, *Through the Iron Bars*, 50.

Von Bissing Attempts to Divide the Nation 195–196

The Germans—and; "Among the German": a memorandum from von Bissing in *General von Bissing's Testament: A Study in German Ideals* (T. Fisher Unwin Ltd., London, n.d.).
"Not being able"; "Germany, who had": Cammaerts, *Through the Iron Bars*, 50.

20. Antwerp and Environs 197–210

Hunt Gets a New Antwerp Delegate 197–198

"Antwerp training": Green diaries and essays, Green papers, Princeton Mudd Library.
Richardson information: Richardson oral history interview by Charles Morrissey, HIA; internet website on Richardson family tree.
When the war: Ibid.
"From the windows"; "We patrolled the": Hunt, *War Bread*, 262–263.

Richardson Reports on the Unemployed 198–201

The numbers were: Hunt, *War Bread*, 304–305.
"In the plans": Ibid., 307.
Richard took less: Richardson, "Report on Chomage in the Province of Antwerp," June 11, 1915, in the E. Coppée Thurston papers, box 1, HIA.
Unemployed assistance details: Hunt, *War Bread*, 304–305; Richardson Report, HIA; monetary conversion from Charlotte Kellogg's *Women in Belgium*, 164, which states that 3 francs equaled 60 cents.
nearly four francs a day: Belgian historian, Roger Van den Bleeken, 10–7–2016 email says "3,80 francs per day," author's archives.
"to require from"; summary of points; all remaining quotes in section not otherwise noted: Richardson Report, HIA.
"secure a certain"; "The Commission was": Hunt, *War Bread*, 306.

The Emotional Toll on the Delegates 201–204

"The conditions of"; "Belgium was like": Hunt, *War Bread*, 262.
"quite a number": Kittredge, *History of CRB*, 153.
"Until late in": Hunt, *War Bread*, 262.
"breathing spells were": Ibid., 263.
"When we spent": Ibid., 264–265.
"soon grew impatient": Kittredge, *History of CRB*, 176.
Tempering the February; "it soon became"; "It was there": Ibid., 178.
"in a companionship": Ibid.
"arranged a series"; all remaining quotes in section: Hunt, *War Bread*, 263, 265, 267–268.

Hunt's Impact on the Bunges 204–206

Internally, however, she; all quotes in section: Erica Bunge's diary, author's archives.

The Germans Create a Deadly Border 206–210

Unless otherwise noted, all details, statistics, and quotes within section: Van den Bleeken, *Cappellen*.
"In order, it": Toynbee, *The Belgian Deportations*, 57–58.
Maurice Lippens: de Gerlache de Gomery, *Belgium in War Time*, 207.

21. Brussels and Environs 211–230

The CRB Is Drawn into the Workers' Fight 211–214

"The Belgians had"; issued two decrees; all quotes in section: Hoover, *American Epic*, 154–158; including reprint of Sir Edward Grey letter to Walter Page, September 22, 1915.

Von Bissing Restricts the CN 214–215

Von Bissing letter to Whitlock and related quotes: Gay and Fisher, *Public Relations*, vol. I, doc. 36, 56, 40, 64.

Delegate Duties and the 1915 Harvest Lead to a Battle for Control 216–218

"the first phase": Gay and Fisher, *Public Relations*, vol. I, 55.
As to the harvest: Ibid., vol. II, "The Belgian Harvest of 1915: March–July 1915," 522–550.
Hoover, working through: Ibid.
Francqui had weighed: Ibid., doc. 331, 531–532; Kittredge, *History of CRB*, 198–199.
"had no right": Kittredge, *History of CRB*, 199.
Hoover told Francqui; "At first in": Ibid.
June conferences: Ibid.; Whitlock to von der Lancken, Gay and Fisher, *Public Relations*, vol. I, doc. 344, 546.
"Francqui showed a": Kittredge, *History of CRB*, 199.
July 7, 1915, letter from Marquis of Crewe to Page: Gay and Fisher, *Public Relations*, vol. I, doc. 341, 539–542.
"The whole yield": Hoover, *American Epic*, 147; Gay and Fisher, *Public Relations*, vol. I, doc. 38, 61–62.
"I assign to": Gay and Fisher, *Public Relations*, vol. I, doc. 343, 544.
"sole right to": Hoover, *American Epic*, 148.
A direct benefit; 54,000 tons: Gay and Fisher, *Public Relations*, vol. I, 549.

Should the Retirement of the CRB Be "Considered"? 218–222

"With the organisation": Kittredge, *History of CRB*, 199–200.
"Many important decisions": Ibid.
"It is perfectly": Hoover, *American Epic*, 99.
Hoover had come; "Francqui's attitude was": Kittredge, *History of CRB*, 200.
"Adjustment of Functions": Gay and Fisher, *Public Relations*, vol. II, 65.
Hoover's handling of; *procès-verbal*; "if the time"; list of four items: Gay and Fisher, *Public Relations*, vol. I, doc. 41, 66–69.
The official record; "it was impossible"; "should retire"; "The Comité National"; "Therefore, the Comité": Ibid.
"ravitaillement [relief] and care": Ibid.
"the whole question": Kittredge, *History of CRB*, 202.
"We are here": Gay and Fisher, *Public Relations*, vol. I, doc., 42, 70–71.
"The view of": Kittredge, *History of CRB*, 204.
The delegates were: Gay and Fisher, *Public Relations*, vol. I, doc. 42, 70–71.
"the attitude of"; "The relation of": Ibid.
"This memorandum did": Kittredge, *History of CRB*, 204.
"The tension at": Hunt, *War Bread*, 314.

La Libre Belgique Grows 222–227

The first 13; all dates and quotes in section: Millard, *Underground News*, 51–52, 54, 56–62, 67–68, 78–84.

German Raids Catch Two Important People 227–230

Within a month; composing room story: Millard, *Underground News*, 83–86.
The Germans came; Baucq's arrest: Ibid., 86–88.
A little more; Edith Cavell details: Multiple sources of the Edith Cavell arrest and trial, including Whitlock, *Belgium*, vol. II, 81–158.

22. Northern France 231–237

Northern France statistics: Kittredge, *History of* CRB, 154.
Two French areas: Gay and Fisher, *Public Relations*, vol. I, doc. 287, 421–426.
In December 1916: Kittredge, *History of CRB*, 137, asterisked footnote.
a minimum ration: Gay and Fisher, *Public Relations*, vol. I, doc. 287, 421–426.
Even though the: Ibid.

The German "Nurses" Become Personalities 232–235

Partial list of names and districts: No complete list has ever been prepared. This list, prepared by the author, was compiled from numerous sources, including Joe Green's "German Begleitsoffiziere" essay, Green papers, Princeton Mudd Library; HHPLA photo captions, box 13, 1916: 26–50.

All quotes regarding the German officers not otherwise noted: Green, "German Begleitsoffiziere" essay, Princeton Mudd Library.
"Of all the": Maurice, *Bottled Up in Belgium*, 99.
"by two or": Ibid.
"a fine-looking"; "rendered loyal service": Whitlock, *Belgium*, vol. II, 779.
"debonair" and could: Maurice, *Bottled Up in Belgium*, 85.
"witty and philosophical"; Winkie story: Simpson, *Random Notes* (self-published, 1969).

NELSON AND HIS PRO-GERMAN VIEWS 235–237
Illustrated magazine info: Wikipedia.
Nelson's details and quotes about Weber: Nelson, *Letters and Diaries*, letter to mother, April 28, 1915, Nelson.
"a solemn, bullet-headed": Green, "German Begleitsoffiziere" essay, Green papers, Princeton Mudd Library.
Nelson's details and quotes about Captain Weber: Nelson, *Letters and Diaries*, letter to mother, April 28, 1915.
Nelson leaving and returning to Oxford: Ibid., letter to family, Aug. 18, 1915, and letter to father, Oct. 5, 1915.
All Nelson quotes about change in his view: Ibid., letter to father, Oct. 5, 1915.

23. London 238–241

CHANGING TIMES DICTATE A CHANGE IN PR MESSAGING 238–241
"The fact, however": Gay and Fisher, *Public Relations*, vol. II, doc. 576, 267–268.
"I regret intensely": Ibid.
"appealed for foodstuffs": Ibid., vol. II, doc. 577, 268–270.
"in order to"; "material no longer": Ibid.
"Announcements of importance": Ibid.
"but, above all": Ibid.
As Hoover was; "personal publicity"; "great nervous strain": Hoover, "Bates Episode," HIA.
"In the late": Kittredge, *History of CRB*, 211.
The wedge came; paragraph quotes: *Saturday Evening Post*, August 1915.
There was no: Hoover, "Bates Episode," HIA.
Hoover did not; all paragraph quotes: Ibid.
"Our experience of"; remaining quotes: Gay and Fisher, *Public Relations*, vol. II, doc. 577, 268–270.

24. Elsewhere in Belgium 242–246

A NEW DELEGATE COMES TO HAINAUT PROVINCE 242–246
In late August: Hilda Bunge Tuck, oral history, Nov. 25, 1966, HHPLA.
The SS *St. Louis*: Passenger list of the ship, Aug. 15, 1915, Ancestry.com; Hilda Bunge Tuck, oral history, HHPLA.
Tuck learning of the CRB and meeting Hoover: Hilda Bunge Tuck, oral history, HHPLA; the author's knowledge of first-class sailing from multiple primary sources and his personal experience.
The initial opinion; "Tuck had just": Hunt, letter to Princeton dean Howard McClenahan, Nov. 22, 1915, box 312, HIA.
Tuck description: Official CRB photograph and the author's oral history of Tuck, who was the author's great uncle. Tuck married Hilda Bunge, sister of Erica Bunge Brown (the author's grandmother).
Tuck called Friar Tuck: Joe Green's letters to Tuck, Green papers, Princeton Mudd Library.
Tuck's various assignments within the CRB: Delegates' work list, Arrowsmith papers, HIA.
Description and statistics about Mons and Hainaut: Baedeker's *Belgium*, 213–215.
(probably Georges Heupgen): In Memoriam, William Hallam Tuck, with Hilda Bunge Tuck's oral history, box 24, HIA.
"a delightful man"; all details and remaining quotes in section: Tuck, "Duties of the American Representative in the Province," Gilchrist Stockton papers, box 5, HIA.

25. Antwerp and Environs 247–254

More Than Food Is Needed 247–250

"The lack of"; "Appeals for clothes": Hunt, *War Bread*, 301.

The Belgians had: Milton Brown, *Clothing the Destitute*, author's archives.

Approximately 3 million destitute in Belgium and 1 million in northern France: Ibid.

In Antwerp a: Hunt, *War Bread*, 357; Brown, *Clothing the Destitute*, author's archives.

Hunt, as Antwerp's: Hunt, *War Bread*, 357.

The city had: Ibid.

"piled with boxes": Ibid.

"nine hundred girls": Ibid.

All these people: Kellogg, *Women of Belgium*, 149–157.

Those who worked; "personal hygiene, domestic"; "the literature and": Brown, *Clothing the Destitute*, author's archives.

The result of: Hunt, *War Bread*, 358.

While most if; remaining details in section: Brown, *Clothing the Destitute*, author's archives.

Antwerp Says Goodbye to a Special Delegate 250–253

Hugging the Scheldt; description of city and city hall: Baedeker, *Belgium*, 177–178.

On Saturday, October: translation of an article in Rotterdam's *Nieuwe Rotterdamsche Courant*, Oct. 18, 1915, in Hunt, *War Bread*, 372–373.

"by his devotion"; all details of the event: translation of an article in Rotterdam's *Nieuwe Rotterdamsche Courant*, Oct. 18, 1915, in Hunt, *War Bread*, 373.

usual number of delegates: Hunt stated, "Our normal number was five," which included himself (Hunt, *War Bread*, 262).

Number of delegates in Antwerp in Oct. 1915: Delegates work list, Arrowsmith Papers, HIA.

Hunt also came; all remaining quotes; Hunt poem: Erica Bunge's diary, Feb. 21, 1915, author's archives.

Erica Bunge and the Dairy Farm 253–254

Besides overseeing the; all details in section: Van den Bleeken, *Cappellen*.

26. London 255–259

The Bates Issue Can No Longer Be Ignored 255–257

Bates memorial to his son: *New York Times*, Sept. 15, 1915, 4.

Edgar Rickard wondered: Rickard cable to White, Sept. 27, 1915, CRB correspondence, box 4, HIA.

"For political reasons": Hoover cable 212 to Bates, Sept. 22, 1915, CRB correspondence, box 4, HIA.

On October 1: CRB–New York office cable 198 to Hoover, Oct. 1, 1915, CRB correspondence, box 4, HIA.

He could not: Hoover, *American Epic*, 161–162.

seven-page document; "gives a Barnum"; "There is no"; "small corner in"; "it will be": Hoover to CRB–New York office, Oct. 13, 1915, CRB correspondence, box 4, HIA.

"For the future": Ibid.

"As I have": Ibid.

"If anyone in": Ibid.

A day before: Hoover cable 251 to Bates, Oct. 15, 1915, CRB correspondence, box 4, HIA.

"one of the most": Hoover, *American Epic*, 164–165.

The First Year's Summary 257–259

Statistics in section: Gay and Fisher, *Public Relations*, vol. I, 119–127; Kittredge, *History of CRB*, 235–236.

"piratical state organized": Gay and Fisher, *Public Relations*, vol. I, v (Preface).

approximately 40,000 workers: Ibid., 66.

"included also a": Kittredge, *History of CRB*, 235.

"That will make"; remaining quotes: Smith, "The Feeding of Belgium," Princeton Mudd Library.

27. NYC and D.C. 260–266

Hoover Confronts His Old Friend Bates 260–261

Cablegram to Hoover; related quotes: Copy in Hunt papers, box 15, HIA; the eight who signed the cable were Hunsiker, Connett, Sengier, Young, Shaler, Rickard, Honnold, and Kellogg.

The next day: Hoover, "Bates Episode," HIA.

Charges of Treason Leveled against the Chief 261–266

When Bates had; quotes in paragraph: Hoover, "Bates Episode," HIA.

Hoover was at: Ibid.

"Mr. Bates was": Ibid.

On Thursday, October; "with a grin": Ibid.; Hoover, *American Epic*, 162.

"its representatives acting": Lansing cable to American Embassy, London, Oct. 15, 1915, RG 59, microfilm 675, roll 52, NARA.

Senator Lodge had: Henry Cabot Lodge to William Phillips, Oct. 22, 1915, RG 59, 855.48/389, NARA.

"because our negotiations": Hoover, *American Epic*, 161.

He responded with: Hoover to William Phillips, Oct. 30, 1915, RG 59, 855.48/395, NARA; copies in CRB correspondence, box 4, HIA.

"extraordinary esteem and"; "atom of moral": CRB correspondence, box 4, HIA.

"Even in these": CRB correspondence, box 4, HIA.

Hoover's words worked: Hoover, "Bates Episode," HIA.

He headed back: Ibid.

"a streak of": Hoover to CRB-London office, Nov. 2, 1915, HIA.

"There is a": Goode cable to Page, Nov. 1, 1915, London American Embassy, 848 Belgium, Great Britain, RG 84, vol. 700, NARA.

"The Commission for": Page cable to secretary of State Lansing, Nov. 2, 1915, London American Embassy, 848 Belgium, Great Britain, RG 84, vol. 700, NARA.

The same day: Hoover, "Bates Episode," HIA.

Much to Hoover's: Ibid.

"upset by virtue"; "were a little": Ibid.

Meeting with Wilson; all quotes: Ibid.

Wilson CRB press release: Ibid.; CRB news clippings (New York office), vol. 10, 42, HHPLA.

The President also: Hoover, "Bates Episode," HIA.

Senator Lodge letter to the State Dept.: RG 59, Microfilm 675, roll 52, NARA.

"an energetic campaign": Kittredge, *History of CRB*, 211.

Cable from Hoover to London CRB executives; their reply; Page's letter to Honnold: London American Embassy, 848 Belgium, Great Britain, RG 84, vol. 700, NARA.

"I was able"; all remaining quotes in section: Hoover, *American Epic*, 162, 169, 148–149.

28. Brussels 267–297

Baucq, Cavell, and Others Stand Trial 267–268

"treason in time of war": Whitlock, *Belgium*, vol. II, 83.

"Everyone must be": Princess Marie de Croÿ, *War Memories* (MacMillian and Co., London, 1932).

The following day: multiple sources; the German *affiche* announcing the sentences.

"No. I am English.": de Croÿ, *War Memories*.

General Sauberzweig's explanation: See this book's section "Hoover Fights for the Life of the CRB," 457–462.

Gibson and Villalobar Get Involved 268–275

"a noble woman": Whitlock, *Belgium*, vol. II, 83.

Two days later; "admitted that she": Ibid., 88.

"The long strain": Ibid., 81.

The news of; Gibson's telling of the story and related quotes: Gibson's official report to Whitlock, copy in Whitlock, *Belgium*, vol. II, 117–121.

"kept the minister's": Gibson papers, letter to Bell, Nov. 1, 1915, box 80, HIA.

Later, Gibson related; quotes in paragraph: Ibid.
"the German Authorities": Ibid.
"this was a": Ibid.
"I also avoided": Ibid.
"the morning after": Laurence Wellington, oral history, by Raymond Henle, Feb. 9, 1968, HHPLA.
"It would have": Whitlock, *Belgium,* vol. II, 147–148.
Edith Cavell had: and "I have seen": Ibid., 138–139.
"Even the Germans": Ibid., 118–119.
"The world has": Cammaerts, *Through the Iron Bars,* 59–60.

La Libre Belgique Honors Baucq and Cavell 275–276

"with every issue"; all details and quotes: Millard, *Underground News,* 99–101.

Spies, Spies, Everywhere Spies 276–278

"the man who": Gibson, letter to his mother, Nov. 14, 1914, box 31, HIA.
On Friday, November: Hoover, *American Epic,* 148–149.
Baron von Bissing: Gibson to State Dept., Jan. 3, 1916, and Jan. 7, 1916, RG 84, correspondence, American Legation Brussels, 1916, vol. 181, file 848, Relief, NARA; Hoover, *American Epic,* 148–149.
Description of spies and informers; all remaining quotes in section: Hugh Gibson, speech "German Rule in Belgium," Gibson papers, box 73, HIA.
Estimates were as: Green, spies essay, Green papers, Princeton Mudd Library.

Those Accused of Spying Are Revealed 278–281

"These are busy": Gibson to his mother, Nov. 25, 1915, box 31, HIA.
Green's personality: Brown letters and family oral history, author's archives.
"It is impossible": Milton M. Brown to Erica Bunge, April 21, 1917, author's archives.
Green's description: the author's family oral history.
Gibson's offer to hire Green: Joe Green letter to his parents, Jan. 14, 1917, 7, Green papers, Princeton Mudd Library.
"was not noted": Ibid., Green papers, Princeton Mudd Library. Green does not name Vernon Kellogg as the director who told him to leave Belgium, but Kellogg served as director of the Brussels office from Sept. 1915 to Nov. 1915. Mid- to late November would have been when Green was told to leave. It is true that William Poland did write a letter in November that offended von Bissing and many say he was director at the time of writing, but the CRB record shows Poland was assistant director of the Brussels office from Sept. 1915 to Nov. 1915. Poland only became director of Brussels in Dec. 1915, after the charges were leveled in November. It is obvious from Green's letters and diaries that he did not think highly of Kellogg and did think very well of Poland, leaving the strong impression that Kellogg was the person who told him to leave Belgium.
"anxious weeks"; "spies, male and": Ibid.
Restaurant de la Monnaie: Joe Green in diary entry with no date but just before the Wednesday, Oct. 13, 1915, entry (Princeton Mudd Library), spells the restaurant as Restaurant de la Mounoie; Baedeker's, *Belgium,* 91, says, "Restaurant de la Monnaie, Rue Leopold 7, behind the theatre" [Theatre de la Monnaie], which is "in the central part of the Lower Town" and on the Place de la Monnaie.
John Brodhead Van Schaick: Vernon Kellogg's CRB delegate list reads "Broadhead" for the middle name, while all other references are "Brodhaead," including the New York Social Register, April 1909, 586.
Hoover arrived in: Letter from Gibson to Whitlock, Dec. 1, 1915, Gibson papers, box 65, HIA.
Joe Green's account of meeting with Hoover: Joe Green speech he gave to the Washington Literary Society in the 1970s, Green papers, Princeton Mudd Library.
Nov. 30 meeting with von der Lancken: Letter from Gibson to his mother, Dec. 1, 1915, Gibson papers, box 31, HIA; Gay and Fisher, *Public Relations,* vol. I, doc. 43, 73–74.

Hoover, Gibson, and Von Der Lancken Discuss the Spy Charges 282–286

The next day; all dialogue in the Dec. 1 meeting was created using the exact words attributed to each speaker in Gibson's memorandum: Hugh Gibson's six-page memorandum, dated Dec. 1, 1915, detailing a meeting in Brussels with Gibson, Hoover, and von der Lancken regarding the spy charges and Poland's insulting letter, Gibson papers, box 72, HIA. This memorandum is not mentioned nor listed in Gay and Fisher's *Public Relations.* Listed in that book are three documents pertinent to the spy charges: Doc. 43, a memorandum written by Gibson about his Nov. 30 meeting in Brussels with von der Lancken; Doc. 44, a memorandum by Vernon Kellogg about a Dec. 2, 1915, in Brussels meeting between Kellogg, Caspar Whitney, Hoover, von Kessler, Wengersky, and Uhl; Doc. 45, a memorandum by Hoover about a conversation he had with von der Lancken on Dec. 4, 1915, the entire event was also covered by two dispatches by Gibson to the State Dept., dated Jan. 3, 1916, and Jan. 7, 1916, which are found in RG 84, correspondence, American Legation Brussels, 1916, vol. 181, file 848, Relief, NARA.

"If the three": This one quote comes from Joe Green in a speech to the Washington Literary Society, Green papers, Princeton Mudd Library.

As Gibson summed: Gibson to Whitlock, Dec. 1, 1915, Gibson papers, box 65, HIA.

"In accord with": Gibson to his mother, Dec. 1, 1915, Gibson papers, box 31, HIA.

"threatened to withdraw": Brand Whitlock mentions in his diary that Gibson, when acting in Whitlock's absence, had "threatened to withdraw" over the CRB and how the Germans were using that as one of the items that gave them cause to want Gibson removed from Belgium in Feb. 1916; Nevins, *Journal,* 234.

"we might as": Gibson to State Dept., Jan. 7, 1916, RG 84, correspondence, American Legation Brussels, 1916, vol. 181, file 848, Relief, NARA.

Hoover Turns to the German Military for Help 286–290

"For some time"; German civil government supervision of relief: Gay and Fisher, *Public Relations,* vol. I, 72.

Conrad Uhl: Gibson to mother, Dec. 1, 1915, Gibson papers, box 31, HIA.

"the relations of": Gay and Fisher, *Public Relations,* vol. I, doc. 44, 75–77.

He then proceeded; all quotes in paragraph: Ibid.

As for the; "he was a": Vernon Kellogg memorandum of the meeting, Dec. 2, 1915, in Hoover, *American Epic,* 152; Captain Uhl from America is also described in Gibson's letter to his mother, Dec. 1, 1915, Gibson papers, box 31, HIA.

Hoover could not; "the incident was": Hoover, *American Epic,* 152–153.

A "Benedict" Is Uncovered 290–291

"out of consideration": Hoover, *American Epic,* 149.

Erdlets as the "Benedict": Letter from Capt. Lucey to J. B. White, box 316, Lucey folder, HIA; George Nash, in *The Life of Herbert Hoover,* says Erdlets was removed from Rotterdam office in Jan. 1916 and went to London, where he talked to the British and caused more trouble for Hoover. Gibson talks about Erdlets, without naming him, on numerous occasions to various people.

"had come to": Hoover, *American Epic,* 149.

Hoover to Rotterdam; Henry van Dyke: Gibson to mother, Dec. 9, 1915, Gibson papers, box 31, HIA.

Erdlets pulled from Rotterdam: Hoover, *American Epic,* 150.

"to work in": Ibid., 152.

What happened to the delegates: Delegates work list, Arrowsmith papers, HIA; Erica Bunge's diary entry, Dec. 1915, "Van Schaick had to leave on account of Boches in December," author's archives.

Social Obligations Begin to Mend Fences 291–295

"He did not"; "devoted to the": Hoover, *American Epic,* 48.

"extraordinarily brilliant": Ibid., 48.

"For the past": Gibson, Dec. 1, 1915; letter to his mother, HI, box 31, HIA.

Edmond de Wouters: Hoover, *American Epic,* 43.

Hoover left December 10: Gibson to mother, Dec. 9, 1915, Gibson papers, box 31, HIA; a Hoover schedule later created shows he left on Sunday, Dec. 12, HHPLA.

A Routine Ride Turns Ugly 295–297

"It was snapping": Hugh Gibson to mother, Jan. 27, 1916, Gibson papers, box 31, HIA.

All details of the ride and the dialogue: Gibson to mother, Dec. 9, 1915, Gibson papers, box 31, HIA.

29. London 298–306

Hoover Asks the British for More Imports 298–302

By December 1915: Hoover, *American Epic*, 179.
"The monthly consignments": Gay and Fisher, *Public Relations*, vol. I, doc. 66, 121–122.
"arbitrary restrictions placed": Ibid., 135.
80,000 tons for: Hoover, *American Epic*, 179.
"minimum supplement of": Gay and Fisher, *Public Relations*, vol. I, 128.
35,000 tons per: Hoover, *American Epic*, 182.
Even with such; "The available native wheat"; "Maize is used": Gay and Fisher, *Public Relations*, vol. I, doc. 71, 129–136.
"the imports desired"; "this is the": Gay and Fisher, *Public Relations*, vol. I, 132.
126,400 tons per: Hoover, *American Epic*, 179–180.
35,000 tons: Ibid., 182.
French support Hoover's proposal to British: Ibid., 183.
Sir Edward Grey was later Viscount Grey of Falladon: Ibid., 44.
"Allied military authorities"; "Those agencies were"; "In a country"; "the Belgian ration": Ibid., 171–173.
Most of these: Ibid., 173.
black market description: Ibid., 171.
One example was; related quotes: Ibid., 173–174.
He acknowledged that: Gay and Fisher, vol. I, doc. 71, 134–135.
In the end; "The burden of": Hoover, *American Epic*, 175.
On Friday, New; "evoked an explosion": Hoover, *American Epic*, 180.
"as patron, in"; "A very critical": Gay and Fisher, *Public Relations*, vol. I, doc. 73, 136.
Grey then went; all following quotes from Grey's letter: Ibid., 136–138.
"Sir Edward's action": Hoover, *American Epic*, 181.

New Recruits Head for Belgium 302–306

All Clare Torrey biographical material: oral history, box 24, HIA; Torrey family tapes, author's archives.
Torrey appearance: Official CRB delegate photo; family descriptions.
He wrote Hoover; all Torrey details and quotes: Torrey papers, box 317, folder 26, HIA; Torrey oral history, box 24, HIA.
Milton Brown, all details and descriptions: family oral history and author's archives.

30. Brussels 307–308

A German Agent Begins Hunting *La Libre Belgique* 307–308

When the underground; all details and quotes: Millard, *Underground News*, 138–142.

Section III: Crises, 1916

31. London 311–324

No Fresh Start 311–313

The New Year's: Gay and Fisher, *Public Relations*, vol. I, doc. 73, 136–138.
"I need not": Ibid., 79.
"I must therefore": Ibid.
"we shall reconsider": Ibid.
Hoover illness: Gibson to mother, Jan. 14, 1916, Gibson papers, box 1, HHPLA; Hoover letter to Gibson, Jan. 18, 1916, RG 84, American Legation in Brussels, vol. 181, NARA.
"I have not": Ibid.
"opposition to our"; looked "rather black": Gibson to mother, Jan. 20, 1916, HHPLA.
"to meet the": According to Gay and Fisher, *Public Relations*, vol. I, footnote 18, 136, the reorganization of the Inspection and Control Department was a direct result of Grey's Dec. 31, 1915, letter to Page. The department was being reorganized "to meet these British objections."
Bureau of Inspection and Control details: Hoover, *American Epic*, 172, 176.

Ongoing Problems with Finding Good Delegates 313–319

"We are badly"; "We want people": Hoover to Galpin, Nov. 24, 1914, Galpin papers, box 1, HIA.

"inability of judging": Milton M. Brown, diary #44, 260–270, author's archives.

At least six: The six recorded by Galpin as having gone into Belgium in the second wave of Oxford students, but who are not listed on any official CRB lists, are George B. Noble, Francis L. Patton, William H. Mechling, Clyde Eagleton, Alexander R. Wheeler, and Clarence A. Castle; Galpin to CRB London office, Dec. 4, 1914, Galpin papers, box 1, HIA.

" 'Fired' at once"; "no good": Membership lists, CRB personnel files, box 312, HIA.

"a lot of": Whitlock to Hoover, Dec. 17, 1914, RG 84, correspondence, American Legation Brussels, 1914, file 848, Relief, NARA.

"are half-baked": Gibson to Millard K. Shaler, Dec. 1914, 194, RG 84, correspondence, American Legation Brussels, 1914, file 848, Relief, NARA.

"secure for us": CRB London office to CRB New York office, July 10, 1916, CRB personnel files, Dawson, HIA.

"You know, this": John Simpson, oral history, HIA.

"The requirements were": Ibid.

For those who; "he would be 'promoted' "; "needed in London": Ibid., HIA; Prentiss Gray, *Fifteen Months in Belgium: A C.R.B. Diary* (edited and complied by son Sherman Gray, grandson Prentiss S. Gray, and great-grandson Zachary S. Gray, Nov. 19, 2009, given to the author to use by Sherman and Prentiss Gray in Princeton, NJ, in 2013), 99.

No such respect; all quotes not otherwise noted: Gilchrist Stockton, "The Flock's Black Sheep," Stockton papers, box 9, HIA.

He supposedly told: Milton Brown, "A Day in the London Office (for Members of the C.R.B.)," author's archives.

"Yesterday in San"; "disagreeable person": both Kellogg letters to White, Jan. 18 and 31, 1916, box 316, Vernon Kellogg folder 1, HIA.

CRB membership lists: All lists made by official CRB sources have numerous errors and/or omissions; this author's list, which includes names and photos, can be found at http://www.jbmwriter.com/CRB-Delegates-Names-and-Photos.html.

"We don't need": Hoover cable to New York office, Nov. 22, 1916, John Simpson papers, box 317, HIA.

Gunn details and photo: Passport issued Sept. 1, 1915, ancestry.com; CRB membership lists and photo, Arrowsmith papers, HIA.

"decided some time": Gibson to Edward Bell, U.S. embassy London, Jan. 16, 1916, RG 84, correspondence, American Legation Brussels, 1916, vol. 181, file 848, Relief, NARA.

"extended chat with": Poland to Gibson, Jan. 3, 1916, RG 84, correspondence, American Legation Brussels, 1916, vol. 181, file 848, Relief, NARA.

At the frontier: Ibid.

Lucky for Lathrop: Ibid.

After a half: Ibid.

"The whole occurrence": Ibid.

"publish certain data": Ibid.

"The other members"; "recently been much"; "Naturally, the Germans": Gibson to Hoover, Jan. 4, 1916, RG 84, correspondence, American Legation Brussels, 1916, vol. 181, file 848, Relief, NARA.

"There need be": Hoover to Gibson, Jan. 11, 1916, RG 84, correspondence, American Legation Brussels, 1916, vol. 181, file 848, Relief, NARA.

"I am full": Ibid.

"Volunteers always get": Hoover to Gibson, Jan. 25, 1916, RG 84, correspondence, American Legation Brussels, 1916, vol. 181, file 848, Relief, NARA.

A Delegate's Journey to Acceptance Is Representative 320–324

Brown's acceptance process, all following letters and quotes: CRB personnel files, Milton Brown, Box 313, HIA.

"I was leaving": Brown's first CRB diary, author's archives.

On Wednesday, January; descriptions of the six onboard delegates: Brown to family, Jan, 26, 1916, author's archives.

"The more I": Ibid.
"is a lightweight": Eckstein to his mother, Jan. 28, 1916, Eckstein papers, HHPLA.
"We all take": Brown to family, Jan. 26, 1916, author's archives.
"acknowledged the possession": Arthur Bartlett Maurice, *Bottled Up in Belgium*, 22.

32. Brussels 325–342

Description of New Year's Day and all quotes in section: Gibson to mother, Jan. 3, 1916, Gibson papers, HHPLA.

New Delegates Arrive for the New Year 326–328

Prentiss Gray biographical details and all quotes in section: Gray, *Fifteen Months.*

Van Doren Plays with Fire 328–333

"Even if the"; all quotes in section: Millard, *Underground News*, 125–126, 121–122, 127, 131–132, 134–142.

Whitlock Returns and Intrigues Follow 333–335

Less than two; all details and quotes not otherwise noted: Gibson to mother, Jan. 14, 1916, and Jan. 20, 1916, Gibson papers, box 1, HHPLA.
Gibson would have; all partial quotes in paragraph: Nevins, *Journal*, 229.

A Belgian/American Wedding Brings a Welcome Distraction 335–338

"The air was"; all quotes about wedding and all quotes not otherwise noted: Gibson to mother, Jan. 27, 1916, box 31, Gibson papers, HIA.
Charles H. Carstairs details: Various CRB personnel documents, HIA and HHPLA.
Helen Guinotte details: Gibson to mother, Jan. 27, 1916, HIA.
All details and quotes regarding Raoul Warocqué: George F. Spaulding, "The CRB and the Chateau de Mariemont," unpublished, in the Alan Hoover papers, box 8, HHPLA.
"weeping and wailing"; "All the family": Gibson to mother, Jan. 27, 1916, HIA.
Horseback ride; "out of bed": Ibid.

The Reorganization of the Inspection and Control Department 338–342

"one of the finest": John Simpson, oral history, HHPLA.
From October 15; "commercial sides of"; "systematised"; "properly supervised"; "I had just": Green memorandum, May 21, 1917, Green papers, Princeton Mudd Library; also in Joseph C. Green papers, box 20, HIA.
At his new; "three-cornered fight"; "which really left": Ibid.
Such success led: Ibid.
"Outstanding among all": Hoover, *American Epic*, 43.
"It is a curious": Green, "Some Portraits, Emile Francqui," Green papers, Princeton Mudd Library.
Green's introduction of; "I have never": Ibid.
As for Francqui's; "Some of them": Ibid.
When it came; "His constant opposition": Ibid.
"He constantly intrigued": Ibid.
What made the; "his feelings and": Ibid.
As Green met; "He stormed for": Green memorandum, May 21, 1917, Green papers, Princeton Mudd Library.
When Francqui came: Ibid.
All findings and: Hoover, *American Epic*, 172.
"left to work"; Within a few; the new Inspection: Green memorandum, May 21, 1917, Green papers, Princeton Mudd Library.
"This was the": Ibid.
A big hurdle; "he had no": Ibid.
"trustworthy Belgians, whose": Hoover, *American Epic*, 172.
"These energetic American": Ibid.
This was critical; "consisted of records"; "We were able": Ibid., 172–173.
During this time; all remaining quotes in section: Green, "Some Portraits, Emile Francqui," Green papers, Princeton Mudd Library.

33. Northern France 343–355

Lille explosion: Multiple references of this well-known event.

The Delegates for Lille and Valenciennes 344–346

The Duke nickname: Numerous references in many fellow delegate papers, including those of Clare Torrey, Fred Eckstein, and Francis Wickes, HIA.

He was one: Galpin to CRB telegram, Nov. 29, 1914, Galpin papers, box 1, HIA.

Wellington's assignment: delegate work list, Robert Arrowsmith papers, HIA.

Duke's sick mother: Francis Wickes oral history, HIA.

Duke quickly learned: Joe Green, German "Begleitsoffiziere" essay, Green papers, Princeton Mudd Library.

Because the trenches; details of the house arrangement: Wellington oral history, HHPLA.

House story; "In this garb": Ibid.

Billiards story: Ibid.

Not being allowed to visit the Lille explosion site: Both Wellington and Richardson mention this in their oral histories, HIA.

"When it was": Wellington, oral history, HIA.

The German "Nurses" Get a Name Change 346–348

Change in German officer name: Gay and Fisher, *Public Relations*, vol. I, doc. 315, 502.

The reality had: Green, German "Belgeittsoffiziere" essay, Green Papers, Princeton, Mudd Library.

The changing role of officer and CRB delegate: Kittredge, *History of CRB*, 152.

"took very seriously": Ibid., 153.

This left the; "The [Brussels CRB]"; "supreme insult"; "North of France": Gay and Fisher, *Public Relations*, vol. I, doc. 315, 497–498.

"really did most": Green, German "Belgeittsoffiziere" essay, Green Papers, Princeton Mudd Library.

"Effort and accomplishment": Gay and Fisher, *Public Relations*, vol. I, doc. 315, 497–498.

"realized that American": Kittredge, *History of CRB*, 326.

"the most violent": Ibid.

"It's trench warfare": Gay and Fisher, *Public Relations*, vol. I, doc. 315, 502.

Pink Simpson Takes On the Germans and Northern France 348–355

Nickname of Pink: John L. Simpson, oral history, Sept. 20, 1967, HHPLA.

migrant worker cases: Clare Torrey, oral history, author's archives.

FTC position: John L. Simpson papers, box 317, folder 9, HIA.

"Mr. Simpson is": Torrey papers, box 317, folder 26, HIA.

Story about Simpson and Torrey chosen; Hoover cable: Torrey and Simpson papers, box 317, HIA.

Simpson's personality: Numerous third-party sources including Clare Torrey, Milton Brown, Prentiss Gray, and Erica Bunge, as well as Pink's own recollections in his HHPLA oral history and in two self-published books, *Random Notes, Recollections of My Early Life: Europe without a Guidebook*, and *A Holiday in Wartime and Other Stories.*

A fellow delegate: Milton M. Brown, author's archives.

"Erica Bunge and"; "You can't believe": John L. Simpson, oral history, HHPLA.

Roman "legionnaire": Simpson oral history, Bancroft Library, University of California, Berkeley, 46.

"the Americans were": Ibid.

"the vistas of"; all remaining quotes in section not otherwise noted: Gay and Fisher, *Public Relations*, vol. I, doc. 315, 492–507.

"perhaps the most": Ibid. The quoted retort was attributed to Alfred C. B. Fletcher by Arthur B. Maurice in his book, *Bottled Up in Belgium*, 88–92, but Fletcher arrived too late in Belgium (Feb. 1916) to be credited as the source of this well-known quote.

"considered very pleasant": Simpson oral history, Bancroft Library, University of California, Berkeley, 37.

The process to: Kittredge, *History of CRB*, 329.

"even though they": Ibid.

"Many of the": Ibid.

34. Elsewhere in Belgium 356–357

The Germans Put Pressure on the Belgians to Work 356–357

They had developed: Gay and Fisher, *Public Relations*, vol. II, 42.

Details about Rochefort: Baedeker, *Belgium*, 230.

On Monday, February: Gay and Fisher, *Public Relations*, vol. II, doc. 413, 42–44.

Torrey's report and all related quotes: Ibid.

35. Brussels 358–363

The Germans Seek Revenge on Gibson 358–362

Whitlock Feb. 7, 1916, details and quotes relating to meeting with von der Lancken not otherwise noted: Nevins, *Journal*, 234–239.

The five items against Gibson: From multiple sources, including Nevins, *Journal*, 234; Gibson letters to mother, Gibson papers, box 31, HIA; Robert M. Crunden, *A Hero in Spite of Himself: Brand Whitlock in Art, Politics, and War* (Alfred A. Knopf, New York, 1969), 315–318, and extensive footnotes, 466–468.

Gibson demanded that; "dignified"; "advanced to the": Whitlock cable to Secretary of State, Feb. 10, 1916, RG 59, file 123, G31, 146, G35, 253, box 1374, NARA.

Gibson said he; "rather sharply, indeed"; "needed no instructions: Nevins, *Journal*, 235.

"I have had"; "black hand crowd"; definition of black hand: Gibson to his mother, Feb. 21, 1916, Gibson papers, box 31, HIA; Wikipedia on "black hand."

Either way, he: Gibson to mother, Feb. 21, 1916, Gibson papers, box 31, HIA; cable from State Dept., Feb. 14, 1916, RG 59, file 123, G31, 146, G35, 253, Box 1374, NARA.

A Response Is Negotiated; A Plot is Hatched 362–363

"English Tories are"; all quotes in section: Nevins, *Journal*, 229–230, 238.

36. London 364–381

Gibson arrived in: State Dept. cable, Feb. 21, 1916, that Gibson had arrived in London "yesterday," RG 59, file 123, G31, 146, G35, 253, Box 1374, NARA.

"From the first": Hoover, *American Epic*, 41.

"playmate of Washington": Gibson to mother, Feb. 21, 1916, Gibson papers, box 31, HIA.

"The bad one": Ibid.

"I can better": Crunden, *A Hero*, 313, footnoted by Crunden, "House diary, January 5, 1916, House Papers, Yale University."

"have done me": Gibson to mother, Feb. 21, 1916, Gibson papers, box 31, HIA.

While he enjoyed: Gibson cable dated March 9, 1916, RG 59, file 123, G31, 146, G35, 253, box 1374, NARA.

"be particularly glad": Ibid.; Page cable date March 10, 1916.

A few days; "Gibson's return here": Ibid.; Whitlock cable to State Dept., March 13, 1916.

The British Finally Reply to Hoover's Request for Increased Imports 366–367

Ten days before; "it seemed absurd": Hoover, *American Epic*, 195.

After getting back; letter from Percy; list of tons: Gay and Fisher, *Public Relations*, vol. I, doc. 76, 140–141.

"The British Foreign"; remaining quotes in section: Hoover, *American Epic*, 186.

Is the CRB Really Necessary for Relief to Continue? 367–371

The first was: Nevins, *Journal*, 236–237.

"the basis of": Kittredge, *History of CRB*, 104.

"Mr. Hoover is": Smith, "The Man in Action," Robinson Smith papers, HIA.

"Hoover does not": Gibson to mother, Feb. 21, 1916, Gibson papers, box 31, HIA.

"There had developed"; all quotes from his postwar diplomatic description: Hoover, *American Epic*, 196–197.

This was blatantly: years of reading CRB-related primary source documents, letters, journals, and diaries of those involved.

Most documents support: Ibid.

"Francqui left for": Green memorandum, May 21, 1917, Green papers, Princeton Mudd Library.

Reportedly, Lambert went; "nice young college"; all remaining Whitlock quotes in section: Nevins, *Journal*, 244.
Not to be outdone; Gibson had gotten: Hoover, *American Epic*, 200.

Hoover Gets Fed Up—The CRB Resigns 371–375

"By the end"; "required working twelve"; related details and quotes: Hoover, *American Epic*, 198.
The following nine points and all related quotes: Hoover, *American Epic*, 198–202.
"You know . . .": Hoover, *American Epic*, 203; Gay and Fisher, *Public Relations*, vol. I, doc. 54, 92–93.
"The harmony which"; related quotes: Gay and Fisher, *Public Relations*, vol. I, docs. 54–57, 92–95.
The Germans were: Hoover, *American Epic*, 204–205.

The Threat of Resignation Improves German Guarantees and Imports 375–376

As Ambassador Gerard; all details and quotes: Hoover, *American Epic*, 205, 216–219, 222–225, 230–232.

Attacks Continue from the British Admiralty and Military Intelligence 376–379

"leakages of food"; "The requests that"; all remaining quotes: Hoover, *American Epic*, 206–213, 221–222.

The *Sussex* Pledge Helps CRB Shipping 380–381

On Wednesday, April; telegram of Wilson speech; all related quotes: cable from State Dept. to London embassy, April 21, 1916, RG 845, Diplomatic Posts, Belgium, Legation correspondence, 1916, Relief, vol. 183, file 848, NARA.

37. Elsewhere in Belgium and Northern France 382–395

The Bunges, Their Dairy Farm, and a CRB Delegate 382–385

"we had been"; von Bissing stopping CRB from buying milk cows: Hoover, *American Epic*, 220–221.
"It is obvious": Gay and Fisher, *Public Relations*, vol. I, 550.
Feeding for the: Roelands, *Oude Gracht.*
Brown letter about the Bunges; all remaining quotes in section: Brown, letter to father and mother, March 12, 1917, author's archives.

Von Bissing Takes Another Step toward Separation 385–387

"suddenly espoused": Cammaerts, *Through the Iron Bars*, 30–31.
"If we are": Ibid.
Before the war; all quotes not otherwise noted: Whitlock, *Belgium*, vol. II, 236–245.
"extraordinary ability to": Brown diary #42, 50, author's archives.

Pink under Pressure to Return to America 387–388

For Hoover, it; all quotes in section: Simpson files, box 317, folder 9, HIA; cable and letters, April 25, 1916, RG 84, Diplomatic Posts, Belgium, Legation correspondence, vol. 183, 1916, File 848, NARA.

Deportations Come to Northern France 388–391

The most congested: Gay and Fisher, *Public Relations*, vol. II, doc. 434, 76.
The food supplied; Roubaix riot: Ibid.
The German military: Ibid., doc. 433, 73.
"saw-mills, roadways": Kittredge, *History of CRB*, 318.
"evacuate"; "volunteers would be": Gay and Fisher, *Public Relations*, vol. II, doc. 433, 73.
"while in principle": Ibid.
Part of the plan: Ibid., doc. 434, 76.
As imagined, the: Ibid.
When the time: Ibid.
On April 22: Ibid.
"candles or other": Ibid., 318.
Eyewitnesses to the; all quotes in paragraph: Gay and Fisher, *Public Relations*, vol. II, doc. 434, 77.
"had orders to": Ibid.

While the stated: Kittredge, *History of CRB*, 321–322.
"Girls of good": Gay and Fisher, *Public Relations*, vol. II, doc. 434, 78.
"Every household, whether": Ibid., 77.
"Naturally, the American": Ibid.
Poland was horrified: Kittredge, *History of CRB*, 319.
"in the maelstrom": Kittredge, *History of CRB*, 317.
In a stroke: Ibid., 317–319.

A Bombshell Makes a Tea Party Memorable 391–395

Major-General Zoellner: Hoover, in *American Epic*, 109, says incorrectly that he was the quartermaster general; Kittredge, in *History of CRB*, 148, says he's the chief of staff of the quartermaster general; Kellogg, in *Fighting Starvation in Belgium*, 186, says he represents the Supreme Command of the German Army in France; Wikipedia states he is a major-general on the staff of the quartermaster general.
On the train; "promised him that"; "ornaments"; "in connection with": Kittredge, *History of CRB*, 319.
In attendance: Gay and Fisher, *Public Relations*, vol. II, doc. 433, 74; in numerous books, personal journals, diaries, and correspondence there are numerous spellings of Neuerbourg, including Neuerberg, Neuerburg, and Neuburg. Fritz is actually Friedrich H. Neuerbourg.
"sympathetic nature, revolting": Kittredge, *History of CRB*, 319.
"The proper opportunity": Gay and Fisher, *Public Relations*, vol. II, doc. 433, 74.
"A bombshell bursting": Kittredge, *History of CRB*, 319.
Poland went on: Gay and Fisher, *Public Relations*, vol. II, doc. 433, 74–75.
"proper and satisfactory": Ibid.
"the French people": Kittredge, *History of CRB*, 319.
"Oberleutnant Fritz Neuerbourg": Gay and Fisher, *Public Relations*, vol. II, doc. 433, 75.
"Of all the": Kittredge, *History of CRB*, 319.
"expressed himself as": Gay and Fisher, *Public Relations*, vol. II, doc. 433, 75.
"proved himself, however,": Kittredge, *History of CRB*, 319.
"was much affected": Gay and Fisher, *Public Relations*, vol. II, doc. 433, 75.
Major-General Zoellner: Kittredge, *History of CRB*, 320.
After the tea: Gay and Fisher, *Public Relations*, vol. II, doc. 433, 75.
Nonetheless, in the; "Any avowed attempt": Ibid., doc. 434, 76–80.
Most did return: Kittredge, *History of CRB*, 323.
Wellington was able; the following dialogue between Wellington and the mayor: Gay and Fisher, *Public Relations*, vol. II, doc. 434, 80.
Wellington ended his; "It is known": Ibid.
Gardner Richardson was: Delegate work list, Arrowsmith papers, HIA.
Caspar Whitney, who; "he was never": Kittredge, *History of CRB*, 325.
The story of: Gay and Fisher, *Public Relations*, vol. II, footnote 27, 73.
"German frightfulness": Ibid., 80.
"The Commission and": Kittredge, *History of CRB*, 323.
To clarify the; "It is our"; "The incident is": Gay and Fisher, *Public Relations*, vol. II, doc. 435, 81–82.
In May 1916: Cammaerts, *Through the Iron Bars*, 49.

38. Brussels 396–423

Petit Is Tried; German Raids Take Their Toll 396–406

Gabrielle Petit—the: Millard, *Underground News*, 127.
Gabrielle Petit story: Ibid.; Sophie De Schaepdrijver, *Gabrielle Petit: The Death and Life of a Female Spy in the First World War* (Bloomsbury Academic, 2015).
On Saturday morning; all details and quotes remaining in section: Millard, *Underground News*, 127, 134–135, 141–157, 159–172.

The Human Side of the Chief 406–407

In April 1916; following story about Torrey's fiancée: Torrey, oral history, box 24, HIA.
"Yes. Deborah"; remaining quotes and details from article: *The Call*, box 317, HIA.
In a British-reserved; the following Hoover/Torrey story: Torrey, oral history, box 24, HIA.

GREEN GETS TO WORK ON INSPECTION AND CONTROL 407–410

"We [Americans] have": Green letter to parents, Jan. 14, 1917, Green papers, Princeton Mudd Library.
"Our Inspection work": Ibid.
Green felt his; overreach by the Comité National: Ibid.
Some provinces, such; "The American representatives": Green memorandum, May 21, 1917, Green papers, Princeton Mudd Library.
In Hainaut Province: Ibid.
In Limbourg Province; "exceedingly rudimentary"; "delayed all progress,"; "put in good": Green memorandum, May 21, 1917, Green papers, Princeton Mudd Library.
"slow at getting": Ibid.
Even so, success; quotes in paragraph: Gray, *Fifteen Months*, 81.
Adding to the; "never could get"; "and succeeded in": Green memorandum, May 21, 1917, Green papers, Princeton Mudd Library.
In the all-important; "was more interested": Ibid.
Each American representative: Ibid.
"My Belgian colleagues"; remaining quotes in section: Green letter to his parents, Jan. 14, 1917, Green papers, Princeton Mudd Library.

CLOTHES BECOME AN IMPORTANT PART OF RELIEF 410–413

"In the first": Kittredge, *History of CRB*, 369.
By spring of: Hunt, *War Bread*, 357–358; Kellogg, *Women of Belgium*, 137–157; Hoover, *American Epic*, 407–411.
In late 1915: Brown, *Clothing the Destitute*, 13, author's archives.
On following through; "turned to imports": Hoover, *American Epic*, 407.
The CRB placed; "forwarded as fast": Brown, *Clothing the Destitute*, author's archives.
Before reaching Belgium: Hoover, *American Epic*, 407–408.
Donated items were: Ibid.
"everyone is crazy": Brown to mother, Sept. 25, 1916, author's archives.
"When the C.R.B.": Kellogg, *Women of Belgium*, 139–140.
"When we opened": Ibid.
"They did not": Ibid.
That thoughtful gift; "a corrugated zinc": Ibid., 140–141.
"Useful as these": Hoover, *American Epic*, 409.
"distributed under the": Gay and Fisher, *Public Relations*, vol. I, doc. 86, 160.

BROWN FINDS HIS PLACE—JUST NOT IN FOOD RELIEF 413–416

Brown's description: Passport issued July 31, 1917, ancrestry.com, and author's recollections.
When Brown had; "spoken for him"; "one of the": Brown to mother, Feb. 4, 1916, author's archives.
In a short: Green memorandum, May 21, 1917, Green papers, Princeton Mudd Library.
Brown was asked: Brown to grandmother, Feb. 15, 1916, and to Bruce, March 1, 1916, author's archives.
"On Thursday morning": Brown journal, 23–24, author's archives.
After the regular; "delivered Mr. Hoover's": Ibid.
The next night: Ibid., 24–25.
"This one weekend": Brown to father, March 26, 1916, author's archives.
"You told me": Ibid.
"we are so"; "Finally comes a": Earl Osborn to Mr. Brown, April 30, 1916, author's archives.
"That is one": Brown to mother, March 19, 1916, author's archives.
Brown also discovered; the scene of walking in Brussels at night: Brown journal, author's archives.
Before long; Hoover had established: Hoover, *American Epic*, 407; mention of the CN's clothing board in multiple letters and diary entries of Milton Brown in the author's archives.
"clothing was never": Brown, "Recommendations on the Purchase of the Accompanying Order," author's archives.
"The provision of": Hoover, *American Epic*, 407.
"requested to check": Kittredge, *History of CRB*, 369.
"said to be": Nevins, *Journal*, 262.
"not a mere": Brown to mother, April 19, 1916, author's archives.

Belgian Efficiency at Its Best 417–420

The four major components; all details and quotes: Brown, *Clothing the Destitute,* author's archives.
Pôle Nord/Palais d' Eté: Baedeker's, *Belgium,* 95, 132; internet website, http://www.retroscoop.com.
Watching over the: Kellogg, *Women of Belgium,* photo, 144–145.
"pieces, yards and pairs"; hundreds of thousands: Kellogg, *Women of Belgium,* 138.
"So efficient were": Hoover, *American Epic,* 408.

"Determined Opposition" Stymies Brown 420–421

"encountered determined opposition": Kittredge, *History of CRB,* 369.
Brown detailed the: Brown, *Clothing the Destitute,* author's archives.
"It was not": Ibid.

Belgian Lace Making Is Revitalized 421–423

Belgium was famous; convent schools produced; Approximately 50,000 women: Hunt, *War* Bread, 364; Kellogg, *Women of Belgium,* 159.
While the vast: Hunt, *War Bread,* 364.
A few years: Kellogg, *Women in Belgium,* 158–159.
It's honorary president: Ibid., 17.
When the CRB: Hunt, *War Bread,* 364.
In early 1915: Hoover, *American Epic,* 410.
"They agreed on"; Brown quotes: Brown, "A Final Word to My Family," March 16, 1917, author's archives.
No person was; all figures and quotes in paragraph; Each lace worker: Kellogg, *Women of Belgium,* 164, 160.
Some of these: Brown, oral history, HHPLA.
As an example; "as many as": Evelyn McMillan, "Gratitude in Lace: World War I, Famine Relief, and Belgian Lacemakers," *Piecework* magazine (May/June 2017). The tablecloth is on display in the Lou Henry Hoover Room of the Hoover Tower on the campus of Stanford University.

39. London 424–426

Francqui Starts Another Round 424–426

"one of the longest"; details and quotes not otherwise noted: Kittredge, *History of CRB,* 378, 365, 367.
Once again, the; "There would seem": Gay and Fisher, *Public Relations,* vol. I, doc. 58, 86–99; Kittredge, *History of CRB,* 367–368.

40. Elsewhere in Belgium 427–443

Gray Experiences Different Sides of Belgium 427–432

Gray's experiences, all information, and quotes not otherwise noted: Gray, *Fifteen Months,* 103–104, 99.
"situated on the": Baedeker, *Belgium,* 169.
In the northern: Map of Antwerp, Baedeker, *Belgium;* Gray, *Fifteen Months.*
"a town with": Baedeker, *Belgium,* 88.

The Mass Trial in Charleroi 432–434

At 6:00 a.m.; all details and quotes in section: Millard, *Underground News,* 172–176.

Gray Faces Promotion and Pain in June 434–436

On June 3; all details and quotes in section not otherwise noted: Gray, *Fifteen Months,* 121–126.
"In order not": Brown to Francis and Bob, June 19, 1916, author's archives.

A Weekend at Chateau Oude Gracht 436–440

"The work has"; details and quotes: Brown to his father, July 3 and 4, 1916; Brown to mother, June 22, 1916; Brown to grandmother, June 26, 1916; Brown diaries, all in author's archives.

A New Delegate Comes to Hainaut Province 440–443

Maurice Pate biographical information and senior yearbook: Pate papers, "Biography," box 6, folder 6, Princeton Mudd Library.
"meals with a": Alexander Leitch, *A Princeton Companion* (Princeton University Press), 1978.

He wrote to; all quotes in section not otherwise noted: Pate diary, box 13, folder 4, Princeton Mudd Library.
Tournai details: Baedekers, *Belgium*, 82–85, 215.
The two men: Pate, "A C.R.B. Delegate's typical day," Pate papers, Princeton Mudd Library.
"Would you actually": Pate to Richard Pate, July 25, 1916, Pate papers, HIA.
across the street; "All correspondence, etc.": Pate to Richard Pate, July 25, 1916, Pate papers, HIA; Pate diary, Pate papers, Princeton Mudd Library.
Hainaut Province delegates: Delegate work list, Robert Arrowsmith papers, HIA.
The Tournai District: Pate to Richard Pate, July 25, 1916, Pate papers, HIA.

41. Brussels 444–452

The Paper Skips a Beat but Does Not Fail 444–447

For the first; all details and quotes in section: Millard, *Underground News*, 177–187.

Cardinal Mercier Stirs Up Patriotism 447–450

Knowing the importance; all quotes in section not otherwise noted: Mercier, *Own Story*, 232–248.
The Belgians couldn't; "The Belgians have": Nevins, *Journal*, 280.
somehow word had; "Even the dogs": Ibid.

Hoover's Quick Stop in Brussels 450–451

While in Brussels; "Belgian sources"; "I am certain": Kittredge, *History of CRB*, 370.
"Hoover in; a": Nevins, *Journal*, 282.
Mr. Hoover, just": Pate diary, Pate papers, Princeton Mudd Library.
"insisted firmly that"; As Hoover left: Kittredge, *History of CRB*, 370–371.

Brown's Heart in Two Places 451–452

Brown's assistants; details and quotes: Brown to mother, Sept. 25, 1916, and Aug. 16, 1916; Brown to Bruce, Oct. 8, 1916; Brown to father, July 3, 1916; Brown to Harry, Aug. 21, 1916, author's archives.

42. Berlin 453–462

The Northern France Harvest Leads to Crisis 453–457

Hoover had seen: Kittredge, *History of CRB*, 314–315.
In Lille, Hoover; "Salvation can only": Kittredge, *History of CRB*, 315.
April 1, Hoover; "degenerating into a": Kittredge, *History of CRB*, 314–317.
In an effort: Hoover, *American Epic*, 227–228.
Hoover also pointed; four separate "classes": Ibid.
By early August; von Sauberzweig signed Cavell execution orders: Ibid., 238–239; Britain's *Daily Telegraph*, Feb. 6, 1917, "Von Sauberzweig, the officer directly responsible for the execution of Edith Cavell," clip books, HHPLA.
"the Germans insisted"; details and quotes not otherwise noted: Hoover, *American Epic*, 193, 238–239, 240.
Unfortunately, von Sauberzweig: Ibid.; Kellogg, *Fighting Starvation*, 58–65.

Hoover Fights for the Life of the CRB 457–462

When the group; "The conference was": Hoover, *American Epic*, 240–241; Kellogg, *Fighting Starvation*, 58–65.
"We were disappointed": Ibid.
At 4:00 p.m.: Ibid.
"Extremely violent speeches"; "no worse for": Ibid.
"bellicose speakers"; "The feeling all": Kellogg, *Fighting Starvation*, 58–65.
Kellogg's account, which; "just one ray"; "if the request": Ibid.
"This was our": Ibid.
"there came one": Hoover, *American Epic*, 241.
"apologetically mentioned that": Ibid.

Hoover and Kellogg: Ibid.; while Hoover stated, "I expressed sympathy for this tragedy," there is no doubt that Kellogg, with his gentlemanly ways and sophistication, would have done so as well.
Taking another drink; all quotes by Hoover in section: Hoover, *American Epic*, 241.
Kellogg's account explains; "We argued here";"The long story": Kellogg, *Fighting Starvation*, 58–65.
"hasten the formulation": Ibid.
"The crisis was": Ibid.
By the end; "as the year": Kittredge, *History of CRB*, 338.
By September the: Gay and Fisher, *Public Relations*, vol. I, 590–605; Hoover, *American Epic*, 227–250.
One critical behind-the-scenes; "One important condition": Gay and Fisher, *Public Relations*, vol. I, doc. 379, 596.
A sad footnote; "consequently the Commission": Kittredge, *History of CRB*, 342.
With von Hindenburg; "The Commission made": Ibid., 342–343.

43. Brussels 463–464

"Hoover very bitter": Nevins, *Journal*, 284.

Green Feels the Heavy Hand of Francqui 463–464

Only a day; all following bullet points: Kittredge, *History of CRB*, 371.
"naturally very indignant": Ibid.
The Kelloggs decided: Gray, *Fifteen Months*, 179.
"The meal nearly": Ibid.
"rather inconclusive meetings"; "The difficulties with": Kittredge, *History of CRB*, 371. 370.

44. London 465–474

The British Get Involved in the CRB/CN Conflicts 465–469

Whitlock had given: Nevins, *Journal*, 308.
Hoover letter to Page, Oct. 16, 1916: Kittredge, *CRB* History, 371; Nevins, *Journal*, 308.
Hoover letter to Percy, Oct. 18, 1916, RG 84, American Embassy, Relief, 848, 1916, vol. 805, NARA.
Only two days; Hoover's letter to Percy: Kittredge, *History of CRB*, 371–372.
"I am this": Hoover letter to Page, Oct. 18, 1916, RG 84, American Embassy, Relief, 848, 1916, vol. 805, NARA.
"During the whole": Ibid.
"Without going too": Ibid.
The ambassador also: Ibid.
Still, on October; "It seems to"; "while I sympathise": Page letter to Whitlock, Oct. 18, 1916, RG 84, American Embassy, Relief, 1916, vol. 805, NARA.
"I am trusting": Ibid.
Lord Grey's Oct. 20, 1916, letter and all related quotes in section: Kittredge, *History of CRB*, 372–374.
Oct. 20, 1916, letter from Lord Robert Cecil to Page and all related quotes in section: Gay and Fisher, *Public Relations*, vol. I, doc. 62, 108–109.
Page wrote that; "the whole thing"; "any action taken": Ibid., doc. 61, 106–108.
"reports coming out"; Page maintained it: Ibid.
"The action of": Ibid.
"The Comité National": Ibid.
"I do not": Ibid.
"It seems unfair": Ibid.
As if this; "would be impossible": Kittredge, *History of CRB*, 375.

Hoover Again Requests an Increase in Imports 469–472

"remained heartbreakingly": Hoover, *American Epic*, 222.
From all that; "impressive": Ibid., 29.
As covered by; related quotes: *Field*, Nov. 25, 1916, clip books, HHPLA.
"With the aid": Hoover, *American Epic*, 28–29.
Hoover letter, Sept. 15, 1915; all bullet points: Gay and Fisher, *Public Relations*, vol. I, 164–165.

"The imports of": Ibid.
He followed this; "Coffee is now": Ibid.
Lord Percy's memorandum; all items and tons: Hoover, *American Epic*, 173–174.

Gibson Finds a Home and Makes a Move 472–474

Gibson's temporary, then finalized posting: State Dept. cables, May 16, 1916, and July 15, 1916, RG 59, file 123, G31, 146, G35, 253, box 1374, NARA.
Gibson reported that; "A good part": Gibson to mother, May 7, 1916, Gibson papers, box 34, HIA.
Officially his title: Ibid.
"The tearing to": Ibid.
"Among other things": Gibson to mother, Aug. 5, 1916, Gibson papers, box 34, HIA.
"keep a closer": Gibson to mother, May 7, 1916, and Dec. 30, 1916, Gibson papers, box 34, HIA.
Torrey had decided; Torrey personal details: Torrey, oral history, author's archives.
Gibson surprised Torrey; He received his; quotes in paragraph: RG 59, General Records of the State Dept., box 252, NARA.
"I went to": Torrey, oral history, box 24, HIA.
A couple of; Page letter to State Dept.; "troublesome Transatlantic case": RG 59, General Records of the State Dept., box 252, NARA.
"No one whom": Wellington, oral history, box 25, HIA.

45. Elsewhere in Belgium 475–478

The All-Flemish University of Ghent Opens 475–476

Through the summer: Whitlock, *Belgium*, vol. II, 249; Cammaerts, *Through the Iron Bars*, 30–32.
Von Bissing and: Ibid.
When the school; "The God of": Ibid.
"With one hand": Cammaerts, *Through the Iron Bars*, 31–32.
Differing accounts have: Whitlock, *Belgium*, vol. II, 249; Cammaerts, *Through the Iron Bars*, 30–32.
"I was told": Whitlock, 16-page memorandum to the State Dept., Aug. 10, 1917, RG 84, Diplomatic Posts, Belgium, Legation correspondence, 1917, vol. 191, file 703, NARA.
"Von Bissing had": Kellogg, *Headquarter Nights*, 66–67.
"are obliged to": Cammaerts, *Through the Iron Bars*, 31–32.
"in spite of": de Gerlache de Gomery, *Belgium in War Time*, 2.

Delegate Pate Doesn't Want to Leave 476–478

By autumn 1916; "I have acquired": Pate to father, Aug. 24, 1916; to mother, Sept. 1916; to Ann, Sept. 14, 1916; all in Pate papers, Princeton Mudd Library.
"Started for Mons": Pate diary, Pate papers, Princeton Mudd Library.
"if anything are"; "This side does": Pate to mother and father, July 11, 1916, Pate papers, Princeton Mudd Library.
"enter the social"; "tennis is very": Ibid.
"It may seem": Ibid.
"At nearly all": Pate to Richard, July 25, 1916, Pate papers, Princeton Mudd Library.
"Fortunate for me": Pate diary, Pate papers, Princeton Mudd Library.
"the most fertile": Pate to Richard, July 25, 1916, Pate papers, Princeton Mudd Library.
"It seems impossible": Pate diary, Pate papers, Princeton Mudd Library.
"Spent morning visiting"; "At each place": Pate diary, Pate papers, Princeton Mudd Library.
"The present occupation": Ibid.
What did change; "I do not"; "During three and": Pate to mother and father, Oct. 25, 1916, Pate papers, Princeton Mudd Library.

46. Brussels 479–488

The CRB and *La Libre Belgique* Must Stay Apart 479–480

"Throughout the entire"; all details and quotes in section: Kellogg, *Mercier*, 58–66.

Autumn Falls Heavy on *La Libre Belgique* 480–483

Madame Massardo, who; all details and quotes not otherwise noted: Millard, *Underground News*, 190–193, 200–208.

"Editors Counsel the": *New York Times*, May 21, 1915.

"The daring little": *London Times*, Nov. 24, 1916, clip books, HHPLA.

"The paper contains": Hugh Gibson, "German Rule in Belgium," Gibson papers, box 73, HIA.

"It is difficult": Ibid.

Brown Finds Points of Trouble within the Clothing Operations 483–486

The largest delays; all details and quotes in section not otherwise noted: Brown, *Clothing the Destitute*, 12, author's archives; Brown, "Recommendations on the Purchase of the Accompany Order," 1–6, author's archives.

Shipping and receiving: Milton Brown to Erica Bunge, April 21, 1917, author's archives.

"For months and months": Ibid.

Emmanuel Janssen was: Ibid.

One autumn night; all quotes related to the airplane story: Brown to mother and father, Nov. 16, 1916, author's archives.

"the dearest friends": Ibid.

Hoover Tries One Last Time with Francqui 486–488

"Hoover comes tomorrow": Nevins, *Journal*, 310.

"Hoover, by his": Ibid., 311.

Three days after: Kittredge, *History of CRB*, 375.

"full of fight": Nevins, *Journal*, 311.

Francqui was just; "defiant and unyielding": Kittredge, *History of CRB*, 375.

"It appears . . . that": Nevins, *Journal*, 313.

Still, Francqui's perception: Kittredge, *History of CRB*, 375.

"It is useless": Ibid.

Milton Brown recorded: Brown memorandum, Nov. 9, 1916, Brown diary #43, Nov. 9, 1916, author's archives.

"We are not"; "Just to show"; "been linked up"; "To do this": Ibid.

"the danger of": Ibid.

"Hoover was worn"; "the arrival of": Nevins, *Journal*, 313–314.

"a rage, banging"; "since the American"; "with a black"; "It is Hoover": Ibid., 314–315.

"The more one": Ibid., 322.

47. Coercion Turns to Mass Deportations, Autumn/Winter 1916 489–509

The Process Evolved in Stages 489–493

"That the German": Gay and Fisher, *Public Relations*, vol. II, doc. 407, 34–35.

"that the Governor-General": Ibid.

"no technical violations"; "disastrous effects . . . not": Ibid., 44–45.

"civil officials and": Ibid.

In early September: Ibid., 44–46.

When conscription and: Ibid.

"setting the Belgian": Cammaerts, *Through the Iron Bars*, 55.

October 3, 1916, decree; following quotes: Toynbee, *The Belgian Deportations*, 41; "Belgian Note to Neutral Powers," *London Times*, Nov. 16, 1916.

Within the Army: Toynbee, *The Belgian Deportations*, 15–16.

"Great Headquarters had": Gay and Fisher, *Public Relations*, vol. II, 45.

At stake were; the German plan and statistics: Van Den Heuvel, *Slave Raids in Belgium*, 2; Jens Thiel, in a speech he gave on Mar. 24, 2014, "'Slave Raids' during the First World War? Deportation and Forced Labor in Occupied Belgium," stated the figure was 500,000.

General Hurt, the; "Where the Communes": Cammaerts, *Through the Iron Bars*, 53.

With or without: Toynbee, *The Belgian Deportations*, 15–16.
"turn its attention": Gay and Fisher, *Public Relations*, vol. II, doc. 427, 63–66.
After numerous discussions: Ibid.

THE AMERICANS BEAR WITNESS 493–495

"The delegates were": Whitlock, *Belgium*, vol. II, 628.
St. Ghislain details: Baedeker *Belgium*, 215.
"The women had": Whitlock, *Belgium*, vol. II, 628.
When it came; "Indeed," Whitlock noted: Ibid.
"not allowed even": Ibid.
"marched off to": Ibid.
Recommended capacity of cattle cars: "The Agony of Belgium," *London Times*, Nov. 21, 1916.
"sick with horror": Whitlock, *Belgium*, vol. II, 628.
"rushing back and": Gade, article in *Heart's Magazine*, October 1917.
"Ever-swelling, anxious"; "men read the"; "mob could easily": Ibid.
Tuck and Gade; "the Regional and": Gay and Fisher, *Public Relations*, vol. II, doc. 427, 63–66.
"Mr. Tuck and I": Ibid.
They immediately took; "vigorously, especially when": Ibid.
The officers in; "every man provided": Ibid.
"The officers of": Ibid.
In utter frustration; None, the man: Ibid.
"Down the many"; "endless rows of": Gade, article in *Heart's Magazine*, October 1917.

THE WORLD AND BRITAIN REACT 496–499

"slave raids": A term used to describe the forced deportations of Belgian workers that began in 1916 and continued into 1917. The term was used many times in multiple sources; one example, "Slave Raids in Belgium," *London Times*, Nov. 8, 1916.
In America, protests; "packed to capacity"; "as long as": *New York Times*, Dec. 16, 1916.
The main speaker; "The question is": Ibid.
"The manhood of": *Daily News*, Nov. 27, 1916, clip books, HHPLA.
"This crowning infamy": Ibid.
"This development of": Ibid.
"no sudden or": Britain's *Daily Telegraph*, Nov. 28, 1916, clip books, HHPLA.
Despite the worldwide; Dec. 2, 1916; "very childish judgment": Gay and Fisher, *Public Relations*, vol. II, footnote no. 15, 45.
One editorial, titled; "Have the neutrals"; "They have. . . .": *Birmingham Daily Post*, Nov. 27, 1916, clip books, HHPLA.
"As matters stand": Ibid.
"We suppose the": Ibid.
"In effect," Hoover: Hoover, *American* Epic, 254.
Lord Percy referred; British stipulations to: Ibid., 255.
"You should take": Ibid.
In effect, this: Ibid.
Lord Percy went; "the criterion that": Ibid.
"impossible to impose"; "We could not": Ibid., 256.

HOOVER PUSHES FOR AN OFFICIAL PROTEST 499–502

"food should not": Hoover, *American Epic*, 256.
"at this time"; "It is common"; "should accept this": Ibid., 256–257.
"England has reduced": Toynbee, *The Belgian Deportations*, 19–20; *New York Times*, Nov. 12, 1916, by Cyril Brown, 1; *London Times*, Nov. 16 and 21, 1916.
The governor general; "Hundreds of people": Gay and Fisher, *Public Relations*, vol. II, doc. 427, 63–66.
On Monday, October; October 30 meeting details: Gray, *Fifteen Months*, 192.
"we had not": Ibid.
"these men who": Ibid.

"sat in the": Ibid., 192–193.
"at the end": Ibid.
Having no success; "loath to act"; Hoover's full letter that follows: Hoover, *American Epic*, 273.
Whitlock became more; "was positively ill": Any of Whitlock's writings around this time indicate his agitation; Kellogg, *Mercier*, 158.
Besides Whitlock's usual; Whitlock's reasoning for not making an official protest: Hoover, *American Epic*, 273.
In this regard; The two critical: Gay and Fisher, *Public Relations*, vol. II, doc. 419, 50–51.
"Thus far our"; The one exception: Ibid.
"cut at the"; "constrained to protest"; "in all probability": Hoover, *American Epic*, 277–278.

A Belgian Moral Voice Rings to the Rafters 502–506

"Any German statesman": Moritz Ferdinand von Bissing, *General von Bissing's Testament: A Study in German Ideals* (T. Fisher Unwin Ltd., no date).
"If the Cardinal": Kellogg, *Mercier*, 152.
"In the name": Ibid., 153–154; Whitlock, *Belgium*, vol. II, 499–500.
"Do not talk": Whitlock, *Belgium*, vol. II, 496.
"familial virtues"; "The working classes": Ibid., 509.
"Knowing that fear": Kellogg, *Mercier*, 156.
"in the name": Mercier, *Cardinal Mercier's Own Story*, 315.
"An Appeal to": Kellogg, *Mercier*, 156.
"The unvarnished truth": Mercier, *Cardinal Mercier's Own Story*, 318.
"We, shepherds of": Ibid., 320.
Back in Belgium: Ibid., 308–350.
A particularly detailed; "It consisted of": *New York Times*, Dec. 15, 1916.
"a thundering chorus": Ibid.
"I found myself": Ibid.
and reportedly played: Jean Massart, *Under the German Eagle*, (E. P. Dutton, New York, 1916), 308.
"the transport of"; "has taken its"; "state that after"; "the good care": *Kölnische Zeitung*, Nov. 9, 1916, Green papers, HIA.
Gray's description of the King's Fete Day: Gray, *Fifteen Months*, 195–200.
"In spite of": Mercier, *Cardinal Mercier's Own Story*, 332.
"We must leave": Ibid., 334.

Hoover's Deadly Dilemma 506–509

More than 1,000: 991 "men taken having cards" and 63 "men taken entitled to cards but not having received them," from Gay and Fisher, *Public Relations*, vol. II, doc. 427, 63–66.
"The Commission for": Ibid., 63–69.
"The Allies must": Hoover, *American Epic*, 278–279; Britain's *Daily Telegraph*, Dec. 4, 1916, clip books, HHPLA.
"The Allies have": Hoover, *American Epic*, 278–279.
"it will be"; "appeal to the": Ibid.
"Should we risk": Ibid., 283.
"It seemed to": Ibid.
He put the: Ibid.
Four bullet points: Ibid., 283–284.
"that he thought": Ibid., 284.
"bring pressure on": Gay and Fisher, *Public Relations*, vol. II, 45–46.
"after what he": Whitlock, *Belgium*, vol. II, 628; family oral history of the author (Hallam Tuck married Hilda Bunge, sister of Erica Bunge, who is the author's grandmother).
"Our C.R.B. men": Kellogg, *Mercier*, 158; the family oral history of the author.
Tuck did leave: Pate, daily journal, 39, HHPLA.
"The experience was": Tuck, "Duties of the American Representative in the Province," Gilchrist Stockton papers, box 5, HIA.
"Department would be": Gay and Fisher, *Public Relations*, vol. II, doc. 428, 66–67.

48. London 510–517

Francqui and Hoover Play Their Final Cards 510–516

Hoover return to London Nov. 20, 1916: Hoover calendar prepared by Miss Schulte at HIA.
When Hoover returned; He immediately sent: Kittredge, *History of CRB*, 375.
"As to that": Nevins, *Journal*, 335.
Lord Percy's letter to Hoover, dated Nov. 25, 1916: Author's archives.
"first for the": ibid.
"responsible for many": Ibid.
"You came in": Ibid.
"We have got": Ibid.
"On my honour": Ibid.
"I regard myself": Ibid.
"We have received": Whitlock letter to Page, Nov. 29, 1916, RG 84, Diplomatic Posts, Great Britain, vol. 805, 1916 Relief, 848 Belgium (cont.), NARA.
"Since then relations": Ibid.
"An important factor": Ibid.
"I send you": Ibid.
"This was shown": Ibid.
when the Belgian: Kittredge, *History of CRB*, 376.
In the end: Ibid.
Back in Belgium: Ibid.
"made a secret": Nevins, *Journal*, 341.
Tracy Kittredge, in: Kittredge, *History of CRB*, 376–378.
Hoover added his: Hoover to Whitlock, Dec. 29, 1916, RG 84, American Legation, Brussels Correspondence, 1917, vol. 70, file 848, NARA; copy correspondence box 7, HIA. The author of *WWI Crusaders* would like to thank Hoover biographer George Nash for helping him locate a copy of the Hoover-Whitlock letter.
"the neutral and"; "changes in form"; "Hoover immediately accepted": Kittredge, *History of CRB*, 377.
Francqui said he: Ibid., 376.
"If this contract": Hoover to Whitlock, Dec. 29, 1916, RG 84, American Legation, Brussels correspondence, 1917, vol. 70, file 848, NARA; copy correspondence box 7, HIA.
Hoover was taken; "attitude in Brussels": Kittredge, *History of CRB*, 376; Hoover to Whitlock, Dec. 29, 1916, RG 84, American Legation, Brussels Correspondence, 1917, vol. 70, file 848, NARA; copy correspondence box 7, HIA.
"I did not wish"; To Francqui it: Ibid.
Hoover—finding himself; "protested vigorously to": Kittredge, *History of CRB*, 376–377.
"The reason was": Hoover to Whitlock, Dec. 29, 1916, RG 84, American Legation, Brussels correspondence, 1917, vol. 70, file 848, NARA; copy correspondence box 7, HIA.
Not to be; "made my own": Hoover to Whitlock, Dec. 29, 1916, RG 84, American Legation, Brussels correspondence, 1917, vol. 70, file 848, NARA; copy correspondence box 7, HIA; Kittredge, *History of CRB*, 376–377.
"sledge hammer to": Hoover to Whitlock, Dec. 29, 1916, RG 84, American Legation, Brussels correspondence, 1917, vol. 70, file 848, NARA; copy correspondence box 7, HIA.
"I would use": Ibid.
"We thereupon agreed": Ibid.
"expressed the fear": Ibid.
"We had no"; "common circulation": Ibid.
Hoover and Francqui signings: Gay and Fisher, *Public Relations*, vol. I, footnote 16, 115.
"None better than": Kittredge, *History of CRB*, 378.
"The admiration which": Hoover to Whitlock, Dec. 29, 1916, RG 84, American Legation, Brussels correspondence, 1917, vol. 70, file 848, NARA; copy correspondence box 7, HIA.
"If I were": Ibid.; Kittredge, *History of CRB*, 377.
It was true: Kittredge, *History of CRB*, 377–378.
"I was only": Green, letter to parents, Jan. 14, 1917, Princeton Mudd Library.

"Mr. Hoover decided": Green, oral history, HHPLA.
document-heavy *Public Relations*: George I. Gay and H. H. Fisher, 2 volumes (Stanford University Press, Stanford University, California, 1929).
"He is pretty": Gibson to mother, Nov. 16 and 17, 1916, Gibson papers, box 34, HIA.
"It was, of": Kittredge, *History of CRB*, 378.

AN END-OF-THE-YEAR REVIEW 516–517
Overall, the end: Gay and Fisher, *Public Relations*, vol. I, 174.
One of the: Ibid., 174, 347.
Greater demand for; shipping cost details: Hoover to Whitlock, Jan. 28, 1916, RG, Diplomatic Posts, Belgium, Legation correspondence, 1916, vol. 182, file 848, Relief, NARA.

49. Elsewhere in Belgium 518–523

DECEMBER MOMENTS AT CHATEAU OUDE GRACHT 518–523
Early in the month: Pate diary, Pate papers, Princeton Mudd Library.
"The Bunges keep": Ibid.
"spent a quiet": Ibid.
The next day; "We made part": Ibid.
When the group; "filled with collections": Ibid.
For Pate, the; "millionaire many times": Ibid.
"Here," Gray noted: Gray, *Fifteen Months*, 204.
Gray's living conditions; "took out his": Ibid., 205.
"The evening party": Ibid., 208.
Brown's Christmas spent with the Bunges and all following quotes: Brown to mother and father, Dec. 25, 1916, author's archives.

WINTER RAINS TURN SEVERE 523
By late December; "on account of": Pate diary, Pate papers, Princeton Mudd Library.

50. Brussels 524–526

THE CRB LOSES A MEMBER WHO WAS "TRUE AS STEEL" 524–526
Baron Lambert dinner details: Whitlock, *Belgium*, vol. II, 676.
song about him: Whitlock, "Belgium: The Deportations," *Everybody's Magazine* (Nov. 5, 1918, no. 5, vol. 39), 11.
At the end: Whitlock, *Belgium*, vol. II, 676–677.
"chief secretaries"; "the breakdown of": *Pall Mall Gazette*, Jan. 2, 1917, clip books, HHPLA.
"There seemed to": Whitlock, *Belgium*, vol. II, 678.
"It was a": Pate diary, Pate papers, Princeton Mudd Library.
"was one of": Brown to grandmother, Jan. 3, 1917, author's archives.
"We buried him": Whitlock, *Belgium*, vol. II, 678–679.
"every one I": Ibid.
"For one morning": Ibid.
"A great crowd": Ibid.
"During all his": Gray, *Fifteen Months*, 209A (missing from the author's copy but found in HHPLA).
"bedecked in silver": Ibid.
As the crowd: Ibid.
"As we stood": Ibid.
"He was one": Gibson to his mother, Dec. 30, 1916, Gibson papers, box 34, HIA.

SECTION IV: FAREWELL, JANUARY TO MAY 1917

51. London 529–532

GIBSON GETS ENTANGLED IN MORE THAN RELIEF 529–530
He had also; all Gibson details and quotes in section: Gibson to mother, Dec. 30, 1916, Gibson papers, box 34, HIA.

"Elizabeth Asquith announced": *Margot Asquith's Great War Diary 1914–1916: The View from Downing Street,* footnote 3, 275.

Duke Wellington's wedding: newspaper clipping, RG 59, General Records of the State Dept., box 266, NARA.

Only two days; "Gibson's health requires": Page cable to State Dept., Jan. 8, 1917, RG 59, file 123 G31, 146, G35, 252, box 1374, NARA.

Two days later; Gibson was going: Ibid.; SS *Philadelphia's* first-class list, ancestry.com.

HOOVER'S TAKE ON THE DEPORTATIONS 530–532

Hoover's letter to State Dept.; all related quotes in section: Hoover, *American Epic,* 279–282; Gay and Fisher, *Public Relations,* vol. II, doc. 429, 67–68.

Hallam Tuck leaving the CRB because of the deportations: Whitlock, *Belgium,* vol. II, 628; Kellogg, *Mercier,* 158; the family oral history of the author.

"I do not": Hoover letter to Secretary Lansing, Jan, 27, 1917, in Hoover, *American Epic,* 281.

"The Belgian people": Ibid.

"It is useless": Ibid.

"Although the deportations": Gay and Fisher, *Public Relations,* vol. II, 68.

On Saturday, January; Hoover sailing and identification: SS *Philadelphia's* first-class passenger list, ancestry.com. The list shows a departure date of Jan. 13. Some CRB sources show Hoover sailed Jan. 15. The ship was probably held up because of German submarine activity.

52. Brussels 533–541

THE DEPORTATIONS COME TO BRUSSELS 533–536

Whitlock letter of protest to von der Lancken: Gay and Fisher, *Public Relations,* vol. II, doc. 430, 69–70.

Whitlock reminded von; "not only has": Ibid.

When the Germans; all Whitlock quotes not otherwise noted: Whitlock, *Belgium,* vol. II, 688, 692, 696, 692–694.

The day the; the scene of the Brussels deportations: Ibid., 690–691.

Description of *uhlan* crowd control: Milton M. Brown, *Gloria Victis,* author's archives.

CRB Director Warren: Whitlock, *Belgium,* vol. II, 694.

That first day: Nevins, *Journal,* 346.

The deportations continued; but the weather; "At last even": Whitlock, *Belgium,* vol. II, 695.

"did not suffer": Ibid.

"lighted a fire": Whitlock's official report as recorded in "One of the Foulest Deeds in History," *London Times,* May 18, 1919.

"Saddest of all": Nevins, *Journal,* 345.

PEACE FEELERS HAVE LITTLE IMPACT 536–537

"the generals down"; "the military party"; "The Germans felt": Whitlock, *Belgium,* vol. II, 695.

"frowned down upon"; "Acropolis of Brussels": Hunt, *War Bread,* 165.

"To the delight": Whitlock, *Belgium,* vol. II, 696.

"acted a comedy!": Ibid.

"These days, the": Ibid.

"on very urgent": Nevins, *Journal,* 347–348.

BROWN'S CLOTHING EFFORTS FINALLY GET A BREAK 537–539

"The British Government"; "He finally came": Brown to Erica Bunge, April 21, 1917, author's archives.

"And then—after": Ibid.

At that critical; Brown as chief delegate of Namur Province: Brown to father, Jan. 16, 1917, and Brown to Harry, Jan. 21, 1917, author's archives.

"very drastic action": Brown, *Clothing the Destitute,* author's archives.

He also knew; "very considerable"; remaining quotes in section: Brown, *Memorandum for the Foreign Office,* author's archives.

THE BELGIANS CONTINUE THEIR PASSIVE RESISTANCE 539–541

"We had not"; all Percy quotes: Percy, *Lanterns on the Levee* (Alfred A. Knopf, New York, 1941), 166, 162.

Nowhere was Belgium's; all remaining details and quotes in section: Millard, *Underground News*, 207, 209–212.

53. Elsewhere in Belgium 542–543

FLOODING FOLLOWED BY ARCTIC COLD 542–543

On New Year's; "in a rowboat": Pate to Richard, Jan. 4, 1917, Pate papers, Princeton Mudd Library.
"The weather has": Gray, *Fifteen Months*, 217–219.
"The most important": Pate diary, Thursday, Jan. 25, 1917, Pate papers, Princeton Mudd Library.
"an entirely new": Pate to mother and father, Feb. 28, 1917, Pate papers, HHPLA.
The approximately 100,000: Pate to mother and father, Feb. 28, 1917, Pate papers, HHPLA.

54. Brussels 544–550

A NEW DEVASTATING GERMAN POLICY IS ANNOUNCED 544–546

Arriving diplomatically early; details and quotes of the scene in von der Lancken's office: Whitlock, *Belgium*, vol. II, 699–700.
known only as: Whitlock, in *Belgium*, vol. II, 700, lists Dr. Brohn; Nevins, in *Journal*, 348, lists Dr. Rohn.
"Gentlemen, I have": Nevins, *Journal*, 348.
Von der Lancken: Ibid.
German statement on relief; "the Imperial Government"; all remaining quotes in section not otherwise noted: Whitlock, *Belgium*, vol. II, 701–704.
the group decided; Francqui's actions: Nevins, *Journal*, 349.
"It is hard": Whitlock, *Belgium*, vol. II, 700, 703. The quote is attributed to Dr. Brohn in *Belgium*, while in *Journal*, 348, the man in attendance is identified as "Bucher."
"Villalobar remaining as": Nevins, *Journal*, 349.
"What madness, what": Ibid.

ANOTHER MASS TRIAL—LE ROUX'S TIME IS UP 546–549

On Tuesday, February; all details and quotes in section: Millard, *Underground News*, 219–223, 212–216.

A NEW MAN HELMS THE UNDERGROUND NEWSPAPER 549–550

In this case; all details and quotes in section: Millard, *Underground News*, 224–232.

55. Hoover in America 551–557

TRYING TO KEEP RELIEF AFLOAT 551–554

Hoover had returned; "expressed his great": Hoover, *American Epic*, 284–285.
11 ships damaged or sunk in 1916: Gay and Fisher, *Public Relations*, vol. I, 343.
For Hoover and; bullet points: Ibid., 344.
"I could not": Hoover, *American Epic*, 287.
Initially, Hoover quickly; "conclusions reached": Ibid., 287–288.
On February 3; "the Secretary's view": Ibid., 290.
Hoover's replacement plan: Gay and Fisher, *Public Relations*, vol. II, doc. 465, 128–130.
It also stated; "Think it extremely"; all other quotes in section not otherwise noted: Hoover, *American Epic*, 290, 287–288, 292, 293, 296.
"shrank from the": Ibid., 41.
The Germans agreed; new route: Gay and Fisher, *Public Relations*, vol. I, 344.
"the Commission was": Ibid., 345.
Overall, though, the: Hoover, *American Epic*, 296.
It was only: Ibid., 296–297.

VON BISSING AND VON DER LANCKEN CREATE A CRISIS 555–557

On Sunday, February; Villalobar and Francqui message; "could no longer": Gay and Fisher, *Public Relations*, vol. II, doc. 468, 133; Hoover, *American Epic*, 302.
Walter Page in; "close the Commission's"; "America can now"; "I await Department's": Hoover, *American Epic*, 304.

"I did not": Hoover, *American Epic*, 304.
"The American members": Gay and Fisher, *Public Relations*, vol. II, doc. 473, 137.
While Hoover was; details and quotes not otherwise noted: Hoover, *American Epic*, 304–310, 314.
Most notably, an: *New York Times*, April 12, 1917, 1 and 2; *New York Times*, April 22, 1917, Section 1, 17.

56. Brussels 558–562

"The Best Diplomat of All of Us!" 558–562

Initially, however, all: Whitlock, *Belgium*, vol. II, 708.
A short time: Ibid., 712.
"I am in": Nevins, *Journal*, 352.
"the minister is"; "I never saw": Gray, *Fifteen Months*, 221–222.
Gregory, anticipating trouble; "took advantage of": Kittredge, *History of CRB*, 414.
"Listening to him": Nevins, *Journal*, 353.
"terribly blue": Ibid., 354.
"jokes, those flashes": Whitlock, *Belgium*, vol. II, 786.
"I have read": Nevins, *Journal*, 355.
Whitlock working on his novel: Hoover, *American Epic*, 41.
Whitlock's admission on leaving Belgium that he was taking his novel, Nevins, *Journal*, 374.
On Monday, February; "It was perfectly": Gray, *Fifteen Months*, 228.
On Valentine's Day; Hoover's bluff: Nevins, *Journal*, 356–358.
Later that day: Ibid., 357.
Gregory explained that: Whitlock, *Belgium*, vol. II, 714.
"It was plain"; "It is sure": Nevins, *Journal*, 358; Whitlock, *Belgium*, vol. II, 730–731.
"Hoover is the": Whitlock, *Belgium*, vol. II, 730-731.
"many changing varying"; all remaining quotes: Nevins, *Journal*, 360–362, 367.

57. Elsewhere in Belgium, Rotterdam, and Northern France 563–570

The Deep Freeze Breaks but Hunger Persists 563–566

All tons imported to Belgium and northern France: George L. Gay, *The Commission for Relief in Belgium: Statistical Review of Relief Operations* (Stanford University Press, California, 1925), 192–193, 196–197.
On Sunday, February: Pate diary, Pate papers, Princeton Mudd Library.
"The Rotterdam office"; all Gray quotes in section: Gray, *Fifteen Months*, 227–228.
In late February; the family description: Pate report, Mons, Feb. 28, 1917, Pate papers, HHPLA.

Brown, Eckstein, and the Bunges 566–570

"I believe I"; all Brown quotes in section: Brown to mother and father, March 12, 1917, and Brown to father, March 13, 1917, author's archives.

A Planned German Withdrawal Brings a Flood of Refugees 570

"The result was": Hoover, *American Epic*, 315.

58. Brussels 571–592

A Final Blow Decides the Issues 571–574

"The country is": Nevins, *Journal*, 364.
"Everybody laughing at"; "The annals of": Ibid., 364–365.
"cold again, winter"; "very blue, very"; "the prospect of": Ibid. 366.
In a gathering; "We decided to": Ibid., 367.
For Gregory, at; "I know that": Whitlock, *Belgium*, vo. II, 786;
"I know that"; Gay and Fisher, *Public Relations*, vol. II, doc. 469, 134.
"The members of": Ibid., doc. 470, 135.
Throughout this highly: Nevins, *Journal*, 368; Whitlock incorrectly spells Rene's last name Janssen rather Jensen.
"I gave this": Ibid., 368.

"It is a": Ibid., 370.
A much smaller: Ibid., 370.
In the meantime; delegate names: Kittredge, *History of CRB*, 417; Maurice, *Bottled Up in Belgium*, 169.
Percy memoir; "I at once": Percy, *Lanterns*, 163.
"doubted if they": Nevins, *Journal*, 371.
On March 19: Kittredge, *History of CRB*, 417.

THE CONFUSION STIMULATES DELEGATE PLANS AND DECISIONS 574–578

"When you speak": Brown to mother and father, April 19, 1917, author's archives.
One of those; Brown's plans to escape: Noted later in letters and documents in author's archives.
"taking many precautions"; all details and quotes: Brown, "A Final Word to My Family," March 6, 1917; Brown to Erica Bunge, April 21, 1917; Brown to mother and father, March 12, April 4 and 19, 1917; Brown to father, May 1, 1917, author's archives.

A GERMAN DECREE DIVIDES BELGIUM 578–580

In early March: Whitlock, *Belgium*, vol. II, 754–755.
As reported by; all Chancellor von Bethmann-Hollweg quotes: Ibid., 770–779.
Most in Belgium: Ibid., 756.
La Libre Belgique: Millard, *Underground News*, 232–233.
When the new: Ibid.
Throughout Belgium, the: Whitlock, *Belgium*, vol. II, 765–778.
A protest letter; "We consider this": Ibid., 775.
"The atrocities, the": Ibid., 754.

EVACUATION ORDERS FINALLY COME FROM WASHINGTON 580–582

"in view of": Kittredge, *History of CRB*, 418.
"At the request": Nevins, *Journal*, 371–372.
The direct, explicit; "distinct relief": Ibid., 372.
The seven CRB; "The farewell dinner"; Oberlieutenant Lüdert: Kittredge, *History of CRB*, 422; Maurice, *Bottled Up in Belgium*, 177.
Percy's description of dinner and train station scene; related quotes: Percy, *Lanterns*, 164–165.
"Our last glimpse": Gray, *Fifteen Months*, 250.

WHITLOCK'S LAST IMPRESSIONS OF BRUSSELS 582–586

"flew at once"; all Whitlock quotes in section not otherwise noted: Whitlock, *Belgium*, vol. II, 795, 736–738, 779, 737, 780, 744, 802, 805.
"coming to go": Maurice, *Bottled Up in Belgium*, 163–164.
That same day; all details and quotes: Kittredge, *History of CRB*, 421–422.

WHITLOCK HAS A FINAL MOMENT WITH VON BISSING 586–587

In the morning; "I can not": Nevins, *Journal*, 372.
Eugene was Whitlock's driver: Whitlock, *Belgium*, vol. II, 809.
His dilemma was: Nevins, *Journal*, 372.
Because Whitlock's German; "an ass, placed": Ibid.
As Whitlock's motorcar; "feeble and haggard": Ibid., 373; Whitlock, *Belgium*, vol. II, 810.
Whitlock was seated; "You are going": Nevins, *Journal*, 373.
"in a kind"; "boomed out across": Ibid.
Whitlock laughed and: Ibid.
"in rather questionable": Ibid.
Shortly after, von: Ibid., 374.
"Governor-general von": Kellogg, *Headquarter Nights*, 61–65.
With his farewell: Nevins, *Journal*, 374.

BROWN'S LAST TWO DAYS IN THE OFFICE 587–589

All quotes in Brown's departure: Brown to Erica Bunge, April 21, 1917, author's archives.

THE AMERICAN SPECIAL 589–592

After Brand Whitlock; "very sad and"; "most precious of": Nevins, *Journal*, 374.
"There had been": Whitlock, *Belgium*, vol. II, 812.
"It was very"; "All our friends": Ibid.
"I nearly broke": Nevins, *Journal*, 374.
With German guards; "were all silent": Ibid.
All quotes in Brown's departure: Brown to Erica Bunge, April 21, 1917, author's archives.
The Whitlocks had: Nevins, *Journal*, 374.
According to Whitlock: Whitlock, *Belgium*, vol. II, 808.
Staying behind with: Nevins, *Journal*, 376.
Villalobar was the: Ibid., 375; Whitlock, *Belgium*, vol. II, 813.
"Far across the": Ibid., 813.
"I shall never"; "Nor shall I": Brown to Erica Bunge, April 21, 1917, author's archives.
"We waved our"; "A sense of": Gray, *Fifteen Months*, 251–252.
"You lucky beggars": Ibid.
"As we entered": Ibid.
Fearful of German; "awful oppression of": Ibid.
Long after the; all remaining details in section: Nevins, *Journal*, 377–378.

59. Elsewhere in Belgium and Northern France 593–596

BELGIUM'S MORAL VOICE RISES AGAIN 593–596

On January 24: Mercier, *Cardinal Mercier's Own Story*, 336–337.
von Bissing had: Whitlock, *Belgium*, vol. II, 686.
As the cardinal: Mercier, *Cardinal Mercier's Own Story*, 344–345.
"with heavy hearts": Ibid., 345–346.
"Your Imperial Majesty": Ibid., 346.
"the undersigned, representing": Ibid.
The first signer: Ibid.
Dated February 14: Ibid., 346–348.
On Friday, March: Ibid.
On March 14; "Certain Belgian notables: Ibid.
The Emperor had; "careful examination"; "given orders to": Ibid.
Nothing had been; the reported 10,000 to 13,000: Jens Thiel, in a speech he gave on March 24, 2014, titled " 'Slave Raids' during the First World War? Deportation and Forced Labor in Occupied Belgium," stated there were "approximately 13,000 recruited Belgian civilian workers—*who were not forced laborers per definition.*" Britain's *Daily Telegraph*, on Feb. 6, 1917, reported "It is true that in the case of the voluntary enlistment of the Belgian labourers for war work, a very small number—only some 10,000 out of the 350,000—were driven by hunger to accept the proposals made to them" (clip books, HHPLA).
Still, it was; more than 120,000: Toynbee, in *The Belgian Deportations*, 14, 69, states, "The latest accounts of all place the number already deported at 100,000"; Belgian historian Jens Thiel, in his March 24 speech, stated, "between October 26, 1916, and February 10, 1917, approximately 60,000 Belgians were deported to Germany for forced labor" from the portion of Belgium controlled by Governor General von Bissing, while another 60,000 were Belgian and Northern French who had been deported to other parts of both countries. Hoover, in *American Epic*, footnote no. 1, 281, states, "The number of deportees who returned to Belgium and France after the German surrender in November, 1918, exceeded 700,000. This was not the total deported, however, because many had died in Germany." (Most experts now discount Hoover's count.) Britain's *Daily Telegram*, on Feb. 6, 1917, quotes a figure of 350,000 total deportees (clip books, HHPLA).
"The deportations ceased": Mercier, *Cardinal Mercier's Own Story*, 348.
"I saw trainloads"; "This was only": Percy, *Lanterns*.
"Today a trainload"; all remaining quotes in section: Gray, *Fifteen Months*, 246–247.

60. London **597–599**

HOOVER ARRIVES BACK IN LONDON 597–599

Hoover cable to Wilson: Dated April 4, 1917, in Arthur S. Link, ed., *Papers of Woodrow Wilson*, vol. 41, 543.
"proved troublesome and"; all remaining details and quotes: Hoover, *American Epic*, 317–328.

61. Brussels **600–604**

VON BISSING LEAVES THE STAGE 600

When von Bissing; "unconcealed satisfaction"; "worn out and": Millard, *Underground News*, 233.
As if the; "Take this. My": Ibid., 235–236.

THE FINAL DAYS OF THE AMERICANS IN BELGIUM 600–604

Still remaining and: Kittredge, *History of CRB*, 423–424.
Also remaining were: Ibid.
Promotion of Poland; "Following Hoover's traditions": Ibid., 442.
Fernand Baetens's position; "had been far": Ibid., 440.
On April 23: Ibid., 440–441.
By May 1; "Delegates had gone": Ibid.
It was time: Ibid., 423–424.
Baron von der: Gray, *Fifteen Months*, 271–280.
Leaving Belgium through: Kittredge, *History of CRB*, 423–424.
The train was; all remaining quotes not otherwise noted: Gray, *Fifteen Months*, 271–280.
Kittredge ended a; "So came to": Kittredge, *History of CRB*, 424.
"the greatest thing": Brown to Junior, April 29, 1917, author's archives.
"tremendous privilege rather": Brown to Erica Bunge, April 21, 1917, author's archives.

62. London **605–610**

BROWN BEGINS WORK IN LONDON 605–607

All details and quotes in this section: Brown to Erica Bunge, April 21, 1917; Brown to mother and father, April 19, 1917; Brown to mother, April 29, 1917, author's archives.

HOOVER HEADS HOME FOR A NEW CHALLENGE 607–610

"The country is": *New York Times*, Oct. 12, 1916.
Hoover farewell dinner: Nelson, *Letters and Diaries*, April 24, 1917.
"You people in": Brown to Harry, April 21, 1917, author's archives.
Also in attendance: Nelson, *Letters and Diaries*, April 24, 1917.
Description of the farewell dinner and all related quotes: Nelson, *Letters and Diaries*, April 24, 1917.
Details of America Day in London: *The Illustrated London News*, April 28, 1917.
The St. Paul's event; all details and quotes not otherwise noted: Nelson, *Letters and Diaries*, April 24, 1917.
"The King and": Brown to mother and father, April 19, 1917 (later day entries within it), author's archives.
The singing of three songs: *The Illustrated London News*, April 28, 1917.
The next day: Nash, *The Life of Herbert Hoover*, 361.
List of those also traveling on same ship as Hoover: The passenger list of the SS *Philadelphia*, Ancestry.com.
Dining at the Hoover table: Nelson, *Letters and Diaries*, April 24, 1917.
"owing to a"; Hoover playfully suggested; Hoover ultimately "balked"; "merely descriptive passages": Ibid.
That same day; all following quotes in paragraph: Ibid.
Ben Allen talked; all following quotes in paragraph: Ibid.
The ship's delayed departure and extended time at sea: Ibid., April 24 and 27, 1917.

EPILOGUE

Wrapping Up the Major Stories **611–626**

A SHORT SUMMARY OF AMERICA'S ENTRY INTO THE WAR 611–612

Details within this section not otherwise noted: Multiple public history sources.
Hoover's firm belief; Hoover also understood: Years of reading and analyzing Hoover material.

The Relief Continues through the War and Beyond 613–615

On May 1; all details and quotes in section not otherwise noted: Hoover, *American Epic*, 329–333, 355–356, 376, 380.

"performed with devotion": Gay and Fisher, *Public Relations*, vol. II, 174.

"In the face": Ibid.

The State of the Belgians and Northern French 615–617

The average daily; all details and quotes in section not otherwise noted: Hoover, *American Epic*, 346–347, 340, 350, 351, 356, 381, 383, 376.

After the war; Elaborate three-panel presentation piece, author's archives.

The Fate of *La Libre Belgique* 618–623

"suggested that the"; all details and quotes in section: Millard, *Underground News*, 238, 245–247, 239–240, 250, 252–257, 259, 262–268, 272–287.

The Deportations 623–624

"By 1918 the": Gay and Fisher, *Public Relations*, vol. II, 71.

"The number of": Hoover, *American Epic*, footnote no. 1, 281.

The Flemish/French Issue 624–625

Baron von Falkenhausen: Whitlock, *Belgium*, vol. II, 777.

Shortly after von; "highest officials of": Whitlock, *Belgium*, vol. II, 777; Mercier, *Cardinal Mercier's Own Story*, 386.

The German response: Whitlock, *Belgium*, vol. II, 777.

With the past: Ibid.; Mercier, *Cardinal Mercier's Own Story*, 386.

Cardinal Mercier protested; "I beg of": Whitlock, *Belgium*, vol. II, 777; Mercier, *Cardinal Mercier's Own Story*, 389.

The new governor: Mercier, *Cardinal Mercier's Own Story*, 389.

The CRB Clothing Department and the Belgian Lace Industry 625–626

Brown's activities, clothing report, and quotes in section not otherwise noted: Brown's papers, including his final report, author's archives.

"These reports and": Hoover, *American Epic*, 409.

"Of the 24,384": Ibid.

Warehoused lace: Ibid., 411.

What Happened to Them? 627–638

All details in this section not otherwise noted: Multiple history books, sources already listed elsewhere, and online sources including ancestry.com and Wikipedia.

Herbert C. Hoover 627–629

Hoover's quotes from the July 1958 speech: Hoover, *American Epic*, 450–454.

In 2018, the: The website for the Belgian American Educational Foundation.

Milton M. Brown 629–631

All Brown material: Author's archives.

The Bunges 631

All Bunge material: Author's archives.

William Hallam Tuck 631–632

Tuck material not in public sources: Author's archives.

Hugh S. Gibson 632

Arrival back in America: Gibson cable to State Dept., Jan. 21, 1917, RG 59, File 123 G31, 146, G35, 253, box 1374, NARA.

"special duty for": Ibid., cable from State Dept. to London embassy, April 9, 1917.

"class one": Ibid., cable from State Dept. to Gibson, Aug. 24, 1917.

Reported to embassy in Paris: Ibid., various State Dept. cables.

Prentiss Gray 632–633

Gray details and quotes in section not otherwise noted: Gray, *Fifteen Months*.

P. N. Gray & Co. employees: An ad for the P.N. Gray & Co., author's archives.

Joseph C. Green 634

"J. C. Green": Kittredge, *History of CRB*, 442.

Green details: Multiple sources including ancestry.com, census lists, and an Aug. 5, 1978, *Washington Post* obituary.

Edward Eyre Hunt 634–635

David T. Nelson 635

Walter H. Page 635

"The C.R.B. would": Hoover, *American Epic*, 356.

Clare M. Torrey 635–636

Brand Whitlock 636

Émile Francqui 636–637

Marquis de Villalobar 637

"He could treat": Whitlock, letter to the editor, *The Spectator*, Sept. 11, 1926.

Baron Oscar von der Lancken 637

Maurice Pate 637–638

Pate details: "Scope and Content Note," Maurice Pate papers, HHPLA; "Biography," Pate papers, Princeton Mudd Library.

"the most effective": Alexander Leitch, *A Princeton Companion* (Princeton University Press, 1978).

A Final Note about the CRB Delegates 638

Sources

CRB Official Reports and Books

"Balance Sheet and Accounts, French Government Accounts, Belgian Government Accounts, Supporting Schedules, Covering Six Years from Commencement of Operations, October, 1914, to 30th September, 1920." No location: CRB, 1921.

Gay, George I., and H. H. Fisher. *Public Relations of the Commission for Relief in Belgium: Documents*, 2 vols. Stanford, CA: Stanford University Press, 1929.

Gay, George I. *Statistical Review of Relief Operations: Five Years, November 1, 1914, to August 31, 1919, and to Final Liquidation.* Stanford, CA: Stanford University Press, n.d.

Institutional Collections

I studied the papers of more than 50 CRB delegates that I found in numerous research libraries and institutions. Three critical archives and the primary papers I read within them are:

Herbert Hoover Presidential Library Archives (HHPLA), West Branch, Iowa: Ben S. Allen, Hugh Gibson, Prentiss Gray, Joseph Green, Herbert C. Hoover, Edward Eyre Hunt, Maurice Pate, George Spaulding (found in the Alan Hoover papers), and Brand Whitlock. Also extremely useful were the comprehensive clip books, which contained hundreds of CRB-related newspaper clippings from the United Kingdom, and the oral history interviews.

Hoover Institution Archives (HIA), Stanford University, Stanford, California: Ben S. Allen, Robert Arrowsmith, Perrin C. Galpin, Hugh Gibson, Emil Holman (original spelling Hollmann), Edward Eyre Hunt, Robert A. Jackson, Tracy B. Kittredge, David T. Nelson, Maurice Pate, Robinson Smith, Gilchrist B. Stockton, and Robert Withington. Also extremely useful were the oral history interviews and the more than 500 boxes of files under the name Commission for Relief in Belgium.

National Archives and Records Administration (NARA), College Park, Maryland: Extremely helpful were the General Records of the State Department (RG 59) and the Records of the Foreign Service Posts of the State Department (RG 84), particularly the files of the American Embassy in London and the U.S. Legation in Brussels.

Author's Archives Are Available

My archives are open to any legitimate researcher. They include hundreds of letters and a diary written by my grandfather, Milton M. Brown, while he was a CRB delegate (January

1916 to April 1917), as well as an extensive final report he wrote on the clothing department. From my grandmother, Erica Bunge Brown, I have a small diary (edited by my mother) and numerous photos she took during the war. In addition, I have from my great grandfather, Edouard Bunge, his extensive personal account, "What I Saw of the Bombardment and Surrender of Antwerp" which details his participation in the surrender of the city to the Germans. For more information about my archives or to obtain access, contact Jeff Miller at jbmwriter@aol.com or 303-503-1739.

Primary and Secondary Books

The most important books sourced in writing *WWI Crusaders* have been cited in the text and/or in the Notes. Because I researched extensively the CRB, Belgium, and World War I (fulltime from 1986 to 1988 and from 2012 to 2018), a comprehensive list of sources would be excessive. I have included here only the critical books I used. To see my full list, go to www.WWICrusaders.com and click on the "Research" button.

Cammaerts, Émile. *Through the Iron Bars (Two Years of German Occupation in Belgium).* London: The Bodley Head, 1917.

Gibson, Hugh. *A Journal from Our Legation in Belgium.* New York: Doubleday, Page and Co., 1917.

Gray, Prentiss; Sherman Gray (son) and Prentiss Gray (grandson), eds. *Fifteen Months in Belgium: A CRB Diary.* Princeton: Self-published, 2013.

Hendrick, Burton J., ed. *The Life and Letters of Walter H. Page,* 4 vols. New York: Doubleday, Page and Co., 1924.

Hoover, Herbert. *An American Epic, Introduction, The Relief of Belgium and Northern France, 1914-1930,* vol. 1. Chicago: Henry Regnery Co., 1959.

Hunt, Edward Eyre. *War Bread: A Personal Narrative of the War and Relief in Belgium.* New York: Holt and Co., 1916.

Kellogg, Charlotte. *Mercier, The Fighting Cardinal of Belgium,* New York: D. Appleton and Co., 1920.

Kellogg, Vernon. *Fighting Starvation in Belgium.* New York: Doubleday, Page and Co., 1918.

Kellogg, Vernon. *Headquarters Nights: A Record of Conversations and Experiences at the Headquarters of the German Army in France and Belgium.* Boston: Atlantic Monthly Press, 1917.

Kellogg, Vernon. *Herbert Hoover, The Man and His Work.* New York: D. Appleton and Co., 1920.

Kittredge, Tracy B. *The History of the Commission for Relief in Belgium, 1914–1917.* Unpublished, n. d.

Millard, Oscar E. *Underground News, The Complete Story of the Secret Newspaper That Made War History.* New York: Robert M. McBride and Co., 1938.

Nash, George H. *The Life of Herbert Hoover, The Humanitarian, 1914–1917.* New York: W. W. Norton and Co., 1988.

Nelson, John P., ed. *Letters and Diaries of David T. Nelson, 1914–1919.* Iowa: The Amtndsen Publishing Co., 1996.

Nevins, Allan, ed. *The Letters and Journal of Brand Whitlock,* 2 vols. New York: D. Appleton-Century Co., 1936.

Toynbee, Arnold Joseph. *The Belgian Deportations.* London: T. Fisher Unwin, Ltd., n.d.

Whitlock, Brand. *Belgium: A Personal Narrative,* 2 vols. New York: D. Appleton and Co., 1919.

Withington, Robert. *In Occupied Belgium.* Boston: The Cornhill Co., 1921.

Index

Made in the USA
San Bernardino, CA
14 July 2018